COMPARATIVE COMMUNISM

COMPARATIVE COMMUNISM

The Soviet, Chinese, and Yugoslav Models

Gary K. Bertsch and Thomas W. Ganschow

UNIVERSITY OF GEORGIA

W. H. Freeman and Company
San Francisco

Library of Congress Cataloging in Publication Data

Main entry under title:

Comparative communism: the Soviet, Chinese, and
      Yugoslav models.

      Includes bibliographies and index.
      1. Communism—20th century—Addresses, essays,
          lectures.
      2. Communism—Russia—Addresses, essays, lectures.
      3. Communism—China—Addresses, essays, lectures.
      4. Communism—Yugoslavia—Addresses, essays,
          lectures.
      I. Bertsch, Gary K.   II. Ganschow, Thomas W.
HX40.C735   335.43′4   75-20464
ISBN 0-7167-0733-0
ISBN 0-7167-0732-2 pbk.

Printed in the United States of America

9 8 7 6 5 4 3 2 1

CONTENTS

PREFACE

This selection of readings has been compiled to introduce students to comparative communism. Our objectives have been to provide the readers with some understanding of the rich variations found in Communist societies, and of the reasons for such diversity in what many observers at one time considered a united and homogeneous "Communist world." In planning the book and choosing the readings to be included, we tried to determine what students approaching communism for the first time knew about this subject, and then what instructive materials would best facilitate their learning more.

Our primary interest, therefore, is in teaching, and the book is intended as an instructional tool to help the reader compare and contrast three interesting and important Communist societies. It is our hope that it will prove useful to many students, both undergraduate and graduate, as well as interested laymen, who want to know more about the rich and complex diversity one finds in the Soviet, Chinese, and Yugoslav systems. It should be noted at the outset, however, that genuine comparison must be made with care and organization, and that confusion among the initiates, as well as among the experts, can result from and in haphazard comparison. The introduction that follows sets out the comparative framework for the book, denotes the "whys" and "hows" of comparison, and explains the methodology for making the final comparative selections.

In preparing the book, we had the assistance of twenty or thirty colleagues, and several hundred university students. Our students proved to be the severest critics, and in the years from 1970 to 1974, all of the readings included in this book—as well as about 150 alternatives—were subjected to student opinion. The type of information we sought can be summarized as follows: Which readings and essays about the Soviet Union, China, and Yugoslavia best informed them about these countries, challenged their previously held stereotypes and misconceptions, and enabled them to acquire specific information for making more accurate and intelligent comparisons. Although the students' critical and often caustic evaluations, objections, and suggestions led to some important changes in the book, we maintained certain criteria of our own and therefore assume ultimate responsibility for the readings and essays included in the volume.

As we look back on the early development of the book, we feel that it was initially shaped by three important influences. The first was a series of conversations between ourselves, in which we exchanged ideas based on years of research, travel, and living experience in the three countries treated in the book. In discussing these diverse societies and states that all classify themselves as Communist, we decided that one could learn much more about the meaning of communism by comparing its origin, development, and effect within such different societies. Why had the ideology evolved in one particular fashion in one society and another in the second? Why was one "class"—for example, the peasantry—more important to the Communist revolution in one country than in another, even though theoretically there should have been no difference? How and why did the economy of one of the three countries allow a mixed "free-market" type of economic system while the others did not? What can explain the variation in control over such groups as students, writers, and other intellectuals and artists? We felt that these types of patterns could be most clearly explained by comparative study.

The second influence was our growing recognition of the important effect that the separate histories and contemporary features of these societies had on the Communist experience of each. A full understanding of Communist development, in our estimation, benefited from the perspectives of both history and political science. Since we specialized in these two disciplines (Bertsch in political science, Ganschow in history), we felt our different backgrounds and training could help us examine more effectively both the historical and modern influences that helped shape the present political systems.

The third was the dramatic sequence of political events that took place in the early 1970s. To be sure, the 1960s had already seen the twilight of monolithic communism, if it ever really existed. However, the media coverage of former President Nixon's visits in the 1970s to Yugoslavia, China, and the Soviet Union demonstrated to millions of American citizens that the cultures and societies of these three nations were indeed dramatically different from one another. Even though all three subscribed to a doctrine of communism, they had significantly divergent political, economic, and social systems. The student of contemporary political life should be sensitive to these differences and the reasons for them, and he should be able to gauge their impact upon the domestic as well as international situations. It is our ultimate hope that students will formulate their own critical assessments of these countries, but only after understanding the values for which they stand, the objectives for which their people work, and the resultant product of their labors.

We would like to point out certain features in the format and composition of the book. First a selected bibliography is included at the end of each section of readings. These short bibliographies include some of the most important books on the topic for each of the three socialist states. In addition, the following should be noted. (1) Books and articles that are cited in the text are not repeated in the bibliographies. (2) Although we have not included the writings of Marx, Lenin, Mao, Tito, and other Communist ideologues, readers are advised to peruse them. Translations of past and current thought and policy are readily available in public and university libraries. (3) Finally, articles in periodicals are not cited in the selected bibliographies, simply because of the limitation of space. But a large number of periodicals and scholarly journals on Communist issues in the Soviet Union, China, and Yugoslavia is available. *Soviet Studies, Slavic Review, Problems of Communism, Studies in Comparative Communism, The China Quarterly, Asian Survey, Yugoslav Survey,* and *Socialist Thought and Practice.* The interested reader is encouraged to consult these and other sources.

The footnotes to the previously published materials varied widely in number and purpose between selections, and the greater proportion have been retained. However, where editorial policy permitted, our strategy was to delete those footnotes that we did not consider to be of particular significance for readers of this book. Most foreign language sources, and references to highly specialized or more esoteric materials have been deleted. Our basic goal was to include only those footnotes which would contribute to the general reader's understanding of the subject being covered. Also, in certain articles, minor modifications in punctuation, spelling, and capitalization have been made in order to maintain stylistic uniformity within the book as a whole.

We have already mentioned the fact that this volume was prepared with the assistance and cooperation of many colleagues and students. But we would be remiss if we did not express our special gratitude to the following for their help: to Dr. Ronald Rader, Professor of Russian History, and Dr. Han S. Park, Professor of Political Science, at the University of Georgia; to Mr. Dwight Hunter, Mr. Ted Chylak, and Mr. Thomas Soo, all able graduate assistants who spent much of their time and energy on the book; and to the secretaries in both the history and political science departments who typed much of the manuscript. Finally, of course, behind this book were our wives, Joan and Lisa, who waited patiently (if sometimes skeptically) for its appearance, and expedited its final publication in innumerable ways.

September 1975

Gary K. Bertsch
Thomas W. Ganschow

COMPARATIVE COMMUNISM

INTRODUCTION

THE COMPARATIVE STUDY OF COMMUNIST POLITICAL SYSTEMS

Winston Churchill once referred to Russia as "a riddle wrapped in a mystery inside an enigma." Indeed, these words might be aptly used to express the confusion, uncertainty, and insecurity that so many westerners have felt about Communist states in general. When Nikita Khrushchev's first reminiscences were released in 1970, interested observers throughout the world expressed renewed hope of gaining some broader understanding of developments within the Communist world. But the results were disappointing, and in a *Newsweek* review of the memoirs, Geoffery Wolff commented, "the man who speaks in these pages is as slippery as Proteus." After the subsequent expansion of detente in the 1970s, the various meetings that took place between East and West—specifically, between American presidents and such Communist leaders as Brezhnev, Mao, and Tito—were expected to increase our understanding of Communist states. But the information conveyed on our television screens and in other media, though interesting, did little to contribute to a deeper comprehension of political affairs in Communist party states. What chances, then, do we have of making some progress toward a broader comprehension of society and politics in the various Communist countries of both hemispheres?

If we were to catalogue, count, and weigh the materials on communism in our libraries, we might be led to believe that we know a great deal about this ideology. Voluminous materials are available on the Soviet Union, on Mao's China, and on communism in Eastern Europe and other parts of the globe. But how much do they reveal on what we want and need to know about communism?

What we know about communism today is largely a result of the efforts of "area specialists," that is, those scholars who concentrate on a certain geographical area. Such efforts are usually carried on at centers or institutes established within certain universities to facilitate instruction and research in a particular area. Although these area specialists have provided us with scholarly, exhaustive studies of important aspects of many Communist countries, they have been limited to describing communism within their own special geographical area. This limitation obviously does not contribute to a broader understanding of political phenomena, an understanding that can only be attained through a *cross-national* comparative approach to the study of communism. Certainly, if we restrict ourselves to the area studies approach, we cannot formulate generalizations and laws about political phenomena that might obtain in all Communist states irrespective of geocultural setting. But if we are to expand our efforts beyond the single area, what should those efforts be?

It is our belief that what the comparativist should seek is an understanding of communism as it exists across different societies and cultures, and as it has evolved through different time periods. For example, whereas the area specialist would wish to describe with minute detail, say, the rise of the Chinese Communists to power, the comparativist, guided by the broader interests of the social sciences, wishes to understand the advent to power in all Communist systems. That is, he asks why the contemporary Communist states have turned to communism rather than some other ideology or system of politics? However, although numerous articles, monographs, and books focusing on communism in one country are available, few attempts have been made to gather and synthesize these materials in order to allow the student *to formulate and test these kinds of generalizations across the various systems.* We feel, therefore, that at this stage in the field of comparative communism it is incumbent upon the comparativist both in his research and teaching to take the materials and findings produced by the area specialist and integrate and synthesize them in a manner permitting systematic comparison across the different systems.

Before making such a study of Communist systems, the comparativist must answer the following questions: What do we compare? How do we compare? What we compare might be grouped into two sets of factors: first, the historical factors that have influenced the rise of communism; and, second, the contemporary factors—the ideological influences and the various social and political processes. In this book we are concerned with both areas, the purpose of comparison throughout being to discover the

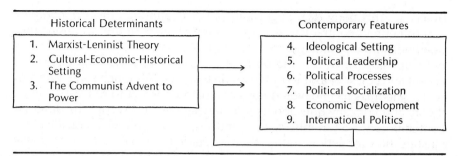

Figure 1.   Comparative framework.

conditions under which certain phenomena take place. The topics we have selected for comparison will be discussed in more detail subsequently.

The question "How do we compare?" is more easily answered after we have determined "what" we will compare. For the present, however, we can note that once the important phenomena have been identified, the student takes the body of materials on separate systems—most of which is the work of area studies scholars—and combines them to provide equivalent information on the same phenomena across the various systems. However, since Communist systems have arisen at different times and at different stages of development, the student must be aware that certain intervening influences may affect the phenomenon being investigated. Obviously, in any study, the investigator must be certain that he is comparing the same phenomena at the same historical stage in all systems.

The comparative framework within which we have organized the contents of this book (See Figure 1) consists of two major and interrelated components: historical influences and contemporary features. Sections One, Two, and Three are concerned with the first component, a set of historical conditions that have significantly influenced the nature of contemporary communism and so help to explain the features of contemporary political life in China, the Soviet Union, and Yugoslavia. Sections Four through Nine, are concerned with the contemporary features and, though considered to be dependent upon the historical determinants, are themselves individually causal in nature. For example, a change in political leadership in a particular Communist country may be current, but it must also be considered of causal significance because of the effect it is likely to have upon other features, such as international politics. Therefore, while all of the contemporary features described in Sections Four through Nine are considered dependent variables, they are also more than that as suggested by the feedback arrow in the diagram. This arrow indicates that these features are also determining variables and must be given this status when one is conceptualizing the interplay of the historical and contemporary features.

In Section One of the book, for example, we examine the theoretical and ideological basis of communism as prescribed by Marx and as first applied by Lenin. This body of thought and practice, although diverse, complex and sometimes contradictory, is the source of many of the commonalities one finds in the contemporary features of Communist party states. This is not surprising, since it is the body of doctrine that all Communist states accept and consider as the central guide to action. Although some Western social scientists have devoted considerable discussion to Marxist-Leninist theory and critically question its role and significance within the different contemporary Communist states—(indeed, some observers consider it a "justification for action" rather than a "guide to action"), it is safe to say that the theoretical basis of communism is an important "historical influence" of many of its contemporary features. For example, in Section Four in the book, when we consider and attempt to evaluate the effect of number 1 in the diagram (Marxist-Leninist theory) on number 4 (the contemporary ideological setting), we will note the number of common ideological threads that permeate the features of all present-day Communist states. In each, outlooks on social classes and social change, capitalism, and imperialism all have common roots in Marxist-Leninist thought. Furthermore, in each of these nations, there has been a conscious effort to follow Marxist-Leninist doctrine in the planning, organization, and functioning of the Communist state. The diagram shows that this first determinant affects such affairs of the state as political leadership (number 5) and political processes (number 6). Marxist-Leninist doctrine provides specific guidelines on "who should govern" and "what political conflict should be permitted." In brief, we believe that, by studying the thought and work of Karl Marx and Lenin's application of his thought to revolutionary Russia, we gain some important insights into present-day communism.

The second influence in the diagram is of no less significance. In all Communist states, the cultural, economic and historical setting that preceded the coming of communism has proven to be of major importance not only to the advent of communism, but also to the formation of its contemporary features. Therefore, in Section Two, we will examine the settings that existed in the three different states, and attempt to identify those elements that influenced the coming of communism as well as contemporary features within each. For example, what effect did Confucianism in China, or tsarism in the Soviet Union, have upon the eventual seizure of power by the Communists? Furthermore, how do these two historical determinants currently influence contemporary events in these two states? Why have the political leaders of China and the Soviet Union tried to destroy all remnants of Confucianism and the tsarist element? The answer would seem to be that such features of the past have an important influence upon present-day politics. Hence, when the effect of such factors is judged to be negative—as is that of Confucianism in present-day China—the leaders strive to eliminate it. The readings in Section Two provide us with important information about the past—the conditions that prevailed in each country before the rise of communism—so that we may further our understanding of the present.

Section Three is concerned with the last historical influence in the comparative framework, the Communists' advent to power in the three states. There is sufficient evidence to suggest that the revolutionary experience of a state is of considerable importance in explaining postrevolutionary behavior. For example, the very fact that Mao and the Chinese Communists were engaged in thirty years of constant struggle before finally attaining power may help to explain contemporary features in the Chinese ideological or international realms. Similarly, Tito and the Partisans' national liberation movement may have strongly influenced various features of the social and political processes that exist today in Yugoslavia. The revolutionary experience, then—the means by which revolution occurred and the actors who implemented it—is an important historical determinant.

For the first three sections of the book, we have selected readings on these three historical influences that will provide you with a solid background for each country. The readings in the first section will give you some basis for drawing your own conclusions about the role and influence of Marxist-Leninist theory in each of the three states. When you then gain an understanding of the historical settings (Section Two) and advents to power (Section Three) in the three states, you will have a good foundation for analyzing the features that make up the contemporary component of the comparative framework.

Each of the contemporary features (numbers 4 through 9) has been chosen because of its crucial importance in defining the nature of politics and society in the modern nation-state, Communist and non-Communist alike. First, the ideological setting consists of those values and objectives that guide the behavior of both elite and mass sectors. Although all three of the Communist states with which we are concerned have accepted the Marxist-Leninist doctrine, it is evident that significant differences in ideology exist between the three states. Much of this variation can be explained by an evaluation of the historical influences.

For example, to illustrate how the comparative approach in this book might be used, let us think about the following example. In the study of the "ideological setting" in Section Four, one is struck by the ideological differences characterizing the three states, and in particular by the Chinese variant of Maoism. When reviewing the historical influences, we come to a number of conclusions on pre-Communist China, including the following: (1) Mao, and the Chinese Communist movement in general, was guided by Marxist-Leninist thought. Mao and the other Chinese leaders were in every respect Marxist-Leninists (and Stalinists) and followed this body of doctrine with a fervid sense of dedication (Section One). (2) The cultural-economic-historical setting of China was in many respects unique and quite unlike that in which Marx expected socialism to take hold and flourish. Instead of an industrially developed, urbanizing society, we find an underdeveloped, Confucian oriented peasant society. Therefore, this societal setting was quite different in many important respects from that which Marx envisioned, and from those in which communism had taken hold or would subsequently arise (Section Two). (3) Because of the historical features that marked twentieth-century China, the Communists advent to power was both long and complex. Owing to the relative absence of an urban-based proletariat, Mao and his associates had to generate and lead a "proletarian revolution" without a proletariat. Replacing the proletariat was the peasant, the backbone and ultimate weapon accounting for the Chinese Communist victory (Section Three). If some general comparisons were made to the Soviet and Yugoslav cases, we would find some basis for accounting for contemporary ideological differences. But although these three sets of historical influences certainly provide some basis for an explanation of the ideological setting in China, they may not be sufficient.

To work towards a fuller explanation, one should consider the effect of the contemporary features as demonstrated by the feedback arrow in Figure 1. Consider, for example, the effect that political leadership (number 5) might have upon the ideological setting. An obvious example is Stalin's influence upon Marxism-Leninism. During the years of Stalinist rule, ideology was revised so extensively that it bore little resemblence to the original doctrine. Subsequent leadership struggles and changes—for example, the regimes of Khrushchev and later Brezhnev—have also altered the function and content of Soviet ideology.

Other modern determinants influence contemporary forms and uses of ideology in similar ways. The methods a state uses to educate and socialize its populace, and the extent to which its efforts are successful, will also have an important influence on the ideological setting. Such processes will be studied in the readings on political socialization (Section Seven), which are concerned with the transfer of political values from the revolutionary elite to broader mass sectors of the population. A cursory examination of the various socialization strategies and results suggests that some methods, and some states, have been more successful than others. These variations, in exerting a causal influence upon the ideological setting, account for some of the contemporary differences that we find.

As we examine each of the features listed in the figure, we follow the same method of comparison. Each section is concerned with a particular feature, and the readings illuminate the ways in which that feature has manifested itself in the Soviet, Chinese, and Yugoslav systems. For each of these determinants, you will probably note both similarities and differences among the three systems. As you study each successive feature, you should draw upon what you have learned of the others in preceding sections. It is our hope that, when you have finished the book, and thereby worked your way through every component of the comparative framework, you will have a comprehensive understanding of contemporary communism—its origins, the reasons for its rise in different geocultural settings, and the reasons for its variation from system to system.

In conclusion, by selecting the Soviet, Chinese, and Yugoslav models of communism for study and comparison, we endorse, at least in part, the widely held viewpoint that Communist countries have more similarities than differences, sharing as they do a number of important characteristics that allow us to designate each nation as "Communist." However, we also challenge the view that communism is monolithic—that similar motives, leaders, and structures can be attributed to each state, and that the actions and functionings of each are therefore highly predictable. Rather, in China for example, the Stalinist form of communism was imported to a social and cultural setting vastly different from that prevailing in the Soviet Union. What evolved was a unique mode of communism in which the power of a strong charismatic leader merged with the cultural order of a Confucian peasant society. In the Soviet Union, we encounter what the Soviets would like to call "orthodoxy" in the Communist world. Being the first to interpret and apply Marxism, the Kremlin has viewed itself as the father and guardian of orthodox communism. Finally, the innovators from the Balkans, the Yugoslavs, have blended nationalism with Tito's strong leadership to experiment with what is truly a distinct national approach to communism. These three countries, all dedicated and established Communist states, provide three ideal models for comparative study: all subscribe to a common Marxist-Leninist doctrine, but their individual modes of interpretation and application reflect differences that are significant indeed.

IDEOLOGICAL FOCUS: MARXISM AND LENINISM

Marxism-Leninism, the ideological basis of communism, has had a greater impact on our twentieth-century world than any other modern philosophy or creed. Whatever one might think of communism as a way of life—the very clash of opinion on this subject testifies to its import—it is distressing to realize how little Americans really know about the ideology itself, or about the countries practicing it. The reasons for this shocking ignorance in a nation with as high a literacy rate as ours are many and varied. One would be the mutual mistrust and fear that have existed between the Communist countries and the United States, preventing—until recently—scholars and visitors from even crossing one another's borders. Another reason was the hostile climate that prevailed in America, particularly during the eras of the "red scare" in the 1920s and the McCarthy "witch hunts" in the 1950s, when rational discussion about communism was almost impossible, in the schools or anywhere else—in fact, it was dangerous to be caught with a book on the subject. A final factor contributing to this ignorance was American indifference to the study of communism as the result of a smug belief that America's way of life was best not only for this country but for every other as well. Only in times of crisis has the indifference been replaced by a more serious consideration of existing alternate systems. It is our hope that the ignorance, indifference, and fear are past history, and that Americans—particularly in the schools and universities—are ready and able to give serious attention to the important and complex subject of communism.

This readiness to undertake a fresh approach is manifested by the recent introduction of comparative and area studies programs in the schools, by augmented coverage of Communist nations in the mass media, especially television, and by intelligent and concerned criticism of America by some of her own people. A closer examination of three models of communism chosen for this study reveals great ideological diversity as well as the seeming contradictions between theory and practice. In the two readings of this section, Peter H. Vigor and Theodore H. Von Laue illuminate the roots of these contradictions but, perhaps more importantly, they also show that the diverse actualizations of modern communism stem from a common source: the philosophy of Karl Marx and the political strategy of V. I. Lenin.

To be sure, neither Marx nor Lenin were the originators of the communist idea. The concept of a communal life, in which sharing and community ownership were valued over individualism and the acquisition of private property, is expressed in the earliest institutions and writings of civilized man. The Greek *polis* inspired Plato to write about his ideal society in the *Republic,* which is one of the earliest examples of Western literature that advocated the sharing of possessions and families. Even in the Judeo-Christian tradition a form of communism has been significant. The Essenes, a Jewish sect existing before Christ, observed communistic practices, and the monastic orders of the Middle Ages adopted certain communistic ways that they thought allowed them to serve God most effectively. Since then, in the course of Western history, numerous prominent individuals, inspired in part by the teachings of Jesus Christ recorded in the New Testament, have added their voices to those preceding them in advocation of the communist society. Among the better known of the precursors of modern communist thought are Sir Thomas More's *Utopia* (1516), Tommaso Campanella's *City of the Sun* (1623), and Gabriel Bonnet de Mably's *On Legislation* (1776). The social and economic frustrations of the nineteenth century, combined with the philosophical romanticism of the time caused a host of writers to express their views on communism and socialism: Henri de Saint-Simon, Charles Fourier, Louis Blanc, William Godwin, and Robert Owen, to name a few. Consequently, when Karl Marx began to express his ideas on the subject, he had a long and established tradition behind him. But Marx did not intend simply to add his name to the list of those endorsing communistic ideas; rather, he wished to be distinguished from them. Whereas others had seen their utopian hopes fade with the passage of time, Marx was convinced that his "scientific" approach would ensure success.

The nineteenth-century German society in which Marx lived was undergoing the same growing pains that so many others had endured throughout history: the struggle between the traditional and the new, the mutual distrust of the old and young, the contradictions between one way of life and another. Marx applied a logic to these various confrontations that, in his view, explained not only why and how they occurred but exactly how they would be resolved. Frustrated at the failure of the French Revolution to fulfill its promises of Liberty, Equality, and Fraternity, many intellectuals absorbed Marx's prediction of peace, unity, and happiness, formerly reserved for life after death, into their visionary philosophies. The French Revolution, Marx reasoned, had failed to achieve the goals expected because it had given rise only to the imperfect bourgeois society; he further proposed that not until the inevitable Proletarian Revolution had taken place, would human struggle and strife cease to exist and be replaced by the new utopia—the communist society. With this theory, Marx attracted to his future "City of Man" not only the intelligentsia but also the downtrodden who might provide the "manpower" for political revolution.

The chaotic political and social conditions of the nineteenth century Western world were further complicated by the technological revolution. Whatever other effects the "machine age" can be said to have had, it did indeed cause the capitalist system to flourish, especially in the United States. There seemed to be no limit for a man who wanted to fulfill a dream, enact an idea, or build his own invention into a personal fortune. Thousands of ambitious and innovative young people struggled up the ladder of success, thus giving living testimony to the merits of the capitalist system. But capitalism also wrought less desirable change on millions of others in the society: first, the gap between the rich and the poor widened more than ever before; also the massive movements into urban settings caused deeper anguish and hardship, for the teeming city did not provide an impoverished family with enough land even to grow food for itself. Little was done to relieve the people in these lower classes from their suffering. Moreover, the system generally fostered the belief that each person demonstrated his real worth by the amount of material wealth he could acquire in a lifetime. Also, the unwillingness to associate with the class out of which one had moved (lest it pull him back into the mire) made it even more difficult to correct injustices and abuses.

The cultural lag was growing as fast as the technical and material life. Marx believed that the capitalist mode of production inevitably produced the alienated worker and conflicting economic classes, but he failed to understand that the source of man's alienation was much more complex than the mere separation of the worker from the product of his labor. The disintegration of the family system, the displacement of religious values with scientific and rationalistic ones, and the chaotic life of the large metropolis were some of the other contributing factors.

When Marx viewed the abysmal working conditions and the grinding poverty of an increasing percentage of the population, he concluded that the very nature of capitalism produced such conditions. He further contended that only revolution, with its power to raise man to a higher level, could remedy the situation. Though we might differ with his conclusions, we cannot negate the genuine humanity of Marx who assumed the Promethean task of speaking to the lords of capitalism on behalf of the impoverished workers. He himself suffered poverty, personal tragedy in his family, and other hardships in return for his conviction that the destruction of capitalism would produce the long-sought utopian society. The narrow confines of Marx's analysis of what motivates man, how society achieves progress, and what influence the methods of economic production have on the formation of society make him vulnerable to valid criticism and, perhaps even more importantly, to the inevitable fluctuations communist doctrine has undergone since his death. But there is enough truth in his writings, enough suffering and poverty in the modern world, and even enough faults in the capitalist system to continue to attract many disciples to his doctrine. One such disciple whose ideas became part of the creed itself was Vladimir Lenin.

If Karl Marx is the ideologue and theorist of modern Communism, Lenin is its strategist and tactician. A dominant principle of Lenin's might have been expressed as follows: "if theory does not agree with the measures necessary for action, let us dispense with theory." Lenin instructed his comrades to regard Marxism not as inert dogma but as an impetus to action. If Lenin did not violate Marx's ideas in the process of implementing them, he certainly altered them permanently.

Lenin was an astute observer of conditions of the times in which he lived. He was, in one sense, more scientific in his approach to man and history than his mentor had been. The anger that was supposed to be seething in the alienated proletarian and his growing class consciousness that inevitably was to culminate in the Proletarian Revolution in the capitalist countries were but words in Marx's writings. The symptoms actually existed but the results were not taking place. Workers, Lenin observed, were not revolting against the "shackles of capitalism." Furthermore, after being enticed into trade unions, they were using collective bargaining and the threat of strikes to obtain wage increases, better working conditions, and shorter hours from their bosses. Marx might speak philosophically about spontaneous revolution, but Lenin was determined to see that revolution came about. In order to head off a drift to reformism, revisionism, and economism, he wrote polemics for his comrades; he organized the tightly knit, highly disciplined vanguard of the proletariat, the Communist party; and he aspired to foment revolutions wherever he deemed them possible, even outside the industrialized countries of the west. A successful revolution, then, was necessary for salvation of the oppressed classes of the world, and his efforts to accomplish his goal would suggest that he believed that the end justified whatever means were required. Indeed, in the words of Leonard Schapiro, "Lenin could veer, prevaricate, intrigue and sow confusion, seeking support from the devil himself if it offered, without for a moment imagining that his conduct might in itself be considered of any importance when judged in relation to the ultimate end."[1] In addition, in the course of his improvisation, Lenin irremediably split the Communist party and also prepared the way for the totalitarian excesses of Joseph Stalin when he assumed power after Lenin's death. Although Lenin hated the oppressiveness of the tsarist regime in which he was raised, this environment had taught him that the wielding of power, strict control, and discipline had effective results, and he applied the methods he had learned to his concept of the Communist party. Consequently, Leninism imposed on the proletarian a state system that was not going to wither away quickly. Lenin himself had written that the state was a class concept, "an organ or apparatus of force to be used by one class against another. So long as it remains an apparatus for the bourgeoisie to use force against the proletariat, so long can the slogan of the proletariat be only—the destruction of this state. But when the state has become proletarian, when it has become an apparatus of force to be used by the proletariat against the bourgeoisie, then," he concluded, "we shall be fully and unreservedly for a strong state power and centralism."[2] The extreme to which power and force were implemented both in the party and the government marks a dramatic departure from the original Marxist theory.

Lenin, then, was concerned with practical details, and he contributed the following concepts to modern communist thought: the importance of a highly disciplined, united Communist party; the necessity for a professional, dedicated elite of revolutionaries that would lead the party and be in charge of implementing revolution; the procedures for indoctrination and education of the proletariat; a proposal for the increased power of the dictatorship of the proletariat and the socialist state; and the importance of obtaining the support of the underdeveloped, colonial areas of the world in the struggle against capitalism and imperialism. In his article "Leninism," Theodore H. Von Laue deals briefly but lucidly with Lenin's interest in the colonial peoples of underdeveloped countries, and his prophecy that they too would join in the anticapitalist uprising. In his publication *Imperialism: The Highest Stage of Capitalism* (1916), Lenin thus proposed new revolutionary possibilities, unforeseen by Marx and Engels, by extending the vision from the advanced industrial centers to the colonial and semicolonial societies, which he described as subjected to ruthless exploitation by international capitalism. It is ironic that when his prediction actually became a reality in China, Stalin, because of an internal struggle for power and his ignorance about China, neglected the opportunity to assist the Chinese Communist party in its efforts at revolution. As a consequence, the way was opened for a new edition of modern communism, written by Mao Tse-tung.

---

[1]Leonard Schapiro, *The Communist Party of the Soviet Union* (New York: Vintage Books, 1971), p. 25.

[2]V. I. Lenin, *Collected Works* (New York: International Publishers, Vol. XXI, Book 2, 1932), p. 39.

1

A Guide to Marxism

Peter H. Vigor

Karl Marx was born at Trier in Germany in 1818, the son of a Jewish lawyer who later became Christian. At the age of seventeen he left the local school and went to study law [at] the University of Bonn; but after a year he moved to the University of Berlin. While there, he became attracted by the works of Hegel--to such an extent, indeed, that he abandoned his legal studies and immersed himself in philosophy; but . . . , he was influenced also by Feuerbach, to whose works he owed the inspiration for some parts of his later theories.

His career as a political writer may be said to have begun when, in 1842, he joined the staff of the democratic paper *Rheinische Zeitung,* of which he soon became the editor; and, from then until his death, political writing, and the study necessary to obtain the materials for his political writing, occupied the greater part of his time.

In 1843, in protest at some legislation introduced by the Prussian Government, he moved to Paris and began to make a serious study of socialism. His stay there proved to be extremely important for him; for not only was he able to study socialism in what was more or less its birthplace, not only did he there make the acquaintance of such prominent Socialist thinkers as Proudhon and Bakunin, but it was there too that he began his collaboration with Friedrich Engels, a collaboration which was to last until his death.

Engels was the son of a wealthy cotton manufacturer from the Rhineland. As a young man, he became interested in social questions, and in 1845 published his *Condition of the Working Class in England,* a masterly study of British labor conditions. Although clearly not as profound a thinker as Marx, he succeeded in making an important contribution to their partnership by means of his gift for clear statement and his tremendous powers of application in the collection of factual evidence. Indeed, it was he who first drew Marx's attention to the importance of such evidence, and thereby rescued him from that nebulous generalizing which is characteristic of so much German philosophy, and which is to be found also in Marx's early work.

Nor was this Engels' only contribution to the partnership. Marx had no private means; and radical political journalism, which was his main activity, is seldom very lucrative; it was Engels, possessed of a comfortable income from profits of his father's business, who was largely responsible for the maintenance of Marx's household. All

From Peter H. Vigor, *A Guide to Marxism* (New York: Humanities Press, 1966), pp. 11–15, 17–21. [Reprinted with permission from the publisher.]

in all, Marx could not have done without him; and indeed the collaboration between the two of them was so close, so intimate, and so fruitful that Marxism should more properly be called "Marxism-Engelism," as Marx himself acknowledged.

One of the first fruits of their partnership was *The Communist Manifesto,* which appeared in 1848. It has often been described as the creed of the Communist party; and it is certainly one of Marx's and Engels' most important works. It was soon to be followed by others.

In 1848, revolts broke out in many countries in Europe; and Marx supported the rebels in his own country by publishing an appeal to all Prussian citizens not to pay their taxes. He was, as it happened, in Prussia at that moment; and he was arrested by the Prussian Government and tried for sedition. The jury acquitted him; nevertheless, in 1849 he was expelled from Prussia, whereupon he came to England [and stayed there] for the rest of his life.

He spent his time in Britain in politics and in political writing, and in study in the Reading Room of the British Museum. For some years, he acted as correspondent for the *New York Daily Tribune* in an effort to earn enough money to support himself and his family; and between 1863 and 1871 he was extremely active, first in helping to form, and then in directing, The Working Men's International Association (The First International). He died in 1883, at the age of sixty-five, and was buried in Highgate Cemetery.

As well as *The Communist Manifesto* of 1848, his chief works are: *Theses on Feuerbach* (1845); *The German Ideology* (1846); *The Critique of Political Economy* (1859); *A Critique of the Gotha Programme* (1875); and, of course, *Das Kapital,* of which the first volume appeared in 1867, but the second and third not until after his death—the third, indeed, being largely written by Engels from the notes which Marx had left. On top of that, he wrote numerous articles and political broadsheets, many of which contain passages [that] are of the very greatest importance for an understanding of Marx's thought; and these cover the whole of the years of his creative life.

It will be seen, then, that his major works span the heyday of nineteenth-century Europe, a Europe which was marked politically by a growing despotism and economically by Victorian *laissez-faire.* Marx had strong personal reasons for disliking both the despotism and the *laissez-faire;* and it is probable that it was this dislike which gave him the stimulus needed to conceive and carry out his work.

Marx's work can be divided into five main categories. There are the elaborations of philosophic doctrines mostly derived from Hegel (in which group come, *inter alia,* the dialectic, the concept of alienation, and the theory of knowledge); there is the attempt to discover scientific laws governing evolution of all human societies in all epochs, from the most primitive to the most advanced and from the earliest in time to the latest—an attempt in which Marx claimed to have been successful; there is the detailed analysis of the working of the capitalism of his day; there are the economic theories which Marx evolved, and in particular the theory of surplus value; and there is the advice on how to destroy capitalism, how to set up the ideal society (communism) in its stead, and hints (though no more than hints) on what sort of characteristic that ideal society should have.

Although these elements, taken together, form an extremely tightly woven philosophic system, rigorously thought out and abundantly documented, yet there is no one work of Marx in which they are presented as a whole; so that a man reading only *Das Kapital,* for instance, misses a great deal of the preliminary thought which has gone into *Kapital's* construction, and a man reading only *The German Ideology* learns nothing of Marxist economics. It is for this reason that I have felt at liberty to introduce my own order into the exposition of his theories; since, by doing so, I have contrived (as I hope) to present them in the most logical, and hence in the most comprehensible, manner. . . .

There are two other points about Marx's work which should be made clear at the outset. The first is that he believed that he had evolved a theory of human societies which was true for all time and all place: it was (he insisted upon it) a *scientific* theory. It was thus far removed in spirit from those agglomerations of platitudes and generalizations, spiced with the author's particular emotional and moral prejudices, which were almost all that the world had seen till then in the way of large-scale works on sociology. Marx's work, being (as he thought) scientific, was to discover and lay bare to the inspection of mankind the laws of human development (for unless it discovered such laws, it could make no claim to science); and the evidence it was to adduce was not to be appeals to right thinking nor to the moral sentiments of the reader; it was to be evidence taken from the figures issued by responsible government departments; it was to be evidence which, to a large extent, was factual and therefore (in so far as the figures were accurate) unimpeachable.

This, of course, still makes it possible for Marx to have drawn from this evidence conclusions which were not logically justified, or to have made assumptions without supporting evidence (and in this connection it must be remembered that in Marx's lifetime statistics were in their infancy): nevertheless, he was one of the first writers on politics and sociology to have used this evidence at all; and it gives his work a solidity and intellectual respectability which is not to be found in the writings of so many political philosophers.

Not that statistics and government blue books were the only evidence he used. His reading at the British Museum was designed to supply him with, in addition, the knowledge of the history, customs, and commerce of as many civilizations as possible, and in as many eras of human existence as possible: it ranged, therefore, from feudal Europe to the Polynesian Islanders, from the India of the Moguls to the Incas of Peru; and its purpose was to marshal in front of him all that had been done by men anywhere, and at any period in history; so that, by scanning all this material, he could (as he hoped) detect the laws which govern men's actions and the development of their societies.

The second point to be mentioned is that in Marx's lifetime the trades unions had little power. Even in England, they did not achieve proper legal recognition until 1871; and that was only twelve years before Marx's death. Most of his major work had already been published by then, including the first volume of *Das Kapital;* and even though the other two volumes were not to be published until after he was dead, the bulk of the research for them had been done some years before, and most of the notes written. In other words, by 1871 his theories had already assumed their final form; it would have needed strong factual pressure to make him alter them; and nothing that the trades unions were to do in the twelve years that remained to him was to make him think that any such alteration might be necessary.

This circumstance is often cited in their support by those attempting to show that Marx has been outdated by events. The argument runs as follows: Marx did not foresee modern trades unionism; this trades unionism, by winning concessions from the employers, has contributed greatly to the contentment of the working class, and thus made revolution much less likely; by making revolution much less likely, it has falsified important sections of Marx's theory; Marxism, as a theory of revolution, is therefore obsolete (at any rate in the West).

This argument, however, would not be accepted by Marx, if he were alive today; for he would point out that it assumes that the diminution of the likelihood of revolution in the West has been largely due to the activities of the trades unions in wresting concessions from the employers; and he would go on to say that he had always held that such an activity would tend to such a result; that therefore he had continually urged the trades unions to make this kind of activity purely secondary; and that, in his opinion, they should have devoted their main effort to destroying capitalism completely. Marx wrote little enough about the trades unions in any of his works; but here is a passage from *Wages, Price, and Profit*, published in 1865, which will illustrate what I have been saying:

Trades unions work well as centres of resistance against the encroachments of capital. They fail partially from an injudicious use of their power. They fail generally from limiting themselves to a guerrilla war against the effects of the existing system, instead of simultaneously trying to change it, instead of using their organized forces as a lever for the final emancipation of the working class, that is to say, the ultimate abolition of the wages system.

In view of this, the present unlikelihood of revolution in the West cannot be taken as a final proof of the falsity of Marx's theories: it may be strong evidence against them, but it cannot be said to *disprove* them. For one thing, Marx set no time limit to his prophecies; and the fact that the West is capitalist [now] does not mean that she is bound to be so in [25 years]. For another, it could be urged that the present comparative stability of Western capitalism is due to the fact that the trades unions have *not*, as a whole, obeyed Marx; they have [for the most part] concentrated upon winning concessions from the employers, and not upon trying to abolish capitalism. Should they change their tactics in the future, things might perhaps be different. . . .

I have prowled along the frontiers of Marxist criticism in this instance simply because it is one which is not only commonly cited as some sort of disproof of Marx; but also is one in which, when cited, the distinction between fact and inference is all too often forgotten. For although it is possible to draw a large number of inferences, there are only four *facts* in the case, and they are these:

1. The rise of modern trades unionism dates from only a few years before the death of Marx.
2. Western trades unions have (on the whole) used their power to win concessions from the employers.
3. Marx thought that this should be a secondary activity, and that the main effort of the trades unions should be devoted to abolishing capitalism.
4. Marx died in 1883, prophesying the doom of capitalism; now, eighty-one years later, capitalism is still with us.

What inferences you may care to draw from these facts are purely a matter for you: the important thing, when you have drawn them, is to remember that they *are* inferences. Myself, I would be concerned, not so much [with drawing] an inference, as [with asking] four questions:

Why is it that the western trades unions have chosen to ignore Marx's advice? Would it have made any difference if they had not done so? Are they likely to continue to do so in the future? If they are, what are the prospects for the destruction of capitalism?

No firm answers, only opinions, can be given to any of these questions—which means that the value of Marxist theory on this particular question must still remain a matter of belief.

Before starting on an exposition of Marx's theory, it may be convenient to give an outline of it first.

Briefly, it consists of a survey of the capitalist system and of a prophecy of that system's doom. It sees two causes for the collapse of capitalism, of which one is capitalism's own inherent inefficiency, and the other the superiority of communism not only as a way of life, but also as an instrument for dealing with the social and economic problems of the new technological age. That atomic energy, for instance, should from the very beginning have been state-owned in all countries, even the most capitalistic of them, not only explains the sort of thing that Marx was thinking of, but also (to a Communist) proves him right.

The rest of Marx's theory consists of an examination of the means by which the doom of capitalism would be achieved. He gives us, as it were, not only the destination and the route, but also a detailed description of the working parts of the car. As he surveyed the whole history of mankind in the course of his years of reading in the British Museum, and observed the enormous changes that had taken place, he analyzed these changes and isolated from among them that which seemed to him to be the one constant and basic motive force. This, in his view, is economic self-interest.

He did not, of course, say that economic self-interest is the *only* human motive, nor did he deny that there are individuals who are almost completely unaffected by it. What he did say is that they, being individuals (and rare individuals at that), are not powerful enough to affect the course of history. History as a whole, he felt, is determined by the "big battalions." Marx lived before there was ever such a science as statistics; but if he had been born a hundred years later, he would, I am sure, have reveled in the phrase "statistically significant."

Men who are "statistically significant" are, by definition, in groups; and Marx therefore focused his attention upon groups. [Owing to] his preoccupation with the importance of economic self-interest, he used this as a criterion with which to allot men to their groups; men, that is to say, are to be classified . . . according to the sort of economic self-interest that possesses them.

However, although it is possible to think of a number of different sorts of economic self-interest (that of the buyer, for instance, as distinct from that of the seller, or that of the cotton-spinner as distinct from that of the manufacturer of artificial fibers), Marx considered that only one sort was important; and this he derived from the relationship in which each man stands to what he termed the "factors of production." The phrase will be explained later: for present purposes, it is enough to say that, in a modern society, the relationship in question *roughly* corresponds to the difference between "employer" and "employed." It is on this basis that Marx allotted men to their groups; and groups classified in this way are called "classes" in Marxist terminology.

In his view, all traditional societies (such as, for instance, capitalist ones) are divided into two main classes. Other classes often do exist; but, as compared with the two principal ones, they are of little importance. Since the economic self-interests of these two main "classes" are opposite and utterly irreconcilable, it follows that such societies must inevitably be a prey to a desperate internal struggle, which Marx called "the class struggle." Such a struggle necessarily weakens the society in which it rages, and is a prime cause of its inefficiency; but since it is called into being by the mere existence of the two "classes," only the abolition of *all* "classes" can bring it to an end. The goal, that is to say, is a wholly classless society.

This new society will therefore be superior to capitalism on two counts: Firstly, it will be free of the "class war" and all the hatred, injustice, and waste of effort which that implies. Secondly, since the economic self-interest of the whole of the community will be identical, the ship of state can sail in a definite and mutually agreed direction.

Such a ship will be planned, purposeful, disciplined and well-organized; and, as a result, the voyage will be profitable to every single human being on board (and profitable not merely in the monetary sense, but in the widest possible sense, including morals, ethics, and social harmony).

The capitalist ship, on the other hand, is distinguished by having a large number of officers and no captain. The officers frequently quarrel among themselves about their destination and must, in any case, spend a great deal of their energies in preventing a mutiny among the crew. [The crew], having no real incentive to do more than they are obliged to do and feeling not the slightest community of interest with the officers, work when they must, and at other times hang apathetically about the forecastle, where they while away the tedium of the voyage by drinking or playing cards.

The birth of the new society, however, will not be a matter of an automatic historical process. The ruling class of the old society has enjoyed a lot of privileges (money, leisure, etc.); and the advent of the new one will mean that these must come to an end. Clearly, they will not be forfeited without a struggle; and the struggle to extinguish these privileges—to extinguish, indeed, the whole privileged "class"—will be what is known as the revolution. Since the new society is *fated* to supersede capitalism, and since it cannot come into existence without the revolution, it follows that the revolution has equally been decreed by fate: its coming can be hastened or retarded, but not stopped. No man of good will would wish to retard the coming of the millennium; it is clearly the duty of all such to do everything they can to hasten it. That is to say that all Marxists are committed to the furtherance of the revolution or, in those countries where it has already taken place, to its preservation.

The details of the new society which is to follow the revolution are not, however, known. Marx was content to prophesy its coming, and to let those who acted as midwife settle the details. He stated that in it men would "live abundantly"; that "he who will not work, neither shall he eat"; and that demand for, and payment of, work should be along the lines of "From each according to his abilities, to each according to his needs." . . .

It should be noted that the word "abundantly," . . . is a key word in any description of society under communism. Communism could not come, so Marx believed, in a primitive or poor society. Admittedly, he held no brief for nineteenth-century capitalism; but he said that capitalism, as well as breaking the restrictive fetters of feudalism, had allowed the productive powers of men to flourish and increase, until now, in its turn, it was acting as a check to progress. In other words, in the Marxist view, capitalism had been a good thing in its day; it was Marx's case that by the middle of the nineteenth century that day was over.[1]

The next step was to be socialism, and on through socialism to communism; but it is important to see that, in Marx's view, the move forward to socialism and communism was possible only from capitalism, since capitalism was the only form of society to be found in human history which had succeeded in creating that abundance which was, Marx thought, the prerequisite for the change.

---

[1] It is absolutely essential for any student of communism to acquire this "relativity" view of history; and to see that, if a Marxist were to invent a time machine and go backwards and forwards in history propagating the opinions of his master, he would damn the capitalists in the twentieth century but, when he got back to the fifteenth century and feudalism, he would turn round and extol capitalism for all he was worth. Similarly, when he got a bit more ambitious and went further back in time to the slave states of ancient Greece or Rome, he would become a devoted preacher of feudalism.

This explains why, in the early days of the Russian Revolution, many Russian Communists were so worried. The party considered prerevolutionary Russia to be feudal; consequently, it could not attain communism without first becoming capitalist. This led to a great many of the Bolsheviks at first working together with, and for the support of, the undeniably "bourgeois" Provisional Government. It took the whole weight of the drive and authority of Lenin (who was much less interested in theories than in power) to alter this state of affairs, and to get his fellow Communists to devote themselves to the Provisional Government's downfall.

I cannot conclude this brief outline of the theory without a few words of my own. It is a matter of sheer historical fact that the revolution has not yet broken out in any but poor and backward countries. So, far from having that abundance which Marx said was essential for a transition to communism, they have all been characterized by poverty; so, far from being capitalist (which implies being industrial), they have all been semi-feudal and agricultural. This means that one of the three following propositions about them must be true:

1. Marx was wrong.
2. They are not truly socialist, let alone communist.
3. The difficulties and near disasters, the privations and the miseries, the oppressions and the persecutions, which all these societies have admittedly suffered, stem from the one fact that Marx was right; and that they should not have launched the revolution when they did, but should have waited until they had achieved a strong, stable, and prosperous capitalism before embarking on communism.

2
Leninism
Theodore H. Von Laue

As the Russian intellectuals steeped themselves in Marxism . . . , it became clear that their creed, so largely based on western European precedent, did not readily fit Russian realities. The exact location of their Russia in the Marxist chart of history was—and still is, to Soviet historians—a tough theoretical problem. Autocracy, Marxists would agree, was a feudal rather than a bourgeois institution. Russian capitalism was still weak. Marxism thus might seem to require that its followers first strive for a capitalist Russia—a preposterous suggestion; to a Russian Marxist the rise of "capitalism" in Russia always signified the rise of the proletariat as a revolutionary force and a step toward socialism. They were always one step ahead of history.

Russian Marxists thus could not, as this shift in emphasis implied, strictly subscribe to the laws of dialectics as laid down by Marx. This was made clear—unwittingly, no doubt—from the outset. As Plekhanov, the father of Russian Marxism, wrote in one of his early tracts (1883) concerning the role of the individual in Marxist philosophy:

> For us the freedom of the individual consists in the knowledge of the laws of nature, and in an ability to submit to these laws, that is, among other things, to combine them in the most advantageous way.

The freedom to submit and not to submit to the laws of nature (or of history) attracted most strongly the revolutionary activists over the protest of the orthodox Marxists. But, after all, had this not been one of the freedoms of Marx himself?

And was the proletariat to be tool or master of the revolutionary intelligentsia? Seasoned Marxists answered that naturally the proletariat fashioned its own mentality (or "consciousness," according to their lingo) and thus shaped its destiny. The revolutionary intelligentsia merely acted as a vanguard which took its orders and its very outlook from the main force. Yet would the revolutionary hotspurs be willing to mark time if the "consciousness" of the proletariat was not ready for either revolution or socialism? And was its "consciousness" ever to be trusted? These doubts led to a spate of further questions regarding the relationship between the vanguard and the main

From Theodore H. Von Laue, *Why Lenin? Why Stalin?* 2nd ed. (New York: J. B. Lippincott Company) Copyright © 1964, 1971 by Theodore H Von Laue. pp. 86-99. [Reprinted with permission from the publisher.]

host, the character of leadership, the timetable for revolution, and innumerable details of strategy and tactics.

In the bitter disputes that arose over these issues, two distinct points of view emerged, the "soft" and the "hard." Both were advanced by revolutionaries familiar with the vicissitudes of their calling. For years the difference was one of emphasis and inclination, not of fundamentals. Only gradually did the rift [widen] into schism. By 1912 the breach was complete, by 1917 it was irrevocable.[1]

The "softs" inclined toward the liberal-humanitarian strains in Marxism. They were willing to listen to the views of the industrial workers (but never of the peasants!) and to adjust themselves to their spontaneous activities. They cheered when the workers formed the St. Petersburg Soviet in 1905. For the same reason they preferred a party structure allowing a maximum of mass participation, after the model of the German Social Democratic party. They looked forward to the day when all their work could be legal. Necessity drove them underground, but they never felt comfortable with the conflict of ends and means which ensued; they shrunk from fanaticism. Since in their estimate Russia was not ready for socialism—it would come to Russia only after it had been achieved in the West—they leaned toward patience and tolerance. Their goal was the overthrow of autocracy and the establishment of a liberal-democratic regime with a strong labor party and a powerful trade union movement. This called for an alliance with liberalism and for continued close ties with Western Europe, to which the spokesmen of this faction looked with genuine admiration and where some of them, like Plekhanov, felt rather at home. Under special conditions there might even be need to support the existing autocratic government. This was Plekhanov's attitude after the outbreak of war.

The "soft" position was generally adopted by the faction called Menshevik (the minority), so named after an entirely unrepresentative ballot at a party congress in 1903, when it had lost out to the "hards." With a quick eye for the propaganda advantage, the latter forever thereafter hailed themselves as Bolsheviks (the majority), although in fact the Mensheviks always had a larger following right down to March, 1917, when they formed the second largest faction in the Petrograd Soviet.

The "hard" position was the creation of Vladimir Ilich Ulianov (1870–1924), better known as Lenin, one of the great political figures of the twentieth century. From Western and native sources he fashioned the first great Western anti-Western movement, with a style suited to the temper of the outer marches of the urban-industrial West.

Historical evidence has as yet found no trait in the Ulianov family that need have pushed their two eldest sons into the revolutionary movement. As a supervisor of schools in the chief towns of the lower Volga region, Lenin's father had risen high in the ranks of the Imperial bureaucracy, advancing even into the hereditary nobility. If his sons turned rebels after his death it was, presumably, because of the discrepancy between their humanitarian ideals, innocuously—and perhaps too ardently—cultivated in their home, and the harsh reality of the autocratic regime. For his protest, Lenin's older brother soon paid with his life. While a student at the University of St. Petersburg he took part in a plot against the Tsar's life and was executed in 1887. His fate committed the younger boy to the same cause.

In constant trouble with the authorities from the start of his university studies, Lenin was trained as a lawyer. In 1893 he moved to the capital and at once immersed himself

---

[1]Among the rank and file, however, the split was not final until May–June, 1917. Many simple workers indeed never understood its reasons; they often resented it.

in the revolutionary agitation among the factory workers, who welcomed the solicitude of the intelligentsia (although not necessarily their revolutionary extremism).[2] In a short time he assumed a position of respect in the Marxist circles. Inevitably the police began to take notice, and in December, 1895, he found himself arrested. Sentenced after some delay, he was exiled to a village in the depths of Siberia, whence he called himself Lenin, presumably after the river Lena (although he had been sent no further than the Yenissei). Neither jail nor exile diminished his prodigious capacity for work. Barred from all revolutionary action, he wrote an impressive scholarly tome on *The Development of Capitalism in Russia* and translated Sidney and Beatrice Webb's volume on trade unionism, not to mention many pamphlets, articles, and letters. In Siberia he married a fellow revolutionary from St. Petersburg, likewise under sentence of exile, named Krupskaia—she continued to be called by her maiden name—who served him as a devoted and selfless companion to the end of his days. She bore him no offspring— how could they have fitted children into a revolutionary career?

After his release in 1900, Lenin went to Western Europe, soon to be followed by his wife. There they stayed until 1917, with the exception of a brief Russian interlude during the Revolution of 1905, rootless aliens, unwanted and unassimilated. When Trotsky after his first escape from Siberia visited Lenin in London, Lenin showed him the sights. "This is *their* famous Westminster," he said, pointing at the Houses of Parliament. Alas, to Lenin the good things of Europe were all *theirs,* the capitalists' and exploiters'. Ill at ease amidst their comforts, Lenin never acquired an inside view of Western democracy or of "capitalism." He remained close to his Russian heritage, a secret Slavophile in the Marxist ranks. With the single-mindedness of genius he pined for Russia, for revolution, and for getting the better of the "capitalists'" easy superiority.

By 1902, the revolution seemed as distant as ever. Two generations of revolutionaries had passed and accomplished nothing. Their accumulated failures now taught a still more impatient third generation, of which Lenin made himself the spokesman, to become yet hardier and craftier professional revolutionaries.[3] More intensively than even Chernyshevsky's "monster," Lenin armed himself to the depths of his personality for this task. Softness in any form was the supreme sin. As he once observed to Maxim Gorky:

> I can't listen to music too often. It affects your nerves, makes you want to say stupid nice things and stroke the heads of people who could create such beauty while living in this vile hell. And now you must not stroke anyone's head—you might get your hands bitten off.

The previous generations of revolutionaries had had their hands bitten off by being too emotional, too kind, too careless of their impulses. By contrast Lenin permitted himself only the most rational and cold-blooded calculations of revolutionary opportunity. In case of failure he allowed no despair, but counseled self-criticism, analysis of the mistakes, and a new and still more earnest beginning. In case of success he shunned exultation—that too was a form of weakness and courted disaster.

What counted "in this vile hell" was discipline, method, accuracy, precision, and infinite patience with detail in all the black arts of revolution. A revolutionary had to

---

[2]The most advanced elements in the Russian working class were not eager to risk their hard-won pittance of prosperity in constant revolutionary warfare. The revolutionary surge originated more commonly with those working class elements that remained close to the village.

[3]The extraordinary length and depth of the revolutionary tradition was another peculiarity of the Russian setting, distinguishing it from any other.

be *toujours en védette*, ready to advance when possible and to retreat when necessary, to endure above all and to preserve intact the vital revolutionary resolve. Throughout his life, Lenin retained an almost masochist fierceness toward the gentle voices that might weaken this hard-won determination, whether generosity, sentimentality, or any form of what he called "petty-bourgeois" morality. The only moral guide which a revolutionary recognized, he preached, was success in his calling. Considering the emotional and undisciplined ways of the Russian intelligentsia in which it had its origin, Lenin's code was a remarkable monument to the human will. Yet it still remained a product of human flesh and blood. It could be upheld—and the doubts suppressed—only by the utmost exertions of fanaticism. Thus rationality of purpose was carried to the point of a rigid irrational compulsion.[4] And human nature demanded a price for such outrage. All too often Lenin, who in his heart remained tuned to the music of kindliness, complained that his nerves played him tricks which kept him from working. Revolutionaries with coarser temperaments, of course, would have better nerves. And the fourth generation—the commissars—would laugh at such weakness; the trend favored the primitives like Stalin. The natural pull of Russian life, however, continued to run in the opposite direction (which, by way of compensation, perpetuated the need for Lenin's inhuman discipline).

The code of thought and feeling which Lenin prescribed for himself and other revolutionaries was accomplished by a set of rules for the organization through which they must work. These rules again can best be understood as a response to past failures. The revolutionaries had had their hands bitten off, Lenin charged, because they had been amateur organizers. Their desire to imitate the mass organizations of the German Social Democratic party had allowed the police to penetrate their ranks. What had been created with heroic effort was thus wiped out in short order; the best revolutionaries were sacrificed for nothing. His plea therefore was for a revolutionary organization capable of outsmarting the police (which at this time, under the direction of an ex-revolutionary, Colonel Zubatov, was beginning to apply the methods of modern crime detection to the revolutionary movement).

Survival—not to mention success—under these conditions was impossible, Lenin argued, [as long as] the Russian Marxists believed that the revolution must proceed from the workers themselves. He angrily proclaimed the contrary view. "The history of all countries shows that the working class, exclusively by its own efforts, is able to develop only trade union consciousness."

Revolutionary consciousness, Lenin proceeded, could be carried to the workers only from without, by the revolutionary intelligentsia, an altogether different category. Whether this was universally true may be questioned. But who could deny that the Russian workers were singularly unsuited to cope effectively with the complex tasks of bringing socialism to Russia? The antinomy between the vanguard and the proletarian host remained a crucial ingredient in Lenin's political theory. It betrayed his ineradicable suspicion of all spontaneous, unorganized humanity, even of genuinely proletarian organizations like the St. Petersburg Soviet of 1905. This secret contempt of spontaneity sheltered him from the influences of the western democratic model, yet it also perpetuated the old cleavage between the educated classes and the Russian masses. (Could there have been a more disdainful approach to the man in the street

---

[4]The closest European parallel can be found in the traditions of Prussian militarism, as established in the eighteenth century (with very different connotations, to be sure). Both *Junkers* and Communists refused to recognize the term "impossible."

than this heartless collective term, "the masses"?) Physically and spiritually, Lenin (like Marx) always kept aloof from the workers. There is no evidence, for instance, that he ever set foot inside a factory.

Revolution, then, was the concern first and last of the revolutionary leaders, the heirs of both the Russian and European revolutionary tradition and the masters of the scientific laws of historical development. They alone possessed the proper "consciousness." They devised the appropriate policy for every new set of circumstances and formulated what eventually became known as "the party line." It had to be defined precisely so as to avoid misunderstanding and to enable the members of the party to carry it out to the letter. The elite, Lenin further insisted, must be organized like a miniature army, a human machine expressly designed for revolution, disciplined and loyal to the commander. He therefore demanded that the party's Central Committee have plenary power over the entire organization, like a commanding general over all officers and troops in the field. And like a general in time of war—war and revolution were much akin—the revolutionary leader could not afford to be choosy in his methods.

> Revolution is a difficult matter [Lenin wrote in 1907]. It cannot be made with gloves and manicured fingernails. . . . A party is no girls' dormitory. Party members should not be measured by the narrow standard of petty-bourgeois morality. Sometimes a scoundrel is useful to our party precisely because he is a scoundrel.

During the low years after the failure of the Revolution of 1905, Lenin even approved of bank robbery, euphemistically called "expropriation," as a means of financing the Russian Social Democratic party. The most spectacular of these "ex's" was carried out in Tiflis under the supervision of Stalin. Later, during the war, he had no scruples about taking German money for his faction. All means were fair so long as they promoted the revolution. Needless to say, Lenin's conception of what a Russian Social Democratic party should be, so contrary to the liberal-humanitarian tradition of Marxism, did not go unchallenged. As early as 1903, Trotsky predicted what would happen if Lenin's views prevailed:

> The organization of the party takes the place of the party itself; the central committee takes the place of the organization, and finally the dictator takes the place of the central committee.

This, precisely, was the way in which the Bolshevik Party evolved (and after the summer of 1917 even with Trotsky's active support).

Lenin, however, would never see the danger. He believed that in the comradeship of the common struggle no conflict could arise within the party. The flow of commands from above would be modulated by the flow of information and suggestion from below; no constitutional safeguards were needed.[5] At all events, his chief reply to his critics was unanswerable. Under autocracy—and he never believed that the October Manifesto made any difference—only a secret and highly trained organization of militant revolutionaries could prevail. It was either that or catastrophe again. Under Russian conditions, he further contended, the masses could be properly won to the party and made conscious of their role only if the party attained the quality of a tight-knit revolutionary elite. Striking workers, he wrote, would hardly risk their lives for an unwieldy, spy-ridden mass organization. They needed efficiency and the leadership of

---

[5]Here again Lenin carried a *narodnik* argument into Russian Marxism. [Editors' Note: Narodniks were nineteenth-century Russian "populists" whose basic goal was agrarian socialism based on the peasant commune.]

reliable underground agents to guide their work in street and factory. Successful mass action indeed depended on the expert core.

This was the way, then, in which Lenin proposed to combine the highly centralized leadership of the revolutionary elite—of himself, had he been frank—with large-scale action in an age of mass politics. The secret of success in this squaring of the circle lay in constant agitation by the elite among the masses. By propaganda and a thousand other forms of directing revolutionary discontent, including irrational means of mass manipulation, the revolutionaries were to shape the "consciousness" of the masses. Lenin early recognized the benefit of slogans and other simplified appeals geared more to the emotions than to the understanding of the man in the street. Thus the Bolsheviks learned the techniques of modern mass politics under the frontier conditions of revolutionary warfare. Never, so Lenin preached, could they afford to lose touch with the masses. In this lay their strength.

Yet, in the last analysis, the identification was never quite complete. With all their skills of manipulation, the Bolsheviks could never lure the masses into the proper consciousness. The gap between spontaneity and revolutionary consciousness remained unbridged—the circle, after all, could not be squared. The Bolsheviks thus shared the predicament of the tsars. Unlike the other opposition parties which bowed, in theory as well as practice, to the will of the people, they could not admit the population into the political decision-making process, which is the essence of democracy. By his own theory Lenin was cast into the role of a counter tsar, and the Bolshevik faction into that of a counter autocracy. Thus did the tsarist regime perpetuate itself, illegitimately, yet with improved skill; for despite the innate flaw, Bolshevik political practice was vastly superior to that of the tsars, who had never learned to work with an aroused populace.

One other strand tied Lenin, however obliquely, to the tsars—his nationalism. As one reads his famous pamphlet of 1902, *What Is To Be Done?* which sets forth the basic concepts of Leninism, one is struck by his allusions to the superiority of the Russian revolutionary movement. Fighting the most reactionary government in Europe, it was the vanguard of the international revolutionary proletariat.

> The role of the vanguard fighter can be fulfilled only by a party that is guided by the most advanced theory. To have a concrete understanding of what this means, let the reader recall such predecessors of Russian Social Democracy as Herzen, Belinsky, Chernyshevsky, and the brilliant galaxy of revolutionaries in the 1870s, let him ponder over the world significance which Russian literature is now acquiring; let him . . . but be that enough.[6]

The incomplete "let him" speaks volumes for the soaring national pride in Lenin, who yearned for world recognition, not on behalf of the Empire—that was moribund—but for revolutionary Russia. His thought leaped far ahead into the future. Lenin undoubtedly was guilty of what Trotsky once called "that national revolutionary messianic mood which prompts one to see one's own nation state as destined to lead mankind to socialism." And he forcefully expressed the burning hope for an escape from backwardness which we have noted earlier among Russian intellectuals. In Lenin, nation-

---

[6]Russian literature, incidentally, was not revolutionary in its greatest representatives. Lenin was running out of proofs of superiority—which obviously did not thwart his ambition. In part, this ambition, incidentally, was a hand-me-down of German origin. Kautsky, the German Marxist, had just encouraged the Russian revolutionaries to think of themselves as the vanguard of the international proletarian revolution.

alism and the Marxist foreknowledge of history combined in a powerful stimulant to the Russian ego. Let "capitalist" Europe beware!

Proper revolutionary organization was one leg of success, proper theory the other. In the realm of theory, one can again see Lenin's impatience at work, combining the laws of history in a way most advantageous to those who wanted revolution at once and at any price. In none of his speculation was he concerned merely with the replacement of autocracy by a bourgeois democratic regime—bourgeois democracy was for the rich only. He aimed at the next revolution thereafter, the socialist revolution. The obvious objection to such far-reaching plans, according to Marxist theory (as well as to common sense), lay in the fact of Russian backwardness. Russian "capitalism" would not have run its appointed course for a long time. But for a third-generation revolutionary such perspectives were intolerable and, fortunately for him, not entirely supported by the evidence. As the events of 1905 showed, Russia possessed a revolutionary thrust that might well carry it quickly beyond a purely bourgeois phase.

Marx already had advised the revolutionary vanguard to take any available revolutionary force as its ally. Lenin expected no help from the Russian *bourgeoisie*, a class far weaker than its Western counterpart. At least one stratum of that class had been bought off by the October Manifesto; the others had not acted vigorously enough (and never could, by their very nature.) It was rather the peasantry—to omit here the revolutionary potential of national and religious dissent—which had accounted for the revolutionary ground swell. And to the peasants Lenin turned in 1905, despite the fact that Marxist theory rated them as hopeless, Marx himself having spoken of the "idiocy of the countryside." Whatever the economic convictions of the peasants—Lenin always remained suspicious of their "petty-bourgeois" bent of mind—the explosive impact of Black Partition was invaluable revolutionary capital, too important to be spurned. Thus he began to speak, over the protest of the "softs," of a revolutionary democratic dictatorship of the proletariat and the peasants (the poorer peasants particularly), which was to emerge from the overthrow of autocracy.

The new perspectives also implied an adjustment of the normal Marxist pattern of social progress to Russian conditions. The peculiarities of Russia prevented a clear-cut succession from feudalism to capitalism and from capitalism to socialism. In Russia, as in other backward countries, a combined development was apt to be the rule. Feudal elements mingled with capitalist and socialist ones; a weak *bourgeoisie* and a powerful proletariat existed side by side, even under autocracy. Thus, Lenin foresaw that after the overthrow of autocracy, the toiling masses would already have the upper hand, giving the new government the character of a powerful revolutionary democratic dictatorship rather than of a bourgeois democracy in the western style. Such a regime, he thought, might also have a startling effect outside Russia. It might act as a spark, setting off the proletarian revolution in the advanced "capitalist" West, riper for socialism than Russia. Having created a socialist society of its own, the West would then rush, with socialist zeal, to introduce socialism into Russia, well in advance of the natural course of its development. Trotsky, who was gradually drifting closer to the Bolshevik position, formulated an even more articulate theory—the theory of "the permanent revolution"—for those who wanted to leap forward into socialism regardless of whether Russia was ready or not. Such implacable revolutionary determination in theory and practice, incidentally, ranged the Bolsheviks on the side of the irrationalists in European politics, despite their guise of Marxist rationalism.

When war broke out in 1914, Lenin watched with choking rage the collapse of international socialist solidarity. Workers now fought workers for the defense of their national interest, for their *bourgeoisie*. During these bitter months, after settling down in cheap lodgings in Zurich, he set the basic concepts of Bolshevism into the largest possible context of global politics. Russian revolutionary theory had traditionally suffered from its ignorance of the realities of power politics. Lenin, in his famous pamphlet *Imperialism the Last Stage of Capitalism* (1916), now remedied this deficiency. In that last stage, he argued, giant capitalist monopolies competed all over the world for new markets. In their rivalry they set nation against nation, people against people. Thus they had caused the First World War. Yet the very violence of the imperialist competition advanced the revolution in a double movement. The war, Lenin predicted, would make the European proletariat rise against its masters. Ever since the outbreak of hostilities, he himself had urged the European socialists to convert the international war into a civil war. Yet—and this was a new feature—it would also drive the colonial peoples, who in the period of imperialism had been enslaved by "capitalist" rule, to rise against their exploiters (among whom Lenin included Imperial Russia). This grand conception of imperialism provided a ridiculously distorted account of both "capitalism" and the origins of the war. Yet it contained a prophetic insight. In it Lenin fused the traditional socialist revolutionary movement in Europe with the incipient antiwestern global revolt, which he had keenly eyed for several years. The "internal" and the "external" proletariat, the industrial workers of Europe and the backward peoples, were joining forces against the western ruling classes then locked in mortal combat. Posing the question of what he would do if the party of the proletariat came to power during the current war, Lenin [in 1915 had] confidently replied:

> We should have to prepare and undertake revolutionary war, that is, not only should we fully carry through in the most decisive ways our entire minimum program but we should systematically begin to draw into revolt all peoples now oppressed by the Great Russians, [and in addition] all colonies and dependent countries of Asia (India, China, Persia, and so on), and also—and primarily—the socialist proletariat of Europe.

It was a sweeping vision of a counter power to the great outpouring of Western civilization, a counter power centered around the revolutionary potential of the European proletariat. Thus Leninism helped to carry the seed of the French Revolution into the non-European world. Liberty, equality, and fraternity—the revolutionary quintessence of European civilization—now were set to work against the Western domination of the global community.

Before March, 1917, however, all of Lenin's plans for effective revolutionary action in the imperialist age remained a matter of theory. They merely reflected his effort to keep Marxist analysis —the correct version—abreast of the rapidly unfolding events. However crucial for the political education of the "hards," they did not advance the cause. Representing the extreme left of the Russian Social Democratic party and counting few adherents, the Bolsheviks were even more unsuccessful and divided than the other opposition groups. Despite Lenin's talk of the superior efficiency of his revolutionary elite, the secret police had succeeded in planting an agent, Roman Malinovsky, in its inner circles; he enjoyed Lenin's confidence. Paradoxically, the Bolsheviks became an effective political force only after the collapse of autocracy.

At the time of the March Revolution, the Bolsheviks were still a negligible group. Their leaders were scattered: Lenin in Switzerland, Stalin in Siberia, Trotsky (whom we may henceforth include among the "hards") in New York. They possessed but a handful of delegates in the Petrograd Soviet. Yet when Lenin heard of the fall of autocracy, his mind was made up. A socialist revolution in Russia—and perhaps world revolution too—was within reach. The Provisional Government of Russia, he wrote,

> is in no condition to escape collapse, for it is impossible to tear ourselves out of the claws of that terrible monster begotten by world capitalism—the imperialist war and the famine—without leaving the soil of bourgeois relations, without going over to revolutionary methods, without appealing to the greatest historical heroism of the proletariat of Russia and the whole world.

He arrived in Petrograd toward the end of April, 1917, after having crossed Germany with the assistance of the German government. At once he set the course of his small band of followers toward the seizure of power in the name of the proletariat, staking all on the monstrous effects of the war.

Selected Bibliography

Berlin, Isaiah. *Karl Marx: His Life and Environment.* 3d ed. New York: Oxford University Press, 1963.

Bober, M. M. *Karl Marx's Interpretation of History.* Rev. ed.; Cambridge, Massachusetts: Harvard University Press, 1948.

Drachkovitch, Milorad M., ed. *Marxism in the Modern World.* Stanford, California: Stanford University Press, 1965.

Gray, Alexander, *The Socialist Tradition: Moses to Lenin.* London: Longmans, Green, and Co., 1946.

Hook, Sidney. *From Hegel to Marx: Studies in the Intellectual Development of Karl Marx.* Ann Arbor, Michigan: University of Michigan Press, 1962.

Hunt, R. N. Carew. *The Theory and Practice of Communism.* 5th ed. Baltimore: Penguin Books, 1963.

Lichtheim, George. *Marxism: An Historical and Critical Study.* 2d ed. New York: Praeger, 1965.

Marcuse, Herbert. *Reason and Revolution: Hegel and the Rise of Social Theory.* Boston: Beacon Press, 1960.

Meyer, Alfred G. *Leninism.* Cambridge, Massachusetts: Harvard University Press, 1957.

———. *Marxism.* Ann Arbor, Michigan: University of Michigan Press, 1963.

Page, Stanley W. *Lenin and World Revolution.* New York: McGraw-Hill, 1972.

Schapiro, Leonard, and Reddaway, Peter, eds. *Lenin: The Man, the Theorist, the Leader.* New York: Praeger, 1967.

Shub, David. *Lenin.* Rev. ed.; London: Penguin Books, 1966.

Wetter, Gustav A. *Dialectical Materialism.* Translated by Peter Heath. New York: Praeger, 1958.

Wilson, Edmund. *To the Finland Station.* Garden City, New York: Doubleday, 1953.

CULTURAL BACKGROUND AND HISTORICAL SETTING

Having examined the philosophical roots and the origin of modern communism, let us now examine its initial formation and development in the three countries selected for this study. A historical approach is essential here, because only by studying the traditional living patterns that prevailed before the twentieth century in Russia, China, and the nations that today make up Yugoslavia are we able to understand the recent foothold Marxism-Leninism has gained in these countries. But, perhaps more importantly, an examination of the cultural background and historical setting can provide us with insights that help explain the present diversity in the type of communism these three countries expound.

The most striking fact about the conditions existing in Russia, China, and Yugoslavia before the advent of communism is their dissimilarity to Karl Marx's description of those advanced, industrialized countries teeming with alienated factory workers who would be ready to rise against their exploiters. In contrast, in all three countries the great majority of the people were peasant-farmers, dependent on agriculture for their livelihood, and there was only a minimal amount of industry. Moreover, in none of these countries was there an economy that even remotely resembled a developed capitalistic system—the necessary and inevitable stage on the road to communism. Indeed, when the Communists came into power all three economies were still more similar to ancient feudal systems than to capitalism.

If Marxist theory is to be taken as a guideline, then, it was the wrong time, the wrong place, and the wrong stage of economic development for Communist revolutions in Russia, China, or Yugoslavia.

Nevertheless, within a century after Karl Marx's death, all three of these "unprepared" countries claim to be Communist systems. How can these contradictions be explained? Were there common factors in all three countries that prepared the ground for revolution in general? And what were the historical and cultural components present in each country that acted as catalysts or deterrents for the growth of Marxism-Leninism in particular? Finally, can we discern other variables in the history of each country that may account for the present differences among the three communist systems? These questions, of course, are complex and cannot be conclusively answered within the available space, but at least some suggestions can be advanced.

In the essays of this section, the traditional cultures of Russia, China, and Yugoslavia are briefly but succinctly described, and the cohesive and divisive forces at work in their pre-Communist societies are highlighted. For example, it is interesting to note that democratic traditions were lacking in all three countries. Instead, each government could be labeled as elitist-authoritarian structures in which the masses of people had little or no voice in the political decision-making process. To the majority of peasants the central government—represented by the emperor, tsar, or king—seemed as remote and awesome as heaven itself. A Chinese folk poem expresses what must have been the political sentiments of the common people in all three countries:

> We work when the sun rises,
> We rest when the sun sets.
> We dig wells for drink,
> We plow the land for food.
> What has the Emperor to do with us?

Nature, then, was the peasant's guide to life and, as such, nature prescribed a definite hierarchy of order: there were the strong that ruled, and the weak that were ruled. In Russia and China, it was believed that the select few who governed the many had been chosen by divine mandate. The coronation (itself a ceremony of deep religious significance and symbolism) and the many other ritualistic acts and ceremonies that a ruler was obliged to perform throughout his reign—a Russian tsar in particular, but a Chinese emperor as well—must have made the conscientious rulers acutely aware of the divine significance of their power and the accompanying responsibility. The lowly masses were expected to follow silently along, because it was taken for granted that they would not know anything about the rights and responsibilities of authority. By the end of the nineteenth century, as a result of the growth of education and the influence of foreign ideas, especially in the sciences, the mystique of the rulers of these countries had been considerably de-emphasized, though their power was still extensive.

In the various nations that today make up Yugoslavia, numerous kings and princes, too, wielded considerable power, though they possessed little of the aura of "divine right." Rather, many of them had gained power as a consequence of the decline of the Turkish or Austro-Hungarian empires, and they continued to retain their power by military might.

The age of democracy had little effect on the rulers of Russia, China, and the various South Slavic nations. All ruled their states with an autocratic hand and only token democratic reforms. The traditional governments of China, Russia, and Yugoslavia might be figuratively described as a pyramid: at the pinnacle stood the often remote and autocratic ruler; below him were a variety of ministers, counselors, representatives, magistrates, and others who made up a vast centralized bureaucratic structure; at the base were the millions of people who supported the upper levels through their sweat and their allegiance. Centuries of custom and tradition, years of training, and, of course, the military strength of the ruling class had combined to fashion a populace that was devotedly loyal to the ruler, and also apparently impelled to preserve the traditional ways for the sake of civilization itself. Therefore any individual who proposed to deviate from the customary way of doing things was considered dangerous not only to the smaller community in which he lived but even more so to the principles of society at large.

Conformity and resignation, then, earmarked the lives of the largely illiterate peasants in each of the three pre-communist countries before the twentieth century. The similarity of the lives of these peasant-farmers was due, in part, to their agricultural occupation, which was determined by the rhythm of the seasons, and which required that anyone gaining his living from the land do his arduous work at certain specified times of the year in order to insure good crops. But this conformity was imposed also by the harshness of subsistence living. The peasants of Russia, China, and southeastern Europe plodded through life, bodies bent over in the fields where they sowed and gathered in wealth for their lords and landlords, who in return might offer them some promise of security. Change for the peasant masses took such forms as release from serfdom, (for the Russian peasants in 1861) or the development of better agricultural tools so that the field work could be done more efficiently. Unfortunately for the many, change did not effect a release from illiteracy, disease, malnutrition, or the entrenched poverty that impeded them from altering their own situation. The peasant's world revolved around his land, his family, and his religion—in these he found his joy and happiness. Whoever would guarantee their security and continued sustenance could expect the peasants' support and following, but whoever endangered or abused these precious treasures provoked their wrath and enmity.

Peasant revolts occurred in all three countries. Particularly in the lands now constituting Yugoslavia, where a large variety of ethnic and national groups existed, internecine wars and political revolts were numerous. Toward the end of Turkish rule in the nineteenth century, especially, revolts and rebellions seemed to be endemic among the Slav peasants. Localism and division, though certainly present in China and Russia, seemed even more exaggerated in the Balkans because these states lacked both a strong central ruler and a cohesive, unifying philosophy.

In Russia and China, too, peasant uprisings occurred, but most of them were attempts to improve the harsh conditions around them or to replace an unusually incompetent or rapacious ruler. It appears that it was not until the nineteenth century that the peasants of China and Russia decided to strike at the traditional system itself by revolting.[1] By the end of that century the peasants had become even more rebellious as increasing numbers of people taxed the already overworked land, and the inroads of Western culture, especially industrialism and technology, challenged centuries-old ways and customs.

The impact of the West and its technology not only threatened the complacency and conformity of the peasants' lives but also endangered the entire traditional political pyramid. Western imperialism, bolstered by its modern industry and armored navy, exposed the decay and effeteness of the old regimes, whose ruling elite seemed unable to cope with the challenge of modernization. In China, for example, private enterprise had developed by the turn of the twentieth century, but the Confucianists continued to generate a deep mistrust of the business class, maintaining that merchants were parasites on the economy, who distracted the peasant from the worthy occupation of farming. Consequently, advocates of modernization and industrialization were suspect, and their ideas remained on the periphery of Chinese life.[2]

Russia, in contrast, had been successfully experimenting with technology and science for several decades before 1917: mines were opened, oil wells were drilled, and railroads were built. Russia, unlike China, seemed anxious to join the industrial age. But this promising movement was darkened by the very low wages of factory workers, their wretched living and working conditions, and the frequent incompetence of the ruling Tsar himself.[3] In any case, it would not be the disorganized proletariat out of the broader population that Marx had predicted would finally topple the old regime. The revolutionary spark resided in a chosen few.

In all three countries, what finally provoked the movement for sweeping change was the fact that by the beginning of the twentieth century the political, economic, and social conditions in Russia, China, and southeastern Europe had rapidly deteriorated. The crisis that ensued was the

---

[1]This will be discussed further in Section Three.

[2]See Albert Feuerwerker, *China's Early Industrialization* (Cambridge, Massachusetts: Harvard University Press, 1958) and Samuel C. Chu, *Reform in Modern China* (New York: Columbia University Press, 1965).

[3]Theodore H. Von Laue, *Sergei Witte and the Industrialization of Russia* (New York: Columbia University Press, 1963) and M. S. Miller, *The Economic Development of Russia, 1905–1914* (London: P. S. King and Son, Ltd., 1926).

clash between the inertia of the past and the impetus of change. The innovations sought included the following: the surrender of power by a few to the wishes and concerns of the majority, the redistribution of wealth and land to the impoverished majority, and modification of the basic political system and the philosophy that had sustained it. Indeed, those persuaded of the urgency of these measures vowed to accomplish them by force if necessary.

Thus far, in this introductory essay, we have emphasized the following common factors in the histories of Russia, China, and Yugoslavia: (1) a farming economy made up primarily of peasant-farmers, rather than an advanced industrial state composed of proletariat; (2) each had an elitist-authoritarian type of government administered by a ruler with almost absolute political power; (3) the peasants, making up 90 percent or more of the population, shared a hard life of poverty and conformity to a specified way of life; (4) despite the harshness of their life, the peasants shared a common interest in land, family, and their own forms of religion; (5) internal decay and ossification of the traditional system were heightened and more sharply exposed by the incursion of the Western Powers and the subsequent impact of industrialization and modernization. These common features aside, the three countries have distinct cultural heritages, each of which is elucidated by the readings in this section.

In "The Russian Legacy" Herbert McClosky and John E. Turner begin by suggesting that although a given system of communism cannot be understood apart from Marxian ideology, neither can it be understood apart from its own history and cultural heritage. The authors examine the traditional absolutism of the Russian Tsar and the lack of individualism and freedom among the Russian populace—characteristics that have counterparts in Chinese and Balkan history. Also described are three special cultural features that are unique to Russia. The first of these unique characteristics was the existence of serfdom; though the landlord system in China and the Balkan kingdoms often provided the same conditions for the peasants of those countries—excessive land rents and inherent poverty—the Russian serf, before 1861, could find no respite. Unlike his Chinese or South Slavic counterpart who could move (though with difficulty) to another part of the region or country for a new start, the Russian peasant remained tied to a landowner and his land, no matter how much he suffered. Though he might take the drastic step and revolt when the situation became too unbearable, such uprisings were against one's immediate ills and antagonists, rather than efforts to uproot the Tsar and the traditional system.

The second characteristic, the Russian *mir*, as described in "The Russian Legacy" has some interesting parallels to some periods of Soviet communism. The *mir* was a communal institution that was in general an extremely conservative, if not reactionary, force in Russian life. As McClosky and Turner point out, there are some interesting parallels between the *mir* and certain stages of Soviet communism, but they also remind us that early Communists were deceived by the analogies they thought they had perceived between the two, and that therefore the influence of the *mir* must be examined carefully. In fact, rather than fostering the development of communism after the Revolution of 1917, the *mir* often proved resistant to change and had to be eliminated.

One of the cultural values the *mir* did foster and sought to preserve was the third characteristic unique to Russian heritage—the religious nature of the people. Russian religious expression ranged from the majestic pomp of the Russian Orthodox Church, which was synonymous with the state creed, to the mysterious and superstitious cults that varied from locality to locality. Whatever one's particular conviction happened to be, religion was apparently so strongly rooted in the Russian personality that one wonders whether an ideology that espouses atheism can become, even in the course of time, as deeply embedded?

In "The Chinese Pattern," John K. Fairbank, the dean of American scholars on China, suggests that the traditions and social mores of China's past still present formidable challenges to the present Communist government in Peking: the abiding respect the Chinese people formerly had toward the family and the once ubiquitous influence of the scholar gentry are two examples. Fairbank suggests that the institutions of family and gentry jointly safeguarded the ancient values—agriculture, the classics, Confucian ethics—and provided the mortar that gave China its long, cohesive history. In spite of periods of great hardship, caused by famines, civil war, or internal uprisings, the Chinese culture survived and was even renewed, largely owing to these loyal guardians of the system. The gentry, the family, and the central government were conservative forces that collaborated to preserve the traditional system and the philosophy in which it was rooted.

Ironically enough, it was these same forces in Chinese history that helped open the door for the Communists' successful attainment of power. Mao Tse-tung and his followers have labeled the traditional Chinese family, gentry, and government as reactionaries who strove to preserve widespread illiteracy, the unequal division of land and wealth, and the elitist system that benefited a few rather than the many. The relationships between these institutions and the Communist system that replaced them will be examined in greater detail in Section Three.

Perhaps the most striking feature of Yugoslavia's political and cultural history, as discussed in "The Yugoslav Setting," is that the six Slavic republics of Serbia, Croatia, Slovenia, Bosnia-Hercegovina, Montenegro, and Macedonia were a colorful mosaic of culture patterns, language groups, and established mores. Gary K. Bertsch and George Zaninovich point out that not only was this variety a challenge to past attempts to attain unity and centralized rule, but also that it remains a complex problem for the present Communist government administered by Tito and will probably continue to be one for his successor. Though the Communists skillfully incorporated the previous attempts at unification to strengthen their own efforts to achieve unity, the possibility remains that it was the Second World War, and not agreement among the six republics, that was the key to the Communists' initial success. Consequently the following question is yet to be answered: how successful have the Communists been in persuading or forcing traditionally antagonistic groups to lay aside their differences and divisive pride in order to build an enduring unified state?

In conclusion, then, as we examine the cultural heritages of these three diverse Communist systems, we will want to ask ourselves which traditions have been eradicated by the new system, which have in some way been reinforced, and what the effects of these changes have been on the uniqueness and vitality of each culture.

3

The Russian Legacy

Herbert McClosky and John E. Turner

If the Soviet system cannot be understood apart from the influence of Marxian ideology, neither can it be understood apart from its Russian heritage. The Bolshevik leaders made their revolution in the name of international communism, and they believed that they were making a complete break with tsarist society. But recognition of the fact that the Bolshevik revolution was, after all, a *Russian* revolution is essential to any analysis of the Soviet Union.

To some extent the nature of every revolution is determined by the society that gives rise to it. The new order it establishes is never completely free of the old order it replaces. Ancient cultures are not easily extinguished, and no society, however revolutionary, can escape from carrying forward some of the traditions, habits, and patterns of organization of the previous social order. Once transplanted in the new society, the customs of the past tend to persist and to reinforce themselves. They are known and familiar and often adaptable to the purposes of the revolutionary government. In the case of Russia, we shall see that in many respects the new Soviet society closely parallels traditional tsarist patterns.

Origins of Absolutism

Geography placed Russia on the boundary between Europe and the Orient. At first her history gave promise that a society along Western lines might emerge. By the ninth century the Slavic principality of Kiev, a forerunner of the Russian state, had come into existence, and the decentralized nature of its government enabled the trading centers and local principalities to enjoy a measure of autonomy. While the political system could hardly be characterized as democratic, it was more aristocratic than absolutist, and a feudal pattern not unlike that of the West began to develop. Although the Kiev state turned to the Orthodox Christianity of Byzantium rather than to the religion of Rome, it maintained contact, peaceful and otherwise, with its European neighbors.[1]

From Herbert McClosky and John E. Turner, *The Soviet Dictatorship* (New York: McGraw-Hill, 1960), pp. 21–28. [Reprinted with permission from the publisher.]

[1]For the Kiev period see V. O. Kliuchevsky, *A History of Russia,* E. P. Dutton & Co., Inc., New York, 1911, vol. I, chaps. 5–12.

Discord among the principalities and a series of foreign wars weakened the Kiev state, and the Kievan period came to an end in the thirteenth century, following repeated invasions by Eastern tribes. Russia eventually fell under the control of the Asiatic Mongols or Tartars, whose domination lasted for more than two centuries (1238–1452). During this period Russian contact with the West was virtually cut off, and Russian life was predominantly influenced by Oriental culture. The Mongols lived in Russia as conquerors, bringing with them an Asiatic pattern of central absolutist government which left its imprint upon later Russian regimes.

Destined to cast out the invader and to conquer all of Russia, the principality of Moscow emerged during the period of Tartar control as the nucleus of the new Russian state. The victory of Moscow resulted from several factors: its strategic location, the ruthlessness of its princes in the struggle for power, and their opportunistic dealings with the Mongols. Favored both by geography and by its conquerors, Moscow was able to extend its authority over rival principalities and to gain the support of nobles and church authorities who sought refuge in its territory. As the Moscow state grew in strength, its princes became the symbol of Russian nationality and of the Orthodox faith. Eventually they were able to establish a dynasty that was to prevail over all competitors.

The departure of the Mongols did not result in a reduction of absolutism. Not only did the pattern of authoritarian control persist, but it was strengthened by the intervention of the Orthodox Church, whose leaders soon declared the Moscow princes to be governors by divine right. After the fall in 1453 of Constantinople, the old center of orthodoxy, Moscow was proclaimed the guardian of the true Christian faith and was ultimately designated the "Third Rome." To the Moscow rulers was assigned the task of "saving" mankind through the preservation and extension of "true Christianity." Thus the acts of the Moscow autocrat came to be regarded as divinely inspired and beyond human challenge.

The centralization of state power was further reinforced by military policies of the Moscow rulers. Imperialist ambitions and the rivalries of hostile monarchs kept them continually at war, and this in turn impelled them to expand their authority over internal affairs. Independent power was not even permitted to the nobility, who were pressed into the service of the autocrat and whose position became contingent upon that service. Thus, in contrast with Britain, for example, there never developed a nobility with rights against the central authority. Likewise the mass of the population was required to give service directly either to the state or to the aristocracy—a condition which encouraged the rise of serfdom. Facing the costly burden of incessant war, the state also extended its power over the economy. To facilitate the collection of taxes and the requisitioning of military supplies, it fixed men both in their locale and in their service. These encroachments by the state hastened the development of a hierarchical society based upon "orders" or estates, each with its set of obligations and privileges. In its many military encounters with the Tartars, Poles, Turks, Swedes, Ukrainians, and others, the Russian state annexed vast territories, eventually becoming the largest country in the world. In recognition of the expanding power of the Moscow rulers, Ivan IV (the Terrible) adopted in 1547 the title of Tsar (emperor).

Nature of the Tsarist Autocracy

The main outlines of tsarist autocracy were already established by the sixteenth century. Except for occasional modifications, especially by Peter the Great (1682–1725), the pattern of government remained fairly stable until the nineteenth century.[2] Its most striking feature was the single and omnipotent authority of the Tsar. The theory upon which his power rested left no room for the principle of accountability; in law, as well as in practice, he was answerable to no man. The Tsar was mystically united with God and the people, a union which justified his absolute leadership in the fulfillment of Russia's destiny. Described as the "Little Father," God's appointed ruler on earth, he wielded an authority which was regarded as sacrosanct. He had jurisdiction over the spiritual as well as the secular and was the defender of the faith as well as the nation. In exercising his power, he was not merely a titular sovereign but an actual ruler who personally directed the affairs of the state.

The scope of state power naturally gave rise to a vast bureaucracy, but like all governing agencies, it was entirely subordinate to the Tsar. Rudimentary legislative bodies, based primarily on the landowning classes, came into existence from time to time, but they had little power beyond advising the crown. The monarch's authority reached even to the level of the village. Of course, the power of the central government was limited in practice by distance and by the lack of effective communication. Many local problems were, by custom or necessity, handled by the peasant communes and the provincial nobility without reference to the central authorities. Nevertheless the Tsar and his ministers did not encourage local autonomy, and effective institutions of local government did not develop until the nineteenth century.

The Tsar's power was limited only in the way that all autocratic power is limited. He was dependent upon subordinates to carry out his will, and he could not entirely disregard the customary rights and privileges of the various classes. Occasionally he had to grant concessions to such powerful groups as the landed nobility and the church. These limitations could not be enforced by law, however, as there were no regular procedures for delimiting the Tsar's prerogatives or for redressing grievances against him.

No area of life was secure against tsarist intervention, the range of controls resembling in some respects that of a modern dictatorship. Except for the church, no association could exist without the government's permission. Freedom of speech, press, and other basic liberties were either absent or feebly exercised. The state controlled the movement of its people through such devices as police registration and internal passports. The regime demanded conformity and by a system of censorship and police controls sought to prevent alien ideas from taking root.

Under tsarism there was little opportunity for individuals or voluntary associations to influence public policy. Not until the closing years of the regime were there political parties, elections, and other forms of popular participation. The state was often the principal initiator of economic activity, building railways and factories and encouraging domestic and foreign capital to invest in favored projects. The state also farmed great areas of land and managed various types of industry. It was the largest single employer, directing a huge bureaucracy and commanding the involuntary services of many of its subjects, including state serfs. Even those areas of the economy left to private operation were expected to gear their activities to the state's military and economic needs. Thus,

---

[2]On the nature and development of the tsarist system, see G. Fedotov, "Russia and Freedom," *Review of Politics,* January, 1946, pp. 12–36. Interesting observations on tsarist Russia in the nineteenth century by a French traveler are to be found in Phyllis P. Kohler (ed. and trans.), *The Journals of the Marquis de Custine: Journey for Our Time,* Farrar, Straus and Cudahy, Inc., New York, 1951.

under tsarism the state grew at the expense of its citizens, establishing a pattern of absolutism upon which the Communists were later to build.

Social Structure under Tsarism

Throughout its history, tsarist Russia was a rigidly stratified society. At the top of the social pyramid were the landed nobility, the upper clergy, and state officials, comprising in the late eighteenth century less than 3 percent of the male population. Further down the pyramid were merchants, artisans, and urban workers (approximately 3 percent of the population), while at the base were the peasants (over 90 percent of the Russian people), engaged chiefly in rural but not exclusively agricultural occupations.[3] Political and economic power was centered in the nobility, who, because of their hereditary privileges, education, control of the land, and style of life, stood as a class apart. Although the noblemen were never able to gain independent power, they held important positions in civil and military administration and were largely responsible for governing the millions of serfs attached to the landed estates. They enjoyed a wide range of privileges, including a unique status in law and a special voice in governing local affairs. In the eighteenth century, they were legally freed from obligatory service to the state, although they continued to claim such service from their serfs. While the nobility and gentry were in many respects a leisure class, many of them were narrowly cultured, exhibiting the cruelty common to many slave-holding classes. There were others, however, more cultivated and humane, who felt guilty about serfdom and their own extraordinary privileges. To them tsarism became repugnant, but most noblemen remained loyal to the system until the end.

The middle classes developed slowly in Imperial Russia. The landed aristocrats were generally hostile toward the merchants, and the system of state-directed enterprise hindered the growth of small-scale entrepreneurs. Moreover, the shortage of free labor held back the development of a capitalist economy of the sort found in the West. The merchants were further harassed by special tax levies from which the higher orders of society were exempt.[4]

At the bottom of the social hierarchy were the peasants who, by virtue of their overwhelming numbers, influenced the character of tsarist society. By the sixteenth century most of the peasants had been reduced to serfdom and were in service to the landed nobility or the state.[5] The authority of the landowner over his serfs was virtually without restriction. He could demand compulsory labor; he could punish or sell them, control their marriages, or banish them to remote regions. Many serfs were treated well, of course, but many more suffered brutality and privation. Peasant discontent mounted steadily and uprisings against the landlords became increasingly frequent. By the time serfdom was abolished in 1861, many Russian leaders had become convinced that reform from above was necessary to prevent revolution from below.

Serfdom left its strong imprint on tsarist society. It condemned the peasant to poverty and ignorance and engendered habits of subservience which reinforced the power of

---

[3]See Alexander Kornilov, *Modern Russian History,* Alfred A. Knopf, Inc., New York, 1916, vol. I, pp. 25–26. For general treatment of the tsarist social system see Maxime Kovalevsky, *Russian Political Institutions,* University of Chicago Press, Chicago, 1902, chap. 2, and Geroid T. Robinson, *Rural Russia under the Old Regime,* Longmans, Green & Co., Inc., New York, 1932, chaps. 1 and 2.

[4]Kornilov, *Modern Russian History,* vol. I, pp. 30–32.

[5]See Robinson, *Rural Russia under the Old Regime,* chaps. 3 and 4.

the autocracy, prolonging its life. The peasants were prey to primitive and superstitious beliefs, looking forward to the day of "black reconstruction" when they would be delivered from their misery, avenged against the landowners, and given possession of the land.

However, the serf's anger against the landlord and the injustices of the tsarist order did not extend to the Tsar himself. The monarch remained for them a "father figure," in whose authority and justice they trusted implicitly. They thought of him as a "savior," through whom the earthly millennium would be established. It was a common belief among the peasants that the "Little Father" wanted to relieve their suffering and had previously decreed their emancipation but that his wishes were being frustrated by his advisers and the landlords.

Serfdom also contributed to the general backwardness of the Russian economy and culture. With so many people employed as serfs, the nation was slow to take advantage of the technology and economic organization developed in the West. In agriculture, serfdom helped to perpetuate ancient, wasteful methods of farming, such as the three-field system and the practice of dividing the land into long, narrow strips. Furthermore, it deprived the nation of much potential talent. A population that remained largely illiterate, pitifully unlearned, and with little opportunity for initiative, could hardly be expected to create an advanced culture. Recognition that it was an inefficient system eventually helped to bring about its abolition.

An analysis of the social structure of Imperial Russia would be incomplete without mentioning the *mir,* or commune, into which the majority of the peasants were organized.[6] The mir was a communal form of village association through which the peasants regulated their mutual affairs. Communes varied in size but were usually composed of a group of families who had hereditary rights to membership. Land holdings, pastures, forests, etc., were owned cooperatively, but cultivation of the land was done on a family basis. The mir allocated strips of land to each family, periodically redistributing them to give everyone a chance at the best fields. The form of political organization was patriarchal, the heads of the various families constituting the ruling group. This group decided when to redistribute the land, which fields to leave idle, and when to begin planting and harvesting the crops.

In the nineteenth century, many Russian intellectuals defended the mir as a type of peasant communism superior to any form of social organization developed in the West. They thought of the mir as the natural unit upon which to build the communal society of the future. The mir did give a collectivist cast to much of Russian village life. But it also served to forestall important changes that would have enabled the peasant to improve his position and the economy to become more productive. In reprospect, the mir appears to have been an inefficient, custom-ridden type of organization which often prevented the introduction of more efficient farming methods and held back the peasant in his individual development.

Membership in the commune also made the peasant more accessible to state control. The central authorities held the mir responsible for the collection of taxes in the village, and since it was forced to pay the assessments of absent or delinquent members, the mir naturally discouraged emigration. Many peasants did flee the commune, of course, migrating to the frontier or to the city, though usually without the approval of the

---

[6]See Maxime Kovalevsky, *Modern Customs and Ancient Laws of Russia,* David Nutt, London, 1891, chap. 3.

government. The system of internal passports—later adopted by the Soviet government—was often used to prevent the unauthorized migration of peasants from their villages.

Like the Soviet collective farm, the mir served the state as an agency of control. It lent stability to agrarian life and made the patterns of land tenure more secure. By retaining the forms of collectivist life, the mir impeded the progress of Western individualist ideas and contributed to the popularity of communal ideologies in Russia.

The Consecrated State

Political power in Russia rested upon religious as well as social and economic institutions. From the Orthodox Church the autocracy received both political support and doctrinal inspiration.[7]

Christianity came to Russia, not primarily from Western Europe, but from Byzantium, the holy center of which was Constantinople. Unlike Western monarchs, the Byzantine emperors had refused to tolerate an independent papacy, and after a series of struggles they established their personal supremacy over the church as well as the state. They considered themselves to be simultaneously emperors and popes, divinely chosen to rule both the spiritual and temporal realms. Under their control, the Eastern church accommodated itself to subordinate status as an arm of the state, developing a tradition of service to the imperial power from which it never escaped.

At first the introduction of Eastern orthodoxy into Russia did not produce a parallel theocratic pattern. During the Kievan period and for a time under the Tartars, the church continued to give its loyalty to the Byzantine emperors rather than to the Russian princes. For many Russians, Byzantium, not Russia, was the true Christian state and the seat of culture. However, as Tartar control tightened, the links of the Russian church with Constantinople grew weaker, and with the rise of Moscow, religious leaders turned to the Russian princes for support. Following the fall of Constantinople, the Eastern church was moved to Russia. Moscow came to be regarded as the "Third Rome," its princes inheriting the power that formerly belonged to Byzantium. Orthodoxy now served the Russian tsars as it had once ministered to the Byzantine emperors. The attachment of the church to Moscow stimulated the tsars to fashion their power in the theocratic and messianic image of Constantinople. Thus Russia became a Christian state in the Byzantine style—a fact of major importance for its subsequent development.

Orthodoxy in Russia was a highly dogmatic religion—formal, mystical, and elaborately ritualistic.[8] It considered itself the "true church" and regarded its adherents as divinely chosen to carry on God's work. Conformity was central to its entire outlook, deviation being looked upon as sinful. Its authority was thought, moreover, to extend to all aspects of life, the temporal as well as the sacred. Orthodoxy was a communal religion, deemphasizing the individual conscience. God's truth resided with the congregation and could be shared by the individual only as a member of the congregation. These characteristics, together with its extreme emphasis on suffering and the renunciation of the world as means to salvation, contributed to the development of a narrow and messianic culture.

---

[7]See Nicolas Berdyaev, *The Origin of Russian Communism,* Charles Scribner's Sons, New York, 1937, pp. 1–15; Hans Kohn, "The Permanent Mission," *Review of Politics,* July, 1948, pp. 267–289.

[8]Thomas G. Masaryk, *The Spirit of Russia,* The Macmillan Company, New York, 1919, vol. II, chap. 16, pp. 487–491.

The identification of tsarism with Orthodoxy produced among many Orthodox Russians the sense of being "chosen" or "appointed." They thought of themselves as a consecrated people in a consecrated—and hence justifiably autocratic—state. In the words of Berdyaev:[9] "The consecrated kingdom is always a dictatorship of a world outlook, always requires Orthodoxy, always suppresses heretics. Totalitarianism, the demand for wholeness of faith as the basis of the kingdom, fits in with the deep religious and social instincts of the [Russian] people."

The union of Orthodoxy with tsarism had the effect of intensifying Russian nationalism. The Pan-Slavic policy pursued by the Russian leaders, for example, was to some extent an expression of their messianic outlook and of their desire to create a great Slavic empire under a single ordained ruler. Russification reflected the same impulse in its attempt to impose Russian customs, institutions, and language on non-Russian peoples. Orthodoxy alone cannot explain the spread of nationalism, of course, but it contributed to it through its tendency to identify human salvation with Russian destiny.

The Orthodox religion seems also to have influenced the utopian outlook which has been so prominent in Russian politics and literature. Under the spell of Orthodoxy, the Russians became a passive and mystical people, inured to suffering. They endured suffering because of the promise of salvation, placing their faith in mystical rather than natural processes, in millennial hopes rather than concrete possibilities. Many anticipated divine intervention; others dreamed of a sudden, violent overturning by revolution. A mystical faith in ultimate deliverance from the ills of the world seems to have pervaded all levels of Russian culture. Bolshevism came to exhibit many of these same tendencies, thus combining two messianic and utopian strains, the Marxist and the Russian.

Orthodoxy was also in part responsible for the cultural backwardness of Russia. Throughout Russian history the Eastern church remained essentially medieval in doctrine and outlook, extolling ancient forms of social organization and perpetuating superstitious beliefs.[10] Its emphasis on submission discouraged the masses from taking effective action on their own behalf. Orthodoxy was a force for the preservation of traditional modes, helping to create an environment that was hostile to science and reason, to commerce and industry. It showed little concern for the welfare of the masses; many leading clerics were actually opposed to the abolition of serfdom. As late as the closing years of the nineteenth century, Orthodox leaders like Konstantin Pobedonostsev actively resisted measures, such as popular elections or a free press, that would have led to more enlightened government.[11] The church never doubted that the Tsar and the Holy Synod were wiser than the people and that it was the sacred obligation of the masses to obey the central power.

The Russian state, supported by orthodoxy, regarded itself as not only different from but superior to the nations of the West, which had adulterated Christianity and succumbed to false doctrines. Many Russians believed that they had achieved a unique culture which should not be contaminated by Western influences. Thus orthodoxy combined with geography to isolate Russia from the mainstreams of Western thought and development, producing attitudes of insularity and suspicion. Many of the early tsars discouraged contact with the people of other nations, and Russian citizens were fre-

---

[9]Berdyaev, *Origin of Russian Communism,* p. 172.

[10]See B. H. Sumner, *A Short History of Russia,* Reynal & Hitchcock, Inc., New York, 1943, part 4.

[11]See, for example, the analysis of Pobedonostsev's political philosophy in Masaryk, *Spirit of Russia,* pp. 197–207.

quently prevented from traveling abroad. Except for brief lapses, a strong distrust of foreigners became characteristic of Russian life.

East and West

Geography, politics, and religion had combined to isolate Russia from the West, but the separation was never complete. Especially after the seventeenth century, Western ideas were known to the ruling and educated classes of Russia. The effect of this contact was to produce among many Russian leaders a sense of the backwardness of their own country. Often this feeling of inferiority expressed itself in the form of hostility toward Western ideas and institutions, although, in fact, the Russian attitude toward Europe seems to have been somewhat ambivalent. While disparaging the West, Russian leaders emulated European practices in their effort to catch up with and overtake their neighbors.

The Western impact on Russia was especially pronounced in the early eighteenth century during the reign of Peter the Great.[12] Driven by military needs and the desire to build a great empire, Peter introduced a number of advanced Western institutions. He initiated conscription and fashioned an army on the European model. He sponsored new industries, constructed factories, and welcomed technical experts from the West to assist in developing the economy. He expanded education, established trade schools, and encouraged scientific work. He also reorganized his government and introduced Western practices into administration. To secure manpower for these ambitious efforts, he opened the door to talent from the lower classes, basing his appointments on service to the state rather than social origin. On the whole, Peter's reform program brought Russia into closer contact with Europe and marked an important break in the continuity of ancient Russian institutions.

Some of the later monarchs, particularly Catherine the Great (1762–1796) and Alexander II (1855–1881), carried the process of westernization even further.[13] Catherine, who followed with great interest the work of the French Encyclopedists, helped disseminate the ideas of the Enlightenment, although her government's policies hardly corresponded with her professed beliefs. In the 1860s Alexander introduced a number of social and political reforms that were markedly Western in nature. Obviously, Russia could not ignore the economic changes, the political revolutions, and the intellectual movements that were taking place in Western Europe during the eighteenth and nineteenth centuries.

But imitation of isolated ideas and practices was not sufficient to transform Russia into a society of the Western type. The great developments that were so significant in shaping the culture of the Western world were felt in Russia only as tremors. The Renaissance, the Reformation, the Industrial Revolution, the development of free-enterprise capitalism, the growth of science, the rise of democracy—these did not wholly bypass Russia, but they had little effect on the essential character of Russian life. In the West these developments had greatly modified the medieval patterns, giving rise to a preponderantly secular and urban culture based on science, commerce, advanced technology, and an ever-increasing division of labor. Intellectual and artistic life flourished, the social order became more fluid, and new classes emerged. Habits of toleration and the "open mind" were encouraged, and individualism was given wider scope. The

---

[12]See Kovalevsky, *Russian Political Institutions*, chap. 4.
[13]*Ibid.*, chaps. 5–9.

masses came to play an increasingly greater role in government, the economy, education, and the arts. Despite variations from country to country, life in the West came to be distinguished by a widened range of possibilities for the individual.

In Russia, on the other hand, there were few comparable developments. There had been a schism in the church, but no Reformation. There had been sporadic uprisings, such as the peasant revolts led by Stenka Razin in 1667 and by E. I. Pugachev in 1772, but until 1905 no political revolution had altered the system of power in any basic way. Before the nineteenth century there were few important developments in science, technology, and economic organization; not until then did Russia begin to approach the West in the quality and quantity of its intellectual and artistic output. Even with the appearance of large-scale capitalism, the economy remained essentially handicraft and agricultural. Until the declining years of the empire, neither the *bourgeoisie* nor the proletariat was large enough to be politically significant. Comparatively few cities existed, and even these were not highly industrialized. Throughout most of its history, tsarist Russia remained predominantly agrarian in economy and culture, rigidly stratified, slow-changing, and narrowly restricted in the opportunities afforded for the development of the individual. Liberal attitudes were held by relatively few and had only slight effect on the pattern of Russian life. Habits of rationalism, toleration, and free enquiry never developed on a large scale. The democratic conception of man as a rational being, free to pursue his own ends in his own way, was not deeply rooted in Russian thought. Instead, a theocratic order identified the purposes of the individual with those of the state and proclaimed authority and obedience to be among the highest human values.

Wherever Western ideas did influence Russian life, they tended to bring about the disintegration of established forms and to disrupt the integrity of Russian culture. The rapid growth of capitalism in the nineteenth century, for example, expanded the middle and working classes, strengthened the desire for parliamentary government, gave rise to Marxist revolutionary parties, weakened the village commune, and reduced the economic power of the landed nobility. The influence of Western science and technology gave a secular and materialist cast to intellectual efforts in many spheres, unsettling the modes that Orthodox theology had imposed on philosophy and ethics. Wherever the West impinged on Russian culture, it challenged existing values and offered new ones as substitutes. The eventual breakup of the tsarist order may thus be attributed in some degree to the inroads of Westernism.

In spite of this impact, East and West remained, as they do even today, widely separated and to a considerable extent alien to each other. Despite its Marxist roots, the Communist society erected by the Bolsheviks must be understood as deriving in part from a Russian tradition that was fundamentally at variance with Western values and habits. It is impossible to state accurately how much influence the Russian tradition has had on the Soviet system, for historical influence is difficult to measure. Nevertheless, Soviet society parallels so many of the traditional Russian modes that the influence of the latter appears to be significant. Among these parallels, the separation from and antagonism toward the West is one of the most striking.

Modifications in the Tsarist System

Although the tsarist system was not overthrown until 1917, signs of its disintegration were already visible in the nineteenth century. With the spread of Western influence, the tempo of Russian life was quickened and liberal ideas, long resisted, began to take hold more firmly. The abolition of serfdom and the growth of capitalism introduced significant social changes and led to demands for the modification of the political order. As censorship was relaxed, voices of protest were raised in the arts and education, and intellectual life took on new vigor. These stirrings gave promise of a sharp break with the past.

Abolition of Serfdom.   The emancipation of the peasants by Alexander II in 1861 was a dramatic sign that the integrity of the old order could no longer be maintained.[14] With the growth of capitalism and the demand for free labor, serfdom had become both an economic and political liability.

Not that emancipation was uniformly beneficial, for some peasants found themselves worse off than before. As a class they were allocated more land, but they were also faced with new taxes and with the burden of having to pay a redemption to their former landlords. To meet their indebtedness many were forced to continue in the service of their old masters. Some, owing to the complexities of the emancipation edict, had their holdings reduced and were compelled to lease additional fields from the landlords at exorbitant rates. Nor did emancipation completely revise the system of orders. The peasants were subject, as before, to special legislation, including a higher rate of taxation. Many of them were still attached to the mir, which remained collectively responsible for the tax liabilities of the individual member and therefore restricted his mobility.[15]

Some of these difficulties were alleviated in the decades following emancipation. The Stolypin reforms, beginning in 1906, were designed to free the peasant from the mir and to establish a class of independent smallholders. Peasant banks made loans to those who wanted to own their farms, and many peasants were allowed to leave agriculture and to seek employment in the cities. In 1905 redemption payments were canceled, reducing the peasants' financial burden. Thus by 1917 Russian agriculture had shifted toward an economy based primarily on individual peasant holdings.

There still remained, however, cause for discontent. In many areas rapid population growth created a serious land shortage, increasing peasant resentment toward the gentry who possessed holdings. With the growth of a capitalist money economy, rural communities lacking cash found themselves at a disadvantage in the marketplace. Many peasants felt themselves exploited by an emerging class of wealthier peasants (*kulaks*), whose energy and shrewdness enabled them to take advantage of the new opportunities to increase their holdings and gain domination over their fellows. At the time of the revolution, the Russian peasants still held the lowest place in the social pyramid. They remained subject to the arbitrary authority of government agents sent to supervise their villages; they were inadequately represented in the newly established parliament; and they continued to suffer discriminatory legislation. Considering these grievances, it is not surprising that, despite the agricultural reforms, many peasants were willing to make the most of the revolution when it came.

Alexander's Political Reforms.   Other changes accompanied the abolition of serfdom, as Alexander II, stung by defeat in the Crimean War, decreed a number of reforms intended to revitalize his country. He relaxed censorship, enlarged freedom of movement, and reduced restrictions on commerce. The courts, previously subject to administrative

[14]Robinson, *Rural Russia under the Old Regime,* chaps. 5–7.

[15]Kornilov, *Modern Russian History,* vol. II, pp. 65–69, 119–122, 196–206.

control, were made more independent and their procedures were modernized. Citizens were guaranteed the right of counsel, equality before the law, and public trial by jury. Alexander also granted a larger measure of autonomy to the universities and extended opportunities for popular education.

An outstanding reform of this period was the introduction of a system of local councils (*zemstvos*) designed to allow more self-government to the inhabitants of the rural areas. Although the peasants were represented on these bodies, the zemstvos were dominated by the gentry and professional classes, who were favored by the election laws. Nevertheless, the councils became key agencies for improving the welfare of the people and for stimulating the growth of progressive opinion. Utilizing the powers accorded them by the Tsar, they built schools, libraries, and hospitals, improved sanitation methods, undertook programs of public works, and administered to the poor. The zemstvos also sought to educate the peasants in modern methods of agriculture, establishing model farms for instruction and experimentation. They extended credit to agricultural producers and made farm implements available. Most important, they provided an opportunity for the development and expression of public opinion and served as a training ground for political leadership. It was in these local councils that liberal attitudes were fostered and hopes for constitutional government were engendered. Despite limited powers and inadequate budgets, the zemstvos became, in the decades prior to the Revolution of 1905, an influential political force in Russia—a significant break in the absolutist pattern of tsarist organization.

Growth of Capitalism.   Equally fundamental in altering the character of tsarist society were developments associated with the growth of modern capitalism. In the period between emancipation and World War I, industrial expansion in Russia rivaled that of the United States after the Civil War and Germany after 1870. Production increased especially in such basic industries as coal, metallurgy, oil, machinery, and textiles. Industrial output between 1862 and 1882 was approximately doubled, and from 1885 to 1913 the index of industrial production rose from 20.57 to 100.[16] In the 1890s, the rise averaged 8 percent each year. In a little more than a decade the rate of railway construction increased fivefold.

Much of the new industrial activity was sponsored by the state which granted subsidies and tariff protection to Russian capitalists. Foreshadowing the Communists, the tsarist state became an entrepreneur on a vast scale, building and operating railroads, factories, and banks. To help finance its industrial program it invited foreign capitalists to invest in Russian enterprises. These state-sponsored activities had the effect of hindering the growth of a powerful and independent *bourgeoisie*. While many capitalists became critical of the tsarist system and yearned for constitutional government, they never gained sufficient strength to become a dominant class or to achieve their political objectives fully. This helps to explain why the Bolsheviks rather than a bourgeois party seized control of Russia after tsarism was overthrown.

The expansion of industrial capitalism brought Russia into closer contact with Europe, exposing her still further to Western ideas. This contact also had the effect, ironically, of intensifying Russian competition with the West. Impelled by xenophobia and by their sensitivity to Russia's backwardness, her leaders were driven by a desire to catch up with Europe—to compress within a few decades the scientific and technolog-

[16]Alexander Gerschenkron, "The Rate of Industrial Growth in Russia since 1885," *The Tasks of Economic History* (suppl. 7), 1947, pp. 145–146.

ical progress that had taken other nations centuries to achieve. Drawing upon European experience, Russia was able to leap quickly from an economy still medieval in many respects to one employing the most advanced methods of production. Thus the Russian rulers, like their Soviet successors, were encouraged in their ambition to overtake and outstrip Western economic achievements.

But rapid industrialization could not be accomplished without seriously disrupting Russian society. The shift in economic power from the rural areas to the cities weakened the nobility and impoverished many peasants. Industrial pressures unsettled life in the mir, encouraging the ascendancy of the kulak class and driving farm laborers into the ranks of the proletariat. The growth of a class of city workers, badly exploited and shaken loose from many of their traditional ties, created new problems of housing, education, and wages for which the government was poorly prepared. Even the middle class, despite its predominant loyalty to the monarch, was in outlook and style of life only partially integrated into tsarist society. Thus the Revolutions of 1905 and 1917 were to some extent expressions of the social disorganization resulting from the rise of capitalism.

These economic and social changes also stimulated the development of liberal institutions. The old system of estates began to decay as social classes became more fluid. The 1905 Revolution, as we shall see, achieved modest concessions in the direction of parliamentary government, along with greater freedom to speak, to publish, and to organize political parties, trade unions, and cooperatives. Imperial Russia, especially after 1860, was thus moving, albeit slowly, in the direction of an "open" society, enlarging opportunities for individual development.

These advances did not always proceed smoothly, however, for the tsarist government remained on most scores traditional and narrow in outlook. The later tsars, especially Alexander III (1881–1892), were unable to accommodate themselves to the spirit of the liberal reforms or to the rapid changes in the economy and social structure. They endeavored as much as possible to govern in the spirit of "Autocracy, Orthodoxy, and Nationalism," by which the tsars had ruled for centuries. But the foundations of tsarism had become so weakened in the last decades of the empire that continuation in its old form appears to have been unlikely, even without a revolution.

Constitutional Reform

Although attempts had been made from time to time to modify the forms of tsarist government, no significant break in the absolutist pattern occurred until the Revolution of 1905. Rudimentary legislative bodies to advise the Tsar had come into existence as early as the sixteenth century, but none of these had ever succeeded in making inroads on the system of absolute monarchy. The autocrat remained until the twentieth century the single source of political authority, sharing *functions* but not *powers* with the other branches of government.[17]

The Revolution of 1905[18] forced Tsar Nicholas II to recognize the principle of limited government. To halt the uprising he proclaimed a set of Fundamental Laws (or constitution), establishing a national parliament with legal power to share in the lawmaking

[17]For a description of the political institutions of the first three Romanov Tsars, see Kovalevsky, *Russian Political Institutions,* chap. 3.

[18]See Kornilov, *Modern Russian History,* vol. II, pp. 293–336; George Vernadsky, *History of Russia,* Yale University Press, New Haven, Conn., 1951, pp. 183–192.

process. The members of the lower house, or *Duma,* were popularly elected under a restricted franchise; half the delegates to the upper house, or *State Council,* were appointed by the Tsar himself, while the remaining members were chosen by the church, the nobility, the universities, and the provincial councils.

The new parliament was authorized to initiate and adopt legislation and especially to control the budget. In practice, however, its powers were severely limited, for most bills were drawn up and introduced by the Council of Ministers, and the Duma was prevented from considering important budgetary matters. Only the monarch, moreover, could initiate changes in the Fundamental Laws. No legislation could be enacted without the approval of the Tsar and the State Council, a body he easily dominated. He also controlled the sessions of the legislature, being empowered to convoke and dissolve the parliament as he pleased so long as he summoned it at least once a year. Thus he dismissed both the first and second Dumas shortly after they were convened because they exhibited "radical" tendencies. In 1907, before the election of the third Duma, the Tsar issued a decree which weighted the electoral system in favor of the landed nobility and the propertied classes, reducing accordingly the representation of peasants and workers. Hence the third and fourth Dumas, indirectly elected on the basis of unequal suffrage, were relatively conservative in composition and more amenable to control by the Tsar and his ministers. The Fundamental Laws also entitled the monarch to declare a state of emergency and to issue executive decrees during periods of crisis—a practice frequently resorted to by the regime in its declining years.

Under the reforms brought about by the revolution, the Tsar retained control of the executive power. The Council of Ministers was accountable to the monarch alone and bore no responsibility to the Duma beyond having to answer questions (interpellations) in parliamentary debate. The Fundamental Laws gave the Duma no checks upon the Tsar himself; they referred to him, in fact, as the Supreme Autocrat. Furthermore, the Tsar's power of appointment remained untouched, ensuring his continued domination of the powerful bureaucracy.

Concessions were also made to civil liberties. In addition to extending the franchise, the regime officially proclaimed the rights of free speech, assembly, worship, and mobility. Censorship of the press was to be relaxed, and political parties were to be allowed to organize freely. Members of parliament were to be granted immunity for statements made in legislative debate. Impressive though these concessions were in law, however, they were often denied in practice. When occasion required it, the regime continued to ban radical newspapers and to outlaw political associations. It persecuted minority nationalities and arrested or exiled radicals, even including socialist members of the Duma.

Nevertheless it would be a mistake to assume that the Revolution of 1905 failed completely to modify the Tsarist political system. Even though the Duma was prevented from exercising its legal powers, it provided a forum for the presentation of alternative views and the airing of criticism. It stimulated the development of public opinion and helped train opposition leaders. If radical newspapers were suppressed, the moderate press, at least, enjoyed a limited opportunity to discuss public questions and inform its readers. If the Bolsheviks were imprisoned or driven into exile, less radical parties were allowed to organize and express their views. The changes introduced by the Revolution of 1905 did not bring democracy to Russia, but they registered an advance in that direction.

4

The Chinese Pattern

John K. Fairbank

Mao Tse-tung's real claim to immortality lies in his effort to smash the ancient ruling class tradition. His bucolic distaste for the evils of city life and bureaucracy is deeply felt. It rings a bell in the Chinese mind and touches feelings that go far back; for the old China was the world's great example of upper-class government from the city over the countryside, by the few over the many.

Social Structure

Since ancient times there have been two Chinas: the myriad [of] agricultural communities of the peasantry in the countryside, where each tree-clad village and farm household persists statically upon the soil; and the overlay of walled towns and cities peopled by the landlords, scholars, merchants, and officials—the families of property and position. There has been no caste system, and the chance to rise from peasant status has not been lacking. Yet China has always remained a country of farmers, four-fifths of the people living on the soil they till. The chief social division has therefore been that between town and countryside, between the 80 percent or more of the population who have stayed put upon the land and the 10 or 20 percent of the population who have formed a mobile upper class. This bifurcation still underlies the Chinese political scene and makes it difficult to spread the control of the state from the few to the many.

If we look more closely at this inherited social structure, we note that the upper levels have included really several classes—the landowning gentry, the scholar-literati, and the officials, as well as the merchants, the militarists, and their hangers-on. This composite upper stratum has been the active carrier of China's literate culture in its many aspects. Within this minority segment of the Chinese people have been developed most of the literature and the fine arts, the higher philosophy, ethics, the political ideology of the state, the sanctions of power, and much of the wealth that accompanied them. Culture has filtered down to the masses.

The Peasant: Family and Village. Even today the Chinese people are still mostly peasants tilling the soil, living mainly in villages, in houses of brown sun-dried brick,

From John K. Fairbank, *The United States and China* (Cambridge, Massachusetts: Harvard University Press, 1971, 3d ed.), pp. 16–30, 49–61. [Reprinted with permission from the publisher.]

bamboo, or whitewashed wattle, or sometimes stone, with earth or stone floors, and paper, not glass, in the windows. At least half and sometimes two-thirds to three-quarters of their meager material income is used for food. The other necessaries of life, including rent, heat, lighting, clothing, and any possible luxuries, come from the tiny remainder. They lack even the luxury of space. Peasant dwellings have usually about four small room sections for every three persons. Sometimes family members of both sexes and two or three generations must all sleep on the same brick bed. There is little meat in the diet, and so simple a thing as iron is scarce for tools or for building. The per capita consumption of steel in the United States is several hundred times that in China. Manpower still takes the place of the machine for most purposes. In this toilsome, earthbound existence the hazards of malnutrition and disease until recently have given the average baby in China, as in India, little more than twenty-six years of life expectancy. Human life compared with the other factors of production is abundant and therefore cheap.

To an American with his higher material standard of living the amazing thing about the Chinese peasantry is their ability to maintain life in these poor conditions. The answer lies in their social institutions which have carried the individuals of each family through the phases and vicissitudes of human existence according to deeply ingrained patterns of behavior. These institutions and behavior patterns have been the oldest and most persistent social phenomena in the world. China has been the stronghold of the family system and has derived both strength and inertia from it.

The Chinese family has been a microcosm, the state in miniature. The family, not the individual, has been the social unit and the responsible element in the political life of its locality. The filial piety and obedience inculcated in family life have been the training ground for loyalty to the ruler and obedience to constituted authority in the state.

This function of the family to raise filial sons who would become loyal subjects can be seen by a glance at the pattern of authority within the traditional family group. The father was a supreme autocrat, with control over the use of all family property and income and a decisive voice in arranging the marriages of the children. The mixed love, fear, and awe of children for their father was strengthened by the great respect paid to age. An old man's loss of vigor was more than offset by his growth in wisdom. As long as he lived in possession of his faculties the patriarch possessed every sanction to enable him to dominate the family scene. According to the law he could sell his children into slavery or even execute them for improper conduct. In fact, of course, Chinese parents were by custom as well as by nature particularly loving toward small children, and they were also bound by a reciprocal code of responsibility for their children as family members. But law and custom provided little check on parental tyranny if they chose to exercise it.

The domination of age over youth within the old-style family was matched by the domination of male over female. Chinese baby girls in the old days were more likely than baby boys to suffer infanticide. A girl's marriage was, of course, arranged and not for love. The trembling bride became at once a daughter-in-law under the tyranny of her husband's mother. In a well-to-do family she might see secondary wives or concubines brought into the household, particularly if she did not bear a male heir. She could be repudiated by her husband for various reasons. If he died she could not easily remarry. All this reflected the fact that a woman had no economic independence. Her labor was absorbed in household tasks and brought her no income. Peasant women were universally illiterate. They had few or no property rights. Until the present century their subjection was demonstrated and reinforced by the custom of foot binding. This crippling practice by which a young girl's feet were tightly wrapped from about age five to prevent normal development seems to have begun about the tenth century. The "lily feet" so produced, with the arch broken and lesser toes curled under, meant the suffering of hundreds of millions of young girls but had great aesthetic and erotic value for men. During a girl's childhood and adolescence she endured the pain in her feet in order to attract a good husband. Daily care of her feet—washing them, cutting the nails, maintaining circulation—was a very private matter since she kept them constantly bound and covered. Eventually a husband's interest in these small sensitive objects made them genuinely erogenous—still another Chinese invention! In daily life bound feet, stumping about on one's heels, also kept womankind from venturing far abroad.

The inferiority of women imposed upon them by social custom was merely one manifestation of the hierarchic nature of a society of status. It exemplified an entire social code and cosmology. Philosophically, ancient China had seen the world as the product of two interacting complementary elements, *yin* and *yang*. *Yin* was the attribute of all things female, dark, weak, and passive. *Yang* was the attribute of things male, bright, strong, and active. While male and female were both necessary and complementary, one was by nature passive toward the other. Building on such ideological foundations, an endless succession of Chinese male moralists worked out the behavior pattern of obedience and passivity which was to be expected of women. These patterns subordinated girls to boys from their infancy and kept the wife subordinate to her husband and the mother to her son. Forceful women, [which] China has never lacked, usually controlled their families by indirection, not by fiat.

Status within the family was codified in the famous "three bonds" emphasized by the Confucian philosophers; namely, the bonds between ruler and subject (prince and minister), father and son, and husband and wife. To an egalitarian Westerner the most striking thing about this doctrine is that two of the three relationships were within the family, and all were between superior and subordinate. The relationship of mother and son, which in Western life often allows matriarchal domination, was not stressed in theory, though naturally important in fact.

Within the extended family every child from birth was involved in a highly ordered system of kinship relations with elder brothers, sisters, maternal elder brother's wives, and other kinds of aunts, uncles, and cousins, grandparents, and in-laws too numerous for a Westerner to keep in mind. These relationships were not only more clearly named and differentiated than in the West but also carried with them more compelling rights and duties dependent upon status. A first son, for example, could not long remain unaware of the Confucian teaching as to his duties toward the family line and his precedence over his younger brothers and his sisters.

Chinese well habituated to the family system have been prepared to accept similar patterns of status in other institutions, including the official hierarchy of the government. The German sociologist Max Weber characterized China as a "familistic state." One advantage of a system of status (as opposed to our individualist system of contractual relations) is that a man knows automatically where he stands in his family or society. He can have security in the knowledge that if he does his prescribed part he may expect reciprocal action from others in the system. It has been observed that a Chinese community overseas gains strength by organizing its activities to meet new situations in a hierarchic fashion.

The life cycle of the individual in a peasant family is inextricably interwoven with the seasonal cycle of intensive agriculture upon the land. The life and death of the people follow a rhythm which interpenetrates the growing and harvesting of the crops. The peasant village which still forms the bedrock of Chinese society is built out of family units; village, family, and individual follow the rhythm of seasons and crops, of birth, marriage, and death.

Socially, the Chinese in the village have been organized primarily in their kinship system and only secondarily as a neighborhood community. The village has ordinarily consisted of a group of family and kinship units (clans) which are permanently settled from one generation to the next and continuously dependent upon the use of certain landholdings. Each family household has been both a social and an economic unit. Its members derived their sustenance from working its fields and their social status from membership in it.

The Chinese kinship system is patrilineal, the family headship passing in the male line from father to eldest son. Thus the men stay in the family while the girls marry into other family households, in neither case following the life pattern which Western individuals take as a matter of course. Until recently a Chinese boy and girl did not choose each other as life mates, nor did they set up an independent household together after marriage. Instead, they entered the husband's father's household and assumed responsibilities for its maintenance, subordinating married life to family life in a way that modern Americans would consider insupportable.

From the time of the first imperial unification, before Christ, the Chinese abandoned the institution of primogeniture by which the eldest son would have retained all the father's property while the younger sons sought their fortunes elsewhere. The enormous significance of this institutional change can be seen by comparison with a country like England or Japan where younger sons who have not shared their father's estate have provided the personnel for government, business, and empire. By the abolition of primogeniture, the Chinese created a system of equal division of the land among the sons of the family. They left the eldest son only certain ceremonial duties, to acknowledge his position, and sometimes an extra share of property; otherwise the land was divided. This constant [parcellation] of the land tended to destroy the continuity of family landholding, forestall the growth of landed particularism among great officials, and keep peasant families on the margin of subsistence. Under this system the prime duty of each married couple was to produce a son who could maintain the family line, and yet the birth of more than one son might mean impoverishment.

Contrary to a common myth, a large family with several children has not been the peasant norm. The scarcity of land, as well as disease and famine, set a limit to the number of people likely to survive in each family unit. The large joint family of several married sons with many children all within one compound, which has usually been regarded as typical of China, appears to have been the ideal exception, a luxury which only the well-to-do could afford. The average peasant family was limited to four, five, or six persons. Division of the land among the sons constantly checked the accumulation of property and savings and the typical family had little opportunity to rise in the social scale. The peasantry were bound to the soil not by law and custom so much as by their own numbers.

Yet Chinese peasant life was richly sophisticated in folklore and the civilities and happenings of an ancient folk culture. Life was not normally confined to a single village but rather to a whole group of villages that formed a market area.

The Market Community.   Even today this pattern can be seen from the air—the cellular structure of market communities, each centered on a market town surrounded by its ring of satellite villages. The old Chinese countryside was a honeycomb of these relatively self-sufficient areas. Each one . . . centered on a market town from which footpaths (or sometimes waterways) radiated out to a first ring of about six villages and continued on to a second ring of, say, twelve villages. Each of these eighteen or so villages had perhaps 75 households and each family household averaged five persons— parents, perhaps two children, and a grandparent. No village was more than about two and a half miles from the market town, within an easy day's round trip with a carrying pole, barrow, or donkey (or a sampan on a waterway). Together, the village farmers and the market town shopkeepers, artisans, landowners, temple priests, and others formed a community of roughly 1500 households or 7500 people. The town market functioned periodically—say, every first, fourth, and seventh day in a ten-day cycle— so that itinerant merchants could visit it regularly while visiting the adjoining markets five miles away in similar cycles—say every second, fifth, and eighth day or every third, sixth, and ninth day. In this pulsation of the market cycle, one person from every household might go to the market town on every third day, perhaps to sell a bit of local produce or buy a product from elsewhere, but in any case meeting friends in the tea shop, at the temple, or on the way. In ten years he would have gone to market a thousand times.

Thus while the villages were not self-sufficient, the larger market community was both an economic unit and a social universe. Marriages were commonly arranged through matchmakers at the market town. There festivals were celebrated, a secret society might have its lodge meetings, and the peasant community met representatives of the ruling class—tax gatherers and rent collectors.

The Gentry Class

The gentry dominated Chinese life, so much so that sociologists have called China a gentry state and even ordinary people may speak of the "scholar gentry" as a class. But do not let yourself be reminded of the landed gentry with their roast beef and fox hunts in merry England, for "gentry" in the case of China is a technical term with two principal meanings and an inner ambiguity. It requires special handling.

Non-Marxists generally agree, first of all, that the gentry were not a mere feudal landlord class, because Chinese society was not organized in any system that can be called feudalism, except possibly before 221 B.C. While "feudal" may still be a useful swear word, it has little value as a Western term applied to China. For instance, an essential characteristic of feudalism, as the word has been used with reference to medieval Europe and Japan, has been the inalienability of the land. The medieval serf was bound to the land and could not himself either leave it or dispose of it, whereas the Chinese peasant both in law and in fact has been free to sell and, if he had the means, to purchase land. His bondage has resulted from a press of many circumstances but not from a legal institution similar to European feudalism. Nor has it been maintained by the domination of a professional warrior caste. Avoidance of the term feudal to describe the Chinese peasant's situation in life by no means signifies that it has been less miserable. But if the word feudal is to retain a valid meaning for European and other institutions to which it was originally applied, it cannot be very meaningful in a general Chinese context.

The Chinese gentry can be understood only in a dual, economic and political sense, as connected both with landholding and with officeholding. The narrow definition, following the traditional Chinese terminology, confines gentry status to those *individuals* who held official degrees gained normally by passing examinations, or sometimes by recommendation or purchase. This has the merit of being concrete and even quantifiable—the gentry in this narrow sense were degree-holders, as officially listed, and not dependent for their status on economic resources, particularly landowning, which is so hard to quantify from the historical record.

Yet in an agrarian society one can hardly ignore the importance of landholding as one source of upper-class strength. The main point about the gentry as individuals was that they were public functionaries, playing political and administrative roles, in addition to any connection with the landlord class. Yet, being Chinese, they were also enmeshed in family relations, on which they could rely for material sustenance. This political-economic dualism has led many writers to define the term gentry more broadly as a group of *families* rather than of individual degree holders only. Both the narrow and the broad definitions must be kept in mind.

Looked at descriptively, the gentry families lived chiefly in the walled towns rather than in the villages. They constituted a stratum of families based on landed property which intervened between the earthbound masses of the peasantry, on the one hand, and the officials and merchants who formed a fluid matrix of overall administrative and commercial activity, on the other. They were the local elite, who carried on certain functions connected with the peasantry below and certain others connected with the officials above.

For the peasant community the gentry included the big landowners, the economic base of the great ruling class. Their big high-walled compounds enclosing many courtyards, replete with servants and hoarded supplies and proof against bandits, dominated the old market towns. This was the type of "big house" celebrated in both Chinese and Western novels of China. As a local ruling class the gentry managed the system of customary and legal rights to the use of land. These ordinarily were so incredibly diverse and complicated that decided managerial ability was required to keep them straight. The varied tenant relationships, loans, mortgages, customary payments, and obligations on both sides formed such a complex within the community that many peasants could hardly say whether they were themselves mainly small landowners or mainly tenants. In general, the peasant's loss of title to his land was more likely to make him a tenant and decrease his share of its product than to make him a displaced and homeless wanderer. Peasant poverty was reflected sometimes in the increase of landless laborers in the villages, but it was marked chiefly by the increased payment of land rent.

There have been two schools of thought about China's rural poverty. One school has stressed the exploitation of the peasant by the ruling class through rents, usury, and other exactions, resulting in a maldistribution of income. This idea of landlord class exploitation has of course fitted Marxist theory and is now an article of faith concerning the old China. The other school . . . has stressed the many reasons for the low productivity of the old farm economy: farms of two acres per family were too small; even these tiny plots were improperly used; peasants had insufficient capital and limited access to new technology; there was little control over nature; primitive transport increased marketing costs. Supporters of this interpretation point to the fact that most Chinese farmers owned their land, some were partly owners and partly tenants, and only about one quarter or one fifth were outright tenants, so that landlord exploitation of tenants was far from the general rule and less of a problem than the general lack of capital and technology compared with labor.

Without attempting final judgment, we may suggest one rule: that social status and class prerogatives must have figured in the rural scene along with all the agronomic factors, and any explanation must be social and historical as well as economic. For example, as in all farming, the seasonal need of capital permitted usurious interest on loans, which ran as high as 12 percent a month, depending on what the traffic would bear. Since capital was accumulated from the surplus product of the land, landowners were usually moneylenders. The gentry families thus rested in part upon property rights and money power, as well as social prestige. In the early twentieth century, they still dominated the back country in most provinces. Modern developments like absentee landlordism strengthened rather than weakened their position, by stressing economic claims untempered by personal relations.

For the officials of the old China the gentry families were one medium through whom tax collections were effected. By this same token they were, for the peasantry, intermediaries who could palliate official oppression while in the process of carrying it out. The local officials dealt with conditions of flood or famine or incipient rebellion and the multitude of minor criminal cases and projects for public works, all through the help of the gentry community. It was the buffer between populace and officialdom.

The economic role of the gentry families was no more than half the story, for they had very important political-administrative functions in the Chinese state which made them unlike any group in Western history. Here we meet a problem of historical interpretation, created by the ambivalence of the term gentry, which in the present literature on China may refer either to landowning families or to degree-holding individuals. Unfortunately for the clarity of the term, the latter group was not entirely included within the former. Peasants without landlord-family backing occasionally rose through the examination system to become degree holders and officials. Thus a poor man, by his educational qualifications alone, could become a member of the gentry in the narrow sense used above, even though he was not connected with a gentry family. This fact makes the term "gentry" ambiguous and therefore subject to dispute.

The view taken here is that the degree-holding individuals were in most cases connected with landowning families, and the latter in most cases had degree-holding members. Until the subject is clarified by further research we can only proceed on the assumption that, in general and for the most part, the gentry families were the out-of-office reservoir of the degree holders and the bureaucracy. The big families were the seed-bed in which officeholders were nurtured and the haven to which dismissed or worn out bureaucrats could return.

In each community the gentry had many important public functions. They raised funds for and supervised public works—the building and upkeep of irrigation and communication facilities such as canals, dikes, dams, roads, bridges, ferries. They supported Confucian institutions and morals—establishing and maintaining schools, shrines, and local temples of Confucius, publishing books, especially local histories or gazetteers, and issuing moral homilies and exhortations to the populace. In time of peace they set the tone of public life. In time of disorder they organized and commanded militia defense forces. From day to day they arbitrated disputes informally, in place of the continual litigation which goes on in any American town. The gentry also set up charities and handled trust funds to help the community, and made contributions at official request to help the state, especially in time of war, flood, or famine. So useful were these contributions that most dynasties got revenue by selling the lowest literary degrees, thus admitting many persons to degree-holding status without examination.

While this abused the system, it also let men of wealth rise for a price into the upper class and share the gentry privileges, such as contact with the officials and immunity from corporal punishment.

The local leadership and management functions of the gentry families explain why officialdom did not penetrate lower down into Chinese society. The Imperial government remained a superstructure which did not directly enter the villages because it rested upon the gentry as its foundation. The many public functions of the local degree holders made a platform under the imperial bureaucracy and let the officials move about with remarkable fluidity and seeming independence of local roots. Actually, the Emperor's appointee to any magistracy could administer it only with the cooperation of the gentry in that area. All in all, in a country of over 400 million people, a century ago, there were less than 20,000 regular imperial officials but roughly one and a quarter million scholarly degree-holders.

Continued domination of the gentry families over the peasantry was assured not only by landowning but also by the fact that the gentry mainly produced the scholar class from which officials were chosen. . . .

The Confucian Pattern

Confucius and Karl Marx had even less in common than the ideologies which bear their names, and the differences between Confucianism and Marxism-Leninism-Maoism are as great as the similarities. Yet both traditional China and Communist China have stressed the role of ideology, and no one can understand Chiang Kai-shek or even Mao Tse-tung without knowing something of the Confucian tradition.

Superficial Western observers, looking only at the texts of the Confucian classics, have been impressed with their agnostic this-worldliness and their ethical emphasis upon proper conduct in personal relations. In its larger sense as a philosophy of life, we have generally associated with Confucianism those quiet virtues so artfully described in Lin Yutang's *My Country and My People:* patience, pacifism, and compromise; the golden mean; conservatism and contentment; reverence for the ancestors, the aged, and the learned; and, above all, a mellow humanism—taking man, not God, as the center of the universe.

All this need not be denied. But if we take this Confucian view of life in its social and political context, we will see that its esteem for age over youth, for the past over the present, for established authority over innovation, has in fact provided one of the great historic answers to the problem of social stability. It has been the most successful of all systems of conservatism. For most of two thousand years the Confucian ideology was made the chief subject of study in the world's largest state. Nowhere else have the sanctions of government power been based for so many centuries upon a single consistent pattern of ideas attributed to one ancient sage.

Naturally, in the course of two thousand years many changes have occurred within the broad limits of what we call Confucianism—periods of decline and revival, repeated movements for reform, new emphases and even innovations within the inherited tradition. The range of variety may be less broad than among the multiple facets of Christianity but it is certainly comparable. Consequently the term Confucianism means many things and must be used with care.

As a code of personal conduct Confucianism tried to make each individual a moral being, ready to act on ideal grounds, to uphold virtue against human error, especially against evil rulers. There were many Confucian scholars of moral grandeur, uncompromising foes of tyranny. But their reforming zeal, the dynamics of their creed, aimed to reaffirm and conserve the traditional polity, not to change its fundamental premises.

That Confucian ideas persist in the minds of Chinese politicians today should not surprise us. Confucianism began as a means of bringing social order out of the chaos of a period of warring states. It has been a philosophy of status and consequently a ready tool for autocracy and bureaucracy whenever they have flourished. Unifiers of China have been irresistibly attracted to it, for reasons that are not hard to see.

When Chiang Kai-shek on Christmas Day, 1936 was released by the mutinous subordinates who had forcibly held him at Sian, he returned to Nanking amid unprecedented national rejoicing. Yet four days later he submitted his resignation. "Since I am leading the military forces of the country, I should set a good example for my fellow servicemen. It is apparent that my work failed to command the obedience of my followers; for otherwise the mutiny . . . would not have occurred . . . I sincerely hope that the central executive committee will censure me for my negligence of duties. After the Sian incident, it is no longer fit for me to continue in office."

Nine years later in his famous wartime book, *China's Destiny,* Chiang Kai-shek said: "To cultivate the moral qualities necessary to our national salvation . . . we must revive and extend our traditional ethical principles. The most important task is to develop our people's sense of propriety, righteousness, integrity, and honor. These qualities are based upon the Four Cardinal Principles and the Eight Virtues, which in turn are based on Loyalty and Filial Piety."

These two examples could be multiplied. They demonstrate the degree to which China down to recent decades remained a Confucian state. In the first case no one wanted Chiang to resign, nor did he intend to do so, and his resignation was elaborately declined. In the second case no one expected that China's national salvation in the midst of Japanese aggression, blockade, and inflation could be achieved through moral qualities alone, nor did Chiang think so. But in both cases his words delineated the traditional Confucian way.

Countless Chinese leaders before Chiang Kai-shek have quoted Confucius while fighting off rivals or alien invaders, who, like the Japanese, have invoked the Sage on their part while trying to take over China. Peking today sings a different tune, but there are Confucian overtones in the Marxist-Maoist orchestration. The crucial role of ideology under communism lends particular interest to China's ideological past.

Confucian Principles

The principles of Confucian government, which still lie somewhere below the surface of Chinese politics, were worked out before the time of Christ. Modifications made in later centuries, though extensive, have not been fundamental.

First of all, from the beginning of Chinese history in the Shang and Chou periods (from prehistoric times before 1400 B.C. to the third century B.C.) there was a marked stratification into the classes of the officials and nobility on the one hand, and the common people on the other. Thus the term "hundred names" *(pai-hsing)* referred originally to the clans of the officials who were in a category quite different from the common people *(min.)*. It was not until much later that the modern term "old hundred names" *(lao-pai-hsing)* became transferred to the populace. This difference between the ancient ruling class and the common people gave rise to a particular type of aristocratic tradition which has been preserved and transmitted through Confucianism down to the present. The Confucian aristocrat has been the scholar-official, and Confucianism his ideology.

In the result, this Confucian aristocracy of merit or talent came closer to the original Greek idea of aristocracy, "government by the best," than did the subsequent European hereditary aristocracies of birth. In the era of warring states, when the empire was not yet unified and philosophers flourished, Chinese thinkers of all major schools turned against the principle of hereditary privilege, invoked by the rulers of the many family-states, and stressed the natural equality of men at birth: men are by nature good and have an innate moral sense. . . . This means that man is perfectible. He can be led in the right path through education, especially through his own effort at self-cultivation, within himself, but also through the emulation of models outside himself. In his own effort to do the right thing, he can be influenced by the example of the sages and superior men who have succeeded in putting right conduct ahead of all other considerations. This ancient Chinese stress on the moral educability of man has persisted down to the present. It still inspires the government to do the educating.

Government by Moral Prestige.   The Confucian ideology did not, of course, begin with Confucius (551–479? B.C.). The interesting concept of the Mandate of Heaven, for example, went back to the early Chou period (ca. 1027–770 B.C.). According to the classic *Book of History,* the wickedness of the last ruler of the preceding dynasty of Shang, who was a tyrant, caused Heaven to give a mandate to the Chou to destroy him and supplant his dynasty, inasmuch as the Shang people themselves had failed to overthrow the tyrant. As later amplified this ancient idea became the famous "right of rebellion," the last resort of the populace against tyrannical government. It emphasized the good conduct or virtue of the ruler as the ethical sanction for preserving his rule. Bad conduct on his part destroyed the sanction, Heaven withdrew its Mandate, and the people were justified in deposing the dynasty, if they could. Consequently any successful rebellion was justified, and a new rule sanctioned, by the very fact of its success. "Heaven decides as the people decide." The Chinese literati have censored bad government and rebels have risen against it in terms of this theory. It has also reinforced the belief that the ruler should be advised by learned men in order to ensure his right conduct.

Confucius and his fellow philosophers achieved their position by being teachers who advised rulers as to their conduct, in an age when feudal princes were competing for hegemony. Confucius was an aristocrat and maintained at his home a school for the elucidation and transmission of the moral principles of conduct and princely rule. Here he taught the upper class how to behave. He emphasized court etiquette, state ceremonies, and proper conduct[1] toward one's ancestors and in the famous five degrees of relationship. One of the central principles of this code was expressed in the idea of "proper behavior according to status" (*li*). The Confucian gentleman or *chün-tzu* ("the

---

[1]"When he [Confucius] was in his native village, he bore himself with simplicity, as if he had no gifts of speech. But when in the ancestral temple or at court, he expressed himself readily and clearly, yet with a measure of reserve . . . At court, when conversing with the higher great officials, he spoke respectfully. When conversing with the lower great officials, he spoke out boldly . . . When he entered the palace gate, he appeared to stoop . . . When he hastened forward, it was with a respectful appearance . . . When the prince summoned him to receive a visitor, his expression seemed to change . . . When his prince commanded his presence, he did not wait for the carriage to be yoked, but went off on foot . . . He would not sit on his mat unless it was straight." Translated by D. Bodde from *Shih Chi* [Historical Records].

superior man," "the princely man") was guided by *li,* the precepts of which were written in the classics.

It is important to note that this code which came to guide the conduct of the scholar-official did not originally apply to the common people, whose conduct was to be regulated by rewards and punishments rather than moral principles.

This complex system of abstruse rules which the Confucians became experts at applying stemmed from the relationship of Chinese man to nature. . . . This relation had early been expressed in a primitive animism in which the spirits of land, wind, and water were thought to play an active part in human affairs. The idea is still prevalent in the practice of Chinese geomancy or *feng-shui* ("wind and water"), which sees to it that buildings in China are properly placed in their natural surroundings. Temples, for example, commonly face south with protecting hills behind them and a water course nearby. In its more rationalized form this idea of the close relation between human and natural phenomena led to the conception that human conduct is reflected in acts of nature. To put it another way, man is so much a part of the natural order that improper conduct on his part will throw the whole of nature out of joint. Therefore man's conduct must be made to harmonize with the unseen forces of nature, lest calamity ensue.

This was the rationale of the Confucian emphasis on right conduct on the part of the ruler, for the ruler was thought to intervene between mankind and the forces of nature. As the Son of Heaven he stood between Heaven above and the people below. He maintained the universal harmony of man and nature by doing the right thing at the right time. It was, therefore, logical to assume that when natural calamity came, it was the ruler's fault. He might acknowledge this by issuing a penitential edict, like that of Chiang Kai-shek quoted above. It was also for this reason that the Confucian scholar became so important. Only he, by his knowledge of the rules of right conduct, could properly advise the ruler in his cosmic role.

The main point of this theory of "government by goodness," by which Confucianism achieved an emphasis so different from anything in the West, was the idea of the virtue which was attached to right conduct. To conduct oneself according to the rules of propriety or *li* in itself gave one a moral status or prestige. This moral prestige in turn gave one influence over the people. "The people are like grass, the ruler like the wind"; as the wind blew, so the grass was inclined. Right conduct gave the ruler power.[2]

On this basis the Confucian scholars established themselves as an essential part of the government, specially competent to maintain its moral nature and so retain the Mandate of Heaven. Where the Legalist philosophers of the Ch'in unification had had ruthlessly efficient methods of government but little moral justification for them, the Confucianists offered an ideological basis. They finally eclipsed the many other ancient schools of philosophy. As interpreters of the *li,* they became technical experts, whose explanations of natural portents and calamities and of the implications of the rulers'

---

[2]In the *Analects* Confucius said: "When a prince's personal conduct is correct, his government is effective without the issuing of orders. If his personal conduct is not correct, he may issue orders but they will not be followed." [See Chiang Kai-shek's statement earlier in this selection.] In the *Great Learning* it was said: "the ruler will first take pains about his own virtue. Possessing virtue will give him the people. Possessing the people will give him the territory. Possessing the territory will give him its wealth. Possessing the wealth, he will have resources for expenditure. Virtue is the root, wealth is the result." Compare Chiang Kai-shek in *China's Destiny:* "So long as we have a few men who will set an example, the people in a village, in a district, or in the whole country will unconsciously act likewise. As the grass is bent by the wind, so the social tone is influenced by the example of such men."

actions could be denied or rejected only on the basis of the classical doctrines of which they were themselves the masters. This gave them a strategic position from which to influence government policy. In return they provided the regime with a rational and ethical sanction for the exercise of its authority, at a time when most rulers of empires relied mainly upon religious sanctions. This was a great political invention.

Early Achievements in Bureaucratic Administration.   Theory, moreover, was matched by practice in the techniques of government. The bureaucratic ruling class came into its own after the decentralized and family-based feudalism of ancient China gave way to an imperial government. The unification of 221 B.C., in which one of the warring states (Ch'in) swallowed the others, required violent dictatorial methods and a philosophy of absolutism (that of the so-called Legalist philosophers). But after the short-lived Ch'in dynasty was succeeded by the Han in 206 B.C., a less tyrannical system of administration evolved. The emperors came to rely upon a new class of administrators who superintended the great public works—dikes and ditches, walls, palaces, and granaries— and who drafted peasant labor and collected the land tax to support them. These administrators supplanted the hereditary nobility of feudal times and became the backbone of the imperial regime. They incorporated many of the Legalist methods in a new amalgam, imperial Confucianism.

In the two centuries before Christ the early Han rulers firmly established certain principles. First, that political authority in the state was centralized in the one man at the top who ruled as Emperor. Second, the Emperor's authority in the conduct of the administration was exercised on his behalf by his chief ministers, who stood at the top of a graded bureaucracy and who were responsible to him for the success or failure of their administration. Third, this bureaucracy was centralized in the vast palace at the capital where the Emperor exercised the power of appointment to office. His chief task became the selection of civil servants, with an eye to the maintenance of his power and his dynasty. For this reason the appointment of relatives, particularly from the maternal side, became an early practice. (Maternal relatives were the one group of persons completely dependent upon the ruler's favor as well as tied to him by family bonds, in contrast to paternal relatives who might compete for the succession.) Fourth, the early Han rulers developed the institution of inspection which later became the censorate, whereby an official in the provinces was checked upon by another official of lower rank, who was sent independently and was not responsible for the acts of his superior.

In this and in many other ways the central problem of the imperial administration became that of selecting and controlling bureaucrats. It was here that Confucianism gained strength from certain Legalist methods, and ancient China . . . led the world in developing the basic principles of bureaucratic government: namely, the impersonal use of specifically delegated powers in fixed areas of jurisdiction by appointed and salaried officials who regularly reported their acts during limited terms of office. For more than two thousand years this system of territorial bureaucracy has been epitomized in the walled administrative city of the district of *hsien* (in recent years also called "county").

To find the talent for officialdom the Han emperors subsidized schools and began to set written examinations. This practice continued, and when the imperial structure was reinvigorated under the T'ang dynasty (A.D. 618–907), the examination system became firmly established as the main avenue to office. For more than a thousand years, [until] 1905, this imperial institution produced administrators who had established their qualifications for official life by thoroughly indoctrinating themselves in the official orthodoxy—surely another of the great political inventions.

The Classical Orthodoxy

The Confucian doctrines were transmitted through the Chinese classics. As might be expected, these ancient books have formed a canon, the texts of which have been interpreted and reinterpreted through the centuries. In this process later texts, sometimes written for the purpose, have become canonized as more ancient, and books of early importance have fallen into obscurity. In the early Han period the classics usually mentioned were the *Book of Changes* (for divination), the *Book of History,* the *Odes* (ancient folk poems), the *Book of Ceremonies and Proper Conduct,* and the *Spring and Autumn Annals* (chronicles of Confucius' own state of Lu, in Shantung province) with their commentaries. It was not until the T'ang that the ancient book of the philosopher Mencius (fl. 324–314 B.C.) was elevated to the position of a classic. By degrees there was accumulated a canon of thirteen classics, which with their commentaries today fill some 120 volumes. In order to simplify this unwieldy corpus of ancient texts, scholars of the Sung (A.D. 907–1279) selected the famous Four Books (the *Analects of Confucius,* the *Book of Mencius,* the *Doctrine of the Mean,* and the *Great Learning*), which were so brief that any gentleman could master them.

The apothegms and aphorisms of the Four Books depict paternal government as the key to social order and the defense of the state. "If your Majesty," says Mencius to King Hui, "will indeed dispense a benevolent government to the people, being sparing in the use of punishments and fines, and making the taxes and levies light, so causing that the fields shall be plowed deep, and the weeding of them be carefully attended to, and that the strong-bodied during their days of leisure shall cultivate their filial piety, fraternal respectfulness, sincerity, and truthfulness, serving thereby at home their fathers and elder brothers and, abroad, their elders and superiors—you will then have a people who can be employed, with sticks which they have prepared, to oppose the strong mail and sharp weapons of the troops of Ch'in and Ch'u."[3]

Though eminently rational in form, this official doctrine had its religious side, expressed in the official rites at the Confucian temples, the pantheon of sages and their tablets, and the ritual veneration of them—all forming a state cult closely allied to the veneration of ancestors in the people's homes below and the Emperor's ritual acts above. While not anthropomorphic, this was a religious cult. One might call it a cult of state humanism, based on faith in the power of virtuous conduct to capture men's hearts and so lead them in the path of order under wise and benevolent authority.

The vicissitudes of the Confucian creed, like those of Catholicism, are a most instructive study and show how deeply it has penetrated Chinese life. In the third to sixth centuries after Christ, during the decline of central authority which followed the Han Empire, Confucianism was all but eclipsed by Buddhism. But in the second great imperial period of China's long history, under the T'ang and Sung dynasties of the seventh to thirteenth centuries, the Confucian system was re-established and remolded into a form more stable and enduring than ever.

The revival of Confucian government under the T'ang was part of a general revival of Chinese society in politics, administration, literature and art as well as thought.

---

[3]As Chiang Kai-shek put it 2250 years later in his book *Chinese Economic Theory,* "the government's duties are to support the people on the one hand and to protect them on the other. National plans for the support of the people are plans for the people's livelihood. But since this livelihood must also be protected, plans for livelihood become plans for the national defense . . . From the Chinese standpoint, therefore, Western economics is merely the study of private enterprise or of market transactions, whereas Chinese economic theory is a combination of the people's livelihood and national defense."

The T'ang rulers in the seventh century and until the middle of the eighth century extended their control in all directions, into Korea and Annam and over the nomad tribes and the settled oases of Central Asia. Meanwhile the T'ang capital at Ch'ang-an (modern Sian) became a metropolitan center of almost two million persons and a focus of travel and trade from Byzantium and all the Middle East.

It is interesting to note that in the early period of T'ang strength, when the state and the economy were expanding and both the legal system and the examinations were functioning vigorously, the revived Confucian bureaucracy was remarkably tolerant of foreign creeds. Foreign visitors brought with them all the variety of medieval religions: Judaism, the fifth-century Christian heresy known as Nestorian Christianity, and Manichaeism and Zoroastrianism from Persia. But when the first great rebellion threatened the dynasty in the middle of the eighth century, and its problems of revenue and military control continued to grow more pressing, the self-confidence of Chinese power was evidently shaken, and the cosmopolitan spirit declined with it.

After the collapse of the T'ang and the successive incursions of barbarian rulers on the northern frontier, the Sung dynasty failed to recapture the international position which the early T'ang had achieved. Chinese rulers throughout the Sung were on the defensive against the peoples of the steppe. Handicraft production and domestic and overseas trade brought financial well-being to the government, but they were offset by military weakness. The later Sung became a great commercial empire whose exports of copper cash, silk, and porcelain reached all of Eastern Asia and spread into Indonesia, India, the Middle East, and Africa. The Sung period saw the development of a highly sophisticated urban life, the perfection of landscape painting, and the use and abuse of paper money long before its introduction in Europe. But through all this period China's reaction to the invaders from Inner Asia remained rather unwarlike. Chinese influence abroad was based on commerce and culture rather than on military power.

This experience of foreign aggression in the Sung period of the eleventh and twelfth centuries (and the Mongol conquest which followed it in the thirteenth century) strengthened in Chinese society an ethnocentricity which has remained one of its chief characteristics. Of course many other factors also influenced the thought of this period, but during it the Confucian orthodoxy was reinforced and never lost its grip thereafter.

5
The Yugoslav Setting

Gary K. Bertsch
and M. George Zaninovich

The cultural history of Yugoslavia is really the history of a diverse set of nationalities who have been influenced by a variety of external and domestic forces. In this essay, our concern is with one basic question—namely, were there features of South Slavic culture and history that might have encouraged the advent and growth of communism in Yugoslavia? In other words, was the coming of communism simply a matter of chance, or was it a natural outgrowth of conditions that were already well established?

In a consideration of the establishment and growth of any particular ideology, then, one should probe into the culture and history of the people to obtain some broader understanding of the reasons for its success. For example, in a study of Yugoslavia, it is both interesting and instructive to ask what features of early South Slavic[1] history might have been linked to the coming of communism. To this end, we propose to examine in the following discussion certain significant features of South Slavic development.

Historical Developments

A study of the people of the South Slavic lands reveals a diverse mosaic of national or ethnic groups whose separate cultures and traditions have been interwoven over the centuries and who now inhabit this geographically variegated area of Southeastern Europe known as Yugoslavia. In the course of their history, their surrounding European neighbors—the Byzantines, Magjars (Hungarians), Rumanians, Austro-Germans, Italians, and Turks—have at one time or another tried to influence and control these proud people.

The South Slavs have enjoyed a unique geographical situation. Positioned at the crossroads of Europe, they have occupied an area that is convenient for expansion and influence. Geographically, Yugoslavia stretches southward from its Austrian border and the Julian Alps in the north to within a hundred kilometers of the Aegean Sea. On the west its border winds along 2000 kilometers of the Adriatic coastline, from the

---

[1]The term South Slav is used most often to refer to the five Slavic groups making up contemporary Yugoslavia—the Slovenes, Croats, Serbs, Montenegrins, and Macedonians—*and* the Bulgars of Bulgaria. In this essay, however, the term South Slav will be used to refer only to the five Yugoslav groups. (Note also that in Serbo-Croatian, *Jug* means "south"; hence the name Jugoslavija.)

Gulf of Trieste in the north, southward to the border of Albania. On the east it extends for 1716 kilometers along the Hungarian, Rumanian, and Bulgarian borders. Consequently, throughout history, the peoples of this strategic and attractive region have been susceptible to the influence of numerous European, Latin, and Oriental cultures.

Early History (600–1917).[2]   When viewing the history of the South Slavic peoples, we see that despite the early influence of their European neighbors, distinct Slavic cultures have remained. Although examples of acculturation and assimilation can be found, many features of contemporary life can be traced back to the original Slavic groups that migrated into the Balkan lands in the sixth and seventh centuries. The early Slavs who entered this region of Southeastern Europe originally consisted of three major groups. In the North were the Slovenes, who, according to most historians, appear to have arrived first. Next came the Croats who settled in the area just to the south of the Slovenes. Further to the south were the Serbs. The early differences among the three groups were minimal, but geographical, cultural, and religious influences were soon to change all of that. The two most northern groups, the Slovenes and the Croats, came under Western influence, accepting the Roman Catholic religion, and adopting the Latin alphabet in their separate languages. The Serbs to the south, underwent the influence of the Orthodox Church and Constantinople, and came to use the Cyrillic alphabet in their language. The consequence was three distinct South Slavic groups—each with separate cultures, languages, religions, and traditions. In addition, other smaller Slavic groups, whose distinct national culture and traditions are somewhat more difficult to identify, arrived and established themselves in this general region. Also, the Slavic newcomers encountered certain indigenous populations—for example, Italians, Morlachs, and Albanians. Thus the early heritage of the present, multinational Yugoslav state is diverse indeed.

However, once the extensive sixth- and seventh-century Slavic migrations had taken place, the possibility of a state based upon an alliance of Slavic-speaking groups emerged. Three subsequent attempts to coordinate these groups are particularly noteworthy. The first was an effort to form a "League" extending from the Polabian Sorbs in the far North to the more southern Slovenians of present-day northern Yugoslavia. The moving force behind this loosely arrayed confederation was a leader referred to as Samo, who was of unknown origins and stood at the head of the Slavic tribes for 35 years (623–658). However, under intense pressures from the Avars and assorted teutonic tribes, the early Slovenian "League" of Samo rapidly disintegrated after his death. During the centuries to follow, and before the second major attempt to build a unified South Slavic state, the individual tribes were to be so divided by geography and religion that several distinct cultural and national groupings developed.

The second major attempt at organizing a Slavic state in this area of the Balkans was undertaken by the Croatians under the leadership of Tomislav (910–928), who extended his rule over the most of what is today Croatia and Bosnia-Hercegovina.[3] The success of Tomislav and his heirs forced both Hungarian and Serbian leaders to

---

[2]For a comprehensive yet concise review of Yugoslav culture and a history from early times to the present, consult Stephen Clissold (ed.), *A Short History of Yugoslavia* (New York: Cambridge University Press, 1966).

[3]Bosnia-Hercegovina is one of the six republics of present-day Yugoslavia and is inhabited by a diverse representation of various Slavic groups.

forgo their aspirations regarding the same territories. With his primary base of territorial power in coastal Croatia and Dalmatia, Tomislav extended his rule over Pannonian Croatia along the Danube and eastward toward Serbian lands. At the height of his power, Tomislav declared Croatia to be a kingdom (rather than a princedom) and himself to be the first Croatian king. However, owing to pressures from the Byzantine Empire on the east, the Venetian republic on the northwest, and the Hungarians from the northeast, his successors found it increasingly difficult to maintain the young Croatian kingdom. These external pressures coupled with internal struggles for power among the Croatian nobility, resulted in an agreement (the *Pacta Conventa*) between the Croatian leaders and the Hungarians. The designation of Koloman—the head of the Hungarian ruling house—as the King of Croatia-Dalmatia (1102) included, as a part of the pact, the retention of specific rights for the Croatian nobility, the most significant feature of which was the continuation of the parliament of Croatia-Dalmatia under the Hungarian crown. Such an arrangement, although always in a state of fluctuation, was to continue until the final collapse of the Austro-Hungarian empire after the First World War.

The third and most powerful Balkan Slavic state to emerge during this early period was the Serbian empire of Tsar Dusan (1331–55). Since the seventh century, these Slavic-speaking peoples designated as "Serbs" had occupied the present-day Yugoslav republics of Serbia, Macedonia, and parts of Bosnia-Hercegovina. For a time, they fell under the rulership of the Bulgarian tsars in the east or the Croatian princes and kings in the west. In the ninth century, however, Serbian power under tribal chiefs began to emerge. Stronger coordination among these tribes was achieved in the tenth century, resulting in the formation of an early Serbian state known as Raska, under the leadership of its Grand *Zupan*, Radoslav. A period of disorder followed, and the Byzantine Empire overran Serbian Raska late in the tenth century.

Serbian hegemony did not again become effective until the rise of the Nemanja dynasty with its founder Stevàn Nemanja (1168–1196). The Serbian medieval state under the Nemanja family continued as a major Balkan power and reached its zenith under Tsar Dusan (1331–1355). During this period, the Serbian state declared itself an "empire" with Dusan as emperor, incorporating, in addition to Serbia itself, Macedonia, Montenegro, much of Dalmatia, Bosnia-Hercegovina, and Bulgaria. The reign of Dusan also saw the publication of the first South Slavic law in 1349, which was based upon Serbian practices and customs. After the death of Dusan, however, the power of Serbia rapidly declined. Two crucial battles took place between the Turks and the Serbians (Maritsa in 1371, and Kosovo Polje in 1389), and the outcomes firmly established Ottoman (Turkish) superiority over formerly Serbian territory.

But domination by the Turks did not signify the end of the Serbs. What allowed the Serbian and Slavic national consciousness to survive for the next four centuries under Ottoman rule were the legends of heroism associated with the epic battle of Kosovo Polje and with the medieval Serbian state that had once flourished so strongly. Then in 1878, in the aftermath of the last Russo-Turkish war, Serbia was once again declared independent and remained so until the end of World War I.

In addition to these three experiments in early South Slavic unification, a number of small principalities were established for shorter periods of time and with less success (for example, those of George Brankovic, Despot of Serbia, and Trpimir Ostojic, King of Bosnia). The function of these early kingdoms was to provide a precedent or rationale for the restoration of what was later to become a greater Slavic state in that part of the Balkans.

Interwar History (1918–1945).   The first truly South-Slavic state was established in 1918 from the ruins of World War I, and was designated as the "Kingdom of Serbs, Croats, and Slovenes." The implicit goal of the new leadership and the Royalist government under King Alexander was to create a union of the South Slavs, similar to the earlier but less extensive efforts at restoration. This new multinational South Slavic state—which included the minority groups found in contemporary Yugoslavia as well as the three major nationalities designated in the name of the new state—was designed to give expression to what was considered as a partnership of all of the South Slavic peoples. However, despite the formal recognition of the various ethnic groups and religious sects, the practical effect of governmental policy during the interwar period was to create hostility and distrust among nearly all of the participating nationalities. A crucial reason may have been that those institutions which had existed prior to World War I and were adopted by the new state were Serbian (since Serbia had been an independent state, whereas the other nationalities had been under foreign rule and occupation in the period before the War). Consequently the Serbs had an important advantage in that Yugoslav institutions were little more than transformed Serbian structures, and, in addition, dissident national groups (for example, Croats and Macedonians) had some justification for alleging that they were in effect merely second-class citizens within a "Greater Serbia." Indeed, the population census published by the interwar Yugoslav regime designated all six groups—Macedonians, Montenegrins, Bulgars, and Slavic Moslems, as well as Serbs and Croats—under the sweeping linguistic-ethnic category of Serbo-Croats. As a result, it became apparent that the centralized structure of authority being utilized in the new multinational state was in conflict with the national self-interests expressed by various South Slavic groups.

A basic issue confronting the interwar regime was that of deciding which national groups were to be given formally acknowledged status. A particularly sensitive aspect of this question was the position of the Macedonian Slavs, who had been somewhat offhandedly classified with the Serb-Croat sector in the country. Having lived for centuries under Turkish domination and control, the Macedonians were largely divided in their ethnic loyalties, some being inclined to maintain a rather vague Slavic identity and others to consider themselves either as Serbs or as Bulgars. In fact, their folk culture is replete with stories and anecdotes of families that were divided by the conflicting ethnic orientations. While the interwar Yugoslav regime was busy trying to convince itself, as well as others, that these southerners were simply "old Serbs" with a somehow forgotten identity, important segments of the Macedonian Slav population were striving through IMRO (Internal Macedonian Revolutionary Organization) to assert a separate Macedonian identity and a basis for a Macedonian nation-state. The reasons for IMRO patriots' intrigues varied: some were sympathetic to a Bulgarian movement to recover the independence of that state; others were quite seriously committed to the interwar Yugoslav Communist party. Despite the seriousness of this movement, the interwar policy of the Yugoslav Royalist government toward these southern regions of the country remained the same—namely, an insistence on the existence of a historic and ethnic link between Macedonia and the predominant Serb group, as well as continued refusal to recognize a Macedonian Slavic nationality. This and similar policies tended to divide even further an already fragmented state.

Perhaps the most far-reaching problem that immediately became apparent in the Kingdom of Serbs, Croats, and Slovenes was the question on the degree to which the various nationalities were to be allowed some form of political expression. Since no system of territorial political representation of the different nationality groups had been formally established, the tendency was for political parties themselves to form according to narrow regional-ethnic and religious affiliations. The resulting activities of such organizations as the Serb Radicals, the Croat Peasants, and the Slovene People's Party, caused the internal political environment of the young South Slavic state to become seriously fragmented into nationalistic groups. The growing tension among nationalities reached its climax with the assassination of the Croat Peasant Party leader, Stjepan Radic, in 1928 on the floor of the Royal Yugoslav parliament. The immediate result was the assumption of full dictatorial power by King Alexander since he feared the growth of widespread civil disorders in which one nationality group would be pitted against the other. To mitigate further the strong feelings of national conflict, a territorial reorganization of the Yugoslav kingdom was also instituted. The country was to be divided into new districts, which would cut across nationality groupings and traditional provincial boundaries. Each district was to have its own governor, appointed by the King. The Royalist regime hoped that this manuever would undercut the more provincial national ties and would help strengthen the "Yugoslav" or "pan-slavic" characteristic of the country.

In a final move to quell nationalistic uprisings, King Alexander issued a series of edicts in 1929, terminating what semblance of democracy had hitherto existed in the country: the assembly was dissolved, political parties (including the Communist party) were banned, and freedoms of speech and assembly were severely curtailed. Consistent with the purpose of undermining the power of regionally based nationality groups, the official name of the new country was also changed to the Kingdom of Yugoslavia.

These attempts at integrating the various Yugoslav groups into a united Yugoslav state met with no success. Separatist movements developed, terrorist activities continued, and the Serb-Croat antipathies attained a new intensity. In general, the pattern of rulership in Yugoslavia from 1929 through the beginning of World War II continued to aggravate both sociopolitical unrest and regionally based conflicts and tensions among nationalities. In attempting to remain above the social problems and regional-ethnic conflicts, the Yugoslav monarchy had succeeded only in alienating nearly all parties.

Interwar Yugoslavia, then, had rapidly digressed and was on the verge of collapse. In its final years, the Royalist government became little more than a police state under Serbian administration. Even though the government made some attempts at parliamentary democracy during the interwar years, the masses achieved little, if any, political representation. In general, it is accurate to say that the majority of the population enjoyed neither legal security nor economic and political freedom in any meaningful sense. The problems confronting the various sectors of the broader population were severe. The peasantry, making up about 70 percent of the broader society, became increasingly frustrated by a deteriorating agricultural economy and by marked increases in taxes. Both problems were being exacerbated by the worldwide depression which was crippling all agricultural economic systems, such as the Yugoslav. In addition, Yugoslav industrialization was posing another threat to the peasant: capitalism, after destroying the traditional peasant-based economic system, left the peasant farmer without a means to improve his economic lot. Together, these forces established the setting for a revolutionary spirit among this large and important sector of Yugoslav society.

The social unrest of the country was expressed also in the cities. Although much smaller than the peasantry, this sector of the population had a more vocal and organized leadership which was now beginning to espouse and promote socialist and communist ideals. One young organizer, Josip Broz, who later became known as Tito, was only one of many members of the proletariat who were capitalizing on the discontent and unrest in the factories in an attempt to build a truly revolutionary movement.

Therefore, not only did King Alexander's dictatorship fail to alleviate the national disunity in the country, but also it neglected to address itself to the growing conditions of social and political unrest. It would not seem unwarranted to suggest that the ensuing collapse of the Yugoslav regime in 1941 in response to German pressure was due, in large part, to a variety of internally unresolved problems, issues to which the Yugoslav Communists were later to apply a blend of Marxism-Leninism class doctrine and "Titoist pragmatism."

Forces of Disunity and Revolution in Pre-Communist Yugoslavia

The elements of animosity that existed among nationalities in interwar Yugoslavia had a firm historical basis in the ethnic and religious complexity of the past. Throughout the centuries, ethnic and religious differences had degenerated on more than one occasion into vicious struggles between regional-ethnic groups who placed blood, faith, and localisms over democratic form or constitutional precept. Then, as we have seen, the absence of an effective and broadly based value consensus during the interwar period meant Yugoslavia was more a nominal union, administered by a narrow and authoritarian government, than it was a genuinely integrated political community. Although the existing government may have had a monopoly on the instruments of force, it lacked the support and confidence of the masses necessary to achieve cooperation without intimidation. Ideally, what the young multinational country needed was a constituted authority, buttressed by a unified historical past that all nationality groups might share, an authority that would be committed to social values as a philosophical foundation for ordering human relations. Pre-Communist Yugoslavia was not so structured, and as a result actualization of a fully effective "Yugoslav idea" (that is, cross-national community and cooperation) was impossible.

A common problem in a multiethnic and multireligious setting, such as the Yugoslav, is that norms of behavior tend to be viewed as applying only to a specialized community or brotherhood. Those individuals unable to share in the "historical consciousness" of such a community tend to feel neither privileged nor accepted. In Yugoslavia, it is evident that the Serbs, the Croats, and the Slovenes believed themselves to possess traditions, historical epics, and behavioral norms that were not only distinct from those of the other nationalities, but also superior (and therefore largely incompatible). Such ethnic consciousness, combined with visible religious and cultural differences, provided a basis for magnification of what may in fact have been lesser distinctions.

Thus the absence of a shared and integrated historical past resulted in the growth of variegated belief systems and a fragmented political culture. It was to be expected that the Macedonian Slavs, in the course of centuries of subservience to Turkish rule, would develop a political culture somewhat different from that of the Slovenes, who had lived for a millennium under Hapsburg domination. Accordingly, it would have been unrealistic to demand that one such Slavic group identify and share in the more specialized historical and revolutionary tradition of another group within a new Yugoslavia. The Slovene and the Croat, for example, found little reason to respond to the historic battle between the Serbs and the Turks at *Kosovo Polje* as a genuinely "Yugoslav" epic tragedy, since it was a Serbian (rather than a Slovene or Croat) defeat by the Turks, and therefore a Serbian tragedy. In some of the groups in particular, there resided a sense of ethnic integrity and a hope for political autonomy, encouraging the creation of a separate historical tradition, even if the actual traditions of certain groups were less than stirring or colorful. Therefore, to identify closely with the Serbian revolutionary tradition of the nineteenth century was a form of cultural treason for both the Croat and the Slovene; to exalt Serbian epics and traditions as "Yugoslav" was to negate the heritage of one's own people.

Political affiliations, then, were determined primarily by religious identification and ethnic localisms, and only secondarily, if at all, by enlightened transregional class or professional interests. Consequently any attempt to obtain a nationwide consensus and to generate a dominant Yugoslav consciousness, founded on shared common values and traditions, elicited only resistance and suspicion from the minority groups. Such efforts at unity, then, would be greeted with charges that one was striving for a greater Serbia or a greater Croatia by eroding the culture and traditions of other groups.

So the situation remained until the Yugoslav Communists came to articulate and defend the idea of a shared South Slavic revolutionary movement against the conservative forces from "within" and the Fascist invaders from "without." Since the sense of a common historical experience and set of traditions was almost totally absent, the foremost task facing Tito and his Partisans was the creation of a united South Slavic resistance movement. It was necessary to convince members of the various nationalities —workers, peasants, and intelligentsia alike—that Marxist-Leninist ideology, combined with a revolutionary resistance strategy and guerrilla tactics had meaning and appeal to all South Slavs, and as such, could serve as an integrating, revolutionary force capable of uniting a formerly exploited and downtrodden state.

The prevailing conviction that guided the Yugoslav Communist leadership during World War II, then, was that theirs was genuinely a movement for the founding of a new political structure. Like so many other revolutionary organizations, it had to create its quasi-mythical heroes standing in bold contrast to just as clearly delineated enemies. Tito and his entourage felt that even a firmly administered Communist Yugoslavia could not survive without some basic unifying traditions and a shared historical experience that would bring all divisive forces within the country together into an integrated socialist community. As well as generating a basis for brotherhood and unity by stressing the equal share by all nationality groups in a new Marxist-Leninist experience of "national liberation," the Partisan leadership also recognized the need to underscore what semblance there was of the older "Yugoslav idea" of cooperation among ethnic groups. Indeed, the masterstroke of the Yugoslav Communist leaders during the war resistance was the grafting of mass participation in a "national liberation struggle" onto a traditional and well established "Yugoslavism."

During World War II the immediate integrative force was a shared experience of guerrilla warfare and resistance against the German invader, or, in the words of the Partisans, a revolutionary movement against Fascist imperialism. For the Communists, the ethnic or regional background of a potential convert was insignificant; the only type of association emphasized was that of class affiliation. This posture, by its very detachment from any ethnic group, gave Tito and the Partisans a definite recruiting advantage over the more narrowly nationalistic resistance groups. In contrast, a Mihailovic Chetnik, for example, belonged to a distinctly Serbian resistance movement, and by this very association he openly declared himself a Serb (and in no sense whatever a Croat or a South Slav) and furthermore a Serb who supported the restoration of the Serbian monarchy.

Out of the dramatic experience of World War II developed a Partisan "myth of solidarity," arising from a common dedication to "national liberation." Bolstered by the realities of passion and suffering, this myth strengthened the bonds among leaders of the Communist movement, solidified the non-Communist rank-and-file behind a common "Yugoslav" and socialist cause, and de-emphasized the relevance of nationality distinctions within the context of the resistance experience. As in any such political movement, an entire body of myths was necessary as a principal support of the authority structure that the leaders intended to impose. Contributing to the construction of this postresistance mythology was the new literature, both fictional and factual, that burgeoned to describe "the heroic struggle against the invader." Combined with this glorification of the immediate past was an extensive denunciation of interwar Yugoslav political parties and their leadership as separatists, traitors, and collaborators. This process culminated in the eventual outlawing of movements that opposed the Communist-dominated Popular Front, the purpose being to undermine regional-ethnic bases of political power.

Therefore, the Communist wartime experience should not be viewed simply as a successful movement of military resistance against the Germans, since such an outlook would tend to ignore its critical domestic impact on the psychology and the attitudes of the Yugoslav citizenry. One should also recognize that the resistance generated a shared value-base for a *founding myth,* which served to delimit the foundation of the new postwar structure of Communist authority and to override the traditional regional-ethnic divisiveness. A genuinely "Yugoslav" nation-state, it was felt, could not have an effective basis until all *jugo-slaveni* (i.e., all nationality groups in Yugoslavia) had somehow shared in the sacrifice that would bring it into existence.

The Communist Partisan literature had, from the very start, magnified, and probably even exaggerated, the revolutionary resistance as an achievement of "Yugoslav peoples." The formal histories as well as the fictional novels that followed in the wake of "national liberation" glorified such qualities as individual heroism, brotherly sacrifice, and a unified effort against "the invader," and thereby strengthened the founding myth. This literature appealed to seemingly irreconcilable regional-ethnic and religious elements in the immediate postwar phase; and, as an expression of a broader "Yugoslav socialist patriotism," founded on the older "Yugoslav idea," it provided the basis for a more extended cooperative effort. This sense of Partisan cooperation made the Marxist socialist forms somewhat more acceptable to the wider Yugoslav population.

However, as evidenced by recent national conflicts within the country, all is not well within the Yugoslav socialist community. Despite the cooperation that has been engendered by the Partisan experience, and despite significant postwar integrative efforts, underlying forces—evoked by the varied historical experiences and differing levels of economic development—persist as sources of internal dissatisfaction and conflict. In other words, the irreconcilable nationality problem led to the collapse of Royalist Yugoslavia, and thus to the advent of its Communist successor; but the problem remains and, unless it is controlled, it may ultimately contribute to the demise of the successor state as well.

Conclusion

In trying to analyze the effects of Yugoslav history on the coming of Communism, it will be instructive to summarize the developments by asking ourselves two basic questions. First, what was it about the culture and history of Yugoslavia that caused the government preceding the Communist regime to collapse? In attempting to answer this question, we should bear in mind the Marxist explanation: a conventional Marxist would argue that the capitalist system of interwar Yugoslavia had simply outgrown its usefulness and led to its own destruction; that it had left peasants without the means of economic survival; that it had brought laborers to the cities and into the factories where they could be mobilized into the Communist movement. According to the Marxist perspective, such developments could be expected to produce the disintegration of the Royalist government. This explanation has reasonable though limited validity. It is quite true that the economic situation in the 1930s was bleak, that the peasants were overtaxed and underemployed, and that the laborers were overworked as well as underpaid. But these factors alone do not explain the disintegration and subsequent collapse of the pre-Communist regime. Instead, it seems clear that an additional and perhaps equally important factor leading to the demise of the Royalist government was the unresolved nationality problem, rendering the government paralyzed and unable to govern. When the country was threatened and subsequently attacked by the Nazi invaders, the government did not have the support to integrate the people behind common goals and a united struggle. The country was therefore almost totally fragmented and unable to weather the shock of war. Ultimately the regency collapsed because it could not govern, and it could not govern because it had not solved the most basic problem of a multinational state.

The second question is this: why was the successor state Communist rather than another ideological form? To answer it, we must briefly examine the Yugoslav Communists' revolutionary strategy. Tito and his Partisans did not lead a revolutionary movement against internal capitalists, but rather a war against the foreign imperialists. The Partisans were aware that the most immediate problems confronting the country were not those coming from within the system, but rather from outside its borders. What the Communist struggle represented, then, was not a revolutionary movement against the capitalist overlords, but rather a Yugoslav resistance against the Fascist invaders. Communism came to power, then, and took the form that it did because of its appeal to Yugoslav nationalism, democracy, and its policy of unmitigated hostility and resistance against the outside invader. Although Tito and the Partisan leadership were dedicated Communists fighting for the establishment of a workers' state, they deemphasized the Marxist goals and ideological orientation and concentrated on leading a united resistance movement, founded on a definite strategy for throwing out the Nazis and healing the nationalist divisions of the past. They addressed themselves to the most critical problems facing the people, and this meant that their foremost objective was to drive out the foreign invaders. This goal required the cooperation of all national groups in Yugoslavia, a goal that had the effect of ameliorating, at least temporarily, the nationality divisions of the past. The other major resistance movements—the Chetniks and Ustashe—were exclusively Serbian or Croatian and were thus incapable of generating a broadly based resistance movement. Thus, the Communists, with their effective resistance strategy and guerrilla tactics succeeded where the other groups had failed.

The end of the War found Tito and his Partisans in control of the reins of power. Their success in retaining the power, however, would be dependent upon their capacity at dealing with those elements in the culture and history of the South Slavs that had led to the collapse of the previous regime. To date, the Communists' ability to do so is still being tested.

Selected Bibliography

Soviet Union

Blum, Jerome. *Lord and Peasant in Russia from the Ninth to the Nineteenth Century.* Princeton, New Jersey: Princeton University Press, 1961.

Dmytryshyn, Basil, ed. *Modernization of Russia under Peter I and Catherine II.* New York: Wiley, 1974.

Karpovich, Michael. *Imperial Russia, 1801–1917.* New York: Henry Holt, 1932, Reprinted 1959.

Masaryk, Thomas G. *The Spirit of Russia.* Translated by Eden and Cedar Paul, 2 vols. New York: Macmillan, 1955.

Mosse, W. E. *Alexander II and the Modernization of Russia.* Rev. ed. New York: Collier Books, 1962.

Pares, Bernard. *A History of Russia.* 5th ed. New York: Knopf, 1949.

Vernadsky, George. *A History of Russia.* 5th ed. New Haven: Yale University Press, 1961.

Wallace, Donald MacKenzie. *Russia on the Eve of War and Revolution.* Edited by Cyril E. Black. New York: Random House, 1961.

China

Dawson, Raymond, ed. *The Legacy of China.* London: Oxford University Press, 1964.

Elvin, Mark. *The Pattern of the Chinese Past.* London: Eyre Methuen Ltd., 1973.

Fung Yu-lan. *A Short History of Chinese Philosophy.* Edited by Derk Bodde. New York: Macmillan, 1960.

Goodrich, L. Carrington. *A Short History of the Chinese People.* 3d ed. New York: Harper and Row, 1959.

Li, Dun J. *The Ageless Chinese.* 2d ed. New York: Scribner's, 1971.

Loewe, Michael. *Imperial China: The Historical Background to the Modern Age.* New York: Praeger, 1966.

Meskill, John, ed. *An Introduction to Chinese Civilization.* New York: Columbia University Press, 1973.

Mote, Frederick W. *Intellectual Foundations of China.* New York: Knopf, 1971.

Munro, Donald J. *The Concept of Man in Early China.* Stanford, California: Stanford University Press, 1969.

Yugoslavia

Clissold, Stephen, ed. *A Short History of Yugoslavia*. Cambridge, England: Cambridge University Press, 1966.

Dvornik, Francis. *The Slavs: Their Early History and Civilization*. Boston: American Academy of Arts and Sciences, 1956.

Erlich, Vera St. *Family in Transition*. Princeton, New Jersey: Princeton University Press, 1966.

Heppell, Muriel, and Singleton, Frank B. *Yugoslavia*. London: Ernest Benn, Ltd., 1961.

Pavlowitch, Stevan F. *Yugoslavia*. New York: Praeger, 1971.

West, Rebecca. *Black Lamb and Grey Falcon*. 2 vols. New York: Viking, 1940.

THE REVOLUTIONARY YEARS: THE ADVENT OF COMMUNISM

The word "revolution" has perhaps inspired and/or terrified all of us at one time or another. It may have been as we studied the writings of Thomas Paine, the exploits of Crispus Attucks, or the heroics of George Washington at the time of the American Revolution; or it may have been during our own direct involvement in one of the various movements that have taken place since the early 1960s—such as the Black Revolution, Women's Liberation, or the antiwar protests. But it is possible that none of us have ever been embroiled in the type of revolution to be discussed in this chapter: the violent overthrow of the traditional political and economic system, the attempted destruction of certain classes in the society, the uprooting of their philosophy and religion, and finally, the establishment of communism. To evaluate how successful such revolution has been in Russia, China, and Yugoslavia, it is necessary to compare the origin of the revolution of each, the course it has taken, and its results. We will also try to determine, in brief, the point at which the society feels it is necessary to use the drastic action of revolution to produce change.

First, let us read excerpts of what the authors of modern communism themselves thought about the reasons for and the nature of revolution. Writing in 1847, at a time when he thought the flames of revolution were about to sweep across Western Europe, Karl Marx declared in his book, *Poverty of Philosophy:*

> Would it, moreover, be a matter for astonishment if a society based upon the *antagonism* of classes should lead ultimately to a brutal conflict, to a hand-to-hand struggle as its final *dénouement?* . . . It is only in an order of things in which there will be no longer classes or class antagonism that *social evolutions* will cease to be *political revolutions.* Until then, on the eve of each general reconstruction of society, the last word of social science will ever be: "Combat or death; bloody struggle or extinction." It is thus that the question is irresistibly put.[1]

Lenin, an even more enthusiastic proponent of the use of violence to destroy the old and build the new, especially extolled the virtues of expanded world revolution:

> Uneven economic and political development is an absolute law of capitalism. Hence, the victory of socialism is possible first in a few or even in one single capitalist country taken separately. The victorious proletariat of that country, having expropriated the capitalist and organized its own socialist production, would rise against the rest of the capitalist world, attract to itself the oppressed classes of other countries, raise revolts among them against the capitalist, and, in the event of necessity, come out even with armed force against the exploiting classes and their states.[2]

But for those who have gotten enraged enough at their government to expound violence, it might be well to read Mao Tse-tung's sobering caveat on revolution. Mao, in his "Report on an Investigation of the Peasant Movement in Hunan," warned the peasant masses and other would-be revolutionaries that, after they were organized and had initiated revolts against the "local tyrants and evil gentry," some people would complain that they were going too far. Mao insisted otherwise:

> Such talk may seem plausible, but in fact it is wrong. First, the local tyrants, evil gentry and lawless landlords have themselves driven the peasants to this. The most violent revolts and the most serious disorders have invariably occurred in places where the local tyrants, evil gentry and lawless landlords perpetrated the worst outrages. . . . Secondly, a revolution is not a dinner party, or writing an essay, or painting a picture, or doing embroidery; it cannot be so refined, so leisurely and gentle, so temperate, kind, courteous, restrained and magnanimous. A revolution is an insurrection, an act of violence by which one class overthrows another.[3]

Is total destruction—not only of a structure of a system but of human lives as well—inevitable (as Communist thinkers have contended) in order for the masses to attain greater peace, equality, security, and happiness? And at what point is such violent action deemed necessary by a significant segment of a society? There is no simple answer to either question.

Certainly, severe material deprivation, such as the lack of food, clothing,

---

[1] Karl Marx, *Poverty of Philosophy* (New York: International Publishers, 1964), pp. 146–147.
[2] Quoted in David Shub, *Lenin* (New York: New American Library, 1948), p. 189.
[3] Mao Tse-tung. *Selected Readings* (Peking: Foreign Language Press, 1967), pp. 24–25.

shelter, is an important factor contributing to violent uprising. Though human beings may not "live by bread alone," empty stomachs and purses have proven, time and time again in history, to be salient causes for political and social insurrections. In Russia, China, and Yugoslavia, too, large masses of people suffered severe deprivation at different periods. However, it was not until the twentieth century that the traditional philosophy and government prevailing in each failed to survive whatever discontent or disorder may have ensued. Thus it would appear that more than material deprivation is required to turn people against the valued traditions of their country.

A related but even more important condition helped to engender revolution in these three countries: this was the deep disappointment in the traditional political and social system, a despair that was felt throughout each society. The government and the ruling class had long promised to improve conditions, but unfulfilled promises were no longer enough to retain the faith and confidence of the majority of the people in the government or the doctrines and myths that had sustained and revitalized the culture century after century. In other words, throughout history the poor and helpless had survived without equitable division of land, fair distribution of the national wealth, the alleviation of crushing taxes, and the opportunities to improve themselves in education and work. Peasant uprisings and political revolts occurred, but their purpose was to improve conditions, not to uproot the traditional ways, for they were the basis of life itself. Total upheaval, then, came only when spiritual or moral despair over the basic system itself shattered the traditional myths.

Yet another factor was needed, however, for the success of Communist revolutions, and that was strong leadership. Already, in pre-communist China, Russia, and Yugoslavia, there had been periods in which the society had seemed ripe for deep-seated insurrection, but the right leader for completing the task was missing. For example, in China's Taiping Rebellion (1850–1864) at least twenty million lives were lost, but total revolution still did not take place; nor did the Russian Revolution of 1905—when hundreds of workers were killed and wounded by the Tsar's troops on Bloody Sunday—develop into a full-scale insurrection; then, again in 1918, the new state known as the "Kingdom of Serbs, Croats, and Slovenes" (later Yugoslavia) was created from the chaos of World War I, but it too failed as a total revolution, partly because strong leadership was lacking.

No doubt, Lenin, Mao, and Tito each took advantage of the "right time and place" to attain success, but they also exhibited the leadership ability to organize the already committed as well as to publicize their cause to those still uncommitted. Tightly disciplined organization, then, has been important to the Communists, not only in their means of retaining power, but also in their initial efforts to attain it. The pattern of governing has generally been one of dictatorial leadership, penetration into society at large, imposition of Communist party control over the masses, and the use of military and police force. But while promoting revolution and striving for power, Communist leaders made use of various propaganda techniques to gain large numbers of followers by inciting them to action against the prescribed enemy. Through impassioned speeches and rousing literature, the leaders would try to convince the general populace of the need for violent action, glamorizing the role the common man would have in the insurrection, and, vaguely, the new society that would emerge once the revolution had finished. Such ubiquitous propaganda intensified the discontent that already existed: people became more conscious of the need for material relief, their disillusion with the existing system, and the yearning for a better tomorrow. This restlessness was articulated and popularized in such slogans as "Land to the Tillers," "Power to the Workers," "Kick the Imperialists Out," and others. However, one final spark was needed in Russia, China, and Yugoslavia before a successful Communist upheaval could be realized. What was it that finally set off the revolution and swept in the Communists? In each country, the single but important causal factor was a major, destructive war.

In Russia, then—as Michael T. Florinsky points out in "The Emergence of Russian Communism,"—the disaster of World War I brought the effete Tsarist regime to its knees and allowed the revolutionary factions the chance to stand in its place. Past conflagrations with foreign nations, such as the Crimean War and the Russo-Japanese War, had already exposed the glaring political, economic, and military weaknesses of the old regime, but it was this "Great War" in particular that drained the morale of the Russian people and diverted its loyalty and support from the Tsarist government. As Florinsky demonstrates, whether one agrees that World War I was the major cause for the collapse of the Tsarist regime, the fact remains that it did put the government to a severe test, which it failed. Any progress that had been made toward reform in the course of the previous decades—and some had taken place in several areas—was virtually obliterated by the killing, suffering, and destruction caused by the War.

In China also, the trauma of war may have allowed the Communist revolutionary forces to enter and eliminate the old regime. Unlike the events in Russia, however, several decades of struggle would pass in China before the Communists would gain power and be in a position to begin national reforms. As in Russia, China too suffered from the battering aggression of the imperialist powers: she too had lost territory, men, and much of her treasury to the rapacious foreigner. Her humiliation was even more intensified by the so-called Unequal Treaties during the last half of the nineteenth century, and by her defeat at the hands of her former protégé, Japan, in the Sino-Japanese War (1894–95). As a result of these humiliations a Chinese nationalist who had been educated in Western medicine as well as in the Chinese classics, Dr. Sun Yat-sen, launched China's revolutionary course. After a number of failures by both his own and other revolutionary organizations, Sun's efforts to topple the Manchu regime and establish a republic for China came to a fruition in October, 1911. Though this non-Communist revolution had destroyed the dynastic political system, it barely affected the social, economic, and philosophic traditions that were the very foundation of the ancient dynasties. Further challenges were inevitable, and they came from two sources: one from within China herself, with the establishment of the Communist Party in July 1921 (succinctly described by Michael Gasster in "The Rise of Chinese Communism"); the other from without, as incursions by the Japanese continued.

In July 1937, four years before the involvement of the United States, World War II began for China and provided the basis for Mao Tse-tung's ascendency to power. The war with Japan presented Chiang Kai-shek—the leader of China and the *Kuomintang* (the Nationalist party)—with a crucial question, and his decision would be vitally important to his and China's future: Which threat should he try to eliminate first—the Japanese threat, which he referred to as a disease of the skin and body, or the Communist menace, which he described as a disease of the heart and spirit? He decided to try and destroy the Communists first. While this effort was being made, the nation lost all the main seaports—its arteries for supplies—to Japan, all the major established industrial cities that supplied the war machine and the economy, as well as large areas of territory and millions of people needed to infuse men, money, and essential morale into the government and the military.

The Communists, meanwhile, under the leadership of Mao Tse-tung at Yenan, were busily building up their own strength in men and arms, organizing Communist cells and guerrilla war units behind the Japanese lines, and propagating their cause among the people with promises of land reform and social equality. One can imagine how difficult it must have been for the ordinary Chinese to understand why the leader of their country, Chiang Kai-shek, was engaged in trying to exterminate fellow Chinese, who were labeled by many as "agricultural reformers," and why he was not making a greater effort to destroy the common enemy, Japan.

In any event, China's war with Japan destroyed the efforts of reform and improvement that the Nationalist government had successfully launched, especially in the economic area, between 1927 and 1937. World War II severely exacerbated such problems as inflation, malnutrition and disease, and the serious landlord-peasant problem, the last of which the Communists had already begun to confront. But the war gave Mao and his followers time and opportunity to strengthen their position and to take advantage of Chiang Kai-shek and the Nationalists' weakened position. Just as World War I had brought about the downfall of tsarist Russia, then, World War II was an important reason, perhaps the main one, for the Communist victory in China.

It is an irony of history that out of a fanatic Serbian patriot's assassination of Archduke Francis Ferdinand, heir to the throne of the Austro-Hungarian

Empire, and the holocaust of war that followed, came the collapse of the Austro-Hungarian Empire and the birth (1918) of the Kingdom of Serbs, Croats, and Slovenes (later called Yugoslavia). Born out of the nationalistic urgings of nineteenth-century South Slavs, and of the idealism that had prevailed during World War I, monarchical Yugoslavia quickly succumbed to the turmoil and conflicts of the real world. Within its short lifespan of little more than three decades, the new nation was marked by a series of crises and perpetual conflict, arising from both internal fighting and external aggression. J. B. Hoptner, in a perceptive study on Yugoslavia, sums up the major problem of the new nation after World War I in this way:

> Many forces contributed to its disunity. Under the Wilsonian star of self-determination three national groups with divergent and often conflicting historical, administrative, and cultural backgrounds found themselves joined together in one kingdom. Their debates over the nature of the new state promptly revealed the centrifugal nature of its political forces. From the outset the conflict that raged between the Croats who argued for federalism and the triumphant Serbs who insisted on centralism warped the growth of democracy in Yugoslavia.[4]

Under such circumstances, the constitutional monarchy moved progressively from a parliamentary democracy that on occasions worked tolerably well, to a centralized police state in which terror was the order of the day. These years of political turmoil, moreover, did little to alter the economic and social problems that had been brewing even before the establishment of an independent country in 1918.

Perhaps in a desperate attempt to solve the many problems facing his divided nation, and convinced that the traditional political method would be the best one, King Alexander, in January 1929, invalidated the Constitution, dissolved the parliament, and established a dictatorship. The tension only increased, however, and, though the King issued a new Constitution in September, 1931, he was assassinated three years later. This event left Yugoslavia both to the danger of civil war and to the menace of Hitler's expanding Germany.

Naturally, in such a chaotic milieu, numerous individuals, factions, and parties began promising the people relief from their serious troubles. Among the parties that arose was the Communist Party of Yugoslavia, which had emerged after the Russian Revolution of 1917. Like its counterpart in China, it at first existed on the edge of extinction owing, in part, to oppressive government measures, and it survived largely as an arm of the more powerful Communist Party of the Soviet Union, which after 1928 was led by Stalin. It was again World War II that provided the impetus for the Yugoslav Communist Party to thrust itself into the political headlines (as it soon would for the Chinese Communists). On April 6, 1941, the Nazi

---

[4] J. B. Hoptner, *Yugoslavia in Crisis 1934–1941* (New York: Columbia University Press, 1962), p. 293.

Juggernaut overwhelmed the Yugoslav army, totally disintegrating it, and a reign of terror and warfare settled on the land.

A resistance movement began immediately, and its important activities are described in the reading "Tito and the Yugoslav Partisan Movement" by N. J. Klones. It need only be said here that Marshal Tito (originally Josip Broz) emerged as leader of the Partisan resistance movement. During this national liberation period, a time during which Tito and the Communists waged a heroic guerrilla war against the Nazis, the country was ravaged by bombing, invasion, suffering, and death. The conditions being what they were, the Communist leadership de-emphasized its ideological orientation and Marxist goals. Propaganda was focused on Yugoslav nationalism, democracy, and hostility to the invaders. Interestingly, it was the Western allies, especially Britain and the United States, that supported Tito both morally and materially, whereas little assistance was provided by Stalin and the Communist Party of the Soviet Union. Finally, the Nazis were driven out of Yugoslavia, and Tito and his Partisans moved into the capital of Belgrade to assume and consolidate governmental power under the banner of communism. During the ensuing years of socialist construction, Tito's job as leader of Yugoslavia would be hindered and complicated by Stalin's continued suspicion and distrust of him. Indeed this distrust was not unfounded, for the Yugoslavs, having won power independent of the Soviet Union, resisted Soviet intervention in Yugoslav affairs, and ultimately Stalin expelled the Yugoslavs from the Cominform in 1948. These and subsequent events were the beginnings of the Yugoslav "road to socialism."

6

The Emergence of Russian Communism

Michael T. Florinsky

The Downfall of the Empire

The events of February–March, 1917, which led to the abdication of the [Tsar] and the creation of the Provisional Government, while generally anticipated, took a form which no one had foreseen. It will be remembered that the imminence of the catastrophe was almost openly discussed everywhere. At the end of 1916 and early in 1917 the possibility of a revolutionary change in the regime had been canvassed behind closed doors by a small group of men representing the Progressive Bloc, the Unions of Zemstvos and of Towns, and the war industries committees. Simultaneously a discussion of the same question was undertaken by another group which included some of the military leaders and was inspired by General Krimov. Both groups arrived quite independently at the same conclusion: the [Tsar] must abdicate in favor of his son, with the Grand Duke Michael Alexandrovich, the [Tsar's] brother, as regent. They also prepared a tentative list of the future ministers and many of their nominees were actually called to take office in March, 1917.

In spite of these preparations, the Revolution came as a surprise to both the liberal and the revolutionary leaders of Russia. It was at first a popular movement which started in Petrograd, probably as a result of a shortage of foodstuffs, the importance of which rumors had much exaggerated. It began on February 23 as a strike of some 70,000 or 80,000 men employed in the metal industries. At first it gave no reason for any great anxiety, and few realized at the time that the fate of the Imperial regime was at stake. Soon, however, it grew in volume and was joined by the troops of the Petrograd garrison. The first desertion among the troops occurred on February 27 when the Volhynsky regiment of the foot guards refused to obey orders and joined the revolutionary populace. It was soon followed by other military units. From that moment the fate of the monarchy was sealed. . . .

The Duma, which assembled on February 27 only to learn that it had been prorogued, was confronted with a situation of extreme seriousness, and appointed a Provisional

From Michael T. Florinsky, *The End of the Russian Empire* (New Haven: Yale University Press, 1931), pp. 237–249, 256–258, 261–266. Reprinted with permission from the publisher.

Committee to take command of the situation. Its leadership, however, remained largely nominal, events pursuing their own course independently of the confused and often contradictory counsels issued from the Taurida Palace. The Taurida Palace itself was soon invaded by a revolutionary mob of soldiers and workmen, [and this development] put an end to all attempts to transact business in an orderly manner. With the new and unruly elements which came to the surface apparently from nowhere, Russian liberals, with their balanced minds and good intentions, had little in common. On March 1, the eve of the abdication, Rodzianko, heading the Provisional Committee of the Duma, telephoned directly to General Ruzsky, commanding the north front. "I am hanging by a mere thread," he told him,[1] "the control of events is slipping from my hands. . . . I am afraid, the worst is still awaiting us." As a matter of fact, he had never had any control of events.

Revolutionary circles were taken by surprise just as much as the liberals. Their organizations at the time, it will be remembered, were practically nonexistent. The majority of their leaders were abroad or in local prisons, or in Siberia. Those still at liberty apparently failed to play any important part in the movement. It was, indeed, said by one of their own writers that "the Revolution found them sleeping, like the foolish virgins."[2] They soon realized, however, that their day had come; and they organized in the Taurida Palace the Soviet of Soldiers' and Workmen's Deputies which played so important a part in the later period of the Revolution.

The spontaneous nature of the movement of February 23–March 2 is generally recognized. Professor Miliukov, a leading figure in the Duma and later for a time Minister of Foreign Affairs in the Provisional Government, admitted that the movement was "entirely chaotic. . . . It was clear that it had nothing to do with the prorogation of the Duma. The two events merely happened to coincide."[3] General Klimovich, a former director of the State Police, also expressed the opinion that "the Revolution was a spontaneous movement . . . it was not the fruit of party propaganda."[4] "The whole of Russia appeared to me like a stormy ocean," said Protopopov,[5] "and where were the social groups that were satisfied? There were none. Where were the social groups one could trust, that one could depend upon? There were none."

The movement [that] led to the abdication of the [Tsar] and the establishment of the Provisional Government was purely local and was limited to the capital. The arrests of the members of the Imperial Cabinet and the seizure of public buildings were carried out by the rebellious troops and by the populace of Petrograd; but the success of the Revolution obviously depended on the support, inarticulate at first, that it received throughout the country. The movement itself had no organization, no leaders, and, at the beginning, it would seem, even no definite purpose. Like a snowball rolling down the slope of a steep hill, it grew in size and gathered strength on its way. It would hardly be correct to say that the Imperial regime had been overthrown: it merely collapsed because it had nothing to rely upon. The news of the abdication of the Tsar was received everywhere either with satisfaction, even with enthusiasm, or with fears for the future and a recognition of its inevitability. The Revolution was the outcome of the work of the disintegrating forces set in motion by the War. The end of the monarchy came with

---

[1]*Fevralskaya Revolutsya 1917 Goda (The Revolution of February 1917)*, in *Krasni Arkhiv*, XXI, 59.
[2]Quoted in Nolde, *L'ancien régime et la révolution russes*, p. 124.
[3]Evidence of Miliukov in *Padenie Tsarskago Rezhima*, VI, 352.
[4]Evidence of Klimovich in *Padenie Tsarskago Rezhima*, I, 98.
[5]Evidence of Protopopov in *Padenie Tsarskago Rezhima*, I, 149.

an ease which few would have ventured to predict. This event, however important in itself, was merely the beginning of an infinitely more fundamental and far-reaching readjustment.

We will not attempt to tell again, with details, the familiar story of the political revolution. It will suffice to recall the fact that Nicholas II, out of affection for his son, refused to abdicate in favor of the Tsarevitch Alexis, as he was urged to do by the emissaries of the Duma, Guchkov and Shulgin, and nominated his brother, the Grand Duke Michael Alexandrovich, as his successor. But by the time Guchkov and Shulgin had returned to Petrograd, the situation had already changed, and antidynastic feelings had greatly increased in intensity. At a conference called by the Provisional Committee of the Duma on March 3, the necessity of preserving the monarchical form of government, with the Grand Duke on the throne, found no supporters except Miliukov and Guchkov. The Grand Duke accordingly declined to accept the Crown, and put the future organization of the Russian State in the hands of a Constituent Assembly to be elected by popular vote. In the meantime the work of government was to be carried on by a Provisional Government, which was to be appointed by the Provisional Committee of the Duma.

This was, indeed, an unforeseen development. Instead of a mere change of sovereign and the establishment of a regime of constitutional monarchy with a boy-emperor under the regency of a benevolent and effaced Grand Duke, the liberal leaders unexpectedly found themselves vested with what amounted in theory to dictatorial powers, and had to face the prospect of elections to a Constituent Assembly in an illiterate country in the midst of a war. The Constitutional Assembly was, to say the least, an unknown quantity, and those coming elections lent to the Provisional Government, resting on the uncertain legal foundation of a revolutionary *coup d'état,* a character of the temporary which was fraught with danger.

The Provisional Government

The Provisional Government, especially the Provisional Government of the first period, was flesh of the flesh of the Russian liberals. It was headed by Prince Lvov, president of the Union of Zemstvos and one of the most popular men in liberal circles. Prince Lvov's long and untarnished record of public work, his close association with the institutions of local government, his eminent services to the country—during both the war with Japan and the [ongoing] War gave him an exceptional position and practically pointed to him as to the logical leader of the new Government. The men who joined his administration were chosen from the more prominent figures of the former opposition. With a few minor exceptions they seemed particularly well qualified for the task they had undertaken. Professor Miliukov, for instance, the new Minister of Foreign Affairs, was not only an eminent scholar and historian, known throughout the world, but also one of the Duma's foremost spokesmen on foreign affairs and a trusted friend of the Entente. A. J. Guchkov, the new Minister of War and the Navy, was a leader of the war industries committees and one of the Duma's experts on military questions. A. J. Shingarev, Minister of Agriculture, was the rapporteur of the budget committee of the Duma, [and his] erudite expositions of the country's financial problems were always listened to with the greatest respect. The socialist elements were represented in the first Provisional Government by A. F. Kerensky, Minister of Justice, an eloquent young lawyer without much practical experience, temperamental and self-confident, but not really extreme in his views or unmanageable. All things considered, the first Provisional Government embodied a realization of the dreams of the Russian liberals when they pressed the Tsar for a government enjoying the confidence of the nation.

It is obviously idle to speculate on what the fate of Russia would have been if Prince Lvov and his colleagues had been called to power by the Tsar, but not as any result of a revolutionary *coup d'état*. Enough that under revolutionary conditions their administration brought nothing but disappointment. We shall not endeavor here to describe the political struggles of the Provisional Government, struggles that made necessary six important changes in its constitution in the course of eight months, and the resignation of Prince Lvov, who was succeeded by Kerensky. It is true that none of the members of the Provisional Government proved to be men of large caliber. Prince Lvov was completely lacking in the determination and aggressiveness of a national leader in an emergency. The gentleness of his nature and disposition, coupled with an inborn inability to make rapid and clear-cut decisions, markedly disqualified him for any position at the head of a revolutionary government. Indeed, in the light of his postrevolutionary activities, his immense popularity in the prerevolutionary period must seem something of a miracle. Kerensky succeeded him in July, and was an even less fortunate choice than his predecessor. The peculiar position he occupied in the Provisional Government as the only link between that body and the Soviet of Soldiers' and Workmen's Deputies resulted in giving him an entirely false and grossly exaggerated idea of his own importance. He sincerely believed himself to be the chosen leader of the nation, and proceeded to carry out a program of re-establishing the morale of the army by a campaign of speech-making. Indeed, he was fully confident that his mere presence was sufficient to imbue the troops with an invincible will for victory. This preposterous idea was naturally doomed to disappointment. A poignant and essentially correct characterization of Kerensky is given by Leon Trotsky.

Lenin called Kerensky a "petit braggart" [he writes]. Even now there is little one can add to that. Kerensky was and still is an adventitious figure, a ruling favorite of the historical moment. Every mighty wave of revolution, as it draws on the virgin masses not yet trained to discrimination, inevitably raises on its crest such heroes for a day, heroes who are instantly blinded by their own effulgence. . . . His best speeches were merely a sumptuous pounding of water in a mortar. In 1917, the water boiled and sent up steam, and the clouds of steam provided a halo.[6]

The Divorce Between the Educated Classes and the Masses

It would be a mistake, however, to attach too much importance to the personalities of the men who happened to be at the helm. . . . The real source of the difficulties of the Provisional Government lay much deeper than mere personalities and must be sought in the divorce between the educated classes and the masses. After the tumultuous days of February–March the rebellious troops and the workingmen of Petrograd had been prevailed upon, not without difficulty, to return to their barracks and their factories but they refused to resign themselves to their prerevolutionary, passive attitude and to allow any well meaning liberals and moderate socialists to arrange the future

---

[6]Trotsky, *My Life* (New York, 1930), p. 289.

according to their particular ideas. The Petrograd Soviet, supported by other local Soviets which rapidly sprang up all over the country, was a constant and most active reminder of the new factor in Russian politics. The Petrograd Soviet itself was steadily moving toward the Left. The relatively moderate composition it had had in the first days of the Revolution, with its mere handful of Bolsheviks, had been gradually replaced by elements much more radical. Against this rising tide of the social revolution in its most extreme forms the Provisional Government waged a losing battle.

Professor Miliukov and his colleagues in the Government [on the one side, and] the masses of the Russian peasants and workmen [on the other], only now awakening from their secular sleep and seeking redress from the grievances that had accumulated in the course of centuries, did not speak the same language. Since the beginning of the War the liberals had staunchly advocated the cause of the Entente and fought the Imperial Government on the ground that it was putting in jeopardy the cause of victory. They refused to admit that this was not the attitude of the masses. The spontaneous movement of the people of Petrograd (exasperated by the privations of a war the purpose and necessity of which they had never understood), a movement which was primarily a protest against war, was officially interpreted as the desire of the masses to establish a regime which would bring the country to victory.

With the supreme contempt for facts of a professor turned politician, Miliukov expounded the theory that the Revolution was primarily a protest against the slackness of the Imperial Government in conducting the War and the prospect of a separate peace with Germany. . . . And this at a time when the garrison of Petrograd, "the glory and pride of the Revolution," refused to leave for the trenches, and the disorganization of the army, with its thousands of desertions, was proceeding at full speed! The liberal intellectuals and moderate socialists who succeeded in high places to the bureaucrats of the Imperial régime were thinking, like their predecessors, in terms of Russia's international obligations, her position among the Great Powers, her national honor. They were irresistibly attracted by the long-coveted prize of Russian diplomacy—the Dardanelles—which was at last within their reach. Partly as a matter of expediency and partly on grounds of social justice, they were willing to make real concessions in the land problem, to transfer to the peasants the large estates, the land for which they had so long and so passionately been hungering. But this transfer was to be carried out legally. The question was to be decided by the Constituent Assembly. And in the meantime no interference with the right of private property was to be tolerated.

The peasant—in his cottage, in the trenches, in the workshop—approached the problem from a very different point of view. To him the international obligations of Russia, her position among the Great Powers, her national honor, were equally meaningless. The Dardanelles was merely a foreign word conveying nothing. The Constituent Assembly was just another strange and suspicious innovation. While Professor Miliukov extolled the necessity of bringing the War to a victorious end, and Prince Lvov and Kerensky pictured the millennium which the Constituent Assembly was to bring about, the long-suffering, ill-treated, illiterate peasant stubbornly thought of that particular estate of a few hundred acres near his native village the division of which among his fellow villagers had always appeared to him to be the one solution of all his problems, and an act of social justice long overdue. "The sole preoccupation of our soldiers," wrote General Selivachev in his diary, on March 13, 1917,[7] "is whether they will receive

---

[7] *Iz Dnevnika Generala V. J. Selivacheva (From the Diary of General V. J. Selivacheva)* in *Krasni Arkhiv,* IX, 117.

additional allotments from the estates belonging to private owners, the appanages, and the monasteries; this is their chief desire." And then came the terrible thought that the redistribution of land might take place before they had time taken by others. What was the fate of the Great War, the loss of international prestige, the abandonment of Constantinople, when compared with this fearful possibility?

The conflict between the attitude of the masses and that of the educated classes, with the exception of the extreme radical wing, was fundamental, insoluble, fatal. It was as impossible for the educated classes to renounce the ideas and principles in which they had been brought up and accept the peasant's point of view, as it was for the [peasant] to understand that [certain objectives] might be more important than the increase of his allotment. There was no room for compromise between the two points of view, and the conflict had to be fought out to its bitter end. In this struggle victory was naturally on the side of the masses.

The members of the Provisional Government were, of course, not unaware of the general drift of events. Prince Lvov, for instance, while maintaining an extremely optimistic attitude in his official pronouncements, frankly admitted to General Kuropatkin in a private conversation that circumstances had carried them much farther than they intended to go. "We are tossed about," he said, "like debris on a stormy sea."[8]

The parties of the extreme Left, whose ranks were strengthened by the return of exiles from Siberia and [expatriots] from abroad, were in a much more favorable position. There was nothing in their political outlook to keep them from adopting the only slogans which the masses could understand and rally to: immediate peace for the soldiers, land for the peasants, abolition of private ownership of the means of production for the workers—and then the overthrow of the whole social hierarchy and the confiscation of all private wealth. In a country like Russia, where the well-to-do and educated groups represented an infinitely small minority, where the bulk of the population lived in extreme poverty, and the potential forces of social discontent were immense, no other policy had any chance of success. In 1917 the Bolsheviks had just as little control over the masses as the other parties. But they rightly understood the underlying factors of the situation, and their watchwords corresponded [to] the inevitable course and development of the Revolution.

Professor Miliukov, who displays infinitely better judgment as a historian than as a statesman, rightly points out that the masses of the people were not, as is sometimes maintained, passive witnesses of the revolutionary storm. "The masses," he writes, "accepted that part of the Revolution which corresponded with their desires; but they opposed a wall of stubborn passive resistance as soon as they began to suspect that events were taking a turn unfavorable to their interests."[9] This is, indeed, one of the lessons of the Russian Revolution.

Economic Decay

The eight months of the rule of the Provisional Government were characterized by a steady decline in every department of the national economic life. The process of the elimination of the bourgeois state, and the substitution for it of the then still untried Communist rule found its external expression in the struggle between the Provisional

---

[8]*Iz Dnevnika A. N. Kuropatkina (From the Diary of A. N. Kuropatkin)* in *Krasni Arkhiv*, XX, 66. Entry under the date of April 25, 1917.

[9]P. N. Miliukov, *Istorya Vtoroi Russkoi Revolutsii (History of the Second Russian Revolution)* I, Part I, 6.

Government and the Soviet of Soldiers' and Workmen's Deputies on the one hand, and the movement of both alike toward the Left, on the other. The Petrograd Soviet came into being simultaneously with the Provisional Government. It was a self-appointed body modeled on the Soviet of 1905. An idea of the conditions which prevailed in it at the start may be gathered from the following description by an eyewitness.

> It was, in the beginning, a confused and mixed assembly [writes M. Labry] towards which the people turned nevertheless as to something that really represented them. It became the meeting place of soldiers who had escaped from their barracks, of workmen on strike, of domestic servants, of cab-drivers. . . . It was the refuge, the port, the pound. One went there to palaver, to drink, to smoke, even to sleep. It truly was the house of the people.[10]

Soon, however, the Soviet grew into a kind of popular parliament.

In spite of its extremely loose organization it had a firm hold over that section of the populace which carried out the *coup d'état* of February–March, the workers and the garrison of Petrograd whose interests it represented. Even in its early days, the Petrograd Soviet, while still quite a conservative assembly as compared with the same body in the autumn of 1917, was nevertheless infinitely [bolder and more] radical than the Provisional Government. Supported as it was by the revolutionary soldiery and workmen of the capital, it proceeded at once to carry out—partly through pressure upon the Provisional Government, and partly by "revolutionary" methods —a policy of radical social reforms, especially in the field of labor legislation and organization. . . .

We may now turn our attention to the effects of this policy and the Revolution in general upon the economic condition of the country. As may well be expected they were nothing short of disastrous. The output of practically every industry suffered a drastic reduction. At the Putilov Works, for instance, a comparison of the production in June, 1916, and June, 1917, will stand out in the following figures. Mild steel decreased from 240,185 [poods (Russian pounds)] to 69,104; cast steel, from 357,676 to 118,325; pig iron, from 70,301 to 45,279. In one of the biggest iron foundries of the Donets Basin the output of pig iron fell from 460,000 [poods] in June, 1916, to 280,000 in June, 1917. Of a total number of 65 blast furnaces in the south, only between 34 and 44 were working, and not even all of these were producing at full capacity. Of 102 Martin furnaces, only 55 were in use in October, 1917. The rail-rolling mills reduced their output by 45 percent.

In the coal mining industry the situation was somewhat different. For the first four months of 1917 the mines of the Donets Basin showed an increase of 70,000 [poods] over the same period in 1916. No sharp decline appeared until May; and the decrease for the first eight months of 1917, as compared with 1916, was only 15,000,000 [poods], the respective figures being 1,052,000,000 and 1,066,400,000. Production, however, remained considerably below prewar figures (in 1917, by 73,000,000 [poods]). The relatively high output of the coal mines was purchased at a heavy price: the number of miners increased substantially while the output per miner steadily fell. From the average monthly figure of 710 [poods] in January, 1916, it dropped to the notably low level of 410 in August, 1917. The same decrease in the output per workman occurred in the metal industry; and in each case it was accompanied by a drastic increase

---

[10]Raoul Labry, *L'industrie russe et la révolution* (Paris, 1919), p. 12.

in wages. M. Labry quotes figures which indicate that at the Putilov Works the outlay in wages for the production of one [pood] of steel increased 14.5 times from June, 1916, to June, 1917 (from 14 copecks to 2.24 rubles).

Even more ominous was the decline in the quantity of coal transported by rail. Here, too, a downward movement manifested itself, beginning with May, 1917. In January, 1916, some 112,000,000 [poods] were loaded in the Donets Basin. In August, 1917, the corresponding figure is only 80,000,000 [poods]. The reason for the decline lay in the shortage of rolling stock and the rapid disorganization of the railroads.

It seems hardly necessary to multiply these examples. The fall in industrial production was merely one of the forerunners of the approaching nationalization of industry. Labor demands, it will be remembered, were no longer directed to the defense of their professional interests but were aimed at the elimination of the class of capitalistic employers. The Provisional Government at its best was capable of giving lip service to the employers, but could offer them no real protection. The position of owners, directors, managers, and engineers became impossible. In the summer of 1917 the Provisional Government received a number of requests from the foreign owners of industrial concerns to take over the management of their works. The leading British and French manufacturers in Russia informed the Government that under existing conditions they could be no longer responsible for the management of their enterprises. They suggested the adoption of the British system of control of industry, which the Provisional Government, more than ever under the influence of the extreme elements, could not possibly accept.

The breakdown of industry was naturally accompanied by other manifestations of an acute economic crisis which are so familiar a feature of the history of postwar Europe, by inflation, depreciation of currency,[11] and a rise in the cost of living. It does not seem necessary to dwell here on these aspects of the situation. The index number of prices for 1917 . . . was computed as 673 (1913 = 100) an increase of 470 over the 1916 figure. Although extreme caution is urged in accepting this figure, there is no doubt that the rise in prices in 1917 proceeded by leaps and bounds. . . .

The Army

The Revolution of February–March, 1917, dealt the last blow to the army, the demoralization of which, as we have seen, was already well advanced in 1915 and 1916. The troops of the Petrograd garrison had had an important part in bringing about the downfall of the Imperial regime and sent their representatives to the Petrograd Soviet of Soldiers' and Workmen's Deputies. One of the first measures of this body was to issue an order which completely upset the recognized principles of military discipline. The essential provision of this order established in every military unit committees of men and officers the functions of which were not clearly defined. We shall not here go into the details of the bitter controversy which arose around this order. The really important fact was that as early as March, 1917, the system of committees was introduced into the army; and military hierarchy, which seems to be one of the essential conditions in the

---

[11]The depreciation of the ruble on foreign markets in the course of 1917 was catastrophic. The par exchange of a pound sterling was £1 = 9.46 rubles. The average London quotation for the second half of 1916 was £1 = 15.53 rubles; in October, 1917, it was £1 = 34.00 rubles.

organization of a military force, was shaken to its very foundations. The army was now thrown open to political propaganda, which was made not only legitimate but even necessary by the fact that the soldiers were to vote in the elections to the Constituent Assembly. "There was everywhere a passion for speech, the right to which has been so long denied," writes General Knox describing the conditions in March, 1917,[12] "and a moment of silence seemed to everyone a moment lost."

It is undoubtedly true that the sweeping tide of revolutionary oratory was an important factor in bringing to the fore the profound discontent which had accumulated in the army [between] 1914 and 1916. However, additional factors explaining the breakdown of the army were . . . an immense fatigue, from uninterrupted military reverses, the insufficiency of supplies, the War's lack of purpose, as seen by the peasant-soldier, and his growing hostility to his leaders, [as well as] . . . that all-absorbing interest in the approaching redistribution of land which was the only consequence of the Revolution with which the peasant-soldier was really concerned.

The command of the army found itself in the same predicament, in the same inescapable situation, as the Provisional Government and the whole of the educated classes. Shortly before the Revolution, at the conference of Chantilly in November, 1916, and at the conference of Petrograd on February 16, 1917, the Russian High Command had given the Allies a definite guaranty to take part in a joint offensive against the Central Powers. In a letter written on March 12, ten days after the abdication of the Emperor, to Guchkov, then Minister of War, General Alexeev, the Commander-in-Chief, was forced to admit that Russia was no longer in a position to meet such an obligation, at least for some time to come. The tragedy of the High Command and the army officers lay in the losing struggle they were pledged to wage, as against the steadily growing determination of the peasants to bring the War to an end.

The full effect of the Revolution upon the army did not appear at once. Some of the commanding officers reported to Headquarters that the army's fighting spirit and discipline were not adversely affected by the abdication of the Tsar. General Danilov, commanding the Second Army, and a few others went even so far as to maintain that the troops under their command were in better fighting condition than ever. One may well question the sincerity of this official optimism. Any expression of doubt as to the beneficial effects of the new regime was treated in those days as disloyalty to the Revolution, and the changes in command were sweeping. There is little question that the grandiloquent promises to defend Russia and the Revolution against the enemy embodied in the resolutions passed by innumerable army units were not always taken at their face value.

> For three days the regiments of the reserve have been calling on me to express their willingness to fight to the bitter end [wrote on March 29, 1917, General Dragomirov in "strict confidence" to General Ruzsky]; they promised to obey my every order and die for the country. Nevertheless it is difficult to make them obey orders that send them to the trenches. One gets no more volunteers for the simplest military operation, even for a mere reconnaissance, and no one can be induced to move from our trenches in the direction of the enemy. The fighting spirit has dwindled away. Not only have the soldiers no desire to advance, but their will even to defend themselves has been so terribly shaken that it is a real menace to the issue of the War. All the thoughts of the common soldiers turn towards home. Their only desire is to leave the trenches.[13]

---

[12]Major-General Sir Alfred Knox, *With the Russian Army, 1914–1917,* two volumes (New York, 1921), p. 575.

[13]*Razlozhenie Armii v 1917 Godu,* document No. 27, p. 31.

The patriotic declarations of the first days soon gave place to demands for peace without annexations and contributions, to refusals to fight for the benefit of British and French capitalists, and to promises to defend the existing front, which were now accompanied by refusals to participate in any attempt to break the enemy's line. This, of course, was nothing but a slightly disguised demand for immediate peace. The ball which had started rolling could no longer be stopped. . . .

It is hardly necessary here to mention the Kornilov episode which had no practical bearing upon the general trend of events. Kornilov, a gallant general with a brilliant war record and Commander-in-Chief in August–September, 1917, endeavored to save the Provisional Government against its own will by restoring discipline in the army and establishing a regime approaching that of a military dictatorship. It would seem that Kerensky, who for a time lent his support to the scheme, deserted Kornilov at the last moment, and the General was arrested by the very men he was trying to save. It was just one more ephemeral attempt to restore order that was doomed in advance. In the meantime the army was rapidly degenerating into an unruly mob which became the terror of the districts adjoining the front. . . .

The Growth of Bolshevism

It will be remembered that the Bolsheviks had no immediate part in bringing about the downfall of the Empire. In February, 1917, their organization among the working people was negligible; practically all of their prominent leaders were either in Siberia or abroad. Lenin was still in Switzerland, engaged mostly in literary work, and Trotsky had Union Square in New York for the chief field of his activities. Even after the downfall of the Empire, in the Soviet of Soldiers' and Workmen's Deputies—that vanguard of the revolutionary forces—the Bolsheviks were represented at the beginning by a mere handful of men who exercised very little influence. Until the arrival of Lenin via Germany on April 4, 1917, the Bolshevik chieftains in Petrograd were entirely unconscious of the events which were to make them the masters of Russia within eight short months.

> Not one of those leaders of the party who were in Russia [writes Leon Trotsky] had any intention of making the dictatorship of the proletariat—the social revolution—the immediate object of his policy. A party conference which met on the eve of Lenin's arrival and counted among its members about thirty Bolsheviks showed that none of them even imagined anything beyond democracy. . . . Stalin was in favor of supporting the Provisional Government of Guchkov and Miliukov and of merging the Bolsheviks with the Mensheviks![14]

Even with the arrival of Lenin, followed a month later by Trotsky, the prospects of the Bolsheviks seemed anything but bright. The extreme doctrines of Lenin, his demands for an open declaration in favor of communism and class war were given a cool reception by the Social-Democrats. . . .

Undoubtedly, with the arrival of Lenin and Trotsky the revolutionary movement found its real leaders. The organization of the party was enlarged and improved. In the first two weeks after the Revolution, according to Shlyapnikov, one of the Soviet leaders, the burden of all the party work, as well as that of participation in the deliberations of the Soviet, was carried by only three men. But even six months later, it was a

---

[14]Leon Trotsky, *My Life* (New York, 1930), pp. 329–330.

party still inefficient and loose in the extreme. Speaking of the situation at the end of October, after the successful *coup d'état* which brought the Soviets to power, Trotsky says: "Three weeks ago we had gained a majority in the Petrograd Soviet. We were hardly more than a banner—with no printing works, no funds, no branches."[15]

The forces which worked for the Bolshevik cause were not, as it is sometimes imagined, their superior skill in rallying the masses by creating a powerful secret organization. It consisted merely in the fact that the Bolsheviks were the only political party which had openly proclaimed as their program the sole ideas which the immense majority of the country could understand and was longing for: the immediate end of the War, the land for the peasants, "the taking back of what had been taken away," that is, the right to take immediate possession of all private wealth. And the fulfillment of this program was promised through the dictatorship of the proletariat, embodied in the sacramental sentence "All power to the Soviets," accompanied by a merciless class struggle. In this program the "latent socialism without a doctrine" of the masses at last found its expression. And what did the Russian liberals and moderate socialists [propose in opposition] to this program: the myth of the Constituent Assembly and "war to a victorious end"! What chance of success did a program of that kind have in a country which had reached the degree of demoralization we find in Russia in 1917?

The great service of Lenin to the Bolshevik cause consists in his recognition of the importance of the peasant revolution in a country constituted as Russia is. While the more orthodox Marxists shrank from the idea of an agrarian revolution, Lenin boldly accepted it as a stepping stone to the social revolution, and the course of events in 1917 proved that he was right.

> In the life of the country and in the life of the individual, those were extraordinary days [writes Trotsky]. In social passions, as well as in personal powers, tension reached its highest point. The masses were creating an epoch, and their leaders felt their steps merging with those of history. On the decisions made and the orders given in those days depended the fate of the nation for an entire historical era. And yet those decisions were made with very little discussion. . . . they were almost improvised on the moment. . . . The pressure of events was so terrific, and the work to be done so clear before us, that the most important decisions came naturally, as a matter of course, and were received in the same spirit. The path had been predetermined; all that was required was to indicate the work. No arguments were necessary, and very few appeals. Without hesitation or doubt, the masses picked up what was suggested to them by the nature of the situation. Under the strain of events, their "leaders" did no more than formulate what answered the requirements of the people and the demands of history.[16]

If the analysis offered by this volume truly reflects the course of events in Russia during the War it seems impossible not to agree with Trotsky. The overthrow of the Provisional Government and the establishment of the Soviet rule was merely the completion of the process which started with the outbreak of the War, shattering, as it did, the fragile structure of Imperial Russia. The next stage was reached in February–March, 1917, when the long rule of the tsars was brought to an end and the forces of discontent and social hatred, so long suppressed, were suddenly set free. The result of this new process was the establishment of a regime adhering to principles such as those

---

[15]Ibid., p. 366.
[16]Ibid., p. 334.

proclaimed by Lenin. With complete contempt for the rather flattering theory of a sinister and powerful Soviet conspiracy, Trotsky frankly admits that "it was impossible to tell in advance whether we were to stay in power or be overthrown." And he also confesses that the work of the Soviet Government in the first months was nothing else but "an immense legislative improvisation," an exposition of the party program "ir. the language of power" rather than a constructive policy of political and social reforms.[17] But it flattered the masses, encouraged them to follow a line of conduct on which they had already set their mind; and it was only a government supporting such a policy that could maintain itself in the midst of the revolutionary upheaval. Under the conditions which prevailed in Russia in the second half of 1917, it would seem hardly correct to picture the Bolsheviks as mere usurpers.

Conclusion

If we . . . attempt to appraise the forces which brought about the fall of the tsars and paved the way for Bolshevism, all Russia in 1914–1917 will appear as an uneasy sea gradually lashed to fury by the winds of the approaching revolutionary storm. The source of the catastrophe which overcame the Empire may, undoubtedly, be traced far back in the history of the Russian people. As long as the country was not asked to make the supreme and heroic effort imposed upon it by the War, it managed to trail, and not without a certain degree of success, behind the other European countries along the road of economic development and progress. But the Great War put the whole framework of the Empire to a severe test. The obsoleteness and the imperfections of its political, social, and economic structure could no longer be concealed and ignored. Following the example of England, France, and Germany, who, reacting from the blows they were receiving, made superhuman efforts to meet the emergency, Russia, or rather her educated classes, tried to organize their country for the War; but their attempts were sporadic, uncoordinated, and almost pathetic in their helplessness. A ship without a captain and manned by an unskilled and undisciplined crew, Russia drifted along an uncharted course.

Few are the instances in the history of the human race when the impotence and inadequacy of a political regime revealed themselves with such striking force. None of the elements of the Russian state proved equal to the burden which was thrown upon them. The [Tsar] was a weak and obstinate man, a mere tool in the hands of an unbalanced woman guided by vulgar adventurers. The bureaucracy was senile, unadaptable, and helpless in an emergency. It soon lost whatever virtues it might have possessed before the War. The Duma was sadly lacking in authority and leadership. The educated classes, in spite of their honest desire to champion the cause of the people, were crippled by the opposition of the bureaucracy and their aloofness from the masses. There was no organized labor, no real self-government on a broad democratic basis, no real tradition of public service. The economic and educational standards of the masses were appallingly low. And beneath the thin layer of refined European culture one could feel the subdued, heavy breathing of the millions of peasants, inarticulate, ignored, and often forgotten in their snowclad cottages in the immensity of the Russian plains. The menacing murmur which rose at times from the countryside reminded those in power that

---

[17]Ibid., pp. 342–343.

everything was not well. But the machinery of the bureaucratic state is slow, and the "peasant question" presented so many interesting problems that had to be threshed out before a decision could be reached!

The War—the losses in men, territory, and wealth, the economic hardships, the flagrant impotence of the ruling clique when faced with crisis, the degeneration of autocracy itself—all brought to the top the powers of discontent and social antagonism which had been gathering beneath the ominously quiet and peaceful surface. Who will be bold enough to determine which was the factor that played the leading part in bringing about the Revolution? Was it the folly of the [Tsar] . . . ? the decay of the Government? military losses? the secular grievances of the peasants? the starving conditions of the cities? the weariness with the war? We cannot answer these questions, just as there is no way of determining, when the storm bursts, which of the many streams pouring into a river is responsible for the breaking of the dam and the flooding of the country below, or which handful of snow started the avalanche that buries in its deadly path the villages and pastures of the hard-working mountaineers. One thing, however, is clear. When the swollen river breaks the dam or the avalanche begins its descent into the valley, there is no human power which can stop it until the elementary forces of nature, over which men have no control, have exhausted their destructive energies. The same may be said of the Russian Revolution. Here the landslide which started in March, 1917, did not reach the bottom of the valley until the establishment of the Soviet rule.

7

The Rise of
Chinese Communism

Michael Gasster

Around 1900 China paused at a fork in the road. Looking over its shoulder along the path of traditionalism, the government could see forty years of defeat. Ahead, clearly in view, lay almost certain disaster, for at that very moment China seemed about to be carved into bite-sized colonial portions. The Peking authorities decided to explore a new route, one that seemed to skirt the West by way of Japan. After 1901 Chinese modernization began to follow Japan's example.

Between 1895 and 1905 Japan had smashed China; thrown off some of the most obnoxious features of the unequal treaties that the Western powers had imposed on her; consummated an alliance with Great Britain, the world's leading power, on a basis of equality; and thrashed another prominent imperialist power, Russia, in a bloody war. It was a decade's work that aroused Chinese envy, particularly since Japan seemed to have borrowed a great deal from the West without sacrificing her own unique cultural identity. Japan had combined industrialism, modern military methods, and at least the appearance of constitutional-parliamentary government with a strengthening of the emperor's position and the destruction of feudal power. This combination made the enfeebled Ch'ing government, harassed for decades by the loss of its power to provincial military regimes, dream once again of restoring central authority and shoring up its defenses against the West.

Beginning about 1901, therefore, the government intensified its efforts to modernize the armed forces, build railroads and other modern means of transportation and communication, streamline its bureaucracy, promote modern education, and develop industry and mining. Some of its most enterprising steps were prompted by Japan's example. Among the most significant measures were the dispatch of thousands of students to Japan and the decision, reached in 1905 and 1906, to adopt a constitution. The students were to provide trained personnel for the government's modernization program. The constitution was a defensive measure undertaken in a spirit resembling nineteenth-century self-strengthening. The Empress Dowager reasoned that "the wealth and strength of other countries are due to their practice of constitutional government,

From Michael Gasster, *China's Struggle to Modernize* (New York: Alfred A. Knopf, 1972), pp. 19-21, 25-39, 71-95. [Reprinted with permission from the publisher.]

in which public questions are determined by consultation with the people." For her, constitutionalism was not intended to guarantee individual rights or to limit government or to divide power or for any of the other purposes known in Western democracies; instead, its object was to make China wealthy and powerful. After several months of study the government decided to follow closely the kind of constitution adopted by the Japanese, who had borrowed theirs from Prussia. In the Empress Dowager's eyes, the artful combination of elected representation with strengthened imperial prestige and power was among the most attractive features of the Japanese constitution.

The decision to study foreign governments in order to determine what kind of political system would be best for China represented a remarkable change of attitude. Of their many great achievements, none had given the Chinese greater pride than their form of government, which for lengthy periods had functioned efficiently and justly, despite premodern conditions and problems of immense area and population. For the Chinese now to confess so openly that they had something to learn from foreigners about the art of government was an about-face of the first magnitude.

Thus, as the twentieth century began, the rotting Ch'ing dynasty was moving further than ever before toward rejecting Chinese tradition and adopting Western practices. But even as it quickened its pace along the new path, the government was already being overtaken by more radical competitors. To understand the new steps taken by the government and the still newer ones called for by others, we must look into the backgrounds of the new movements.

Intellectual Foundations of Modern China

It is easy now to forget how novel and how enormously revolutionary—in the West as well as in Asia—was the idea that rapid social change is both desirable and possible. That life *should* be very different from what it had always been was an idea that people were beginning to accept in late nineteenth-century China. Still, the conviction persisted that great changes, even if they were desirable, were not really possible; it was difficult to see that life *could* be very different from what it had always been.

Sun Yat-sen (1866–1925), the founder and moving spirit of the revolutionary movement, came to his calling by a peculiarly winding route. His early life was scarcely different from that of tens of thousands of other farmers' sons. But in 1879 Sun joined his older brother in Hawaii. The next fifteen years included education in a British missionary school in Hawaii, a return to his home village during which he offended the villagers by destroying some wooden idols, further British education in Hong Kong culminating in graduation from a medical school, and medical practice in Macao. Throughout the fifteen years Sun's professional education was his major concern, but his interest in social and political problems followed closely behind. He soon abandoned his medical career and spent the last thirty-one years of his life as a full-time professional revolutionary.

Sun tended to think in terms of contemporary Western (especially American) standards of nationhood and government. He usually emphasized the need for China to achieve full national sovereignty, to be independent of all foreign control, and especially to develop a sense of national community. He was later to stress that the Chinese people were "scattered sand," granules of families and clans with no cement of national spirit. Sun's education and temperament did not equip him to formulate a coherent or profound political philosophy, nor was his career as a revolutionary conducive to the development of systematic ideas; but to the extent that he was able to think out a program, it was one of nationalism, democracy, republicanism, and economic modernization.

Nationalism meant to Sun driving out the Manchu rulers and creating a Chinese-controlled nation-state; democracy meant a representative system with a strong executive branch and a system of checks and balances much like that of the United States; and economic modernization meant a dimly perceived compromise between socialism and capitalism that he hoped would avoid the evils of both. Only to a relatively small extent did he attempt to explain the relevance of his program to Chinese needs and conditions; Sun's idea for adapting democracy, for example, was simply to add to the legislative, executive, and judicial branches two other branches of government that had functioned in traditional China: One was to administer the civil service bureaucracy and the other, to be known as the "control" branch, was intended to inspect the entire government for signs of malfunctioning.

On the basis of this program Sun regularly appealed to foreign governments to support his movement, and in his anxiety to obtain foreign aid he occasionally made rather extravagant promises of economic concessions in return. For a long time he remained convinced that the Western democracies would welcome and help a Chinese democratic movement. With only a few modifications, his followers, although resentful of Western imperialism, allowed their admiration for Western strength and prosperity to outweigh their resentment.

Sun's ideas were influenced not only by his Western education but also by his early home life and, probably more profoundly, by the overseas Chinese with whom he lived and among whom he traveled for much of his later life. The Chinese in Hawaii, Hong Kong, Japan, Southeast Asia, and all over the world lived in tight communities of their own, islands of industrious immigrants struggling to maintain themselves and at the same time earn something extra to send home. Their settlements remained largely isolated within the countries in which they lived; and without the protection of his family and clan, a Chinese who lived overseas relied on the secret society organizations that had protected commoners in China for centuries. Hence Chinese secret societies, which were essentially mutual aid and mutual protection organizations with mystical-religious ideologies, had active branches in the overseas Chinese communities.

Sun's early revolutionary organizations depended heavily on money contributed by Chinese who lived abroad, especially businessmen. Many of Sun's earliest political associates and most trusted allies were secret society men, often from societies that had branches overseas. His own organizations had initiation rituals, oaths, slogans, sworn brotherhood, and other secret society characteristics. Indeed, one of Sun's recurring problems was that, like a secret society leader, he often insisted on the unquestioning obedience of his followers; he exercised a very personal, cabalistic, almost occult kind of leadership.

Sun's style of leadership found few followers. A poor organizer and an inept tactician, Sun spent an unhappy decade fruitlessly promoting revolution. In the summer of 1905, however, his fortunes changed. And so did the course of modern Chinese history. Sun now became caught up in a swelling tide of revolution that was already changing China more than anyone could see at the time.

Several currents intersected to produce this tide. One was the reform program of the Ch'ing government, which in 1905 not only charted a new political course for China, but also initiated fundamental social changes. Its most important measure was the abolition of the traditional civil service examination system. This measure opened the way for the destruction of the elite group of scholar-gentry, whose social status and privileges had sharply distinguished them from everyone else in China. Similarly, the old educational system, which had been designed to prepare students for the civil service, received a crippling blow, and so did the entire body of Confucian principles that the old education had taught.

The major beneficiaries of these changes were the thousands of students who were sent abroad, mostly to Japan, to receive a new education. From a few hundred in 1902, the number grew to fifteen thousand in 1906. The government hoped they would return to employ their new skills in the service of a modernized Ch'ing state and of the new army it was also attempting to create. But the students, sensitive to the changing intellectual climate in 1901 and 1902, were already listening more to Yen Fu and Liang Ch'i-ch'ao[1] than to the Empress Dowager. When they arrived in Japan the students were dazzled by what they discovered. Japan was on the march. The country bustled with confidence. A militant nationalism spun the wheels of social and economic change, producing goods, weapons, and national pride. Relations with Russia happened to be worsening at the time, and war fever swept the land; when Japan's victory came in 1905, thousands of Chinese students participated vicariously. An Asian nation had demonstrated that it could quickly develop a modern army, navy, economy, and government, and thereby subdue a major Western imperialist power. Reasoning that if Japan could do it, so could China, the students decided that the time had come to dedicate themselves to China's future and to organize for concerted revolutionary action on a large scale.

By 1905 the students' ideas had outraced those of Liang Ch'i-ch'ao, who was lowering his sights precisely when the students were raising theirs. In the absence of other attractive leadership, the students decided to unite behind Sun Yat-sen. But this was not entirely a decision by default. Sun had great personal magnetism, and in ten years of devoted revolutionary work, he had cultivated a wide range of very useful contacts, including secret societies, overseas businessmen, and foreign adventurers and politicians. Some of his exploits had earned him a considerable reputation abroad. A persuasive speaker, he could be useful in future negotiations with the imperialist powers; meanwhile, he could raise money and impress foreigners enough to enhance the reputation of the revolutionary movement. As a medical doctor and at least a nominal Christian, he had qualities no other Chinese leader could match; and there was nothing he wanted more than to overthrow the Ch'ing dynasty and make China a republic, aims that suited the students.

The revolutionary alliance that was forged in the summer of 1905 toiled mightily for six years in behalf of anti-Manchu republicanism, and in that time it grew into a broad coalition of discontented groups. Between October, 1911 and February 1912 this rather loose coalition saw its efforts rewarded at last. A revolution overthrew the Ch'ing government and ended the Chinese empire. The alliance between Sun and the students contributed a good deal to the fall of the Ch'ing dynasty and the founding of the Republic of China; most important, it infiltrated the imperial army and weakened the soldiers' will to fight in behalf of the dynasty, and it effectively spread ideas of democracy and republicanism.

Still, the alliance was not solely responsible for the momentous events of 1911 and 1912. Among the several other forces that combined to terminate the ancient imperial

---

[1]Yen Fu (1853–1921) was an advocate of modernization in China who translated works by Thomas Huxley, Herbert Spencer, Adam Smith, and many other Western intellectuals. Liang Ch'i-ch'ao (1873–1929) was a leading intellectual and writer who advocated reform for China.]

system, two must be mentioned here. Ironically both played their roles after being called on stage by the Ch'ing court. The government created the first when, as part of its plan to introduce a limited form of constitutionalism, it decided also to permit elections. Held for the first time in 1909, the elections produced assemblies in each of twenty-one provinces. Few members of the assemblies were revolutionaries, but many were highly critical of the central government, and their vocal demands put added pressure on Peking. Then a national assembly, initiated in 1910, harassed the court still more. But in addition to undermining the authority of the central government, the assemblies provided rallying points for many protesters. Through the assemblies it became possible for landowners, businessmen, educators, journalists, and even some ordinary citizens to become active in politics and to make their voices heard. These people found both their nationalist sensibilities and their economic aspirations outraged by a government railway nationalization plan that favored foreign investors. The assemblies protested but were unheeded, and the members' loyalty to the government evaporated. Thus, new interest groups and new instruments of power, which had been allowed to exist by the Ch'ing court in the hope that they would modernize the government, appease its critics, and strengthen its claim to rule and its ability to enforce that claim, now decided they could better promote their interests by throwing off Ch'ing rule and creating a republic. When the opportunity came in the autumn of 1911, fifteen provincial assemblies declared their independence, and China began to break up into provincial regimes.

In a last-ditch effort to stave off disaster, the Ch'ing court called upon General Yüan Shih-k'ai[2] (1857–1916), whose help had been decisive in the Empress Dowager's coup of 1898. He had been in retirement since her death in 1908, but his army, which was the best-equipped and best-trained army in China, had remained intact. Yüan negotiated terms with the court that were favorable to himself, entered the fray, fought until a stalemate was created among the revolutionaries, the various provincial regimes, and himself, and then maneuvered adroitly until he managed to obtain the Manchus' abdication. Thus the Ch'ing government committed unintentional suicide by sending students abroad, initiating constitutional and representative government, and inviting back into power the very man who finally forced it to step down.

Yüan Shih-k'ai, by compelling the Manchus to abdicate, persuaded his other rivals for power to accept a compromise. In exchange for ending the empire, he was to become president of the Republic of China, but he in turn was to permit free elections, a parliament, and a system of constitutional government providing for checks and balances and a sharing of power. Sun Yat-sen and his allies accepted a compromise with Yüan because they feared division in the country. Inexperienced, disorganized, woefully lacking in mass support, and afraid that continued disorder might lead the foreign powers to intervene, the republicans chose not to prolong the struggle by military means. They agreed to recognize as president a military man they distrusted and to count on a constitution and their strength in the parliament to control him. Perhaps a bit intoxicated by their own propaganda about the merits of republicanism, they were unduly optimistic that democratic institutions were taking root in China. They lost the gamble. Many of them thereupon renounced political activity in disgust; some even left the country. Speaking for his generation, one émigré explained in a letter to a friend: "Politics is in such confusion that I am at a loss to know what to talk about."

---

[2]Pronounced *Yew-on Shr-kie* (as in "pie").

New Culture and Nationalism

Governing authority after 1912, and increasingly so between 1916 and 1926, devolved upon "warlords"—military men of narrow vision, limited objectives, and, with few exceptions, mediocre abilities. Each warlord controlled as much territory as he could without taking great risks, taxed as heavily as the people could bear, governed minimally, expanded his army, and maneuvered cautiously to maintain his security vis-à-vis other warlords. All relied heavily on armies whose numbers fluctuated due to the soldiers' unreliability, but which were intended to be personally loyal to an individual warlord. Some had small forces of no more than a few thousand men, but major warlords had armies that occasionally numbered more than a quarter of a million. Some controlled small areas no larger than a county; others controlled several provinces. Some nourished vague ambitions of greater glory, perhaps even a throne; many sought and some obtained aid from foreign powers; a few carried out, usually on a modest scale, social reforms such as attempts to discourage vice or promote education and public works. Some warlords even paid attention to national problems, but for the most part they were concerned only with their own immediate welfare and security.

After the death of Yüan Shih-k'ai in 1916, China had no political leader of national stature; the republic, crippled from the very first, now almost ceased to exist. Its officers and agencies functioned at the whim of whichever warlord managed to hold Peking. That warlord handled China's diplomacy in the name of the republic, but in China his writ extended only to the territory of the neighboring warlord. China was divided among countless satrapies and for a long time after the republican revolution had anything but a modern government. Intellectuals began to think that little had changed despite the fall of the monarchy. They felt that the introduction of reforms over the last fifty years in the armed forces, schools, government, and economy had brought China no closer to being a strong and prosperous nation.

When Japan in 1915 presented to China a set of Twenty-one Demands, the intellectuals' frustration turned to rage. The demands were so far-reaching that it was humiliating merely to be presented with them; only to a country held in utter contempt could Japan have dared to present so naked a claim for virtual colonization. China managed only narrowly to avert full accession to the Japanese demands, and the entire incident provoked immense anger among patriotic Chinese. The day Japan delivered her final ultimatum (May 7) became National Humiliation Day, almost a day of mourning, but also a day of commemoration and rededication. It was in this atmosphere—the failure of republicanism, the renewal of foreign imperialism, and the frustration engendered by failure and weakness—that a handful of Chinese intellectuals undertook to re-examine the problem of modernizing their country.

The intellectuals who surveyed the wreckage of the 1911 revolution were led by men who had not played an important part in it and who felt no stake in justifying it or rationalizing it. They evaluated the revolution coolly and ruthlessly, judging it to have produced a "pseudorepublicanism" under which

> we have experienced every kind of suffering known to those who are not free. These sufferings remain the same regardless of political changes or the substitution of one political party in power for another. When politics brings us to such a dead end, we have to arouse ourselves and realize that genuine republicanism can never be achieved until politics is initiated by the people. In order to get the people to initiate politics, we must have as a prerequisite an atmosphere wherein a genuine spirit of free thought and free criticism can be nurtured.

With this ringing denunciation of the republic and call for more popular initiative in politics, China's struggle to modernize entered a new phase. Intellectuals retained continuity with Yen Fu by reaffirming the doctrines of struggle for existence, natural selection, and survival of the fittest, and they demanded a "new culture" much as Liang Ch'i-ch'ao had called for a new people; but the leaders of the New Culture Movement went further than Yen and Liang by condemning all of Chinese tradition. Liang had criticized "those who are infatuated with Western ways and . . . throw away our morals, learning, and customs of several thousand years' standing"; to Ch'en Tu-hsiu[3] (1879–1942), who by 1915 was on his way to becoming the most influential writer in China, Chinese tradition resided in an antiquated Confucianism that "did not go beyond the privilege and prestige of a few rulers and aristocrats and had nothing to do with the happiness of the great masses." Evaluation of the 1911 revolution led men like Ch'en to conclude that Chinese tradition accounted for the republic's failure. In particular, Confucianism, with its subordination of the young to the old and the individual to the family, stifled the freedom of thought that the people needed in order to bring about true republicanism. Thus New Culture Movement leaders not only continued to uphold ideals of Western democracy and science, but they also promoted those ideals even more fervently and uncompromisingly than earlier modernizing movements; and they went beyond earlier movements in their antitraditionalism and in their appeal for mass participation and even for popular initiative in political action.

In 1915 Ch'en Tu-hsiu founded a magazine called *Youth,* which for the next five years was probably the most widely read and influential publication in China. For the first issue Ch'en wrote a "Call to Youth," in which he urged young people to assume responsibility for eliminating "the old and the rotten" from Chinese life and replacing it with science and democracy. Ch'en's theme was this: "If we expect to establish a Western type of modern nation then the most basic step is to import the foundation of modern Western society—the faith in the equality of men."

Ch'en's "Call to Youth" was heard, and the response was immediate and powerful. Within a few months many of the men who soon dominated Chinese intellectual life were writing tributes to Darwin, the scientific method, the experimental spirit, and liberty, equality and fraternity. Ch'en's magazine changed its name to *The New Youth* and, symbolically, later adopted a French title, *La Jeunesse.* To the English and American influences fostered by Yen Fu, Liang Ch'i-ch'ao, and Sun Yat-sen, China's new youth had added the scientific and French revolutions.

The young people's burgeoning activism was furthered early in 1919 by developments at the Paris Peace Conference. China had entered World War I after much debate. One of the most convincing arguments for participation in the war was that a contribution to victory would entitle China to share in the rewards; the Chinese hoped that at the very least they would regain from the losing powers whatever holdings the losers had in China. Thus the Chinese negotiators at Paris were confident of obtaining the return of Germany's concessions, and, hearing the worldwide proclamations of "territorial integrity" and "national self-determination," they had hopes of obtaining much more. Perhaps even the Twenty-one Demands would be reversed. These hopes were shattered by the revelation at Versailles of secret agreements Japan had made years before with Britain, France, and the warlord government of China; they had been promised to Japan. Japan's position in China was not to be weakened, but strengthened.

---

[3]Pronounced *Chuhn Doo-shyo.*

Details of these agreements had trickled into public view during 1918, but at first aroused only small and scattered protests. The protests grew in size and frequency and were supported by new social and economic groups as well as by the intellectuals. The Chinese economy expanded considerably due to the war, and embryonic classes of merchants, industrialists, and workers began to grow. Demonstrations against foreign domination began to bring them into contact with each other and with students and teachers. The minor outbursts of 1918 and early 1919 turned out to be rehearsals for the volcanic political eruption of May 4, 1919.

On May 1 reports from the Chinese delegates revealing that they had lost the diplomatic contest began to appear in the Peking press. Readers were dumbfounded, unbelieving, outraged. Despite all signs to the contrary the public had not been able to believe that the effort to secure China's rights would end in failure. Wilson and others had spoken too well; the world could not ignore the truth and beauty of such noble principles. The disappointment was cataclysmic. One student recalled:

> When the news of the Paris Peace Conference finally reached us we were greatly shocked. We at once awoke to the fact that foreign nations were still selfish and militaristic and that they were all great liars. I remember that the night of May 2 very few of us slept. A group of my friends and I talked almost the whole night. We came to the conclusion that a greater world war would be coming sooner or later, and that this great war would be fought in the East. . . . Looking at our people and at the pitiful ignorant masses, we couldn't help but feel that we must struggle!

The struggle burst forth almost at once. The students had planned a demonstration for May 7, National Humiliation Day, but government repression made them decide to move more quickly. Student leaders hurriedly called a meeting for the evening of May 3 and passed a number of resolutions, including one for a mass demonstration the next day. On Sunday morning, May 4, some three thousand students met, drew up manifestos, and marched. Spectators cheered, some wept, and even Western observers were impressed. John Dewey and his wife, who had arrived only a few days earlier to begin a visit that was to last more than two years, wrote home in wonder: "To think of kids in our country from fourteen on, taking the lead in starting a big cleanup reform politics movement and shaming merchants and professional men into joining them. This is sure some country."

As Dewey observantly noted, this was not merely a student demonstration in Peking. It became nationwide, both geographically and socially. A sixteen-year-old high school boy in Ssu-ch'uan, 1,000 miles from Peking, recalled the day he heard the news:

> Only a month was left before my graduation. We were having our examination period. And suddenly, like a black Japanese bomb, the Fourth of May exploded over our heads.
>
> Busy with our noisy studying we did not see the teachers running hurriedly to the office of the director. The servants who carried tea to the conference whispered in our inattentive ears: "A letter. . . . Important. From Peking. They don't know whether or not to show the students."
>
> . . . The secretary pasted a long letter on the black announcement board. A thick crowd of students, panting with excitement, gathered quickly around the board. Our best orator, who had a ringing voice and clear enunciation, read every sentence of that remarkable letter. . . .
>
> The letter upset us completely: Boycott . . . Union . . . Constitution . . . Organization . . . Collections . . . All these were strange words. The weight of important political action was laid upon our narrow boyish shoulders.

. . . That night we could not sleep. Our meeting rumbled loudly in the light of oil lamps, and the timid sparrow-like twitter of the younger boys mingled with the harsh breaking voices of the sixteen-year-olds.

. . . Noise, exciting speeches. One student after another came up on the platform. When had they learned to speak? When had they found these ardent gestures—these boys who only yesterday were engaged in childish scuffles. Where did they learn to make those exalted, convincing speeches, to which teachers, directors, and the representatives of merchants now listened so attentively, nodding their heavy heads in time to the angry shouts of their sons and pupils?

The three boys' high schools dedicated themselves, down to the last person, to the anti-Japanese boycott.

. . . Every word of every orator fell into the crackling fire of applause. The treasurer reported the rapid growth of Union funds. I, the secretary, waving over my head a blueprint map of the town, announced how we were going to carry out the boycott.

"All Japanese merchandise must be destroyed," I shouted. "Not a single Japanese object must be hidden. For this, you must elect people whose hands are clean. The Peking comrades summon us to join the strike!"

"The strike!"

The May Fourth incident created an unprecedented wave of patriotism in China. Boycotts, strikes, and demonstrations erupted all over the country and continued for more than a month. Government attempts at repression failed. Rumors circulated that police and soldiers were going to side with the students, merchants, and workers. Several cabinet members resigned. And finally, on June 28, under pressure from Chinese students and workers in France who surrounded its headquarters, the Chinese delegation at Versailles defied its government's instructions and refused to sign the treaty.

But the May Fourth incident was only a partial victory. The secret treaties were not abrogated, and China still had to confront the militant and aggressive Japanese. The confrontation, however, was now on a different basis. The masses were far from mobilized, but nationwide political organization and action had taken place on a scale never before seen in China. A new intelligentsia that had been developing at least since the early 1900s, when thousands of students had gone abroad, had become a major force in Chinese life. Their own organization spanned the country. They had discovered that organized propaganda and demonstrations could bring results. They had tasted the excitement of political activity and some fruits of success. They had made contact with big industrialists and clerks, merchants and laborers, college presidents and janitors, university professors and professional politicians. They had created a pattern for future action and a basis for a new feeling of national commitment, a beginning of a national community and a sense of nationalism. In future confrontations with outside powers China would stand more as a nation than ever before. The combination of freedom and cohesion sought by Yen Fu, the devotion to the public interest called for by Liang Ch'i-ch'ao, the cement of national spirit yearned for by Sun Yat-sen—this common goal of the last twenty years seemed attainable in 1919. The question was whether the new sense of nationhood could be harnessed to the cause of building a new culture. The answer, soon given, was that cultural change was to be subordinated to political action.

Kuomintang Revolution

Following the May Fourth Movement, political activists struggled to organize themselves. The only existing party that seemed to offer any immediate promise was the

Kuomintang[4] (KMT), also known as the Nationalist party. Led by Sun Yat-sen, it had grown out of the 1905–1911 revolutionary movement. Since that time Sun had been struggling with only minimal success to keep the party together as a potent political force. From 1920 to 1923 he was nominal head of a nominal KMT government in Canton; in actuality he was little more than an appendage of the local warlord regime, and his position was extremely precarious. Thus he was again looking for firmer sources of support precisely at a time when many Chinese were bent on political action; KMT ranks began to grow accordingly.

Sun, as usual, was anxious for foreign help. It turned out that the only place from which help was forthcoming was the Soviet Union. At the same time, Chinese intellectuals were also beginning to pay closer attention to the Soviet Union. Their interest in Russia, which had grown slowly after the Bolshevik Revolution of 1917, snowballed in the post-May Fourth atmosphere. The Bolsheviks helped to encourage this interest (with policies we shall explain later), but equally important encouragement came inadvertently from the West and Japan. The imperialist powers had already alienated the Chinese at Versailles. Then they created a bond of sympathy between China and Russia by invading Russia and supporting anti-Bolshevik forces and regimes. As the West turned its demonic side to China once again, Chinese ambivalence shifted away from its admiration for Western-style democracy and toward anti-imperialism. The availability of an alternate foreign model doubtless facilitated the renewal of Chinese anti-Westernism. Scores of Soviet-oriented groups of many kinds sprouted in 1920 and 1921. In July 1921 the Chinese Communist Party (CCP) was formally organized, and Ch'en Tu-hsiu became its head. In 1923, thanks to the tireless efforts and adroit maneuvering of the Soviet Union, a KMT-CCP united front was set up. . . .

The Beginnings of Marxist Influence

When Western thought made its first deep and lasting impact on Chinese intellectuals, it impressed them with the ideas of struggle and progress. As Yen Fu had remarked, "unity and progress result from diversity and competition." Western devices for securing social cohesion seemed not to interfere with the pursuit of individual interests; national unity, wealth, and power seemed compatible with pluralism. In the early 1900s many Chinese intellectuals believed that representative government and constitutionalism ensured the best combination of unity and diversity, for Western-style democracy created strong, prosperous states and also upheld the ideals of liberty, equality, and fraternity. Hence, even though many prominent Chinese intellectuals paid attention to the Russian revolutionaries, felt some kinship with them, and became superficially acquainted with Marxism, only a few were attracted to Marxist ideas of dialectical materialism and progress by means of class struggle. The Chinese could not yet see any relationship between Marxism and national power.

Between 1912 and 1919 the intellectual and political climate changed. Because many Chinese considered that China's experiment with Western-style constitutional democracy was a dismal failure, their admiration for Western institutions wavered. The precarious balance between envy and resentment of the West tipped once again toward resentment when Westerners and Japanese violated China's territorial integrity at Versailles. Intellectuals still desperately longed for China to be both powerful and

---

[4]Pronounced *Gwaw-min-dong*.

democratic, but as the failures of the republic mounted after 1912, and especially after Versailles and May Fourth, Western-style democratic politics lost much of its appeal.

During this disillusionment in China, Russia in 1917 threw off its antiquated autocracy, proclaimed scientific socialism, issued a call for world revolution, and prepared itself for both civil war and resistance to Western and Japanese efforts to crush the new Soviet regime. The Chinese watched these events as closely as they could; a few, such as the Peking University history professor and chief librarian Li Ta-chao[5] (1889–1927), soon commented favorably on the Bolshevik Revolution, but most were not yet touched by the events in Russia. Li began to study Marxism and to discuss it with small groups of students; among the young intellectuals who met in Li's office (which quickly became known as the "Red Chamber") was Mao Tse-tung[6] (1893 ————). Even Li, however, was still uncertain of his ideological convictions and of his estimate of the prospects for revolution. As late as spring of 1919 the mood of the intellectuals, including the most radical of them, was overwhelmingly one of curiosity, probing, and experimentation. But within a year a substantial number had turned unequivocally to Marxism-Leninism.

Founding of the Party

Among the many reasons for this shift, three are particularly relevant to our story. The first was the renewal of political organization and activism fostered by the May Fourth Movement, with its heated anti-imperialist and antiwarlord sentiment. This two-edged nationalism, one slashing at the foreign powers and the other at the warlords who blocked the unification of China, found new meaning in Marxism-Leninism. In 1919 Lenin's writings were just beginning to become readily available to Chinese intellectuals. Works such as *Imperialism, The Highest Stage of Capitalism,* which Lenin had written only a few years before, gave the Chinese appetizing food for thought. The notions that imperialism was a necessary stage in the development of capitalism and an inherent part of capitalism and that imperialism marked the final step in capitalism's growth before it met destruction drew a deep response from the bitterly anti-imperialist intellectuals. The intellectuals' determination to find new political weapons to use against the warlords made Leninist concepts of political organization highly attractive, for the very core of Leninism was the idea of a disciplined, elite party of revolutionary intellectuals. In brief, May Fourth produced among many Chinese intellectuals sentiments that were uniquely receptive to Leninist ideas.

Another reason for the sudden growth of Marxism-Leninism in China was the Soviet Union's timely appeal to Chinese anti-imperialism. In the summer of 1919, the Soviet foreign minister declared that his government was prepared to renounce all privileges obtained from China by previous Russian governments. Later Soviet denials that the renunciation was total and revelations that the Russians were bargaining with the warlord government in Peking impressed the Chinese much less than the first and unequivocally anti-imperialist pronouncement. Praise for the Russians and salutes to the new era that had dawned in international relations filled the press. Even moderate intellectuals began to investigate Marxism, and Marxist study societies flourished as never before. Some Chinese intellectuals now sensed that Marxism-Leninism resolved

---

[5]Pronounced *Lee Dah-jow* (as in "now").
[6]Pronounced *Mow* (as in "now") *Dzuh-doong.*

one of their most agonizing dilemmas: how to be modern, Western, and scientific in their outlook and at the same time be uncompromisingly anti-imperialist, and therefore nationalist, and therefore Chinese. "Scientific socialism" in Lenin's anti-imperialist state (which was in those very years under attack by Britain, France, the United States, and Japan), offered a combination that earlier foreign objects of Chinese admiration (English liberalism, the French Revolution, United States republicanism, and Japanese modernization) could not match.

Finally, Marxism-Leninism gained impetus from the arrival of agents of the Communist International (Comintern) almost precisely when the Soviet anti-imperialist declaration was made public. With the ground already well prepared, the agents had no difficulty in persuading Ch'en Tu-hsiu to take the lead in organizing a small Communist group in Shanghai in May 1920. Other groups followed in at least five more Chinese cities, plus Tokyo and Paris. The Shanghai branch soon founded a Sino-Russian news agency, two journals, a youth corps, and a foreign language school, all aimed at recruiting and training cadres. Some cadres were later sent to the Soviet Union for advanced schooling. Only a little more than a year later the Chinese Communist Party (CCP) held its first congress, signifying the formal establishment of the party, with twelve or thirteen delegates representing an estimated fifty-seven members.

The early history of the CCP was marked by Marxist orthodoxy, adherence to a Soviet model, and subservience to outside authority. Having originated largely from the example and with the encouragement of the Soviet Union, the CCP organized itself under the watchful eyes of two Comintern representatives who attended the First Party Congress. According to one participant, the Comintern also sent a Russian worker who represented the Red International of Labor Unions and spoke to the Chinese about its aims and activities. The delegates agreed to learn from the experience and example of the Communist party of the Soviet Union. They also adopted a program that reads, appropriately enough, like a Marxist primer. To show that they meant what they said, the Communists immediately applied themselves to overthrowing "the capitalistic classes" by organizing labor unions and converting the workers into a class-conscious proletariat of which the party members might then be the vanguard. The new party set industriously to work in conventional Marxist fashion.

Perhaps the clearest indication of the CCP's lack of independence was its allegiance to the Comintern. It is likely, though not certain, that a formal affiliation between the CCP and the Comintern took place at the First Party Congress. Formally subservient or not, the CCP felt compelled to accept when the Comintern decided that the time had come to adopt a new strategy. The Comintern insisted upon an alliance with the KMT in 1923 because it believed that the CCP could in this way isolate its major enemies, the warlords and the imperialist powers; the CCP was too weak to fight alone. The Chinese Communists submitted even though they despised the KMT and were baffled by the Comintern's departure from Marxist orthodoxy. The KMT, Moscow explained, did not represent one class, the bourgeoisie; it was a coalition of all classes. Communists could therefore join it and still retain their leadership of the laboring masses. But the CCP knew it had both committed Marxist heresy and strayed from the Bolsheviks' path to power.

What sweetened this bitter pill for at least some members, including Li Ta-chao and Mao Tse-tung, was that the alliance with the KMT was aimed at ridding China of imperialism. From this point of view, subservience to the Comintern was in the larger interest of Chinese nationalism. Soon, however, Stalin relegated Chinese nationalism to a lower priority. Not merely Russian or even Comintern interests but those of Stalin himself took first place; Stalin, who was grappling with Trotsky for the right to succeed Lenin, had championed the united front policy against Trotsky's objections. Worrying less about the CCP's fate than his own, Stalin clung to the policy until Trotsky was no longer a threat to him. This, however, was a little too long for the Chinese Communists, many of whom were still clinging to it as they fell before Chiang Kai-shek's guns in 1927. Nevertheless, as Lyman P. Van Slyke has neatly put it:

> It can be argued that the disaster of 1927 hid the successes that preceded it. . . . The extent of the defeat may well have been a measure of how much was attempted. . . . The CCP's rapid growth from a membership numbering a few dozen intellectuals to a mass party seriously competing for national power was an impressive accomplishment. Perhaps no set of policies could have achieved complete success in so short a time.

To build on its successes and remain a serious competitor for national power, however, the CCP found it necessary to break further with Marxist orthodoxy, Soviet models, and Comintern authority than it was able to do by 1927.

Seedlings of CCP Independence

Much of Chinese Communist history centers on its transformation from a foreign-dominated movement to an essentially indigenous one. It was a twisting and erratic process in which parts of the scattered movement skidded from one pole to another like iron filings drawn this way and that by a revolving magnet. Indigenous elements were powerfully present in the beginning, and foreign influences persist to this day. But the general trend over these fifty years has been for the Chinese Communists to shape their movement to their own circumstances, take control of their own destiny, and develop their own brand of Communism.

The Chinese Communist revolution was not simply a peasant revolution; it was a revolution in which intellectuals who were disposed toward both Western and Chinese values, standards, styles of life, and conceptions of history and social relationships learned they had to bring the two together in a new way. It is not yet clear that they have done this successfully, but it is clear that they have enjoyed more success in dealing with this central problem in modern Chinese history than anyone else who has confronted it since the middle of the nineteenth century. One key to the Communists' success has been their flexibility. They have learned hard lessons and profited from them. They have formulated different types of appeals to different segments of the population and have adjusted the content and delivery of the appeal and their method of organization to changing circumstances in different parts of the country. The creativity of the Communist leadership revealed itself more in this general respect than in specific insights, such as the discovery of the revolutionary potential of the peasantry.

The importance of the peasantry had been recognized by Lenin and was perhaps seen even more clearly by Asian Communists such as the Indian M. N. Roy, who pleaded at the Second Comintern Congress in 1920 for emphasis on "mass struggle" in which peasants as well as workers would be organized by Communist parties. The Comintern itself, although often inconsistent or vague on this point, advised the CCP in May 1923 that the peasantry was "the central problem of our whole policy." In 1925 the Comintern's chief agent in China, Michael Borodin, told the KMT that organizing the peasantry for a solution of the land question would determine the success or failure of the revolution. The Comintern usually stressed, however, that the proletariat must take the lead. The question of who made the crucial intellectual breakthrough is unanswerable, but it is beyond dispute that many people realized the potential of the peasantry before anyone did much to translate that realization into political and social action, and that only after years of perseverance did the Chinese intellectuals overcome the deeply ingrained attitudes that walled them off from the Chinese masses. The difficulty of this prolonged effort, which continues even now, has profoundly influenced the Chinese Communist movement.

The work began in the 1920s, when the first serious efforts at mass mobilization were made; by turning to peasants more than to urban workers, a few pioneering Communists blazed a trail toward independence from the Comintern. The first Chinese Communist to devote himself to organizing the peasants was an intellectual who seems to have taken this course of action with little of his colleagues' hesitation. P'eng P'ai[7] (1896-1929) was the son of a wealthy landlord. He spent three years as a college student in Japan, where he joined a socialist group that devoted itself to agrarian problems. After graduation he returned home, joined the CCP, and soon began organizing peasants. Between May and September 1922 he organized a village peasant union with more than 500 members; four months later he organized a *hsien* Federation of Peasant Unions that claimed 20,000 members. By May 1923 he led a Kuang-tung Provincial Peasant Union which, after a temporary setback in 1924, grew to an estimated 210,000 or more, covering twenty-two *hsien*. Due partly to P'eng's success, the KMT (by now allied with the CCP) founded a Peasant Department, in which he became the most prominent individual.

These startling gains received little or no encouragement from the CCP, which was preoccupied with consolidating its alliance with the KMT and renewing its emphasis on orgnaizing labor. This preoccupation was not entirely due to Marxist orthodoxy and Comintern instructions, however, for in 1924 and 1925 the labor movement expanded rapidly. There was, in other words, a good practical reason for the CCP to concentrate its efforts on urban workers—the field seemed fertile. The many strikes of 1924 and 1925 testify to the Communist organizers' success.

May Day 1925 coincidentally found both the trade unions and the peasant unions convening in Canton. The Second Labor Congress, however, dwarfed the Peasant Congress, for it represented 166 trade unions that claimed a membership of 540,000. The Peasant Congress acknowledged its subordinate role by adopting a resolution in which it affirmed that "our struggle must be concentrated in the city, because the political center is located in the city; therefore the working class must strive to lead the peasants to participate in this struggle."

By this time the CCP was beginning to take more note of the peasant movement in Kuang-tung. Party headquarters urged that peasant unions and peasant self-defense corps be organized. Such moves were invariably checked, however, because the alliance with the KMT still had top priority, and to keep that alliance the CCP had to avoid offending landlords. Hence the 1925 Peasant Congress did not dare to declare itself in favor of rent reduction. But P'eng P'ai, who did not attend the Peasant Congress, refused to accept party restraint. A few months later he urged the peasants to take matters into their own hands. They did, and many landlords and others, both innocent and guilty, lost their lives as well as their property. Reforms were at first limited to rent reduction, but soon the tenants in P'eng's area abolished rents altogether and took

---

[7]Pronounced *Pung Pie.*

over the landlords' holdings. CCP membership grew from 700 in December 1926 to 4,000 only three months later, and Communist cells were created in 330 villages. Somewhat ironically, in view of the Russian desire to concentrate on the urban workers and bourgeoisie, P'eng P'ai's headquarters came to be known as "Little Moscow." More cruelly ironic was P'eng's eventual capture and execution by the KMT in Shanghai in 1929.

Earlier, however, the influence of P'eng P'ai's peasant revolution had spread north to Hu-nan. Mao Tse-tung had grown up there on a small farm that he later said had evolved to "middle peasant" range by the time he was ten years old and to "rich peasant" status later on. In 1924 Mao happened to leave his party work temporarily to return to Hu-nan; there he discovered the revolutionary potential of the peasantry and turned to rural organization work. Thanks mainly to Mao's efforts, Hu-nanese soon began to pour into P'eng P'ai's Peasant Movement Training Institute. By the autumn of 1925 Mao himself had become active in the institute, and early in 1926 he was beginning to sort out his own ideas on the relative importance of the workers and peasants. A young, inexperienced, and groping Marxist, Mao was unsuccessful in these early intellectual efforts. His writing shows a deep preoccupation with the peasants' revolutionary power, but he considered them to be only a "semi-proletariat" and held that "the industrial proletariat, though small in number, has become the major force of the national revolutionary movement."

Nevertheless Mao continued to work with the peasants, and from May to October 1926 he served as principal of the Peasant Movement Training Institute. In that capacity he once took the entire student body on a two-week visit to P'eng P'ai's headquarters to let them see firsthand a rural revolution in the making. Early in 1927 he was back in Hu-nan, where he witnessed so active a peasant movement that he predicted:

> In a very short time in Central, South, and North China, several hundred million peasants will rise like a mighty storm, a hurricane, a force so swift and violent that no power, however strong, can restrain them. They will break all the shackles that bind them and rush forward along the road of liberation. All imperialists, warlords, corrupt officials, local tyrants, and bad gentry will be sent to their graves by the peasants. All revolutionary parties and comrades will stand before them to be tested and either accepted or rejected as they decide.

Mao then asked rhetorically: "Are we to march at their head and lead them? Or trail behind them, gesticulating and criticizing? Or stand in their way and oppose them?" The growth of the peasant movement in 1926 and 1927 gave Mao and a few others the answer to this question, but the Russians and the CCP leadership saw only a dilemma. To promote the peasant movement was to risk a split with the KMT; to try to check it or to find some compromise was perhaps to miss an opportunity that might not come again. The CCP managed at last to turn toward a peasant emphasis, but the shift came slowly and only at the cost of party unity. The shift was not decisive until the early 1930s when Moscow's hand was removed and the Chinese were freer to experiment. Until that time the CCP managed to resist any temptation to exploit fully the huge reservoir of rural discontent that P'eng P'ai and Mao Tse-tung had revealed.

This important point should not be allowed to obscure the breakthrough that Chinese intellectuals in general, and the Communists in particular, made in the 1920s. Although elementary Marxist orthodoxy seemed to demand that Communists concentrate on organizing the urban proletariat, it took only a little sophistication in Marxism-

Leninism to justify a policy of mobilizing the peasants; and although the Soviet experience and Comintern leadership tended to direct the Chinese to the cities, these guidelines were not fixed, and it was still possible for men like P'eng P'ai to work in the countryside and make the Comintern reconsider its strategy. The Comintern was aware of the peasants but decided its immediate interests lay more in maintaining the united front with the KMT.

The Chinese Communists had to overcome some obstacles that were inherent in Marxism-Leninism, Soviet models, and Comintern discipline, but they also had to address themselves to a central problem that all revolutionaries had to face in China: how to relate rural and urban movements to each other. In this regard their own elitism and, above all, their own inexperience and uncertainty hobbled them as much as outside control. Some, such as P'eng P'ai, found it easy to go among the peasants; most found it difficult. Mao Tse-tung himself, after having lived in cities for fifteen years, confessed that he had learned to despise rural life. Communist intellectuals found it easier to go among the workers, perhaps, but probably most of the workers were peasants only recently come from the countryside. The deeper problem was how to go among the masses, urban and rural, and mobilize them for revolution. Opportunity lay on all sides, as the huge growth of labor unions and peasant unions demonstrated. The challenge was to turn the opportunity to the service of the revolution.

In the 1920s the CCP began to meet this challenge, but the party was still too weak and inexperienced to take advantage of the opportunity, and Comintern leadership was unable to teach what the Chinese needed to know. Perhaps the mass movement was not yet large enough and the Communists' rivals, Chiang Kai-shek and the KMT, were still stronger than the CCP. Thus the CCP subordinated itself to the Comintern and gave priority to maintaining a united front with the KMT, hoping to control the KMT and, through it, to carry out a "revolution from above." But in the 1930s the CCP grew more experienced and much stronger. It freed itself of outside direction and once again rose to rival the KMT for state power, this time by mobilizing the masses in a "revolution from below."

The Rise of Mao Tse-tung

More than a decade after the Communists entered Peking and made it China's new capital, their foreign minister was to say: "Soviet communism has bloomed a Soviet flower and Chinese communism a Chinese one. Both are equally communism, but their flowers are of different hues." It is not clear precisely when seedlings such as those of P'eng P'ai and Mao Tse-tung blossomed fully enough to be identifiable as Chinese, but a trend toward Chinese Communist independence from Moscow is clearly identifiable in the late 1920s and thereafter becomes increasingly plain. CCP independence went hand in hand with the rise of Mao Tse-tung to leadership of the party.

Mao's rise was erratic, and his ideas as well as his strategy and tactics changed several times. Much as the nineteenth-century reformers, the earlier revolutionaries, and the Kuomintang government had shifted their ground, baffled but determined, so Mao probed and backtracked and sidestepped and probed again. One biographer has aptly characterized Mao in the late 1920s as an "apprentice Leninist." Most students of his career would agree that his apprenticeship lasted rather a long time, and hostile critics find little evidence of sophistication in his thinking to this day. But other students of his thought see remarkable growth beginning in the 1930s. A prominent feature of that growth was his departure from Russian models and influence.

In 1927 Chiang Kai-shek's coup left the CCP leaders no choice but to seek their own way. Comintern policy was thrown into confusion by Chiang's move, and by the time it recovered the CCP was splintered into many fugitive groups. By the beginning of 1930 there were fifteen Communist bases scattered across half of China. Each had to survive as best it could.

Mao's struggle took him first to Hu-nan where, in September 1927, he participated in a disastrous defeat that may have been the most valuable learning experience he had yet undergone. In an attempt to regain the initiative from Chiang Kai-shek, the CCP decided to attack major cities, including Changsha in Hu-nan. Mao anticipated optimistically that the fall of Changsha would lead to a successful nationwide revolution like Russia's in 1917. But until the key city fell, Mao thought, there was no point in promoting the rural movement. A shattering reversal at Changsha told him a new strategy was needed.

Limping into the mountains on the border of Hu-nan and Chiang-hsi,[8] Mao established a base in October 1927 and began to organize it according to what he termed his own "clumsy inventions." For about three years thereafter Mao's inventions were challenged by instructions from the Comintern and the CCP Central Committee. Mao objected more than once; and, although in crucial situations he followed orders, he did so only up to a certain point. The best example is a disagreement that matured in 1929 and 1930. By this time Mao's experience had convinced him that the CCP's chief needs were to establish base areas, systematically construct a political structure, promote agrarian revolution, and build up the Red Army by slow stages beginning with local militia. He also cautioned against "revolutionary impetuosity" and urged patient, but confident, preparation; he was beginning to work out the concepts of "despising one's enemy strategically, but respecting him tactically" and of surrounding cities from the countryside. The CCP leadership, however, scoffed at Mao's ideas, and the Comintern still stressed that the vital task of the CCP was to lead the struggles of urban workers. Despite this head-on collision of views, when the order came to march in a major attack on three cities, Mao and his military commander, Chu Teh[9] (1886–   ), reluctantly accepted it. But when it was evident to him that the attack was a failure, Mao did not wait for instructions to disengage. He pulled back to the Chiang-hsi base in September 1930, and from that time forward he developed and followed his own conception of how to carry the revolutionary potential of China's hinterland into her cities.

Alternatives to Mao's conception and challenges to his growing authority in the Communist movement were powerful in the years that followed. Mao was overruled on occasion, and not always to the detriment of the movement; in early 1933 Maoist tactics were abandoned, and a major victory was won by a direct frontal assault on KMT troops. Mao was criticized, and some of his adherents were vigorously attacked by the party leadership. Only in January 1935 did Mao finally gain the upper hand and make his policies those of the CCP.

Mao's policies developed in several stages, but the fundamental elements were already present by 1929 and 1930. Perhaps the innermost core of his policies was a belief in organization. A leading student of Mao, Stuart Schram, has speculated that in Mao's personality was a natural Leninism, that is, "a certain intuitive understanding of the

---

[8]Pronounced *Jee-yong-hsee.*
[9]Pronounced *Joo Duh.*

importance of organization that is one of the reasons for his emergence as the leader of the Chinese Communist Party." Hints of this predilection appear in Mao's writings on labor organization as early as 1920 and emerge more clearly in his 1926 and 1927 writings on the peasantry. On several occasions in the 1920s he also demonstrated a taste and talent for analyzing organizational problems. And in Mao's own account of his efforts in 1929 to build up a base area, he recalled that the "bad tendencies" he had to correct in his followers had included "lack of discipline, exaggerated ideas of democracy, and looseness of organization." Another tendency that had to be fought was " 'vagabondage'—a disinclination to settle down to the serious tasks of government, a love of movement, change, new experience and incident." Mao had little use for spontaneity and improvisation.

Mao's remarks were directed at his troops, but he did not intend them to apply only to military organization. One of the most prominent characteristics of his outlook was the interpenetration of military and political strategy. In 1929, for example, Mao explicitly condemned what he termed "the purely military viewpoint." He explained:

> [The Red Army] is an armed group for carrying out political tasks of a class nature. In order to carry out this task, particularly in present-day China, the Red Army must not merely fight; besides fighting, it should also shoulder such important tasks as agitating among the masses, organizing them, arming them, and helping them to set up political power. When the Red Army fights, it fights not merely for the sake of fighting but exclusively to agitate among the masses, to organize them, to arm them, and to help them establish political power; apart from such objectives, fighting loses its meaning, and the Red Army the reason for its existence.

Mao then went on to explain why "absolute equalitarianism" in the army was essentially the same as "extreme democratization in political matters" and equally reprehensible. In brief, similar principles governed military and political matters, and the purpose of military organizing was to create political organization. The classic and by now the most familiar expression of these concepts is Mao's statement in 1938 that "political power grows out of the barrel of a gun." The statement continues: "Our principle is that the Party commands the gun: the gun shall never be allowed to command the Party. . . . Anything can grow out of the barrel of a gun. . . . As advocates of the abolition of war, we do not desire war; but war can only be abolished through war—in order to get rid of the gun we must first grasp it in hand."

Since Mao was engaged in war almost continually from 1927 to 1953, this experience inevitably molded his thinking and infiltrated his idiom. Mao's stress on military power and his use of military terminology is in no way surprising. More remarkable is the persistent reference to the political context of military affairs. Even during the life-or-death struggle against Japan, Mao said: "Any tendency among the anti-Japanese soldiers to belittle politics, to isolate war from it, and to make war an absolute, is erroneous and must be corrected." Although Mao conceded that "war has its special characteristics and in this sense it is not identical with politics," he insisted,

> such a gigantic national revolutionary war as ours cannot succeed without universal and thoroughly political mobilization. . . . The popular masses are like water, and the army is like a fish. How then can it be said that when there is water, a fish will have difficulty in preserving its existence? An army which fails to maintain good discipline gets into opposition with the popular masses, and thus by its own actions dries up the water. In this case, it naturally cannot continue to exist. All guerrilla units must thoroughly understand this principle.

Thus Mao closed the circle around his core ideas. Base areas were the water in which he would find his fish and from which he would feed them. A revolutionary land program would attract peasant support, and disciplined troops would preserve it. Soldiers recruited from the peasantry would feel they had a stake in protecting the base areas; indeed, a local defense corps would provide a way of initiating peasants into organized activity and solidifying their sense of common purpose. Mao insisted that *all* people had to be included, even bandits and other unreliable elements, of whom there were many in Mao's original force. Not only were they to be included, they were to be given education and made to feel deeply involved. It was not enough for people to learn of the war by being subjected to enemy action. The people needed the positive message of the Red Army, not merely the negative one of the Japanese. Finally, "with the common people of the whole country mobilized, we shall create a vast sea of humanity in which the enemy will be swallowed up, [we shall] obtain relief for our shortage in arms and other things, and secure the prerequisites to overcome every difficulty in the war."

The actual course of the Chinese Communists' rise to power followed Mao's policies with considerable precision, although deviations were inevitable under the harsh and changing conditions of those years. In Chiang-hsi in the early 1930s there were also disagreements within the party that interfered with consistency, especially at this early stage in the process of building a base area. But by 1935 the rise of Mao and the rise of Chinese communism had become irrevocably meshed.

Yenan Communism

After the Chinese Communists were forced by Kuomintang military pressure to flee the Chiang-hsi area, they took refuge in the northwest. The relocation required what came to be known as the "Long March," an epic trek of a full year over some 6000 miles of fiercely hostile terrain. Along the way the Communists fought at great loss against pursuing government armies and local warlord forces, but Mao claimed that they had also "sown many seeds in eleven provinces, which will sprout, grow leaves, blossom into flowers, bear fruit and yield a crop in future."

The Long March began the next stage of CCP history, commonly called the "Yenan[10] period." Yenan did not become the CCP's northwest capital until January 1937, but the Yenan period is usually delimited by the end of the Long March in 1935 and the end of the civil war in 1949. During that time Mao consolidated his power within the party and promoted new ideological emphases on the power of the human will to do the seemingly impossible and on the distinctiveness of the Chinese revolution. These emphases characterize the "Yenan spirit," to which the Long March is a fitting prologue. The march was an extraordinary test of endurance, will power, determination, and self-reliance. It brought the CCP into direct contact with parts of the country that few party members had ever seen and ended by putting the CCP in a position to fight against the invading Japanese, on whom they had declared war in April 1932. Thus the march stimulated patriotic feeling by providing the Communists with a broader knowledge of their country and an opportunity to fight for it. It is entirely possible that the Yenan spirit was born as a result of the Long March.

---

[10]Pronounced *Yeh-non*, the first syllable resembling "yet" without a "t."

The first clear indication of new emphases in Mao's thinking came very shortly after the Long March. In 1936 Mao wrote an essay on China's strategic problems in which he minimized the value of Russian experience as an example for the CCP.

> Although we must value Soviet experience, and even value it somewhat more than experiences in other countries throughout history, because it is the most recent experience of revolutionary war, we must value even more the experience of China's revolutionary war, because there are a great number of conditions special to the Chinese revolution and the Chinese Red Army.

These special conditions determined that the Chinese revolution would be distinctive. First, China was a semicolonial country, controlled by several imperialist powers; Mao refrained from pointing out that Russia, far from being colonized, had been imperialist herself. Second, China was unevenly developed politically and economically. It had only small classes of industrial workers and capitalists but vast numbers of peasants, only a few semimodern industrial and commercial cities but "boundless expanses of rural districts still stuck in the middle ages." Warlords and warlord armies divided the country, but the KMT was strong and gaining in strength. Above all, the KMT held "the key positions or lifelines in the politics, economy, communications and culture of China." These conditions compelled the CCP to lead China in a revolutionary war different from the relatively brief civil war in the Soviet Union after the 1917 Revolution. China had to plan for a protracted war. Furthermore, the Chinese Red Army had to face two enemies, Japan and the KMT, both of whom had armies that were far larger and more modern than the Communists' force. The Red Army could win, Mao said, "because its men have sprung from the agrarian revolution and are fighting for their own interests, and because officers and men are politically united." According to Mao's estimates the CCP could win by relying on itself; it needed neither foreign aid nor models. But he stressed that the war would be long and difficult and might even be lost.

From 1936 on, Mao concentrated on developing a winning strategy. The problem of fighting the Japanese and simultaneously preparing to fight the KMT absorbed him completely. He reasoned that, to fight well, the Red Army had to be a people's army, and to be a people's army it needed a program uniquely suited to Chinese conditions.

The conditions Mao outlined were not entirely unique to China; Russia's Red Army, for example, had also faced both foreign and domestic troops that possessed superior numbers and equipment. But China's economy was far less developed than Russia's had been in 1917, and China had a far smaller urban working class; still more important, the Chinese Communists had failed to gain a foothold in the cities, whereas the Bolsheviks' power was rooted in Moscow, Petrograd, and a few other industrial cities. Finally, and perhaps most important of all, the Bolsheviks gained followers by calling for peace in World War I and surrendering to Germany huge pieces of Russian territory; the Chinese Communists gained followers by calling for resistance to Japan and leading the fight to defend Chinese territory.

Thus one of the most important differences between China and the Soviet Union emerged only after Mao made his analysis. The Chinese Red Army grew from roughly 80,000 to about a million during the war against Japan, and in addition to these regular troops the CCP by 1945 commanded guerrilla forces and militia that amounted to several million more. These huge forces were unlike any soldiers the Chinese masses could remember. The people were accustomed to soldiers who looted and raped. The Red Army became famous for its honesty and discipline. Relying exclusively on volunteers, it became a people's army in the fullest sense of that term. And because its training was at least as much political as military, the Red Army was a school in which countless peasants learned to read, think about national goals, and work for the victory of communism as well as China.

In 1938 Mao wrote:

A communist is a Marxist internationalist, but Marxism must take on a national form before it can be applied. . . . We must put an end to writing eight-legged essays [old-fashioned essays that have perfect form but no substance] on foreign models; there must be less repeating of empty and abstract refrains; we must discard our dogmatism and replace it by a new and vital Chinese style and manner, pleasing to the eye and to the ear of the Chinese common people.

To reach the eye and ear of the common people in a Chinese manner, the CCP during the Yenan period adopted a variety of policies that shifted according to time and place; Mao and his followers continued to demonstrate a flexibility that was vital to their success. The policies were based on patriotic resistance to Japan, a program of land reform that concentrated on reducing rents and interest rates, and a system of local government that resembled, at least in form, parliamentary democracy. These policies of moderation helped the CCP to earn a reputation as nationalists and democratic "agrarian reformers."

To carry out these diverse policies, Mao relied heavily upon a single technique, the "mass line." The idea underlying this technique has been summed up most simply by Chalmers Johnson: In order to find out what kind of political program the masses will support, a political leader goes among them and asks them. The concept of the mass line is itself fundamentally simple, but the CCP's efforts to implement it reveal an enormous complexity. The massline policy requires CCP members to reconcile what the masses *will* support with what the party in its Marxist-Leninist wisdom thinks they *should* support; once these two rarely matching designs have been stitched together, party members must take the finished products back to the people and, in the words of one leader, "explain and popularize them, and arouse the masses to support these policies *so they will act on them as their own.*" Italics have been added to indicate it was in this respect that the CCP did the most to refashion in its own way what is in reality a rather common notion; and, by so doing, the CCP grew by leaps and bounds during the Yenan period. Through its highly imaginative formulation and skilled execution of a mass-line technique adapted to Chinese conditions, the CCP came to power.

Following the mass-line technique, the CCP sent agents into countless villages. There the agents listened, learned the peasants' grievances, gained their confidence, and tried to explain why the grievances existed and what could be done to erase them. With the party's active encouragement, peasants found the courage to pursue their own interests whether those interests were to regain land they had lost due to usury or high rents, take revenge on a corrupt official, or resist the Japanese occupation. As they corrected old abuses and mobilized to defend their homes, the peasants accepted CCP leadership and organization. Some began to absorb communist ideas, for the CCP taught many people to read and did so with heavy doses of propaganda that began in the early lessons. Creating new organs of local government, peasant associations, cooperatives, youth and women's organizations, and militia, the Chinese Communists drew unprecedented numbers of the Chinese people into purposeful action.

The CCP was not the only group to perceive patriotism, anti-imperialism, land reform, mass education, and political democracy as desirable ends. Throughout the twentieth century one movement after another had proclaimed these and other laudable goals. But no other group so carefully defined goals with an eye to what the masses of people wanted, and no other group so assiduously cultivated the ability to mobilize the masses in pursuit of those ends. Here is where the Communists are most clearly distinguished from all other political groups in modern Chinese history, for it was the CCP in the Yenan period that at last, even if only temporarily, bridged the gap between city and country, modern and traditional, Western and Chinese, rulers and ruled. As a result, China made a fresh start in her struggle to modernize.

During the eight years of war against Japan and, concurrently, intermittent fighting against the KMT, the CCP's strategy and methods were put to a severe test. Genuine unity still required that Western-oriented modern urban intellectuals come directly to grips with the problems of rural and still largely traditional China. New personnel problems appeared as Communist influence expanded to reach more than 100 million people in 1945, at least one hundred times more people than it reached in 1936. The Communist areas virtually amounted to a huge, sprawling nation (the population of the United States in 1945 was about 140 million). Numerous Communist enclaves were scattered over vast areas, and it was nearly impossible to maintain contact between them and Yenan; local party workers had to be reliable because they often had to work without instructions. The Communists needed more manpower to carry out the mass line; hence party membership grew from 40,000 in 1937 to over 1,200,000 in 1945. According to CCP historians, 90 percent of the new members were from "petty bourgeois" backgrounds. Precisely when the party needed experienced and reliable cadres, it also had to grow rapidly, and it had no choice but to admit untested members and try to train them quickly; both quality and quantity were urgently necessary. A party leader warned that "nonproletarian classes" were influencing the CCP in "ideology, living habits, theory, and action." By 1940 CCP membership had shot up to about 800,000; party organization and mobilization of the masses were in danger of being crippled by excessively rapid expansion. Setbacks in 1941 and 1942, due to Japanese offensives and a Kuomintang blockade, heightened the sense of urgency and the need for cadres who were dedicated enough to start their work again after a defeat. The leadership followed two courses. One was to slow down party recruitment, weed out the less desirable members, and indoctrinate intensively those who remained. The other was to simplify administration, develop local leadership, and introduce new social and economic institutions, such as cooperatives, on an unprecedentedly wide scale. The first worked from the top (government) down; the second worked from the bottom (villages) up.

Indoctrination was undertaken on a massive scale from 1942 to 1944, based on a small body of written materials, mostly Mao's, which were widely disseminated, studied, and discussed. The central theme was a reaffirmation and strengthening of Mao's 1936 statement that the Chinese revolution posed its own unique and concrete problems and that men had to engage those problems in hand-to-hand combat. The bedrock of the entire new movement was Mao's demand, stated in a lecture he gave in 1942, for "a theory in accordance with China's real necessities, a theory which is our own and of a specific nature." Another leader, Liu Shao-ch'i[11] (1900–), explained further the Chinese effort to "make something real of Marxism." The CCP, he said,

has passed through many more great events in these twenty-two years [since 1921] than any other Communist Party in the world and has had richer experience in the

---

[11]Pronounced *Lee-oo Show* (rhymes with "now") -*chee.*

Chinese revolutionary struggle. If we treat the experience of our Party's struggle in these twenty-two years of great historical change lightly, if we do not diligently learn our lessons from these experiences, but only learn the lessons of the revolutionary experience of comparatively distant foreign countries, we will be turning things upside down and will have to travel many tortuous paths and encounter many more defeats.

Artfully invoking the authority of Stalin, Liu quoted a lengthy statement in which the Russian leader's point was that "true Marxists" are only those who are "guided by methods and procedure in keeping with their environment" and who "do not find their instructions and directives from comparisons and historical analogies," but from "research on surrounding conditions" and from their own "practical experience."

The stress on "practical experience" served to underline the uniquely Chinese emphases of the CCP leaders, and it also honed the blade Mao used to lacerate the intellectuals: "I advise those of you who have only book knowledge and as yet no contact with reality, and those who have had few practical experiences, to realize your own shortcomings and make your attitudes a bit more humble." Humility was taught not only with Mao's advice, but also by means of a "to the village" movement that followed the indoctrination. After mastering the selected texts, intellectuals were sent to the countryside, sometimes to work in the fields, sometimes to teach and to aid in local administration. At all times, Mao warned, such "outside cadres" must take care to "cherish, protect, and constantly assist local cadres" and "not ridicule or attack them"; and all cadres "must actually learn from the people."

An excellent example of the CCP's emphasis on practicality and mass initiative can be seen in its educational system. At first, schools in the Communist areas followed familiar Western practices. In the border area of Shen-hsi, Kansu, and Ningsia-hui, however, the masses protested that education did not suit their needs. The CCP investigated in order to determine what kind of schools people wanted, and the result was the establishment of "people-managed" schools in which each village decided what should be taught. Problems of many kinds were inevitable—some villages even wanted to stress the Confucian classics, and in such cases the authorities had to persuade the village committee that classical learning was impractical—but the system proved to be so popular that in 1944 it spread quickly throughout the Communist areas. Literacy, arithmetic, and vocational subjects predominated, the general rule being that mass education "should keep to the knowledge needed by the home and the village." Cadre education, which stressed leadership in both warfare and production, was conducted by "people who actually have experience of the armed struggle or production."

This educational system also exemplified the CCP's determination to dispense with foreign models that did not suit Chinese conditions. Party directives criticized the KMT for copying Western and Japanese education, referring frequently to the differences between China and countries that were wealthy, industrialized, capitalist, and at peace. One crucial difference, for example, was China's extensive adult illiteracy, which impaired her ability to increase production rapidly and at the same time carry on a protracted people's war. Since adults had greater responsibilities than youth, the CCP decided to give adults priority over children in the mass education campaign.

The success with which these principles were carried out in the Yenan period is indicated by the dramatic reversal of the Communist-Kuomintang balance. A bedraggled remnant in 1935, the CCP scratched at the barren soil of the northwest and looked out from its caves upon a future as bleak as the land; meanwhile, the resurgent KMT seemed capable of destroying its enemy with only another blow. Ten years later the CCP not only was in a position to challenge the KMT for power and win, but it had tangible skills and intangible momentum and spirit to carry it into the postrevolutionary era.

The spirit may have developed most of all from the war effort, which was the immediate objective of all other policies. Many of the policies, including mass propaganda and village organization, were implemented through the army, especially in the early years of the war. As trained party workers were produced, they took up more of the burden. But whoever was responsible for the implementation of policy, the spirit was essentially the same. Peasants who had been intimidated by the air power and tanks of Japan's war machine learned to their astonishment that it was possible to fight back by guerrilla methods; at the same time, many learned to read, to command troops, to govern, and to produce more than ever from their land. Mao taught that nothing was impossible for men who combined practical experience, understanding of Marxism-Leninism and the thought of Mao Tse-tung, and the will to undertake awesome tasks in a spirit of optimism: "So when we see the enemy, whether he is many or few, we must act as though he is bread which can satisfy our hunger, and immediately swallow him." This kind of confidence flourished in the climate of patriotic resistance to invasion. Peasants and intellectuals knew what they were fighting for and became certain they would win. Differences of social class, wealth, and education were outweighed by a new unity of purpose. . . .

In the civil war that followed from 1946 to 1949, the Chinese Communists won a victory that was even more their own than the victory over Japan. Two stunning military successes against huge mechanized armies vindicated the strategy of people's war. But . . . the strategy had also unleashed a social revolution. Would the Communists carry it forward in the pattern of the preceding decade? If so, Mao's strategy would undergo its severest test yet, for it would have to adapt the techniques of people's war to the tasks of government.

8

Tito and the Yugoslav Partisan Movement

N. J. Klones

In the European theater, the earliest organized large scale guerrilla activity recorded began in Yugoslavia on May 10, 1941. On that day, only three weeks after the Yugoslav army had capitulated, a colonel named Drago Mikhailovich organized his first guerrilla band in the village of Ravna Gora.

In recounting the World War II guerrilla activities in Yugoslavia, it is impossible to separate the purely military operations from the paramount political issues of the period.

In retrospect, one has to conclude that the creation of Yugoslavia after World War I raised difficult issues. The Yugoslav state not only lacked homogeneity, but included mutually antagonistic elements within it. The Croat underground organization, the Ustashi, was active for almost 20 years prior to 1941. Its leaders, Pavelich and Kavaternich, had planned the assassination of King Alexander in Marseilles in 1934, although the triggerman was not a Croat, but a Bulgarian member of the IMRO named Valdimir Georgiev-Chernozemski.[1]

On March 25, 1941, the Yugoslav government of Regent Prince Paul signed the Tripartiate Pact, thus joining the Axis. Less than 48 hours later, the Yugoslav army revolted, deposed the government and repudiated the pact. In that revolution, the army had the wholehearted support of the Serb people; however, it did not have the support of the Croats. When the German army attacked Yugoslavia, the Croat units mutinied and thus became the prime factor in the Yugoslav army's collapse. The local communists also participated actively in the numerous acts of treason that doomed the Yugoslav army.

Following the conclusion of the campaign, the Germans allowed the Italians and Bulgarians to occupy most of Yugoslavia and created the independent state of Croatia under the Ustashi leader Pavelich. The new state included within its borders a substantial minority of Serbs. The Croat government proceeded to exterminate the Serb

From N. J. Klones, "Tito and the Partisan Movement," *East Europe* (Vol. 21, No. 4, 1972), pp. 20–24. [Reprinted with permission from the publishers.]

[1]IMRO was a Bulgarian underground organization established around 1900. IMRO and Ustashi had for a long time cooperated against their common enemy, the Yugoslav state; IMRO's last leader, one Ivan Mihailov found asylum in Zagreb in 1943.

minorities employing methods similar to those used by the Germans in murdering Jews. It appears also, that there was no dissenting opinion to this policy of extermination and that the majority of the Croats, including the intelligentsia and the Catholic clergy, approved or tolerated it. The reaction among the Serbs was one of bitterness and violence. Mikhailovich and his Chetniks concentrated their efforts on attacking the Ustashi and rescuing the Serbs in the disputed areas rather than harassing the Germans. Although he did not go on record as advocating it, Mikhailovich probably felt that it was time to dissolve the unhappy union of the Yugoslav state. Nor was he alone in this thought. President Roosevelt is reputed to have favored a homogeneous United Serbia to a heterogeneous disunited Yugoslavia.

In spite of the heavy odds against him, the Mikhailovich organization grew substantially. Chetniks, meaning "irregular fighter" or "guerrilla" in Serbo-Croat, was used for the Serb guerrillas who participated in the revolutions against the Turks in the previous century and the underground wars against the Bulgarian Komitadjis between 1903 and 1914. Mikhailovich was promoted to general and made Minister of War of the Yugoslav Government in Exile in London. The allied radio and press, including the Russian, heralded his successes daily to the free world. During those days (1941 and 1942) allied military successes were few and far between; the existence of an active guerrilla movement in occupied Europe was, therefore, a psychological warfare factor of paramount importance.

The Partisans in the Picture

Suddenly, Radio Moscow in July 1942 announced that there was a guerrilla movement in Yugoslavia under someone called Tito. Why [were] Tito and his Partisan movement ignored by Moscow until 1942? One theory has been that Tito, or Josip Broz, having been one of the organizers of the International Brigades during the Spanish Civil War, was on Stalin's black list as were all of the Communists involved in that affair. This could well be true. It has been established that the majority of the Communist leaders who returned to Russia from Spain were executed during the purges of 1937 and 1938. However, we do not have sufficient authentic information on these intraparty struggles to verify this theory. It is more likely that Tito had been ignored by Radio Moscow until July 1942 because the Partisan movement was late in getting organized, and it did not have a substantial following.

Tito's apologists, of course, deny both of these counts. However, it has been established that none of the Communist underground movements in Europe got underway until after Germany's attack on Russia. By virtue of this fact alone, it is a simple matter of arithmetic to establish that Mikhailovich preceded Tito in the field by at least 48 days. This assumes that Tito got started the day of the German attack on Russia, which, from a practical view, is unlikely.

As for Tito's mass following, it developed after 1944, when it became apparent that the Allies were favoring his organization over the Chetniks. In the beginning, the Partisans could not possibly have had any substantial following outside the proletariat, and since the labor force in prewar Yugoslavia was very small, this following could not have been anything but negligible.

The Partisan movement could not have any appeal to the middle class or the peasants among any of Yugoslavia's ethnic groups. What issue could attract the peasantry to Tito? The Croat peasantry had already committed itself to cooperation with the Axis while the Serb peasants, naturally, supported the Chetniks.

The slogan "land for the peasants" could not have the appeal in Yugoslavia it had in Russia in 1917. Yugoslavia, like other Balkan countries, in spite of their backwardness in other fields, had few landless peasants or farm laborers; the vast majority of peasants owned their own small plots. If anything, the Communists would take "land from the peasants" and force them into collectives. For this reason, the Communist following among the Balkan peasants has always been meager. As a matter of fact, opposition to communism among the peasants has been fierce and effective. . . .

The military activity of the Partisans was concentrated on attacking the Chetniks rather than harassing the Germans. The Chetniks defended themselves and the result was civil war. The Partisans moves against the Germans, whenever they did operate, consisted of hit-and-run tactics. This is a usual guerrilla method, although the attacks were carried out against relatively unimportant targets. After the withdrawal of the Partisans, the local inhabitants were left to face the German reprisals. This method of guerrilla warfare is catastrophic to the non-combatants. A conservative estimate of the Yugoslav losses among non-combatants in World War II reached the staggering number of 800,000 out of a population of 16 million. The losses inflicted on the Germans was estimated at 16,000. This ratio of 50 to 1 was unjustifiable [and] yet the British, from their Middle East Headquarters in Cairo, encouraged it.

After 1942, many operations conducted by the Chetniks were credited to the Partisans by British broadcasts. For instance, . . . the three railroad bridges over the river Lim on the Uzice-Vishegrad line were blown [up] in September 1943 by Chetniks under the command of a Colonel Ostoyich. That operation was conducted on orders of the British Middle East Headquarters. BBC radio reported that the bridges were blown [up] by Partisans and, in spite of protests by Brigadier Armstrong (British) and Colonel Seitz (American), the two Allied liaison officers present at the operation, BBC did not correct the error. Very little mention was also made of the fact that the Chetniks, at considerable loss, rescued 552 downed American and British airmen who had bailed out over Yugoslav territory.

In contrast to the Partisans, the Chetniks were organized along territorial lines. Their units, although not entirely static, were operating within territorial regions composed of inhabitants of these regions. The members of the units were in the villages and pursued their normal activities until they were alerted for a specific operation. They were on hand to defend the villages against attacks by the Germans, Bulgarians, Italians, Ustashi, or Partisans.

It can generally be said that during 1942, the Chetniks were much the stronger of the two guerrilla groups, but their activities were largely confined in Serbia with a few peripheral units operating in Montenegro, Bosnia, and Herzegovina. The last two were in part under Croat administration. Tito, in 1942, was unable to establish himself militarily in Serbia although in the summer the Partisan organization made a concerted effort to do so. Towards the end of the year, Tito gave up and retreated with his few followers into Bosnia where he tried to establish a new guerrilla base.

While the two guerrilla groups were thus competing with each other, the Germans took the attitude that this was a case of "dog eats dog" and left them alone. However, with the coming of 1943, undisputed control of communications, particularly of the rail line running South from the Austrian border to Salonika through Zagreb and Belgrade, became for the Axis forces a matter of vital importance. In November of 1942 the Allies had landed in North Africa, and the German High Command was desperately trying to maintain a bridgehead in Tunisia and Tripolitania. A large volume of supplies for the Axis forces in Africa was passing through this line. So between January and March of 1943 the Germans conducted a series of operations intended to clear the areas adjacent to the line between Zagreb and Belgrade. The Germans used a total of seven divisions in this operation, but they were never simultaneously engaged. Some of the units employed were Italian, Croat, and Bulgarian, of relatively low proficiency. This combined Axis operation was generally successful. Tito's followers suffered'the brunt of this offensive because they happened to be in this area, whereas the Chetniks were operating mostly south and west-southwest of Belgrade. The Germans, however, have reported that they met more stubborn resistance from the Chetniks than from the Partisans. This may indicate that Mikhailovich was becoming preoccupied with retaining territorial control, a fatal error in guerrilla warfare, whereas the Partisans were prudently withdrawing to fight another day.

In the summer of 1943 the Germans sent a reinforced mountain division against the Partisans. These special troops moved away from the communications lines and attacked the Partisans in their hideouts. For a time it looked as if the guerrilla movements in Yugoslavia were on their last legs. The Partisans would be finished in a few weeks and then the Germans could, if they so decided, turn their strength against Mikhailovich and the Chetniks. But radical changes were taking place at the fronts. The Axis forces were thrown out of Africa in April and [then] the invasion of Italy took place. In September, Italy capitulated. The Italian capitulation not only saved the Partisans from probable annihilation, but provided them with the material means to overwhelm their adversaries; . . . the Chetniks. The Partisans had made up their minds that the Chetniks would be their long-range enemies after the Allied victory.

The equipment of ten Italian divisions, including some of the artillery, was turned over to the Partisans. The Italian equipment which the Chetniks were able to acquire was of insignificant quantities. The reason for this imbalance can be found in the intervention of the British Middle East Headquarters. The terms of the Armistice provided for the Italians to surrender their weapons to the nearest Allied forces. The Italians were only too happy to do just that and get out. But where were the nearest Allied forces? British Headquarters, through its mission in Yugoslavia, indicated the Partisans as the intended recipients.

Helping the Partisans

The acquisition of artillery gave the Partisans a decisive advantage over the Chetniks from then on. In the areas evacuated by the Axis forces, conventional engagements were bound to develop between the Partisans and the Chetniks for control of the territory, with artillery as the decisive factor. Tito wasted no time in capitalizing on this new advantage. In October his forces attacked the Chetniks in Montenegro. The Chetniks were commanded by General Djukanovich and Colonel Stanishich. They retreated to the Ostrog Monastery where, after a short siege, they capitulated. At the same time, Bulgarian occupation forces in South Serbia began openly to favor the Partisans and succeeded in expelling the Chetniks from the area. The territory under the influence of Mikhailovich was rapidly shrinking.

In 1944 the German reactions to guerrilla activities in Yugoslavia became progressively more passive. German troop shortages were becoming severe. They were unable to launch offensive operations against the guerrillas. In January they sent the First Brigade of the Kozak Cavalry Division to clear the area near Karlovach, southwest of Zagreb. The Brigade consisted of the first Kozak Regiment (Don) and the third (Kuban). It was engaged by superior forces and went on the defensive in the forest near Vojnits. Later the Germans sent the second Kozak Regiment (Sibirsk) with one artillery battery as reinforcements and the whole force managed to extricate itself and retreat toward Zagreb.

The last major operation against Tito took place on May 24. The Germans dropped a battalion of paratroopers on Tito's headquarters at Dvar after their intelligence was able to locate the Headquarters. Tito took to the hills and was later rescued by a British aircraft which flew him to Bari, Italy. After a few days in Italy, Tito set up a new headquarters on the Dalmatian island of Vis protected by British troops. This operation is important because it is the first one on record where airborne troops were used against guerrilas. . . .

It is known today that the Western leaders sincerely hoped for postwar cooperation with the Soviet government. They also feared the possibility of a separate treaty between the Nazis and the Soviets who, after all, had consummated such a rapprochement once before in 1939, in the Ribbentrop-Molotov agreement. To avoid such a calamity the Western leaders were prepared to make all kinds of concessions and trade others' territory. In making these concessions, they were helped greatly by the numerous members of the "lost generation" of the 30s who . . . believed that the world would be better off with increased Soviet influence. Many such persons were located in positions of responsibility (usually away from the fronts) and were able to influence major decisions.

In Yugoslavia's case in particular, the decisions were greatly influenced by the reports of the British Military Mission with Tito, headed by Brigadier Fitzroy Maclean. Instrumental in these decisions also was the head of the intelligence section in the British Headquarters, Middle East—Major Kluggman, who, after the war, became Director of Education for the Communist party of England.

A second factor, no doubt, was the opportunistic attitude of British foreign policy [founded on a] belief that concessions to the Russians in Yugoslavia would induce them to relieve the pressure on other parts of the Empire, such as India (still a Crown Colony) and the Middle East.

On the American side, a concerted effort to sway American public opinion to Tito's side was made by the avowed Croat communist Louis Adamic, but he had little influence in official circles. . . . [The United States] abandoned Mikhailovich with reluctance. But Churchill at the Quebec conference in September 1944 insisted that the United States withdraw its mission from Mikhailovich and Roosevelt complied. . . .

Evaluating the Guerrilla Role

The attempt to assess the effectiveness of guerrilla warfare in Yugoslavia [entails a comparison] of two different groups of guerrillas. However, a fair assessment has to take into consideration the political and military objectives of the two groups and of the Allied High Command.

The Allied objective was to inflict as much material damage as possible to the Axis forces regardless of what casualties the guerrillas and civilians suffered. There were no immediate political objectives manifested by the Allied High Command; the tendency was to subordinate or defer political problems.

The Partisans' objectives were principally political. As good Communists, they looked ahead to control of the Yugoslav government after the war. To this objective they subordinated military operations.

The Chetniks' objectives, at first, coincided with those of the Allies. But as they realized that they were being caught in the middle between the Axis forces and the Partisans, their objectives gradually changed and became preoccupied with establishing their control over Serbia, Bosnia, and Herzegovina.

Militarily, from the Allied point of view, the guerrilla operations in Yugoslavia were a partial success. The material damage inflicted on the Axis forces was small. But the potential threat of the guerrillas to the Axis communications lines compelled the German High Command to maintain in Yugoslavia a large number of combat formations at the expense of other theaters; this, in spite of the fact that very substantial forces from the German satellites were also available for occupation and security missions in Yugoslavia.

The military and political objectives of the Partisans were completely attained whereas those of the Chetniks were a complete failure. The reasons can be found in Allied, particularly British, intervention favoring the Partisans over the Chetniks.

Selected Bibliography

Soviet Union

Charques, Richard. *The Twilight of Imperial Russia.* Fairlawn, New Jersey: Essential Books, 1958.

Footman, David. *Civil War in Russia.* New York: Praeger, 1962.

Pares, Bernard. *The Fall of the Russian Monarchy.* New York: Knopf, 1939.

Reed, John. *Ten Days that Shook the World.* Foreword by V. I. Lenin. New York: International Publishers, 1967. (1st ed., 1919.)

Seton-Watson, Hugh. *The Decline of Imperial Russia, 1855–1914.* New York: Praeger, 1952.

Treadgold, Donald W. *Twentieth Century Russia.* 3d ed. Chicago: Rand McNally, 1972.

Trotsky, Leon. *A History of the Russian Revolution.* Translated by Max Eastman, 3 vols. New York: Simon and Schuster, 1932.

Wolfe, Bertram D. *Three Who Made a Revolution.* Rev. ed. New York: Dell, 1964.

China

Barnett, A. Doak. *China on the Eve of the Communist Takeover.* New York: Praeger, 1963.

Chow Tse-tsung. *The May Fourth Movement.* Cambridge, Massachusetts: Harvard University Press, 1960.

Clubb, O. Edmund. *20th Century China.* 2d. ed. New York: Columbia University Press, 1972.

Crowley, James B., ed. *Modern East Asia: Essays in Interpretation.* New York: Harcourt, 1970.

Franke, Wolfgang. *A Century of Chinese Revolution, 1851–1949.* Translated by Stanley Rudman. New York: Harper, 1970.

Harrison, James Pinckney. *The Long March to Power. A History of the Chinese Communist Party, 1961–1972.* New York: Praeger, 1972.

Johnson, Chalmers. *Peasant Nationalism and Communist Power.* Stanford, California: Stanford University Press, 1962.

North, Robert. *Moscow and Chinese Communists.* Stanford, California: Stanford University Press, 1963.

Schwartz, Benjamin I. *Chinese Communism and the Rise of Mao.* Cambridge, Massachusetts: Harvard University Press, 1958.

Seldon, Mark. *The Yenan Way in Revolutionary China.* Cambridge, Massachusetts: Harvard University Press, 1971.

Snow, Edgar. *Red Star Over China.* New York: Random House, 1938.

Teng Ssu-yu and Fairbank, John K., eds. *China's Response to the West.* Cambridge, Massachusetts: Harvard University Press, 1954.

Wright, Mary C., ed. *China in Revolution: The First Phase, 1900–1913.* New Haven: Yale University Press, 1968.

Yugoslavia

Auty, Phyllis. *Tito.* New York: McGraw-Hill, 1970.

Colakovic, Rodoljub. *Winning Freedom.* Translated by Alec Brown. London: Lincoln-Prager, Ltd., 1962.

Dedijer, Vladimir. *Tito Speaks.* London: Weidenfeld and Nicolson, 1953.

———. *With Tito Through the War.* London: Alexander Hamilton, 1951.

Dragnich, Alexander. *Tito's Promised Land—Yugoslavia.* New Brunswick, New Jersey: Rutgers University Press, 1954.

Hoptner, Jacob B. *Yugoslavia in Crisis. 1934–1941.* New York: Columbia University Press, 1962.

Maclean, Fitzroy. *The Heretic: The Life and Times of Josip Broz-Tito.* New York: Harper, 1957.

THE IDEOLOGICAL SETTING

Even before his death in 1883, Karl Marx's ideas and writings had gained currency among European radicals. Quickly, however, disagreement on the correct or orthodox interpretation of Marx arose. The ideas and intellectual ferment that surrounded the dispute about the true meaning of Marxist thought were soon put to test, after a number of Marxist parties were established, and a Marxist regime was subsequently constructed in the wake of the Bolshevik victory in Russia. As a result of the victory, Russian communism (and, more specifically, "communism" as defined by those Soviet leaders in power at that particular time) became equated with orthodox Marxism. Like all ideologies, the Marxist movement in Russia developed left and right wings, each accusing the other of betrayal, but both being at the mercy of the power in the center. Those deviating to the right or left—that is, Marxists in disagreement with more powerful Marxists—were accused of ideological betrayal and branded as "revisionists."

To the average observer, the disputes among Marxists might seem strange indeed since various defenders and advocates of the doctrine have on occasion called it an ideology of "scientific absolutes." And how, one might ask, can right-thinking men argue over scientific absolutes? Most Marxist theorists would contend, however, that if there are scientific elements to Marx's doctrine, they are in the area of a science of capitalism and societal change, but not in the nature and governing of the socialist society. As noted in Section One, Marx had described in detail the nature of the capitalist system and prophesied its inevitable doom, which he maintained would be due to the irreconcilable conflicts inherent in the system. Marx concentrated on explaining historical and dialectical materialism, economic determinism, and the nature of capitalism, but he did not discuss at length the new socialist system that was to arise from the ruins of capitalism. Thus his followers and advocates were left with very little guidance for constructing and developing the new socialist state. The obvious consequence was improvisation and experimentation by national Communists, a practice not particularly conducive to ideological unity within an international movement.

Lenin, the first to have the opportunity to apply Marxism, was forced to improvise even before the revolution began. In the last few years preceding the revolution, Lenin questioned the nature of the dialectic and the resultant revolution effectuating the expected change to socialism in Russia. Although he was dedicated in 1905 to the necessity of achieving socialism by following a change pattern leading through political democracy and the bourgeois revolution, his ideological prognostications came back to haunt him in 1917. In spite of his fear of oversimplification, note that when the opportunity for the triumph of Communism occurred, Lenin omitted the stage of bourgeois capitalist development and launched directly into the socialist revolution—a major revision indeed.

The institution that was established to implement this accelerated revolutionary process was called the "party of the new type," better known as the Communist party. Lenin and the Bolsheviks contended that this organization would enable the working class to take power "before their time," because the organizational planning would compensate for what was lacking in dialectical development. Highly centralized, militant, and closely knit, the Communist party did indeed become the instrument needed to bring the class consciousness to the worker and to mobilize him for political action. As history shows us, Lenin was successful and the Bolsheviks soon found themselves in control of revolutionary Russia.

With the success of the Bolshevik takeover, Lenin the revolutionary became Lenin the state-builder. But what did Lenin do to establish and to further the cause of Russian communism and how much guidance did he receive from the tenets of Marx? When this new leader of the Russian people turned to Marxism for solutions to the problems confronting Russia, the answers were not forthcoming. In addition, the war years that followed were not conducive to the stabilization and development needed to bring about a smoothly functioning socialist system, and instead the tragic experiences of World War I and the Civil War left the country in a state of social and economic chaos. Although Lenin set out to solve these critical problems by embellishing, revising, and adding to the doctrine of Marx, he did not live to see the results and succumbed after a series of strokes on January 21, 1924. Against the better judgment and advice of Lenin, Stalin was allowed to become the new architect and the guardian of the subsequent building years. He introduced yet further ideological deviations from Marxism, and by the mid-1930s differences in degree had grown into differences in kind. The "dictatorship of the proletariat" became the "dictatorship of the party," which eventually, one might contend, developed into the "dictatorship of one man"—Joseph Stalin.

Although Stalin encountered obstacles on his way to dictatorial power —for example, the battle with Trotsky's "Leftist Deviation" and Bukharin's "Rightist Group"—they were temporary, and ultimately overcome. Stalin's basic strategy became a conservative one, whereby the primary objective was the preservation of the Soviet socialist state. To rationalize and justify his behavior, Stalin proposed the doctrine of "socialism in one country" which directly conflicted with the Trotskyite position of "international revolution." This allowed Stalin to work toward the preservation of communism in one country, through the use of increasingly totalitarian based tactics, rather than extending the Communist revolution abroad. Because of his "deviant" views, Trotsky became *persona non grata* in the Stalinist state and was exiled in 1929, taking refuge in Turkey, France, Norway, and finally Mexico, where he was assassinated in 1940.

The significance of "Stalinism" lies in the totalitarian model of government and the set of practical precepts for controlling power that were established. These ideological tenets were applied by Stalin's successors at home, and they were imported by Communist leaders abroad as guidelines for the early formative stages of Communist development in their own states. For example, although Mao Tse-tung learned to suspect Stalin, the respect he bore for the man he referred to as the "great eagle of communism" was reflected by the influence of Stalinist ideology on his own strategies, both before and after the Chinese Communists' victory over the Nationalists in 1949. Similarly the Partisan Communists of Yugoslavia adopted the Stalinist strategy, and during the initial phase of development (1945–50) the nation became known as a "police state," a "totalitarian dictatorship," and inevitably, "the most Stalinist of the Stalinist states." Although this stage was only temporary, Stalinism had left a definite imprint upon the Titoist state.

However, in both countries, certain historical events and circumstances allowed (or we might say "forced") the leaders of the Chinese and Yugoslav states to begin to define their own paths of ideological development. The first such event was Stalin's dispute with Tito, which resulted in the Yugoslavs' expulsion from the international Communist organization, the Cominform, in 1948. The reasons for Stalin's dissatisfaction with the Yugoslavs were many, but the foremost seems to have been Tito's stubborn independence and foremost concern for Yugoslav sovereignty. This event signified the dawn of a new era in Eastern Europe, where international adherence to the "absolutes" of Marxism-Leninism proved much too weak to compete with the quest for national identity and autonomy. Nationalism became of primary importance—a development that reflected the changing relationships within the Communist world and, ultimately, defeated the ideal of a united Communist movement.

Upon the Yugoslav expulsion from the Cominform, a new stage in ideological development began for the Communists from the Balkans, although the first few years of independence proved a lonely, costly experience. What developed was an extended period of de-Stalinization that began in the early 1950s and has endured into the present. As a consequence, there exists in Yugoslavia today a more humane form of socialism that allows greater freedom and autonomy for the individual and groups within the society.

A subsequent event that would appear to have lent greater credibility to Yugoslav independence was Khrushchev's "secret speech" of 1956, in which he denounced the errors of the Stalinist years and admitted the past failures of the Soviet regime. In this speech, he refuted the infallability of the Soviet ideological form and, by inference, seriously questioned the Soviet party's role as the sole definer of orthodox Marxism-Leninism.

Then a few years later, a series of political, military, and economic disputes led to increasing disagreement between the Soviet and Chinese Communists, a conflict that came to be known as the Sino-Soviet dispute. This conflict between two Communist powers produced greater disunity within the ideological movement and a new and distinct body of thought—now called Maoism—emerged.

What is important to remember about communist ideology, however, is that it is a doctrine purporting to explain social behavior of the world. This doctrine has its roots in Marxism, but it continues to be embellished, revised, and changed in a variety of ways by the leaders of the different Communist states. As a result, these doctrines have become distinguishable from one another, and each variant must be carefully examined in the Chinese, Soviet, and Yugoslav cases in order to gain an insight into the inner workings of that particular system.

In each political system, then, there is an identifiable body of doctrine governing political, social, and economic life. These bodies of doctrine share many common features, but the ideological setting of each varies from system to system. The differences have been influenced by numerous factors—historical circumstances, cultural conditions, personalities, and political expediency being some of the most important. In the readings to follow, the authors attempt to describe the ideological settings, identify some of their major determinants, and evaluate the effect that these different settings have upon the political systems.

In "The Functions of Ideology in the Soviet Political System," Alfred G. Meyer defines the meaning of ideology, its role and functions in Communist political systems, and raises some serious questions about future trends in the nature and meaning of ideology in the Soviet system. Next, in "Changes in Chinese Political Ideology," Han Shik Park discusses the philosophical foundation of the Chinese ideology and suggests implications for the future policy of China. Then, in "Chinese and Leninist Components in the Personality of Mao Tse-tung," Stuart R. Schram examines the ideological interpretations and thoughts of Mao. Schram addresses himself to the controversy on the relative influence of Chinese tradition and Leninist directives on contemporary Chinese ideology and behavior. Finally, in "Marxism Belgrade Style," Dennison I. Rusinow describes the ideology of the innovators from the Balkans, and provides us with a fresh and intriguing insight into the functions and meaning of Yugoslav ideology.

9

The Functions of Ideology in the Soviet Political System

Alfred G. Meyer

Ideology as used in this paper is easily defined. I mean by it the body of doctrine which the Communist party teaches all Soviet citizens, from school children to the higher party leadership. On such different levels, there are, of course, variations in intensity and duration of instruction, in sophistication as well as in detail. But the contents and indeed the vocabulary are remarkably uniform, whether we examine the agitation material intended for the masses or the guidelines put out in theoretical journals intended only for party leaders. This doctrine consists of the following parts: (1) a philosophy called Dialectical Materialism; (2) generalizations about man and society, past and present, called Historical Materialism; (3) an economic doctrine called Political Economy, which seeks to explain the economics of capitalism and imperialism on the one hand, and of socialist construction on the other; (4) a body of political thought, or guidelines, now called Scientific Communism, which deals, first, with the strategy and tactics of communist revolutions, and, second, with political problems of socialist states; and (5) the official history of the CPSU. To this one might add the shorter-range pronouncements made by the party interpreting current affairs and determining goals and priorities.

For the Western student of Soviet society, the official ideology is strange, forbidding material; and many have hesitated to get tangled up with it. This applies particularly to scholars reared in the Anglo-Saxon traditions of empiricism and pragmatism. For them, the Hegelian form of Soviet ideology renders it difficult to grasp. Indeed, they find it so strange to their ears that the pronouncements of Soviet ideologists appear to them similar to the chants and litanies of some esoteric religious cult; and, just as some scholars assert that religious beliefs are irreconcilable with reason and modern science, so some western students of Soviet society find it difficult to believe that obviously intelligent people such as those in charge of the Soviet government and the Communist party could possibly take their own ideology seriously.[1]

From Alfred G. Meyer, "The Functions of Ideology in the Soviet Political System," *Soviet Studies* (Vol. XVII, No. 3, January 1966), pp. 273–285. [Reprinted with permission from the publisher.]

[1]This works the other way around as well. Wolfgang Leonhard tells the wonderful story of the Catholic prelate who found himself in a Soviet labour camp. Once his jailers learned that he had been at the Vatican and knew the Pope, they gave him V.I.P. treatment; and a delegation from the Central Committee even came down to chat with him. One of the first questions, after they had ascertained that he really knew the Pope, was, "Tell us, does the Pope really believe in Christianity?"

In addition, the study of ideology and its relation to social action is one of the most difficult and tricky branches of social science. Here again the empirical bent of contemporary social science impels many of us to leave such obstreperous material alone and turn to more quantifiable and researchable problems. The present essay may convince the reader that I, too, should have stayed away.

My remarks will concern themselves with three problems very much related to each other, although in exceedingly complicated fashion, and all of them puzzling.

The first of these is the apparent ambivalence of the party leadership to the ideology. I have the impression . . . that the party depends very much on the ideology and yet regards it also as a source of great embarrassment, and that, moreover, this is a very old attitude. The need for the ideology is attested by the great attention which the party has always devoted to problems of ideological training and to the careful elaboration of all parts of the doctrine. In the most recent years, we have witnessed a grandiose reorganization of the entire *agitprop* machinery, under the direction of Mr. Il'ichev, for a seemingly unprecedented job of indoctrination. Yet in observing Mr. Il'ichev gird his loins for this task, I wondered whether we might not apply to this effort Professor Parkinson's law about buildings. According to this law, the magnificence and elaborateness of an organization's premises are inversely related to its efficiency. I suspect that the new ideological apparatus of the Central Committee may be a hollow shell. Whether the people in the Central Committee perceive it thus, and whether they are pleased by it, is a very much more difficult question to answer.

A second problem that concerns me very much is a curious unity of opposites characterizing Soviet ideology. I am speaking about the dialectics of rigidity and flexibility in communist doctrine, a phenomenon with which we are all familiar, and about which many of us are puzzled. Precisely what is rigid and what is flexible in this body of dogmas? Can we make generalizations about this dialectics for the entire Soviet period, or has the relationship between rigidity and flexibility changed from Lenin's time to Stalin's, or from Stalin's to his successors'? What does it mean when Stalin is called a dogmatic cynic, or Khrushchev a flexible believer? Does it mean that the former clung to the letter of the Marxist-Leninist holy writ, denying its spirit, and that in Khrushchev this relationship was reversed? Obviously, matters are not nearly so simple. But precisely what they are remains to be investigated.

Finally, no sovietologist can get away from a question very closely linked with our last problem, namely, that concerning the relation between the Soviet regime's official ideology and its actual performance. This is the old question of whether Marxism-Leninism functions as a guide to action, i.e., whether it motivates the rulers of the country, or whether it is a mere public relations device. Those who advance the first hypothesis subscribe to ideological determinism. They characterize the ideology as the master plan of Soviet politics and say, with the Reverend Fred Schwartz, "You can trust the communists—to do exactly as they say". Those who subscribe to the latter hypothesis believe that ideology is no more than post-hoc rationalization of policies: they say, with Robert V. Daniels, that "action has become a guide to theory."

I have for a long time been inclined to prefer the latter view; but I am no longer certain about it. Indeed, I think it is as one-sided as the former. For either hypothesis there is a good deal of supporting evidence. At the same time, neither is subject to convincing verification: it is impossible to state firmly that any policy being pursued is or is not in accord with the ideology; and it is equally impossible to convict the Soviet leadership of cynical disbelief in their own dogmas. Indeed, the earnestness with which the vast indoctrination machinery is operated, and even more the intellectual problems the regime has willingly endured for the sake of maintaining doctrinal orthodoxy, attest to a commitment far more intense than is suggested by a theory of purely machiavellian manipulation. The problem, rationalization or guide to action, may therefore be a false one.

Let me relate the issues I am raising to yet another problem of social science which I feel has not been explored sufficiently. I have in mind the complex nature of the phenomenon we call revolution. I would define a revolution as two or three distinct processes which often are lumped together. One is the destruction of the old order or the old political system; another is the creation of a new one; and a third is the inevitable period of chaos that comes in between the two. The fallacy of seeing these three distinct processes as one lies in regarding all destruction as the creation of something new. Yet the false starts and abortive undertakings of the interregnum dramatize the break between the destructive and the constructive phases. So does the leadership turnover: the creators are usually people other than the destroyers. Indeed, before the new system is built, the destroyers themselves are usually destroyed.

There are two links between the old system and the new one which have served to obscure the break: organization and ideology. The Communist party, it can be argued, helped to administer the final blow to tsarism and was also the sovereign ruler over the new order which it itself created. Similarly, Marxism-Leninism is not only an ideology of destruction, but also incorporates a blueprint for the future which, one might argue, has remained as a programme, or at least as a beacon or guiding star for the Soviet leadership.

Against this I would maintain, first of all, that the organization which Lenin had created was also destroyed and had to be built anew before Stalin could use it for the purposes of system building. Secondly, I submit that the ideology was also profoundly altered. Its functions within the party underwent fundamental changes; its content was drained; only the hollow forms of the terminology remained. These forms or formulations have become rigid. They have crystallized into that esoteric jargon which to the outsider appears either meaningless or unrealistic, delusory, and self-deceptive. Yet the Soviet citizen talks this language; and I am sure that every reader who has been in the USSR got an initial jolt when he found that people actually talked to him like *Pravda* editorials.

In another place I have summarized this draining of content as the withering away of utopia, and the creation of an authoritarian ideology of conservatism based on verbiage which includes tautologies, circular reasons, question-begging, and other devices of word magic. While retaining and using the words of Marx, this ideology stands Marxism on its head and thus "negates" it. No doubt such a transvaluation of ideology is to be expected whenever a theory of revolution turns into a theory of state, or, to use Mannheim's terminology, whenever utopias turn into ideologies.

The purpose of this essay is to try to pull the strands of these various paradoxes together by discussing the different and conflicting functions of the ideology within the Soviet political system.

Let me begin with the exceedingly trite observation that ideology is the language of politics in the USSR. This statement itself has several meanings. It connotes, first, that the ideology serves as the frame of reference for all individuals in the society. It is their set of concepts for perceiving the world and its problems, hence their means of orienting themselves in the universe. Now it is generally accepted that every conceptual framework in its own fashion aids cognition: and at the same time every such framework injects its own distortions into perceived reality. Conceptual frameworks both aid and hinder realistic self-orientation in the environment. In physics and related sciences, it may be possible at times to measure the cognitive benefits and drawbacks of one conceptual framework against those of another. But in the social disciplines (and Soviet ideology is primarily a special view of society) we ought to be very hesitant to make such judgments. If they are made at all, they usually reflect the judge's own conceptual framework, with all the limitations and blindspots this implies.

Speaking from the point of view of my own biases, then, let me argue that Soviet ideology seems to me to have serious limitations as a cognitive self-orientation device. In this it is similar to political ideologies in most or all established systems. To me, many assumptions of Soviet ideology appear highly unrealistic. Again, one would have to say the same thing about other political ideologies. They, like the Soviet ideology, are, at least in part, designed to distort or conceal reality, as Mannheim pointed out some decades ago. Hence I would maintain that they are characterized by a certain quality which we might call unrealism, or one might refer to a gap between ideology and life, or between ideology and reality.

This gap doubtless creates a strain in all political systems, because the need for realistic self-orientation must be very persistent in human beings in our time. This strain must be felt, if only vaguely, by many Soviet officials. I am thinking foremost of the top leadership of the party, where realistic appraisals must continually be straining against orthodox formulas, and where ideology may appear as a hindrance or a drag which can retard the policy makers in coping with new problems and new phenomena. The repeated efforts made by younger Soviet social scientists today to attack policy problems in a more empirical fashion and to draw firm boundaries between ideology and social science doubtless are a response to this strain. In western political systems there are similar conflicts due to analogous attempts of social scientists and other citizens to shine beacons of illumination through ideological smokescreens. One might add to this also that in ages where official ideologies were clothed in metaphysical or even theological dogmas, the strain between ideology and reality was infinitely greater than it is today in the USSR.

Now, self-orientation means not only the attempt to comprehend the world, but also to define our role in it. It has normative as well as analytical connotations. Soviet ideology, also, seeks to define the citizens' values, expectations, rights, and duties. Its contents in this regard might be summarized as the continual and cumulative attempt to tone down expectations, and to define roles so as to ensure everyone's unquestioning collaboration with the party. It is this which I call the withering away of utopia.

Here too there is a strain, because the radical humanism of original Marxism is not so easy to explain away altogether; and in many ways it clashes with the ethics of contemporary communist ideology. We can, I believe, expect such clashes to become, if anything, more intense. The lingering memory of the utopian elements in Marxism is bound to persist as long as Marx's writings are regarded as holy writ. Marxian ideas thus function as the bad conscience of the Soviet political élite. This, too, may serve, or may have served, as a drag on hard-nosed, pragmatic decision making; and in the long run the managers of the system must feel it to be a really intolerable hindrance. Yet they are very strongly committed to the letter of this holy writ.

Even more tritely, ideology serves also as the code of communications. Every political system has such a code, which to the outsider sounds esoteric, whereas the insider speaks it with ease. In American society, it is inconceivable that anyone could be successful in politics without being able to sound off about democracy, liberty, the Constitution, or the Founding Fathers. Similarly, the upward-mobile Soviet citizen and functionary must know how to say the right things at the right time. He must be able to communicate with peers, superiors, and subordinates, in the accepted language. Again, the USSR is not the only society communicating in an esoteric code. In the United States everybody knows that "States' rights" often means white supremacy; "free enterprise" means administered prices, and so forth.

Lest I have implied that the esoteric code is used primarily by subordinates for their communications with superiors, let me stress that it is of particular importance in downward communications. Ideological pronouncements in the USSR are probably the single most important method by which the party informs its subleaders and members of current policies. Many students of the Soviet system have remarked on the surprising independence of the middle-range bureaucratic chief and the political center's great reluctance to interfere with his autonomy and responsibility. Professor William McCagg, in a recent paper, has called my attention to the incredibly tight restriction on important communications within the system, especially downward communications. Hence the importance of policy guidelines which the party supplies by its programmatic formulas.

I would sum this up by saying that every public figure in the USSR is *ex officio* an ideologist. Now I have already referred to a gap between theory and reality, to the unreality of the language of politics. The abstruseness of the language, it seems to me, is one token of that gap. The greater the gap, the more abstruse the language and the more difficult to understand. Yet being a code of communications, it must be understandable. Hence it seems to me that its very "unreality" leads to pressures for making it even more rigid and inflexible. It then becomes a mere code, the "realism" of which becomes immaterial.

In addition to being the language of politics, ideology functions as a legitimizing device. It is to convince the citizenry that the party and its leaders have a legitimate claim to rule them. More broadly, it is to convince the people that the entire system of government is legitimate. Ideology is thus an exercise in salesmanship or public relations. It seeks to persuade the Soviet citizens that theirs is the best of all possible societies.

Now, given the obvious inadequacies of the Soviet system in its early decades, this has for a long time been a [nearly] hopeless undertaking; and we can be pretty sure that the party leadership has been aware of this. Yet every revolutionary regime desperately needs legitimacy if it wants to accomplish anything or even simply stay in power. Let me return to the process of revolution I talked about earlier. I referred to the last phase of it as the fashioning of a new political system. This is the task Stalin tackled. On a comparative basis, political system building has not yet been studied very thoroughly. But I suggest that one of its essential processes is the primitive accumulation of legitimacy—a concerted effort on the part of a new ruling élite to sell the new order to the constituents. The typical methods for the primitive accumulation of legitimacy are a combination of terror and indoctrination, or indoctrination backed by terror.

But here, too, doctrinal rigidity must develop, if only because the regime had to make sure that elements of the ideology would not make themselves independent, and that a total restructuring of the citizens' thinking was achieved. Soviet doctrine had to turn into a rigid catechism chanted compulsively in ritual affirmations of loyalty and approval. Uttering the proper phrases was to become a conditioned reflex.

I think this compulsive and dogmatic form of indoctrination is related not only to the need for accumulating legitimacy, but also to the difficulty of this task. Let us face it: convincing the Soviet citizens that theirs was the best of all possible worlds was difficult. Hence the ideology became implausible. The effect of this is not only increased rigidity, but the further intensification of the indoctrination effort. We might formulate this as a law (I am not sure whether it is verifiable in the form in which I state it): The intensity of indoctrination and the rigidity of official dogma are inversely proportional to the credibility of the doctrine. Moreover, these elements mutually reinforce each other.

One might refine the observation that ideology is a public relations device by distinguishing between the function of legitimization and that of socialization. The former is designed to make the citizen accept the system; the latter, to accustom him to his own status and role within the system. Here too there may be a strain: legitimization must seek to link the present regime with the past. Hence it must keep alive a carefully screened memory of the Russian past, of Marxist-Leninist writings, and of the revolutionary goals. Socialization, on the other hand, must adjust the citizen to the non-utopian reality of the present. Thus the promise of the revolution must be kept alive and yet emasculated. Similarly, the party leaders feel obliged to play two conflicting tunes in their world wide public relations. On the one hand, they seek to "socialize" other governments for coexistence by stressing coexistence themes; yet at the same time they feel compelled to assure other publics, or at least themselves, that they will, in the end, and quite soon, bury us.

The idea of ideology as a public relations device is by no means new. For decades, scholars have studied Soviet propaganda, which is but another name for public relations. But after making reference to some things with which we are all very familiar, I would like to add something a little unfamiliar: I think we are mistaken if we conceive of Soviet ideological output as aimed primarily at various publics, be it ourselves or the Soviet citizenry. I have the feeling that in sounding off in ideological fashion, Soviet leaders are not talking to us or to the "masses," but are talking to each other or, much more important, primarily to themselves. Soviet ideology is not only communication with others. It is also a monologue in which the leaders compulsively engage. We might refer to this mass monologue as a process of self-legitimization, a continual attempt on the part of the rulers to convince *themselves* of their legitimacy.

If this self-legitimization function of ideological production leads to the systematic distortion of reality, then the above observations would imply that Soviet ideology is not so much deceptive as self-deceptive. This gives a novel twist to the cynical statement of Talleyrand that "language is a means to hide our thoughts." The sly diplomat did think of language as a deceptive smokescreen to be used skillfully by a cynical manipulator of words. But ideology in the sense in which I have used it takes in the very users of the words, in accordance with the proverb "believing is seeing."

I believe that the conception of ideology as a collective monologue applies not only to the Soviet political system, but to many if not all other systems. But I also think that the compulsion to engage in it is particularly strong in the USSR, for the following reasons.

First of all, the Soviet regime is comparatively new. The revolution by which it established itself occurred within the memory of living people. The regime, moreover, was highly unpopular for decades. Within the elite, there is a sharp competitive rat race. All these factors create a feeling of intense insecurity, which must be allayed by repeated reassurance and self-legitimization.

We can relate this, furthermore, to both the unrealism and the rigidity of the ideology. Here I would like to make the following points:

First of all, let me go back to the ideological transformation which I have called the withering-away of utopia. I may have implied that this change was made more or less deliberately, in order to tone down the citizens' expectations. But we can see it also as one imposed by circumstances. Soviet ideology has been *compelled* to tone down its own expectations. During the revolutionary euphoria of the first years in power, the party members expected the millennium. Instead, they got coexistence with capitalism and with the many persistent non-Communist features of Soviet society. For this coexistence, the party has never really been ready. Ideologically and, perhaps, psychologically, it has been unable to face the facts which caused this state of affairs. It therefore had to fashion for itself an illusory image of why things went wrong or why they are as right as they could possibly be. The clinician would probably call the image somewhat paranoid. Both the unreality and the rigidity fit the syndrome. Like all other ideologies, that of the USSR appears [insane] to the outsider. . . .

To this one might add a sociopsychological dimension: the bureaucratic authoritarian system which Stalin created and his successors are now managing seems, like all similar systems, to bring to the fore considerable numbers of compulsive, ego-weak, authoritarian personalities, whose psychological needs include the strong urge for firm guidelines such as are provided by a rigid and comprehensive ideology. The greater their insecurity, the more they may cling to it. Hence inability or unwillingness to adjust to changing circumstances or to other threats to routine is likely to express itself (in those bureaucrats afflicted with this insecurity) in recourse to certainties of the doctrine. Orthodoxy is an armour plate, or corset, for insecure authoritarians.

It seems to me that we can learn a great deal about the Soviet Union from studying bureaucratic organizations anywhere. One observation often made by students of large, complex administrative organizations is the urge which such structures manifest for suppressing all dissent and conflict, because disunity threatens the control which the bureaucratic managers seek to exercise. In fact, however, conflict is ever-present; hence the urge to achieve unity turns into the mere concealment of conflict and an outward show or pretense of unity. Or so it seems to the outsider. The hierarchs that run bureaucratic machines may well convince themselves that the continual show of unity reflects reality. Pretense becomes magic. Things are so because everyone repeats again and again that they are so. The concealment of conflict behind a pretense of agreement thus contributes to their emotional balance and assures them that they are in control.

One of the methods for pretending unity is the continual expression of identical views, goals and principles—the ritual incantation of a standardized ideology. The paradox of the situation is that conflicts nonetheless persist and must, of course, be expressed. Several observers of Soviet politics (Leonhard, Bialer, McCagg, Rush) have told us how the paradox is resolved: conflicting views are expressed between the lines, by means of slight variations in the standard formulas—so slight, indeed, that only the initiates have even an inkling that conflicts are in fact being voiced. As McCagg has formulated it, conflicts express themselves in the competitive rehearsal of identical jargon. They can thereby remain subconscious; and in the insecure world of bureaucratic politics, this pretense of unity makes rational debate possible, even though it may at the same time distort rationality.

If my points are valid, then it becomes clear why the indoctrination effort becomes more intense and prolonged, the higher we rise in the party hierarchy: the people closest to the center of power must not only be initiated into the language of political discourse and the *arcana imperii* which this language must convey. They also have far greater need for recurrent self-legitimization.

One further generalization about modern bureaucracy may support my hypothesis. In *The Organizational Society,* (Robert Presthus describes different modes of psychological adjustment to bureaucratic systems.[2] Those he calls *upward-mobile* accept elite values positively and actively. A large body of people whom he characterizes as *indifferent* are relatively passive in their attitude towards the prevailing ideology. Anyone who overtly *rejects* the system and its ethos is likely to be eliminated and can therefore be disregarded. Finally, Presthus asserts that all bureaucratic systems contain their share of creative individualists, whom he calls *ambivalent.* If in fact these different personalities can be found in all large and complex modern organizations, then it is plausible to assume that the only people who are truly indoctrinated, the only ones who fully sub-scribe to the prevailing ideology, are the upward-mobile persons, who are likely to be found in positions of authority. Those whose acceptance of the ideology is perfunctory or who are passively rejecting it are likely to be apathetic and resigned—products of fear and habit rather than true indoctrination. If this applies to the USSR, then perhaps Soviet ideological work may have no greater effect upon the minds of the masses of citizens than American advertising. Again, one is led to assume that the educational effort of Soviet ideology functions primarily for the elite, i.e., the upper 5 or 10 percent of the population, while the vast majority of people are left languishing in relative indifference as long as they are rendered harmless by control, incentives and other devices.

One might add to this that the ideology, in turn, helps to create and educate those upward-mobile figures of authority (the New Soviet Men) needed by the administrative machinery. The Soviet political system requires people who are disciplined, productive, compulsive, authoritarian organization men. To train them, it requires an ideology in which content may be irrelevant, but consistency ("rigidity") matters a great deal; and so does the manner in which it is learned and repeated—compulsively, unquestion-ingly, in cathechismal, automaton fashion. In turn, ideological conformity becomes one of many tests used in recruiting the young elite of company men.

Ideology in the Soviet Union faces many challenges today. A rebellious younger generation is questioning the authority of its elders. The myth of the party's infallibility has been shattered by the trauma of destalinization and by galloping polycentrism. Professional experts in a host of endeavors no longer find Marxian concepts fully ap-plicable to their respective fields. In a world of revolutionary change, an ideology based on the experiences of the 1840s may no longer satisfy the rulers' urge for realistic self-orientation. The result of these and other challenges is a tendency which many scholars have called the erosion of ideology. I like to discuss this trend together with another one which, for want of a more euphonious term, I . . . call the routinization of in-doctrination. In this connection, let me make the following rather disconnected observations:

As the Soviet regime manages to fulfill some of its promises and redefine others, the ideology has a tendency to become more credible than before. By the same token, and also from mere longevity, the system is acquiring more and more legitimacy with the population. These two trends decrease the need for frantic, perpetual, and total indoc-

---

[2]Robert Presthus, *The Organizational Society* (New York: Knopf, 1962).

trination, even though they do not eliminate the many other reasons for clinging to a rigid doctrine.

At the same time, compulsive indoctrination has by now become ingrained in the Soviet system. It will not easily be abolished or even de-emphasized. But I believe that it is beginning to turn more and more into routine. Ideology is in the process of becoming a ritual akin to Sunday sermons or Independence Day oratory. Solemnly voicing the old truths will remain a marginally important means of refreshing the citizens' loyalty, devotion, and identification with the regime. But, as a mere ritual, ideology will tend to be almost as removed from actual life and its activities as Sunday sermons. When Mr. Khrushchev preached coexistence as a serious aim, but added his customary strictures against ideological coexistence, he was implying that life is life, and ideology is ideology. Let us be aware that for those who preach them, Sunday sermons are important, just as I have tried to show that, for the Soviet leadership, ideology is meaningful and important. We might add that the warning against ideological coexistence must be seen also as an effort by the party to stave off the domestic threats which global dealings with capitalism conjure. The unwillingness to coexist ideologically attests to the rulers' aim to isolate their citizens from ideological contamination. Whether in the long run it will be possible thus to coexist selectively is another question.

I said earlier that every public figure is *ex officio* an ideologist. However, Soviet society is faced with a growing complexity of tasks, and the division of labor gets ever more refined. In this process, ideology finds itself somehow separated from politics, if only because the active politician or manager can no longer keep up. His phrases must become more general and vague. Meanwhile, ideology itself becomes too complex for the party generalists to handle. The hierarchs superior to the ideologists may lose control, and the ideology experts gain autonomy. This is one of the trends behind the sharpening conflict between ideology and science in the USSR.

In short, as the USSR develops into a complex and heterogeneous society, the party leadership faces the ever more difficult task of weighing and aggregating conflicting views and interests impinging on it from a host of professional experts or their spokesmen within the party. Policy pronouncements, while couched in the jargon, are likely to be the results of stimuli which the Central Committee receives from many different agencies in response to political events and situations. Current revisionist or erosive trends are thus the result of the effort to accommodate the various group interests in the USSR and the Communist commonwealth while maintaining the party's prerogative of ultimate decision making, an effort to achieve realism and flexibility while maintaining doctrinal rigidity.

I want to end these observations on an inconclusive note. The trends and countertrends I have indicated, even if their existence could be fully verified, are not, I think, subject to quantification. If there is a theme which ties my remarks together, it is perhaps the following: Compulsive indoctrination and doctrinaire rigidity, like the so-called totalitarian style of government with which they are associated, are typical symptoms of the crash program phase of political development. Stalinism as a political system can, I think, be defined as a crash program of industrialization, of the so-called cultural revolution, and of political system building. On the whole, the initial leap has now been made. The system can probably settle down. The question which remains is whether the USSR will recover from Stalinist ideology any faster than we in the west have recovered from the Victorian ethic of self-denial and competition which accompanied our own crash program of modernization. But even this parallel should not be overdrawn.

One final remark: we all know that the Catholic prelate told his hosts from the Central Committee, quite truthfully, that the Pope indeed believes in Christianity. Similarly, I have tried to show that the leaders of the Communist party really do believe in communism, as they understand it. Another question would be much more difficult to answer: are they really Communists? I am not sure whether it should even be asked.

10

Changes in Chinese Political Ideology

Han Shik Park

The nature of communism and its role in world politics seem to be ultimately related to the nature of political ideology in general. When totalitarian communism emerged as a reality in the course of the Cold War decades, extreme polarization of totalitarian socialism and pluralistic democracy, and confrontation between the two blocs, followed. Since the early 1950s ideology has been the myth by which many civil and international wars have been justified. Unlike most of the wars in the past, wars of these two decades have been fought for the alleged defense of ideologies. An immense tension among the major powers has contributed to the enormous wasting of material resources and sacrifice of human lives—all legitimized in the name of ideology.

Consequently, to ask about the nature and meaning of political ideology is both significant and timely. This question seems to be particularly relevant in view of the apparent reshuffling of the world power structure that has been suggested by the Peking conference, Moscow summit talks, China-Japan peace treaty, and the growing ethos for political reunification in Germany and Korea.[1]

Political Ideology

The term "ideology" has had diverse meanings in the course of its conceptual evolution. To identify them all would be impossible, but we might safely classify them into three categories: ideology as philosophical conviction, ideology as way of life, and ideology as institution. These categories are by no means clearcut and pure. Almost any ideology that we have seen is, in fact, a combination of all three. Nonetheless, each ideology belongs more to one category than to either of the others.

This paper was originally written for delivery at the Southeastern Regional Conference of the Association of Asian Studies held at Appalachian State University, Boone, North Carolina, on January 26-27, 1973. The author wishes to thank Professor Thomas W. Ganschow of the University of Georgia for his insightful suggestions and comments on Communist China.

[1]In addition to the mutual recognition of East and West Germany, Korea opened a dialogue between South and North in 1972 for the first time since their separation.

Ideology as Philosophical Conviction.   The ideologies of the first type are the prescriptions and guidelines for political activities and social change. Such an ideology defines an "ideal" form of government and often sets out specific guidelines for achieving such government. Plato's political philosophy of the Republic was a classical example of a political ideology in which an "ideal" form of government was prescribed. Both Machiavelli and Hobbes posited what they considered to be inevitable forms of government, as opposed to the "ideal" forms based on their own analyses of human nature and natural law. Indeed, most of the political ideologies that evolved in the West until early modern times, including the medieval ecclesiastical doctrines, were based on philosophical dogmas and the basic beliefs about human nature and social order, and it was these that paved the way for the establishment of the tyrannical rules.

The outburst of *laissez-faire* capitalism and political liberalism in the early modern times was a cry against tyrannical order and the immoral justification of human inequality. However, the poor development and corruption of the economic and political liberalism provided the motivation for the French Revolution, and the basis for the growth of Marxist and non-Marxist socialism in the late 19th and early 20th centuries.

Both liberalism and socialism, unlike the philosophy of tyrannical government, were founded on a moral conviction that all humans were equal. This doctrine of human equality has been cited as the basis of legitimacy by most of the modern regimes— though they might operate under such divergent ideological labels as nationalism, socialism, democracy, and totalitarianism. All these ideologies justify political power in the name of "people's consent."

Ideology as Way of Life.   Once the moralistic interpretation of human nature and the credibility of man's capability became irrefutable, and the doctrine of "social contract" secured a firm basis of legitimacy for all forms of government, philosophical doctrine became a meaningless justification for claiming the superiority of a government. Consequently a new basis for claiming superiority was sought, and one founded on the second conception of ideology. This conception was expediently established during the Cold War era.

Differences were not those of political legitimacy, but rather of life style: private life versus communal life, mutual adjustment versus central coordination, contractual legitimacy versus functional effectiveness, and process versus outcome. Those differences were unlikely to be resolved by bargaining or negotiation, because the central issue was not one of "more" or "less," but of "right" or "wrong." The dialogue between the two sides of the "iron curtain" and the ideologically justified wars, cold or hot, were thus between enemies who stood for irreconcilably different modes of life style. As long as wars are fought between "right" and "wrong" or "just" and "injust", they are not likely to be permanently resolved through peaceful means, although long-term truces of uncertain duration may occasionally be agreed upon as in Korea.

Ideology as Institution.   As technological development causes the world to become smaller both physically and culturally, and as different societies become increasingly interdependent, and as more countries seek the common objective of industrialization, economic development, and prosperity, the concept of ideology is again in the process of change.

As a result of the more widespread use of technology, men of different ideological orientations have begun to confront similar problems in similar ways. Solutions have thus been technical rather than ideological, and have contributed to the decline of ideology as a motive force in modern society.[2] No serious observer of world politics would deny that the bipolarity of world power is being overpowered by its multipolarity, that the great powers are seeking "companions" rather than "subordinates," or that the idea of a Cold War has lost its ominous significance.

Most of the developing nations today are willing and ready to accept any system of norms, values, and doctrines that appear to contribute to their modernization. As Paul Sigmund observes, the ideologies of the developing nations, no matter what their official names may be, can be called "modernizing nationalism."[3] It does indeed seem that most of the developing nations place "ideological" emphasis on what they can *do*, rather than on what they *are*. In other words, they have shifted ideological significance from content to function.

Contemporary ideology focuses on the function in achieving the goal of "national interest" rather than on its philosophical content, and in this sense ideology is an institution just like other social institutions, such as the family, the school, religious organizations, and economic groups. These institutions emerge to perform a certain function, for instance, to maintain the coherence of a society over time. So does political ideology. It is one of the institutions that helps the political system attain its goals. Just as the family structure differs in nature and function from one society to another, the content of ideology can also be expected to vary from one sociocultural setting to another. As long as an international conflict does not occur because of, say, the simultaneous presence of the extended family system and the conjugal family structure in different parts of the world, international war is unlikely to break out based on ideological diversity. The agreement between Nixon and Chou En-lai on "respect for mutual ideologies" could never have been attained during the height of the Cold War.

In the post colonial era, when a nation is assured of sovereignty and each is concerned with economic development, ideology is no longer important as a goal itself. The limited liberalization of "private" economy that has inevitably evolved in Russia and China, not to speak of Yugoslavia and the East European nations and the unavoidable expansion of welfare policies in the United States and Canada (as well as in the Scandinavian countries) are examples of necessary measures that have deprived ideology of the status of an end alone. In short, ideology today is simply an institutional means to achieve the common goal of "national interest." But what is this national interest that has become so important that ideology is meaningless without it? Can we find a national interest that is universally applicable?

National Interest

To be sure, the national interest of a specific nation depends on the emergent problem(s) of that country. But, in the course of a country's development as a nation, three stages appear to be reasonably universal: governmental stability, political integration, and economic development.

First, as soon as a nation attains independence, the ruling element attempts to establish governmental stability by which it can build the legitimacy for control and

---

[2]For a good discussion along this line, see Clark Kerr, et. al., *Industrialism and Industrial Man* (Cambridge, Mass.: Harvard University Press, 1960), pp. 1–13.

[3]Paul E. Sigmund, ed., *The Ideologies of the Developing Nations* (New York: Praeger, 1971), p. 36. See also the introduction in the same work for a good summary of the character of the ideologies in developing areas.

formalize the rules for the allocation of values. Once governmental stability is assured, the government seeks to accomplish at least some degree of political integration, so that the interests of all segments of the society are coordinated (and regime stability can be perpetrated). Once these two goals of governmental stability and political integration are attained, a country can be said to have attained the status of a nation, and economic development emerges as its primary objective. Although economic development is important throughout all the stages of nation building, it is emphasized only after governmental and political stability are secured. These three stages are found to occur in the development of most nations, in order of priority and urgency.

Ideology and Political Behavior

It has already been suggested that political ideology is an institution that is used to further a country's national interest. The existing ideologies vary from pluralist democracy to communist socialism, and a specific national interest may be defined as whichever nation-building stage is being highlighted in the political system at a given time. On the basis of these two variables—ideology and national interest— a typology of international conduct can be constructed that may be applied to the analysis of contemporary world politics.

According to this typology (Figure 1), there are four general patterns of international conduct: cooperation, coordination, coexistence, and conflict.

When nations share the same emergent national interest and also an ideological leaning, as do such pairs as the United States and Britain, Japan and Canada, or China and North Korea, their pattern of conduct toward one another tends to be one of cooperation. Cooperation is bilateral, or reciprocal, rather than unilateral. However, if nations sharing a similar ideological doctrine differ in their conception of national interest (owing to different stages of national development), as do China and North Vietnam, or the Soviet Union and the Arab states, they are likely to seek a relationship that is maintained by *coordination.* Coordination is manifested by such unilateral interactions as the bestowing of foreign aid. If two nations have different ideologies but similar national goals, a competitive *coexistence* would be facilitated, such as that maintained by the United States and the Soviet Union, or by China and France. Finally, the predominant mode of interaction tends to be one of *conflict* when nations diverge in both national interest and ideology, as did the United States and China in the 1950s and the United States and North Vietnam in the 1960s.

National Interest

	Same	Different
Same (Ideology)	COOPERATION	COORDINATION
Different (Ideology)	COEXISTENCE	CONFLICT

Figure 1. Types of international conduct.

It is important to recognize that ideology as an institution is not static. Changing priorities in national interest naturally produce change in the norms and values predominant in the society and, eventually, in the content of political ideology itself. In the long run, a nation will adopt ideologies in accordance with its emergent national goal. When a nation lacks independence and sovereignty, an ideology of political conviction, such as nationalism, that will enable it to attain political and economic independence, is desperately needed. The ideologies of nations that have not yet attained independence are appropriate examples. But when a nation is in urgent need of regime stability and political integration, ideology becomes a way of life, maintained by an authoritarian power structure and the charisma of an individual, as we have seen in many newly independent nations and as we saw in Communist China once independence from Chiang Kai-shek was achieved. At the next stage, that of striving for economic development, many nations tend to be more indiscriminate in the types of economic structure and the political ideologies they choose, as India and many of the African nations have been. At this point, the nation will be increasingly less ideological and more practical. An ideology that is hostile to foreign powers can be an effective tool for the early stages of nation building (i.e., regime stability and political integration), but such an ideology may not be as useful for economic development, particularly in a global economic system. All in all, the apparent rapprochement between nations that were staunch adversaries throughout the Cold War would appear to have been a logical and predictable development. The wine toast of Nixon and Chou was of more serious import than mere diplomatic courtesy.

In the context of the preceding theoretical framework, let us now analyze Chinese communism and suggest the direction in which Chinese foreign policy toward her former enemies, including the United States, will evolve.

Ideology and Communism in China

Political ideology as an institution, just like other social institutions, is expected to emerge from an indigenous society in which dedication to an ideology is believed essential for achieving the emergent collective goal in an effective way. When an ideology is transplanted, instead of emergent, it tends to be ineffective and often dysfunctional as exemplified by the ideological confusion prevailing just after World War II in the new nations whose independence was granted rather than earned.

The success of Chinese communism lies primarily in its reliance on social and cultural heritage and its emphasis on nationalism. From its beginnings as an initial movement of socialism in China, Marxism has been carefully modified to coincide with Chinese nationalist sentiment. The dynamic force of the Chinese communist revolution is not founded in Marxist mysticism or in any other philosophical doctrine alien to Chinese culture. In fact, Chinese communism has never been consistent with the concept of class polarization and the theory of class struggle, which are so central to Marxist theory. Instead, the unbearable humiliation of the proud Han Chinese produced by a series of defeats beginning with the Opium War of 1839, and the profound crises resulting from forced Westernization, paved the way for the collaboration of communism and nationalism, and eventually for political consolidation under Mao Tse-tung.[4] The revolutionaries and their enemies were distinguished under Maoist rule, not by the

---

[4]For an excellent discussion on the social conditions before the revolution, see A. Doak Barnett, *China on the Eve of Communist Takeover* (New York: Praeger, 1963).

Marxist criterion of their affiliation to the mode of production, but by national interest. Any class that contributed to the emergent national interest of nation building, even the bourgeoisie, was considered a necessary part of the revolutionary force.

The theory of two stages of revolution, which obviously is not derived from Marxist socialism, is little more than a theory of comprehensive Chinese nationalism. The first phase of revolution, directed toward abolishing foreign intervention in Chinese affairs, was an antagonistic movement to regain political initiative and governmental stability. This stage was comparable to nationalist movements in many of the emerging nations in Africa and Latin America. Unlike the Third World leaders, however, Mao Tse-tung correctly sensed that antagonism alone was not enough for building a nation. Rather, he felt, it had to be converted into a positive spirit that would be directed toward China. This transition was the beginning of the second phase of revolution, a revolution in which the internal contradictions are to be resolved, that is, the conflicts between such segments as urban and rural, industry and agriculture, and military and civilian, rich and poor, old and young, and above all, between political center and periphery. In other words, this phase of revolution is a positive movement for regime stability by political centralization and social integration. In short, it is geared to nation building.[5]

As mainland China becomes unified under a charismatic leader and the society becomes sufficiently integrated around the center, the primary and emergent national interest can be expected to shift to economic growth. This shift, moreover, is highly probable because economic development has always been a concern of Mao's. He is a thorough realist. As he himself has repeatedly stated, he started the revolution not for Marxist utopia but for food. It is, therefore, reasonable to anticipate a concerted effort by China to explore maximum opportunities for economic development.

Not only is Chinese communism ideologically nationalistic, but also it has, at least at the early stages, closely conformed to the inherited social structure and political culture. It would be safe to say that the revolution would not have been successful if there had been no correspondence between revolutionary programs and the socio-cultural setting. The smooth establishment of the Mutual Aid Program and the Agricultural Producers' Cooperatives during the First Five-Year Plan, for instance, was the direct reflection of the positive influence of the traditional heritage. Thus the natural boundary of the extended family structure was easily converted into a collective farm. The norms of mutual assistance and cooperation within the extended family system were simply given a new name of Mutual Aid. The disastrous outcome of the Great Leap Forward and large scale communalization in the late 1950s illustrates the types of problems that result from the destruction of traditional societal norms with political force.

However, recognizing the difficulty of achieving political innovation without social and cultural transformation, China launched a massive war, called the Great Proletariat Cultural Revolution, against the tradition—particularly the cultural values and social structures—associated with Confucianism. Although the full consequences of the Cultural Revolution are still unclear, we suggest here that cultural change is beyond politics, rather than subject to it, and little conclusive evidence has as yet emerged to negate this thesis.

---

[5]For the theory of two stages of revolution, see Mao Tse-tung, "On Contradiction" and "External and Internal Contradictions—The Bourgeosie Between Imperialism and Revolution," in S. Schram, *The Political Thought of Mao Tse-tung* (New York: Praeger, 1969), pp. 194-235.

Conclusion: The Ideology and Its Implications

We can draw the following conclusions from the foregoing discussion.

(1) The concept of political ideology has had a variety of meanings. Contemporary ideologies such as communism and democracy are the institutional means to achieve the collective desire of a nation.

(2) The institution of political ideology has its goal, just as any other social institution does. The common goal for all the ideologies today is "national interest."

(3) A national interest is three-fold, and includes political stability, social integration, and economic development. These three objectives are pursued by all nations regardless of their ideological leanings. A regime tends to feel that a state of emergency exists if political stability is endangered. Social integration is only a secondary concern to such a nation. Social integration, however, is desperately sought as soon as political power becomes stabilized. Economic development, although it is considered important throughout all the phases of nation building, becomes the primary goal only after political stability and social integration are reasonably assured.

(4) Generally, four different types of international conduct can be classified: Co-operation, Coordination, Coexistence, and Conflict. The model is based on the nation's similarities and differences in the institution of ideology and the content of national interest defined by the stage of national development.

(5) The People's Republic of China, being reasonably assured of political stability and integration, will place much stronger emphasis on economic development than ever before. She will explore all possible means to induce foreign capital investment and economic cooperation. Political ideology will bear only a marginal significance, if any, for her foreign conduct.

11

Chinese and Leninist Components in the Personality of Mao Tse-tung

Stuart R. Schram

The relative importance of Leninist ideology and of traditional factors in determining the behavior of the Communist leaders is a favorite subject of controversy. In the past, two extreme viewpoints have sometimes been expounded. One of these has seen Stalin as a new Peter the Great and Mao Tse-tung as a new Liu Pang, whose actions were explainable entirely in terms of geopolitics or "national psychology," without any reference to Leninism whatsoever. The other has suggested on the contrary that the policy of Moscow or Peking could be predicted in all its details from a careful reading of Marx and Lenin. A variant of this second approach, in the case of the Chinese Communists, has seen the latter as mere puppets of the Soviets, and looked for the explanation of their behavior not in Leninist doctrine, but in the orders received from Moscow.

The events of the past thirteen years have adequately demonstrated the falsity of all such one-sided views. As adherents of Marxism-Leninism, all Communists attempt to make use of certain ideas and categories to understand society and to change it. As Russians or Chinese, they are influenced in the way they go about applying Leninism by the fact that patterns of thought and action inherited from the past have marked not only the societies with which they must deal, but the revolutionaries themselves. As the rulers of two great empires, their ideological positions are also influenced by considerations of prestige and power. The common commitment to world revolution, and the ideal of "proletarian internationalism," no more suffice to eliminate conflicts and rivalry than the clear injunction, "Let them be one, as I and my father are one," has prevented Christians from quarreling for 2000 years regarding the correct defini-

From Stuart R. Schram, "Chinese and Leninist Components in the Personality of Mao Tse-tung," *Asian Survey* (Vol. 3, No. 6, June 1963), pp. 259–273. [Reprinted with permission from the publisher.]

tion of their faith, or even massacring one another in a struggle to decide who should enjoy the authority to fix doctrine and to rule over the organization of the Church.

After the events of the last few years, and especially of the last few months, there are not many people who still venture to dispute these obvious verities. The quarrel is no longer about whether Chinese communism bears any relation to the historic entity, China, but rather about which factor is of primary importance: Leninist doctrine, or traditional attitudes. I would suggest that the qualitative aspect of this problem is at least as important as the quantitive aspect. We must ask ourselves not only whether "communism" or "China" is more important in the combination of the two, but *how* the two mesh together, both in present-day Chinese society in general, and in the minds of its leaders.

In his report to the Sixth Plenum of the Central Committee of the Chinese Communist Party in 1938, Mao Tse-tung discussed the problem of combining Marxism-Leninism and the Chinese inheritance in the following terms:

> Today's China is an outgrowth of historic China. We must not mutilate history. From Confucius to Sun Yat-sen, we must sum it up critically, and we must constitute ourselves the heirs of all that is precious in this past. Conversely, the assimilation of this heritage itself turns out to be a kind of methodology which is of great help in the guidance of the revolutionary movement. A Communist is a Marxist internationalist, but Marxism must take on a national form before it can be applied. There is no such thing as abstract Marxism, but only concrete Marxism. What we call Marxism is Marxism which has taken on a national form, that is, Marxism applied to the concrete struggle in the concrete conditions prevailing in China, and not Marxism abstractly used. If a Chinese Communist, who is a part of the great Chinese people and is bound to his people by his very flesh and blood, talks of Marxism apart from Chinese peculiarities, this Marxism is merely an empty abstraction. Consequently, the sinification of Marxism—that is to say, making certain that in all of its manifestations it is imbued with Chinese peculiarities, using it according to the peculiarities of China—becomes a problem which must be understood and solved by the whole party without delay. . . . We must put an end to writing eight-legged essays on foreign models . . . ; we must cease our dogmatism, and replace it by a new and vital Chinese style and Chinese manner, pleasing to the eye and to the ear of the Chinese common people.[1]

It is clear from this passage how complex and ambiguous is the meaning of "the sinification of Marxism," even in Mao's own mind. On the simplest level, it involves, as the last sentence quoted above suggests, the use of a *language* accessible to the average Chinese, enlivened with popular proverbs and colorful turns of phrase, with an occasional classical quotation to give it added weight. Mao is an extremely skillful practitioner of this kind of sinification. But the kind of "sinification" germane to the subject of this paper is the sinification of the substance rather than the form of Marxism—though obviously the two things cannot be separated completely.

---

[1]This passage has been so modified in the current edition of the *Selected Works* that it is hardly worthwhile to cite the reference; Vol. II, pp. 258–261. For the original Chinese text, see *Lun Hsin Chieh Tuan*, (Chieh Fang She, 1944), pp. 125–129. (Only a short extract from Mao's very long report to the Sixth Plenum is included in the current edition of his works.) An extract from this report, translated from the original version, is included in the anthology of Mao's writings which I have compiled . . . [*Political Thought of Mao Tse-tung* (New York: Praeger, 1969, rev. ed.), pp. 172–173]. . . . This volume will be cited below whenever the examples I mention are included in it, and are not available elsewhere in a satisfactory translation. The above message is from text II A of this anthology.

The ultimate in "sinification" would be the production of an ideology in which the very concepts and methods of Marxism had somehow become peculiarly Chinese. It is extremely doubtful whether Mao has "sinified" Marxism in this sense.

One would expect to find such a contribution, if anywhere, in Mao's analysis of Chinese history and society. In fact, if we look at the most detailed and lengthy piece of writing of this kind, the first part of "The Chinese Revolution and the Chinese Communist Party," we find that Mao has changed his views since 1939, but neither the original nor the current version can be said to break new ground theoretically.

In the original version of this text, Mao affirms that traditional Chinese society has been completely stagnant for centuries, and was only prodded into motion by the impact of the West. In the current version, he has inserted the thesis, more flattering to his countrymen, that changes were already at work which would have led to the birth of capitalism in China even without foreign intervention.[2] But far from advancing any original theoretical ideas to elucidate the unique traits of Chinese society, he endeavors, like any Soviet historian of the period, to force Chinese society into the Procrustean bed of the schema "primitive communism—slave-owning society—feudalism—capitalism—socialism" which Marx himself had clearly said was not necessarily valid for all societies.[3]

A second and somewhat broader meaning for "sinification" would be the adaptation of Marxism-Leninism to the conditions of China as an underdeveloped country which had undergone the experience of Western domination. This is referred to by Mao himself in the above passage as the application of Marxism to "the concrete struggle in the concrete conditions prevailing in China." Liu Shao-ch'i, in his well known interview with Anna Louise Strong in 1946, defined this type of ideological development somewhat more precisely:

> Mao Tse-tung's great accomplishment has been to change Marxism from a European to an Asiatic form. Marx and Lenin were Europeans; they wrote in European languages about European histories and problems, seldom discussing Asia or China. The basic principles of Marxism are undoubtedly adaptable to all countries, but to apply their general truth to concrete revolutionary practice in China is a difficult task. Mao Tse-tung is Chinese; he analyzes Chinese problems and guides the Chinese people in their struggle to victory. He uses Marxist-Leninist principles to explain Chinese history and the practical problems of China. He is the first that has succeeded in doing so. . . . He has created a Chinese or Asiatic form of Marxism. China is a semi-feudal, semi-colonial country in which vast numbers of people live at the edge of starvation, tilling small bits of soil. . . . In attempting the transition to a more industrialized economy, China faces . . . the pressures . . . of advanced industrial lands. . . . There are similar conditions in other lands of southeast Asia. The courses chosen by China will influence them all.[4]

It is my own conviction that Mao Tse-tung *has* made significant changes in the substance of Marxism which were suggested to him in the first instance by his experi-

---

[2]This theory regarding the existence of "sprouts of capitalism" in China as early as the Ming dynasty was the subject of a vast debate among Chinese historians a few years ago.

[3]For the original version of "The Chinese Revolution and the Chinese Communist Party," see *Chung-kuo Ko-ming yü Chung-kuo Kung-ch'an-tang,* (Chieh Fang She, n.d.), 36 pp. For the current version, see *Selected Works,* Vol. III, pp. 72-101. K. A. Wittfogel has dealt with the variants between these two versions in a recent article. [*China Quarterly,* no. 10 (December 1962).] For a further discussion of my own views, see the introduction in Schram, *Political Thought of Mao Tse-tung.*

[4]Anna Louise Strong, "The Thought of Mao Tse-tung," *Amerasia* (6, June 1947), p. 161.

ence in China, but which actually represent adaptations to the conditions of the under-developed countries in general. I would cite in this context the model for the conquest of power based on guerrilla warfare and agrarian revolution, which Mao did not create out of whole cloth, but on which he has placed his stamp, even if Lenin pointed the way. I would cite the accent on ceaseless and perpetual change extending to infinity, which characterizes recent [periods] in Chinese Communist ideology—the period of "permanent revolution." I would cite the theory of the people's democratic dictator-ship, with its suggestion that one can go all the way to communism under the joint dictatorship of the four classes—even if real power belongs to the Communist party as the "party of the proletariat." In all of these instances, Mao elaborated his ideas on the basis of Chinese experience, but the factors which underlie these theories—agrarian discontent, impatience with existing conditions, national solidarity in the face of the West—are to a considerable extent present in many Asian, African, and Latin Ameri-can countries.

There is a third type of "sinification" which consists in making Marxism more com-prehensible and meaningful to the Chinese, not only by clothing it in Chinese language, but by relating it to ideas and events of the past. It is primarily this third dimension of "sinification" which will be dealt with in this essay, and here the precise degree of innovation on Mao's part is of little importance. For whether his thought is drawn almost word by word from the writings of Lenin and Stalin, as some claim, or whether it represents a distinctive variant of Leninism, there is no doubt that Mao Tse-tung stands firmly in the Leninist tradition, which is a Western tradition radically alien in many respects to Chinese ways of thought. The Leninist core of Mao's thought, whether it be orthodox or heretical, therefore requires a certain mediation in order to make it accessible to the Chinese masses.

On the one hand, Mao's references to the national past are not merely neutral "illus-trations" of Marxist-Leninist verities—they are charged with values, which may become intertwined with Leninism to produce, not a modification in the substance of the latter, but a kind of amalgam in which the consciously held ideology gradually becomes bound up with accretions from the past, which may add to its appeal, and at the same time distort it. On the other hand, there is involved not merely the mediation between Marxism-Leninism and the Chinese masses by the leaders of the Party, in their capacity as high priests of the ruling ideology, but the mediation between what Marx and Lenin actually thought and Mao's or Liu's ideas of Leninism by minds trained in a non-western tradition. In a word, Marxism is consciously "sinified" by the leaders for the masses; it is also unconsciously sinified for the leaders themselves by the very manner in which they perceive it.

The aspect of this problem with which I have chosen to deal here is Mao's use of language, metaphor, and example from the Chinese past as part of his style of leader-ship. I shall present a few instances of this, and attempt, on this basis, to draw some tentative conclusions as to the extent to which Mao simply exploits images of this type for purposes completely alien to their original meaning, and the extent to which, on the contrary, he uses them because they are a part of himself and actually influence his own thought.

Mao Tse-tung and Orthodox Tradition

It is well known that Mao Tse-tung's outlook in early years was tradition-oriented and relatively conservative. He has said himself in his autobiography that in 1910, at the age of 16 or 17, he still "considered the Emperor as well as most officials to be honest, good, and clever men" who only needed the help of K'ang Yu-wei"'s reforms.[5] And as late as the winter of 1916–1917, when he was 23, he still showed himself remarkably respectful of China's traditional worthies, going so far as to refer to his great Hunanese compatriot Tseng Kuo-fan by his posthumously bestowed title "Wen-cheng."[6]

In fact, if one were to characterize Mao's mind on the eve of the May Fourth movement, the two most deeply etched traits appear to have been a vigorous nationalism, which had long led him to mourn the loss to China of such territories as Annam and Burma, and an emphasis on courage and the martial spirit, which expressed itself among other things in an admiration for Han Wu-ti.[7]

Obviously, Mao's views have not remained unchanged over the past 45 years. In the current revised version of Mao's report to the October 1938 Party Plenum, there is a reference to two methods of selecting cadres, according to merit and according to personal relations. The first is described as honest, the second as dishonest.[8] Here only a few lines remain of what was originally a very interesting and suggestive passage, worth quoting at length:

> With regard to this question of making use of cadres, in the history of our nation there have always been two lines, reflecting the opposition between the depraved and the upright. One was "appointing men according to merit," the other was "appointing men according to personal relations." The first was the policy of sagacious rulers and worthy ministers, the second was the policy of despots and traitors. Today, when we discuss the problem of making use of cadres, we look at it from a revolutionary standpoint, fundamentally different from that of ancient times, and yet there is no getting away from this standard of "employing men according to merit." It was wrong in ancient times, and is still wrong today, to pass judgment according to one's likes and dislikes, to reward fawning flatterers and to punish the honest and forthright."[9]

An English translation cannot convey the full force of this passage, which results partly from the use of traditional four- and six-character clichés. As far as the substance of this passage is concerned, Mao clearly implies in it that there are certain universal moral standards which apply to political behavior everywhere, independently of the historical or class context. This is a curious position for a Leninist. Secondly, he does not hesitate to use traditional expressions having not only a moral but a political connotation in order to get across his point. To be sure, he does not refer to himself as a *ming chün* (enlightened ruler), nor to, let us say, Chou En-lai as a *hsien ch'en* (faithful minister), but he does denounce Chang Kuo-t'ao not only in Leninist terms as a builder of factions, but in traditional terms as one who rewards flatterers and punishes the honest and forthright.

Another interesting instance of the use of traditional expressions incrusted with many layers of meaning is to be found in an editorial of July 1945. In the current version

---

[5]Edgar Snow, *Red Star Over China* (New York: Random House, 1937), p. 121.

[6]In his article "T'i-yü chih yen-chiu" ("A study of physical education"), published in *Hsin Ch'ing Nien* in April, 1917. For a full French translation of this article see Mao Ze-dong, *Une étude de l'éducation physique* (Paris: Mouton, 1962); extracts in English translation are contained in Schram, *Political Thought of Mao Tse-tung.*

[7]For references, and an analysis of Mao's thought in its pre-Marxist phase, see my introductions to *Une étude de l'éducation physique* and Schram, *Political Thought of Mao Tse-tung.*

[8]*Selected Works,* Vol. II (New York: International Publishers, 1954), p. 252.

[9]*Lun Hsin Chieh-Tuan* (Chieh Fang She, 1944), pp. 114–118.

of this article, Mao affirms that the Chinese people demand "independence, freedom, and unity." In the original text, the enumeration included "independence, freedom, democracy, unity, and *fu ch'iang*," (literally "rich and powerful"—a contraction for a phrase meaning "to make the country rich and militarily strong," earlier identified with the legalists, and much used in the late nineteenth century).[10] It would be far-fetched to use this as evidence in favor of the well known thesis that the Chinese communists are latter-day legalists, but there is unquestionably in it an echo of the late nineteenth-century conservative nationalism to which Mao was exposed during his youth. Incidentally, he also stated in his speech at the Moscow airport on November 2, 1957, that the October revolution had enabled the Chinese people to find the way to emancipation, prosperity, and *fu ch'iang*. I do not know what the Soviets made of this expression.

Among the most interesting references to the rulers of the past are those in Mao Tse-tung's poetry. Here I shall mention only two poems, "Snow" and "Peitaiho."

The first is the well-known one purportedly written in the airplane carrying the author to Chungking for negotiations with Chiang Kai-shek in 1945. Here Mao appears to regard the past as over and done with, and largely unrelated to the present—except for the perennial beauty of the Chinese landscape:

. . . Ch'in Shih Huang and Han Wu Ti
Were rather lacking in culture . . .

To find men truly great and noble-hearted
We must look here in the present.

Whether "great men (or man)" here refers to modern man in general, as the official translation would indicate, to Mao himself, as hostile critics have suggested—an interpretation scarcely admissible if one considers the context in which the poem was written —or to Mao and Chiang as the two greatest men of the age, . . . Mao expresses here a clear preference for the present. "Peitaiho" sounds a rather different note:

More than a thousand years in the past
The Emperor Wu of Wei brandished his whip;
"Eastward to Chiehshih," his poem, remains.
"The autumn wind is sighing" still today—
The world of men has changed!

The deliberate citation of two lines from a poem by Ts'ao Ts'ao has been taken as evidence that Mao Tse-tung identified himself with that ruler, or even with the caricature of him which has been popularized by the *Romance of the Three Kingdoms*. This is obviously reading too much into a passing reference. But one can deduce from this poem a certain feeling of community with a man who contemplated the same scenes in ages past, and who knew, like himself, the servitudes of power.

In reality, the two poems just cited are not contradictory, but illustrate different aspects of Mao's attitude toward his country's past. The first one displays the critical attitude of a revolutionary toward the grandeur of the past; the second, written after he came to power, emphasizes rather the continuity with the past. It is impossible to make any sense of Mao or of Chinese communism in general if one does not take into account both of these tendencies.

---

[10]*Chieh Fang Jih Pao*, July 13, 1945; *Selected Works*, Vol. IV (New York), pp. 328–329. See Schram, *Political Thought of Mao Tse-tung*, text IX F, pp. 401–402.

Mao Tse-tung and the Tradition of Peasant Revolt

The evaluation of Mao Tse-tung's attitude toward the legitimate holders of power and their ideology in prerevolutionary China poses delicate problems, for whatever sentiment of continuity he may have there are limits to the extent to which he can openly identify himself with this particular past. The problem is obviously quite different as regards peasant insurrections and other forms of revolt against imperial authority. Here the Chinese communists openly proclaim themselves the heirs of all such movements. An extreme and highly picturesque example of this is Mao's appeal to the Ko Lao Hui (the well known secret society, very influential among the peasantry, which played a certain role in the ferment leading to the 1911 revolution) in July 1936, a few sentences of which read as follows:

Brothers of the Ko Lao Hui!
. . . In the past you were partisans of restoring the Han and exterminating the Manchus; today we are partisans of resisting Japan and of saving the country. You are partisans of striking at the rich and helping the poor; we are partisans of striking at the local bullies and dividing up the land. You despise wealth and defend justice, and you gather together all the heroes and brave fellows (ying-hsiung hao-han) in the world; we do not spare ourselves to save the country and the world, we unite the exploited and oppressed peoples and groups of the whole world. Our standpoints and our positions are therefore quite close . . .[11]

To be sure, this is obviously a manipulative test designed to serve a political purpose, and I do not mean to suggest that Mao Tse-tung actually thought that Marxism-Leninism and the ideas of the Ko Lao Hui were substantially identical. But there may well be a residue of genuine feeling of fellowship here, which ought not to be overlooked.

Another curious resemblance between Mao Tse-tung's style of leadership and the ways of the past lies in his constant use, during the civil war, of exhortations to surrender and even to come over to the side of justice, addressed to enemy generals. He continued this practice down to 1949 and beyond. One can hardly imagine Lenin or Trotsky addressing the lieutenants of Kolchak or Denikin in exactly the same way, though an appeal was made, of course, to the patriotism of former Tsarist officers, especially, during the Polish campaign of 1919. Mao is building here upon a very characteristic Chinese tradition of exhorting, insulting, and expostulating with one's adversaries on the eve of a battle.

Once again, I do not wish to overstress the import of these echoes of the past. A very large proportion of such references unquestionably represents merely an attempt to sinify the *language* of Marxism, to the exclusion of any substantive modification or even any smuggling in of elements foreign to Marxism. For example, if Mao Tse-tung in an appeal of September 25, 1931, castigated the *Kuomintang ti tiao cheng-fu*[12] (this term will be familiar to all readers of *Shui Hu Chuan*), this can hardly be taken as proof that he identified himself with, for example, Lu Chih-shen; he was merely seeking an insult that would strike the imagination of his audience. Moreover, even while appealing

---

[11] *Tou Cheng* (no. 105, July 12, 1936), pp. 3b–5a; Schram, *Political Thought of Mao Tse-tung,* text IV G, pp. 260–261.

[12] "A Letter from the Chinese Workers' and Peasants' Red Army to our Brothers and Officers and Soldiers of the White Army on the Subject of the Forced Occupation of Manchuria by Japanese Imperialism," *Su-wei-ai Chung-kuo,* pp. 60–64; Schram, *Political Thought of Mao Tse-tung,* text III F, pp. 217–220.

to strands in the experience and tradition of the past, he clearly adopts a critical attitude toward them.

A good illustration of this, which will serve as a transition to the third part of my presentation, is provided by Mao's treatment of the *lumpenproletariat* or vagrants (*yu-min*). On the one hand, he praises these elements, and links them in colorful fashion to the protest movements of a traditional type. At the same time, he criticizes them.

> The *lumpenproletariat* . . . can be divided into soldiers, bandits, robbers, beggars, and prostitutes. These five categories of people . . . each have a different way of making a living: the soldier fights, the bandit robs, the thief steels, the beggar begs, and the prostitute seduces. But to the extent that they must all earn their livelihood and cook rice to eat, they are one. . . . They have secret organizations in various places: for instance, the Triad Society . . . the Ko Lao Hui . . . the Big Sword society. . . . These serve as their mutual aid societies in the political and economic struggle. . . . These people are capable of fighting very bravely, and if properly led can become a revolutionary force. . . .[13]

> The lumpen-proletarians form the majority of the Red Army soldiers. . . . As a result . . . there has arisen . . . a political mentality of roving insurgents. . . . But the type of large-scale actions by roving insurgents carried out by Huang Ch'ao, Li Ch'uang and Hung Hsiu-ch'üan are no longer permissible in imperialist-ruled China, . . . into which advanced weapons . . . advanced methods of communication, . . . and of transportation have already been imported. . . . The mentality of the roving insurgents seriously hampers the Red Army in accomplishing the great tasks which the revolution imposes on it; thus the elimination of this mentality is one of the most important aims of the ideological struggle. . . .[14]

These passages have been so extensively re-written in the current edition of Mao Tse-tung's *Selected Works* as to be unrecognizable, in the direction of removing some of the overly picturesque description of the *yu-min*, minimizing their role in the Red Army, and emphasizing their weaknesses. Nonetheless, it is clear that even in the 1920's Mao's sympathy for the outlaws and castoffs of traditional China did not lead him to identify himself with them.

The "Natural Leninism" of Mao Tse-tung

Hitherto I have stressed, with some reservations, the links which bind Mao Tse-tung to the Chinese past. This is, in my opinion, an important aspect of the truth about a very complex personality; but it is only an aspect of the truth, and not the whole. In years past, when the Chinese communist leaders, in order to adapt themselves to a position of weakness and dependence, undertook to minimize their own originality and to stress their conformity to the letter of Stalin's teaching, some people were misled into actually taking Mao and his colleagues for colorless Soviet puppets. Today, when news of the Sino-Soviet conflict fills the headlines, we should not fall into the opposite error of viewing them merely as Chinese nationalists with a Marxist veneer. Leninism may be, and indeed is, radically foreign to traditional Chinese culture; it may have,

---

[13]"An Analysis of the Various Classes of the Chinese Peasantry and their Attitudes toward Revolution," *Chung-kuo Nung-min* (Vol. 1, no. 1, 1926). Schram, *Political Thought of Mao Tse-tung*, text IV B, pp. 241–246.

[14]Resolution written for a conference of the Communist Party organizations of the Fourth Red Army, December 1929, in *Chung-kuo Kung-Ch'an-tang Hung-chun Ti-ssu-chün Ti-i-tz'u Tai piao Ta-hui-i Chüeh-i-an* (Hongkong: Hsinmin Ch'u'pan'she, 1949), pp. 14–15. Schram, *Political Thought of Mao Tse-tung*, text V D, pp. 272–275.

and indeed did, take Mao Tse-tung a long time to master it. But there is no doubt that he did master it [in the late 1930s] in Yenan, and that he was deeply committed to it as a revolutionary creed long before he learned to use it effectively as a method of analysis. Moreover, there can be detected in his thinking from a very early date a kind of "natural Leninism," analogous to the "natural morality" of the theologians, i.e., a certain bent of mind congenial to the Leninist approach. This is particularly the case in the domain of leadership techniques, which is, of course, the heart of Leninism.

As early as 1920, when he had only just become converted to Marxism, and had not even begun to understand the Leninist strategy for revolution in the underdeveloped countries, Mao Tse-tung put forward ideas regarding the importance of organization in the labor movement which may be regarded as very close to the Leninist conception of democratic centralism. In his view, the labor unions should have democratically formed executive organs entrusted with full powers, for if authority were too much divided, the result would be unsatisfactory. Some of these conceptions may have grown out of his experience as a labor organizer, but he also seems to have had a kind of intuitive understanding of the importance of organization which is no doubt one of the reasons for his emergence as the leader of the Chinese Communist Party.

Once again, in the fall of 1926, when he was as yet far from an adequate grasp of Leninist theory, Mao wrote, regarding a peasant uprising in Chekiang: "The reason for the failure of this movement is that the masses did not fully organize themselves, and did not have leadership, so that the movement barely got started and then failed."[15]

During the two decades from 1920 to 1940, Mao Tse-tung thoroughly absorbed the categories of Leninist analysis, and began to speak with precision and confidence, and in impeccably orthodox tones, of the organization of the Communist party and its role in the revolution. But this does not mean that he dissociated himself from the past, as the text of 1938 regarding the "sinification of Marxism" suffices to illustrate. There is no reason, of course, why, as a good Leninist, he *should* have repudiated his national background completely; even Stalin frequently spoke of adapting Marxism-Leninism to national conditions, though Mao claimed a degree of latitude in this respect going well beyond what the leader of the world communist movement was inclined to admit. The question which interests us here is to what extent Mao Tse-tung, as a Leninist revolutionary, dominated his Chinese background, and to what extent it dominated him.

The balance in this respect was undoubtedly influenced by the fact that for nearly a quarter of a century the context in which Mao Tse-tung had to apply his Leninist theories was that of peasant-based guerrilla warfare. In this situation, the example and traditions of the past, especially those of the innumerable peasant uprisings in Chinese history, were closer and more immediately meaningful than they would have been in any other. And yet, Mao Tse-tung made continuous and determined efforts to impose a Leninist mentality and a Leninist system of democratic centralism on the army of dubious and mixed class composition which he commanded.

At the same time, the fact that Mao Tse-tung accepts the theories of organization and leadership developed in the Soviet Union does not mean that he accepts the Soviet application of these as a model to be blindly followed. As a matter of fact, he clearly affirmed, as early as 1936, that although the Soviet Union and its leaders were worthy of emulation, Chinese communists should pay even more attention to their own

---

[15]"The Bitter Sufferings of the Peasants in Kiangsu and Chekiang, and their Movements of Resistance," *Hsiang-tao* (no. 179, Nov. 25,1926), pp. 1869–1871, (signed with Mao's *tzu*, Jun-chih). See Schram, *Political Thought of Mao Tse-tung*, text IV D, p. 249.

experience. In the original version of *Strategic Problems of China's Revolutionary War,* he wrote: "Although we must cherish Soviet experience, and even cherish it somewhat more than experiences in other countries throughout history, because they are the most recent experiences of revolutionary war, we must cherish even more the experience of China's revolutionary war . . ." In 1951, he felt himself obliged to stand this passage on its head, writing that "although we must especially cherish the Soviet experiences of war, and have been acquired under the guidance of Lenin and Stalin, we must also cherish the experiences of China's revolutionary war."[16]

This brings us to the question, particularly interesting in the light of recent developments, of Mao Tse-tung's attitude toward Stalin. Throughout the last two decades of Stalin's life, Mao frequently praised the Soviet leader as his teacher and model. This praise was expressed in particularly fulsome tones on the occasion of Stalin's death, when Mao wrote in a commemorative article:

> Since the passing of Lenin, Comrade Stalin has always been the central figure in the world Communist movement. We rallied round him, ceaselessly asked his advice, and constantly drew ideological strength from his works. . . . Everyone knows that Comrade Stalin had an ardent love for the Chinese people and believed the might of the Chinese revolution to be immeasurable. To the problems of the Chinese revolution, he contributed his sublime wisdom. And it was by following the theories of Lenin and Stalin, and with the support of the great Soviet Union . . . that the Chinese Communist party and the Chinese people . . . won their historic victory.[17]

Even at the time, these words can hardly have been written entirely without tongue in cheek, for Mao well knew that Stalin's "sublime wisdom" regarding the Chinese revolution had almost caused its defeat on several occasions. And in 1956, the editorial "On the Historical Experience of the Dictatorship of the Proletariat," in which Mao undoubtedly had a hand, severely criticized Stalin's errors, and his enjoyment of the "cult of his own personality." But in fact, the contrast between this text and Mao's previous utterances regarding Stalin is far less violent than at first appears.

Since 1927 or thereabouts, Mao Tse-tung appears to have had a remarkably consistent view of Stalin. On the one hand, he was clearly conscious of Stalin's errors, for he had been the victim of them. On the other hand, he admired in Stalin the dedicated revolutionary, and also the universal leader whose existence he believed indispensible to the world revolutionary movement. This dual attitude comes through clearly in the editorial "On the Historical Experience of the Dictatorship of the Proletariat," which sharply criticizes Stalin for many failings, and yet continues:

> . . . Some people consider that Stalin was wrong in everything. This is a grave misconception. Stalin was a great Marxist-Leninist, yet at the same time a Marxist-Leninist who committed several gross errors. . . . We should view Stalin from an historical standpoint, . . . Both the things he did right and the things he did wrong were phenomena of the international Communist movement and bore the imprint of the times.[18]

---

[16]The original text (or at least a relatively early version) appears in the supplement to the 1947 edition of the *Hsüan Chi,* pp. 109–112. See Schram, *Political Thought of Mao Tse-tung,* text V E, pp. 430–431. The current version is in *Selected Works,* I, p. 177.

[17]"The Greatest Friendship," Hsinhua Agency Daily News Release no. 1265, March 10, 1953.

[18]*Jen Min Jih Pao,* April 5, 1956.

This last phrase reveals, incidentally, one of the roots of the Chinese leaders' opposition to the extremes of "destalinization" to which Khrushchev [had] gone—apart from resentment against the fact that they were not consulted. Mao Tse-tung is too consistent and too historically-minded a thinker to imagine that the whole epoch of terror initiated in the 1930's can be blamed on one man. To reject it root and branch, he undoubtedly realizes, means to condemn not only Stalin but the system which permitted such abuses. Hence the balanced approach, blaming Stalin and yet recognizing his stature, illustrated by the editorial of April 1956. Moreover, as affirmed in the same text, "Marxist-Leninists hold that leaders play a big role in history. The people and their parties need forerunners who are able to represent the interest and the will of the people, stand in the forefront of their heroic struggles, and serve as their leaders." This conviction undoubtedly occupies a central place not only in Mao Tse-tung's doctrine of leadership, but in his image of his own role.

Conclusion

There is not the slightest doubt that Mao Tse-tung is a faithful Leninist in the dual sense that his conception of the Chinese revolution is drawn from Lenin and Stalin, and that he is loyal to the ideal of a united world communist movement. But, as recent developments have shown, these two strains in Mao's Leninism may ultimately prove contradictory. Lenin's voluntarism expressed itself in the statement that politics takes precedence over economics.[19] In the special conditions of the underdeveloped countries, Mao Tse-tung (or those who speak in his name) has carried this one step further and affirmed that "the subjective creates the objective."[20] This attitude, which has recently been defined as a kind of "voluntarist illuminism,"[21] has obvious implications for leadership techniques. It leads to the "mass line," the great leap forward, and in general to the notion that there are no limits to what the liberated energies of the masses can achieve, or the speed at which they can achieve it. As Mao said in 1945, he believes that "revolution can change everything."[22] Or, as he put it in the fall of 1958, after inspecting a variety of industrial and agricultural enterprises, just as the drive to create the communes was gathering momentum:

> During this trip, I have witnessed the tremendous energy of the masses. On this foundation, it is possible to accomplish any task at all.[23]

The encounter between this *chiliastic* variant of Leninism, born out of the impatience of the non-Western countries with their situation of poverty and inferiority, and the ideology engendered by a highly industrialized Soviet society, which might be defined as "the Leninism of the organization man," was bound to produce a rude shock. This shock could not conceivably incite Mao Tse-tung to abandon Leninism; on the contrary, as is now perfectly clear, it has led him to set himself up as its only true exponent. At the same time, the position of isolation into which his interpretation of Leninism has brought him may reinforce in Mao Tse-tung those national reflexes which link him

---

[19]Lenin, *Sochineniia* (3rd ed.), vol. 26, p. 126.

[20]Wu Chiang, "A Partisan of the theory of the permanent revolution must be a consistent dialectical materialist," *Che-hsüeh Yen-chiu* 8 (1958), p. 28.

[21]Enrica Collotti Pischel, *La Rivoluzione ininterotta* (Torino: Einaudi, 1962), p. 77.

[22]*Selected Works*, IV (Peking), p. 454.

[23]SCMP (no. 1871, Oct. 9, 1958). Translation modified after comparison with the original in *Hung Ch'i* (no. 10, 1958).

to China's past. He may well compromise with the laws of nature and the logic of modern industrial society; he will be less inclined to compromise with the foreigners, whether they be American or Russian. In this he is clearly a true heir to the Chinese tradition.

I have suggested that both Chinese and Western components play a significant role in Mao Tse-tung's patterns of thought and behavior. The question naturally arises: where are the deepest springs of his conduct? Is he, as was Lenin, a revolutionary who merely *used* nationalism for his own ends? Or is he above all a nationalist for whom Marxism-Leninism is merely a convenient slogan?

Most certainly he is neither of these things. He has thoroughly assimilated Marxist categories, and he is deeply committed to world revolution. It would be absurd to say that he is above all a nationalist, who merely used Marxism-Leninism for nationalist ends. Moreover, the very aim of the "war against nature," though Mao Tse-tung may expound it in terms impregnated with Chinese folklore, is a Western idea, radically foreign to traditional Chinese culture, with its ideal of adaptation to nature. And yet, nationalism is certainly not for Mao Tse-tung, as it was for Lenin, simply a necessary evil. The glory of the Han is clearly a living thing to him, a value no less precious than revolution. And though he is thoroughly committed to Leninism, he has stated very brutally that this commitment is of a purely utilitarian nature:

> The arrow of Marxism must be used to hit the target of the Chinese Revolution. If it were otherwise, why would we want to study Marxism-Leninism? . . .
>
> Our comrades must understand that we do not study Marxism-Leninism because it is pleasing to the eye, or because it has some mystical value, like the doctrine of the Taoist priests who ascend Mao Shan to learn how to subdue devils and evil spirits. Marxism-Leninism has not beauty, nor has it any mystical value. It is only extremely useful. . . .[24]

Indeed, it could be argued that, if the categories in which he reasons are basically Marxist, Mao Tse-tung's deepest emotional tie is still to the Chinese nation; and if he is bent on transforming China's society and economy in the shortest possible time, in order to turn her into a powerful modern nation, it is above all in order that she may once more assume that rank in the world which he regards as rightfully hers. In this sense, Mao has "sinified" Marxism indeed.

Mao's use of examples from the past is no doubt in part manipulative, a technique for making his revolutionary theories more comprehensible and acceptable to the Chinese masses. And yet, there is a residue which is spontaneous. Mao Tse-tung's style and techniques of leadership are a mixture of Leninist democratic centralism and the flamboyant moralism and faith in the triumph of a just cause which characterizes the heroes of his favorite novels. Though he has not produced an explicit intellectual synthesis between Marxism and the Chinese tradition, he is himself a living synthesis.

---

[24]Speech of February 1, 1942, launching the rectification campaign. Boyd Compton, *Mao's China*, p. 21; Schram, *Political Thought of Mao Tse-tung*, p. 179, text II B. Most of the above passage does not appear in the current edition of the *Selected Works*.

12

Marxism Belgrade Style

Dennison I. Rusinow

Those who maintain that ideology in general and Marxism-Leninism in particular are not important to the rulers of Yugoslavia either do not read what these rulers and their academic and journalistic apologists write or are overly impressed by the gulf that separates principles and practices. Whether by inclination or because it is expected of them as senior Communists, most party and government officials lard their speeches, writings, and conversation with ideological justifications of the actions they have taken or the policies they are advocating, and if such exegesis is often *pro forma* and more often sophistic, both the quantity and sometimes the quality and originality suggest that the need to be ideological and "scientific" is more seriously felt than is usual in the Western world. At the same time the failure of practice to conform to principles is not peculiar to Yugoslavs, or to Marxists, nor is a continuous two-way interaction between what is done and what is preached, in which each modifies the other, sometimes in unexpected and inconsistent ways and under the additional impact of external influences.

Ideology is important in Yugoslavia as a justification and legitimation, as a frame of reference, even if sometimes unconscious and often badly articulated, and as a manipulative device. Its importance in these functions is one reason why official, academic, and common or garden-variety Marxism have all undergone interesting and significant transformations in the twenty years since the Tito-Stalin quarrel began. It has been necessary for Marxists in power, under constant attack by fellow Marxists, to justify their actions in theoretical terms, and it has been equally necessary for them as "scientific" Marxists to try to bring practices born of expediency into line with some consistent theoretical framework.

In such a process the relationship between changing theory and practice frequently resembles that of the chicken and the egg, and it is difficult, if not impossible, to say which came first.

The circumstances in which the Titoist experiment began had a decisive influence on the direction in which Yugoslav Marxism, as well as Yugoslav institutions, were to evolve. These circumstances included isolation from and condemnation by a still monolithic international Communism, and a consequent dependence on Western aid and diplomatic support for the survival of the regime, an isolation and dependence that

From Dennison I. Rusinow, "Marxism Belgrade Style," *Antioch Review* (Vol. 27, Winter 1967/1968), pp. 477–490. [Reprinted with permission from the publisher.]

were absolute for five years and spasmodic and partial for another eight. They also included a desperate economic situation, partly a result of the Cominform blockade imposed in 1948 and partly the result of domestic mismanagement of the economy during Yugoslavia's own Stalinist years (1945–50). One consequence was an early and wide opening of the country to the example and influence of Western thought, institutions, and technology at a time when a drastic overhaul of the existing economic system was in any case absolutely necessary. Another, related to the first, was that the only *constructive* dialogue with the outside world available to Yugoslav Marxists in these years was with Westerners or the Third World, with either non-Marxists or Social Democrats. A third consequence, vital but often overlooked, was an imperative need to criticize both the Soviet system and Russian Communist ideology and to distinguish their own practice and theory from it, in order to justify to themselves and to other Marxists their defiance of Stalin and the Soviet Union. Finally, it was necessary to strengthen their domestic position by enlarging their base of consent and participation inside the country if they were to survive as a Communist regime without the support of the Soviet Union.

The institutions and their ideological underpinning that emerged from this convergence of real and intangible pressures produced a "Titoism" that was and remains conspicuously different from any other brand of Communism, even if it can be reasonably argued that the practical effects of these differences have been less noticeable than apologists of the regime like to claim. "Workers' self-management"—based on the good, if quickly abandoned, Leninist revolutionary slogan "the factories to the workers"— and a "socialist market economy" became the cornerstones of the Yugoslav theoretical system. The former, evolving over the years into a novel principle for political-legislative as well as economic organization, remains the regime's special claim to uniqueness, both in extent of formal legal powers and in rationale. With "market socialism" it was also said to mark the beginning of the "withering away of the state" and, of more practical importance and at the heart of Titoist criticism of Russian communism, to be the only way of avoiding a degeneration of the socialist revolution into Stalinist bureaucratic totalitarianism.

In such a context, the theoretical role of the Communist party also underwent a change. It became a "League of Communists," whose theoreticians talked continually, if confusedly, of the need to abandon a "commanding role" and a monopoly of political power for an "influential role," if true "social democracy" was to be achieved. With such talk, although they never admitted it explicitly and publicly, the Titoists had moved from an attack on the dogmas of Stalinism to an attack on the dogmas of Leninism, on the Leninist concept of the party. Although icons of Lenin were still ubiquitously displayed, Marxism-Leninism-Stalinism was losing both its hyphenations, in theory if not yet in party practice.

Marx remained, but more as a philosophical and methodological mentor than as an oracle of policies and institutions. Yugoslavs became fond of pointing out that Marx had really said very little that was specific about the organization of Socialist society, and that what he wrote as a critique of capitalism in the nineteenth century should not be construed as a prescription for socialism in the twentieth.

The wider international contacts open to many Yugoslavs in the 1950s played a dual role in this evolution. Directly, there was the influence of early, immediate access to non-Marxist (or heretical semi-Marxist) economics, political science, and sociology, and earlier and wider personal experience of post-Marxian capitalism, political democracy, and democratic socialism in the West. If the admission that one can learn from non-Marxist social scientists is now commonplace among Eastern as well as Western Communists, it had a head start in Yugoslavia and—primarily because of the relatively larger number of all kinds of decision-making Yugoslavs who have enjoyed such contacts—it has penetrated to more levels and branches of the political and economic establishment than in other Communist-ruled states. In Yugoslavia it is not just the intellectual elite that has had access to such influences. Indirectly, there has been the effect of the introduction into the Yugoslav system of Western and non-Marxist (but not necessarily anti-Marxist) principles of business organization, marketing, indicative planning, indirect fiscal instruments for governmental interventions in the economy, and so forth, with a subsequent need to integrate these novelties into Yugoslav socialist theory. The latter has acted as a part of the broader phenomenon of the reciprocal interaction of ideology and practice.

In other words the dialogue with the West, which was rendered possible and even necessary by the quarrel with the East in 1948, made available to the Yugoslavs alternative solutions to their problems—theoretical and technical, political and economic. At the same time isolation from the East and from Soviet dictation freed them to choose among these alternatives, if they should so desire, with a remarkable minimum of external restraints. But to make such choices they also had to strip their own ideology of its Soviet-imposed dogmatic rigidity, and in so doing they opened it to modification, evolution, and eclecticism.

Perhaps the best example of the complex role played simultaneously by expediency, the external and internal ideological dialogue, and the consequent logic of both events and ideas is the curious history of the theory of "workers' self-management," the central premise of the Titoist system and its genuinely original feature. Workers' councils and their associated apparatuses were born of expediency, of a desperate need to broaden the regime's base of participation and consent at a time of stress and external pressure, and in a groping for devices that would escape the economic consequences of Stalinism without abandoning Marxism-Leninism as it was then understood. The new institutions quickly acquired a supporting theory, as already noted: they were proclaimed to be the best, indeed the only, way to build "true" and "democratic" socialism (as contrasted with the "state capitalism"—later called "state socialism"—of the Soviet bloc). But this theory in turn implied a modified theory of the Socialist state, which further demanded a rethinking of the role of the Communist party in such a state. If phrases like "*real* decision making by the *working men* in all public affairs" (a favorite in recent years, emphasis added) were to have any practical meaning, it seemed to Yugoslav theorists that the political organization of society must be based in some way on the workers councils and other organs of "workers' self-management" [that had been] created so casually in 1950. What then of the inherited "bourgeois" parliamentary structure which the Yugoslavs readily admit would be reduced to powerless formal bodies in a single-party state? And what of the party itself?

By the 1960s, when political circumstances made it possible for those Titoists who wanted to give meaning to their theory to raise their voices again after a decade of post-Djilasian ideological stagnation, the logic of this line of thought had assumed specific form. Yugoslavia was to become a nonparty—not a single-party or a multiparty—"self-managerial socialist democracy," governed by a hierarchy of "supreme workers councils" elected by "working men" organized in their place of work. Corporativist or syndicalist chambers would parallel and balance traditional chambers representing "working men" as citizens. Pluralism should be achieved, not through the competition of parties based on class or special interests, but through the competition of institutions representing the differing functions performed by citizens and the interests associated with them. The institutions included [the following]: in parliament, chambers of the economy; in business, economic chambers for industry as a collectivity of enterprises; trade unions for workers as workers; social welfare and educational and cultural chambers; student associations, and so forth. Decision making should be through these institutions in which Communists would be influential but would not command. The final corollary, it is worth noticing, remained deliberately vague in theory, and meaningless in practice until a serious but so far unconvincing attempt to give it a precise definition capable of political implementation began, after the purge of Aleksandar Ranković and his conservative party faction in the summer of 1966.

Advocacy of such a constitution has produced a curious kind of Communist in Yugoslavia. He attacks "statism" and big government, advocates free—but not private—enterprise, and condemns state interventions in the economy in terms that seem to be borrowed from Jeffersonian democracy and nineteenth-century economic liberalism. His attitude toward political parties, including the League of Communists as a party with traditional or even Leninist functions, is that of George Washington. By the winter of 1966–67 he was being openly attacked in the Soviet press, for the first time since 1960, as a betrayer of Leninism and a destroyer of the Leninist Party. Nevertheless, his was a position and a vision that had evolved, through a process resembling the internal "logic of events" and historical inevitability dear to Marxists, from a one-time politically expedient espousal of an expedient Leninist slogan—"the factories to the workers"—into the *raison d'être* of an independent Communist regime.

What concerns us here is not the practicality of this vision, nor is it the extent to which, or even the honesty of intent with which, it is being realized in Yugoslav society. It is rather the extent to which the vision incorporates the past twenty years of Yugoslav experience, in particular the communication Yugoslavs have had with the wider world of non-Marxist as well as Marxist thought.

The links are most obvious in theoretical and applied economics. An admirable if not entirely typical example is a 1964 book by Professor Branko Horvat, Director of the Yugoslav Institute of Economic Research in Belgrade, entitled *Towards a Theory of a Planned Economy*. It was originally intended, the author tells us in his preface, "to clarify some theoretical problems for myself and for my colleagues in the Federal Planning Bureau." It was written with the help of a research grant from the University of Manchester in England, and over four-fifths of the references cited are Western—Marxist, non-Marxist, and anti-Marxist—but the argument, like its author, is undeniably Socialist and Marxist in intent. The same can be said for most Yugoslav writing on economics and much economic organization. Methodology and concepts must be borrowed from the West to a large extent, since Yugoslav socialism is to be built using a quasi-market and indicative planning, not a command economy. The most important consequence, for purposes of the present argument, is that the doors of the conceptual prison in which traditional Marxist economics were confined have been thoroughly sprung.

For Yugoslav economists there is no contradiction between what they are doing and the Marxist label they claim for it. They say that Marx and the early socialists were primarily concerned with a criticism of capitalism and had little to say about *socialist* economics, and contemporary Marxist economists should be unfettered by the critical scriptures of the socialist old testament. Thus, such thorny problems as the labor theory of value are neatly sidestepped: the theory can still be considered valid for an *ex ante*, macroeconomic critique of capitalism, but it is simply irrelevant as a guide or value for microeconomic decision making under socialism, where Keynesian marginal analysis is more useful. On the other hand, other related Marxian concepts can be used intact for contemporary criticism of fellow Communists, as when Titoists argue that it is a matter of basic indifference whether "surplus value" is "expropriated" by capitalists in the West or by an undemocratic state bureaucracy in the Soviet East, both equally evil.

Yugoslav social science is similarly eclectic in its sources. This is also increasingly true, of course, of social science in other Communist countries where Western style sociology and social psychology, formerly derided, are more and more widely applied to problems of "socialist man." But in Yugoslavia the process is older, has penetrated further, and is consequently no longer startling. One indicator that sometimes amuses the Western observer is the widespread incorporation of Western social science terminology, sometimes debased and detached from its academic origins and meaning, into the vocabulary not only of intellectuals and students but also of politicians. Perhaps this is because a Marxist politician must pose as an intellectual, while a Western one must not. It is not uncommon to hear a Yugoslav political figure, addressing an audience of workers or peasants, refer learnedly to "a pluralistic society," "socialist pluralism," "broadening the basis of consent," "informal groups," "social stratification," "elites" or "conflicts of interest groups" (under socialism!) in a kind of terminological counterpoint to continued use of the equally abstruse and more incomprehensible jargon of traditional Marxism.

If semantic philosophers are right in arguing that the words we know are important in determining what we think, then developments like this are significant. The terminological frame of reference has been expanded and altered. When one can talk of social stratification as well as of class warfare, it is easier to conclude, as one Yugoslav theoretician, Veljko Cvjetičanin, recently has done in *Praxis,* January 1967, that under the economic conditions prevailing in socialist Yugoslavia: "Antagonistic social stratification is spontaneously reproduced. . . . The Workers Council, being an organ of self-management for workers in the factory, is a form of representative democracy, and because of varying social stratification the Workers Council may become the prey of a certain social group," so that it becomes "the scene of fierce struggles between social groups . . . which are furthering special interests." Similarly, when one has considered the sociological implications of the concept of a pluralistic society, one may travel confidently to the conclusion that the creation of "the Leninist type of Party" bears "the mark of a relatively backward society" and is therefore a device to be abandoned as a society develops.[1]

A characteristic example of the mixing of terms and usages and the Marxist use of abstruse language even for popular consumption is provided by a quotation from a Radio Belgrade report of a speech made by a member of the Executive Committee of the Central Committee of the League of Communists at a meeting of the commission for party reorganization (April 14, 1967). He is discussing the draft *Theses for the Reorganization of the League of Communists,* drawn up by the commission:

> I would like especially to stress the following idea discussed in *The Theses:* if self-management becomes reality, a social basis for an essentially new and qualitatively different form of social grouping is realized. *The Theses* stress the fact that within such a social framework the decay of the old relationships and social strata begins; their internal differentiation takes place; at the same time, the process of their closer links with the working class also begins. The working class is being integrated with numerous strata of technical intelligentsia, with technicians, and especially with the leaders of noneconomic activities. . . . In this way the process of the creation of a modern working class under the conditions of the self-management system starts.

---

[1]The conclusion of Ivan Perić, in *Naše-Teme* (December 1966).

Within such an expanded terminological and conceptual frame of reference, the intellectuals among the elite have been able to reconsider and shake out for an airing—when they have not abandoned—such traditionally troublesome Marxist or Leninist concepts as the vanguard role of the party, democratic centralism, alienation, the changing (or disappearing?) nature of the working class and class structure "under socialism," and others. Attitudes toward religion, especially in Catholic Croatia where they closely resemble recent developments in Italian Communist attitudes, have become ambivalent enough to alarm the orthodox of both faiths. Again, of course, Titoists are not alone among Marxists, even eastern Marxists, in such rethinking. At the same time, even in Yugoslavia basic criticism of received belief can still bring the publications of the most outspoken of Yugoslav critics under periodic official censure and threat of suppression. Those who are more cautious find more "positive" ways to phrase their criticism, and the limits on what is considered safely "positive" tend to widen slowly, if uncertainly. While only a few have dropped Lenin ostentatiously, others do so quietly. Last year the present writer provocatively asked a senior apologist of the regime who was an opponent of far-out criticism when he and his friends were going to stop talking of Marxism-Leninism and admit that their views were as non-Leninist as anti-Stalinist. He replied that "only a few old-timers continue to use the Marxist-Leninist label," and "we know what it means."

Among academic philosophers, diverse non-Marxist influences are also apparent. The selection varies curiously from one republican intellectual center to another, with inevitable exceptions. Thus in Slovenia one can speak of a Marxism heavily colored by existentialism; in Croatia there has long been an influential school of nonconformist Marxist philosophy lately moving in the direction of what one observer calls "a Marxistically oriented philosophical anthropology"; at the University of Belgrade, at least until recently, the influence on Marxism of latter-day logical positivism has been strongest and is reflected in such book titles as *Formalism in Contemporary Logic* and *The Dialectical Theory of Meaning*.

The most controversial and hence internationally known of these philosophers are the Croatians at the University of Zagreb who edit *Praxis*. This periodical has been publicly attacked by President Tito and by a variety of Croatian Party organizations. It came close to suppression in 1966 when publication was suspended for eight months. With their dedication of "creative Marxism," "Marxist humanism," and "criticism of everything that exists," the Zagreb group have been accused of making neoscholastic use of youthful Marxist texts to destroy not only Lenin but also the mature Marx. Of the original editorial board almost all are lecturers or assistant professors in the faculty of philosophy and members of the League of Communists. Philosophically they have variegated interests: in the infiltration of existentialism into Marxism, in a Sartre-like interpretation of Marxist ethics, in modern logic and neopositivism, in "philosophical anthropology," and most of all and most obstreperously in a criticism of Yugoslav society and politics based on nonconformist "creative Marxism."

When *Praxis* made its reappearance at the beginning of 1967, the unregenerate editors declared again that their "primary task" would be "to fight Marxist dogmatism, socialist conservatism, bureaucracy and etatism" and to support the self-management system and "humanist socialism." This was the first international issue, published in English, French, and German with a new forty-seven-member Advisory Board recruited from Yugoslavia outside Croatia, and from abroad, both West and East. The seven Eastern Europeans on the board represented Poland, Hungary, and Czechoslovakia, and included George Lukacs and the controversial Leszek Kolakowski who created an international stir when he was purged from the Polish party [later the same year.]

The Western world was represented by a variety of Marxists and non-Marxists, twenty-two in all and including such disparate personalities as A. J. Ayer, Erich Fromm, Howard Parsons, and David Riesman.

In the increasingly open debate that has characterized the Yugoslav dialogue in recent years it is increasingly difficult to say with certainty which of the variety of views and interpretations referred to in the preceding pages are "authorized" and which are not. Certain ideological precepts are still decidedly fixed and "official." The dogma of workers' self-management, for example, is publicly untouchable, as are some but not all of its corollaries. Other points of view are clearly unacceptable, such as Mihajlo Mahajlo Mahajlov's explicitly Christian "socialism" and advocacy of a multiparty solution. Most of the rest inhabit a shadow land between the two extremes. Some, like the political philosophizing of the *Praxis* group, stand astride the frontier with one foot dangerously outside the boundaries of the permissible. Others are in whole or in part essential ingredients in the ideological-political platform of the liberal group within the League of Communists that has been in the ascendancy in recent years. These now "official" views include an interpretation of the philosophical and institutional logic of workers' self-management which is fairly radical: however, within the liberal coalition there remain important differences of opinion concerning both the degree of radicalness and timing, based on differences in vested interests as well as on differing premises, mostly unspoken or unformulated. But the very existence of such a large and multicolored shadow land of the hypothetically acceptable is indicative of the openness of Titoist ideology at the present time, and of the variety of influences that are shaping it.

The importance of the expressed ideology, whether "official," academic, or literary, should, of course, not be overestimated. *Praxis* and its kindred are read by a relative handful of intellectuals, both establishment and antiestablishment. The more "official" pseudophilosophical, multisyllabic maunderings of politicans on the hustings or in columns in the daily press are largely incomprehensible to most of their audience and possibly to themselves. Quite apart from the question of whether Yugoslav institutions and practices can or ever could conform to the vision or ideal type that partly motivates some of today's principal actors, it may be just as important to know something about the inarticulate, semiconsciously or unconsciously held vision of the more "conscious" and active of their followers, especially among the youth.

Much has been said and written on the subject of the attitudes of young people, in Yugoslavia as elsewhere. Most of it is impressionistic or speculative, although some attitudinal studies with approved social-scientific methodology have been attempted. It is said that young Yugoslavs are nonpolitical and bored with ideology; it is certain that they are bored with the Partisan generation, their fathers. There is little doubt that they share the malaise of their generation throughout the world, although some people may indecently doubt that their malaise is really greater than that of their predecessors. After all, their Partisan fathers were so sick as youth that they became Communists and made a revolution. The leaders of the League of Communists have been worrying about youthful disinterest for some years, but when they have time left over they worry that youthful interest is hypercritical or downright unsocialist. Presumably, however, some young Yugoslavs, who are not party activists involved with "official" visions, do operate on the basis of some personal ideal type of the society they think Yugoslavia should become.

Perhaps, as a teasing introduction in place of a survey, a fragment from a single conversation may offer an insight into the components of one such vision. It may not be typical except in its confusion and vagueness. It may, however, be representative of the views of a group among the younger, non-party *intelligentsia* that is larger and more significant than is usually supposed: those who are neither anti-Communist nor politically disinterested—the two groups that have attracted most attention—but who qualify rather as critical fellow travelers, accepting too much to be active in opposition, but skeptical of too much to join. Although not of the elite, they are important to it because in Yugoslavia they provide one kind of informal two-way ideological transmission belt—reduction gears seems a better simile—between party members and general public, to both of whom they are often teachers. In this instance we are dealing with a young university instructor whose field is literature. He is intelligent, open-minded, and perhaps atypically idealistic, but untrained and not wildly interested in Marxism or the social sciences. He is old enough to remember the war as a child and therefore perhaps too old to be the "new" generation but too young to be the old.

In the course of the usual postprandial cafe conversation he was asked why he was not a party member, since he seemed to be sympathetic to socialism and no more critical than many inside the party. It is no longer necessary, he replied, for the party is quite big enough and it is no longer an act of courage and faith to join; besides, in Yugoslavia the party has fulfilled its historic function and is no longer needed.

Talk of historic functions led naturally to more general philosophy. By whatever word we choose to call it—"communism," "progress," "the future," "democracy"— this is the future and the inevitable, he thought, and we are moving toward it. Therefore (with interesting logic) we must struggle for it even if it turns out to be evil, unsatisfying. We do not know whether it is bad or good because it does not yet exist, we can only find out when we get there. For example, it does seem to involve industrialization and urbanization, and these are mixed blessings because they raise new problems and contradictions which so far baffle both socialism and liberalism.

Then why work for it? Because we must by a kind of categorical imperative; because communism is "being becoming." But there is another argument: because one believes, as Marx did, that man's liberty is an ultimate value and that it can be completely obtained only in a society so prosperous and so organized that [the slogan] "to everyone according to his need" becomes a reality. (So communism is not so entirely an unknown land as he had just maintained? The inconsistency remained unnoticed.) Communism is therefore what all people in favor of "progress" are moving toward; that is why it is (a) inevitable and (b) already has majority support in the world because most people are in favor of "progress and development." Is progress therefore inevitable? Yes, although we may often take two steps backward and one step forward; progress is uneven, and some individual societies may fail to progress.

There is, however, no reason to suppose that the Socialist countries must necessarily get to communism first, he continued. It is quite possible that the liberal democracies of the West, with their higher standards of living and civil liberties, will arrive considerably ahead. Nevertheless, it is very important that now there are many Socialist countries. When there was only one and it got off the track of progress as the Soviet Union did, great harm could be done; but with a number of them, while several may fall by the wayside, there will always be others making correct choices and advancing toward the goal.

Political democracy and majority rule as practiced in the West may be useful as imperfect guardians of "liberty," he added, but they are neither as central nor as helpful as is believed there. Their democratic purpose is often—perhaps usually—defeated by two factors: by imperfections in the system allowing the intrusion of pressure groups, demagogues, and the like, and by ignorance and stupidity on the part of too large a part of the electorate. The first task is to train the electorate for self-government. This is ignored in the West but concentrated on in Yugoslavia, and until it is complete the genuinely free ballot is meaningless. Ignorant and misled people may too easily be persuaded to vote themselves back into slavery and superstition, retreating from the progress made toward meaningful freedom under an authoritarian regime, as happened in Turkey under Menderes.

One is reminded of a Yevtushenko, surprising Western audiences by declaring after his outspoken and courageous criticism of Soviet society that he believes in "communism." The image that has filtered down to at least some nonpolitical Yugoslavs does not appear dissimilar to his, even as it bears a relationship to vague images of a "great society" circulating in other, nonsocialist countries, those that may "get to communism first." Someone has suggested that for the nonapathetic among the younger Yugoslav intelligentsia, Marxism has come to mean a pragmatic mixture of the Western welfare state with a touch of old-fashioned communist idealism.

The influence of official Marxism on such Yugoslav images is clearly strong, but there have been other inputs as well. Some of them are the same that the Zagreb philosophers of "creative Marxism" have perceived in the "young Marx" whose "humanism" and critical spirit attract them, and who drew upon intellectual dialogues with most of the historic main currents in Western thought for his inspiration, as they would do. They and other Yugoslavs may, of course, end—like Marx himself—by refusing to call themselves "Marxists."

Selected Bibliography

Soviet Union

Bell, Daniel. *The End of Ideology.* Glencoe, Illinois: Free Press, 1960.

Brzezinski, Zbigniew. *Ideology and Power in Soviet Politics.* New York: Praeger, 1962.

Drachkovitch, Milorad M., ed. *Marxist Ideology in the Contemporary World.* New York: Praeger, 1966.

Dux, Dieter, ed. *Ideology in Conflict: Communist Political Theory.* Princeton, New Jersey: Van Nostrand, 1963.

Marcuse, Herbert A. *Soviet Marxism: A Critical Analysis.* New York: Columbia University Press, 1958.

Moore, Barrington. *Soviet Politics—The Dilemma of Power.* Cambridge, Massachusetts: Harvard University Press, 1950.

Stankiewicz, W. J., ed. *Political Thought Since World War II.* New York: Free Press, 1964.

Wetter, Gustav. *Soviet Ideology Today.* New York: Praeger, 1966.

China

Cohen, Arthur A. *The Communism of Mao Tse-tung.* Chicago: University of Chicago Press, 1968.

Hsiung, James Chieh. *Ideology and Practice: The Evolution of Chinese Communism.* New York: Praeger, 1970.

Lowe, Donald M. *The Function of "China" in Marx, Lenin, and Mao.* Berkeley: University of California Press, 1966.

Schram, Stuart R. *The Political Thought of Mao Tse-tung.* Rev. ed. New York: Praeger, 1969.

Schurmann, Franz. *Ideology and Organization in Communist China.* 2d ed. Berkeley: University of California Press, 1968.

Schwartz, Benjamin I. *Communism and China: Ideology in Flux.* Cambridge, Massachusetts: Harvard University Press, 1968.

Soloman, Richard. *Mao's Revolution and the Chinese Political Culture.* Berkeley: University of California Press, 1971.

Wakeman, Frederick, Jr. *History and Will, Philosophical Perspectives of Mao Tse-tung's Thought.* Berkeley: University of California Press, 1973

Yugoslavia

Armstrong, Hamilton Fish. *Tito and Goliath.* New York: Macmillan, 1951.

Dedijer, Vladimir. *Tito.* New York: Simon and Schuster, 1953.

Johnson, A. Ross. *The Transformation of Communist Ideology: The Yugoslav Case. 1945–1953.* Cambridge, Massachusetts: M.I.T. Press, 1973.

Kardelj, Edward. *Socialism and War.* London: Methuen, 1961.

Korbel, Josef. *Tito's Communism.* Denver: University of Denver Press, 1951.

McVicker, Charles P. *Titoism, Pattern for International Communism.* New York: St. Martin's Press, 1957.

Neal, Fred Warner. *Titoism in Action.* Berkeley: University of California Press, 1958.

Stojanovic, Svetozar. *Between Ideals and Reality.* New York: Oxford University Press, 1973.

Zukin, Sharon. *Beyond Marx and Tito: Theory and Practice of Yugoslav Socialism.* New York: Cambridge University Press, 1975.

THE PARTY, LEADERSHIP, AND COMPETITION

In a Communist system, who governs? Is it the one person who stands at the top of the party hierarchy, or is it a group of party members, a collective leadership? Also, are leadership politics of the Communist party states uniform in structure? If so, can this structure be described as one of "stable dictatorship," or is it rather one in "constant conflict?" Furthermore, have the "technocrats"—that is, those more highly educated and specialized party officials—assumed more power than the more orthodox and ideologically motivated party "bureaucrats." And what is the specific relationship between the "technocrats" and "bureaucrats," today, and how will it change as Communist societies continue to modernize and industrialize. These and related questions will be addressed in the following readings on political leadership in Communist states.

In the Soviet Union, Communist China, and Yugoslavia, primary leadership authority has traditionally resided within the Communist party. Guided by "scientific" theory, and controlled by a hierarchical and centralized organization, the party institution has been successful in gaining undisputed power within the political system. Consequently, many observers in democratic systems have tended to equate the Communist party with everything undemocratic in politics, including extreme centralization of authority, ruthless power politics, and overall totalitarianism. Irrespective of the validity of these claims, it should be acknowledged that the centralized revolutionary party came to perform a crucial role during the advent, assumption, and preservation of power in the Communist states under study. As suggested in the first three sections, Lenin molded this "party of a new type" into an organization designed to establish and consolidate political authority in the new state. Early in the revolutionary movement, Lenin used the Russian Marxist newspaper *Iskra* ("The Spark") to express his views on the party, and later, in 1902, he published his work *What is to Be Done?*, in which he explained his plans for the party in greater detail. Although the Russian Communist party had only 20,000 members at the time of the collapse of the monarchy in March, 1917, it increased to ten times that figure by the first of the next year. Its growth in numbers coincided with its growth in power. Under Lenin's adept leadership, the party seized and monopolized power during the ensuing years and became the guiding force of the new Socialist state.

But although Lenin was instrumental in defining the original purposes and functions of the party, it was Stalin who imparted to it those particular forms that have drawn criticism from within the Communist world, as well as from without.[1] Under Stalin, the party recruited, socialized, and advanced people within the political system, and at the same time, monopolized the political process itself. It is perhaps reasonable to conclude that the party controlled both the personnel and the policy, and was therefore of primary influence on the political process. Stalin carried the implementation of control by the party to its extreme, and became the guiding personality of the party organization. This led to the evolution of what some have called a "one-man dictatorship," which replaced what was earlier considered the "dictatorship of the party," which in turn had replaced the "dictatorship of the proletariat." Regardless of whether Stalinist Russia was ruled by an oligarchy (a small number of rulers), or a one-man dictator, the fact remains that the party was placed in a position of primary political power. Then, in order to preserve complete power, Stalin maintained the "purity" of the party by recruiting and purging, a tactic that led to the downfall of some leaders (such as Trotsky), and the rise of others (such as Khrushchev).

After their advent to power, Lenin, Mao, and Tito all used the party to organize and consolidate political authority in the new Socialist states. In these early years of state-building, the internal organization, administration, and behavior of the party were substantially the same. In all three systems, the party was organized along a hierarchical, pyramidal scheme that coincided with the territorial-administrative units of the country. At

---

[1]For a provocative criticism of the party and the "new class" that developed within it, which incidently came from within the Communist world and from one of Tito's closest associates, see Milovan Djilas, *The New Class* (New York: Praeger, 1956).

the lowest level of the hierarchy was the local party cell, and at the top was the central party Presidium or Politburo.[2] Ultimate authority within the party rested with the party Secretary, who was chairman of the Politburo and resided in the state's capital, whereas subordinate regional or provincial units and their leaders assumed positions of considerably lesser importance and power. The power relationships within this pyramidal structure were not unchanging, however, and began to diverge in the three countries as the years passed. Although power tended to remain concentrated at the center in China, and perhaps to a somewhat lesser extent in the Soviet Union, in Yugoslavia it was progressively dispersed to the republic and local levels. In all states, the power distribution is potentially subject to change, and further fluctuations can be expected in the interrelationships of the national, regional, and local administrative levels.

Operating principles and procedures within the party organization are also of considerable interest and importance. In theory, democratic procedures were to be observed at all levels, and such safeguards as the election of all Party officials through a secret ballot were instituted. Also the decision-making process was to be implemented according to the principles of democratic centralism—that is, "democracy under centralized procedures." Democratic centralism was based on the rationale that, once alternative points of view had been considered and the final policy decided, centralism was essential in order to establish a united front. These general guidelines have been deviated from, in both directions, by different Communist states at different periods. For example, in Stalinist Russia, elections and the concept of democratic centralism became empty ideals, whereas Titoist Yugoslavia had, at least for a time, established a pluralistic form of socialist democracy. In general, however, and as the following readings suggest, Communist party leadership does not adhere to democratic ideals.

At the same time, even a cursory examination of recent developments in different Communist systems will indicate that the concept of one-man rule is an oversimplification, and its actualization a political impossibility in contemporary Communist states. Absolute control of the political affairs of a large and complex political system, even if a leader wanted it, would be impossible for any one individual, no matter how competent the First Secretary of a given Communist party might be. This limitation notwithstanding, most leaders at the party summit still attempt to accumulate and maintain maximum political control.[3] But although leadership politics in Communist states (as well as perhaps all other political systems) reveal

---

[2]The terms Presidium and Politburo have been used interchangeably over the years to refer to the highest-level committee of party officials. This small committee is the most powerful policy-making body in Communist states.

[3]Yugoslavia has been far more open to experiments in political decentralization and pluralism than have the Chinese and Soviet systems, although a recent offensive on the part of the League of Communists represents at least a temporary return to more orthodox party centralism in the present-day Yugoslav system.

an unmistakable thirst for increased power among the highest leaders, this thirst is not above or without challenge. As Robert G. Wesson ("The Problem of Soviet Leadership") and Richard C. Thornton ("The Structure of Chinese Politics") point out in their incisive analyses of the political systems of these two states, the positions of the highest leaders are continually challenged by opposing factions. Although the tendency among Western observers has been to assume that a Stalin, Brezhnev, or Mao are protected from political struggle and competition, the analyses that follow suggest almost precisely the opposite. Specifically, both Wesson and Thornton note that such leaders are often in the midst of a process of "constant conflict." They suggest that, although in general leaders would like to avoid political challenge or division, their hopes are largely unrealized. The leadership process in Communist states, therefore, is highly competitive, and even the most powerful leaders sometimes find themselves embroiled in struggle. The resultant tendency has often been a movement toward an oligarchy, that is, a collective leadership within the one-party state.

Not only is the concept of "one-man rule" outdated, but so too are some of our ideas concerning opposition movements in Communist states. In her comparative analysis of opposition movements of the late 1960s within the Czechoslovak and Yugoslav systems ("Yugoslavia: The Case for a Loyal Opposition under Communism"), Barbara Jancar outlines the rise of a rather different type of leadership politics in Czechoslovakia and Yugoslavia. In these two states, the late 1960s were a period of great political diversity and pluralism. Opposition movements—albeit, primarily within the one party structure—increasingly challenged the central party leadership for a share of the power. In both systems, and particularly in Czechoslovakia during the "Prague Spring" of 1968, open discussion on the possibility of genuine opposition parties arose. Obviously, both systems had moved a long way from the highly centralized and oppressive Stalinist type dictatorship. But in each country, a sudden reversal abruptly ended the experiments in increased pluralism. Ironically, just at the time Jancar's article appeared in print (in the summer of 1968), the Soviet Union and participating Warsaw Treaty Organization states swiftly and brutally intervened and ended the Czechoslovak experiment in "socialism with a human face." Then, only a few years later, the scope and intensity of political competition and opposition within Yugoslavia was also curtailed. Here, Tito and the central leadership began to perceive the volatile political climate of the late 1960s and early 1970s as threatening to the unity of multinational Yugoslavia. Their response in the early 1970s was a reassertion of central party control and severe limitations on political diversity.

In all systems, then, conflict and competition within the leadership structure continue to prevail. It is important to note that, for the most part, these competitive forces are neither anti-Communist nor anti-Socialist, but rather the efforts of dedicated Communists to expand their own power in the leadership process. In his analysis of the "constant-conflict" model of Communist leadership, Richard Thornton emphasizes the competitive nature of personal and group relationships within this leadership process. Although the competitors vary—be they personalities (for example, Mao versus Lin Piao) or organizations (for example, the party versus the military bureaucrats versus technocrats)—the basic and underlying leadership struggle is nevertheless ongoing within all states. In this section, our primary concern will be to identify leadership patterns within Communist political systems, and the forces and challenges that affect them. As the following readings demonstrate, these patterns have significant implications for changes in the Soviet, Chinese, and Yugoslav systems.

13

The Problem of Soviet Leadership

Robert G. Wesson

A unique characteristic of the Soviet state is the exceptional flexibility of the power structure at the summit. If a country like Great Britain has domineering prime ministers and others who lead a collegial cabinet government, the Soviet system has had personal leadership varying in strength from the ascendancy of Khrushchev from February 1955 to June 1957 to the firm control exercised by Lenin, and to the despotism of Stalin, as absolute as any in modern history. At other times, the Soviet Union has been headed by committee-style groups, in which no individual was evidently dominant, at three widely separated times in Soviet history. Moreover, these changes have occurred without overt violence and with no disjunction in the Soviet order. For France, for example, to shift from the weak Fourth Republic to the strong presidency of the Fifth required a severe crisis and a change of constitution, but the several Soviet fluctuations from one extreme to the other have been smooth and quiet, with practically no formal institutional change and only slight modification of ideology. Organizational continuity has been unbroken since 1917, and each leadership has been raised up by its predecessor.

In the years since the Revolution of 1917, one-man dictatorships prevailed for about two-thirds of this period. But the lengthy reign of Stalin is not likely to be repeated, unless another revolution should occur, because of the limitations imposed by a single life span. Stalin was exceptional in that he had attained the position of leading party Secretary at an unusually young age. The Soviet system has prospered equally well under oligarchic and monarchic rule. Indeed, it may be surmised that both are essential for the proper functioning of the Leninist state, which has both democratic and undemocratic forms and institutions. Both collective and single leadership are based on personal rather than legal relations, and consequently neither is permanent. Neither is institutionalized, both are useful, and periodically each has to be replaced by the other.

At nearly all times through Soviet history a leader has been improving his apparent position (except for the years 1937–1953 when Stalin had attained the peak of political power). The gradual accumulation of power by Stalin, whereby he built up a loyal machine, eliminated successive numbers of opponents, competitors, or potentially independent persons, and raised his personal cult to virtual deification, is familiar. The similarity of Khrushchev's parallel rise was remarkable, especially in view of the fact that those whom he was pushing aside were well aware of the means by which Stalin had conquered and the danger his power had posed for everyone. The crisis of June 1957 may be seen as their belated reaction. If Khrushchev was actually weakened in his last years of power, he does not seem to have been aware of it, but behaved in an increasingly dictatorial manner. His self-celebration at his birthday in April 1964 befitted a true dictator.[1] Lenin, too, became more and more of an autocrat in the few years available to him. He began as a *primus inter pares* who several times had difficulty imposing his views. Immediately after the Revolution a large faction of the Bolshevik leadership thought he should be sacrificed in the interests of a coalition government. Nevertheless he became unquestioned boss of the monopolistic party in which factions were outlawed, and men hung on his glance as on a tsar's.

Brezhnev has built up his power more gradually and less dramatically than his predecessors.[2] At first, he hardly seemed to outshine his fellows of the Politburo, but the return to the title of General Secretary in March 1966 signaled a considerable advance. Thereafter quotations from Brezhnev increasingly replaced those from Lenin; and Brezhnev's works were published in various languages and millions of copies. Although he appeared to suffer a temporary setback in the early 1970s, today he seems to have no rival in the top group. When visiting the Soviet Union in the summer of 1971, Chancellor Brandt conferred only with Brezhnev, although *Pravda* reported that "responsible members of the secretariat of the General Secretary" participated in the conversations.[3] In May 1972, President Nixon's conversations were chiefly with Brezhnev, and Brezhnev signed as General Secretary both the joint declaration of principles and the arms limitation agreements on behalf of the Soviet Union. In September 1972, Brezhnev conferred with Presidential envoy Kissinger, while Kosygin met American businessmen.

Apparently Brezhnev is not yet an absolute ruler, or perhaps he is judicious enough to avoid offensive prominence. Formally, he has assumed no new powers, and he has pushed no important policies in his own name. Much of his appeal may lie in simply standing for stability. Although Brezhnev has been able to advance several proteges to Politburo status and to ease certain rivals out of the crucial Secretariat of the Central Committee, he has not brought into the inner circle (Secretariat plus Politburo) a corps of newcomers entirely dependent on him alone. Neither has he ousted members of the formerly truly collective leadership, even though it is the first task of a new tyrant to replace former equals by faithful subordinates. It is not known how strong he in fact is, or to what extent he can override opposing views of those around him. But apparently he is becoming increasingly regarded as symbol of the Soviet state.

Soviet experience seems thus to confirm the old axiom that oligarchy is inherently unstable; indeed, throughout history hardly any have endured except those of the small states, such as some of the city-republics of the Middle Ages.[4] Rather, what seems to develop is that one person gradually accumulates authority, and others become accustomed to looking to him for leadership. Consultation is cumbersome, and questions need prompt and decisive decisions which committees are unprepared to produce. Oligarchy is at best a delicate balance, easily overthrown by political stresses. The Soviet oligarchy is intrinsically less stable than historical examples because there is only

---

[1]Much of the politics of Khrushchev's rise is detailed in Howard R. Swearer, *The Politics of Succession in the USSR* (Boston: Little, Brown, 1964).

[2]For an account of Brezhnev's career, see Paul A. Smith, *Orbis* (Vol. XV, No. 2, Summer, 1971), pp. 576–608.

[3]September 19, 1971, p. 1.

[4]Oligarchy is employed here to mean a government by a small, formally recognized group, not one by a small aristocratic class, as in the Aristotelian sense.

a shadow of a constitution, and no legally fixed distribution of authority or regular means of allocating roles, just as in the Soviet bureaucracy no definite tenure, no regular career ladder, and no single line of responsibility exist. There may be understandings, of course; but these lack legal validity and their moral effect is lost as memories of the preceding dictatorship wane, new issues come to the fore, and outlooks change. Committee government is dull, and people may hanker for the movement and excitement of personal rulership as they forget its excesses. In the hierarchy, status is everything, but it is largely undefined; hence anyone is under some pressure to defend his status by seeking to improve it. Power demands its continual increase, and this is always possible in the absence of formal structures delimiting it. The accretion of power is gradual, and in the first crucial stages inconspicuous, and each step is rationalized as response to a specific need. The construction of a basis for dictatorship consists mostly in quietly forwarding friends and in creating conditions that encourage others to stand with rather than against the leader.

In the Soviet state, equilibrium within the rulership is the more difficult to maintain because of imbalance between party and administrative organs. One might assume the principal locus of power and political center of gravity should lie in the governmental apparatus, which has charge of police, armed forces, national revenues, and the economy. The Bolsheviks themselves at first expected decision making to be in the government; Lenin, holding no special party position, became Chairman of the Council of Commissars. But for the Soviet Union, the antithesis of theory and reality of power requires party domination. The party represents a single political will much better than the government, which is more strongly influenced by the multiple demands of the society which it administers. It must of necessity be more responsive to the productive sectors and the important forces in Soviet life, including those like the military, which might conceivably challenge the party monopoly. The party, unburdened by direct administrative responsibilities, is in a better position to override special claims, regional or professional, in the interest of total rulership. The government, in order to function smoothly, must be guided by law and regular procedures; the party can be as arbitrary as necessary for the management of a basically arbitrary system. The government must make at least superficial concessions to pluralism and the facade of democracy; the party can stand unequivocally for the supreme desideratum of unity and demand discipline under the center.

Party domination of the government is thus indispensable, but it is unnatural in that the bulk of material resources lie with the government. Hence if the party is to dominate, governmental power must be split, and that of the party must be concentrated. Governmental power is secured by many devices, such as offsetting the Chairman of the Council of Ministers by the party's Chairman of the Presidium of the Supreme Soviet, direct control of ministries through departments of the party's Central Committee, a special apparatus for management of the armed forces through the Central Committee's Chief Administration, and the like, down to party guidance of local factories and soviets. It is axiomatic, on the other hand, that the party must have a single will. The essential principle of party organization is to bind individuals, through a system of hierarchy softened by consultation and the appearance of some adherence to democratic principles (much less than in the state) so that a monolithic nucleus of political power is created. The party goal, then, is unity; but if the power were to rest with the party as a whole, or with any large representative body, the latent factionalism that always exists below the surface would be legitimized and the growth of pluralism permitted, so that the party's fundamental role would be jeopardized. But authority cannot be concentrated in a Secretariat or Politburo of equals alone, unless these individuals are in total harmony—a human impossibility.

As a consequence, the arbitrarily ruling party can hardly hope to avoid placing itself under a supreme chief. They may wish to prevent sole rulership without permitting dispersal of power but they lack means of doing so. They are not so naive as to fail to realize, after the experience of Stalin and Khrushchev, that a party boss has the levers of potential dictatorship. Stalin's successors apparently wanted to pluralize the party headship, since the post of General Secretary that Stalin had held lapsed with the disappearance of the incumbent. Evidently this pluralization did not work, because, by September 1953, Khrushchev received the title of First Secretary—a designation presumably dictated by the need for a boss coupled with the hope that the post would not resemble the former General Secretaryship. However, in 1966, in the twilight of de-Stalinization, the party returned to the Stalinist title.

The denial of rights to the nonparty ultimately implies negation of rights within the party. If any multiple body held real power or if independent offices were established, political contest could no longer be excluded, and it might spread indefinitely, bring the latent and not so latent divisions of Soviet society into the open, and endanger the entire system. Strong and intelligent men accepted the absolute power of the Tsar, even though he might be mean and contemptible, because he was seen (probably correctly) as indispensable for the unity of the empire and so for their status and way of life. If, as it seems, a single head in the Soviet Union, is required to keep the apparatus on top, the apparatchiks accept him, despite the likelihood that he may become a danger to them. Party dictatorship needs a dictator.

In practice, it is especially necessary to have a final judge to allocate authority in the absence of a constitution. The committee must have great difficulty in settling claims, particularly those between its own members—such as police, council of ministers, trade unions, and so on—who represent chief divisions of the Soviet state and whose jurisdictions inevitably overlap. There is need for a spokesman for the state, one to whom underlings can look up as a fountainhead of wisdom. The ideologically framed empire needs a high priest; the infallible dogma requires an infallible exponent. The oligarchs, unable to agree on significant changes, can only go on repeating old lines which become steadily less relevant and less convincing. Ideological creativity in the Soviet Union has come only from individual leadership, as in Lenin's adaptations, Stalin's transformations, and Khrushchev's updating.

A single final arbiter is most crucially needed for personnel decisions. A committee may be a sound judge of policy, although it tends to make weak compromises; but there is little possibility of compromise in the issues of who is or is not to be advanced. Such a decision is the explicit task of the secretaries throughout the party and of the Central Committee Secretariat at the top; and it is, of course, the key to power, as the leader at the center spreads his political following outward and downward through Central Committee and regional secretaries to local departments and primary groups. The question is especially acute at the summit; the Politburo seems to be, as must be expected, incapable of reconstituting itself. It cannot exclude anyone who remains loyal, it cannot choose between its members without endangering consensus, and it probably regards enlargement of the group as negative for all.

Unlike the fluid entourage of the dictator, the oligarchic governing group must be rather sharply defined. In the Soviet Union, it consists of the full and candidate members of the Politburo plus the secretaries of the Central Committee who are not also Politburo members. This group has been practically unchanged since a few adjustments after Khrushchev's exit. Apparently the members, though willing to countenance some advancements and demotions within the sacred circle, are too mutually protective to authorize the dismissal of anyone from it or to permit new entrants to dilute their power, if not to threaten to overshadow at least the less capable of the group. Unless it changes directions, the collective is headed toward collapse from superannuation.

The party elite is obviously very reluctant to countenance dismissal of its members. The party represents a total dedication; only by giving one's self entirely can one hope to rise within it. Outside of it, there is no status and no life for the faithful. The ruling elite are like bishops of a church, bound together in a special relationship unlike that of ordinary mortals; they are not dismissed lightly—usually only for heresy. The top rank of the party is also like an exclusive club, in which membership is practically indefeasible. As long as one is loyal and observes the rules, he will not be expelled. The party boss can make nominations, but firing someone is an overt, offensive, and generally menacing act; if a boss is to undertake such a measure, it must be for reasons of disloyalty (Stalin's antagonists were usually charged with treason; Khrushchev's, with "antiparty" actions). But since such an action was considered so drastic, both Stalin and Khrushchev had to work for years with people whom they disliked and distrusted, as Brezhnev probably does today. It is more in the Soviet style to shift power than to change personnel, as personal rule has been built more by transferring power to the Secretariat than by taking over the Council of Ministers and Politburo. In his latter years, as Stalin came to distrust his Politburo, he did not replace the old guard with more subservient men but ceased to consult it. Similarly, Brezhnev has kept Kosygin as chief of the government while assuming a large part of his authority.

The power of a leader to disgrace any of those near the top is potentially threatening to them all. There may be some continuing fear that a new absolutism might be physically dangerous. Khrushchev was inhibited by his commitment to de-Stalinization and restoration of "socialist legality," but it is conceivable that a successor might feel it desirable to make an example of those whom he found dangerous. Khrushchev told the Twenty-Second Congress that his beaten opponents feared for their lives. Even if party bosses at all levels have no such fears, they must be apprehensive that a new dictator would rudely disturb them. Khrushchev carried out an extensive renewal of cadres, attempted to limit reelection of leaders, and constantly reorganized party structure (for example, by dividing the party into agricultural and industrial sectors), thus generating uncertainty throughout. Of the Presidium formed after Khrushchev's 1957 victory, only the harmless Mikoyan, the insignificant Shvernik, the underestimated Brezhnev, and the ideologist Suslov were still on hand in 1964.

A single ruler not only detracts from the authority of individuals; in the Soviet system, he reduces the role of the party. The dictator wishes to improve his security by reducing dependence upon the party apparatus. As an aspirant to power, he cannot afford to look at any nonparty groups for assistance, since this would be a threat to the principles of the system; but once on top, he must look afield, both for the cooperation essential for accomplishing his designs and for support to balance against the party machine. Stalin worked through his personal secretariat and used the police and army and the new engineering-managerial class to counter the power of the party as such. Khrushchev went outside of the party for help in fixing policy, as in permitting fairly free debates on such matters as educational policy and economic reform; it was probably a graver affront to the apparatchiks to flood Central Committee meetings with outside experts.[5]

The Soviet system cannot overtly have an autocratic head but must pretend to be popular-democratic just as it must subscribe to an allegedly fact-based ideology as cover for the arbitrary power of the party. The democratic facade is important, as the Soviet state is under strong compulsions to maintain appearances of popular consent and support and of modern, basically Western-style institutions; but the tribute that dictatorship pays democracy has its cost. The formally supreme authority is the power-less Supreme Soviet. Marxism broadly deidealizes and desanctifies by its materialistic philosophy, but autocratic rulers need at least some veil of mystique. Marxism emphasizes material and economic forces in history, downgrading great men as against masses and classes. Only after Communist leaders have attained great power have they incorporated the cult of their personalities into the official ideology, thus over-laying Marxism with Stalinism, for example, or Khrushchevism (as Maoism, Titoism, Castroism, have made their marks elsewhere). The revived idolatry of Lenin exalts the role of the genius-leader, and possibly for this reason the cult of Lenin was exaggerated during the years of Brezhnev's rise; but the canonization of Lenin diminishes the need for an individual to serve as symbol of Soviet authority and unity. Lenin is an ideal who has no frailties and cannot err; consequently he is more acceptable to the people, including non-Russians, than a living oligarch is likely to become.

Personal rulership, then, has no institutional or ideological basis. Rather, it is founded on an individual's character, political acumen, and the aura of success with which he surrounds himself. It is a matter of personality and acceptance, not formal standing, as exemplified by Brezhnev's apparent assumption of the prerogative of sign-ing treaties without explicit authorization. In his lack of legitimacy, Stalin sought always to strengthen his power for fear of losing it; and he continually eliminated those upon whom the slightest suspicion fell. He carried on an enormous unending campaign of self-glorification, built himself up as Lenin's executor, made himself essential by initiating radical transformations of the country, and, after purging everyone suspect of less than total loyalty, kept his followers perpetually insecure by the use of periodic terror tactics against selected individuals. Khrushchev attacked his most obvious rivals by the implementation of de-Stalinization, made himself spokesman for revival of Leninism and the party, forwarded modernization and renewal, proposed a succession of grand schemes as panaceas for the economy, especially agriculture, and set himself up as the architect of the new order of communism.

To justify his unbounded power, the dictator seems to feel impelled to assume un-bounded responsibility. Lenin burdened himself with an endless range of detail—from educational policy to individual housing allotments, including a device for keeping food warm[6]—while directing party and state, directing the Comintern, and writing profusely. Stalin participated in all important activities and pronounced himself on ideology, party organization, foreign affairs, military strategy, economics, literature, music, linguistics, philosophy, and various scientific theories. He inevitably fell into fatuity, such as the proposal in his last work, *Economics of Socialism,* that collective farmers exchange their products directly for industrial wares. One of Khrushchev's

---

[5]Some of these problems are discussed, in regard to the Khrushchev era, by Myron Rush, *Political Succession in the USSR* (New York: Columbia University Press, 1965).

[6]Louis Fischer, *The Life of Lenin* (New York: Harper & Row, 1964), pp. 430–434.

primary criticisms of his deceased master was that of incompetence in various fields. Yet Khrushchev himself dictated policy in diplomacy, industrial priorities and planning, electric projects, chemicals, art, and agriculture, as well as acting as party and government boss. He inevitably made egregious errors, for which he was ultimately made accountable.

In part the stability of the Soviet system may be attributable to the ability to function well under varying types of leadership. While management at the top has alternated between extremes, the party and apparatus have continued to govern, much as the bureaucracy used to carry on through changes from tsar to regency to new tsar. To a considerable extent, each extreme corrects excesses of the other. Collective leadership implies rationality, stability, conservatism, and regular procedures or legalism; single leadership promises innovation and experimentation, rejuvenation of higher echelons, and (at least at first) a housecleaning. The oligarchy hardens institutional lines, the dictator loosens them and makes the power structure more fluid. The oligarchy requires harmony and blandness; the dictator probably prefers men whose views and personalities conflict somewhat so that he can maximize his policy options as well as authority. The oligarchy may give people some relaxation; the single leader is more likely to drive them for some higher purpose defined by himself. But no matter which type of leadership is in control at any given time, the psychological and political environment within which the Soviet leadership operates is in perennial and massive flux. Neither single nor plural rulership can follow closely in the footsteps of its predecessor.

The general effect seems to be a moderation of the potentials of despotism. The settling down of the apparatus makes it more difficult for a leader to build up his personal machine. The bureaucracy crystallizes toward a set of vested interests and becomes intractable, as bureaucracies everywhere. Without a new revolution, no other dictator can come near translating his will into policy as Stalin did. The right of people to continue in their places is accepted now as it was not in the 1950s, or the 1930s. Lenin had a new state to make, and its expansion and transformation offered Stalin countless vacancies to fill. Khrushchev had far fewer vacancies and Brezhnev, when he first came into power, had only a handful of places to which he could easily advance his followers. The leadership ages; not only do older men have less time (and probably less energy) to build up personal power, but riper men are less dedicated followers. Few wish to link themselves irrevocably to the graying figure who wears no halo of historical transformation and who may not be on the stage very long. As the Soviet Union matures, the power struggle is carried on more and more by a group of like-minded persons who share a long period of indoctrination; and, with no stirring changes underway, it is more difficult to discredit people in order to remove them. Much of the instability of the oligarchy that assumed leadership after Lenin arose from the insistence of various leaders and groups on their particular views and policies, which they pushed with the fervor of revolutionists. Stalin's willingness to compromise policies for politics was a major strategic advantage; but now all are willing to compromise. In the "developed socialist society," as Soviet spokesmen describe it, there is little likelihood of there evolving any social change that might result in leadership change.

The erosion of ideology—which began with the revolution and the need to deal with practical problems instead of utopian images—and the ebbing of revolutionary purpose have sapped the foundations of potential arbitrariness. The postmobilization maturity of Soviet society and its changed values and expectations modify and limit the powers of the regime. People must have a cause in which the elite, at least, can believe deeply, if they are to stir things up, unsettle bureaucratic ways, and deal harshly with many people in a modern state. The political contest shifts from passionate principle to personal ambition, but personal ambition implies no full commitment to anyone. The latter-day leaders have been ripened in the Byzantine byways of the party. Stalin out-maneuvered a bunch of revolutionary agitators with little sense of organization politics; a new candidate is surrounded by the most cunning products of the machine.

What Bertram Wolfe called "The Law of Diminishing Dictators"[7] also prevails because of political dynamics. The character of leaders has changed rather consistently with the principle that insecure rulers are reluctant to elevate those with an obvious potential for independence. The succession has thus passed from Lenin, the revolutionary intellectual, through Stalin and Khrushchev, to Brezhnev, the consummate apparatchik. Stalin, who for a long time kept the true extent of his power in the app007ratus inconspicuous, was permitted to advance partly because, as a dull speaker without ideological pretensions, he seemed innocuous. Trotsky, with his revolutionary aura and command of the armed forces, was too obviously Lenin's heir-apparent. Likewise, after Stalin's death, Malenkov was vulnerable because he was his indicated successor. Khrushchev worked himself into the First Secretaryship as the last and least threatening of the inner circle. Although the oligarchs were fooled by Stalin and Khrushchev, they are likely to be more careful in the future. In sum, we are not likely to see a new Stalin. The new dictator is likely to be less a power in his own right and more a trustee for the governing clique, as many Latin American dictators have been—less effective, less admired, and less feared.

These considerations indicate a poor long-term prognosis for the dynamism and progressiveness of Soviet leadership. The Leninist states have no answer for the political problems of the postmobilization, postrevolutionary phase of history.[8]

Hence, although the Soviet state is excellently designed for the control of people, it suffers at the summit a disorder that induces decline of political effectiveness. The suppression of "spontaneity" elsewhere causes more "spontaneity" to emerge at the top, and unchecked power is anarchic. Irregularity at the top is also a corollary of the distance between political forms and realities. The Soviet Union can neither legitimatize autocratic institutions nor implement democratic ones.

The immediate outlook for the future is probably one of continued stability. Party rule is extremely effective, and it is difficult to imagine what developments, economic or political, might break it down as long as it remains functional in political-ideological terms, that is, in securing the firmness of the Russian-dominated realm. In Argentina and many other civilized lands, authoritarian governments much less effectively structured than the Soviet government have been able to retain power for long periods despite multiple failures. But, as a student of the Soviet elite has concluded, "No political system can be considered healthy when it lacks an effective and sure means for circulating the political elite and promoting younger individuals into the elite stratum. The Soviet system has never developed and institutionalized means for circulating elites other than the use of terror. The data we have examined suggest that this failure is resulting in an aging political elite that is unwilling to release the reins

---

[7]"Reflections on the Future of the Soviet System," *Russian Review* (Vol. 26, No. 2, April, 1967), p. 108.

[8]As contended by Zvi Gitelman, "Political Development in Eastern Europe," *Newsletter of Comparative Communism* (Vol. V, No. 3, May, 1972), p. 19.

of power."[9] There is an increasing contradiction between the modernizing society, with an increasingly educated, urbanized, and affluent population, and the incoherent, basically primitive allocation of power.[10] This implies decreasing political effectiveness, which can probably be observed already in a number of aspects, including the inability of the police to repress dissenting opinion as fully as they did a decade ago, not to speak of in Stalin's day, and the widely attested growth of petty corruption. Political underdevelopment may become increasingly burdensome on economic and cultural development.

The lack of a regular way of conferring and withdrawing supreme authority troubles other countries of the Marxist-Leninist mold, such as China. Mao twice appointed successors, Liu Shao-ch'i and Lin Piao, even consecrating the latter's status in the party constitution; but both times the arrangements were disrupted, apparently because of the kind of conflict that frequently arises between an aging autocrat and the impatient heir. In 1972, the heir-apparent of 78-year-old Mao was Chou En-lai, age 74, and number three in the heirarchy seemed to be armed forces chief Yeh Chien-ying, age 73. At the same time, the high echelons of the regime were riddled with vacancies: 15 of the 21 positions on the Politburo (as well as the four alternate posts), three of five seats in the Standing Committee of the Politburo, perhaps half of 30 cabinet minister posts, the headship of state, a large but undeterminable number of seats on the Central Committee were all unfilled at that time. Apparently the advancement of new and younger men to top positions was feared, lest the veterans of the Long March be pushed aside. Chou indicated however, to American newspaper editors in October 1972, that a collective leadership might follow Mao. In Yugoslavia, too, Tito has attempted to engineer the sequence that has occurred of its own accord in the Soviet Union: on May 25, 1972, on the occasion of his 80th birthday, he arranged that a collective presidency of the Yugoslav party would succeed him.

The problem of Soviet leadership is complicated by the fact that it is not acknowledged. Even those who launched the revolution did not consider the issue to be one of leadership: instead they attributed the vices of tsardom entirely to its class structure rather than to the institution itself. The Bolsheviks sought to make a new social order, not a political constitution, and to institute a rough-hewn "dictatorship of the proletariat" to complete the transformation of society. Their aim, in the Russian revolutionary tradition, was not to limit government, but to obtain control of it themselves, and either turn its injustice into justice, or abolish it entirely and replace it with a utopia of anarchistic freedom. The Marxist vision was one of a nonpolitical future society, and its entire approach thereby inhibited consideration of the problem of leadership. In the Marxist view, government was inherently dictatorship by the ruling class, which owned the means of production, and what mattered was to gain class control of the economy. It sufficed that the revolutionaries represented the class of the future and inaugurated the era of socialism. Marxism is not a political but an antipolitical theory.

Since the beginning of Lenin's leadership, there has been no apparent recognition that troubles may be caused, not by minor faults of organization or individual defects

---

[9]Robert E. Blackwell, Jr., "Career Development in the Soviet Obkom Elite: A Conservative Trend," *Soviet Studies* (Vol. 24, No. 1, July 1972), p. 39.

[10]This inharmony is stressed by Zvi Gitelman, "Power and Authority in Eastern Europe," in Chalmers Johnson, ed., *Change in Communist Systems* (Stanford, California: Stanford University Press, 1968), p. 240.

of character, but by unchecked power; there has been no acknowledgment of any need for institutional arrangements controlling the supreme rulership. There has been no public discussion of the means by which anyone has achieved and maintained power.[1] Thus is it assumed that Lenin's primacy was simply the result of his phenomenal virtues. Nor have the means by which subsequent leaders obtained and administered their power been questioned in retrospect. Indeed, even at the height of de-Stalinization, there was no inquiry into Stalin's methods of wielding control, and it was never suggested that his power should have been legally restrained. Neither have the maneuverings of Khrushchev and other subsequently discredited personages been subjected to later scrutiny—not even those alleged as ill-intentioned or anti-Marxist. It thus follows that the means by which Brezhnev and his followers came into power, and their title to authority, are not conceivable subjects of inquiry. In accord with general Soviet approaches, there is no recognition of any legitimate political contest, only an assumption that the party carries out its mission according to the precepts of scientific socialism and that its servants, "the worthiest of the worthy," enjoy authority in accord with their merits and dedication to the cause.

Soviet leaders cannot permit inquiry into their ways of power without encouraging questioning of their legitimacy. Even if they were prepared to consider limitation of their own power, in the absence of free journalism and criticism from outside, they would lack materials for reevaluation. Nor are there independent groups capable of pressing upon the leadership the need for acceptance of restraints. In comparison, the tsarist regime had the advantage of having established a way of changing ministers who had outlived their usefulness (at least in the eyes of the tsar), and of permitting much more discussion and analysis of its institutions.

Reform in this fundamental is a potential threat to the Soviet system. The Soviet Union must be exceptionally fearful of political division because it stands for control by a Russian minority of a synthetic agglomeration of diverse nations. Splitting of power is the basic and necessary condition for its restriction, that is, its regularization; but nothing is more of an anathema to the Communist Party of the Soviet Union. Constitutionalism flows out of pluralism; the more chaotic a society is, the more capable it is of instituting regular methods of changing leadership. It is a virtue of multiparty or representative government that, although misguided public opinion may check or pick the leaders, there are at least orderly and regular ways of selecting them and turning them out.

[11]Academician Andrei D. Sakharov in his memorandum to the Central Committee asked for open selection of cadres and elections wherein the number of candidates exceeds the number of posts to be filled, but he did not touch upon the more sensitive question of how top leaders are to be chosen. Memorandum dated March 5, 1971, published by the *New York Times,* August 18, 1972, p. 29.

14

The Structure of Chinese Leadership Politics

Richard C. Thornton

The past decade has witnessed a general advancement in comparative studies of communism. Yet, in comparing the conceptual development of the Soviet-East European and Chinese Communist fields, one is struck by the peculiarly arrested state of the Chinese side. By comparison, the "Kremlinologists" have produced a veritable storehouse of analytical tools with which they have contributed to the explanation of the nature and functioning of the Soviet political process and Soviet-East European interrelationship.[1] Relatively little conceptual development is discernible in the China field. In this brief essay on comparative developments in the study of communism, I will attempt to compare the concepts which Western scholars have evolved to analyze the politics of the Communist world, account for different approaches, and analyze Chinese political history to determine the most meaningful approach. I speak of the nature and functioning of the political process in a restricted sense—the ways in which leaders interact, how political positions are attained and maintained, and, in general, the structure of leadership politics in the Communist world.

Soviet Studies

In 1964 an important debate reached its climax in the field of Soviet studies over the nature of the Soviet political process. Two schools of thought, which may be termed the stable-dictatorship and constant-conflict schools, represented basically different approaches to the study of post-Stalinist leadership politics in the Soviet Union.[2]

The stable-dictatorship school argued that, once a succession crisis had been resolved, the victorious leader assumed the position of a Stalinist dictator without the dead leader's terror apparatus. The concept posited a two-stage development of the Soviet political process, each stage qualitatively different from the other. During the

From Richard C. Thornton, "The Structure of Communist Politics," *World Politics* (Vol. XXIV, No. 4, July 1972), pp. 498–517. [Reprinted with permission from the publisher.]

[1]The most recent attempt to bring together these analytical concepts is by Sidney I. Ploss, ed., *The Soviet Political Process: Aims, Techniques, and Examples of Analysis* (Waltham, Mass.: Ginn, 1971).

[2]For a summary and bibliography of the debate, see Carl A. Linden, *Khrushchev and the Soviet Leadership, 1957–1964* (Baltimore, Maryland: The Johns Hopkins Press, 1966), pp. 2–7.

succession crisis, conflict over power and policy raged, but, once a victor emerged, a qualitative change took place in the political process, bringing stability to the top leadership. In the second stage a united leadership ruled; conflict no longer occurred at the top but among subordinates, who vied for the favor of the leader.

The stable-dictatorship school assumed the existence of a totalitarian, political monolith. Under such an assumption, the leader was above challenge, and policy became the product of the leader's decree rather than the result of internal pressure and conflict. This school of thought emphasized the formal structure of power which, by definition, gave the leader the necessary authority to ensure his preeminent position and the execution of his policies. The elementary flaw in this conception was the inability to account for the renewal of struggle within the leadership once the stability stage was reached. If the victor were above challenge, how was one to explain repeated challenges to apparent victors? The fall of Khrushchev raised serious doubts about the validity of this concept in explaining the nature and workings of the Soviet political process.

The constant-conflict school, as the term indicates, viewed conflict among the ruling group as a constant factor in Soviet political life. In this conception, Soviet politics was dynamic and unstable, with political struggle shaping Soviet institutions and policies. The accent being on power and policy, a Soviet leader's political position was a delicately balanced combination of factors rather than an assumed entity. Factors which determined a leader's strength were the ever-changing conditions of his political machine, coalitions with others in the leadership who represented political and organizational interests of their own, and the success or failure of the policies he pursued. Ultimately, a leader's power depended upon the extent to which he was able, by virtue of his position, policies, and organization, to reconcile or control the divergent political interests of other leaders. The formal structure of power was considered as only one element in this matrix—the barometer of his success. This school viewed the concept of totalitarianism as essential for understanding the psychological outlook of a Communist leadership and as helping to explain a leader's policies toward society, but hardly adequate for explaining the way in which politics is played within the leadership itself.

The underlying conceptual basis of the constant-conflict school is the theory of games. Communist politics is best described in terms of an n-person game of shifting coalitions under changing circumstances. Theoretically, three kinds of alignments are possible. First there may be a one-person outcome (Stalin's reign most closely approximates this). Second, two groups may coalesce to form a two-person outcome (the current coalition of Brezhnev and Kosygin). Finally, there is the pure n-person outcome with each on his own against the others (a highly unstable situation of "collective leadership" which eventually evolves into some variation of the two-person outcome). The most important possibility is the second, which involves the formation of coalitions. Each player must assume that a coalition may be formed against him and he must therefore attempt to form one himself. This may be the unwritten law of survival in Communist politics: Combine or risk defeat by a rival combination.

Over time, circumstances affect the fortunes of the players and therefore the strength of the coalitions. It is always in the interest, but not always within the capability, of the players to prevent any one of them from achieving complete victory—the one-person outcome. (In the Soviet case, the one-person outcome—the basis of the stable-dictatorship concept—appears to have been ruled out by the mutual consent of Stalin's successors when they disposed of Beria and established collective control over the police apparatus. Control over the secret police is perhaps the decisive element necessary to maintain the one-person outcome.) It remains the ideal solution for all players for which all strive and against which all must guard. The concept of bargaining and pay-offs is implicit here. The players attempt to improve their positions by offering payoffs for support. The player in the dominant position strives to retain and improve that position, offering payoffs to other players, while those outside attempt to build a co-alition capable of challenging the incumbent leadership. The advantage, of course, lies with those in power, but the result is an unstable balance of contending forces.

Such is the general theory of Communist politics that underlies the constant-conflict school. Application of the theory has led to a greater appreciation of the kinds of payoffs, both positive and negative, that are possible in a Communist political system. It has drawn attention to the political effects of institutional, organizational, and ideological change, and to the decisive importance of the structure of power.

Chinese Communist Studies

Something very much like the stable-dictatorship conception underlies virtually all analyses of Chinese Communist politics. The pervasiveness of this concept is not im-mediately apparent because of the existence of a seemingly wide variety of interpre-tations of the role of Mao Tse-tung. But whether one conceives of Mao Tse-tung as a beneficent dictator, revolutionary romantic, cruel despot, aging leader craving for revo-lutionary immortality, or master social engineer seeking the rejuvenation and per-petuation of Chinese society's revolutionary élan, each concept is firmly rooted in the initial assumption of the Chinese Communist political system as a stable, totalitarian dictatorship.[3] Even the cataclysmic Great Proletarian Cultural Revolution failed to foster an alternative analytical concept, although a certain awareness of conceptual in-adequacy is becoming increasingly apparent.[4] In a very real sense, the field has been characterized by the application of Butterfield's "whig" principle of exclusion, by which all focus is on Mao Tse-tung as leader of a highly unified party apparatus, making the troublesome task of examining Chinese Communist history in all its complexity unnecessary.

Although they are similar, the origins of the stable-dictatorship conception for the China field are more complex than for the Russian, the former being rooted in two beliefs about China and communism. First is the "uniqueness" of China's Confucian heritage. A stable, Confucianist social organization gave China a distinction not shared by other societies. Aside from the question of the extent to which contemporary China's social organization is residually "Confucianist" or stable, Communist China is obviously unique in many ways—but not decisively so in its political system. Social organization must not be confused with political organization.[5] Second is the assumption of a mono-

---

[3]Respectively, Benjamin I. Schwartz, "The Reign of Virtue: Some Broad Perspectives on Leader and Party in the Cultural Revolution," *China Quarterly*, No. 35 (July–September 1968), pp. 1–17; Stuart Schram, "The Man and His Doctrines," *Problems of Communism*, XV (September–October 1966), 1–7; Richard L. Walker, *China Under Communism: The First Five Years* (New Haven 1955); Robert Jay Lifton, *Revolutionary Immortality* (New York 1968); Tang Tsou, "Revolution, Reintegra-tion, and Crisis in Communist China: A Framework for Analysis," in Ping-ti Ho and Tang Tsou, eds., *China in Crisis* (Chicago 1968), Vol. I, Book 1, pp. 277–347.

[4]See Parris H. Chang, "Research Notes on the Changing Loci of Decision in the Chinese Com-munist Party," *China Quarterly* (No. 44, October–December 1970), pp. 169–94.

[5]I am not concerned in this essay with the question of the extent of integration between the two, or with social organization, but with the workings of the political system among the leadership.

lithic, totalitarian political system, based on what can perhaps best be described as the cult of Mao Tse-tung and the Chinese Communist Party. However, I believe that to assume an "integrated" leadership based on a Communist Party led by a charismatic Mao is a fundamental misreading of the nature of Chinese Communist politics. To assume unity of leadership and to ignore or to minimize differences as mere expressions of opinion are among the most serious errors a student of Communist politics can make. In studying Communist China, they lead to a focus on the development of the thought of Mao Tse-tung instead of on the system as a whole. This, in turn, leads directly to "oriental whiggism."

The resultant conception of the Chinese Communist political system as a stable dictatorship bears the following outlines. Mao won a prolonged struggle for leadership of the party during the prerevolutionary period, assuming the role of a Stalin-like dictator, who, however, generally abjured the use of terror and force, particularly in regard to early opponents within the party. Since the establishment of the Chinese People's Republic, Mao has been sitting atop a highly integrated, stable party elite. Conflict, if admitted to be serious, was the result of actions by "anti-party" elements (and therefore an aberration from the norm), or by conscious design of Mao himself to "test" the loyalty of his subordinates. Some have gone so far as to assert that the Great Proletarian Cultural Revolution itself was Mao's grandest "test."[6] The elementary flaw in this conception, as in its Soviet counterpart, lies in the inability to explain, in satisfying terms, the eruption of conflict and the breakdown of stability.

What I propose to do in the remainder of this essay is to apply the constant-conflict concept to what is considered to be the most stable period of Chinese Communist history, the first decade. I hope to demonstrate that, far from being an "integrated monolith," Chinese leadership politics exhibited continuous conflict, that several groups vied for political power and advancement, and that Mao Tse-tung, contrary to the dominant impression that he stands above the political struggle, has been deeply immersed in it from the beginning as the leader of one, albeit the dominant one, of these groups.

Primitive Communism, 1949–1954

On the eve of victory, the Chinese Communists were an entity comprising essentially five large, relatively independent armies and a highly developed central party apparatus. Of course, in each of the army systems there existed a party command structure. In fact, the commanders of each army were both military and party leaders. In command of the field armies were: Ho Lung, First Field Army (some sources state it was P'eng Teh-huai); Liu Po-ch'eng, Second Field Army; Ch'en Yi, Third Field Army; Lin Piao, Fourth Field Army. The Fifth Field Army, or North-China Field Army, was presumably under central command.

The initial administrative structure of the Chinese People's Republic derived directly from the military situation as it had evolved during the civil war. At that time there were seven "liberated" areas, each of which was ruled by a military control committee: Northeast, Inner Mongolia, East China, Northwest, North China, Chungyuan, and Chiungya, a small area in Kwangtung province. With the occupation of China after the defeat of the Nationalists, this schema was extended to cover the entire country.

---

[6]See Harry Gelman, "Mao and the Permanent Purge," *Problems of Communism*, XV (November–December 1966), 2–14, and Philip Bridgman, "Mao's Cultural Revolution: Origins and Development," *China Quarterly*, No. 29 (January–March 1967), pp. 1–35.

Inner Mongolia became an autonomous area; North China was placed directly under the Peking government; the Northeast (Manchuria) and East China (Shantung and the east coast) became "Great Areas." Chungyuan was made a province and renamed P'ingyuan, and Chiungya was amalgamated into Kwangtung province. As troops moved outward from the central areas, the Northwest, Southwest, and Central South Great Areas were established. The status of the Great Areas, of which there were five, was formalized in three laws promulgated by the central government: The Organic Law of the People's Central Government (September 27, 1949), the Cabinet Ordinance on Appointments and Dismissals (November 28, 1949), and the Organic Law of the Great Administrative Areas' Governments (December 16, 1949).

The field armies occupied regions which roughly corresponded to the Great Areas, but each army's power position was balanced by a trade-off of military units with other field armies. This arrangement was temporarily upset by the Korean War, in which two-thirds of the People's Liberation Army units eventually saw action, but was restored afterwards. The system of counterbalancing field armies bore the following general outlines. Lin Piao's Fourth Field Army units were assigned to the Northeast and Central South. All units of the North China Field Army, except three corps, were returned to the North China command (Peking) after the war. The remaining three corps were assigned to the Southwest, East, and Northeast regional commands. Ho Lung's First Field Army returned to Sinkiang, but one unit was assigned to Central South. Liu Po-ch'eng's Second Field Army returned to the Southwest, but one unit remained in the Northeast and two others were reassigned to Central South. Of Ch'en Yi's Third Field Army, six corps returned to East China, but one corps remained in the Northeast, while two others were assigned to North China. The placement of these units remained stable until the outbreak of the Great Proletarian Cultural Revolution.[7]

The Peking governmental structure was initially established in September 1949 with the promulgation of the Organic Law and Common Program of the Chinese People's Political Consultative Conference and the Organic Law of the Central People's Government of the People's Republic of China. The Government Council, headed by the Chairman, Mao Tse-tung, and six Vice-Chairmen, Chu Teh, Liu Shao-ch'i, Kao Kang, Soong Ching-ling, Li Chi-shen, and Chang Lan, held supreme state power. Below the Government Council stood five additional organs, all presumably equal in rank—the Cabinet, Military Council, State Planning Committee, Supreme Court, and Procurator-General's office. These five organs functioned directly under the Government Council and wielded not only executive but legislative power.

Theoretically, the Government Council held the power of appointment in the Great Areas, but in practice the regional military commanders were vested with the authority of the central government. The Great Area governments for the most part functioned independently of the central government apparatus. The only direct link between the two was in the Northeast, where Kao Kang held concurrent party, state, and military posts in both the region and central government. Of course, the party's own organizations served to ensure a continuity of policy, but the party's presence varied according to region. In 1950, before the Chinese Communists entered the Korean War, the distribution of party members was roughly as follows: Of a total of 5.8 million, one million were in the PLA; 3.4 million nonmilitary members were in the Northeast, East, and

[7]William Whitson, "The Field Army in Chinese Communist Military Politics," *China Quarterly*, No. 37 (January–March 1969), pp. 1–30.

North China; only 1.4 million were in the vast areas of Central South, Southwest, and Northwest.[8]

It was during the Korean War, when the Great Areas were weakened by the transfer of troops, that the party's organizations in the Areas expanded considerably. The party was organized along the same geographical lines as the Great Area governments, and was directed from regional bureaus. From the start, tension was evident between center and region. For example, as early as March 1950, Peking transferred the taxing power of the Great Area governments to itself, but, because of resistance by regional leaders as well as an inadequately functioning central collection system, part of this authority was returned to the Great Areas the following year.[9] The first step taken by the central government to abolish the Great Areas altogether occurred at the height of the Korean War. In November 1952, Peking decreed that civil rather than military rule should prevail over the Great Areas.[10] At this time the titles changed from Great Areas Peoples' Governments to Great Area Administrative Councils subordinate to Peking. The ministries of the Great Area governments were also reduced in status to departments or offices, some being removed from regional control entirely and placed under the jurisdiction of the Ministries in Peking.[11]

Institutional Regeneration, 1954–1958

The year 1954 is not the best dividing line for the decade 1949–1958. Critical events that affected the second half of the decade had their origins before 1954, but it is from 1954 onward that the almost continuous reorganization of party, state, military, and economic structures from the national to the provincial levels and below took place. These structural changes directly affected the political fortunes of the highest-ranking leaders.

In January 1953, it was announced that a People's Congress would be convened at an early (but unspecified) date to approve the first constitution of the Chinese People's Republic.[12] That same month a drafting committee was set up under the chairmanship of Mao Tse-tung. The congress actually convened over a year and a half later (September 1954); the delay indicates disagreement among the top leaders over the form and substance of the proposed reorganization of the state structure.

By 1953, if not earlier, several high-ranking leaders had become disaffected with Mao's plans and formed a coalition against him and others in top positions. This was the so-called Kao-Jao "antiparty" alliance. As we now know, the coalition consisted of more than Kao Kang and Jao Shu-shih. Numbered among the supporters of Kao and Jao, with varying degrees of commitment, were Chu Teh, P'eng Teh-huai, T'an Chen-lin, Chen Pei-hsien, possibly Tao Chu, several other important figures in the Northeast party and state organizations, and certain members of the Soviet leadership.

The Kao-Jao episode was a matter of coalition politics in action. Several groups, based on the military systems and party organizations, vied for positions in the soon-to-be-reorganized state structure. Mao's group was only one, but clearly the dominant one, in this political constellation. As chairman of the constitution drafting committee,

---

[8]*Jen Min Jih Pao* [People's Daily], July 1, 1950.
[9]*China News Analysis*, No. 43, July 9, 1954, p. 5.
[10]*Hsin Hua Yüeh Pao* [Hsinhua Monthly] (December 1952), p. 3.
[11]*Ibid.*
[12]*China News Analysis*, No. 41, June 25, 1954, p. 2.

Mao had a strong voice in shaping the future structure of the state. Reorganization of the state structure implied changes for the military and party structures and, in fact, greatly affected them.

The main outlines of the struggle within the leadership now seem clear. A new state structure was to be built at the expense of the Great Areas and the military establishment. The entire apparatus would become centralized, resulting in fewer command positions at the regional level. Competition for positions in the central apparatus was therefore keen. Mao sought to undercut Kao's growing power in the Northeast, possibly by excluding him from a top position in the Center. Kao had similar intentions regarding Mao, seeking to persuade or pressure him to relinquish one of his leadership positions—either the top party or state post. The later party resolution condemning the "antiparty alliance" claimed that Kao and Jao, by conspiratorial means, sought "to split our party and to overthrow the leading core—the long-tested Central Committee of the party headed by Comrade Mao Tse-tung—with the aim of seizing the supreme power of the party and the State."[13]

Although the party resolution condemning Kao and Jao was published in 1955, action against Kao had been taken much earlier, probably some time after January 1954. From that date on Kao's whereabouts were unknown.[14] In February 1954, at the Central Committee's Fourth Plenum, Liu Shao-ch'i gave the first official hint that a crisis existed when he said that there were those who "looked on their own region or department as 'personal property or an independent kingdom'" and charged that "those who cause dissension and stir up factionalism will be 'fought mercilessly'; they will be subjected to severe punitive action and will eventually be expelled from the party."[15] By this time Kao and Jao had probably already been defeated.

To the extent that the events can now be reconstructed, Kao had called for the replacement of several top leaders. His choice for the chairmanship of the state post, the one Mao would most likely have given up if necessary, was Chu Teh, hero of the revolutionary war and founder of the Red Army, who was known to be dissatisfied with his subordinate status under Mao. (In 1959 Lin Piao accused Chu Teh, among other things, of wanting to become Chairman in place of Mao.) Kao himself had planned to fill two other positions: General Secretary or Vice-Chairman of the Central Committee of the Party and premiership of the State Council.[16]

To support his claim for advancement, Kao had elaborated the "theory of two parties," the party of the revolutionary bases and army and the party of the white areas (those controlled by the Nationalists).[17] He argued that the party was the creation of the army and that therefore those who represented the party of the revolutionary bases should receive greater consideration for positions of leadership than those who represented the party of the white areas. This interpretation of party history struck directly at Liu Shao-ch'i and Chou En-lai, who had spent much of the war years in the white areas and who occupied the very posts to which Kao aspired.

---

[13]*Jen Min Jih Pao,* April 10, 1955.

[14]The last official mention of Kao Kang occurs on January 1, 1954, when his name headed the list of guests at a banquet feting the visiting Soviet Minister of Metallurgy, I. F. Tevosvan. *Survey of the China Mainland Press,* No. 719, January 1–4, 1954, p. 18.

[15]*Jen Min Jih Pao,* February 18, 1954.

[16]*Ibid.,* p. 6.

[17]*Ibid.*

Kao had also managed to obtain at least the tacit support of P'eng Teh-huai, the hero of the Korean War. (Some charges appeared during the Cultural Revolution which actually attributed to P'eng the leadership of the Kao-Jao coalition.) But he had failed to obtain the support of one other key military man, Lin Piao. Lin declined to support Kao and Jao, siding instead with Mao, Liu, and Chou; for this he was well rewarded. At the meeting which accepted the resolution condemning the opposition coalition, Lin (and Teng Hsiao-p'ing, about whom more will be said below) was elected to the Politburo in the twelfth position (of thirteen).[18] Later that year he was promoted to Marshal, along with nine others, including P'eng Teh-huai who had evidently shifted away from Kao's group in time.

The reasons for Lin's decision to support the Mao group against Kao are undoubtedly numerous, but the history of Lin's relations with Kao provides part of the answer. Kao had become secretary of the Central Committee's Northeastern Party Bureau in 1940, but until 1948 played a subordinate role in that area's affairs. The land reform carried out after 1945 in Manchuria was actually the work of Lin Piao, not Kao Kang. It was only after the collapse of the Nationalist forces in 1948, when, late that year, Lin moved his troops southward toward T'iensin and Peking, that Kao assumed control of the area. Even though part of Lin's forces returned to Manchuria after 1949 (and part were assigned to Kwangtung), Kao remained in command.[19] The elimination of Kao Kang was therefore in Lin Piao's direct interest.

Teng Hsiao-p'ing also played a role in the defeat of the Kao-Jao coalition. Teng led the attack against Kao and Jao at the meeting in March 1955, for which he was promoted, but had evidently opposed this group earlier. Teng's role centered around his opposition to Kao's demands for preferential treatment of the Northeast in the allocation of economic resources. Kao argued that the Northeast had a "special character," being more economically advanced, and therefore deserved high priority.[20] This was in opposition to the view of the Mao group which felt that, while the Manchurian industrial base was to be maintained, as was the East China base, higher priority should be given to North [Central] and West Central China for the industrial development of those parts of the country. Here is one probable reason for Jao Shu-shih's support of Kao Kang, for Jao was chairman of East China as well as a member of the State Planning Committee of which Kao was chairman. In Mao's view, East-China, too, was to receive fewer resources relative to other areas.[21]

The contest over resource allocation in the State Planning Committee suggests that that body was one of the principal organizational vehicles for the Kao-Jao coalition. The subsequent history of the Committee as an organization, as well as that of its members, strongly supports this hypothesis. Membership in the Committee included Kao Kang, Chairman; Teng Tzu-hui, Vice-Chairman; Lin Piao, Jao Shu-shih, Ch'en Yün, Teng Hsiao-p'ing, Li Fu-ch'un, Po I-po, P'eng Chen, Huang K'o-ch'eng, Liu Lan-tao, Hsi Chung-hsün, Chang Hsi, An Chih-wen, Ma Hung, Hsüeh Mu-ch'iao, and

---

[18]*China News Analysis,* No. 80, April 22, 1955, p. 2.

[19]*Ibid.,* p. 6.

[20]*Jen Min Jih Pao,* April 5, 1955.

[21]Jao Shu-shih was also Director of the Organization Department of the Central Committee from 1953, and was accused of having "actively carried out activities to split the Party" in his capacity as Director. Afterwards, the Organization Department was dissolved and replaced by a Control Department.

P'eng Teh-huai.[22] P'eng Teh-huai's appointment to the Committee seems largely to have been honorific, since he was in Korea at this time.

Mao Tse-tung was not a member of the Committee, but managed to obtain sufficient support from its members to defeat the Kao-Jao group there. If promotions of Committee members can be interpreted as a political reward for supporting Mao, then it is clear that the majority of the Committee membership sided with Mao. The promotions of Lin Piao, Teng Hsiao-p'ing, and P'eng Teh-huai have already been noted. Huang K'o-ch'eng was named a General of the People's Liberation Army. P'eng Chen became Mayor of Peking. That same month, January 1953, Teng Tzu-hui, Ch'en Yün, Po I-po, Hsi Chung-hsün, and Liu Lan-tao all were named to the constitution-drafting committee with Mao Tse-tung.[23] In addition, Ch'en Yün became Chairman of the Economic and Finance Committee of the Cabinet, an organization which replaced, in function, the State Planning Committee when the state structure was reorganized in 1954. The State Planning Committee itself was disestablished and reorganized as the State Planning Commission under the Cabinet, losing its formerly independent and equal status. Li Fu-ch'un was named chairman of the Commission.[24] By this reckoning, at least eleven of the seventeen members of the Committee supported Mao Tse-tung against the Kao-Jao group.

The Soviet Role

The issue of resource allocation leads directly to the question of the Soviet role. Stalin had apparently followed the policy of concentrating Soviet aid in the Northeast, possibly in the hope of being able to influence decisions in the area close to Soviet borders. Consequently, he had dealt directly with Kao Kang as well as with Mao Tse-tung. During the initial negotiations for the Sino-Soviet treaty, Kao had preceded Mao to Moscow and signed a separate agreement between the USSR and the Manchurian People's Government. Clearly, Kao permitted the Soviets to exercise a strong influence in Manchuria. Until 1952, the Russians administered the Manchurian railway system and directed the reconstruction of the area's industrial base. Hence, the charge that Kao had maintained "illicit relations with foreign countries" had considerable substance from Mao's point of view.

Stalin's death affected policy toward Manchuria drastically and Kao Kang's position fatally. In the struggle over succession which evolved after the dictator's death, both Malenkov and Khrushchev strove to obtain the support of the Chinese Communists for their respective candidacies. Malenkov apparently sought to perpetuate the Stalinist policy of favoring Manchuria. Khrushchev, in his drive for the support of Mao Tse-tung, recognized that Stalin's Manchurian policy was a liability and turned that realization to political advantage.

In the early months after Stalin's death the Chinese supported Malenkov. In March 1953, in an article eulogizing Stalin, Mao expressed his support for Malenkov, saying "we profoundly believe that the Central Committee of the Communist Party of the Soviet Union and the Soviet Government, headed by Comrade Malenkov, will certainly be able to continue the work of Comrade Stalin."[25] Over the course of the following

---

[22]*Survey of the China Mainland Press,* No. 453, November 15–17, 1952, p. 20.

[23]Biographical data were obtained from *Chung Kung Jen Ming Lü* [Who's Who in Communist China] (Taipei 1967).

[24]*China News Analysis,* No. 80, April 22, 1955, p. 4.

[25]*Pravda,* March 10, 1953.

year, however, the Chinese shifted their support from Malenkov to Khrushchev. An important step was the Khrushchev-Bulganin trip to Peking in September 1954, during which a wide-ranging aid agreement was concluded. The Soviet Union extended a loan of 520 million rubles and raised the number of industrial enterprises it was to build for China from 141 to 156. The Soviet Union was to assist in the construction of two railroad lines linking the two countries, one through Outer Mongolia and one through Sinkiang. Most important, Khrushchev agreed to withdraw Soviet troops from the Port Arthur area by the following May and to abrogate Soviet interests in the four Sino-Soviet joint-stock companies that had been formed in 1950.[26]

Economic assistance undoubtedly helped Khrushchev to gain the support of the Chinese, in particular the Mao group; but it was his position on strategic defense policy, coupled with his willingness to withdraw from Manchuria (and thereby from support of Kao Kang!), which decisively turned them away from Malenkov. Malenkov, at the nineteenth Party Congress in 1952, following Stalin's initiation of the "soft line" toward the West, had asserted that "in peaceful competition with capitalism the socialist economic system will prove its superiority over the capitalistic system more and more vividly year by year."[27] After Stalin's death, Malenkov stated that a nuclear world war would result in the destruction of world civilization and therefore there were "no objective impediments" to the improvement of Soviet-American relations. Shortly thereafter, he moved toward a settlement of the Korean conflict, saying that a "new epoch" had begun in which he saw China as a "mighty stabilizing factor" in Asia, supported by Soviet deterrent strength. Malenkov's "new course" also affected Soviet domestic policy. The easing of tension abroad would permit improvements at home. No longer would heavy industry receive top priority. Now light industries and food industries would develop "at the same rate as heavy industry."

Khrushchev, although he later championed "peaceful coexistence," took an almost diametrically opposite position from Malenkov early in 1954. The Soviet Union, he said, should not merely avoid war but should actively deter it through a strong military posture. A nuclear world war would result only in the destruction of capitalism, not world civilization. He saw the Sino-Soviet relationship as a "powerful factor in the struggle for peace in the Far East." Domestically, Khrushchev called for continued stress on heavy over light industry, at the expense of the consumer sector.

It was obvious which of these two positions Mao and his followers preferred. The Malenkov position of pure deterrence implied acceptance of the status quo, while Khrushchev's hard line indicated a far greater willingness to honor a strategic commitment to China. Early in 1955, Mao publicly endorsed Khrushchev's position that nuclear war would not mean the destruction of the world but only of capitalism; the following year, on the eve of the Twentieth Party Congress, Mao said in a telegram that "the great successes of the USSR in foreign and domestic policy in recent years are inseparable from the correct leadership of the well-tried Central Committee of the CPSU headed by Comrade Khrushchev."[28] But this gets us somewhat ahead of the story.

---

[26]*Sovetsko-Kitaiskie Otnoshenniia 1917–1957, sbornik dokumentov* [Sino-Soviet Relations 1917–1957, a collection of documents] (Moscow 1959), pp. 284–308.

[27]Georgi M. Malenkov, "Report of the Central Committee," in Leo Gruliow, ed., *Current Soviet Policies: The Documentary Record of the Nineteenth Party Congress and the Reorganization After Stalin's Death* (New York: Praeger, 1953), Vol. 1, pp. 105–106.

[28]George Paloczi-Horvath, *Khrushchev: The Making of a Dictator* (Boston: Little, Brown, 1960), p. 193.

The Khrushchev-Bulganin trip to Peking, in September of 1954, came at what was probably the lowest point of Mao's power up to that time. The National People's Congress had just ended, resulting in the reorganization not only of the state but of the military, economic, and party structures, and in the radical redistribution of political power among the Chinese leaders. On the state level Mao had lost considerable power as evidenced by the fact that, at the Congress, he opened and closed the ceremonies with a few words, but gave no major report.

Until 1954, as official head of the Central People's Government, Mao had had the power of "(1) enacting and interpreting the laws, promulgating decrees and supervising their execution. . . . (2) annulling or revising any decisions or orders of the Government Administrative Council not in conformity with the laws. . . . (3) ratifying . . . treaties and agreements . . . with foreign countries. . . . (4) dealing with questions of war and peace, appointing the Premier, members of the Cabinet and all other important officials."[29]

Under the new structure, as Chairman of the Chinese People's Republic, Mao's powers were severely limited by the Standing Committee, whose chairman was Liu Shao-ch'i.[30] Mao could promulgate laws and decrees only "in accordance with the decisions of the Congress, or, when not in session, of its Standing Committee" (art. 40 of the constitution). He could not annul or revise any decision or order of any government organ. He could ratify treaties with foreign states only "in accordance with the decisions of the Standing Committee" (art. 41). He did not have independent power to make appointments to any post.

The Chairman of the Republic "appoints or removes the Premier, Vice-Premiers, Ministers . . . in accordance with the decision of the Congress or its Standing Committee." The only power which Mao exercised independently of the Standing Committee was command of the armed forces (art. 42), and this, too, was qualified. Finally, the Chairman of the Republic had no veto power over the decisions of the Congress and its Standing Committee. The Standing Committee enacted decrees, interpreted laws made by the Congress, and supervised the Cabinet, the Supreme Court, and the Prosecutor-General's office. It had the power to annul laws and to appoint Vice-Premiers and Ministers. When the Congress was not in session, the Standing Committee assumed its prerogatives relating to the negotiation of treaties with foreign countries, proclamations of war, and so forth (arts. 31–33).

Essentially, what had taken place in the state reorganization was that the Standing Committee was interposed between Mao and the major administrative organs of the new state structure. The Standing Committee became responsible for supervision of the day-to-day workings of the Cabinet, Defense Council (even though Mao retained command of the armed forces), Supreme Court, Prosecutor-General, and the General Office. In sum, the reorganization of the state severely limited Mao Tse-tung's power.

The military apparatus was also radically restructured. The six military regions were replaced by thirteen smaller ones. The large field armies were broken up, and each of their approximately thirty-five component units was designated a field army and placed directly under control of the newly established (state) Ministry of Defense and (party) Military Affairs Committee. The redesignated military units remained in place, but the many regional commanders and the Marshals (after 1955) were brought to Peking. The military reorganization stripped military, and therefore political, power from

---

[29]Organic Law of the Central People's Government, art. 7; promulgated September 29, 1949.
[30]Organic Law, National People's Congress, art. 20; promulgated September 28, 1954.

regional commands and centralized it in Peking. The restructuring of the state organization also had its effect on the party. When the Great Areas were abolished, the party's regional bureaus were also reorganized, the line of command now running from Peking direct to the party organizations at the provincial level.

As a result of the major restructuring of the Chinese state, military, and party organizations, there was a significant redistribution of political power among the top leaders. Of the few which I have chosen to note in this essay, two were completely removed from authority (Kao Kang and Jao Shu-shih), several others advanced in the new power structure (Lin Piao, Liu Shao-ch'i, Teng Hsiao-p'ing, P'eng Teh-huai), some made no apparent gains (Chou En-lai, Chu Teh), and one suffered a partial eclipse of power but retained a dominant position (Mao Tse-tung). In the next phase, some of those who had supported Mao against the challenge of Kao Kang and had been promoted for their service used their positions to obtain even greater power at Mao's expense. The party's Eighth National Congress, the first to be held since the establishment of the Communist regime, saw a further realignment of political forces and erosion of Mao Tse-tung's position.

Eighth Party Congress, 1956–1958

The first and second sessions of the Eighth Party Congress, convened eighteen months apart (September 1956 and May 1958), revealed several marked power shifts among the top leaders. At the first session, Mao's position as head of the party was seriously weakened ideologically and organizationally. Aside from brief opening remarks to the Congress, Mao made no major address. The important political report was delivered by Liu Shao-ch'i, and the report on the revision of the party constitution by Teng Hsiao-p'ing, the two leaders who had made the most significant gains at this time.

Ideologically, *collective* leadership was emphasized, which was undoubtedly in part a reaction to the de-Stalinization campaign begun at the Twentieth Party Congress of the CPSU [Communist Party of the Soviet Union] earlier that year. At the first session, the Marxist-Leninist basis of the Chinese Communist Party was emphasized, omitting the phrase "Thought of Mao Tse-tung," which had been incorporated into the 1945 party constitution. Organizationally, several key changes took place. The Central Committee was enlarged from sixty-four to ninety-seven members, and the Politburo from thirteen to seventeen, with six candidate members. (There had been no candidate-member category previously.) Two new organizations were established for the Central Committee and Politburo, clearly reflecting the rise in status of Liu and Teng, and the further weakening of Mao.

Liu had assumed the Chairmanship of the Standing Committee of the reorganized state structure in 1954—his payoff for support of Mao against Kao. He now became senior Vice-Chairman of another newly established organ, the Standing Committee of the Party Politburo. Since 1949, Standing Committees had existed only at the provincial level. The first six men in the Politburo comprised the Politburo Standing Committee. They were: Mao, Chairman; Liu, senior Vice-Chairman; Chou En-lai, Chu Teh, Ch'en Yün, and Teng Hsiao-p'ing. The seventh man was Lin Piao, who did not become a member of the Standing Committee until 1958, when altered political circumstances enabled Mao to enlarge the Standing Committee and bring him in. Clearly, if Chu Teh or Ch'en Yün, for instance, had sided with Liu and Teng on any issue, it would have been impossible for Mao to obtain a majority vote.

Teng Hsiao-p'ing was also advanced in rank at the first session. Placed at the head of the Secretariat of the Central Committee, Teng was charged with "attending the daily work of the Central Committee."[31] It is not clear whether the Secretariat of the Central Committee had existed previously or not, but this was a newly assigned function for that body. In any case, at every level from the national down through the provincial, local, and branch levels, there now existed twin party control mechanisms commanded by Liu Shao-ch'i and Teng Hsiao-p'ing.

It was at this time that the decision to establish the first and second lines was made, a decision which apparently relates to the distinction between policy and command. In a speech in October 1966, Mao asserted that it had been his idea to establish the "two lines" so that Liu and Teng could preside over important conferences and take charge of the party's daily operations.[32] Viewed in terms of the conflict hypothesis, Mao's "idea" indicates an attempt to preserve a policy-making prerogative for himself while relinquishing the power of command to Liu and Teng, rather than an attempt to develop some sort of succession mechanism. Mao also charged in the 1966 speech that Liu and Teng had established "independent kingdoms" like Kao and Jao before them, and that for this reason it had been necessary to initiate the Great Proletarian Cultural Revolution. Mao no longer commanded the power to ensure that his policies would be carried out.

Two major developments occurred between the first and second sessions of the Eighth Congress. First, Mao managed to purge the party organizations, particularly at the provincial level. His speech, "On the Correct Handling of Contradictions Among the People," delivered in February 1957, provided the justification for this move by implying that the party could err. Second, following and perhaps accompanying the personnel shifts, the party as a whole assumed direction of the functions of the state organizations. The "rectification campaign," or purge, also permitted Mao to identify, if not eliminate, his opposition and prepare the ground for the second session of the Eighth Party Congress, in May 1958.

The second session of the Eighth Congress convened from May 5 through 23 and had not been preannounced. Its tone differed sharply from that of the first session. The Congress communiqué, carried in the *People's Daily* of May 25, called it a "cheng-feng reform session." Indeed, the expulsions of eight members of provincial party standing committees, two members of provincial party committees, and one member of a provincial party secretariat were announced. The communiqué also noted the existence of "antiparty groups" among the highest ranks of party members in several provinces, and said that several party provincial leaders were under investigation for "regionalistic" and "nationalistic" activities.[33]

At the first session in September 1956, the creation of the Politburo Standing Committee had seen the transfer of power from the Politburo to the Standing Committee in which Mao had been unable to outvote his opponents. At the second session, Mao, presumably as a result of the purge of the provincial party organizations, was able to enlarge the Politburo and the Politburo Standing Committee. Added to the Politburo at this time were K'o Ch'ing-shih, party First Secretary of Shang-hai city; T'an Chen-lin, member of the Central Committee Secretariat; and Li Ching-ch'uan, party First Secretary of Szech'uan province. Lin Piao was added to the Politburo Standing Committee.

---

[31]Mao Tse-tung, speech to the Central Committee Work Conference, October 23, 1966.
[32]*Ibid.*
[33]*Jen Min Jih Pao*, May 25, 1958.

Whether or not the addition of three men affected the power relationship in the Politburo, the addition of Lin Piao to the Politburo Standing Committee gave Mao at least a four-to-three edge in voting in that body, assuming that Mao, Lin, Chou En-lai, and either Ch'en Yün or Chu Teh voted together. This voting edge was sufficient at the second session for Mao to obtain a favorable decision on his program of the three red banners—the General Line, the Communes, and the Great Leap Forward.[34]

However, the almost immediate and obvious failure of the "Great Leap" gave Mao's opponents the necessary political leverage to pry him out of his post as Chairman of the Republic—one of the objectives which Kao Kang and Jao Shu-shih had sought to achieve a few years earlier. It seems clear that Mao did not step down voluntarily and apparently exerted all his efforts in an attempt to garner sufficient support to beat off the challenge at the Sixth Plenary Session of the Eighth Central Committee, which was held in Wuchang from November 28 to December 10, 1958.

The plenum communiqué, issued one week after the close of the session, pointedly noted that Mao had personally called two meetings, one from November 2 to 10 and a second from November 21 to 27, which "prepared for the plenary session."[35] He had evidently not succeeded in convincing the majority that he should not step down. Eighty-four of the ninety-seven regular members of the Central Committee and all of the Politburo attended the session. Eighty-two of the ninety-eight candidate members also attended. According to the communiqué, the "plenary session approved the proposal of Comrade Mao Tse-tung not to stand as candidate for Chairman of the People's Republic of China for the next term of office."[36] From this point on, as Mao said in a recent talk, Liu (who became Chairman of the Chinese People's Republic) and Teng began to treat him as if he were already dead.

Up to this point, the struggle had not been polarized between two "factions." Several groups had contended. By splitting them, pitting one against another, and allying himself with one against another, Mao managed to remain the leader of the single most powerful group, and in overall control. He has never risen above the political struggle; he has always been deeply involved in it. His political strength has been directly related to his ability to build his own political machine and to prevent the consolidation of opposing coalitions.

The policy decision to embark upon the Great Leap program marked an elemental change in the nature of Chinese Communist leadership politics, for it raised crucial issues for the several contending groups. Representing, as it did, the decision to disengage from Soviet economic dominance, the Great Leap policy posed a central question: What should be the nature of the future Sino-Soviet relationship? Purely domestic problems, such as the type of industrialization program and military system, were directly related to this larger issue, which became the touchstone of the developing process of polarization during the sixties. But that story is beyond the scope of this paper.

Conclusions

The major thesis of this essay is that the structure of leadership politics in the Communist world is essentially similar. The idea that a Communist leader can build a

---

[34]*China News Analysis*, No. 231, June 6, 1958, p. 6.

[35]Communiqué of the Sixth Plenary Session of the Eighth Central Committee," December 17, 1958, in Robert R. Bowie and John K. Fairbank, *Communist China 1955–1959, Policy Documents With Analysis* (Cambridge: Harvard University Press, 1962), p. 484.

[36]*Ibid.*

15

Yugoslavia: The Case for a Loyal Opposition under Communism

Barbara Jancar

In Robert A. Dahl's sense of a group or groups opposing the way those controlling government conduct it,[1] opposition has always existed under communism. Historically, both within and without the party, it has lacked organization and has either been liquidated or in some other way totally suppressed. The logic of Communist ideology and Communist rule refused to permit its continued existence. In the West, the problem of opposition in the Communist system has tended to be understood as opposition *to* Communist rule as contrasted to opposition *under* Communist rule. The distinction is important. The first approach suggests rejection of the system *in toto;* the second infers an acceptance of the system and a willingness to work within it for stated objectives and a renewal of the ruling personnel. While some research has been done in applying group theory to Communist political behavior,[2] little or no thought has been directed toward the crucial question in the modification of Communist totalitarian rule: the possibility of a loyal opposition within the system.[3]

From Barbara Jancar, "The Case for a Loyal Opposition under Communism: Czechoslovakia and Yugoslavia," *Orbis* (Vol. XI, No. 2, Summer 1968), pp. 415–440. [Reprinted with permission from the publisher. Editors' Note: This article was written just before the Soviet intervention (1968) that terminated the Czechoslovak experiment, and a few years before the recentralization of party control (early 1970s) in Yugoslavia.]

[1]Robert A. Dahl, *Political Oppositions in Western Democracies* (New Haven: Yale University Press, 1966), p. 1 ff.

[2]Recent studies suggesting the validity of the group theory approach to communist political behavior include: Zbigniew Brzezinski and Samuel P. Huntington, *Political Power: USA/USSR* (New York: Columbia University Press, 1964); Roger Pethybridge, *A Key to Soviet Politics* (New York: Praeger, 1962); Robert C. Tucker, "The Conflict Model," *Problems of Communism,* November–December 1963, pp. 59–61; H. Gordon Skilling, "Interest Groups and Communist Politics," *World Politics,* April 1966, pp. 434–451; Skilling, *Government and Politics in Communist East Europe* (New York: Crowell, 1966); and Sidney I. Ploss, *Conflict and Decision-Making in Soviet Russia* (Princeton: Princeton University Press, 1965).

[3]The one study which requires mention in this connection is Ghita Ionescu's skillful treatment of political dissent and political checks upon the power of the party apparat in the European communist systems in *The Politics of the European Communist States* (London: Weidenfeld and Nicolson, 1967). . . .

This article develops from the premise that the 1960s have given rise to a new constellation of domestic forces in the countries of the Communist bloc, which urges posing the question whether a genuine, political opposition can exist in a Communist state. Because there is an absence of published theoretical material on this subject, it has been necessary to work out a conceptual approach. The standard studies of Western political parties have been useful in delineating the scope of the problem.[4] Dahl's recent study, *Political Oppositions in Western Democracies*, was particularly suggestive. The terminology used in this article to refer to the various conditions of opposition is almost exclusively that developed by Dahl in the closing chapters of his book, where he elaborates a comparative framework of analysis.[5] All the studies, however, are deficient in the most important respect. They are predicated upon viewing the opposition as a legitimately organized political alternative (primarily, a political party), backed by the sanction of law, able to seek its goals and develop strategies through competitive confrontation with the ruling party or parties at the polls, in parliament, or by influencing public opinion through the channels of mass communication. The emerging pattern of opposition within the Communist states differs sharply from its Western counterparts because a dominant one-party system prevails. Yet, although the myth of Communist party unity for the sake of building socialism is still the official credo, the role of certain social and institutional groups in opposing and thereby modifying official policy possesses a similarity to the role of opposition parties in the West. Equally important, in seeking not only to influence government decisions, but to capture political power, the behavior of dissident factions goes beyond that of an interest group to embrace the ultimate in the determination of the conduct of government.

The case countries for the examination of the pattern of opposition under communism will be Czechoslovakia and Yugoslavia. The choice was deliberate. Perhaps nowhere in the Communist world today does the cleavage between the so-called liberal and conservative tendencies within the Communist party seem so severe, and nowhere has the question of the introduction of a party system been as candidly raised in the press. Communists are challenging the traditional Communist acceptance of the party's leading role in society. Moreover, Czechoslovakia appears at last to be embarking upon a course which Yugoslavia has long since taken. Thus, developments in Yugoslavia provide some indication of the kinds of difficulties the Czechs and Slovaks can expect to encounter.

At the risk of oversimplification, the treatment of the topic will focus on three propositions. The first is considered as a given, and is not under investigation here. The other two form the body of the article.

(1) The deviation from the authoritarian structural pattern of a Communist society has become so great in Czechoslovakia and Yugoslavia that it has fundamentally altered the formerly hierarchical relationship between the party and nonparty institutions, making it possible for various groups within the party to play an ongoing opposition role to the ruling party group.

(2) The two most important general conditions for the evolution and maintenance of an opposition within the Communist system are (a) the interaction of specific sub-

---

[4]Reference is made especially to Maurice Duverger, *Political Parties: Their Organization and Activity in a Modern State* (Second revised edition; New York: Barnes and Noble, 1964), and Sigmund Neumann, editor, *Modern Political Parties: Approaches to Comparative Politics* (Chicago: University of Chicago Press, 1956).

[5]Dahl, *Political Oppositions in Western Democracies*, pp. 332–386.

cultures, and (b) the differentiation of economic and social interests as a result of the decentralization of Communist rule pursuant to the recent social and economic reforms. As regards (a), the subcultures may not necessarily be rival ethnic groups. In Czechoslovakia and Yugoslavia, however, tension between the dominant nationalities, the Czechs and Slovaks, and the Serbs, Croats and Slovenes, is perhaps the central political fact today. Differentiation of economic and social interests refers to the emergence of discrete groups capable of influencing decision making: the intellectuals, economists, economic managers, and workers.

(3) The crucial variables in explaining individual patterns of opposition are formal constitutional and party arrangements and party strategy. My use of the term party strategy, in place of political beliefs, rests on the fact that, as long as the Communist party retains its monopoly of ideology, its strategy—in the sense of an orientation toward action—takes priority before the political beliefs of the country, which are not permitted independent articulation.

At the outset, it must be stressed that the term opposition as applied to the two countries refers to the active opposition within the Communist party. As in other Communist countries, active opposition has originated mainly from within the top echelons of the party hierarchy predicated upon relative degrees of support from the lower party ranks. The passive opposition identified with the population—disaffected workers, students, ethnic groups and other dissident elements—has existed right along. What is new is that, for the first time, a link has been formed between those segments of the population which have traditionally opposed the regime's policy and the groups within the party seeking to modify regime actions.

A further clarification is needed regarding the designation of the opposition. In Czechoslovakia, the liberal victory was won in January 1968. In Yugoslavia, it was achieved in 1964. Technically, therefore, the conservatives (or what has been termed in Yugoslavia "the conservative underground,") now constitute the opposition in both countries. Prior to those dates, however, "the liberals" were in opposition and "the conservatives" were in power. Who controls official policymaking and who does not is not so important to my topic as the fact of opposition itself, how it arose, and why it seems to have acquired permanency. Attention will thus be centered on the *role* of opposition, rather than on a particular coalition of opposition forces.

The prior condition for the tolerance of divergence of opinion in each country was the limitation of the government's right to coerce. The downgrading of terror provided the necessary stimulus for the opposition to become articulate and to mount its challenge to the official leadership. In Czechoslovakia, the first steps were taken in 1963, with open criticism of the arbitrary injustice of the Stalinist period and rehabilitation of the victims of the Stalinist trials of the 1950s. Greater emphasis on socialist legality, however, was not enough to modify substantially the behavior of the Secret Police. One of the first actions of the new First Secretary, Alexander Dubcek, was to work toward the definitive subordination of the Secret Police to the government organs. In Yugoslavia, the initial move toward the modification of the police state was taken in 1951.[6] But it was not until 1966 that the Secret Police (UDB) was finally brought under government control with the dramatic ouster of the UDB's one-time head, Aleksander Rankovic,

---

[6]At the Fourth Plenum of the Central Committee of the Communist Party in 1951, a resolution was adopted demanding a strengthening of "socialist legality," and independence of the legal system generally. . . .

from his posts in the party and government,[7] the subsequent purging of the police organs, and the decentralization of the UDB power structure.

The Dominant Subcultures

The tension between the dominant nationality groups in both Czechoslovakia and Yugoslavia has its roots in the unresolved problems of the interwar period. Both states were artificially created after World War I, from territories inhabited by peoples with radically different experiences of imperial rule. In neither country did an all-national identity exist. In both countries, one of the chief problems was to create it. Nationality differences during the interwar period were exacerbated by different patterns of economic development,[8] and economic unity had to be forged from widely different economic orientations.

Cultural rivalries were the final factor in the stimulation of ethnic rivalry during the two world wars. The Czechs tended to consider themselves culturally superior to the Slovaks, while the Catholic Croats and the Slovenes, the most highly educated of the Yugoslav nationalities, resented an identification with the orthodox Serbs. Cultural cleavage in Yugoslavia was further heightened by the differing previous national experiences of independence. Serbia had been independent since 1878, while tiny Montenegro had enjoyed practical independence for over a hundred years. By contrast, Croatia and Slovenia's hard schooling in constitutional issues under the Dual Monarchy made them unwilling to tolerate a new subjugation to the Serbs.

The centralist constitutional solution to ethnic diversity imposed by the nationality with the largest population in both countries (the Czechs and the Serbs) served to weaken any chance of attaining genuine national unity in the face of the centrifugal pulls exercised from outside on the nonruling nationalities by a Europe plunging headlong toward World War II. On the eve of Munich, Slovakia broke with Czechoslovakia and declared her independence. In the wake of the German invasion of Yugoslavia, Croatian Ustase elements attempted to proclaim a free and independent Croatia. Yugoslavia was partitioned. Croatia became an autonomous province under Italian supervision; Slovenia and Serbia came under German control. By 1942 Czechoslovakia and Yugoslavia had ceased to exist.

This forced abbreviation of the independent existence of the two countries left the nationality problem to be resolved by the Communists. The situation has been complicated in Czechoslovakia by the fact that the Slovak nation had its first taste of independence during the war. In addition, the Slovak Communist Party (CPS) had broken with the Czechoslovak Communist Party (CPCS) in 1939, and operated as an independent unit for the duration of the war. A particular source of tension was the fact that Czech communist activities compared unfavorably with the organized guerilla effort of the Slovak Communists, which ultimately led to the uprising of 1944.

---

[7]Rankovic's fall came at the Fourth Plenum of the Central Committee of the League of Yugoslav Communists (LYC) at Brioni in July 1966.

[8]Bohemia and Moravia entered the new Czechoslovakian nation far more industrially advanced than agricultural Slovakia, and enjoyed economic precedence during the life of the First Republic. In the newly created Yugoslavia, the three dominant nationalities, the Serbs, Croats and Slovenes, found themselves cut off from their former markets in the Balkans, Hungary and Austria, respectively. Moreover, what industry there was, was largely concentrated in the north.

The wartime CPS leaders agreed that union with the Czechs was inevitable after the war, but they saw this union in terms of federation. From 1945 to 1948, during the period of reconstruction, the Slovaks were permitted a considerable degree of autonomy. But after the Communist coup, they were progressively deprived of any independent rights, both constitutionally and politically. The Slovak Communist Party was reunited with the Czechoslovak Communist Party and brought under Czech dominance in 1948. The 1950 trials of the so-called Slovak bourgeois nationalists ended temporarily any chance of Slovak nationalism regaining its former strength. Thus, Slovak complaints multiplied against the Czechs. Slovak Communist grievances were the more intense because the CPS had once known revolutionary élan and a real degree of popular support. As Ladislav Mnacko so well describes in his book, *The Taste of Power,* Slovak Communists remember the war and the period immediately following as a time of heroism and genuine national self-assertion under Communist inspiration against the common enemy.

Similar to the Czech-Slovak confrontation, the Serbian and Croatian Communists have been divided on the issue of centralism or federalism. At its founding in 1918, the Communist party of the Kingdom of the Serbs, Croats and Slovenes was under the leadership of the Serb, Sima Markovic. It was then definitely committed to centralism and secretly to the doctrine that Yugoslavia was a unitary nation. When the leadership of the party passed to the Croat, Tito, [the party] denounced centralism in favor of federalism. However, before the Communist takeover, the party had drawn its main support from peripheral areas and was relatively weak in Serbia. It was feared that if the capital were moved from Belgrade, the Serbs would be further alienated. But in Belgrade, the federal government came increasingly under Serbian influence whose centralist leanings served to spur the resentment of the other nationality groups. In the March 8, 1964 issue of the Belgrade weekly, *Nin,* The Croatian Party leader, Vladimir Bakaric, declared that the Communists had sought to impose "Yugoslav integralism" such as had been tried in the interwar period.

The Eighth Party Congress of December 1964 failed to reconcile the antagonism between the Serbian and Croatian Communists. Edvard Kardelj, the Slovene Party leader, prophetically declared that henceforth the fight between the Slovene and Croat Communists, and the majority of the Serbian Communists, was to be a fight for and against the transformation of the Yugoslav federation into a confederation of semi-independent states. In the context of Serbo-Croat friction, the purge of Rankovic becomes the hard-won victory of the minority ethnic groups under Croatian instigation against the modern variant of the great Serbianism of the interwar period. The pardoning of Rankovic in December 1966 suggests that the Croatian victory was by no means a total one. Indeed, the celebrated language affair of March of the following year[9] may be seen as the product of the conflict between traditional nationalism urging the national Communist parties toward extremism, and the uncertainty of the leadership of the national Communist parties as to the consequences of acceding to national pressure.

---

[9]A group of nineteen Croatian intellectuals and professors published a declaration, accusing the federal government of favoring the Serbian side of the national language, Serbo-Croatian. Two days later, forty Serbian writers angrily replied. In the fracas which followed, seven people were ousted from the party; three Zagreb University professors were expelled, including the Chairman of the Croatian Writers' Union, Vlatko Pavletic. The text of the Croatian declaration may be found in *Telegram* (Zagreb), March 17, 1967; the Serbian reply was published in *Borba* (Belgrade), April 12, 1967.

In this connection, perhaps Tito's greatest single achievement was his success in welding together a Yugoslav spirit to combat the German invader. He remains today the lone symbol of national unity.

At the present time, in both countries, antagonism between nationalities seems to be in the ascendant, a threat to the fragile existence of the two states. It constitutes a permanent condition for opposition, because national grievances within the party are linked with the legacy of ethnic friction inherited from the interwar period. In both cases, support for a nationality opposition within the party awakes a positive response from the corresponding articulate nationality groups in the population at large.

The Differentiation of Social and Economic Interests

The principal political result of all economic reform in the communist countries has been the decentralization of what hitherto was for all intents and purposes a centralized, hierarchical power structure.[10] In both countries, the reforms effected the consolidation of opposition in three principal ways.

In the first place, the reforms intensified the opposition of the national minorities. While Bohemia had been industrialized under the former bourgeois regime, Slovakia's industrialization had taken place for the most part under communist direction. By comparison with the results in the Czech lands, the Slovak party could justly be proud of its economic achievements. By 1965, Slovak industrial production had increased sevenfold over 1945—Bohemia's had increased by only three and a half times—and comprised some 20.7 percent of the total national industrial production. Relative economic progress encouraged the Slovak leaders to press for more rapid industrialization. To succeed in this area, they demanded an end to what they called Prague's economic domination. During 1965 and 1966, the Slovak party pressured for and won from Prague a greater share for Slovakia of the total national investment, and the assignment of priority to Slovak economic growth. There is little question that Slovak resentment of Prague's economic policies toward Slovakia was a major factor in the coalescence of an opposition sufficient to engineer the fall of the First Secretary of the CPCS, Antonin Novotny. The Slovak's essentially negative reaction to official party and government economic policies reinforced those elements in the Czech section of the CPCS that had been demanding a more thorough implementation of economic reform.

In Yugoslavia, there is an even more clear-cut polarization of economic interest along national lines due to the marked imbalance between the northern more advanced regions and the underdeveloped sections in the south.[11] The federal government has tried to rectify the situation by making the southern republics the foremost beneficiaries of federal and republican investment funds and subsidies. The more developed republics have naturally resented their forced participation in the industrialization of the backward areas of the country. In the spring of 1958, 800 Croatian economic specialists sent

---

[10]The Czechoslovak leadership formally inaugurated the New Economic Model (NEM) in January 1965. In July 1965, Tito announced the third and most radical of a series of reforms which started with the introduction of the workers' self-management system in 1950.

[11]In 1965, almost 78 percent of all Yugoslav enterprises employing 78 percent of the total labor force were located in Croatia, Slovenia and Serbia; approximately 41 percent of the enterprises employing about 43 percent of the labor force were in Croatia and Slovenia. In Serbia industry is located in Serbia proper and in the Vojvodina. There is little enterprise in the backward autonomous region of the Kosmet. Federal Institute for Statistics, *Statistical Pocket-book of Yugoslavia, 1967* (Beograd, February 1967), p. 58.

a memorandum to Bakaric, then head of the Croatian government, protesting what they termed the economic exploitation of Croatia by the federal government in Belgrade.

Croatian resentment of Belgrade's economic policies intensified in the 1960's because of the country's mounting economic difficulties. Conflicts and divisions in the party over economic matters sharpened. The reformist wing was headed by Kardelj and Bakaric; Rankovic was the leader of the conservatives. Each accused the other of increasing the country's economic problems. With the victory of the liberals in 1964 at the Eighth Party Congress, reform was assured. The reforms have put Yugoslav enterprises on an essentially profit-making basis, and have given them more say in production decisions. It is expected that enterprises and the banking system will henceforth finance about 70 percent of the total capital investment, compared with some 45 percent in the past. In addition, half of all investment funds are now returned by the component republics to the enterprises, rather than being distributed through Belgrade. These changes naturally make the enterprises in the more developed republics reluctant to invest in unprofitable ventures. In particular, the resentment of the northern enterprises has been directed against Serbia's insistence on higher prices for her raw materials in order to finance her investments.

From the conservative point of view, the drastic reduction of government subsidies to enterprises means that many of the plants in the most backward areas are being forced to close. In other words, Serbia, Montenegro, and Macedonia are the hardest hit by the reforms, and have a strong basis from which to argue that the reform is to the advantage of Croatia and Slovenia only. Thus, the realities of the economic situation are helping to sharpen the antagonism born of traditional national rivalry.

A second consequence of economic reorganization in the two countries has been the differentiation of interest between the managerial and technological elites, including the cultural intelligentsia, on the one hand, and the party apparatchiks, both liberal and conservative, on the other. Reform demanded the replacement of undertrained administrative personnel by trained management cadres. In both countries, the absorption of these elites has been one of the most difficult tasks facing party leaders. Despite the entrance of managerial personnel into the Czechoslovak Party after the Tenth Party Congress in 1954, the percentage of engineers and technicians, according to official statistics in 1966, was only 17.3 percent; scientific workers represented only .2 percent. On the whole, 70.2 percent of the party had a basic education, as opposed to 5.9 percent who had reached the university level. Although intelligentsia representation in the Central Committee was higher than in the party as a whole (22.9 percent), and over 50 percent of the membership had had a university education, the representation from state and party administration continued to predominate. By adding to these statistics the fact of an aging party, the preponderant majority of whose members joined during the 1945–1947 period,[12] it becomes clear why the CPCS, with the possible exception of segments of the Slovak party,[13] has so far been unable to provide the cadres needed to run a technological society.

---

[12]The age structure of the CPCS in 1966 breaks down as follows: under 26, 9.0 percent; 25–35, 18.2 percent; 35–45, 26.7; 45–60, 28.7; over 60, 17.4 percent. In other words, the membership is aging without benefiting from renewal from the ranks of the younger generation.

[13]For example, while only a little more than 16 percent of the Czechoslovak leadership in January 1968 had the equivalent of a university education, over 30 percent of the Slovak leaders had gone on to higher education.

A cleavage within the party between the state and party functionaries and the intelligentsia clearly exists. Another split between the younger and better qualified party members and the old Stalinist-trained bureaucrats has developed. A third division which is only becoming apparent is that between what might be called the liberal functionaries, such as Dubcek, and the reforming intelligentsia. Since 1963, the intelligentsia has managed to run its own press. With the abolition of effective censorship in 1968, the liberal intellectuals gained control of the major channels of mass communication. The press and television's drive for immediate democratization of national life has been in sharp contrast to Dubcek's cautious approach to the solution of his country's problems.[14]

The rift between the intellectuals and managerial cadres and the party apparatus has become well defined in Yugoslavia. Official statistics in 1966 placed the number of white-collar workers in the party at 20 percent of the total membership. Illiteracy still exists among the rank and file. Reports stress that most of the present membership joined the party between 1959 and 1962. Those who joined before 1940 now constitute only a small minority. In other words, the influx of new members cannot be taken to mean an influx of trained personnel. The gulf between the functionary and the intelligentsia of the League of Yugoslav Communists is further apparent from the fact that the core of the wartime party, the Partisan heroes, have had to make way for highly educated technocrats in key managerial and government positions. Finally, even more than in Czechoslovakia, the editorial staffs of the liberal intellectual magazines, such as *Gledista* and *Praxis,* have set themselves up against the bureaucrats and tend to regard themselves and to be regarded as embryonic opposition cadres.

In this connection, a significant exchange of articles appeared in the Yugoslav press last year, re-evaluating Djilas' theory of the new class. A Belgrade professor, Svetozar Stojanovic, published an article in *Praxis,*[15] in which he developed the thesis that the position of the working class in a socialist society is completely the opposite of what ideology says it is. The workers are more subjugated and exploited; they do not even possess those rights conquered by the working class in the bourgeois democratic system. Stojanovic would except Yugoslavia from the general pattern of degeneration of a socialist society into a new exploited class society. Nevertheless, he is convinced that the Yugoslav party, as it is going at the present time, cannot contribute to the building of socialism because its theory and practice are based on outmoded nineteenth-century ideas.

In criticism of Stojanovic's views, Bakaric has argued that prior to the ouster of Rankovic a new bureaucratic class in Djilas' terms had indeed been developing. Since Rankovic's fall, however, the bureaucracy has been transformed into what he termed "our own bureaucracy." In Bakaric's view, the bureaucracy cannot become a new class because it does not possess any rights of ownership. It has only functions. As one of many strata of the population, it is performing the necessary function of the organization of authority. Therefore, Bakaric asserts, the problem of bureaucracy versus self-management is false.

Although he is a university-educated man, Bakaric, as a party functionary, cannot help representing the point of view of the liberal party apparat in terms of its vested interests. Stojanovic and other university professors attack what they term the ideolog-

---

[14]Dubcek's statements that there will be democracy in Czechoslovakia but the party will remain in control give some indication of his approach to the welfare of his country. *New York Times,* April 2, 1968.

[15]Svetozar Stojanovic, "The Myth of State Socialism," *Praxis* (Zagreb), January-April 1967.

ical myths generated by the party, and accuse the party bureaucracy of having carefully cultivated these myths to rationalize their continuance in power. The professors thus support the managerial cadres in their demands for the deprofessionalization of politics and their rejection of the hypothesis that some day all of the working people will definitely decide all key issues concerning the country's development.

The fundamental question that the intelligentsia poses is whether the Communist party is really capable of maintaining its monopoly of power in a modern industrial society. The party functionary would like to answer the question in the affirmative; the intelligentsia argues in the negative. To allow the party apparat to retain undisputed control means to strengthen an unproductive class, which may resort to any means, including arms, to maintain its monopoly of power. While violence may have been necessary at an earlier period, it has to be ruled out for the future. In other words, the managerial cadres must assume their rightful place in the direction of society. The party must step down.

The split between the managerial and technical elites and the liberal apparatchiks, which has developed since the 1965 reforms, cuts across nationality. Both Zagreb and Belgrade have their intellectual periodicals supporting more radical reform than that officially endorsed by the party. Afraid of the consequences of renouncing control, yet unable to endorse the conservative position, the liberal party functionaries have evidently tried to present a case in which they can retain the best of two worlds. Thus, what in 1964 appeared to be a virtually united liberal elite has now divided over the issue of who is to govern. Given the fluid developments in Czechoslovakia today, a similar situation may be anticipated there. The liberal victory is too recent for the conflict between the technocrats and the party liberals to have become fully defined. But that such a conflict is underway is suggested by the persistence of debate over the degree to which the economy should be run by administrative or economic means.

A final consequence of economic reform lies in the shifting patterns of alignments between the conservative party bureaucrats, liberal party functionaries, economic cadres, and blue-collar workers. Essentially, the reformers' appeal is not among the workers but among the higher echelons of the economic bureaucracy. In Czechoslovakia the workers have by no means unreservedly welcomed NEM. Growing worker dissatisfaction at the closing of inefficient enterprises has produced numerous "work stoppages." Strikes in protest of government and party directives have been officially reported. Novotny called attention to the workers' unenthusiastic attitude toward reform in his speech to the Thirteenth Party Congress in 1966. After his ouster as First Secretary in January 1968 and up to his resignation as President of the Republic in March, he apparently tried to capitalize on worker unrest to gather support in a last-ditch stand to mobilize conservative opinion behind him in the party. Parallel abortive efforts to organize the factories in his support was additional evidence of an attempt to set up a conservative coalition. The possibility of a conservative functionary-worker alliance cannot be lightly dismissed.[16]

In Yugoslavia the gulf between the interests of the blue-collar workers and the economic and technical elites seems to be widening. A split between blue-collar and white-collar workers was almost inevitable, precisely because the self-management

---

[16]The liberals are well aware of the danger. In an article in the renamed organ of the Czechoslovak Writers' Union, *Literarni listy,* Editor Ludvik Vaculik holds no illusions about the workers' antagonism to economic reform. In his view, an educational effort to modify their negative attitude is essential to the success of the reform. Ludvik Vaculik, "And What About the Workers?," *Literani listy,* March 28, 1968.

system gives the blue-collar workers ownership of the factories and thus a share in their profits. The arrangement means that blue-collar workers are not on a full salary as are white-collar workers. The pressure for solvency and the need for investment capital produced by the 1965 reforms has forced the enterprises to allocate profits to investment funds rather than putting them into the workers' pockets. Thus, the man who in theory owns the enterprise at times brings home less than half his pay and seldom the whole of it. The white-collar worker can count on full pay every week. It is no wonder that blue-collar workers form the majority of those leaving the party.[17] The increasing number of strikes, which in 1965, by the government's own admission, amounted to 130,[18] is a significant measure of the degree of worker unrest. So intense has been the conflict between the blue-collar and the white-collar groups that the former head of the Yugoslav Trade Unions, Svetozar Vukmanovic-Tempo, has developed what he terms a two-line thesis of antagonism between the worker and management in a socialist society, and has called for the organization of the blue-collar workers into representative councils to pressure for redress of their grievances. What trade unions of Yugoslavia want to achieve, in Vukmanovic's opinion, is the full-fledged implementation of the workers' self-management system. His theory is exemplary of two parallel lines of development in Yugoslavia today: the mobilization of the trade unions in support of the workers' councils, and the attempt by the liberal party functionaries to identify with the workers against management.

The decentralization of the economic structure in Czechoslovakia and Yugoslavia has given rise to autonomous centers of both actual and potential political power, capable of mounting a permanent challenge to official policy. Out of the economic reforms in both countries there have emerged various competing social and economic interests which appeal to different segments of the party for action and to which party groups refer for support. At present, it is impossible to describe an ordered dualism or pluralism of interest in either country. A Croat-Slovene liberal functionary-intellectual-managerial alliance in Yugoslavia in 1964, and a Slovak variant of the same in Czechoslovakia in 1968, suggest the plausibility of other alternatives, such as a Serb- or Czech-conservative functionary-working class alliance, or a Serb- or Czech-liberal functionary-worker alliance.

The Constitutional Variable

The constitutional variable is more important in a communist state in determining the pattern of opposition than it would at first appear to be, because it describes the legal relationship between the various subcultures, defines the legally permissible toleration of diversity of opinion, and provides a framework for the organizational structure of the party.

The 1960 Socialist Constitution of Czechoslovakia effectively completed the socialization of the governmental institutions started in the Constitution of 1948. Although an electoral law in 1964 somewhat modified the conservative constitutional regulations and electoral law of 1960, the liberalization of the electoral system as well as the delegation of any real authority to parliament are still to come. Thus, from the standpoint of the operation of the opposition, the most significant aspect of the constitutional

---

[17]In 1966, 53.6 percent of those leaving the party were workers.

[18]See the account of worker dissatisfaction, based on his personal tour of Yugoslavia, by George Bailey, "Titoism's Failure," *The Reporter*, January 1, 1967, pp. 16–20.

arrangements today is the anomaly of the existence of a quasi-autonomous national unit within a centralist state. The constitution nominally deprives the Slovaks of the last vestige of national rights by relegating Slovakia to mere provincial status. The fact remains, however, that the new Constitution, like the old, provides for a Slovak national administration, and by inference, a Slovak party organization, over which Prague has little direct control.

Slovak pressure on both the party and government in Prague has been based on Slovak control of the policymaking organs in Slovakia. Paradoxically, Slovak participation in the centralist system is a major factor in explaining the present Slovak ascendancy. For the Slovak party and national administration provided the only organized political vehicle which could serve as a basis for consolidating the challenge to Novotny's rule. Another factor in the Slovak achievement has been the solidarity between the Slovak economic and intellectual elites and the party apparatus. With their own national mass media, Slovak reformers could use their mass communications to disseminate liberal views. What is more important, the Slovak party leadership has supported the liberals in return for their cooperation.

The existence of a constitutionally recognized national government and party organization has thus given a certain asymmetry to the pattern of opposition in Czechoslovakia. On the one hand, there is the solidly entrenched Slovak party with all the force of the law behind it; on the other, there are the diverse Czech groups demanding institutional backing. In this connection, one of the more remarkable developments has been the use by the Czechs of nonparty organizations as vehicles through which to press for reform. The most salient example of Czech liberal initiative has been the capture by the liberal writers of the leadership of the Czechoslovak Writers' Union and their use of the union as an organized pressure group. In a similar way, the Economic Institute of the Czechoslovak Academy of Science has provided the institutional base for the Czech reformers. Neither of these two institutions, however, has the same status of authority as that of the Slovak Communist party. The problem is that, although in 1967 the CPS provided a temporary organizational form for the Czech liberals, it can in no way be considered to represent the total interests of the Czech liberals. In the last analysis, Slovak party leaders must support Slovak interests and the Slovak party, among whose membership is a sizeable conservative bureaucratic contingent.

The present Czechoslovak Constitution, therefore, necessarily puts one or the other nation at a disadvantage, since the Czechs have no national organization of their own. Dubcek can rule only with the support of the Czech liberals. Loss of that support would once again reduce the Slovak party to a minority position. The Czechs cannot dominate until they resolve their internal differences, or Dubcek alienates the Czech liberals. A cross-national liberal coalition is out of the question because the Constitution, as an orthodox Communist document, cannot admit political division. But for the liberals to prevail, they must organize politically. Hence, their increasing pressure for civil rights. A more equal constitutional solution may well be one of the most difficult tasks Dubcek will have to face.

Four aspects of the Yugoslav constitutional structure are significant in explaining the complex nature of the opposition in that country today. While federalism was adopted as the solution to the nationality problem in 1946, it is only recently that it has been put into practice on a major scale. The introduction of a federalist format created six republican governments and six republican parties. The institution of the self-management system started the process of decentralization. But it was not until the 1960s that constitutional and party reforms substantially modified the centralist administrative structure in favor of greater republican autonomy.

By 1967 almost all important state and party institutions in Yugoslavia had been confederated. The focus of party power shifted from the federal to the republican executive committees. While the institutional organization of the country moved increasingly toward confederalization, the relative economic, cultural and population strengths of the constituent republics contributed further to the weakening of national unity and the alignment of the nationalities into two rival spheres of influence. If the Croats and Slovenes have fought for greater adherence to the Constitution and the rule of law, it is because constitutionalism benefits their national interests. Federalism made it possible for the two smaller nations to combine and prevail over the more numerous Serbs. On the other hand, because concentration on national rights has tended to separate rather than unite the nationalities, the increasing self-assertiveness of the participant ethnic groups threatens the very existence of the country. A case in point is the Serbian, Croatian, and Slovenian challenge of the federal government's right to set republican tax limits in December 1967. The absence of any firm agreement on the part of the component republics as to the scope of the federal government's power poses a serious problem for the future of the country.

The danger of the disintegration of national unity has no doubt been the major factor in Tito's recent moves to upgrade the role of the Yugoslav Army in the life of the country. The army's 75,000 party members, representing 30 percent of the membership of the armed forces, constitute the most solid and most cohesive group within the party since the demotion of the UDB in 1966. With the partisans forming the hard core, the army can be counted on to be staunchly conservative, loyal to Tito, and thus an effective counterforce to both liberal demands and the centrifugal pressures exercised by the republics.

A second constitutional factor in the pattern of the Yugoslav opposition has been the progressive liberalization of the electoral system, the most recent revision of which went into effect in February 1967, in time for the general elections of that year. The latest legislation reduces the party's control over the elections and provides for more than one candidate to run, thus making a real campaign possible. The new law immediately showed up the weakness of the party liberals' position. In the 1967 elections, many of the candidates chosen by the party to run on a reform ticket failed to get elected, much to the party liberals' disappointment. Elected instead were old-guard revolutionaries and former partisans. The reason for the increased number of conservatives in the post-election legislatures was that liberal strength was unorganized. The conservatives ran their candidates from their strongholds in the highly organized partisan associations. They also found support in the party's bureaucratic contingent, which has been estimated at 40 percent of the membership. As in Czechoslovakia, the liberals had no organization except the party itself, whose control over the elections had been weakened by the liberal legislation.

Decline in the party's centralizing authority has brought to the fore a third development in Yugoslavia's constitutional structure: the possibility that the role of a second party might be played by the Socialist Alliance, the Yugoslav counterpart of the national fronts common to all East European Communist countries. The question of the role of the Alliance under the new reforms has been examined widely in the press since 1966, and attempts have been made to invest it with real autonomy. Party leaders, however, insist on seeing the Alliance as a wider contact between the party and the population: a forum for the airing of public opinion, not an organization independent of the party. Hence, the Sixth Congress of the Alliance, held in June 1966, upheld the principle of party control. Nevertheless, its new statutes made local centers more responsive to local opinion and decentralized the Alliance's organizational structure. Potentially, therefore, if not actually, the Socialist Alliance stands as a possible institutional vehicle for the opposition.

Finally, the impact upon the opposition of the expanded authority of the republican and federal legislatures needs brief mention. One of the consequences of the change has been the emergence of the legislature as a site where the opposition can confront the government, and even bring it down. A dramatic example of this possibility was the resignation of the government of Slovenia over the question of the government's proposal to increase workers' contributions to social insurance. The resignation of the government was permissible under the constitution, but was the first occurrence of its kind in Yugoslavia.[19] The separation of the party and state organizations and the resulting lower representation of party professional apparatchiks in the federal and republican governments give further substance to legislative responsibility.[20] Freer elections, wider powers to the legally elected governing organs, and the resignation of governments upon defeat of their bills are significant steps toward the institutionalization of procedures guaranteeing the tolerance of "loyal" opposition.

The constitutional arrangements operative in a communist state are seen to be critical in determining the distinctiveness of the opposition, its tactics of operation, and the site of its challenge to the ruling group. Federalism in Yugoslavia has resulted in a pattern of opposing national units, confronting each other in the manner of separate governments. The resolution of differences and the formulation of policy on the federal level are consequently fraught with formal questions of principle and national rights. Constitutional and party reforms have reinforced the trend toward the polarization of national conflict around the two predominant subcultures. Freer elections within this context have taken conflict resolution outside the nucleus of the party into a broader arena. In addition, the more liberal constitution has made parliament and the polls effective sites from which to pressure for modification of official policy. In Czechoslovakia the centralist format combined with a less free electoral system and less real authority in parliament has so far kept the management of conflict within the bounds of the Communist party. Since Slovakia is not a federated unit, Slovak and other pressures have been better exerted through informal bargaining and combining within the party itself. The total arrangement of the opposition thus tends to be more fluid, less structured, more one-sided, and less distinctly national than in Yugoslavia.

Party Strategy

The final factor to be considered here as a determinant of the pattern of opposition in a communist country is the crucial matter of party strategy. In this, until recently, the two parties under consideration differed radically. Up to the fall of Novotny as First

---

[19]The vote was forty-four against the government proposal, eleven for, and three abstaining. (Reported over Radio Zagreb on December 6, 1966). News of the Slovenian government's resignation was broadcast over Radio Belgrade on December 7, 1966. It should be noted that the vote against the government was not the first such vote recorded in Yugoslavia or elsewhere in the bloc. Voting against the government has also taken place in Czechoslovakia. What is distinctive is the fact that the government *resigned* as a consequence.

[20]In July 1967 only one-third of the officials in top positions in Yugoslavia were simultaneously party officials. Party functionary representation in the Federal Assembly was stronger than in the Federal Executive Committee. From a report by Zdenko Antic from the Research Departments of Radio Free Europe, July 3, 1967.

Secretary, the Czechoslovak party officially followed a course which did not deflect far from the old Stalinist tactics. Novotny's response to the liberalization of the Soviet line was rigid and orthodox. The consequence of the CPCS' official neo-orthodoxy was that pressure for change and the definition of a strategy of reform came from outside the leadership of the party. In Yugoslavia the situation was reversed. By insisting on a Yugoslav road to socialism, Tito chose the path of innovation and reform. In the face of the increasing bureaucratization of Yugoslavia, Djilas indicted the Soviet bureaucracy as the "new class" of the USSR—thus helping to push the LYC leadership toward a strategy to distinguish its course from that of the Soviets, which Yugoslav leaders considered to be a distortion of socialism.

The two different strategies had different impacts on the emergence and cohesion of the opposition. The Czechoslovak strategy prevented the various party factions for a long time from operating openly and reaching out for popular support. It took ten years for the Slovak Communists to succeed in effecting the rehabilitation of the Slovak "bourgeois nationalists." The first call for freedom of speech was made at the Second Congress of the Czechoslovak Writers' Union in 1956. It was not until 1963 that the writers were able to state their grievances openly and to bargain with the regime for concessions. It took until 1967 for them to counter Novotny's policies with a liberal democratic program of their own. Similarly, the economic reformers did not get a public hearing until 1963, although such discussion was long overdue. The fact that the official line was total party control over society and democratic centralism within the CPCS meant that, unless the opposition factions gained enough strength, they could not challenge that line. But until they could dissociate themselves from official party strategy, they could not hope for popular backing. It is no wonder the writers accused themselves of participating in "a perverted and perverting system."[21]

In this sense, the Slovaks were the best placed of all opposition factions. By 1963 a new generation of Slovak leaders had risen to power, untainted by direct association with the purges of the 1950s, the injustices of which had been firmly attributed to "the cult of personality." These younger leaders were able to use their influence without fear of recrimination and reprisal. In pressing for the rehabilitation of the "bourgeois nationalists," the new Slovak leadership was able to achieve an identification of its aims with those of the entire country. At the same time, it was able to engineer the fall from power of all the Slovak "Stalinists" still in top party and government posts, who had cooperated with Prague in the purges. Feeling most injured by Stalinism, the Slovaks were ideally situated to become the initiators of the revisionist movement. When the Czech intellectuals supported them, the movement was transformed into an all-national opposition to the Prague bureaucracy. Slovak aims remained separate from the aims of the liberal economic reformers and the intellectuals. It was only when these strands of opposition converged to assume sufficient proportions so as to challenge the bonds of party discipline that Novotny's hold over the provincial and municipal party organizations finally broke. Dubcek's accession, however, was founded on orthodox party strategy. He was able to capitalize on the disarray within the Czech section, because he was the only other individual, besides Novotny, who had control of a major group of party secretaryships.

Thus, a party strategy oriented toward maintaining the status quo encouraged a factional, essentially plural opposition. In his failure to reach a satisfactory compromise,

---

[21]Karel Kosik, *Kulturny zivot,* July 13, 1963.

Novotny alienated the dissident Czech elements, who had no other recourse but to ally with the Slovaks. The result was an asymmetrical pluralistic opposition. In the last years of Novotny's rule, factionalism within the party was a fact deriving from the increasing differentiation of interests within society at large. It became obvious that the traditional Communist modes of behavior were inadequate, but the conservative CPCS leadership refused to allow any public discussion of the presence of social conflict within the party.

The accession of Dubcek demonstrated clearly that the character of party rule had fundamentally changed. The strategy of absolute control had been replaced by bargaining. Upholding the status quo had given way to fostering reform. Recent events indicate how risky the new strategy may be. Whereas a year or so ago the intellectuals were merely questioning the leading role of the party and tentatively calling for "an integrated opposition," today, the Social Democratic party can publish a resolution calling for the virtual formation of a party system.[22] Caught between the rising flood of extreme liberalism threatening to burst the bonds of communism, the more moderate elements seeking reform within the Communist framework, and the conservatives desiring a return to the *status quo ante,* Dubcek will be hard pressed to accommodate all interests within the Czech-Slovak antithesis, maintain party control over the direction of the country, and accomplish economic renewal. If the progressives become bolder, the moderates may look anxiously toward the secure familiarity of the conservative position.

A strategy of reform and accommodation has produced a definitive fragmentation of the liberal consensus in Yugoslavia. From 1950 to 1964 the reformers were not effectively in control of policy-making. But because reform was the official party strategy, they were able to pursue their goals more openly than was the case in Czechoslovakia. The question was not whether there should be reform, but what *kind* of reform was required. As in Czechoslovakia, however, the liberals had to develop a united front if they were to succeed. The dilemma of the reformers was that once they had captured political power, they became the official initiators of a change that, when underway, had to undermine their power position if it was to achieve its objective. The draft theses of the LYC, published in April 1967, are indicative of the degree to which the role of the party has already declined in Yugoslav life. Perhaps their most important clause is the assertion that the Yugoslav Communist party is not a political party in the classical sense of the word and has no separate party interest.[23]

It is precisely the diminishing authority of the party in Yugoslavia that is a matter of great moment to intellectuals and party members at the present time. Party functionaries, no matter how liberal, are naturally concerned about the party's loss of control and are hesitant to adopt radical solutions. In 1966 the Macedonian communist leader, Krste Crvenkovski, came out in favor of a permanent "loyal opposition" and the end of democratic centralism within the party. Today he can criticize traditional party behavior, but is silent regarding a solution to the demoralization he believes has come upon the membership. The liberal apparatchiks cannot admit the possibility of a two-party or multiparty system. To Todorovic, it is impossible to have two socialist parties in a Communist country, one ruling and one an organized opposition. Since both are based on Marx's teaching, sooner or later the tolerance between the two would dis-

---

[22]As reported in the *New York Times,* March 10, 1968.

[23]The text of the theses was published on April 27, 1967 in all major Yugoslav dailies.

appear. [He maintains that] only Communist parties can build socialism. The apparat-chiks' immobilism regarding further redefinition of party strategy moves them away from the position of the liberal intellectuals in the direction of the conservative camp.

The liberal intellectuals themselves are sharply divided as to what party strategy should aim for. Views range from a no-party system through a two-party system, a multiparty system, something called socialist pluralism, to Djilas' call for a Western democratic-socialist order. The central problem to all is whether it is possible for a communist country to implement a party system or a political faction system within the party, and yet remain communist. The conservatives answer in the negative. The liberal apparatchiks supported by Tito also say no. Other liberal elements are divided as to what kind of system would have optimum effectiveness. A reformist strategy has thus enhanced division within the ruling government group and cohesion within the opposition.

Conclusions

Several general conclusions are suggested by this survey of the pattern of opposition in Czechoslovakia and Yugoslavia.

(1) The autonomous functioning of an opposition in a Communist system is relative to the degree of tension existing between the dominant subcultures and the degree of economic and political decentralization. The greater the degree of tension and decentralization, the more favorable are the conditions for the emergence and perpetuation of an opposition. In both countries, opposition did not become fully defined until both factors had converged.

(2) The alignment of economic and social interests with the dominant subcultures is not a one-to-one alignment. On the contrary, alliances tend to be fluid. The interaction between party and nonparty groups suggests the development of an informal type of constituency, meriting further study and analysis.

(3) Constitutional arrangements determine how the specific subcultures will confront each other in a formal pattern. Where the federal system prevailed, there was a greater distinctiveness of opposition along nationality lines. Where the centralist system was in force, asymmetry developed, with the sole national party organization acting as the lodestone for the dissident interests of the other nation.

(4) Constitutional arrangements also define the sites from which the opposition may challenge the ruling party group. The more liberal the constitution, the greater is the number of possible sites.

(5) Party strategy acts as an important determinant of the cohesion of the opposition. Where the strategy of democratic centralism and party control over society prevailed, the opposition tended to fragmentation, relative to dominant interest. Where a strategy of reform and greater tolerance of opinion reigned, the opposition was strengthened; the ruling group split on the basis of interests and objectives, thereby initiating a new cycle of division between the ruling moderates and the more radical liberals.

Czechoslovakia and Yugoslavia today are test cases of whether an opposition can survive in a Communist state. The conditions are favorable. The embryo is there. But in order for the groups now competing for political power and influence to resolve their differences in a peaceful and legitimately patterned manner, the leaderships in both countries must see their way to a revolutionary reappraisal of the theory and practice of communism itself.

Selected Bibliography

Soviet Union

Armstrong, John A. *Ideology, Politics, and Government in the Soviet Union.* Rev. ed. New York: Praeger, 1967.

Fainsod, Merle. *How Russia is Ruled.* Rev. ed. Cambridge, Massachusetts: Harvard University Press, 1963.

Gehlen, Michael P. *The Communist Party of the Soviet Union: A Functional Analysis.* Bloomington: Indiana University Press, 1969.

Hammer, Darrell P. *USSR: The Politics of Oligarchy.* Hinsdale, Illinois: Dryden Press, 1974.

Rush, Myron. *Political Succession in the USSR.* 2d ed. New York: Columbia University Press, 1968.

Schapiro, Leonard. *The Communist Party of the Soviet Union.* 2d ed. New York: Random House, 1960.

Tatu, Michel. *Power in the Kremlin. From Khrushchev to Kosygin.* Translated by Helen Katel. New York: Viking, 1968.

Tucker, Robert C. *The Soviet Political Mind.* Rev. ed. New York: Norton, 1971.

Ulam, Adam B. *Stalin, The Man and His Era.* New York: Viking, 1973.

China

Barnett, A. Doak. *Chinese Communist Politics in Action.* Seattle: University of Washington Press, 1969.

Chai, Winberg. *The New Politics of Communist China.* Pacific Palisades, California: Goodyear Publishing Company, 1972.

Hinton, Harold C. *An Introduction to Chinese Politics.* New York: Praeger, 1973.

Houn, Franklin W. *A Short History of Chinese Communism.* 2d ed. Englewood Cliffs, New Jersey: Prentice-Hall, 1973.

Jan, George P., ed. *Government of Communist China.* San Francisco: Chandler, 1966.

Lewis, John Wilson, ed. *Party Leadership and Revolutionary Power in China.* Cambridge, England: Cambridge University Press, 1970.

Lindbeck, John M. H. *China: Management of a Revolutionary Society.* Seattle: University of Washington Press, 1971.

221

Scalapino, Robert A., ed. *Elites in the Peoples Republic of China.* Seattle: University of Washington Press, 1972.

Waller, Derek J. *The Government and Politics of Communist China.* Garden City, New York: Doubleday, 1971.

Yugoslavia

Avakumovic, Ivan. *History of the Communist Party of Yugoslavia.* Aberdeen, Scotland: Aberdeen University Press, 1964.

Barton, Allen H., Denitch, Bogdan, and Kadushin, Charles. *Opinion-Making Elites in Yugoslavia.* New York: Praeger, 1973.

Djilas, Milovan. *The New Class.* New York: Praeger, 1957.

Popovic, Nenad D. *Yugoslavia: The New Class in Crisis.* Syracuse, New York: Syracuse University Press, 1968.

Shoup, Paul. *Communism and the Yugoslav National Question.* New York: Columbia University Press, 1968.

Hoffman, George W., and Neal, Fred W. *Yugoslavia and the New Communism.* New York: Twentieth Century Fund, 1962.

POLITICAL PROCESSES: INTEREST GROUPS AND DECISION MAKING

The memory of Stalin's years of dictatorial rule (1929-1953) has influenced the thinking of American citizens to the extent that "Communist politics" is largely equated with Stalinism and totalitarian rule. No one can deny that Stalin wielded almost unlimited power in a manner and style that placed his rule among the most despotic in modern history. Although Lenin set the guidelines for consolidating political power under the guiding role of the Communist party, it was Stalin, leading observers contend, who brought about major transformations in Marxist thought: thus, that which was once envisioned by Marx and Engels as the "dictatorship of the proletariat," was later revised by Lenin to become the "dictatorship of the party," and became—under one Georgian of humble peasant origin named Josef V. Stalin—the "dictatorship of one man." The long years of Stalinist one-man rule caused many Westerners to think of the political process under communism as nothing more than a totalitarian dictatorship.

By the end of the Eleventh Party Congress on March 1922, Lenin held the Party and state leadership in complete control; however, his strategy of constructing the "new socialist order" was barely in the making when he suffered a severe paralytic stroke. This removal of Lenin from effective leadership left the political process in the hands of the remaining four members of the Politburo: Zinoviev, Kamenev, Stalin, and Trotsky. In

December, Lenin suffered another stroke, after which he decided to dictate his will, which called to the Central Committee's attention the strengths and weaknesses of each of the prospective successors. Yet by early January, Lenin added to his will still another personal note on Stalin: ". . . . he is too rude, and this fault . . . becomes unbearable in the Office of General Secretary . . . find a way to remove Stalin from that position and appoint to it another man. . . ." Lenin eventually succumbed to his third stroke on January 21, 1924. Against Lenin's last wishes and better advice to the Central Committee, Stalin defeated his political rivals and grasped the existing party oligarchy, and transformed it into a centralized elitist organization, led and controlled by the supreme Autocrat at the apex of the party hierarchy. In the course of his years in power, he became General Secretary of the Communist Party, head of the government, and the primary force in constructing a totally socialized and centrally planned economy.

The political process evident during these years—if indeed a process existed—approached a totalitarian extreme, and one man possessed and wielded as much, if not more, power than any other individual in the history of modern political leadership. The totalitarian political system in general—whereby one party, faction, or man largely controls the political system became equated with Soviet, and by inference, with Communist rule. Hence, the study of the politics of Communist states focused upon the "totalitarian dictatorship" and various modes and tactics of political control and manipulation. Throughout the 1950s and 1960s, politics in "the Communist party states" was viewed as the antithesis of the democratic or participatory processes of the Western systems, in which all competing groups were supposedly granted "free access and interaction" in policy making. It was thought that in the Communist system, participation and influence had been denied and successfully eliminated from the political arena. The resultant policy-making process was described as the politics of "totalism," or more commonly, totalitarianism. But it was maintained that, in the Western democratic system, all those who were ambitious, and who were willing to work within the political process would be assured of gaining access, and hence, political influence and power in the making of public policy. This Western form of politics became known as the politics of "pluralism." In recent years, however, there has developed a growing concern that our descriptions of both systems were faulty and not altogether realistic. Increasing numbers of scholars have come to recognize that just as all American citizens do not have equal rights and access to the political process, neither do leading Communist officials formulate public policy in a vacuum totally apart from the rest of society.

Although it is difficult to identify all the reasons for this reassessment, the following factors seem to have contributed to the re-evaluation of the totalitarian model: (1) a growing sensitivity and objectivity on the part of the analysts of Communist affairs, (2) the application of new methods to the study of politics in Communist systems, and (3) a genuine shift in the various Communist states toward increased liberalization and pluralization. First of all, since the late 1950s serious Western scholars have accumulated more and more evidence suggesting that the politics of Communist systems are not "devoid of conflict," and that a one-party system should not necessarily be equated with "totalism" in the political sphere. As early as 1963, Carl Linden wrote of a "continuing battle between powerful and entrenched elements in the party's higher echelons."[1] Then, in 1965 a Communist theorist from Czechoslovakia noted that the socialist system is characterized by conflicts "evoked by the intra-class differentiation of our society, i.e., by interest groups."[2] In addition, Gordon Skilling, in perhaps the seminal piece on the subject, maintained that interest groups in Communist societies had their "own values and interests . . . and all are inescapably involved in conflict with other groups."[3] In other words, the conception of Communist politics as a monolithic system, in which policy making is totally controlled by one man or a party elite, is in large part a myth and should be viewed and suspected as such by serious students of today.

Second, scholars applying new concepts and methods to the study of Communist politics have also imparted significant insights to the concept of "totalism" in the political sphere. Rather than focusing solely on "outputs" (or decisions) within the governmental system, analysts now emphasize "inputs," that is, the various forces affecting the policy-making process—from the demands of the peasantry to the articulation of vested interests by such interest groups as the military-industrial complex.

Third, the marked change brought about by Stalin's death ushered in a period of liberalization and pluralization throughout the Communist world. The fact is that more groups and factions have been evolving in the increasingly complex Communist societies, and conflict between such groups has been on the rise. In an analysis of interest groups in Yugoslavia one observer noted the existence of three major categories of groups competing in the political process: (1) groups participating directly in the governmental process (such as workers' organizations), (2) groups holding "strategic positions" in the process (such as the League of Communists), and (3) special interest groups articulating more particularized interests (such as universities, churches, and unions).[4] Such specialized interest

---

[1]Carl Linden, "How Strong Is Khrushchev?" *Problems of Communism* (Vol. XII, September–October 1963), pp. 27–35.

[2]Michael Lakatos, "On Some Problems of the Structure of Our Political Systems," *Pravny Obzoc* (Bratislava), (Vol. 1, 1965), pp. 26–36.

[3]Gordon Skilling, "Interest Groups and Communist Politics," *World Politics* (Vol. XVIII, No. 3, April 1966), pp. 435–451.

[4]Jovan Djordjevic, "Interest Groups and the Political System of Yugoslavia," pp. 197–228, in Henry Ehrmann, ed., *Interest Groups on Four Continents* (Pittsburgh, University of Pittsburgh Press 1958).

groups also exist in the Soviet Union and China. Suffice it to say that interest groups do exist in Communist systems, they do articulate their interests, and they do have an effect upon the policy-making process.

Today's Communist systems, then, cannot be as rigidly categorized as they were during the Stalin years. Perhaps the most accurate description of contemporary Communist politics is neither totalitarianism nor pluralism. A more meaningful explanatory and descriptive model may be that of "monism," meaning that although many competing institutions and interests are involved, the Communist party is the dominant one. The readings in this section will delve into the subject of politics and describe how different groups and institutions participate within the monistic political system.

A discussion of political processes in Communist states would be incomplete without some mention of the remarkable innovation and experimentation in self-management that has taken place in Yugoslavia. Conceived in the early 1950s as a means to give workers increased participation in the work setting, self-management has been expanded over the years to include every social, political, and economic organization in the society. The Yugoslav idealized goal is a fully self-managing society, a society in which the types of pressure, or interest groups existing in Western systems would no longer be needed. Within this projected self-managing society, all individuals—irrespective of wealth, status, or occupation—would be granted equal access to the decision-making process through a highly innovative system of decentralized, democratic socialism.

In summary, then, additional information, new methods of analysis, and an increased objectivity have caused students of the Communist political process to re-examine previously held assumptions about the totalitarian model and to recognize that some of these views led to unfortunate simplifications if not genuine oversights and inaccuracies. At the same time, the re-evaluation of the totalitarian model has allowed for heightened perception of the kind of political influence and decision making that does in fact exist in contemporary Communist systems. In the readings that follow, the contributing authors provide some valuable background information necessary for an understanding of the processes of political conflict, bargaining, and change in the Communist world.

Perhaps the unifying theme for the readings of Section Six is that Communist officials do not formulate policy in a vacuum; rather, there is considerable influence on policy makers from a variety of groups and individuals. In their selection, "Group Influence and the Policy Process in the Soviet Union," Joel J. Schwartz and William R. Keech use the specific issue of the Educational Reform Act of 1958 to illustrate how much influence such groups as teachers, administrators, scientific personnel, and even factory managers had on both the motivation for educational reform and the actual wording of the Reform Act itself. Apparently a segment of the Soviet citizenry had become concerned with the "increasing stratification of the Soviet society" caused, in part, by defects in the educational system, so that they demanded reform. And while it is certain, according to Schwartz and Keech, that First Party Secretary Khrushchev "clearly identified himself personally with the issue of educational reform," it is also true that the final draft of the Educational Reform Act was not determined by him alone. By accounting for the role played by different groups in developing educational policy in the Soviet Union, the authors suggest that the political process is little different in the formulation of other Soviet policies.

In the selection on China, Michel Oksenberg, while not denying the power of the Communist leaders, dispels the assumption that policy making in China is a monolithic process. Focusing on the important period of the Cultural Revolution, the author describes in detail several major occupational groups in China, their demands, and the ways in which these groups influenced government officials to meet their demands. It is worth noting Oksenberg's procedural remarks on the "four major conceptual underpinnings" of his study: in particular, he reminds us that the very definition of "group" in the the United States is more restrictive than when it is applied to China. In addition, as readers study group influence on the government of China, they might wish to ask the following basic questions: Who are the important groups? What are their demands? How did they pursue their interests? What power did they have before and after they proceeded to make demands? A conclusion one might derive from Oksenberg's article is that interest groups in China, though concerned with short-term goals of solving problems, are even more concerned, in the long run, with attaining power.

Finally, Bogdan Denitch poses these tantalizing questions in "The Relevance of Yugoslav Self-Management." First, what is the relationship between the Yugoslav concept of self-management and such basic Communist principles as dictatorship of the proletariat and democratic centralism? Is the self-management concept consistent with communism's goal to eliminate the entrepreneur, capitalist, and all other classes of society? How did self-management become such an important part of the fabric of Yugoslav communism? Finally, what benefits and also what strains has self-management brought to the political process of Yugoslavia?

16

Group Influence and the Policy Process in the Soviet Union

Joel J. Schwartz and William R. Keech

It has become widely recognized that Soviet officials do not formulate public policy in a vacuum, and that, indeed, their deliberations take into account in some fashion the needs and demands of various elements of the society. Further, it has been observed that social groups of various types play a noticeable, if only rudimentary role in articulating interests to the top of the hierarchy. In fact one author has gone so far as to assert that communist policy making results from a "parallelogram of conflicting forces and interests."[1] While such viewpoints are now far more widely accepted than in the early fifties, relatively little effort has been devoted to illustrating or illuminating how Soviet public policy in general or even a given Soviet policy can be importantly affected by group activity.

We propose here to make a contribution in that direction. Using the Educational Reform Act of 1958 as an exemplary case, we intend to show how and through what process groups can affect policy outcomes, and by identifying circumstances under which this takes place to generate some hypotheses about when such influence is most likely to recur. In their excellent analysis of Soviet policy formation, Professors Brzezinski and Huntington identify what they call "policy groups," which come closest of any nongovernmental groups to participating in policy formation. These groups, such as the military, industrial managers, agricultural experts and state bureaucrats,

> whose scope of activity is directly dependent on the allocation of national resources and which are directly affected by any shift in the institutional distribution of power, . . . advocate to the political leadership certain courses of action; they have their own professional or specialized newspapers which, at times and subject to overall Party control, can become important vehicles for expressing specific points of view.[2]

From Joel J. Schwartz and William R. Keech, "Group Influence and the Policy Process in the Soviet Union," *The American Political Science Review* (Sept. 1968), pp. 840–851. [Reprinted with permission from the publisher.]

[1]H. Gordon Skilling, "Interest Groups and Communist Politics," *World Politics* (Vol. 18, April 1966), p. 449.

[2]Zbigniew Brzezinski and Samuel P. Huntington, *Political Power: U.S.A./U.S.S.R.* (New York: Viking, 1963), p. 196.

In this article we will investigate an instance wherein such groups seemed to influence policy with the result of virtually scuttling one of Khrushchev's own major proposals.

We do not mean to challenge the view that ultimate power in the USSR resides at the top of the Communist party hierarchy. Neither do we mean to infer that the top party leadership was forced by a "policy group" to act against its will. We do not suggest that the instance we cite is modal. Indeed it is the best example we are aware of. We hope that the major payoff in this paper will be in showing why things happened as they did. This is the first step in finding out whether and how often to expect them again.

The first major section of the paper will describe the situation we use as a basis for our speculative analysis about the Soviet decision making process. The second will attempt to explain why things happened as they did, and the third will report some hypotheses about when such phenomena are likely to recur.

Debate over the 1958 Act

A prominent feature of post-Stalin Russia has been the nationwide discussion of certain legislative proposals. This does not constitute a totally new innovation in the Soviet Union. During the preceding period such important laws as the constitution of 1936 received nationwide discussion before enactment. A few differences, however, deserve mention. First, the frequency of these discussions has substantially increased. Second and more important, the impact of these discussions on the proposed legislation has in some instances been far more than peripheral. This especially applies to the debate which surrounded the Educational Reform Act of 1958. A closer look at this debate will afford us an opportunity to consider how the opinion of various "publics" can influence the policy process.

There can be little doubt about whose initiative lay behind the proposed reform. At the Thirteenth Komsomol Congress in April of 1958, First Party Secretary Khrushchev severely criticized the existing school system and demanded fundamental changes. This attack seems to have been motivated by three problems facing Soviet society in the mid 1950s, the cause of which Khrushchev linked to the existing school system.

First, the Soviet press had unceasingly criticized the denigrative attitudes of the younger generation toward physical labor. In the opinion of the First Secretary, the undue emphasis upon classical academic training and the neglect of the polytechnical side of education were largely responsible for this attitude.

Second, competition for admission to higher education had reached an excessive degree and this likewise had caused great concern among political leaders. The competition itself has largely been a by-product of changes in the economic and educational systems.

Prior to 1950 the rapid growth of the economy and the underdeveloped secondary educational facilities maintained the demand for skilled technical cadres at a higher level than the supply. Throughout this period the number of available places in higher education exceeded the number of secondary school graduates. The postwar years, however, witnessed a remarkable acceleration of secondary school facilities and enrollment. In 1949, out of a total enrollment of 33 million pupils, only about one million were in grades eight to ten. Four years later the number of pupils in secondary education had risen to four and one half million. Now the annual supply of secondary school graduates greatly exceeded the number of vacancies in higher education. Since the Soviet regime, for reasons of its own, was unwilling to widen the availability of higher education, the gates of universities were closed to millions of youth regardless of their educational attainment.

An inevitable consequence has been the intensification of competition for the available number of places. The pressures for admission became abnormally high because of the widespread notion that a college degree [represented] the key to individual advancement and entrance into the new class of Soviet intelligentsia. Consequently, those high school graduates initially denied admission refused to accept their fate. Instead of entering the labor force, many of them became perennial college candidates. Very often they applied to schools whose area of specialization was of no genuine interest to them. But in the absence of alternatives they would often enter an agricultural institute just to be able "to study somewhere." Here again Khrushchev charged that the educational system had bred such attitudes. By allowing students to continue their education uninterruptedly and by stressing almost exclusively academic material, the schools naturally generated the expectation that the path to life lay solely through higher education.

The third problem involved the increasing stratification of Soviet society. The notion that higher education was the key to membership in the "new class" had a firm basis in fact. Yet these educational channels for upward social and political mobility were being drastically constricted as a consequence of their preemption by the incumbent political and bureaucratic elites. Khrushchev himself admitted that in the competition for admission to college the influence of parents often proved more important than the merit of the candidates. He further stated that only 30 to 40 percent of the enrolled students in higher education institutions came from worker and peasant backgrounds. The differential access to a prime source of mobility gravely concerned the First Secretary. Both the content and tenor of his statements clearly indicate that Khrushchev sought to eliminate privilege and inequality from the Soviet educational system.

Finally we should mention an additional factor which *may* have influenced the reform movement. At the time of the debate some Western scholars argued that the specifics of Khrushchev's proposals owed much to the serious labor shortage the Soviet economy was about to experience. The argument may be briefly summarized as follows. Because of severe war losses and a declining birth rate in the postwar period the Soviet Union would have one-third fewer people entering the labor force during the late 1950s and early 1960s than normally would have been the case. Consequently the ambitious economic growth program could be achieved only if the vast majority of young people were channeled into the active labor force instead of higher education. It is important to note, however, that the Soviet press never cited a labor deficit as cause for the reform. Other evidence also casts doubt upon the validity of this thesis.

While there is room for disagreement as to what problems motivated the reform, there is no ambiguity regarding Khrushchev's proposals for dealing with them. In September of 1958, the party secretary published his "thesis" on school reorganization. He suggested that continuous academic education be abolished and that all students be required to combine work with study. In effect this meant phasing out the ten-year school which at that time constituted a completed secondary education. After finishing a seven- or eight-year primary school, said Khrushchev, every young person should enter the labor force. Those who wished to prepare themselves for higher education could continue their studies in evening and correspondence schools. Successful students would receive two or three days released time from work to facilitate studying.

The substitution of part-time work and study for full-time education in secondary day schools had, from Khrushchev's point of view, two advantages. First, it would instill in the younger generation a respectful attitude toward physical labor. Second, it would equalize access to higher education. The secondary day schools had become the province of children from the urban intelligentsia. Evening and correspondence schools, on the other hand, recruited most of their students from worker and peasant families. The difference in the quality of education offered by these two divisions gave the day school graduate an obvious advantage. By fusing the two channels into one undifferentiated system, Khrushchev hoped to eliminate the class bias in Soviet education. The road to a higher education would be the same for all irrespective of the positions or jobs which the parents held in society.

Study in higher educational institutions was also to be put on a part-time basis. The student would acquire the first two or three years of his college education through evening or correspondence courses. Thereafter he could complete his training on a full time schedule. Moreover, no individual was to be granted admission to higher education unless he had already worked full time after completing secondary school. Once again we see Khrushchev's determination to de-emphasize the purely academic side of education and to enhance the importance of work experience.

If we compare Khrushchev's September Memorandum with the actual law adopted in December 1958 we find that the two differ not only in detail but in basic principle. To begin with, the old secondary day school was preserved more or less intact both in form and content. Khrushchev's demand that work be combined with study had received token satisfaction by increasing the number of hours devoted to polytechnical training *within* the schools. But the quantity and quality of academic subjects had in no way been sacrificed. The law established an eleven-year day school to replace the old ten-year day school system. The addition of another year permitted greater emphasis upon labor training without simultaneously diluting the quality of academic education. Indeed, the number of hours devoted to purely academic subjects proved to be *exactly the same* under the new system as it had been under the old.

The maintenance of continuous secondary full time education must be seen as a rebuff to Khrushchev's demands. When the new law went into effect, it became apparent that nearly all the former ten-year schools would continue to operate as part of the new eleven-year system. Some figures also suggest that the number of students enrolled in the new system was comparable in size to the two senior grades of the old ten-year school.[3] It is true that Khrushchev recognized in his memorandum the need for *some* full-time day schools. But he envisaged that they would operate only during a transitional period and he expected their number to be sharply reduced right from the beginning of the reform.

While the eleven-year system might have satisfied the demand that work be combined with study, it could not possibly have achieved Khrushchev's other expressed purpose—the elimination of privilege and inequality. The perpetuation of a bifurcated full-time and part-time school system insured that inequality would persist. Nevertheless the disadvantages faced by the evening and correspondence student might have significantly diminished had the law incorporated Khrushchev's suggestion regarding

---

[3]The actual law left this point unclear but later developments indicated that just as many children—about a third of the total—would attend full time high schools as had been the case before the reform. See Thomas Bernstein "Soviet Educational Reform," (M. A. Thesis, Columbia University, 1962), p. 111, and articles in *The New York Times,* September 2, 1959; *Wall Street Journal,* June 29, 1960.

released time for study. Yet in this area as well important modifications were made. The reorganization decree left this question open and subsequent legislation resulted in a far less liberal policy.[4] Under these circumstances the vast majority of college students would continue to come from the full-time secondary schools and an inevitable by-product would be the continuation of class bias in higher education.

The provision for admission to and study in higher educational institutions likewise markedly deviated from Khrushchev's suggestions. Instead of *absolutely* requiring full-time work before admission, the law merely stipulated that *priority* would be granted those with the record of employment or military service. But precedence for people with production experience already existed before the reorganization of the school system. Thus the wording of the law gave only formal recognition to an on-going practice. It cannot be interpreted as a "concession" to the demands made by Khrushchev in his memorandum.

His insistence upon part-time study during the first few college years appears to have been more successfully realized. At least the law accepted it in principle. However, even here some important alterations occurred. The law explicitly exempted from this requirement all students in difficult theoretical disciplines. Similarly, the requirement would be inoperative in both nontechnical higher educational institutions and in arts faculties at universities since "factory work for students cannot in these cases be connected with their future job."[5]

Generally speaking, the education reform failed to implement the most important goals and purposes which Khrushchev had articulated in his memorandum. What factors can account for the observable disparity between the September proposal and the December law? To answer that question we must look briefly at the discussion which ensued during this period of time. The content of that debate clearly revealed that different social groups, or at least some members of them, opposed Khrushchev's reform.

Teachers and administrators identified with the ten-year school obviously wished to preserve and protect their institutional bailiwicks. But a frontal assault on the First Secretary's ideas would not have been good politics. Instead they opposed the reform more deviously. Essentially they argued that to prepare youth for manual labor it was not necessary to send them after the eighth grade to factories or farms. A much better way would be to bring the factories and farms into the schools by setting up first-class workshops. Under these conditions it would be possible to teach pupils the same skills they could learn by entering the labor force. To substantiate their case the proponents of this approach assumed the initiative even *before* the appearance of Khrushchev's September memorandum. Prior to the opening of the school year in 1958, Y. I. Afanasenko, Minister of Education for the Russian Republic, announced that the number of schools giving training in industrial and agricultural skills would double. He further announced that the Russian Republic had begun to experiment with extending secondary schools from ten to eleven years. Under the extended program students would spend half of their time at school and the other half at jobs on farms, in

---

[4]Instead of the two to three days released time from work as suggested by Khrushchev, students in evening schools received only one additional free day for study. See A. I. Shebanova, "O l'gotakh dlia lits sovmeshchaiushchikh rabotu s obucheniem," *Sovetskoe gosudarstvo i pravo* (Vol. 30, November, 1960), pp. 99–102.

[5]This point was made by the Soviet Minister of higher education and was reflected in the final law. See V. P. Eliutin, "Soveshchanie rabotnikov vysshei shkoly," *Vestnik vysshei shkoly* (Vol. 16, No. 10, October, 1958), p. 9.

factories, or at construction sites. He mentioned that fifty schools with this program had operated the last year and this number would increase to two hundred this year. Here, in embryonic form, was the eleven-year school system that became law in December of 1958. Thus, through word and deed, those occupational groups associated with full-time secondary education sought to protect the organization they had built with effort and care.

Other groups opposed to the reform included higher educational and scientific personnel. Their arguments were perhaps more telling. They warned that it would be impossible under the new system to ensure the supply of highly qualified cadres for economic and societal growth. How can we, they asked, perfect and advance scientific knowledge when new entrants to higher educational schools would have only eight years of regular schooling behind them and who, in the following years, would have forgotten the little they had once learned. Several prominent educators and scientists went so far as to assert that a hiatus between incomplete and complete secondary school as well as between complete secondary school and higher education would result in irreparable damage to the state. For creative work in scientific research often manifests itself when the individual has reached his mid-twenties and the acquisition of theoretical knowledge on a large scale demands uninterrupted study.

The warning of experts reinforced grave doubts raised by many parents. The basic argument of the latter was that a shortened basic school program would adversely affect the physical and intellectual maturation of adolescents. Furthermore, it was said that channeling young people into production at an early age does not give them a chance to adequately choose a skill which best suits them. While both of these points had merit, parental views were somewhat suspect because other motives could be readily discerned. As Khrushchev himself pointed out, many parents were determined that their children receive opportunities for maximum education. They saw his plans as a threat to that opportunity and responded by attacking it. To the extent that pedagogical experts echoed parental concerns, as some did, they served as a linkage between public opinion and political decision makers. By articulating the interests of an amorphous group in technical terms, the experts transformed their claims into a politically relevant issue.

A few words must also be said about the attitudes of factory managers. Although their opposition did not find explicit expression in the debate, their behavior left few doubts as to where they stood on the issue. Long before the question of reform had arisen, managers had displayed a reluctance to hire and train juvenile workers. Under the new arrangements they would become responsible for all sorts of educational functions for which the factory was ill prepared. Moreover, the large influx of school children and the necessity to train them would inevitably divert managers from their own duties of production and plan fulfillment. In light of this fact it is not surprising that the reform act failed to implement Khrushchev's suggestions regarding released time from work. That would have greatly complicated the managers' tasks and we can assume that their views were transmitted to the proper authorities.

At this point, our task is to account for the role of groups in forming educational policy in this instance by interpreting a number of facts. The objective facts we must work from are, in summary, that Khrushchev made a far-reaching proposal to deal with a number of educational problems facing the regime, and that the substance of the proposal was radically modified. The major proponent of the reform was obviously Khrushchev himself. The most important—indeed the only—opponents of the changes we can identify are the social groups cited above.

Here we should note that if one quantifies the number of articles which appeared during the debate, the oppositional point of view is clearly a minority. It is quite possible that a "war of memoranda" may have been raging behind the scenes and that during this exchange the minority position was in fact the majority point of view.[6] Whatever may have been the case, it is undeniable that the oppositional arguments were closer to the form of the finally enacted law.

There are several possible interpretations which would explain the outcome of the educational reform debate. One might argue, for example, that the disparity between the September memorandum and the December law resulted from Khrushchev changing his mind. Once the technocratic elites had pointed out the potentially dangerous consequences inherent in Khrushchev's proposals, the First Secretary simply revised his original position. There is no way, of course, to verify or falsify this interpretation. Since we have no knowledge of Khrushchev's preference schedule or to whom he would most likely listen, we must allow for the possibility that anyone who had a position and stated it prior to the outcome might have influenced Khrushchev. If we accept this interpretation, however, we must resolve certain questions which detract from its credibility.

When Khrushchev spoke to the Komsomol Congress in April 1958, he stated that the Party Central Committee had, *for some time,* been discussing the improvement of public education. Presumably, experts had been consulted during the course of such discussions. We might also presume that Khrushchev sounded out experts between April and September when he was preparing a detailed proposal for educational reform. In light of this, it seems unlikely that Khrushchev changed his mind because he heard convincing arguments which had not been made in the far longer period which preceded publication of his memorandum.

It is also important to recall that Khrushchev clearly identified himself personally with the issue of educational reform. He placed his public prestige squarely upon the line. As Richard Neustadt has pointed out, chief executives cannot afford to make indiscriminate public pronouncements. If they are sensitive to the prerequisites of power and influence, they must carefully weigh the consequences which flow from what, when and how they say things.[7] All the evidence we have on Khrushchev's career suggests that he was highly sensitive to the requisites of power and influence. Thus not only did the First Secretary have ample opportunity to consult expert opinion on the educational question, but he also had a vested political interest in doing so before publicly stating his position.

Our own inclination then is to discount, though not categorically reject, the possibility that Khrushchev simply changed his mind between September and December. An alternative interpretation is that bureaucratic groups prevailed over the First Secre-

---

[6]There is some evidence that the opposition was far greater than one would gather from simply reading the official press. For example, relatively few parental criticisms found their way into print. But during 1963–64 when the first author of this paper was conducting interviews in the Soviet Union, it was learned that a very large number of urban middle class parents had strongly criticized Khrushchev's proposals at "PTA" meetings held during the reform debate period. Similarly, Professor William Johnson of the University of Pittsburgh told the same author that opposition among educational officials was far more widespread than the official press revealed. Professor Johnson was in the Soviet Union at the time of the debate and is known to have extensive contacts with Soviet educators.

[7]Richard Neustadt, *Presidential Power* (New York, 1964).

tary and forced him to act against his will. To accept this, however, would demand a rewriting of the literature on political power and resources in the Soviet Union that we think is neither necessary nor appropriate. It is quite easy on the other hand to imagine more important actors prevailing over Khrushchev with the social groups associating themselves spuriously, so to speak, with the stronger actors. In suggesting this interpretation we must argue inferentially because the only direct evidence we have about opposition to the proposal relates to the groups. In the section below we will attempt to account for what happened and to assess the role of the social groups in it.

The Role of Social Groups in Shaping the Act

Brzezinski and Huntington express the orthodox interpretation in arguing that the key political resource in the Soviet Union is control of the party organization, and that such control can be shared only at the top.

> Thus, insofar as there are limits on the power of the top leader in the Soviet Union, they stem from his sharing control of the *apparat* with a small number of colleagues . . . the principal limits on the power of the Soviet leader are inside the Kremlin.[8]

We agree, and we feel that those colleagues were crucially important in defeating Khrushchev's proposal. But the opposition of the groups identified above was not coincidental. We submit that the groups were mobilized after the dispute was left unresolved at the top.

Such an argument forces us to take sides in a dispute among Soviet scholars about whether or nor there is conflict within the Soviet leadership at times other than succession crises. It is the position of the "conflict" school that policy issues such as those on agriculture, heavy industry, consumer goods, foreign affairs, Stalinism, economic reorganization, and education are continuous sources of dispute among the top leadership. When one issue is resolved, another is likely to take its place. We think there is strong evidence for this viewpoint, which became more compelling than ever with Khrushchev's political demise in October 1964.

In this specific case, Khrushchev stated in April 1958, that the Party Central Committee was presently engaged in preparing a resolution on the improvement of public education. But the September "theses" proved to be simply a note by Khrushchev with the "approval" of the Central Committee, instead of a formal resolution by that august body. This suggests that Khrushchev's educational reform was a highly personal document which lacked support among a substantial element of the top political leadership. Esoteric evidence to support this thesis is provided by the unusual silence of the top political leadership during the educational reform debate. Khrushchev appears to have been the only Praesidium member to have played a significant role in the reform discussions and to have clearly and publicly expressed his attitudes. Sidney Ploss has argued that in the context of Soviet politics the silence of leaders on a topical issue must be construed as disagreement with the expressed viewpoint of their colleagues.[9]

---

[8]Brzezinski and Huntington, *Political Power*, p. 145.

[9]See *Conflict and Decision-Making in Soviet Russia* (Princeton: Princeton University Press, 1965), pp. 17–18.

It is also significant that major amendments to Khrushchev's plan were reflected in the Central Committee resolution on education reform which was finally issued on November 16, 1958.

If, as we have argued, the important conflict was on the top leadership level, and if the persons on that level have the power to determine policy outcomes, what role did the social groups play? The answer hangs on the nature of conflict among the leaders. It is well known that such conflict involves elements of power struggle and elements of dispute over policy alternatives.[10] Sometimes these elements operate independently of one another; more often they intertwine. Since Khrushchev had decisively defeated his rivals for power in 1957, we can assume that in the case of the education reforms of 1958 the elements of power struggle were less important than at almost any time since Stalin's death, and that the elements of unadulterated policy dispute were correspondingly more important. Indeed, it is unlikely that Khrushchev would have survived such a defeat as this had this policy dispute involved much power struggle.

Insofar as this was really a policy dispute, it involved numerous problem-solving considerations, as we emphasized above. The problems and policy positions associated with them involved a number of questions of judgment about what courses of action would solve the problem, and what the consequences of such action would have for other goals of the regime. It is here that the groups play an important role. Numerous groups have recognized expertise about [the] problems . . . in their own area. The ten-year school personnel had an authoritative position for a judgment that students could get work experience without radically changing the school organization and curriculum. The scientific community had good claim to special insight into the needs of training scientists. Parents may be viewed as having some legitimate judgment about the needs of adolescents, although this is less apparently expertise. One student of the reform debate has argued that

> The most important factors responsible for the change in Khrushchev's original proposals probably were the arguments of experts—the function of expert opinion was to point out to the leadership the possibly harmful consequences to Soviet society of the literal adoption of Khrushchev's original plans.[11]

It is hard to identify any concrete resource other than their own recognized expertise which the groups might have used in the dispute. Neither money, votes nor popularity were relevant to its resolution. Only the expert judgment was clearly relevant. The only reasonable alternative would seem to be that the regime may have accorded the positions of these groups a certain legitimacy just because they were group preferences, much as an American public official might yield to a constituent's demand simply because he views it as legitimate and because he may view his job as one of servicing such demands when they are legitimate and do not conflict with other goals. We have no reason to believe that Soviet officials view their jobs this way. Communist ideology, unlike democratic ideology, supplies its own policy goals, rather than depending on public expressions of preference to define them. Besides, we have already seen that the goals of these groups conflicted with the goals of none other than the First Secretary of the Communist party. It does seem apparent that insofar as groups influenced the outcome of this issue it was through the communication of their expert judgments to people at the top of the hierarchy who *were* in a position to influence outcomes. The expertise became a resource to be used in making a case that more harm than good

---

[10]See Brzezinski and Huntington, *Political Power,* pp. 267, 269–283, 295–300.
[11]Bernstein, "Soviet Educational Reform," p. 119. See also Brzezinski and Huntington, p. 214.

would result from the proposed reform.[12] We contend that in the Soviet Union policy issues are often decided on the basis of such debates. If such is the case the arguments of persons who are recognized as being knowledgeable can be an important resource for the proponent or opponent of a policy proposal.

One can see elements of ambiguity in this interpretation of the role of these groups as articulators of expert judgment. It may appear, for example, that the ten-year school personnel are looking out for themselves when they oppose changes in their institution. The position of the parents seems even more transparent. There may even have been some self-interest involved in the position of the scientists. The point is that there is no objective way for either Soviet leaders or American scholars to clearly separate the elements of self-interest from those of expert predictions of dire consequences. We would argue that in Western democracies as well there is often an almost indecipherable mixture of preference and prediction in policy debate. For example, social welfare policies in the United States are commonly defended in terms of the prospects of contraction and recession if welfare funds are not fed into the economy. The very ambiguity between preference and prediction may serve to enhance the prospects of group influence through the pressing of interests with the support of expert judgments. The congruence of one's interests with one's predictions is probably less important than the persuasiveness of the predictions and the acknowledged expertness of predictors, no matter whose interests they seem to support.

This almost inevitable mixture of self-interest and expertise provides a channel through which groups in the Soviet Union *may* influence policy when higher powers seek their judgment. We do not know how common this occurence is, but we are confident that expertise is not used in this way to resolve all policy disputes. We will devote the remainder of this paper to an assessment of conditions leading to such a state, and to hypotheses about when to expect it. Our first set of hypotheses deal with what conditions within the current post-Stalin regime will be associated with such group influence. The second set will attempt to identify what it is about post-Stalinist Russia that makes this possible in contrast with the Stalin era.

Some Hypotheses

Leadership conflict has already been cited as an important factor in leading top officials to look to group expertise. It is more than conceivable that monolithic leadership would itself seek expert advice, but we expect that it would do so more surreptitiously than through semipublic debate. More importantly, it could ignore the advice when it chose to rather than in effect being reversed by it. Under conditions of leadership conflict, unresolved disputes may lead some of the participants to broaden the scope of conflict by involving policy groups who might shift the balance. The dynamic involved may be something like the following. There is a split, for example, among the Politburo wherein the First Secretary is about to prevail. Holders of the minority

---

[12]In this instance, many political leaders may have been especially inclined to "believe" these arguments. As primary members of the new class, Communist party cadres had good reason to support the educational *status quo*. They were among the chief beneficiaries of the existing system. Their children enjoyed advantageous access to full-time secondary and higher education. There is no question that such cadres hoped to perpetuate the provision of such education for their children. Khrushchev's proposals surely must have caused consternation among party cadres which other top party leaders would readily have been conscious of. In this respect the party itself was probably an important constituent pressure group which reinforced the doubts Khrushchev's colleagues had about the wisdom of his proposals.

position may react to their imminent defeat by contacting their sympathizers among the "policy groups" and urging them to state their position on the issue in their specialized publications, in hopes that the balance of power will shift in their favor when more actors are involved. Broadening the scope of conflict may change the outcome.

We hypothesize that the more and greater the disputes on the top policy making level, the more likely it is that policy groups will be involved and listened to.

Brzezinski and Huntington point out that policymakers are "more responsive to the demands or aspirations of groups" during a struggle for power, which would seem to bear out our point.[13] They use Khrushchev's struggle as an example but they themselves point out elsewhere that victors in power struggles often reverse themselves and adopt the policies advocated by their opponent.[14] This pattern would seem to reduce the long term impact of group influence in a power struggle. Our own example is of an unreversed policy decided in a period when the heat of the struggle for power had diminished, whether it had completely died or not. Indeed the absence of a threat to his power may well have made Khrushchev more willing to yield. Brzezinski and Huntington say that while policy is the means to power in succession struggles,

> In stable dictatorial conditions, however, the leader may sometimes exercise power in matters that do not affect the security of his position. Then, as with the education reform of 1958, he can tolerate substantial amendments to his original proposal.[15]

It may be, then, that conditions of tranquility lend themselves more effectively to more or less permanent and far-reaching group influence than do power struggles. Leaders are probably more eager to solicit the support of groups when they are trying to secure power or ward off threats to their position, but group influence may be more permanent and real outside of power struggles. We are not prepared to predict that group influence over policy will be greater under power struggles or more ordinary policy conflicts, but we are prepared to argue that under either of these conditions of leadership conflict group influence will be greater than when leadership is relatively monolithic. Such a hypothesis is at the core of our whole argument.

[It has been observed] that the failure of a policy may lead the Politburo to adopt an approach that they recently opposed.[16] Our example does not directly support this observation, although of course it does not conflict with it, but the important point suggested by it is that the nature of the issue may be an important variable. Pursuing the rationale for our argument of group influence in the educational reforms, it is apparent that the problematic character of the issue and the fact that the consequences of a shift were not known with certainty made the judgment of policy groups more important than they would have been otherwise. The obvious implication of this is that the more problematic the consequences of a given course of action the more likely it is that groups would be involved.

A related point that is derived from interest groups politics in Western democracies is that groups are likely to be more influential in policy outcomes when the issue is narrow and technical than when the issue is broad and general.[17] In democratic polities, this is partly because other publics are less likely to be paying any attention, or [less likely] to care when the issue is technical. Thus the field is left relatively open for the

---

[13]Brzezinski and Huntington, *Political Power,* p. 198.

[14]*Ibid.,* pp. 193, 240–252.

[15]*Ibid.,* p. 270.

[16]Raymond A. Bauer, Alex Inkeles and Clyde Kluckhohn, *How the Soviet System Works* (Cambridge: Harvard University Press, 1956), p. 98.

[17]See Harry Eckstein, *Pressure Group Politics* (Stanford: Stanford University Press, 1960).

interested group. A further rationale would be pertinent in the Soviet Union. It is not so much that other actors are or are not concerned; it is rather that technical advice and opinions are at a premium on technical issues.

We hypothesize that the more problematic and technical the issue, the more dependent on expert judgment elites will be. Consequently they will be more likely to consult policy groups, who will thereby be more influential on such issues.

While we hope that the above hypotheses help account for conditions varying *within* the current post-Stalinist regime which we associated with such group influence as we have illustrated, we do not argue that such influence ever occurred in the Stalin era. We know of no such prominent examples. In this final section we will identify several underlying conditions which in part distinguish the two eras and make groups more important in policy formation, or at least potentially so, in the present.

One important change is that the rigid dictatorial one-man rule of the Stalin period has given way to collective leadership. While there may be one dominant leader, his power is shared among several key figures at the apex of the political structure. Under conditions of a diffused power structure, group influence is far more likely.[18] When power is exercised in an autocratic manner, groups must gain the ear of the all-powerful leader if they are to influence the policy process. During a period of collective leadership the access routes to points of decision making become more numerous. Indeed, the very nature of collective leadership may make political leaders more responsive to group demands.

[It has been] argued that the transition from autocracy to oligarchy brings with it a constant struggle for political primacy at the very top. Since no individual is automatically assured of predominant power he must secure that position by winning and holding the support of a combination of societal groupings. His actual or potential rivals, on the other hand, can build their own constituency coalitions by identifying with those elements discontented with an incumbent leader's policy. The politics of leadership struggle then intertwines with the politics of group conflict. It is this interdependence which facilitates group influence on the policy process.[19]

We hypothesize that the larger and more collective the top leadership, the greater the prospects for the sort of disputes that can lead to the involvement of social groups in policy formation.

The attitudes of those leaders and their methods of social control will also have an important bearing on the prospects for group influence. Under a system of terror individuals are frightened into silent submissiveness and live in an atomized state. Unaware that others share common attitudes, grievances and interests, the terrorized citizen accepts his lot and does not attempt to influence the behavior of decision makers. Only when terror subsides does this condition of "pluralistic ignorance" end and the opportunity for interest articulation emerge. For now communication, both through the formal mass media and through informal personal interaction, assumes a more candid and realistic nature. Under these new conditions the communication process itself facilitates group influence. It serves to generate widespread awareness of commonly shared attitudes which in turn becomes a powerful factor inducing groups to influence policy outcomes in their favor.

---

[18]Dispersion of decision making can assume a "personalized" as well as an institutional form. Instead of separation of powers between executive, legislative, and judicial groups one may find a separation of powers between leaders at the top of an outwardly monolithic political structure. . . .

[19]Carl Linden, *Khrushchev and the Soviet Leadership 1957–1964* (Baltimore: Johns Hopkins University Press, 1966), pp. 20–21.

The leashing of terror enhances the prospect for group influence in other ways as well. . . . not all societal claims and demands are converted into policy outputs. Only those which become public issues have this possibility. In any polity this requires the patronage and support of some political authority figure. In a system where terror is no longer all-pervasive individuals may be far more likely to risk identification with unresolved issues since the consequences of poor choices are far less serious. At best it may mean that one's power position remains static. At worst it may mean a diminution in political power and perhaps even demotion. But it does not mean internment or execution as it so often did during the Stalinist period. The individual has lost a political battle but not necessarily the war. He remains on the scene with the possibility of recouping his losses and rising once again to top political positions.

We hypothesize that groups will be influential as technocratic spokesmen only when terror subsides and the regime accords them legitimacy of expression of their point of view.

The kind of expert judgment involved in the interest articulation we have described is a function of the nature of the society. [It has been] noted that modernization increases the significance of groups in the political process. We suggest that the modernization of Russia positively relates to potential group influence in several ways. First, it introduces a functional specialization and differentiation into the society which in turn generates a diffusion of interests competing with one another to write the laws of society to their advantage. During the early stages of Soviet rule the party preempts interest articulation not only because it wants to but also, to some degree, because it has to. The society which the Bolsheviks inherited was largely composed of an undifferentiated mass of peasants who had traditionally played a politically passive role. Thus the task of identifying and articulating interests fell to the party by default.

This is not to say that at the time of Bolshevik ascendancy there were no functionally specialized groups with political experience in the protection of their interests. They existed but they were far fewer and far less significant than in the present period. Furthermore, those groups tended to be stigmatized by their identification with the old regime. Thus any demands put forth by them lacked an essential ingredient for success—the presumption of legitimacy. The a priori belief of the party that such individuals were disloyal deprived them of any political currency which could be used in the process of trading support for recognition of their demands.

The modernization of Russia has fundamentally altered this situation. Not only has it generated a complex economic and social pluralism but it also has provided new cadres to staff these skilled groups.[20] Those who possess scarce technical capabilities are far more likely to exert influence today than in the past. Such technocrats are products of the new system (the new Soviet man) and their loyalty is not impugned. Consequently, their attempts to influence the political process is perceived in legitimized rather than counter-revolutionary terms. The arguments of scientific, educational, and managerial experts may have been motivated by selfish concerns. But, as we noted earlier these arguments were made in the context of what would best serve the interests of the Soviet Union. Given the fact that these experts are the products of the Soviet period, their counsel cannot be ignored on the grounds that the purveyors of such ideas are politically suspect. The handicap which afflicted old specialists simply does not operate in the contemporary period.

---

[20]For an interesting suggestive article on the growth of pluralism in Russian society see Henry L. Roberts, "The Succession to Khrushchev in Perspective," *Proceedings of the Academy of Political Science* (28, April 1965), pp. 2–12.

Stalin's transformation of Russia insured the increased importance of groups in the policy process in yet another way, although the full impact of this development had to await the dictator's death. It was during the 1930s and 40s that the politicization of society reached totalitarian dimensions. As politics came to predominate in all areas of life individuals realized that the protection of their interests could be achieved only by gaining access to and influencing the political structure. Unlike Western political systems where many issues are resolved in the private sector of the society, the struggle over who gets what when and how in the Soviet Union takes place entirely within the public domain. Thus individuals and groups are perforce compelled to focus their attention and pressure on the decision-making process if they hope to maintain or improve their status.

The fourth contribution of modernization stems from the fact that a complex technological society requires stable occupational group membership. As we have already suggested, the behavior of managers, teachers, educators, and scientists was motivated in part by their desire to protect interests derived from their occupational roles. Such a phenomenon occurs, however, only when individuals have an opportunity to firmly anchor themselves in one occupational role so that it becomes for them an important reference group. This connotes, in turn, an absence of the recurring purge so characteristic of the Stalinist period. Stalin purposefully removed leading strata of important groups lest they become too closely identified with the interests of those groups and more specifically lest they use the economic, social and political resources inherent in those groups for the purpose of delimiting the decision making power of the leader.

Now this is a very costly procedure and one that a developed society cannot afford to engage in for very long. Managers, teachers, scientists, and other specialists are not created overnight and their summary purge means not only a loss of experienced and skilled personnel but also the forfeiture of scarce economic resources invested in their education and training. As Soviet society has become more complex and sophisticated this type of gross economic waste proved intolerable. We do not imply, of course, that high ranking Soviet personnel are no longer removed from their positions. The official press is full of accounts concerning the removal of such personnel. We do argue, however, that "the purge" today significantly differs from its Stalinist predecessor. At present leading occupational strata are not removed in the wholesale manner reminiscent of the 1930s and 40s. More importantly their removal is seldom if ever accompanied by internment or execution. Most often they seem to be demoted to a less prestigious and influential job but within the same area of expertise.

We hypothesize that the more modern the society, the more dependent it is on technical expertise, which in turn improves the prospects that groups may influence policy when higher powers seek their judgment.

We have attempted in this article to illustrate that under some circumstances social groups can influence policy formation in the Soviet Union. We have specified those circumstances as clearly as we could, providing hypotheses according to which we expect group influence to vary. If our analysis is sound and valid, we hope that it may provide some guidelines for further research on group influence in the comparative study of Communist political systems.[21] Indeed, we hope that some parts of our analysis may be relevant to the study of the role of groups in policy formation in non-communist political systems as well.

---

[21]See Robert C. Tucker, "On the Study of Comparative Communism," *World Politics* (19 January, 1967), pp. 242–257.

17

Occupational Groups and the Chinese Cultural Revolution

Michel Oksenberg

This article analyzes the interests and power of seven occupational groups in China: the peasants, industrial workers, industrial managers, intellectuals, students, party and government bureaucrats, and military personnel. The evidence comes from two sources: (1) the activities of the members of these groups during the Cultural Revolution; and (2) revelations in the wall posters and Red Guard newspapers about their behavior from 1962 to 1966. The article concludes that the configuration of power and influence among these groups will be an important determinant of Chinese politics in the years ahead.

Analytical Approach

A few years ago, when the totalitarian model of politics in Communist countries was in its heyday, little attention was paid to the ability of various groups in society to influence public policy. The totalitarian model led analysts to concentrate upon the dictator, his whims, the political intrigue among those around him, and the control mechanisms which forced the populace to obey his commands. Barrington Moore and Isaac Deutscher stood out among the analysts of Soviet politics in the early 1950s for their willingness to look beyond Moscow to the power and influence of major groups in society.[1] Now, the totalitarian model has lost its earlier attraction, having proven unable to account for social change. Meanwhile, the approach employed by Moore and Deutscher has begun to win a wider audience, in part because in the early 1950s they suggested the possibilities of significant evolution in the USSR. . . . Barrington Moore's study of the social origins of democracy and dictatorship again has displayed the analytical power of a study of the interrelationships among key groups in society.[2]

From Michel Oksenberg, "The Political Group, Political Participation and Communication," *The Cultural Revolution: 1967 in Review,* Michigan Papers in Chinese Studies, No. 2 (Ann Arbor, Michigan: Center for Chinese Studies, 1968), pp. 1–44. [Reprinted with permission from the author and publisher.]

[1]Barrington Moore, *Terror and Progress USSR: Some Sources of Change and Stability in the Soviet Dictatorship,* Harvard University Press, 1954, and Isaac Deutscher, *Russia: What Next,* Oxford University Press, 1953.

[2]Barrington Moore, *Social Origins of Dictatorship and Democracy,* Beacon Press, 1966.

The Cultural Revolution provided a remarkable opportunity to view the structure of Chinese society in the 1960s. Prior to 1965, that view was obscured by the carefully nurtured image of a monolithic society led by a unified, cohesive elite. In 1966–67, the image was destroyed, revealing that the rulers were deeply divided and locked in bitter struggle. As the rulers lost their ability to provide unified, coherent guidelines to the nation, the various segments of society became more able to pursue their own interests. As a result, the Cultural Revolution made it possible to analyze the concerns of the major groups in society and their relative abilities to achieve their interests.

Before the substantive portions of the paper are presented, its analytical framework should be made clear. The analysis has four major conceptual underpinnings. The first concept involves the nature of groups and the ways they are able to articulate their interests. In common parlance, "group" has one of two meanings. One meaning is an "association," a collection of individuals who are formally organized for a purpose. When "interest groups" are discussed in the United States, people have the "association" in mind—a collection of individuals pursuing their common interests in concert. Another definition, more suited to the Chinese case, considers a group to be an aggregate of individuals with similar attributes, roles, or interests. Whether the members of the aggregate become aware of their similarity and form an association depends upon the context. But it is possible for the members of the aggregate, acting separately, to behave in the same way because of the similarity of their positions. In these terms, then, peasants can react to government policy as a group, that is, as an aggregate of individuals making similar decisions.

A second concept embodied in the analysis is that unorganized groups or aggregates can affect the policy formulation process. In democratic countries, aggregates have little trouble forming associations and gaining access to the key centers of decision making. In non-Democratic countries, aggregates continue to pursue their interests, but since they are unable to organize, they must adopt different techniques. Manipulation of information, passive resistance, noncompliance, and cultivation of friends in high places of government are some of the indirect methods which enable groups to influence policy. The important research question, as far as China is concerned, is to determine how and to what extent each aggregate registers its demands.

A third aspect of the analysis is that some groups in society have a greater ability than others to influence policy. A number of factors determine what groups have the greatest power, but key among them are the degree of their organization, the relationship of these groups to the means of production, the values and attitudes of the particular culture, the international situation, and the interrelationship among various groups. The process of industrialization involves the removal, often violently, of some groups from the locus of power, and their replacement by new groups.

Finally, the fourth underpinning of group analysis is the notion that, to a considerable extent, politics involves the attempts by powerless groups to obtain power, while groups with power struggle to retain it. Moreover, the politics of a country to a large extent reflects the conflicts within the groups that have power. In societies where the military has power, for example, national politics comes to involve inter-service rivalries, conflicts between senior and junior officers, and disputes between central headquarters and regional commands. If one can chart the distribution of power among various groups in a society, then one can predict what some of the important public policies and political issues will be.

The application of these concepts to the events in China in 1966–67 must not be misinterpreted as an attempt to explain the Cultural Revolution. Rather, this paper analyzes the Cultural Revolution for what it tells about one aspect of the structure of Chinese society. The seven broad occupational groups into which the Chinese Communists divide their society—peasants, intellectuals, industrial managers, industrial workers, students, party and government bureaucrats, and the military—are examined briefly and crudely, with the following questions in mind: What were some of the salient characteristics of these groups? What did the members of these aggregates perceive to be in their interest? Did the aggregates have any common group interests, and if so, what were they? How did they pursue their interests? What power did they have to enforce their demands?

These questions are not easily answered. Without the opportunity to do field research, it is difficult to ascertain what people perceive to be in their interests. The activities of the members of different occupational groups during 1966–67 and statements in the wall posters and Red Guard newspapers about their attitudes and behavior provide some clues. In addition, occupational groups appear to have some similar characteristics, no matter what country is under investigation; the literature on the roles and behavior of members of these groups in the developing countries then provides inferences about some of their likely interests in China. Further, some information is available on the perceived interests of different occupational groups in pre-Communist China. By seeking convergence among the different sources of information, the analyst can roughly identify occupational group interests at the present time. It is harder to estimate the ability of these aggregates to articulate their interests and affect public policy, but surely the relevant data here include actual instances of members of these groups influencing important political decisions or public policy clearly reflecting the interests of the group.

An analysis of the activities of occupational groups during the Cultural Revolution admittedly provides only a limited perspective upon the extraordinary complex events of 1966–67. But no single vantage will suffice in interpreting history of such sweeping proportions. Some of the valuable perspectives employed in other essays on the Cultural Revolution and purposefully eschewed here include analysis in terms of elites,[3] bureaucratic phenomena,[4] problems of industrialization,[5] and the Chinese political culture.[6] By approaching the Cultural Revolution from the perspective of occupational group interests, one of the oldest methods of political analysis, one hopefully will acquire additional insights into the structure of Chinese society and its relationship to the Chinese political system.

---

[3]For an analysis stressing this approach, see Philip Bridgham, "Mao's Cultural Revolution," *China Quarterly*, No. 29, January–March 1967, pp. 1–35.

[4]Analyses stressing this approach include: Franz Schurmann, "The Attack of the Cultural Revolution on Ideology and Organization," In Tang Tsou and P'ing-ti Ho, ed., *China's Heritage and the Communist Political System*, University of Chicago Press, 1968 forthcoming, and Chalmers Johnson, "China: The Cultural Revolution in Structural Perspective," *Asian Survey*, Vol. VIII, No. 1, January 1968, pp. 1–15.

[5]Analyses stressing this approach include: John W. Lewis, "The Leaders and the Commissar: The Chinese Political System in the Last Days of the Revolution," in Tang Tsou and P'ing-ti Ho, ed., *China's Heritage, op. cit.;* and Richard Baum, "Ideology Redivivus," *Problems of Communism,* May–June 1967, pp. 1–11.

[6]An analysis stressing this approach is Richard Solomon. "Communication Patterns and the Chinese Revolution," a paper delivered to the annual meeting of the American Political Science Association, September 1967.

Peasants

Peasant Interests. An important desire of most peasants probably is to be free to cultivate, reap, market, and consume their crops; they wish to have less extracted from them, and more goods available for purchase at lower prices. Peasants particularly demand political quietude during the planting and harvesting seasons. They also want their government to protect them from disorder and the ravages of nature. In addition, to the extent that their aspirations have risen, China's peasants also want better educational opportunities for their children, more welfare, greater security, and a standard of living comparable to urban dwellers.

Articulation of Peasant Interests. Peasants have no associations to voice their demands. Nonetheless, the Cultural Revolution provided ample evidence that the peasants had brokers embodying and representing their interests. Recalling the disaster of the Great Leap, when peasant desires had been disregarded, many among the Peking leadership strove to anticipate peasant reaction to proposed policies. Moreover, upon occasion, outbreaks of violence in the countryside forced the officials to pay attention to peasant grievances.

The brokers came primarily from three sources: the officials in agricultural agencies, regional officials whose power stemmed in part from the performance of agriculture in their areas, and military officers. A number of leading agricultural officials, in particular Teng Tzu-hui, T'an Chen-lin, and Liao Lu-yen, were accused in the *ta-tze-pao* of seeking to expand private plots and free markets, to restrict the power of the communes, and to assign brigade plots to individual households, thereby restoring production responsibility to the family. [Editors' note: The *ta-tze-pao* were large posters put up in schools, factories, and public meeting places; they helped communicate the wishes and policies of the leaders of the Cultural Revolution.]

Teng, T'an, and Liao, in effect, were voicing the interests of their peasant constituents. The reason for their action seems clear. The performance of the agencies which they led was judged largely by agricultural production. They depended upon the peasants to fulfill the targets for which the agencies were held responsible. It was in their interest, therefore, to argue for measures and to secure targets congruent with peasant interests.

Similarly, regional officials occasionally represented the interests of the peasants in their area. The purge of Li Ching-ch'uan of Szechuan [was] fascinating in this regard. If the charges against him [were] accurate, Li was keenly aware of the peculiarities of the Szechuan agricultural system, and sought to win exemptions from the uniform, nationwide regulations Peking sought to impose. He took exception, for example, to marketing regulations which Mao had endorsed. He pointed out that (because of the terrain and scattered population) rural markets in Szechuan were different from the rest of the country.[7]

The military also had a vested interest in peasant morale. To the People's Liberation Army [PLA] fell the unpleasant task of suppressing peasant unrest. Moreover, soldiers were recruited in the countryside, and troop morale was adversely affected by disen-

---

[7]Radio Kweiyang, June 28, 1967.

chantment at home.[8] The PLA conducted periodic surveys of troop morale, and monitored letters from home. When the surveys and monitoring revealed disenchantment at home, the military command apparently voiced its concern. As a result of these channels of communication, some military officers became particularly sensitive to the problems of the peasants and upon occasion acted as their representatives. This is precisely what P'eng Teh-huai was doing at Lushan in 1959 when he expressed the discontent of the peasants with the commune system.[9]

In addition to representation by brokers, peasants acted on their own behalf. Such actions included failure to comply with directives—for example, hiding production and concentrating on private plots—and sporadic violence. The *Work Bulletin* described peasant violence in Honan province in 1960, while during the first half of 1967 there were persistent reports of small peasant uprisings and of an illegal influx of peasants into many Chinese cities.[10]

These means of voicing their interests, when combined with surveys measuring rural discontent and the visits by higher level officials to the countryside, added up to a general awareness in Peking of the desires and problems of the peasants.

Sources of Peasant Strength and Weaknesses.   The power of the peasants to enforce their demands, however, was limited by the fact that they had no organization which could be considered their own. One wall poster indicated that some peasants were acutely aware of this problem:

> Workers have their unions, soldiers have theirs, and party workers have a body to represent their interests. Why don't we have unions? . . . .
> The peasants have no voice. They have only "formal" democracy. At the Second Conference of our Poor and Lower Middle Peasants Association, no decisions were made by us. All we had was a few days of free board and lodging.[11]

As anthropologists stress, peasants must overcome innumerable difficulties to become an organized, articulate, enduring political force.[12] Concerned with sheer survival and possessing only limited horizons, most peasants enter the political process rarely or not at all. They must depend upon sympathetic brokers to transmit their concerns to those who control the resources they want; barring that, their only recourse is noncompliance or violence.

This is particularly true in China, where the peasants are now bonded to the land. Owning only a small percentage of the land they till, unable to move without a hard-to-obtain permit, forced to deposit savings in state-regulated credit cooperatives which restrict withdrawals, peasants are largely at the mercy of lower-level party and government bureaucrats.

But it is easy to underestimate the power of the peasant aggregate. China's rulers must be at least somewhat responsive to the demands of the peasants because of their

[8]J. Chester Cheng, ed., *The Politics of the Chinese Red Army,* Hoover Institution, 1966. See pp. 12–19 for example.

[9]See *Peking Review,* No. 35, August 25, 1967, pp. 6–7 and No. 36, September 1, 1967, p. 14; Tokyo *Mainichi,* August 22, 1967.

[10]See *China News Analysis,* No. 645 and 647. For a dramatic account of one such uprising, see Joint Publications Research Service (henceforth JPRS) 44, 052, January 17, 1968, pp. 16–23.

[11]*China Topics,* YB 415, February 23, 1967, part III.

[12]See especially Eric Wolf, *Peasants,* Prentice Hall, 1966, p. 91; and Mehmet Bequirj, *Peasantry in Revolution,* Cornell, 1966, pp. 14–15.

numbers (roughly 80 percent of the population) and their economic importance. Roughly 35 to 45 percent of China's net domestic product, for example, comes from the agricultural sector, and the bulk of China's exports are agricultural and agriculturally derived products.[13]

The Cultural Revolution demonstrated that political power still was rooted to a considerable degree in control over the peasants and agricultural surpluses. The purges of Li Ching-ch'uan, the powerful Szechuan official, and T'ao Chu, the former Kwangtung official, show how these men were somewhat responsive to peasant demands in order to encourage the peasants to develop the potential of their areas. On the other hand, officials in grain-deficit areas, more dependent upon allocations from central government storehouses, were less able to resist Peking directives. Heilungkiang, Shantung, Shansi, Kweichow, Tsinghai, Peking, and Shanghai—all grain-deficit areas—were among the first to respond to Peking's call in early 1967 to establish Revolutionary Committees. (There undoubtedly were other reasons for their response.) Here are indications of the persistence in China of the intimate relationship between power and agriculture. The peasant has not yet lost his crucial role as a source of bureaucratic power.

Peasants During the Cultural Revolution. The course of the Cultural Revolution indicates that by 1967 even the radicals were somewhat sensitive to peasant needs. The two strongest efforts to subdue the Cultural Revolution came precisely at those moments when the peasants probably most desired order. Although earlier efforts had been made, the Red Guards were finally told to cease their marches and return home in early February 1967 on the eve of the spring planting. The PLA received more vigorous orders than usual to assist the peasants in spring planting. These February directives, coming on the heels of widespread signs of peasant unrest, were issued only 45 days after the December 15 directive extending the Cultural Revolution to the countryside.[14] This apparently calmer situation prevailed until early summer, when the turmoil increased. As the fall harvest neared, however, the Peking authorities again recognized the constraints imposed by China's essentially rural character; in late August and early September, they took stringent measures to control the Cultural Revolution.[15]

The peasant desire to be left alone was recognized in other ways. There is remarkably little evidence that the agitational activity which marked the Cultural Revolution in the urban areas spread to the countryside.[16] To judge from the provincial radio broadcasts, the main undertaking of the Cultural Revolution in the countryside was the propagation of Mao's thought, primarily through the organization of Mao-study groups. In spite of all the condemnations, there were very few reports of actual seizure of the private plots or restriction of free markets. The announcements of a good harvest in 1967 further reflected the fact that the Cultural Revolution essentially had bypassed the

---

[13]For summary discussions of the role of agriculture in the Chinese economy, see especially: Alexander Eckstein, *Communist China's Economic Growth and Foreign Trade,* McGraw-Hill, 1966, p. 47; Marion Larson, "China's Agriculture under Communism," in Joint Economic Committee of the United States Congress, *Economic Profile of Mainland China,* Government Printing Office, 1968, Vol. I, esp. p. 205; and Feng-hua Mah, "Public Investment in Communist China," *Journal of Asian Studies,* Vol. XXI, No. 1, November 1961, p. 46.

[14]*China Topics,* No. 415, February 23, 1967.

[15]Crucial here was Chiang Ch'ing's speech of September 5, 1967. An excellent summary of this period is in Chalmers Johnson, "China: The Cultural Revolution in Structural Perspective," *Asian Survey* (Vol. VIII, No. 1, January 1968), pp. 10–15.

[16]John R. Wenmohs, "Agriculture in Mainland China—1967," *Current Scene,* Vol. V, No. 21, December 15, 1967.

rural areas. In short, the evidence strongly suggests that the interests of the peasants elicit a response from China's rulers.

Industrial Managers and Industrial Workers

Since the divergent interests of industrial managers and workers are what strike most Americans, it is wise to recall their common interests in China. Both usually have a vested interest in uninterrupted production, in protecting factory equipment from damage, and in maintaining industrial prosperity and growth. In China, both have a vested interest in the evolving factory management system, in view of the welfare and housing benefits it bestows upon them. Moreover, the deep economic depression following the Great Leap very possibly had underscored to many the commonality of manager and worker interests in resisting attempts by other groups to intrude upon their domain. In spite of common interests, however, industrial manager and worker have rarely joined together to influence the course of Chinese politics.

Against this background, the events from December 1966 to February 1967 [have assumed] historical significance. They suggest that China's industrial sector has begun to come of political age. With a few exceptions, the industrial managers and workers, apparently acting in concert, resisted the efforts by parts of the bureaucracy and organized students to intrude upon areas they deemed to be their prerogatives. Within one month of the decision to extend the Cultural Revolution to the factories, the order was quietly but significantly tempered. If China's rulers had been unified in their support of the spread of the Cultural Revolution to the factories, the ability of the industrial managers and workers to temper its course would have been questionable. But the move was initiated only by a radical segment within the party and government bureaucracy, who required student support. More noteworthy, the considerable opposition within the bureaucracy indicated that since the Great Leap, the industrial managers and workers had acquired strong allies among the top officials.

The exact story of industrial cities in late 1966 and early 1967 has yet to be told, but enough is known to warrant a brief description.[17] In the stormy period following the August 1966 Eleventh Plenum, the Red Guards were repeatedly told that they were not to enter factories without prior approval of the factory employees, nor to interfere with production. One of the strongest warnings came in a November 10, 1966, *People's Daily* editorial, which said,

> Revolutionary students should firmly believe that the worker and peasant masses are capable of making revolution and solving their problems by themselves. No one should do their work for them. Special attention must also be paid to preventing interference with production activities . . . from the outside.[18]

---

[17] As a start, however, see: Evelyn Anderson, "Shanghai Upheaval," *Problems of Communism*, January–February, 1968, pp. 12–22; "Sources of Labor Discontent in China: The Worker Peasant System," *Current Scene*, Vol. VI, No. 5, March 15, 1968; Andrew Watson, "Cultural Revolution in Sian," *Far Eastern Economic Review*, April 20, 1967, April 27, 1967, and May 4, 1967; and Neale Hunter, "The Cultural Revolution in Shanghai," *Far Eastern Economic Review*, June 1, 1967, June 22, 1967, and July 6, 1967.

[18] "More on the Question of Grasping the Revolution Firmly and Stimulating Production," *Jen-min Jih-pao* (People's Daily, henceforth, *JMJP*), November 22, 1966, in *Survey of the Chinese Mainland Press* (henceforth *SCMP*), No. 3825, pp. 1–4.

But by December 9, the earlier policy was reversed and a more radical policy was adopted; the Red Guards were encouraged to enter the factories. In early December, in contrast to the November 10 editorial, a Red Guard newspaper could state,

> Chairman Mao has taught us, "The young intellectuals and young students of China must definitely go among the worker and peasant masses. . . " The cultural revolutionary movement must expand from the young people and students to the workers and peasants.[19]

The formal decision allowing the students to enter the factories, promulgated on December 9, was made public in the important *People's Daily* editorial of December 26.[20]

Five days later, the annual *People's Daily* New Year editorial indicated that there was considerable opposition to the measure. The editorial stated, "Any argument against carrying out a large-scale cultural revolution in factories and mines and in rural areas is not correct."[21] According to the rules of Pekingology, this sentence indicates that a strong debate was being waged. Moreover, by mid-January it was clear that the industrial managers and workers were undermining the December 9 directive. Rather than allowing the Red Guards to enter the factories, which might have led to damage of equipment, the factory managers encouraged their employees to leave the factories and travel to Peking to voice their grievances. Factory managers paid bonuses to their workers, promoted many of them, and gave them travel fare. Protesting Red Guard activities, it appears, factory workers went on strike, probably living off the bonuses paid them by their factory managers.

The joint activities of managers and workers, assisted by some Party and government bureaucrats, were described in an "Open Letter" which stated:

> In recent days. . . , a handful of freaks and monsters have cheated the misled . . . worker masses, to put forward many wage, welfare, and other economic demands to the leadership and administrative departments. . . These administrative departments and leaders, acceding to these demands and not caring whether it is in accord with state policy or not, sign their names to hand out generously a lot of state funds.[22]

Those who encouraged the workers to put forth their economic demands were accused of setting the "revolutionary workers movement onto the devious road of trade unionism."

The situation in Shanghai became particularly critical. The railroad network was partially paralyzed due to a high rate of employee absenteeism, with serious disruptions from December 27 to January 9. Public utility services in Shanghai were disrupted; shipping in the Shanghai harbor was adversely affected. Similar reports came from throughout the country. By mid-January, Radio Peking and the New China News Agency (NCNA) had reported instances of worker's strikes and sabotage in such major cities as Tientsin, Shenyang, Chengtu, Chungking, Sian, Canton, and Hangchow.

Within a month of the December 9 directive, the radical attack upon the industrial sector had produced near chaos. The first response of the leaders of the radical party and government bureaucrats and their Red Guard student supporters was to win allies among the workers and to encourage conflict between managers and workers. Special appeals were made to the temporary factory employees (factories have two types of

---

[19] JPRS 40, 274, p. 34.
[20] For another analysis, see *China News Analysis*, No. 644.
[21] *Peking Review* (No. 1, January 1, 1967), p. 12.
[22] Radio Foochow, January 9, 1967.

employees on their payroll—permanent employees, who are paid according to the set wage scale, receive fringe benefits, and have a regular rank; and temporary employees, who are employed on special contract, receive lower wages, and can be dismissed easily during a recession). To gain the favor of the temporary employees, the radicals blamed Liu Shao-ch'i for originating the temporary employee system. They implied that one of the purposes of the Cultural Revolution was to abolish the distinction between permanent and temporary labor. At the same time, the radicals attempted to isolate the factory managers from their worker allies. The managers were attacked as anti-Maoists; the workers were excused for being duped. A series of student-worker meetings was arranged to build good will.

The tacit alliance, particularly between managers and permanent employees, held firm and the government had to take stringent measures to restore industrial production. On January 15, Chou En-lai cautioned the Red Guards against hasty action. He implied that the action in Shanghai was too rash, adding that "we must . . . see to it that business organizations truly carry out business operations."[23] Two days later, the CCP Central Committee and State Council jointly issued regulations to strengthen urban public security work.[24] On January 28, an article by Mao Tse-tung entitled "On Correcting Mistaken Ideas in the Party," stressing the virtues of discipline and order, was reprinted, while on the next day, the State Council prohibited industrial workers from visiting their rural ancestral homes during the Chinese New Year. The efforts to keep the workers in the city, to keep the chaos in the cities from spreading to the countryside, and to restore urban order were receiving primary attention. To win back the permanent employees, on February 17 the Central Committee and the State Council decided to retain the distinction between permanent and temporary workers.

The stringent measures did not produce immediate results. They were intended to restore the confidence of the industrial worker, but they did little to assuage the fears of the factory managers, former capitalists, trade union leaders, and economic planners. The industrial sector apparently did not begin to return to normal until these groups also were mollified. To restore industrial calm, the vehement charges of "economism" leveled against the industrial managers began to be dampened in February. The press concentrated its attack upon "anarchists," meaning the Red Guards who persisted in their attacks on managers. The slogan so prominent in December and early January, "To Rebel is Justified," gave way to expressions of concern for the sanctity of property.

In view of the tacit manager-worker alliance, and the initial attempts both to split this alliance and divide the workers, the CCP Central Committee letter of March 18 has very special importance. Addressed jointly to the industrial workers and their leaders, the document officially recognized their common interests. Extremely mild in tone, the letter represents an almost total abandonment of the policy outlined in the December 26, 1966 *People's Daily* editorial extending the Cultural Revolution to the factories. The support given to the factory managers in the March 18 directive is worth quoting:

> As masters of the country, all workers *and staff* in factories and mines must, in the course of the Cultural Revolution, heighten their great sense of responsibility and protect State property effectively. . . .

> The Party Central Committee believes that in all factories and mines, the majority of cadres are good or relatively good. (Emphasis added.)[25]

---

[23]*SCMP*, No. 3913, p. 2.
[24]For texts, see *China Topics*, No. 418, March 8, 1967.
[25]*SCMP*, No. 3904, p. 9.

The mere issuance of these instructions did not restore industrial peace. The PLA also was instructed to enter factories to maintain discipline.[26] Workers who had joined the radicals were difficult to control, and factional strife among workers was a frequent phenomenon. Reports of worker absenteeism persisted. The effort to put factory production on a firm footing remained an elusive goal for the rest of the year.

Although these developments were important, the main significance of the events in China's cities from December 1966 to February 1967 should not be lost. In the heat of the Cultural Revolution, the industrial managers and workers, acting together, were able to alter drastically the intended course of the Cultural Revolution. The working class and their managers have moved closer to the center of power in Chinese politics.

Intellectuals

In the broadest terms, intellectuals have three tasks. First, they pass the values and accumulated knowledge from one generation to another. Second, they increase the sum total of knowledge and create new works of art. Third, intellectuals criticize the society in which they live and point out alternative ways of ordering their society. Intellectuals can be distinguished according to the relative emphasis they place upon these roles. Thus, the teacher primarily transmits the knowledge of his generation to his students. The nuclear physicist is responsible for providing new information. The political satirist criticizes his society.

Depending upon the values of the society and the demands of the most powerful groups in the political arena, the particular roles performed by intellectuals command somewhat different rewards.[27] The Cultural Revolution demonstrated the political values of each of these roles in China.

Social Critic.   The social critic was totally vulnerable to political control, as the attacks upon Wu Han and the Three Family Village with which he was associated revealed. To recall briefly, the historian Wu Han wrote on the virtues of the Ming minister Hai Jui.[28] Hai Jui had criticized a Ming emperor's alleged neglect of the peasants, and was removed from office as a result. Mao Tse-tung and those around him charged that Wu Han was using the story of Hai Jui as an allegory to attack Mao and defend P'eng Teh-huai, the dismissed Minister of Defense who had also protested against his leader's peasant policy. Mao, in short, was able to remove Wu Han and others after demonstrating that they were playing the role of social critic. This is not surprising for a society in which the distinction between criticism and disloyalty has often been blurred.

Transmitters of Values and Knowledge.   The Cultural Revolution also showed that the transmitters of values and knowledge serve at the pleasure of the dominant political groups. As Mao's earlier optimism about the fate of the Communist revolution

---

[26]For more detailed chronology see *China Quarterly*, No. 30, pp. 209, 232–233.

[27]For a general discussion, see Edward Shils, "The Intellectuals in the Political Development of the New States," in John Kautsky, ed., *Political Change in Underdeveloped Countries*, John Wiley, 1962, pp. 195–235.

[28]For the editorials attacking Wu Han and the Three Family Village, see *The Great Socialist Cultural Revolution in China* (Peking: Foreign Language Press, 1966–67), pp. 1–3. A collection of the satires attacking Mao which appeared in the Peking Press in the early 1960's was reprinted in Taiwan: *Teng T'o shih-wen hsuan-ch'i* (Taipei: Freedom Press), 1966.

gave way to a more pessimistic appraisal, he became more concerned with the educational process. While optimistic, he could afford to be lenient toward the past, for he believed China would not remain its captive. Later, the accumulated knowledge of the past and those who propagated it became threatening.

Several factors help to explain the political weakness of the propagandists, teachers, artists, and other transmitters of culture and knowledge. First, they had no economic allies, for few people's livelihoods depended upon them. Second, they were divided internally. Some younger "transmitters," such as the idealogues who came to the fore in late 1966—Wang Li, Yao Wen-yuan, Ch'i Pen-yu, and Kuan Feng—apparently were ready to assist in the removal of their superiors. Third, many "transmitters" had strong enemies among their students. Initially, the weight of tradition and knowledge and its concomitant responsibilities rests heavy upon students, and they tend to resent those who place it upon them. Students therefore were ready allies of the political groups who attacked the propagandists and teachers.

Researchers.   At the very moment the critics were condemned and the teachers were attacked, the press pointedly praised other intellectuals for developing nuclear weaponry, synthesizing insulin, and improving medical techniques.[29] The increasing importance of China's scientific community enables this segment of the intellectuals to exert its claims. A reasonable assumption is that many scientists are willing to recognize the supremacy of any political leader, so long as they are able to pursue their intellectual interests. This seems to be the tacit bargain struck during the Cultural Revolution. In the 1966–67 reports of their work, scientists always paid homage to the inspiration they derived from Chairman Mao. In exchange, Mao appears to have made fewer demands upon the time of scientists during this campaign than he did during the Great Leap Forward. For example, the twelfth point of the Sixteen Point Central Committee Directive on the Cultural Revolution specifically exempted the scientists, stating:

> As regards scientists, technicians, and ordinary members of working staffs, as long as they are patriotic, work energetically, are not against the Party and socialism, and maintain no illicit relations with any foreign country, we should in the present movement continue to apply the policy of "unity, criticism, unity." Special care should be taken of those scientists and scientific and technical personnel who have made contributions.[30]

Among China's intellectuals, the scientists fared best in 1966–67. Unlike peasants, industrial managers, or workers, who were able to defend their interests only after an initial attack against them, the scientists saw their interests taken into account *prior* to the Cultural Revolution. Since their role in China's industrialization effort is valued by other groups in society, they appear to have representation at the center of power.

Students

The Cultural Revolution suggests that Chinese students in many ways resemble students everywhere, particularly in the underdeveloped world. Four tendencies among Chinese students seem particularly noteworthy: idealism, deep ambivalence toward authority, highly developed consciousness of their student identity, and low capacity to form associations. These four characteristics must be analyzed at greater length.

---

[29]*Peking Review* (No. 1, January 1, 1967), p. 15.
[30]*Peking Review* (No. 33, August 12, 1966), p. 10.

Student Idealism.   With respect to their idealism, Seymour Lipset put it well in a general essay on the topic: "Educated young people . . . tend disproportionately (to their numbers) to support idealistic movements which take the ideologies and values of the adult world more seriously than does the adult world itself."[31] Lipset's observation seems applicable to China. During the Cultural Revolution, as during the Hundred Flowers Campaign of 1957, the students did not reject the ideals of the adult world, but rather criticized adults for not practicing their ideals. Moreover, as Lipset would predict, many Chinese students adamantly refused to compromise on matters they deemed of principle. Theirs was a movement in pursuit of the millennium.

Several factors seem to have produced their radicalism, not the least of which was that the students had been the target of intensive ideological campaigns, especially from 1962 on. The majority of the Red Guards, it should be remembered, were the first total products of the Chinese Communist educational system.[32] The values transmitted in these schools, glorifying revolution and Mao Tse-tung, apparently had an impact.

Another reason for student radicalism was their limited stake in the status quo. The Red Guards drew a particularly enthusiastic response not from college students but from the younger, middle-school students, precisely the segment of youth which had invested the least time and effort in planning a career. Moreover, in the Chinese cultural context, students can more easily afford to be radical than adults because of their more limited familial obligations. Certainly one of the striking and credible revelations during the Cultural Revolution concerns the familial interests of the older cadres in China. As they matured and assumed demanding adult roles, the former student radicals of the 1920s and 1930s, acting as good Chinese, paid increasing attention to the fortunes of their families. They made sure that their descendents received a good education, and even established special schools for the families of cadres. They saw to it that their children married into decent families and obtained good jobs.[33] And in many instances, the revolutionary leaders of China seem to have enjoyed close, warm relations with their children and grandchildren. These concerns apparently sapped their revolutionary zeal, for rapid social change would have made it impossible for them to assure the continuity of their family. This may be one of the major reasons why students have been so important in China's radical movements. Away from home, with neither children nor dependent parents, students were relatively unencumbered by the net of mutual obligations which confine adult Chinese. They were free to be radical.

Ambivalent Attitudes of Students Toward Older Generation.   Another characteristic of students, their tendency to regard the older generation with deep ambivalence, also helps to explain their idealism and zealotry. On the one hand, the Cultural Revolution indicated that many students seek the emotional support and intellectual guidance of an older authority figure. On the other hand, the Cultural Revolution also showed that many students tend to regard the older generation with distrust. In China, as elsewhere, a generational gap has developed. Some of the causes of the gap can be identified.

Many students apparently resented the fact that the older generation had the jobs and power which they wanted. The Red Guards concentrated their attacks upon those

---

[31]Seymour Lipset, ed., *Student Politics* (Berkeley: Institute of International Studies, 1966), p. 140.

[32]Not all Red Guards were students, it should be noted, nor were all students Red Guards. Though in this section I discuss the student sector of Chinese Society with particular focus upon the more radical students, my remarks may be applicable to Chinese youth in general.

[33]See *China Topics,* No. 427, May 23, 1967, Section F; JPRS, 41, 514.

parts of the bureaucracy which had been most reluctant to promote youth. According to some refugee informants, the party apparatus—particularly the secretariat on each governmental level and the Organization Department—placed the greatest stress upon seniority as a criterion for employment and promotion.[34] At the same time, the PLA and the finance and trade fields appear to have been more willing to reward youth. The PLA, with its "up or out" promotion system, [has guaranteed] to its younger members opportunities for upward mobility in the organization. The finance and trade system, expanding with the economy, probably was somewhat more able to offer employment opportunities to students. Not surprisingly, then, while the students were quick to "bombard the headquarters" of the party apparatus, they were less concerned with bureaucratism in the PLA and the finance and trade system. In sum, their zealous conduct toward the older generation partly reflected a frustration in employment opportunities.

But this was not the only source of generational tensions. The Cultural Revolution also indicated that many Chinese students resented their elders placing unwanted responsibilities on their shoulders. Urban students in particular began to feel these burdens in their high-school days, as they first contemplated the problems of career, marriage, filial obligations, and maintenance of traditions. The student violence toward both teachers and parents in July and August 1966 underscored the hostility with which youth viewed those in charge of disciplining them.[35]

Yet another cause of the generational tensions was the different environments in which the older generation and the students were reared. Many older cadres, Mao included, viewed the younger generation with apprehension, fearful that their education in a peaceful China did not imbue them with a spirit of self-sacrifice and dedication to change.[36] Students also were keenly aware of the gap that separated them from the older revolutionary generation. As early as 1963, an article in the journal *China Youth* put the problem as seen by youth quite well:

> In discussing heroic persons, frequently one hears many youth say such things as, "The era creates heroes," "Only when a drop of water flows down a mountain can it become part of a wave. Our lives are in an era of peaceful construction. We are water on a plain and only can advance slowly and quietly."
> The feelings go to such lengths that some youth believe they were born at an unfortunate time. They say, "If I were born thirty years earlier, I certainly would have participated in the Long March; if I were born twenty years earlier, I certainly would have been a hero in the anti-Japanese war. If I were ten years older, I certainly would have compiled a war record in Korea."[37]

This passage points both to the generational gap which youth perceived, and more significantly, to their desire to narrow that gap. In other words, the [foregoing] quotation reveals the eagerness of some youths to seize an opportunity to "make revolution," and thereby to join the portion of the older generation whose exploits they admire. Under the Communists as well as in traditional times, Chinese moral education makes

---

[34]This point is stressed throughout in A. Doak Barnett and Ezra Vogel, *Cadres, Bureaucracy, and Political Power in Communist China,* Columbia University Press, 1967.

[35]For one discussion of antagonistic student-teacher relations, see Radio Canton, Regional #2, April 3, 1967.

[36]See James Townsend's excellent study, *The Revolutionization of Chinese Youth,* Berkeley: Center for Chinese Studies Monograph, 1966.

[37]*China Youth,* No. 7, 1963, p. 11.

considerable use of models whom students are taught either to follow or shun.[38] Teen-agers are conditioned to search for model men to emulate, and they search for models among older men as well as among youth. Thus, the ambivalent attitude of students toward the older generation becomes understandable. While they resented the burdens the elders place upon them, they depended upon the elders to provide them with models of moral action.[39]

Many students in China, the Red Guards' experience suggests, adopted the model of the Chinese revolutionary tradition, with the romanticism and heroism they associated with it. In this, they follow Mao. Leaders who successfully associated themselves with this tradition and who were sympathetic to problems of youth acquired student support. On the other hand, the students seemed prone to reject the adult's world, of bureaucracy, which to them meant examinations and the need to plan careers. They considered as negative examples the men who, they were told, were responsible for bureaucracy—Liu Shao-ch'i, Teng Hsiao-p'ing, P'eng Chen, and others.

The accounts of Chou En-lai's appearances among the students give the impression of a leader who successfully bridged the generational gap and enjoyed a special rapport with the students. (His support among the students in the early days of the Cultural Revolution, in turn, may have added to his power within leadership circles.) One such account told of a Chou En-lai visit to Tsinghua University. Displaying magnificent command of Mandarin, Chou stated:

> In regard to your school, only by coming into your midst will one penetrate the masses. Nevertheless, now that I have come, I am still barely scratching the surface. (Audience: No!) No? I am sincere, let us think it over. If I do not go to your class room, your dormitory, and your dining room, how can I dissolve the unnecessary estrangement, unnecessary opposition, and unnecessary misunderstanding among you? Yet, you may ask me: Why are you so selfish? I am not! It is not being selfish. I feel bad that the problems were not solved satisfactorily by my talk last time. . . . . . I heard that, after my talk here last time, your problems were not satisfactorily solved, and that you posted three large-letter bulletins about me. They were too few. Reading over my speech again, I feel that you did not post enough large-letter bulletins. Many of your suggestions are correct.
>
> I wish to discuss my views once more. One must ceaselessly examine oneself. As I already mentioned last time, one must work, learn, and reform all one's life.[40]

The speech was delivered in a rain, but Chou apparently refused offers to hold an umbrella over him, saying, "You gave me a Red Guard arm badge. Similar to you, we also steel ourselves in the great storms." At the end of his talk, Chou led the students in singing of "Sailing the Seas Depends on the Helmsman." His was a masterful performance of a 68-year-old man successfully bridging the generational gap. The response he elicited is testimony to the importance of this aspect of the problem of youth in China today.

Student Consciousness.   A third aspect of student life made evident in the Cultural Revolution was its intensity. College students and even many high-school students

---

[38]See Donald Munro, "Maxims and Realities in China's Educational Policy," *Asian Survey,* Vol. 7, No. 4, April, 1967, pp. 254–272.

[39]See Richard Solomon, *The Chinese Revolution and the Politics of Dependency,* MS., University of Michigan, 1966.

[40]JPRS 41, 313, June 8, 1967, pp. 14–21.

lived on large campuses; their dormitories were crowded. In the suburbs of Peking, for example, several large university campuses were in close proximity. In such an environment, as at large American universities, students had little contact with faculty. They formed their own community, and acquired a high consciousness of their identity as students. In fact, some of Marx's observations about the sources of working-class consciousness are applicable to the rise of student consciousness: large numbers of people massed together, in similar positions, having a high rate of interaction. In addition, Chinese students, particularly those attending Peking University and Tsinghua University, were aware of the role of their predecessors in the May Fourth and December Ninth movements. It was therefore, in a sense, natural for the students to respond, as a group, to Mao's initial call for a student movement.

Moreover, student self-awareness probably was intensified during 1966–67. Group consciousness tends to be heightened by the kind of conflict that students experienced in 1966–67. In addition, student consciousness probably developed as their parochial, regional loyalties were weakened through the nationwide marches and "linking up" activities.

Student Inability to Organize.   A fourth characteristic, an especially fascinating aspect of the Cultural Revolution, was the students' inability to form effective associations, in spite of the constant exhortations to do so. Intense factional disputes marked Red Guard activities almost from their inception. While the issues involved in the disputes are not entirely clear, in part they appear to reflect the factional strife among the elite. Mao and the group around him organized Red Guard groups in the summer of 1966 to assist them in their attacks upon perceived enemies in the party and government bureaucracy. Very soon thereafter, other officials began organizing Red Guard groups loyal to them.

As the conflicts between these Red Guard groups intensified and spread throughout the country, particularly from January to August 1967, it apparently became possible for other students to form their own, unaffiliated organizations. The students of China, accustomed to a highly structured environment, suddenly found themselves in a near-chaotic situation. Previously, students were told which organizations were good, which were bad; they had little choice in organizational affiliations. Now, they had to choose among virtually indistinguishable organizations, recognizing that the wrong affiliation could ruin their careers. Little wonder, then, that in such an environment, with little previous experience in forming associations, the students failed miserably. They rapidly degenerated into quarreling, disruptive groups. Unaccustomed to the process of compromise and decision, debates over seemingly trivial issues apparently quickly became problems symbolic of the struggle between the two roads of capitalism and socialism. Coercion became the only way to re-establish order among the youth. The PLA dispatched units to schools; several young rowdies were executed in stadiums and the spectacle televised.

Another related phenomenon also appeared at this time. Unable to associate effectively, some youths simply withdrew from any political activity. . . . [This was] a predictable development. The Red Guards were intended in part to build a sense of community among youth. While undoubtedly becoming more conscious of their identity, instead of acquiring a sense of belonging, the youth probably became more aware of their isolation and their inability to form associations. Moreover, unattainable expectations were probably aroused among some youth in the course of the Cultural Revolution. The sense of isolation and the disappointments appear to have led to alienation or anomie rather than to commitment. . . .

Students during the Cultural Revolution. With the four characteristics of Chinese youth as revealed during 1966–67—their radicalism, ambivalence toward authority, sense of identity, and low capability of association—it is now possible to summarize the ability of the students to affect public policy during the Cultural Revolution. At the outset, the eager students were easily mobilized to attack the bureaucrats in the culture and education system. This occurred by September 1966. Mao and his associates saw that they had forged a powerful organizational weapon. The brutal Red Guard attacks upon defenseless victims in August and September 1966, however, soon made clear that the weapon would not be easily controlled. The mass rallies held from August to October in Peking were perhaps envisioned as a method for providing the youth with an emotional catharsis that would reduce their lust for violence.[41] At the same time, the energy of the youth was tapped by Mao and the radicals around him to attack provincial level party organizations throughout the country.

But for tens of millions of youth demanding participation in revolutionary activity, the dragging out of a couple hundred provincial and municipal level party secretaries only whetted the appetite. The youth appear to have kept pressing for more and bigger targets. In early December 1966, as mentioned earlier, the industrial sector was opened, while on December 15, the rural sector was opened. With the resistance encountered in both these sectors, they were removed from the list of targets in late January. The leaders of China cast about for diversionary targets and in February and March, foreign embassies in Peking bore the brunt of Red Guard hostility. But this too had its limits. Several foreign countries were in no mood to tolerate such diplomatic outrages. In March, the target was narrowed to Liu Shao-ch'i, Teng Hsiao-p'ing, T'ao Chu, and the other "top party persons in authority taking the capitalist road." At the same time, students were encouraged to return to school.

The rebellious force which the leaders had unleashed eight months earlier was not easy to contain, however. In search of new targets, the more radical students next wanted to take on the army. One reason for the increased animosity among many students toward the army was the role it played in quelling factional strife among youth. Following the July defiance of Peking's orders by the Wuhan garrison commander Ch'en Tsai-tao, students apparently increased the pressure to be given the army as a target; some of the ultra-radicals in Mao's entourage supported the student demands. In late August this target was firmly denied to them and new efforts were then made to open schools. By late fall 1967 the Red Guards were less frequently in the news, and in January 1968, a call came for a rectification campaign in Red Guard organizations. The main youth organization prior to the advent of the Red Guard, the Communist Youth League (CYL), rarely mentioned during 1967, began to be mentioned again in early 1968. The radical student movement had run its course, and an effort was being made to re-establish control over youth. In sum, youth were on the periphery of the political arena prior to mid-1966, had been allowed to enter the center by the radicals to wreak their havoc and steel themselves in revolution 1966–67, and were being pushed to the periphery again by the army and the moderates in the party and government in 1968.

Student Potential to Affect Future Policy. Several factors make it unlikely that student interests will be as peripheral to the political process as they were from 1950 to 1965. The memory of the Red Guards will linger on in the minds of bureaucrats, who

---

[41]This theme is suggested in Philip Bridgham, "Mao's Cultural Revolution."

probably will be somewhat more responsive to the demands of youth as a result. In addition, the youth have learned some lessons about voicing their interests which they are not likely to forget. Moreover, demographic trends probably will force the rulers to be particularly sensitive to the problems of youth. Their rapidly increasing numbers place an undeniable burden upon existing educational facilities and force the rulers to provide them with employment.

Further, the leaders will have to cope with the widespread cynicism, alienation and anomie among students, a result of the broken promises of 1966 that idealistic and perhaps opportunistic students soon would be able to make important contributions to the pursuit of Mao's utopian vision. Only months after they made these promises, the leaders were coercing students to return to the same stations they had occupied prior to the Cultural Revolution. . . .

. . . . In view of their deep commitment to building an egalitarian society, the rulers will probably again feel called upon, as they were during the Cultural Revolution, to alleviate the tensions that develop as some youths enjoy upward mobility while others return to the countryside.

As a result of these factors, one aspect of the Cultural Revolution, its emphasis upon the problems of youth, may foreshadow future Chinese politics. In this sense, the Cultural Revolution may have signaled a partial return of youth to the political position they held prior to communist rule.

Party and Government Bureaucrats

Prior to the Cultural Revolution, the Chinese Communists described the organizational trinity that ran their country as the party, the government, and the army (*tang, cheng, chun*). But in February 1967, when Mao and his entourage called for the formation of "Three-Way Alliance" organizations in the provinces and cities, they referred to a new trinity: (1) the party *and* the government; (2) the army; and (3) the revolutionary mass organizations. Although the party and the government retained their separate [identities], the delineation between them, which had been so carefully preserved in theory prior to 1966, was blurred.

The lumping together of party and government in the Three Way Alliance merely gave explicit acknowledgment to a development which students of Chinese politics had long recognized. The overlapping membership in the two organizations, the existence of party organizations within the government, and the close supervision by the party of government activities made it difficult to distinguish between the two.

Mao's placement of party and government in the same category in February 1967 was the logical outcome of the intense party involvement in governmental affairs which began during the Great Leap. In oversimplified terms, the First Five-Year Plan (1953–57) was run by people in the governmental apparatus; the burden of economic development fell upon their shoulders. The party remained a vanguard organization; members of the party apparatus exercised broad control over the government but remained aloof from day-to-day details, in order to preserve their organizational and ideological purity. By 1957 however, the officials in governmental apparatus had become enmeshed in the society they were trying to change. Mao was alarmed by the alacrity with which government officials were increasingly bureaucratized from 1953 to 1957. So, in the Great Leap of 1958–60, he committed his vanguard organization, the CCP, directly to the battle to . modernize China. But by 1965, many members of the CCP also had lost their reformist zeal. Inextricably intertwined with the entire society, the party had come to contain within it all the contradictions, particularist loyalties, and tensions of Chinese society at large. In a sense, by 1966, Mao had used up two organizations in the pursuit of his vision.

In essence, the Cultural Revolution was an attempt by Mao and his associates to remove those government and party cadres whom he perceived to be ineffective and to draw upon a fresh organization—the PLA—in the modernization effort. But such a design obviously did not coincide with the interests of the party and government cadres, who wished to retain their jobs and protect the power of their organizations. (The reaction of the military officers, many of whom also opposed Mao's plans, is discussed below.) By the beginning of 1968, it appeared that most bureaucrats, with the exception of those at the top echelons on each level, had successfully resisted efforts to dislodge them. As a group, the party and government bureaucrats retained their positions of power.

Bureaucratic Power and Vulnerabilities.   What explains the ability of the bureaucrats to withstand the attacks upon their positions? Three obvious factors stand out. The performance of the routine tasks required for society to survive, from preventing epidemics to the merchandising of goods, depended upon the bureaucrats. To attempt to remove them, as nearly happened in Shanghai in early 1967, would result in the total disruption of society. In addition, the network of organizations developed under Communist rule helped to unify the country. As Mao discovered in 1967, a concerted effort to destroy these organizations brought China to the precipice of civil war. Finally, in contrast to other aggregates in Chinese society, such as the peasants, the industrial workers and managers, and the intellectuals, the bureaucrats had their own organizations and enjoyed direct access to the policy formulation process. They were thus better equipped to defend their interests.

While these considerations help to explain why the bureaucrats as an aggregate remained in power, they do not explain the power of individual bureaucrats. Many individuals were able to build positions of considerable strength through their skilled use of personal ties, the manipulation of channels of communication, and the wise allocation of the resources at their disposal. Moreover, the opportunity to act in their own interest was increased by the discretion they enjoyed in making decisions, a discretion that arose in part from the vaguely worded directives they received from Peking. . . .

Several factors made the individual party or government bureaucrat vulnerable to outside control, particularly his dependence upon superiors to provide money and materials and to grant him promotions. . . . But in addition to the commonly mentioned techniques for maintaining discipline within the bureaucracy, two others deserve comment because of their prominence in the Cultural Revolution. First, the thorough files (*tang-an*) detailing their behavior over extended periods of time made individual bureaucrats vulnerable to innumerable distorted charges, all allegedly based on the record. Second, perhaps to an extent previously underestimated in earlier studies, the leaders of China have based their legitimacy upon the ideas and symbol of Mao Tse-tung. The denial of that symbol to an individual bureaucrat made it impossible for him to justify his role. . . .

. . . [The] environment in which Chinese bureaucrats worked needs to be placed in broader perspective. The information obtained during 1966–67 indicates that at least since the Tenth Plenum of 1962, the Central Committee of the CCP was deeply divided over a large number of issues. The disunified elite were unable to provide decisive, bold leadership to the bureaucracy. The divisions among the rulers were smoothed over through the issuance of vague directives. Often these were drafted by erstwhile colleagues of Mao such as Liu Shao-ch'i and P'eng Chen, who based their directives upon Mao's even more vague oral instructions. Examples are several important directives on rural policy issued during the 1960s, which have [since] become available. What characterizes all of them is their ambiguity and sterility.[42] Instead of issuing explicit written orders, the top leaders apparently preferred to shape policy through a series of personal *ad hoc* conferences and trips to the provinces. The denunciations of Liu, Teng, and P'eng, for instance, indicated that these officials made frequent appearances in the provinces to inspect conditions, discuss problems, and deliver instructions. However, it seems that such conferences and appearances usually did not produce more precise directives.

This situation yielded both advantages and disadvantages to the bureaucrat. On the one hand, he was able to interpret the instructions in the light most favorable to his unit. Such behavior should not necessarily be viewed cynically, for most bureaucrats probably considered themselves loyal to Chairman Mao and the party center, and had come to believe sincerely that the interests of their units coincided with the national interest. Yet, while the bureaucrat inevitably tended to bend the vague directives to suit his interests, thereby strengthening his unit, at the same time he was vulnerable to the accusation of deliberately misinterpreting the directives. Moreover, the higher-level leaders who drafted the vague directives were open to the charges that they had violated the spirit of Mao's oral statements.

The conduct of the Four Clearances campaign in China's countryside in 1963–65 provided an excellent example.[43] In late 1962, Mao expressed dissatisfaction with the caliber and honesty of rural, basic-level cadres. However, while calling for a "Four Clearance" campaign to improve the situation, he did not address himself to the problem of standards. Instead, he handed the problem to Liu Shao-ch'i. In 1967, Mao claimed that Liu had violated his instructions by setting standards [that were] too high. Mao accused Liu of wishing to purge an excessive number of basic-level cadres, making them scapegoats for peasant discontent that should have been directed toward Liu. Despite Mao's claims, Liu's directives appear to have been so vague that no standard was clearly stated. The responses to Liu's directive were not uniform. Some provincial officials did not push the campaign, and during the Cultural Revolution they were accused of ignoring the problems of cadre corruption and the spread of capitalism. Other officials placed heavy emphasis upon the Four Clearances, and in 1966–67, they were accused of unjustly condemning local cadres, thereby protecting Liu Shao-ch'i. In sum, the vagueness of the directives meant that when accused of anti-Maoist activity, a bureaucrat was unable to prove that he had not violated them.

The Dossier.   Another source of a bureaucrat's vulnerability was the thorough dossier of his past activities. Rare was the Chinese bureaucrat who, at some point in his career, had not engaged in some form of conspicuous consumption, had not spoken somewhat disparagingly about the political system, had not barked orders to a subordinate rather than employing mass line techniques, or had not associated with "bad elements." Such activities often were recorded in his dossier, and were there to be used against him if

---

[42]The Hoover Institution has a complete file of these directives obtained from GRC authorities in Taiwan.

[43]For discussion of "Four Clearances," see Charles Neuhauser, "The Chinese Communist Party in the 1960's," *China Quarterly* [No. 32]. See Also Richard Baum and Frederic Teiwes, *Ssu-Ch'ing: The Socialist Education Movement of 1962–1966* [Berkeley: Center for Chinese Studies, 1968].

the need arose. Subordinates who disliked their superior but were unable to damage him in any other way could fill their superior's files with charges of misconduct. Also in the dossier were remarks made during periods in which CCP policy was moderate. One such period occurred in 1961-62, when most leaders—again including Mao—stressed the need of restoring the economy through material incentives. But such speeches appeared damning if reproduced out of context in 1966-67, when Mao stressed class struggle and the evils of material incentives.

As the purge swept the bureaucracy, contending factions tried to obtain the dossiers of their rivals in order to gather "black materials" on them. Not surprisingly, during the Cultural Revolution, there were constant reports of illegal seizures of personnel files, and repeated efforts were made to re-establish central control over them. A bureaucrat rightfully feared that his dossier contained enough evidence to condemn him, if it fell into malicious hands. The dossier made the bureaucrat vulnerable to the control of the man who held it.

Bureaucratic Claim to Legitimacy.   Another source of bureaucratic vulnerability stemmed from the nature of the regime's claim to legitimacy. Although in the 1950s China's leaders justified their right to rule by nationalistic and economic appeals, through time they have increasingly based the claims of their legitimacy upon the sanctity of the thought of Mao Tse-tung. Thus, the authority of the bureaucrats was justified, [not] because their commands made the average Chinese more prosperous nor because their actions built a better China, but because their rule was in accordance with the thought of Mao Tse-tung. The power holders in China had equated the right of rule with being a disciple of Mao Tse-tung. Whoever manipulated the symbol of Mao—and when Mao was vigorous, he manipulated it—controlled the bureaucrat's claim to legitimacy.

Once an individual bureaucrat's loyalty to Mao was questioned and his dossier made public, his power—based upon his network of friends, his control over information, and the allocation of his limited resources—gradually eroded. Other bureaucrats sought to disassociate themselves from him, for fear that they might be labeled part of his gang. He became a target for and suffered the humiliation of struggle. He was isolated.

Strategy for Survival.   Working under the intense physical and psychological pressure of the Cultural Revolution and realizing his vulnerability to purge, the individual bureaucrat had political survival as his main objective. The strategies he employed were to cling tenaciously to the source of his legitimacy by claiming that he was a good Maoist, to seal his unit off from outside interference, as much as possible, and to secure the continued support of his loyal subordinates. These tactics were not sufficient to protect all officials, but, given their crucial social role, most party and government bureaucrats weathered the storm and remained in positions of power as the Cultural Revolution subsided in early 1968.

Military

To appreciate the power and influence of the military in Chinese society, one must understand the position of the PLA during the Cultural Revolution. While most analysts agree that the PLA played a crucial role in 1966-67, they differ in their evaluations.

The PLA Rise to Power.   Some analysts stated that the military had taken over. Impressive evidence exists to support this contention. PLA units were dispatched to factories and schools, where the troop commanders assumed important leadership functions. The PLA, already deeply immersed in such tasks as running the railroads and organizing propaganda prior to the Cultural Revolution, increased its responsibilities in these vital areas. When one looked at the top official in each of the provinces, one found that although a few of the new and surviving officials had careers within the CCP, most were former military officers. Some of them, such as Li Yuan in Hunan or Li Ts'ai-han in Kweichow, had risen from obscurity; their names were not listed in the standard biographic guides to China's leaders. In Peking, the national holidays were presided over by military men. Newspaper editorials throughout 1967 stressed the crucial role performed by the PLA in society. In 1967, Mao's closest comrade-in-arms and his likely successor was said to be the Minister of Defense and head of the Military Affairs Committee, Lin Piao. The nationally debated issues reflected the concerns of the military apparatus: the amount of time the army should spend in physical training versus the amount of time spent on the study of Mao's works, the role of the PLA troops stationed in factories and schools, the relations between the military and other sectors of society, the obligations of the regional garrison commanders to obey the center, and even the role of the navy in domestic peace-keeping functions. When the leaders of the country [were] drawn from the military, when the issues debated in the press [were] of particular relevance to the military, and when the military stationed its troops in non-military units throughout the country, the evidence strongly suggests that a military takeover [had] occurred.

Moreover, there were signs that the rise of the PLA was the result of a conscious rivalry with the CCP. The PLA had intimate organizational links with the Red Guards, who led the attacks upon the CCP apparatus. One of the key Red Guard units, for example, came from the Peking Aviation Institute, a school with close PLA connections. Some Red Guard newspapers also spoke of an organizational rivalry between the party and the PLA. For instance, the Ministry of Railways and the PLA shared jurisdiction over the railways. The Minister of Railways, Lu Cheng-ts'ao, was accused of wanting to control the armed railroad personnel, who were under PLA command. Lu allegedly maintained:

> The Public Security Ministry controls its own public security forces. Why shouldn't the Railway Ministry control railway forces?[44]

Lu was accused of "wanting to usurp the power and authority of the PLA."

Invective in a similar vein had been directed earlier against Teng T'o, the dismissed editor of *Peking Daily*:

> We must warn Teng T'o and his ilk that the right to "contend" is not allowed in the PLA, and the fighters of the people will wipe out those who dare to stick their nose into the army under the pretext of contention.[45]

These quotes hinting at a possible PLA-CCP rivalry lend weight to an interpretation of the Cultural Revolution that stresses a PLA takeover from the party.

On the other hand, several factors made it misleading simply to state that the military seized power in China. First, the military apparatus in China lacked clear cut organizational identity and was thoroughly interwoven with the CCP. The commanders of the PLA who acquired power in 1967 probably were also CCP members. The rise to power

[44]JPRS 41, 249, June 2, 1967, pp. 46–67.
[45]Radio Peking, May 24, 1966.

of PLA commanders can be seen as a shift in the balance of power within the party, with CCP members serving in the military sector taking power from those in charge of such internal party work as organization and propaganda.

Second, not all elements in the military enhanced their position in 1966–67. In fact, many leaders of the PLA were purged. The most noteworthy cases included the dismissals of Chief-of-Staff Lo Jui-ch'ing, the head of the Political Department, Hsiao Hua, and Marshal Ho Lung, but the purge extended to garrison commanders, department heads, political commissars, and others.[46] If one is to speak in organizational terms, one cannot speak of a PLA takeover; one must speak of the seizure of power by specific units within the PLA. But here, no discernible pattern emerges, although there are some tantalizing hints. For instance, in recent years three newly appointed regional commanders came from the Shenyang garrison command,[47] Kiangsi province was occupied during the Cultural Revolution by troops dispatched from the Tsinan garrison command,[48] and the Wuhan rebellion was quelled, in part, through the dispatch from Shanghai of a naval force attached to the East China fleet.[49] A hypothesis that merits testing is that several army, navy, and air commands (such as Shenyang and Tsinan), perhaps owing allegiance to Lin Piao, acted together, that forces from these units occupied various areas, and that the newly risen military personnel were drawn primarily from these units. But until firm evidence is uncovered, such hypotheses must be held in abeyance. Thus, the unqualified assertion that the PLA had risen to power glosses over the difficult yet crucial problems of a complex process within the PLA which led to the promotion of some and the purge of other military figures.

A third reason that the image of a "military takeover" needs qualification was its incompleteness. Many government and party officials, even at higher levels, survived. Hunan provides a convenient example. Li Yuan and PLA unit 6900, which had been garrisoned in Hengyang, began to dominate news items from Ch'angsha. But Li appears to be the leader of a group that includes Hua Kuo-feng and Chang Po-sen, both of whom have long records of leadership in Party and government affairs in Hunan. Hua was First Secretary of Hsiang-t'an Special District in Hunan in the early 1950s, served as head of the provincial government's Culture and Education Office and the Party's United Front Department in the late 1950s, and was an active party secretary and Vice Governor in the early 1960s. Chang's tenure in Hunan also dates back to the early 1950s, when he was head of the Provincial Party Finance and Trade Department. The Hunan pattern was observable elsewhere. Leaders of the PLA won positions of power, but their rise was not accompanied by the total removal of leading government and party bureaucrats.

A fourth consideration against labeling the enhanced power of the military as a "takeover" was the noticeable reluctance of some military leaders to assume their new roles in domestic affairs. Military commanders in China were concerned with the capacity of their forces to fight against foreign powers. As the PLA became increasingly involved with domestic functions in the 1960s, of necessity it sacrificed some of its capacity to wage war. Lo Jui-ch'ing apparently was one of the officials opposed to the policy. Moreover, since the PLA automatically created enemies when it tried to restore order between conflicting groups and individuals, local commanders were reluctant to

---

[46]In *China News Summary,* No. 188–194.

[47]*Ibid.*

[48]Radio Nanchang, September 6, 1967 and October 9, 1967.

[49]Radio Wuhan, October 22, 1967.

become involved. If the PLA intervened on the side of one Red Guard organization, the other side became disenchanted. If the PLA tried to work out compromises, then the organizations accused the PLA of not settling the dispute on the basis of principles. During the early part of 1967, many PLA commanders apparently tried to shield their units from the turmoil, but the spreading chaos could be dampened only through military intervention. To a certain extent, it was less that the PLA eagerly seized power than that it reluctantly filled an organizational vacuum.

Sources of PLA Power.   Even with these qualifications, it remains true that the PLA significantly increased its power and influence. Part of the explanation for this rests in Mao's confidence in Lin Piao and the PLA, a confidence inspired by the political program carried out in the army from 1959 to 1965. Because the PLA stood apart from civilian society, ideological indoctrination probably could be carried out more effectively in the PLA than in other institutions in society. The effectiveness of the program in the PLA led Mao, who perhaps failed to discern the inherent differences between military and nonmilitary organizations, to display impatience with the comparatively inefficient indoctrination efforts undertaken by the party propagandists in civilian society, and to replace them with PLA personnel.

Another factor involved in the rise of the military was a personnel policy which enabled it to retain its vigor and extend its influence. Whereas other organizations in Chinese society frequently lacked institutionalized retirement processes, had aged leaders, and suffered from clogged channels of upward mobility, the PLA was able to transfer its older and less competent members to nonmilitary organizations. Not only did the transfer of veterans to positions in government, party, and industry enable the PLA to solve its own internal problems of mobility and retirement, but it also meant that the PLA saturated the nonmilitary organizations with men whose loyalties may in part have belonged to the military.

A further reason for the rise of the PLA was the increased importance of the foreign and domestic functions it performs. In foreign affairs, the leaders of China believed themselves to be encircled by hostile powers. They give primacy to the acquisition of a nuclear capability. In the tense situation of the mid-1960s in East Asia, with problems of national defense a prime concern, it was perhaps natural that military men came to play a more vital role in national politics.

Domestically, although firm documentation is lacking, it appears that the rulers increasingly had to rely on coercive means to control the population. As their ability to elicit a mass response through idealistic appeals diminished and their initial widespread support waned, the leaders administered a more harsh criminal law. With the population growth and the possibly growing gap between urban and rural living standards, the rulers had to exercise increasingly stringent control over population movements. In 1966–67, the situation became acute, and force of arms became a major way of restoring law and order. Those who wielded the instruments of coercion, people associated with the PLA and the public security forces, rose to power as the demand for their skills increased.

Yet another source of military power was its control of rail, air, and major river transport, giving its members and their allies a mobility which people in other organizations lacked. During the rapidly evolving political situation in 1966–67, access to air transport proved especially important. Chou En-lai, for example, was able at several crucial junctures to fly to trouble spots to negotiate or mediate disputes. In other instances, key groups were flown to Peking. One day after the May 6 incident in Chengtu, for instance, several of those involved were already in Peking to discuss the Szechuan situation with Chou, Ch'en Po-ta, K'ang Sheng, and Chiang Ch'ing. Further, to communicate their message to the peasants, perhaps indicating an inability to use a recalcitrant propaganda apparatus, the leadership airdropped leaflets to peasants in Kwangsi and Hupeh province in the spring.[50]

An additional reason for the enhanced power of military personnel may have been their relative self-sufficiency. In contrast to members of other hierarchies, their organization produced a considerable portion of the goods they consumed. Moreover, the PLA had an important role in directing the machine-building industries, the mining and extractive industries, and the agricultural reclamation projects in China's border provinces. When production and delivery schedules fell behind, as happened in early 1967, the army may have been in a better position to sustain itself. (This observation, however, is a logical inference rather than an adequately documented conclusion.)

In sum, the principal reasons for the rise of the PLA were similar to those for the increased importance of the military in many of the economically developing countries.[51] It won the confidence of the national leader. It stood somewhat isolated from society, thereby retaining a vigor and élan which the CCP inevitably lost when it became so involved in societal affairs that its parts came to represent particular interests. The post-service affiliations of former military personnel enabled the PLA to extend its influence to other organizations. Its control of resources enabled it to have an independent base of power. Because the PLA and the public security forces were the coercive agents of the ruler, these organizations came to the fore as the maintenance of the state increasingly rested upon coercion. Moreover, since the reasons for their rise are likely to persist, military personnel seem destined to be at the center of Chinese politics for the foreseeable future.

Conclusion

The power and influence of the major occupational groupings in Chinese society, as revealed in the Cultural Revolution, can now be briefly summarized. The peasants influenced policy indirectly; their interests were voiced by sympathetic government and party bureaucrats and the military leaders. The top policy formulators tried to anticipate peasant reactions primarily because of their economic importance.

In one of the significant aspects of the Cultural Revolution, the industrial managers and the industrial workers displayed their power to act swiftly and to affect policies ruinous to their interests. Members of these occupational groups appear to be acquiring increased power as China industrializes.

Intellectuals, increasingly differentiated in the roles they perform, differed in their ability to alter policy affecting them. Social critics were totally vulnerable to control, and teachers were shown basically to serve at the pleasure of the ruler. Scientific and technical personnel, however, saw their interests taken into account, particularly if they were engaged in research that gained them firm supporters among the military.

The students demonstrated that, when allied with elements of the bureaucracy and the military, they could become a powerful force, but that without allies, they were unable to remain a politically dominant group. Nonetheless, a study of youth suggests that their problems demand urgent attention, and for this reason their demands probably will elicit a continued response from those at the center of power.

---

[50]Radio Wuhan, March 8, 1967; Radio Nanning, February 28, 1967.
[51]See, for example, Lucian Pye, "Armies in the Process of Political Development," in his *Aspects of Political Development*, Little Brown, 1966, pp. 172–187.

Though many government and party bureaucrats were purged, they displayed their ability to survive as an occupational group at the center of power. Their functions proved vital; moreover, they had learned some of the tactics necessary to defend their interests.

Finally, members of the military apparatus moved to the very center of power during the Cultural Revolution. An analysis of the sources of their power and influence indicates that their importance will persist.

This summary, however, has several limitations which should be made explicit. The occupational groups analyzed are broadly defined; in reality, each category includes many kinds of positions. For example, instead of analyzing party and government bureaucrats as one group, a more rigorous analysis would examine the interests and power of the bureaucrats in the various functional systems into which the party and government were divided; finance and trade, agriculture, forestry, and water conservancy, industry and communications, culture and education, law enforcement, and so on. A more rigorous analysis of industrial workers would distinguish among skilled and unskilled workers in large, medium, and small factories. Their attitudes and ability to affect public policy were probably different.

In addition, this article's exclusive focus upon occupational groups neglects other important ways of subdividing the population, such as into geographical, attitudinal, ethnic, or class groups. Indeed, one would gain considerable insight into Chinese politics by asking the question: What does the Cultural Revolution tell us about the relative power and influence of people in different geographic areas in China? Moreover, there is considerable evidence that conflict within the occupational groups was often based upon class and status groups. Among students, apparently, conflict sometimes broke out between children of cadres and children from less favored backgrounds. (The important United Action Red Guards, for instance, reportedly drew its strength from the children of cadres.) The conflict between the permanent and temporary workers was a struggle between two classes. Conflict between bureaucrats often involved disputes between high-ranking and low-ranking cadres. The pro-Maoist leaders apparently tended to draw strong support from the lower classes and status groups, a facet of the Cultural Revolution that does not become clear if one focuses solely upon occupational groups.

Moreover, the Cultural Revolution provides a narrow and unusual time span from which to view the interests and power of occupational groups. They were able to act upon their interests, in part, because of the diminished capacity of the elite to provide effective leadership. (One reason for their reduced capacity, however, was the increased ability of occupational groups to defend their interests. The two phenomena were interrelated.) If the rulers recapture their former strength, or if they resort to different techniques in order to elicit a response (for example, an increased use of material incentives), then the interests and abilities of various groups to affect policy will change.

Finally, another limitation of the exclusive focus upon group interests and power is its neglect of other important subjects, such as the role of ideas. A satisfactory explanation for the persistence of radical thought in China, so crucial for an understanding of the Cultural Revolution, must go beyond an analysis of student radicalism and the interests of occupational groups, for the radicals were found among all of them.[52] Ulti-

---

[52]For sensitive studies of some of the sources of radicalism, see Maurice Meisner, *Li Ta-chao and the Origins of Chinese Marxism*, Harvard University Press, 1967, and Olga Lang, *Pa Chin and his Writings*, Harvard University Press, 1967.

mately, for a thorough understanding of Chinese politics one must integrate group analysis with an analysis of the leaders and the culture and ideas that move them.

In spite of these limitations, however, occupational group analysis enables one to approach China from a fresh vantage point. Transitory factors affecting Chinese politics, such as the power of a particular individual, factional rivalries, or a war on China's border, are blotted out in order to highlight more permanent developments. A clearer picture emerges of the occupational groups that will exercise the greatest demands upon the top leaders, no matter who those leaders might be.

This study suggests that in the years ahead, China's leaders will confront several occupational groups that will effectively articulate their interests: the military personnel, the government and party bureaucrats, and increasingly, the industrial managers and workers. Moreover, the leaders will have to pay urgent attention to the problems of students, and respond to the demands of scientists and technicians. They will face considerable constraints in formulating their policies toward the peasants. It is highly likely that Chinese politics is moving into an era marked by intense bargaining between a weakened central leadership, its authority seriously eroded during the Cultural Revolution, and powerful occupational groups. The leaders will not be in an enviable position, as they attempt to reconcile and mediate the conflicting demands made by these groups.

18

The Relevance of Yugoslav Self-Management

Bogdan Denitch

Yugoslav self-management[1] has been studied both by Yugoslav and foreign scholars for over two decades. The study of Yugoslav self-management, initially begun because of the uniqueness of this institution, which the Yugoslavs themselves were aware was moving them into a hitherto uncharted area, was of particular interest to three groups of Western social scientists. First were those very few Western social scientists who came from a socialist tradition. They sought to find in the system of self-management a solution for problems of alienation with the work process and disenchantment with the authority structure of nationalized industry in the West under social democratic governments—problems which they were all too aware were also present in Eastern Europe and particularly in the Soviet Union. Simply stated, they looked for *social relations* in the economy appropriate to a nonreformist working model of socialism.

The second group studied self-management from a narrower perspective, that of industrial relations and managerial techniques. This group approached the problem of self-management attempting to isolate it from its general political and ideological framework, seeking to discover in self-management that which they thought was applicable to other industrial systems. What they were attracted to particularly was the notion of self-management as a form of codetermination or of workers' participation which would be transferable to industries remaining in private ownership or in owner-ship which was diffused or mixed. For this group, what is particularly interesting about self-management is the question of participation as a method of avoiding conflicts and providing "job enrichment." This group is also interested in productivity and the ticklish and complex problem of the role of technical cadres and management itself within a framework of self-managed industry.

From Bogdan Denitch, "Notes on the Relevance of Yugoslav Self-Management," *Politics and Society* (Vol. 3, No. 4, Summer 1973), pp. 473–489. [Reprinted with permission from the publisher.]

[1]This article is limited to a discussion of self-management as the major force shaping con-temporary Yugoslav society and the most distinct characteristic of Yugoslav socialism. However, one must always insist that, although basic, it is only one of the major forces in that society. A fuller discussion of other forces and institutions—both contemporary and traditional—would require a more extensive presentation.

The third group studied self-management in a more general framework, particularly the economists from the United States and Great Britain who studied self-management as an *aspect* of socialist *market* economy. For them, self-management primarily is conceived as *plant or enterprise autonomy* from the centralized plan; therefore Yugoslavia is most interesting as a unique experiment with socialist market economy. For them the political mobilizing aspect of self-management in industry or democratization of industrial authority patterns is secondary. Self-management is primarily seen as a necessary *instrument* to break down the previous *centralized planning system* which had proved all too inefficient and to establish an economy based on the market and therefore free from the vagaries of political pressure or individual whims.

The same three emphases can be found in the work of Yugoslav sociologists and social scientists who have devoted themselves to the study of self-management. It should at once be stated that the bulk of relevant literature on self-management is in Serbo-Croatian or Slovenian, and very little is therefore accessible to the scholars without command of these languages. The few works that are available in English . . . tend to be dated or based on partial studies, with the possible exceptions of Horvat's *Essay on Yugoslav Society*[2] and the collective papers of the Amsterdam conference on self-management organized by Mr. Broekmeyer.[3] Political scientists such as Robert Dahl from Yale have also addressed themselves to some of the social and political implications of self-management[4] but it is clear from Dahl's own writing that his acquaintance with the system itself is very limited and comes primarily from secondary sources.

I begin with the assumption that self-management in Yugoslavia cannot be isolated from those other aspects of the Yugoslav socialist system which make it unique. Five main characteristics of Yugoslav socialism can be roughly summarized as follows:

1. *In international affairs,* independence and nonalignment;
2. *In the field of economy,* socialist market economy with indicative planning;
3. *Politically,* a multinational state with no dominant nationality, decentralization, and a unique party system;
4. *Historically,* a case of a successful war of national liberation, that is, of guerrilla communism legitimized over three decades of power;
5. *Sociologically,* a new political culture based on self-management in the form of workers' councils, self-managing bodies in institutions and in the communes.

These characteristics exist within a society—and this factor has been of growing importance—marked by a high rate of social and political modernization which has been inexorably slowing down as Yugoslavia has emerged from the mobilization phase dictated by the backwardness of the destroyed traditional society.

It is clear when one considers Yugoslavia that self-management can only be taken as one part of what is an integrated whole, or rather an integrating whole, since the system as yet is in the process of evolution. Self-management itself can be broken down into three component parts: workers' councils or self-management in industry proper; self-managing bodies in social institutions such as schools, quasi-governmental bodies, and the rest; and finally self-management on the level of the commune. All three elements should be considered jointly, as it is all but impossible to treat workers' councils as an isolated phenomenon in Yugoslavia. The workers' councils are perhaps the most interest-

---

[2] Arts & Science Press (White Plains, 1969). This is a translation of a book originally published in Serbo-Croatian.

[3] *Yugoslav Workers' Self-Management,* ed. M. J. Broekmeyer (D. Reidel, Dordrecht, Holland, 1970).

[4] Robert Dahl, *After the Revolution* (New York, 1972).

ing aspect of the Yugoslav experiment and the one which may appear easiest to transfer to other situations, but as the experience of Algeria, India, and other countries has shown, attempts to establish workers' councils in isolation without an accompanying change in the fabric of society itself are likely to lead to a failure and a cumulative inefficiency in the economy and society.

A Historical Note

One of the most puzzling things about the establishment of self-management in Yugoslavia is that it appears to have had no previous roots in the historical experience of Yugoslavia or of the Communist party which led the revolution and directed postwar developments. The Communist party of Yugoslavia became, in the process of the war and revolution, a mass party. However, the predominantly peasant masses who entered the party from 1941 to 1945 joined a party which remained one of the most orthodox . . . in the Communist International even after the dissolution of the International: a party which consciously, perhaps all too consciously, held the Russian model as the only desirable one. While the party had come to power independently, it sought to copy wholesale the political, economic, and military structures from the already existing Russian model. The political writings on which most of the party cadre had been brought up would have to be examined in great detail to discover any references to self-management or workers' councils. One need only note that the most important text in party courses even in the war years had been Stalin's *History of the Bolshevik Party U.S.S.R.* It was the first book set in the printing shops of the first Partisan Republic in Uzice in the fall of 1941; and the unused plates were painfully transported during the retreat that winter.

In the socialist tradition itself, the theme of participation and workers' control weaves through much of the classic literature—from Fourier through Marx, Lenin, the Guild socialists and the various Left opposition groups in the Social Democratic and Communist parties. Lenin himself in *The State and the Revolution* presented a model which was based on directly elected councils, and the very slogan "All Power to the Soviets," before their atrophy, represented an attempt to institute forms of direct democracy as a substitute for traditional state power. The most fully developed theories of workers' control were found in the writings of the Workers' Opposition in the early twenties in Russia,[5] but it would be difficult to trace the influence of the destroyed and vilified Workers' Opposition or its program on the leaders of the Communist party of Yugoslavia in the early 1950s. Furthermore, the grim tasks of the period following World War II, particularly in an underdeveloped society facing the hostility of the Soviet bloc hardly made this the most conducive period to introduce social experiments which had no previous record of success. Therefore, self-management's evolution should be considered as the specific form that Yugoslav socialism took in counterposition to the familiar Stalinist model of development.

This lack of historical roots did not apply to *one* form of self-management, communal self-management. It had been developed during the revolution itself, at least in a nascent form in the National Liberation Councils (N.O.O.) which held wide-ranging authority

---

[5]Robert V. Daniels, *The Conscience of the Revolution* (Cambridge: Harvard University Press, 1960), particularly chaps. 4, 5, and 6, for a summary of the views of the Workers' Opposition.

in the Partisan-held areas and even in the occupied areas. These communal councils harken back to a very active tradition of communal self-government, particularly developed in those parts of Yugoslavia which had been exposed to Turkish influence.

Given the discontinuity between the practice and the immediately preceding organizational tradition that the introduction of self-management presented, it is no wonder that it took over a decade to develop, and that it created a series of stresses and contradictions which are still present in the society. For the classic advocates of workers' control, workers' councils were not a parallel form but the *only* form of organizational power which would exist in a socialist society. In Yugoslavia the workers' councils were initially introduced into an economy still highly centralized with fully developed state administrative organs and a monolithic party structure, all of which had [much] more real power than the councils themselves. This was the case *even* in those matters which, classically, would have been under the jurisdiction of the councils.

It was not until the introduction of the market economy that the councils began to assert at least a minimal enterprise autonomy and it was not until the councils began to dispose of the major part of their income that real economic power began to shift. This "shift" represents a major source of tension, since it of course implies decentralization in economic decision making [that is] hardly consistent with a still powerful centralized state apparatus. In turn this has created continuing pressures to alter political and party structures in such a way that they would reflect the new social relations and modes of political behavior developing through self-management. These pressures of course do not always succeed, if for no other reason than that they are not consciously directed.

Historically, the introduction of workers' self-management within a market economy must therefore be viewed as having the primary role of dismantling the old state apparatus and of shifting the bulk of economic decision making into nonstate bodies. This is why much of the debate about socialist market economy in reality is a debate about workers' self-management in Yugoslavia today. The criticisms directed at the genuine enterprise-egoism which has developed in certain quarters misses the point. In a self-managed society, the workers inside their self-managing institutions have to be *convinced* to make the required sacrifices for the community as a whole. Here of course the role of the League of Communists in developing the needed socialists consciousness would be central. Well-meaning critics find themselves in a posture which often implicitly assumes that societal priorities are better determined by experts, governmental bodies, or for that matter "disinterested" intellectuals than by voluntary participation of the workers themselves. To put it more simply, *they do not trust the workers to self-manage in the interests of the wider community.* Implicit in that is the continual existence of dual power and therefore of a limitation on self-management.

The development of workers' self-management within the framework of a market economy has generated a whole set of real and potential social conflicts. These can be roughly divided between those occurring within the workplace and those between the workplace and institutions and forces outside of it. Within the workplace, two contradictory pressures exist: maximization of production and social organization of work. Efficiency versus humaneness. A workers' council is at the same time the organizational apex of a sometimes increasingly complex organizational pyramid and a town meeting. An obvious conflict exists between the attempts by technocratically oriented managerial strata to stress efficiency and productivity and the natural resistance of the workers toward any attempts to increase the pace of work or alienate them from direct control over the process of production. Increased availability of consumer goods and luxuries has created pressures on the part of the professional strata for greater income differentials. Hiring university graduates from the outside rather than systematically training workers for professional jobs, perhaps by sending them to universities, increases the gap between "experts" and blue-collar workers.

The conflicts between the enterprise and society as a whole are also systemic. The more obvious are the ones posed by narrow self-interests of an enterprise: the scandalous pollution of rivers and parts of the seacoast, production of goods whose social value is dubious, irresponsible pricing, the tendency to regard the enterprise as a form of collective private property, and the like. On the other hand, there are attempts "from the outside" to interfere with the normal prerogatives of self-management in hiring and firing, demands for favors, and the desire of poorer communities to milk the more successful enterprises for general development.

The general reluctance of political structures—local, regional, or national—to permit the development of full autonomy by the self-managing bodies in the economy are always ultimately justified by the need to defend general societal interests. This leaves open, of course, the question of just how "disinterested" are the defenders of general interests.

The Dimensions of Self-Management Today

Before discussing the relevance of Yugoslav self-management to . . . politics, it is useful to examine the extent of popular participation in it at this time. There are three areas of self-management: enterprise, including cooperatives, communal councils and bodies, and social services and institutions. In the economy, where self-management is most widely developed, the numbers of persons involved in various levels are huge. Four specific groups of participants in self-managing bodies can be distinguished in the economy:

1. Workers' councils elected in enterprises large enough to have councils and managing boards: there are 145,488 members of councils in this category.
2. The second group comprises managing boards of smaller enterprises which are too small to have a council and a board: there are 10,016 members of such boards.
3. The third and largest group consists of members of self-managing bodies in *parts* of enterprises. This is a group which can be expected to grow for a number of reasons, one of which is the growth of large complex enterprises in Yugoslavia. There [is] a total of 303,828 persons participating in self-managing bodies on this level.
4. The fourth group consists of self-managing bodies in agricultural co-ops; there are 35,469 persons in these councils.

The grand total for the area of the economy alone therefore comes close to half a million persons participating in various self-managing bodies.

In the field of communal self-government, the communal assemblies (there are 500 communes in Yugoslavia) include 40,791 persons, roughly one-half of whom are elected at large, the other half being elected by the working communities. In addition, there are local community bodies on a lower level which include 92,725 persons, a total of 133,516 persons.

The third area officially defined as "Social Self-Government in Institutions of Social Services" includes: primary and secondary schools; higher schools and universities, scientific institutions; cultural, educational, art, and entertainment institutions; health institutions; and social welfare institutions. The self-managing councils include

210,384 people, of whom roughtly one-half come from the primary and secondary schools.[6]

The point of all these figures is to show the enormous numbers of people involved in one way or another in the institutions of self-management participating with various degrees of intensity and effectiveness in *managing some aspect of their social existence.* (To put it in another perspective, 838,201 persons participate in some type of self-management out of an employed population of approximately four million!) It is important to note that while the largest number are in the enterprises, massive numbers are found in the other two fields. This wide involvement of nonprofessionals in managing major institutions in their society, no matter how limited, obviously affects the entire political culture of the polity over time. *Self-management becomes thus not an instrument of the society but the very fabric of the society.* This is not to say that abuses do not exist, that participation is not sometimes only nominal, and that the general political climate of the society at a given moment does not also have an effect on the workings of these bodies. *All that I am asserting is that the norm of participation is now firmly rooted; and, given the system of rotation which is used in electing representatives to self-managing bodies, this means that a major part of the working population at one point or another participates in running its own institutions.* This however also underlies my earlier point that self-management is not a *partially* exportable system.

Accompanying self-management itself has been a process of decentralization from the federal to the republic and provincial government down to the communes. This process began relatively early in Yugoslavia and can be seen in the decline of personnel in the federal administration from 47,300 persons in 1948 to 10,326 persons by 1956, with the process continuing to this day. There are two underlying theoretical approaches to this process of decentralization. The first emphasizes the sovereignty of the republics and regards decentralization as primarily a reflection of the multinational character of Yugoslavia. The second stresses *structural* decentralization and thus stresses decentralization to the level of the self-managing bodies in the communes and the enterprises. While the two processes are simultaneous, they are in my opinion ultimately contradictory and it is the second process which seems most naturally to flow from the basic needs of a self-managed society. (The emphasis on republics is rooted in the *specific* historical needs of a *multinational Yugoslavia,* not in self-management as a system.) It can however be argued that the first stage of decentralization necessarily required an emphasis on the republics in order to dismantle the central federal structure. I believe that the future will show a greater emphasis on the second process, accompanied in all likelihood by attempts to solidify nationwide institutions such as the League of Communists, the unions, and the unified market.

The two decades of development of self-management have had a profound and long-range effect on the political culture of Yugoslavia. Findings from surveys of workers and the public at large confirm the fact that although there are criticisms of specific practices and abuses in self-management, it is taken at least as the desirable norm and the most characteristic feature of Yugoslav socialism. This was also confirmed in 1968–69 in the study of *Yugoslav Opinion-Makers,*[7] where the leading opinionmakers of the major

---

[6]*Statisticki Godisnjak Jugoslavije 1970,* pp. 66, 67, 68, 69. The figures are somewhat dated (1969–70) but adequate.

[7]Reports on the study are found in: *Svaraoci Jarnog Mnenja u Jugoslaviji* 1–4, Firdus Dzinic, ed. (Inst. Drustvenih Nauha, 1969). A version in English of the major papers in Alan Barton, Bogdan Denitch, Charles Kadushin (eds.), *Yugoslav Opinion Making Elite* (New York: Praeger, 1973).

institutional areas of Yugoslav life were asked, among many other things, what they thought were the major achievements of Yugoslav socialism. The question was broken down into three parts: What were the major achievements of Yugoslav socialism; first, for Yugoslavia itself; second, as an example to developing countries; and third, as a contribution to socialist theory? In all three cases, self-management, either in the economy or in the polity, came . . . first. For Yugoslavia itself, self-management as the first choice ranged from 72.3 percent for legislative leaders, to 53.8 percent for intellectuals, with the second and third choices being not unrelated, i.e., freedom and socialist democracy, and the solution of the national question.

In contrast, they did not view self-management *in industry* as an exportable item for underdeveloped countries. There the answers ranged from 27.3 percent for economic leaders to 16.8 percent for journalists and mass communicators. For underdeveloped countries, it was *political* self-management and economic development which were considered to be the best potential Yugoslav contribution for emulation.

In the field of theory, again self-management was regarded as the major Yugoslav contribution: 58.2 percent emphasizing industrial self-management, and 27.1 percent communal self-management. Interestingly enough, again intellectuals were the least enthusiastic although a substantial majority did pick self-management.

This is a finding which should be taken in its proper context. There is, after all, in most societies a gap between normative descriptions of the system and its performance. However, what is clear is that the leaders of Yugoslav society agreed that the major innovation of Yugoslav socialism was self-management. All major economic, political, and social reforms since that period have basically concentrated on working out the kinks and details of a system to which they are generally committed.

Different Approaches to Self-Management

Self-management means very different things to different groups. *Managers* and *technical* experts . . . stress plant and enterprise autonomy and *their* right to manage without interference of the government or central economic bodies. *Politically conscious workers* regard self-management as *their* right to control the managerial staffs and to make the significant day-to-day decisions affecting their lives. Socialist intellectuals regard self-management as an alternative to a highly structured party-dominated political system which will create new norms and therefore hopefully a new socialist man. These themes, of course, represent ideal types, but what is clear is that although self-management was an unexplored possibility when introduced, it has—at least as a slogan—become attractive to wide publics in both Western and Eastern Europe. What should be stressed is that the slogan is transferred with all of the ambiguities implicit in the different approaches named.

In Hungary and Poland in the mid-1950s, and among the Czech reformers in 1968, very different approaches to self-management were present. In the first two cases, the demand for self-management came primarily *from the workers themselves.* This demand was made more urgent by the fact that they felt that they did not control, or were not represented by, their parties and trade unions. In the case of Czechoslovakia, however, a more ambiguous approach was present among the reformers, many of whom were hesitant about self-management because they wanted to move twoards a greater income differentiation and a society in which managers and experts would be [independent] of the political structure.[8] They rightly assumed that in any industrial situation where genuine power resides in the elected workers' councils, the pressure [would] be towards greater wage equality and against special privileges for the managerial and technical cadres. This is why *partial* self-management in the form of *codetermination* or *joint consultation* is far more attractive to managers and industrial-relations experts who usually reflect the interests of enlightened management among liberal or social-democratic reformers.

A further problem which the discussions about self-management tend to obscure lies in the relationship of other representative workers' institutions to self-management. I refer primarily to the trade unions. Self-management can be related to the trade unions in three typical ways:

1. In some forms of consultation, the union itself represents the interests of the workers on a joint body with managers and technicians. While this implies conflictual interests between management and workers, the practice all too often turns out to be that the trade union representatives on such bodies become more "reasonable" than the rank and file which they represent. They become sensitized to the problem of management and production which often clash with their normative role as the advocates of the *direct* interests of the workers.

2. A second type of relationship is one in which the trade union or, rather, the shop stewards *are* the workers' council. This is the syndicalist model, and at least it has the virtue of simplicity. Managerial and technical staffs at that point work for the workers' council and the problem of representation is solved because of a single line of representation.

3. A third model is one where the trade union is rightly or wrongly perceived as unrepresentative and the workers' council as being more directly representative. This can occur either in situations where a fragmented trade union movement exists divided between politically competing unions *or* in cases where the trade union leadership asserts no independent role from the rest of the hierarchy of the society. In those cases the trade union is not regarded as the instrumentality through which grievances and personnel questions are settled, and often appears on the management side of the table in the managing board. This describes the limited councils in Poland and Hungary, and the early stage of Yugoslav development.

When the trade unions begin to assert greater independence as representatives of generalized interests of the workers, their relationship to the self-governing structure is one where they defend the societal interests of the workers as a quasi-political lobby, while the councils themselves assume the functions which are in part carried out by the shop stewards' committees in some of the unions in Western Europe and the United States. While conflicts exist in these situations, they need not be endemic.

Industrial self-management in Yugoslavia must be distinguished from the classic workers' councils in that it includes the managerial and technical experts as well as a majority of workers. However, self-management *or* workers' control is an increasingly attractive slogan in many different countries and social situations. The content given to that slogan will vary widely. It ranges from those who view the councils as a way of

---

[8]See Ivan Svitak, *The Czechoslovak Experiment 1968–69* (Columbia University Press), particularly pp. 52–59. An excellent discussion of the views of Czech reformers on the question of equality is in Ernest Gellner's "The Pluralist Anti-Levelers of Prague," *Dissent,* Summer 1972, pp. 471–483.

getting participation for workers for the purpose of mediating conflicts, improving productivity, and gaining support for an "incomes policy," to those who view the workers' councils as proto-Soviets, i.e., instruments of revolutionary transformation of a capitalist society (or, for that matter, statist socialism) to a socialist society. It is therefore important to specify very carefully what one means by participation and self-management since those slogans are by now used at least as widely as "democracy." The slogans become most popular in situations where the workers do not feel that their parties and trade unions are sufficiently militant in transforming the conditions and the social organization of work. In these cases economic demands are rare, and one can assume that when wage settlements are determined on a higher level without a direct confrontation of the workers and the employers, the demands for some form of workers' participation on workers' councils will increase. This trend in advanced industrial countries will undoubtedly be strengthened by the increasingly better educated working class and the increasing complexity of work. The old division between the experts on the side of management and the relatively uneducated workers is breaking down, and an intermediary group, sometimes designated as the *new working class*,[9] has arisen. The existence of this stratum in the working class will make the demand for some form of self-management more and more general in advanced industrial societies.

In developing societies, on the other hand, the function of self-management or workers' control is different. To begin with, it represents a major attempt to *mobilize* and involve the newly industrialized peasants in the norms of factory life. It is also an instrument for *recruiting* new managerial strata in societies which are without adequate cadres and, finally, it is *ideologically useful*—even in situations where the power of managers is almost unaffected by the existence of councils—because it justifies, or seeks to justify, the transformation of revolutionary political activists into managers. That transformation is ideologically more acceptable if at least the *form* of participation is maintained. However, forms which do not reflect social reality can prove to be a dangerous luxury. When workers are told that they own the factories and that they are to manage them, they sometimes seek to act as if this were so. *Under these circumstances, conflict can develop between workers operating within the official ideology of the system and the system itself.*

Prospects for Self-Management

The development of self-management in Yugoslavia has had the effect of reviving the entire discussion of possibilities of workers' control in contemporary society. The previous programs, even when they appeared to be spelled out in considerable detail by the anarcho-syndicalists, guild Socialists, and the Workers' Opposition in Russia, were after all abstract models. All assumed, at least implicitly, that the workers' councils themselves would be the focus of governmental power. One could, after observing the Yugoslav experience, outline three possible approaches which flow from the application of self-management to complex politics.

1. The first model would assume a revision of the traditional Marxist definition of the working class, and its replacement by the concept *working people*. In this case the self-managing bodies in the economy and society represent the entire working

---

[9]The best development of the implication of this development is in Serge Mallet, *La Nouvelle Classe Ouvrière* (Paris: Seuil, 1963). Also see B. Denitch, "Is there a New Working Class," *Dissent*, Summer 1970, and Michael Harrington's essay on the same question in the special *Dissent* issue, *The World of the Blue Collar Worker*, which appears as a Quadrangle Book (1972).

population; and therefore, also the managerial, white-collar, and technical strata, as well as blue-collar workers. Implicit in this as well is the notion that there are no major social conflicts within the category "working people" and that harmonious self-managing bodies can represent the group as a whole within a given sector.

2. The second model, which seems to be closer to the classic model, and which is now popular in sections of the French and Italian working classes, conceives of workers' councils as organs of dual power in a class society where the working-class parties do not necessarily rule: that is, workers' councils or shop committees are instruments of struggle for that power and are primarily conceived of as substitutes for the traditional trade union structure. They bargain and speak in the name of the blue-collar workers and their allies and do not necessarily have any connection with the state structure itself.

3. The third model conceives of workers' councils representing the blue-collar working class and its immediate allies running the industry and the economy in a framework where the society itself is ruled by a party of the working class. In this situation the workers' council would hire the experts, managers, technicians, and the rest. It also "hires" the secondary services, i.e., banking, finance, and so on. Here the assumption presumably would be that the party of the working class which rules the society bases itself on the blue-collar workers in self-managing institutions. The party is, simply stated, the society-wide expression of the *conscious will* of the more advanced sectors of the working class with its allies.

The troubling question in all three cases is, of course, the relationship of the workers' councils and other self-managing bodies to the state. In the first case, a model exists which can either be developed within a single or a multiparty structure. What is crucial for it is the conception that there are no specific working-class interests as distinct from those of the other working strata. Therefore, implicit in that model is consultation, coordination, and consensus. The second and the third models imply class conflict and resolve it on different levels. In the case of workers' councils existing as an organ of dual power, the councils themselves are one of the contenders for power and such a situation, particularly if the ownership of the economy is mixed, leads either to the atrophy of the workers' councils and their reduction to mere consulting bodies or to an offensive by the councils for state power. In the third case, while the councils would clearly dominate and control the economy, and the party which rules would reflect their interests, other strata—managers, technicians, private farmers, and so on—would still be represented in the *political* structure, i.e., through their own organizations or even parties.

The Yugoslav model seems to be someplace between the first and the third types. It is therefore, I believe, a model in the process of transition which can either move in the direction of stressing greater enterprise autonomy and the unity of managerial, technocratic strata with the working class, or it can move towards the third category, a possibility which did not exist at the time when the workers' councils were created. It did not exist for the simple reason that there were not enough workers to base industrial and state power on them *as the primary group*.

What is lost in the discussions about the future structure of the working force in modern industrial societies is that, although technical strata and white-collar workers have been expanding at a rapid pace, the blue-collar workers *have not* in any advanced industrial society declined to any statistically significant extent over the past five decades. The percentage of blue-collar workers, even after the massive introduction of labor-saving devices and automation, has remained constant at around 40 percent in most advanced industrial polities. What has diminished has been the percentage of people involved in agriculture, while the increases have been in a growing secondary sector. A change which was not anticipated, however, has been in the sector of technicians and white-collar workers, where massive groups have become proletarianized, at least in the organization of work process and the development of a trade union consciousness.

The point of the seeming digression is that the Yugoslav model, if applied to advanced industrial polities, would more probably be a reflection of a radical working-class program rather than of proposals supported by the economic techno-structure. An instrument of class conflict rather than class conciliation. To put it differently, the aspect of self-management which interests the techno-structures represents a struggle between the classic owners and the managers in private and sometimes in state-owned industry who attempt to buy off the working class by giving it the illusion of participation through consultation while the power stays in the hands of the technically better trained strata. The Yugoslav model, with all of its imperfections and contradictions, is on a different plane. It represents the major historical attempt to create a society based on self-management. The success or failure of this effort may reshape the coming strategy of working-class parties throughout the world.

Conclusions

1. Self-management in Yugoslavia represents an experiment [that has endured long enough] for it to begin to answer some of the basic questions raised, primarily within the workers' movements, about the possibilities of workers' control in modern society. These possibilities in Yugoslavia, however, were limited by underdevelopment, the complex political problems of the postwar state, and the large sector of the population which remained in private agriculture. Thus the experiment was successful, since, even under conditions which were far from optimal, a working system of self-management developed, producing a dynamic economy and a degree of participation hitherto unknown in industrial society.

2. Yugoslav self-management applies to the socialist sector which means that it affects roughly one-half of the working population. Out of the system are three major groups: private farmers, numbering approximately four million, people in the private sector numbering some ninety thousand, and the large number of workers temporarily working abroad (almost one million). Of course, pensioners, housewives, and those not employed are also excluded. Even with these limits, as I have shown, close to a quarter of the relevant population participates at any given time in the institutions of self-management. Since a system of rotation is used, this means that a major portion of the population in the modern sector is involved at one time or another. The other strata, of course, can formally participate through the political process.

3. There is considerable evidence that self-management has entered into the basic value nexus of Yugoslavia and is generally accepted as the desirable social goal, even with the imperfections which exist. The processes of self-management have created new pressures in the society which will in all probability continue to alter the political cultures of Yugoslavia in basic ways. Hostility to Yugoslav socialism—expressed as hostility to self-management—can be expected from a number of sources. In addition to the traditional ones, there will be two major new ones. One will come from the new middle class, seeking to enjoy a living standard close to

that of Western Europe, whose values are increasingly technocratic and managerial. For them what is wrong with self-management is precisely that it *does* involve workers who are viewed as having insufficient *culture* and *expertise* to make major decisions. The second group includes those who identify socialism with centralized planning and a unitary state. They object to the workers' making decisions because they view them as lacking *political* expertise. Both groups of would-be tutors will frame their attacks *within* a nominal support for self-management—only of a reasonable and limited form.

As the society continues to develop, the values implicit in the new set of social relations in the economy will increasingly clash with traditionalist values. These traditionalist values are most often expressed in the form of either nationalism or centralism (or rather statist socialism). This is because the processes of self-management tend to minimize the role of charisma and the special prerogatives of the traditional gatekeepers of societal values. Thus self-management will be viewed with suspicion both by traditionalist political cadres and the humanistic or traditional intelligentsia. The crucial determinant in the future development of self-management, therefore, will be the role and power of the increasingly massive industrial working class of Yugoslavia. It represents the major social group with an unambiguous interest in the *extension* of self-management.

Self-management has launched processes in the base of the society which have not yet produced an appropriate political superstructure. This is, if for no other reason, because the *political structure* has a history and tradition while the *social system* is new. It has, however, begun to shape that superstructure. One of the results is the form of pluralism of institutions now found in Yugoslavia. The continued process of change may take decades, but is in my opinion irreversible without outside intervention, and will basically alter the state and the political institutions. The result can be a model of a democratic socialist society—a model with no real precedent.

Self-management has been too often defended in terms of efficiency and economic rationality rather than socialist principle. This is in part because the spokesmen for it have tended to be "experts" and the result has been that the natural allies of the Yugoslav experiment have not been reached. Much of the discussion about self-management outside of Yugoslavia has been addressed to the wrong audience —to the statesmen, technocrats, . . . economic experts, and "impartial" social scientists, rather than to the workers' movements. This is a mistake since Yugoslavia may well need the sympathy and support of these potential allies, who need a successful model of workers' control and self-management. The continued development of that model requires the survival of an independent Yugoslav socialist state.

Selected Bibliography

Soviet Union

Azrael, Jeremy. *Managerial Power and Soviet Politics.* Cambridge, Massachusetts: Harvard University Press, 1969.

Barghoorn, Frederick C. *Politics in the USSR.* 2d ed. Boston: Little, Brown, 1972.

Gripp, Richard C. *Patterns of Soviet Politics.* Homewood, Illinois: Dorsey Press, 1963.

Hough, Jerry F. *The Soviet Prefects: The Local Party Organs in Industrial Decision-Making.* Cambridge, Massachusetts: Harvard University Press, 1969.

Skilling, Gordon H., and Griffiths, Franklyn. *Interest Groups in Soviet Politics.* Princeton, New Jersey: Princeton University Press, 1971.

Stewart, Philip D. *Political Power in the Soviet Union.* Columbus: Bobbs-Merrill, 1968.

China

Baum, Richard, and Bennett, Louise B., eds. *China in Ferment, Perspectives on the Cultural Revolution.* Englewood Cliffs, New Jersey: Prentice-Hall, 1971.

Oksenberg, Michel, ed. *China's Developmental Experience.* New York: Praeger, 1973.

Pye, Lucian W. *The Spirit of Chinese Politics.* Cambridge, Massachusetts: M.I.T. Press, 1968.

Robinson, Thomas W., ed. *The Cultural Revolution in China.* Berkeley: University of California Press, 1971.

Solomon, Richard. *Mao's Revolution and the Chinese Political Culture.* Berkeley: University of California Press, 1971.

Tsou Tang, and Ho Ping-ti, eds. *China in Crisis.* 3 vols. Chicago: University of Chicago Press, 1968.

Townsend, James R. *Political Participation in Communist China.* Berkeley: University of California Press, 1968.

Vogel, Ezra. *Canton Under Communism.* Cambridge, Massachusetts: Harvard University Press, 1969.

Wei Yung, ed. *Communist China.* Columbus: Charles E. Merrill, 1972.

Yugoslavia

Adizes, Ichak. *Industrial Democracy: Yugoslav Style.* New York: Free Press, 1971.

Blumberg, Paul. *Industrial Democracy: The Sociology of Participation.* New York: Schocken Books, 1969.

Brockmeyer, M. J. *Yugoslav Workers' Self-Management.* Dordrecht, Holland: D. Reidel, 1970.

Horvat, Branko. *An Essay on Yugoslav Society.* White Plains, New York: International Arts and Sciences Press, 1969.

Kolaja, Jiri. *Workers' Councils: The Yugoslav Experience.* New York: Praeger, 1966.

Zaninovich, M. George. *The Development of Socialist Yugoslavia.* Baltimore: The Johns Hopkins Press, 1964.

SECTION SEVEN

BUILDING THE COMMUNIST MAN

Every political system attempts to influence the behavior of its people to some degree. However, more than any other type of contemporary system, the Communist regimes have attempted to mold their citizens in accord with their own expectations: they themselves have dictated what man's goals and needs should be, and the various ways they can be fulfilled; they have diagnosed his deficiencies and formulated various strategies and techniques for removing them. The general objective, then, has been to develop a model Communist man—one who is devoid of such undesirable bourgeois traits as individualism and greed, and who instead embraces the principles of socialist brotherhood. Commenting on this task to the Twenty-Fourth Congress of the Communist Party of the Soviet Union (CPSU), General Secretary Brezhnev said:

> The Party has taken steps to create in our society a moral atmosphere that would help establish respectful and solicitous attitudes toward people, honesty, exactingness to oneself and others, and trust combined with strict responsibility and a spirit of true comradeship in all fields of social life, in work and everyday relations. In short, our aim has been that in our country everyone should live and work better.[1]

At their birth, the infant Communist societies were guided by a group of revolutionary elites who adhered to a set of utopian ideals that would

[1]From the proceedings of the 24th Congress of the CPSU, April, 1971. Quoted in *New World Review*, V. XXXIX (Summer, 1971), p. 59.

ultimately guarantee all citizens a better life. But the leaders theorized that, before this new stage of socialist development could be achieved, the social and psychological values of the old society would have to be changed rather drastically. This necessitated a transformation of the political culture—that is, a transformation or rejuvenation of the behavior and values of the citizenry, which in turn determines the setting in which politics takes place. In other words, the revolutionary leaders believed that a new behavioral and psychological setting would have to be established before the tasks of socialist construction could be fully realized. For example, individuals had to be taught to think and work as comrades, and to put their country before the more particularistic concerns of self, family, region, or ethnic group. In some states, the building task developed into a fanatical drive in which any tactics that would bring about the desired end were used. Then, in some states, if and when the socialist man seemed resistant to the desired changes, the government launched the society into an intensive thought-reform campaign to produce more receptive responses. For example, the Great Proletarian Cultural Revolution that swept China in the late 1960s (1965–1969) marked one of the most dramatic attempts in modern history to reshape the thought patterns of an entire population so that the behavior and life styles of the masses would conform to the goals and expectations of the regime. Although no event quite so dramatic seems to have taken place in the Soviet Union or Yugoslavia, subtler—and perhaps just as effective—methods are being utilized to transform the thoughts, values, and behavior of their societies also.

The central task confronting each of these three Communist systems is to construct a political culture conducive to regime goals and aspirations. To establish this more favorable setting, however, two distinct changes seem to be of primary significance. The first can be described as the attitudes of the Communist citizen, and his corresponding behavior, toward other individuals, social classes, and ethnic groups within the larger social system. As some of the readings in preceding sections have already revealed, all three systems have in the past been marked by vast social cleavages, provincialism, and general disunity. The inabilities of the pre-Communist regimes to bind and unify their countries into modern nation-states proved to be one of the primary factors causing their eventual collapse and the successful advent of communism. Certainly, one of the insoluble problems for the tsarist regime in pre-Communist Russia, was the presence of "Great Russian chauvinism" and the unresolved nationality problem. Indeed, the nationalistic and ethnic attitudes of the diverse Soviet peoples, and their feelings of mutual antagonism plagued, and continue to plague the present regime in its attempt to create brotherhood and unity. It was clear that the Soviet peoples would have to be transformed into a new Communist community before the goals of socialist construction could be realistically advanced. Furthermore, the gaps between social classes in pre-Communist Russia proved to be an obvious source of discontent and resentment. The differences between landowner and tiller, between city and rural dwellers, between exploiter and exploited—all were indications of a disintegrating society.

In modern China, the same condition was equally significant. The problems of provincialism and warlordism led Sun Yat-sen to remark that the Chinese peoples are like "a heap of loose sand," impossible to unite and solidify. Chiang Kai-shek overtly stated his explanation of the phenomenon as follows: "the incapacity to unite is a result of selfishness"; and his subsequent solution was equally straightforward: "the best antidote for selfishness is a public spirit." General Chiang, hindered by the realities of civil and foreign war, as well as by corruption and ineptitude in his own regime, was unable to maintain public support, and ultimately, to develop a new public awareness or consciousness. Eventually, upon the victory of the Chinese Communists in 1949, Chiang's hopes were crushed as he sought refuge on the island of Taiwan. The new Communist regime under the leadership of Chairman Mao immediately set out to destroy the selfishness of the old society and to establish the collective spirit that had long been lacking in China. The strategy has been consistent—the predominance of the collective over the individual. That it continues to prevail is evinced by the leading slogan of contemporary China, "Serve the People."

Finally, the history of the South Slavic groups that make up the population of contemporary Yugoslavia was one of conflict and disputes among various ethnic, regional, and social groups. The controversy among the major nationality groups—the Serbs, Croats, Macedonians, Slovenes, and Montenegrins—was particularly acute. Indeed, although territorially and culturally related, these various groups have found unity more difficult to bear than conflict. Hence, no union or nation of South Slavs was formed until the monarchial state of Yugoslavia was established at the end of World War I. However, this interwar regime had little success in binding the peoples, as evidenced by the almost total fragmentation of the country that occurred upon the outbreak of World War II and the Nazi onslaught.

In all three countries, then serious intergroup conflict was a prevailing tradition, and the new Communist regimes in each were faced with the tasks of transforming and rebuilding the attitudes and behaviors of the individual citizen toward other social, regional, and ethnic sectors in the country. The aspirations of the three regimes were largely the same— namely, to develop a universal ethic and a genuine feeling of comradeship among all of the people. They believed, and reasonably so, that the failure to unite would ultimately cause the collapse of the regime. Although Mao, Tito, and the Soviet leaders were united in their recognition of the severity of the problem and the importance of freeing the citizen of the individualism and provincialism of the past, they have not always adopted similar strategies for doing so. For example, the Soviet strategy appears to be one of building a unilingual, unicultural Soviet commonwealth. But the Yugoslavs have tended to concentrate on developing a new and higher order of

Yugoslav consciousness without sacrificing the identity of the various ethnic groups: indeed, many Yugoslavs contend that national unification and brotherhood can be achieved only by increased political decentralization and ethnic sovereignty. Finally, the Chinese goal is to integrate the nation through centralized ideological and political control emanating from Peking. In summary, the political strategies in each system are complex and often changing, but each regime is guided by the need to alter this first condition—the attitudes of the Communist citizen toward his countrymen.

If the citizen is to be molded into the model Communist man, a second condition also requires change: his attitudes toward the ideology and political system itself. The Communist regimes have maintained that before a new socialist way of life can prevail, the individualistic interests and bourgeois loyalties of the past must be abolished and replaced by a new Communist ethic conducive to the functioning of the worker's state. The characteristics of this ideal citizen are listed in Chapter 20 of this section.

Although the three Communist regimes are agreed on the characteristics required of the individual, the methods employed to develop these traits vary considerably. In the Soviet process, for example, the content of the curriculum is rigidly prescribed and defined. Unlike Western educators, the Soviets maintain that the learning process (at least in social and political areas) should be guided predominantly by ideology, and that it should be implemented by a carefully integrated program: thus the principles to which one is exposed in the schools are reinforced by other institutions, such as youth organizations and the mass media, and the cumulative effect is to impart a strong sense of Soviet patriotism, discipline, and ideological commitment.

The Chinese approach to the socialization process seems to be even more politically and ideologically motivated than that of the Soviets. At the height of the Great Proletarian Cultural Revolution, for example, every occurrence and activity was identified as a function of one or more ideological principles. For example, recent travelers to China have observed that peasant workers are convinced that ideological study has a significant effect on agricultural output. Their ideological commitment was reflected in the chanted slogan: "Higher output through greater study." Similarly, those who study medicine in Peking University, who undertake technical preparation for a job in a Shanghai factory, or who train for service in the People's Liberation Army—all are heavily indoctrinated with political and ideological propaganda. In this way Chinese citizens from every stratum are exposed to the ideological prescriptions of Chairman Mao Tse-tung and his followers.

In Yugoslavia, the building of ideologically acceptable attitudes and behavior is significantly different from that in any other Communist state. In rather sharp contrast to the Soviet and Chinese strategies, the general Yugoslav rationale has been one of "let the individual decide." In the course of the Yugoslav development under communism, the leaders have attempted to depoliticize the society to an extent unheard of in other Communist systems. One of the consequences has been the de-emphasis of ideology in the schools,[2] arts, mass media, and other vehicles of communication.

Instead, the Yugoslav citizen has been exposed to a diversity of opinion, and allowed to form his values and behavior from a wide range of information sources. Although, in Peking or Moscow, it is impossible to find a copy of the New York Times, Newsweek, Der Spiegel, or other Western media, those publications are displayed on newsstands throughout Yugoslavia, even in the most isolated regions. In short, the Yugoslav leadership appears to believe that, if Marxism-Leninism as an ideology, and the Communist system as a state, deserve the support, admiration, and patriotism of the Yugoslav people, they must earn it in the marketplace of ideas. The inevitable consequence is the development of a more sophisticated citizenry that has been exposed to competing ideas, ideologies, and thoughts. However, it should be noted also that the Yugoslav League of Communists is still entrusted as guardian of this marketplace of ideas and is prepared to assert itself if and when the situation requires. In fact, in the early 1970s the political leadership did assert its authority, forcing the Yugoslavs to adopt a more orthodox position on this issue.

That the three Communist systems have utilized quite different strategies to mold the values and attitudes of their citizens is obvious. More difficult to ascertain, however, are the future consequences of the diverse strategies. For example, will the Yugoslav strategy allow its citizens to acquire adverse information and a hostile point of view that will ultimately cause the downfall of the system? Or will this approach produce a more sophisticated and dedicated citizenry better equipped to live and work within a rapidly changing socialist system? Will the prescriptive approach in the Soviet Union lay the foundations for an intellectual revolution that will place great strains upon the social and political system. Or does the Soviet method better prepare its citizenry for the rapidly changing political world? Inherent in the Chinese method of indoctrination, and to a lesser degree in the Soviet's, is the problem of creativity and individuality. Just what kind of people, for example, will emerge from these educational systems? Finally, a question not to be overlooked is one concerning the peoples' dependency on the system—that is, how will they react if the government should falter, if the leader should die, or suddenly be replaced? Although our confidence in predicting the consequences of the diverse approaches is admittedly low, our understanding of the issue should be aided considerably by the readings that follow.

---

[2]Interestingly enough, Tito was quoted as saying during the recent (1972) "cleansing" of the League of Communists that the laxness in Marxist-Leninist education would be brought to an end, and ideological training brought back into the schools.

The readings for this section emphasize how both the theory and practice of communism are inculcated in the youth of the Soviet Union, China, and Yugoslavia. More important, perhaps, are the evaluations by the authors of the degree of success in building the Communist man. Charles D. Cary's article reveals the methodology employed to obtain information about the political socialization of Soviet youth. Not only does he use Western sources on the topic, but also he examines important studies done by Soviet education leaders and social scientists, whose findings confirm the difficulty of indoctrinating youth with values professed by the government. After describing the role of the different youth organizations and the schools in the socialization and upbringing of Soviet youth, Cary offers some conclusions that should be of special interest to the reader: For example, one statement—that "at all grade levels the degree of participation in the various [youth] organizations is high"—contrasts sharply with conditions in the United States. Is this what is necessary to have an involved and committed adult citizenry? Again, Cary suggests that there is a paradox in the answer.

In the second selection, Theodore Hsi-en Chen explores the characteristics of the new Communist man for China, and possibly for the other countries as well. The Chinese communists particularly strove to change "individualistic and selfish persons motivated by feudalistic and bourgeois loyalties." In place of those detestable characteristics, Chen discerns a few qualities of the model Communist man. Among those discussed are absolute selflessness, obedience to the Communist party (which includes adulation of Mao's thought), and dedication to labor and production. The final value not only prepares Chinese youth for Communist adulthood but also benefits the economy of the nation in the process.

As in the other two countries, the government of Yugoslavia also depends upon the schools as the "agents of social transformation." Susan Lampland Woodward concludes that the Yugoslav youth believe they should be prepared for decision making when they enter the workplace after graduation. But how successful are the schools as they train the youth in the theory and practice of self-management? Here, then, is a central issue in the Woodward article.

19

Political Socialization of Soviet Youth and the Building of Communism

Charles D. Cary

Question: Questions about the future of our government disturb me and many other children. What is the exact date of the construction of communism in our country? What benefits will citizens of the USSR enjoy by this date?— Vitia Meshcheriakov, schoolboy

Answer: . . . As it turns out, the point is not "when will communism be declared" but how we approach that time . . . The future depends upon how much the plans of the country become [our own] personal plans. And life will be such as we ourselves will make it.—I. Sergeeva, journalist[1]

All Soviet children are taught that communism is being built in their country. Building communism is presented to them as a very general national goal, in the name of which governmental policies and programs are justified and rationalized. For their part in this task schoolchildren are expected to embrace the goal and to let it motivate their lives and actions. Given these expectations, it seems only natural that a school-child should seek some clarification about the specifics of the construction of communism and should ask some pointed questions about when the building process will end and what the finished product will look like. In contrast to past proclamations and promises about communism, the answer to the schoolboy's questions suggests that the construction of communism is a continuing, possibly interminable process that goes on in accordance with a set of master blueprints. These plans are reviewed

This article is a revised version of a paper delivered at the 1971 Annual Meeting of the American Political Science Association. It is part of a continuing research project by the author on the political socialization of youth in the USSR. The author received research support initially from the Foreign Area Fellowship Program and most recently from the International Research and Exchanges Board. The contents of this paper are the sole responsibility of the author and should not be construed as reflecting the opinions of these funding organizations.

[1]I. Sergeeva, "Ty sprashivaesh' o kommunizme" (You Ask about Communism), *Pionerskaia pravda,* March 16, 1971, p. 1.

publicly at least every five years and each new five-year plan incorporates necessary additions and remodeling.

Since communism may be under protracted construction, those who govern try to persuade each new generation to continue the undertaken task. The rhetoric accompanying these attempts implies the possibility that the job can actually be finished. Thus, each new generation is expected to join the common effort and to make what contribution it can to the completion of the project. The crucial questions for the architects and administrators of society then become the following: (1) Are Soviet youth—the perpetually recurring next generation—prepared to accept their central role in building communism? (2) How positive are their attitudes toward this role. The importance of these questions is revealed by the fact that the continued progress and integration of Soviet society depend upon the answers.

This article is an attempt to formulate some plausible, albeit tentative, answers to these questions. These answers have been inferred from certain data, generated by Soviet educators and sociologists, on the political socialization of Soviet school-age youth and the extent of their participation and involvement in activities that have been contrived to enhance their socialization and to benefit society. The impediments, in the Soviet Union, to independent investigations by foreign researchers and that of Soviet sociological work on schoolchildren has obliged me to rely on such sources and data.

Inculcation of Belief in Communism

If the envisioned transformation of Soviet society is to be effected, then young people must be purposefully—and not haphazardly—socialized to accept the necessity and desirability of building communism, and to acquire the means for the implementing of this goal. More specifically, Soviet youth must be taught, first, to believe that communism can be built and, second, to devote themselves to furthering this task. It would seem that it would be easier to convince one of the wisdom, perhaps even the inevitability, of the future communist state than it would be to instill a personal and wholehearted commitment to its construction.

Whether the future Soviet society takes on the prescribed and predicted shape depends of course upon the personal commitment of citizens to persevere in the building process. If every schoolchild is taught to believe in the building of communism, he must also acquire the willingness and enthusiasm to make his own contribution to the construction. The major problem in this upbringing is not so much one of inculcating an initial, basic willingness and enthusiasm but rather of insuring that this commitment will endure.

The "Moral Code of the Builder of Communism," as formulated in the 1961 Program of the Communist Party of the Soviet Union, translates general belief and commitment into a set of qualities.[2] Other pedagogical materials specify in further detail those orientations and behaviors which should be inculcated in Soviet young people and the manner in which this inculcation should be accomplished. The establishment of uniform or similar socializing experiences in the schools and youth organizations creates conditions that, though perhaps necessary, are by no means sufficient for the realization of

---

[2]See Jan F. Triska, ed., *Soviet Communism: Programs and Rules* (San Francisco: Chandler Publishing Company, 1962), pp. 112–113.

the goals of upbringing. Schools and youth organizations provide an easily supervised environment in which children can be "scientifically" socialized; in addition, these institutions can counteract other agents (e.g., the family, and informal play groups) whose influence on youthful lives may not be as pedagogically proper and positively directed.

Political Socialization and Political Education

Political education pervades the cumulative process of the political socialization of young people, a nation's future full-fledged citizens. Political socialization refers to a broader, more inclusive phenomenon, since it subsumes not only the contrived socializing experiences of political education but also the other socializing experiences of growing up and maturing. Political education includes both civic training and ideological inculcation. The combination of civic training and ideological inculcation in the political education of youth certainly varies among different polities. In the Soviet Union the close connection between the definition of citizenship and the ideological conceptions of society, government, and politics blurs the distinction between civic training and ideological inculcation.

It is appropriate to distinguish here between the concepts of socialization and upbringing, which is the purposeful inculcating of certain habits, ideas, and so forth in the individual. It is included in the entire socialization process, in which the upbringing is reinforced by social activity, such as the individual's own participation in informal groups, and the like. Thus, while socialization and upbringing are related processes of the assimilation of the individual into society, the concept of socialization implies less purposefulness and more randomness than the concept of upbringing.

Although the political consequences of socialization might not be entirely manageable and predictable, a program of political education can counteract or at least offset to some extent this uncertainty. In the Soviet Union the general-education schools and the politically inspired youth organizations in them contrive the kinds of socializing experiences which should promote the upbringing of schoolchildren. The scope of the Soviet version of political education, that is, the range of orientations and behavior which becomes the object of upbringing, is commensurate with the extensively politicized view of the relationship between the individual and society. In Soviet society this relationship envelops virtually all areas and arenas of human endeavor. In fact, the extent of the interface between the individual and society suggests that from the Soviet perspective all socialization is political in nature.

Youth Organizations as Instruments of Political Education

Since the schools and the politically inspired youth organizations in them share the major burden of societal responsibility for molding dedicated "builders of communism," the quality of the relationship of Soviet schoolchildren to these socializing institutions assumes some importance. An examination of the nature of schoolchildren's participation in the activities of youth organizations in particular can provide some data for assessing the function and potential effectiveness of these groups in the upbringing of Soviet youth. Such an examination allows one to estimate, at least tentatively, the degree to which Soviet schoolchildren have acquired the orientations and behaviors necessary for building communism.

Two factors affect the character of schoolchildren's relationships with these youth groups. The first factor concerns the location of the youth group organization. The Octobrist and Pioneer organizations and the units for the school-age portion of the membership of the Komsomol organization are all based in the schools; both formally and informally, they are under the direct supervision of various layers of responsible school personnel. Although the administrative structures of the youth groups and the educational system are distinctly separate, at all levels of the administrative hierarchy these two institutions cooperate extensively. In the context of the school this cooperation becomes a supervisory arrangement.

Given that the school serves as the locus for the organization and supervision of the youth groups for school-age children, the second factor is the function of these groups in the schools. The school's work in upbringing is sponsored and implemented through the youth groups: thus the Octobrist, Pioneer, and Komsomol organizations are the mechanisms of upbringing. At present a period of eight years of formal education is compulsory; in the near future ten years of schooling will become the legal minimum. Educational practice at the primary and secondary levels is centrally coordinated and highly standardized. The coordination and standardization are reinforced by the youth organizations. Hence, by the time that boys and girls have completed at least their minimum, compulsory schooling, they have passed from the Octobrist organization to the ranks of Komsomol and have been exposed to about the same range of in-school upbringing experiences, and of political education.

The social activeness of a Soviet schoolchild is thought to be a reliable indication of the quality of his relationship with his youth organization. The assumption in this literature is that the more a pupil takes part in the activities of his youth organization and the greater his affinity for the organization, then the stronger will be the impact of his involvement. It is a difficult research task to make a strict association between a schoolchild's participation in any given activity and his acquisition of a specific orientation or behavior.

The kinds of activities which are sponsored and implemented by youth organizations are indeed varied. Recommended activities include commemorations of important historical dates, visits to factories and farms, school monitoring duties, choirs, chess clubs, hikes, basketball teams, and many, many others. All activities of the youth organizations should contribute to the proper upbringing of Soviet schoolchildren in one or more of the following broad areas—communist morality, learning and labor, social behavior, aesthetics, and physical training. Indeed, any activity that is sponsored and implemented by the youth organizations is considered to be either "social activity" or "social work."

By definition the Octobrist, Pioneer, and Komsomol organizations are oriented towards benefiting the group or the collective as a whole, whether the "whole" refers to the local unit, the school in which that unit is based, or any other superior, encompassing body, including the national society.

The psychological and organizational principle of upbringing—that is, of accomplishing it through the collective—is manifest in the activities of the Pioneer and Komsomol organizations. The term collective, as used in Soviet pedagogical literature, refers to groups that are organized for the purposes of communist upbringing. The collective in the context of the school is embodied in the units of the Pioneer and Komsomol organizations, which become in effect adult-supervised peer groups promoting the socialization of young people. Upbringing through social activity sponsored and implemented by the youth organizations is supposed to enhance the well-rounded development of the personality and individuality of each and every member, while insuring at the same time a societal directedness in this socializing process. However, a child's mere (though regular and even dutiful) participation in the social activity of the youth organizations only exposes him to an environment that has been established to further his upbringing. Thus, even though large numbers of schoolchildren participate in the youth organizations and derive a reasonable degree of satisfaction from the activities, the findings in this article raise some doubts about their capacity for eliciting earnest commitment from some of their members.

From a social-psychological perspective, the extent of a member's personal commitment to the life of his youth organization should naturally influence the degree to which he is affected by—i.e., socialized by—his participation and experiences. Thus, the development in schoolchildren of a proper set of motives for their participation in social work and in the operation of their youth organizations has become a vital issue for administrators and educators alike.

The Development of Soviet Studies of Political Education. Since 1958 Soviet education leaders have been devoting more and more of their research to the problems associated with the socialization of Soviet young people in the context of the Octobrist, Pioneer and Komsomol organizations. In particular, they have traditionally questioned the prescriptive or normative forms, content, and methods that have prevailed in the upbringing of school-age youth.

One predominant concern has been the quality and nature of young people's involvement and participation in the life of their youth organizations. Although Soviet youth organizations are indeed highly institutionalized and massive, their large memberships (traditionally cited as an indicator of their success and popularity) does not guarantee and may even impair the proper upbringing of young people. It is now recognized that the impact of these youth organizations also depends upon how the individual member relates and reacts to his experiences. Consequently attempts are being made to revamp and revitalize the youth organizations.

The Findings of Soviet Scholars. More specifically, Soviet educationists have been extensively investigating the social activeness of school-children and the ways in which they spend their spare time. Every investigation of the social activeness of Pioneers reports that all pupils in grades 4 through 7 (but girls moreso than boys) take a rather active part in the activities of the Pioneer organization and derive satisfaction from their participation. For example, in one study (of 1533 pupils in grades 4 through 8 of five urban and five rural schools in various locations throughout the USSR[3], 75.5 percent of the respondents (70 percent of the boys, 80 percent of the girls) indicate that they took part in some type of social work; 24.5 percent (30 percent of the boys and 20 percent of the girls) reported that they did not participate at all in social work. Another study (of 641 Pioneers in the fifth grade of some schools in Leningrad, Belgorod, Volgograd, and Orel)[4] revealed that 73 percent of the respondents liked to participate in social activity, 18 percent liked to participate some of the time, 7 percent did not like to

[3]E. S. Sokolova, "Sovremmenyi podrostok i pionerskaia organizatsiia: po materialam konkretnogo sotsiologicheskogo issledovaniia" ("The Modern Teen-ager and the Pioneer Organization: From the Materials of a Concrete Sociological Investigation"), *Sovetskaia pedagogika* (Vol. XXXII, No. 10, October 1968), pp. 19–31.

[4]V. K. Ivanova, "K voprosu ob obshchestvennoi aktivnosti mladshikh podrostkov v pionerskoi organizatsii" ("To the Question about the Social Activeness of Young Teen-agers in the Pioneer Organization"), in *Nravstvennoe vospitanie shkol'nikov v kollektive* (Leningrad: Leningradskii gosudarstvennyi institut im. A. I. Gertsena—Uchenye zapiski, tom 368, 1970), pp. 280–295.

participate very much, and 2 percent did not like to participate at all. The majority of these pupils, 76 percent, were completely or almost satisfied with such activity; the other pupils were either completely or partially dissatisfied with the same activity.

In comparison with Pioneers, students in grades 8 through 10 (who are most likely to be members of the Komsomol organization) are on the whole less active and do not find as much satisfaction in their social activity. In a study of the social activity of 490 ninth and tenth grade students in five Komsomolsk-na-Amur schools, and one Leningrad school[5] almost one-half of the respondents (47 percent) stated that they willingly participated in social activity or work; another 18 percent indicated that they participated without any desire at all. Approximately two-fifths said that they did not participate in social work: some of these plead lack of time, lack of initiative, or lack of desire. Of the same group 39 percent reported that they were satisfied with their social activity, and 56 percent expressed dissatisfaction.

Thus, as schoolchildren progress from the middle grades (5 through 7) to the senior grades (8 through 10), they tend to become less active in social work and derive less satisfaction from their involvement in this kind of activity. Specific reasons for waning participation that were cited by schoolchildren in both middle and senior grades included poor organization of social activity, few opportunities for self-fulfillment, activities that were too time-consuming, and boredom with the prescribed activities.[6] In addition, senior students commented upon their failure to recognize the societal sense of their tasks, the lack of independence in the selection and conduct of these tasks, and the randomness and disorganization of the tasks.[7]

Several investigations of the social activity of Pioneers and Komsomolites include data on the extent of responsibility that schoolchildren assume for the operation of their youth organizations. These studies suggest that most schoolchildren, although they uniformly participate in social work, do not themselves assume the responsibility for the planning and conduct of this kind of activity. Many school units of the youth organizations become divided or polarized into a small permanent active faction and a large stable passive faction. The same few activists occupy the various positions of leadership from one year to the next; the passive majority of the membership continues to participate faithfully in the activities that are organized by the fellow activists.

The willingness to undertake social assignments is considered an indicator of the responsibility that a Pioneer or Komsomolite assumes for his youth organizations. Social assignments differ from social activity or work. If a member of a youth organization simply takes part in an activity such as a waste paper collection, then he is credited with being a dutiful member and with having engaged in a form of social activity or work. But if his participation in the waste paper collection involves something more than just gathering and bundling together old newspapers (such as helping to organize or supervise this activity), then such a pupil is regarded as having carried out a social assignment. In effect those who fulfill social assignments demonstrate a stronger, more responsible link with their youth organization.

---

[5]L. I. Taran, "Otnoshenie starsheklassnikov k uchebnoi i obshchestvennoi deiatel'nosti: opyt izucheniia" ("The Relationship of Upperclassmen to Scholastic and Social Activity: The Results of a Study"), in *Nravstvennoe vospitanie shkol'nikov v kollektive* (Leningrad: Leningradskii gosudarstvennyi pedagogicheskii institut im. A. I. Gertsena—Uchenye zapiski, tom 368, 1970), pp. 193–202.

[6]Ivanova, "The Social Activeness of Young Teenagers," p. 286.

[7]Taran, "The Relationship of Upperclassmen to Scholastic and Social Activity," p. 199.

TABLE 1
Social Assignments: Level of Organizational Responsibility and Extent of Participation by Students in Grades 7 through 10[1]

Organizational Responsibility	*Percent of Students Fulfilling Task by Grade*				
	7	8	9	10	7–10
Assignments in large-scale group activities	53.6%	45.4%	35.2%	53.1%	48.2%
Assignments connected with the organization of small collectives	5.9	5.2	4.0	3.0	5.1
Assignments connected with the organization of big collectives in a definite kind of activity	20.7	25.8	33.7	24.7	24.6
Assignments connected with the organization and supervision of big collectives in various forms of activity	17.6	20.7	20.8	12.3	18.5
Assignments of an instructional-pedagogical character	2.2	2.9	6.3	6.9	3.6

[1]Data are adapted from I. A. Filippova, *Formirovanie obshchestvennoi aktivnosti shkol'nikov podrostkov kak sotsial'nopedagogicheskaia problema (The Formation of the Social Activeness of Teen-age School-children as a Social-pedagogical Problem)* (Unpublished dissertation, Moscow, 1969).

Also a distinction can be made between social assignments that are permanent and those that are temporary. One study indicated that the permanent and temporary activists together outnumbered the passive members, those who did not fulfill any social assignments but merely participated in the various forms of social activity.[8]

In another investigation of 2335 students, grades 7 through 10, the distinguishing criterion between social assignments proved to be the degree of their organizational responsibility, and not whether they were permanent or temporary. The categories of assignments are listed in Table 1, in order of increasing organizational responsibility. As the table shows, the majority of students at each grade level selected those tasks that were merely large-scale group activities that required minimum effort of the individual. In other words, in the context of the given study, these students indicated that they merely participated without assuming organizational or supervisory responsiblility for the various activities sponsored by their youth organizations.

Among the students of grade 7, which is the last full year of membership for pupils in the Pioneer organization, the percentage of passive respondents (those in the first category of Table 1) was greater than the percentage of activists (those in the remaining categories). When they are in grades 8 through 10, students belong to the Komsomol organization, and the proportion of active members varies from year to year. Thus students in the eighth grade were more active than those in the seventh, and ninth-graders were more active still. However, in the tenth grade the percentage of passive students predominates once again.

The following trend is thus apparent: with the exception of the tenth grade, as a student progresses from grade 7 to grade 9, he tends to become more responsible and

[8]Ivanova, "The Social Activeness of Young Teenagers," pp. 289–290.

active, that is, to take on some social assignments. The abrupt reversal of this trend for tenth-grade students may be a direct result of the increased scholastic pressure imposed during the last year of formal schooling at the secondary level. Pupils, especially tenth-graders frequently complain about being overburdened with homework. In addition, the graduating students face final examinations and highly competitive entrance examinations to institutions of higher education. It is reasonable to assume that tenth-grade students, while continuing to participate in social work, may drop the more responsible and demanding assignments in order to conserve time for their studies.

In another study[9] of pupils in grades 7–10, observers first determined the proportion of schoolchildren who had social assignments, the number of them who actually carried out the tasks, and pupil sentiments on social activity in genera. Table 2 presents the relevant evidence from this study of 1491 schoolchildren in Moscow, Kalinin, Smolensk, and Taganrog, and shows the contrast between sentiment and action.

Although most students indicated that they had social assignments to perform, a much smaller proportion actually devoted any time during the week to these assignments. In addition, when the schoolchildren were asked if they were interested in participating in social work during their free time, only a small percentage of each grade level replied that they liked to take part in social activity. Since the findings in Table 2 show that the proportion of students undertaking and completing social assignments was highest for grade 10, there is some conflict between these data and those presented in Table 1. The apparent sense of commitment manifested by these groups of grade 10 students may simply reflect the fact that responsibility for keeping the Komsomol organization running falls automatically to tenth-graders, who have seniority. Tenth-grade students, though possibly taxed by their academic load, cannot entirely shirk social assignments, such as responsibility for the planning and conduct of various upbringing activities.

Organizational Dilemmas of Pioneer and Komsomol Groups

The Pioneers and Komsomolites voice two common complaints about the social work, which constitutes the major activity of each youth organization: these are the ineffective organization of social work and the very nature of the various activities, which basically do not correspond to or match the interests of most schoolchildren. It is possible that these complaints arise out of a fundamental contradiction between expectation and reality—that is, members are expected to assume responsibility for the organization of youth groups and youth group activities, and yet are simultaneously subjected to the authoritarian control of adult personnel.

Such a dilemma is not confronted in the three primary grades, when the school children belong to the Octoberist organization. The Octoberist unit in each class, though formally under the direction of the school Pioneer organization, is nevertheless under the actual guidance of the class teacher. It is after the schoolchildren join the Pioneer organization, either at the end of the third grade or at the beginning of the fourth grade, that they assume at least some semblance of self-direction and self-rule. In both the Pioneer and Komsomol organizations there are various, diversified organs for self-administration.

---

[9]A. Zhurkina, "The Formation of Social Activeness of Older Schoolchildren," *Sovetskaia pedagogika*, Vol. XXXIV, No. 9 (September 1970), pp. 66–71.

TABLE 2
Social Assignments: Sentiment and Action

Grade	Percent having social assignments	Percent carrying out social assignments	Percent liking social work
7	78.3	38.5	2
8	71.6	25	6
9	70.4	41	15
10	84	56	13

If Pioneers and Komsomolites are viewed as capable of assuming responsibility, then they should be treated accordingly and be allowed to govern independently their youth organizations and their activities. If Pioneers and Komsomolites are considered to be not yet capable, then they should be provided with adult guidance and direction, and the Pioneer and Komsomol organizations should become organized peer groups under adult supervision. Although educators recognize the wisdom of treating pupils as responsible and therefore of granting them opportunities to demonstrate initiative, they often retreat from this position by asserting that pupils are still only children and consequently require adult pedagogical leadership.

In practice, school personnel often usurp the opportunities for self-governance that could be utilized in the planning and carrying out of Pioneer and Komsomol activities through the organs of self-administration within the youth groups. In addition, teachers, class leaders, deputy school directors for extracurricular activities, and other adult personnel often assume the same authority roles in the youth organizations that they command in the classroom and in the school. Educators who decree and schoolchildren who want to do their own thing may not agree on the kind of social activity in which Pioneer and Komsomol organizations should engage, or even on how this social work should be implemented. The pervasive, adult supervision of youth organizations by school personnel may be the cause of the boring, time-consuming social activity which Pioneers complain about, and of the lack of freedom to select and conduct social activity that Komsomolites criticize.

Members of both youth groups also object to the poor organization of social activity. This drawback too, may be a consequence of the extensive participation of adult school personnel in the life of the school-based youth organizations. Too much adult interference in the youth groups may actually discourage schoolchildren from taking initiative and responsibility for the activities of their youth organizations. The planning and directing by class leaders and other adults may not evoke the willing and enthusiastic cooperation of the group members, whose interests and desires to run their own show are being frustrated. As a consequence, many activities are undertaken at the urging and behest of school personnel; and many of these turn out to be poorly organized and not to appeal to the rank and file membership.

Conclusion

In this article, we have examined the social activeness of Soviet schoolchildren in grades 4 through 10 by studying their participation in social work, their satisfaction with this participation, their completion of social assignments, and their criticism of social activity. The findings about the various dimensions of social activeness provide a basis for an assessment of one aspect of the upbringing of Soviet young people and for a tentative estimation of the degree to which they are imbued with a revolutionary spirit for the building of communism.

To summarize, it is evident that at all grade levels the degree of participation in the various activities of the Pioneer and Komsomol organizations is high. The Soviet studies examined earlier in the paper show that all pupils in grades 4–7, but girls more than boys, participate extensively in the activities of the youth organizations and derive satisfaction from their participation; children in grades 8–10, in comparison with pupils in grades 4–7, do not take part as much and derive less satisfaction, although the absolute rate of participation remains rather high. In addition, there is an apparent but modest trend—manifested by the kind of social assignments undertaken and the proportion completed—for children in youth organizations to take on more responsible and active roles as they grow older.

However, other data, namely those on the fulfillment of social assignments, suggest that the association of youth with their organizations may be somewhat ritualistic in nature. Although it has been pointed out that young people who have taken on permanent or temporary social assignments outnumber the members who merely participate, it has also been shown by other observers that students at every grade level preferred the passive assignments to large-scale group activities. Furthermore, it has been observed that, of those children who have social assignments, the number who complete them is small. Finally, the previously noted trend for older children to take on more responsible and active roles in their youth organizations is accompanied by a division of the membership into stable contingents of active and passive participants, an oligarchical tendency found in many organizations.

It is premature to predict specific consequences of the findings about the social activeness of Soviet youth, either for the Pioneer and Komsomol organizations or for Soviet society. A perfunctory participation in activities for political education would seem to be of minimal benefit to the upbringing of Soviet children, and therefore a largely ineffective substitute for dedicated, responsible, and active participation. Although participation itself in the activities of youth organizations is stressed and viewed by educators as an important and possibly even a necessary condition for inculcating in each new generation the qualities necessary for building communism, the findings presented in this article imply that perhaps not all Soviet youth are acquiring from their experiences in youth organizations an exuberant revolutionary desire to develop their society. Whether the Soviet political system in its present form is capable of absorbing these builders of communism—that is, active, imaginative, responsible citizens who would be the ideal products of a Soviet program of upbringing or political education—is a separate question and beyond the scope of this article.

Social activity, as currently implemented through the youth organizations in the school, may no longer be the best means for the upbringing of Soviet youth. In fact, Soviet education leaders are currently discussing the advisability of moving the youth organizations out of the schools and into the housing projects where the children live.

Other problems of upbringing currently confront Soviet society. One broad problem is that of social and ethical behavior; and the questions of education in the subjects of etiquette, family, and sex. Another problem appears to be diminishing knowledge of and respect for the nation's laws. These problems may originate at least in part from the nature of the relationship between Soviet youth and their youth organizations. These developments have apparently caused the Soviets to question the socializing capabilities of the youth organizations in general. The gravity with which the problems are viewed is evidenced by the widely discussed proposals for incorporation into the curriculum of the general-education school of specialized courses devoted to each up-bringing program. These actions would bypass the traditional route of reliance on social activity in youth organizations for the upbringing of the model Soviet citizen. Concern and innovative planning by Soviet educators may indeed produce a reorganization of activities for the political education of Soviet youth. It remains to be seen whether such reorganization will more successfully imbue the young with a revolutionary spirit, and more effectively equip them to meet the opportunities and challenges of building communism.

20

The New Socialist Man

Theodore Hsi-en Chen

The Communist revolution is a total revolution aiming to establish a new society and a new way of life. A new society presupposes new men with new minds, new ideas, new emotions, and new attitudes. Before a new way of life can prevail, the old way of life must be abolished. While the new generation is being molded according to the Communist ideology, older people with old minds and hearts must be remolded. The making and remaking of new men therefore becomes a fundamental task of the Communist revolution and the central aim of education.

According to the Communists, the old society breeds individualistic and selfish persons motivated by feudalistic and bourgeois loyalties. They think of personal benefit and personal ambitions. Their narrow family loyalties encourage selfishness and the neglect of what is good for the general public or the state. The new man must be a collectivist, utterly selfless and ever mindful of his obligations to the revolution and the Communist party. Until the old man is replaced by the new, the proletarian way of life can not prevail and the new society must remain a dream.

There are many facets to the internal turmoil in Communist China today. One of the major issues under dispute is whether economic construction and collectivization should be pushed to the extent of alienating the masses, who show little enthusiasm for work that brings no tangible reward. While the more realistic and pragmatic Communists recognize the need for material incentives to stimulate public cooperation, the ideologues argue that the new man should be educated in such a way that he will not expect personal benefits but will find reward in the increase of production, the fulfillment of state plans, and the success of the proletarian revolution. If socialism does not work, according to the ideologues, it is not because the system is not good, but because human nature has not been changed to conform with the new system. Instead of modifying the system, it is more important to change man.

Methods of Making New Men

To popularize the attributes of the new man, the Communists select model citizens from various walks of life—model laborers, model peasants, model women, model youth.

From Theodore Hsi-en Chen, "The New Socialist Man" in *Aspects of Chinese Education.* C. T. Hu, ed. (New York: Teachers College Press, Columbia University Press, 1969), pp. 88–95. [Copyright *Comparative Education Review,* University of Wisconsin, Madison. Reprinted with permission from the publisher and author.]

In the campaign for the collection of fertilizers, for example, a diligent collector of night soil was highly praised as a "model" for all to emulate. A number of famous heroes and heroines of recent years were not recognized as such until after death. One such was Lei Feng, a soldier killed in an automobile accident, who was praised after his death as a dedicated revolutionary. In a nation-wide "Learn from Lei Feng" campaign, many stories were told of his deep love for Mao Tse-tung and his writings, and his determination to do whatever the Communist party wanted him to do.

Various forms of emulation campaigns have been used to promote the desired virtues of the new man. School children are led to strive to become "good pupils of the age of Mao Tse-tung." Girls and women are encouraged to become "good daughters of the Communist party." Specific goals are projected for such patterns of behavior as "three good" for students, "five good" for youth, "five good" for families, "five good" for commune members, and so on. For example, the "five-good youth" is supposed to be obedient to the party, diligent in work, able to overcome difficulties, good in protecting public property and maintaining the unity of Youth League members. "Five-good workers" are supposed to be good in political thinking, good in fulfillment of tasks, good in observing discipline, good in regular (political) study, and good in unity and mutual aid.

A major vehicle for remolding behavior is "thought reform," commonly referred to as "brain-washing." Thought reform for the purpose of exposing the errors of old ideas and attitudes is of special importance in the effort to change the outlook of China's intellectuals. Individualism, liberalism, professionalism, neglect of politics, lack of class consciousness are considered the common faults of intellectuals, who are the constant targets of attack as obstacles to the establishment of the proletarian outlook and way of life.

Characteristics of the New Man

From the virtues extolled in indoctrination and propaganda and from the various "models" selected to publicize desired modes of behavior, it is possible to discern a few major characteristics of the model man envisioned by the Communist planners.

(1) *Absolute selflessness.* The new man has no ambitions beyond that of serving the revolution. He seeks no personal fame or glory. He seeks neither comfort nor reward for himself or his family. He makes no personal plans that can not be completely identified with the revolution. Furthermore, he is always ready to sacrifice his own interests for the good of the revolutionary cause, and he gladly sacrifices his life when necessary.

(2) *Obedience to the Communist party.* The Communist party is the standard-bearer of the proletarian-socialist revolution and the symbol of collectivism. To be a collectivist is to accept the leadership of the Communist party. Loyalty to the revolution and loyalty to the Communist party are one and the same thing. Moreover, since the Communist party represents the collective interests of the "masses," the only effective way to serve the people is to serve the Communist party.

The party stands behind the state and determines its policies. As far as the people are concerned, there is little difference between the party and the state. No matter what the party-state wants, the individuals are obliged to comply. In every form of group life—in schools, factories, or business enterprises—there is a Communist party representative known as the "Leadership." Obedience to the Leadership is an indispensable characteristic of good citizenship. Young people consult the Leadership about marriage and other personal problems; teachers seek the advice of the Leadership in their personal as well as professional activities.

In one of the recurrent campaigns to rectify the thinking of China's intellectuals, the Communists demanded pledges of "heart surrender," in which the intellectuals vowed to "surrender their whole heart" to the Communist party. Acceptance of the leadership of the Communist party is expected of all citizens and is not necessarily equated with membership in the party.

Students before graduation are urged to pledge their willingness to accept any task assigned to them by the party-state. They may be assigned to jobs unrelated to their interests or to places far away from home; but good socialist men obey the call of the party-state. Young married couples have been assigned to jobs in places so distant from each other that they could meet only during leaves of absence, but no change is possible without the authorization of the party-state.

Recent years have witnessed an escalating campaign to exalt Mao Tse-tung to a position of unparalleled height and authority. More and more, love of Chairman Mao is preached as the best way of serving the revolution. Reverence for Mao is now inseparable from obedience to the Communist party as a basic attribute of the socialist man. Pre-school children as well as older children are taught to sing songs to express their worship of Mao. The well-known song "East Is Red" praises him as follows:

The east is red,
The sun rises.
China has brought forth a Mao Tse-tung.
He works for the people's happiness.
He is the people's great savior.

Chairman Mao loves the people,
He is our guide.
He leads us onward
To build the new China.

The Communist party is like the sun,
Wherever it shines, there is light.
Where there's the Communist party,
There the people will win liberation.[1]

(3) *Class consciousness.* The Communists equate political consciousness with class consciousness. A person of high political consciousness is keenly aware of class distinctions and ready to engage in the class struggle. He sees the need of a continuing struggle against the landlords and the "bureaucratic bourgeoisie" and their "bourgeois ideology." He avoids relationships that may blur the line of demarcation between friends and enemies of the revolution. For this reason, the Communists caution young people of worker-peasant class origin against marriage with persons from the landlord and bourgeoisie classes. To have close relationships with the bourgeoisie is to expose one's self to the evil influences of "bourgeois ideology."

Participation in the class struggle is necessary for the socialist man. One of the major complaints the Communists make against the intellectuals is that they do not appreciate the significance of the class struggle. In the agrarian reform of earlier years, the intellectuals heartily supported the distribution of land to the peasants, but were generally unenthusiastic about waging a class war against the landlords. They flinched from what

---

[1]English translation from *Peking Review* (English bi-weekly published in Peking), October 6, 1967.

they considered to be unnecessary cruelties in the treatment of the landlords and reactionaries. To overcome their aversion to the class struggle, the Communists required them to go into the rural areas to participate in the agrarian reform of 1950-1951. The intellectuals were asked to take part in the denunciation of the landlords, even in attacking them personally and demanding their physical liquidation. Upon returning from the rural struggle, they were each asked to write a personal testimony of what they had learned from actual participation in the class struggle.

The major targets of the class struggle are the "feudal" elements at home and the "imperialists" abroad. In recent years, the Communist leaders have been troubled by what they consider to be signs of waning enthusiasm for the class struggle. They fear that the young generation—the younger members of the Communist party as well as the non-Communist youth who have grown up under the new regime—are too far removed from the scenes of earlier battles to appreciate their significance. Without the experience of bitter struggle, the younger generation lacks ideological firmness. Concern over the question of "heirs to the revolution" has led to a renewed emphasis on "class education," to make young and old alert to the continued presence of class enemies and ready to attack all persons and ideas that endanger the progress of the socialist revolution.

(4) *Ideological study.* The new man must be guided by a correct ideological outlook, which depends on unceasing "study." "Study" in the Communist lexicon usually means political or ideological study. The Constitution of the Chinese Communist party stipulates that the first duty of party members is "to study Marxism-Leninism and unceasingly raise the level of their understanding." Similarly, the Constitution of the Chinese Communist Youth League states that every member must "exert himself in the study of Marxism-Leninism," and the Constitution of the Young Pioneers states that its aim is "to unite youth and children, to study diligently . . . to become builders and protectors of Communism." Factory workers, office personnel, as well as students and adult learners attend classes devoted to ideological study.

In recent years, the speeches and writings of Mao Tse-tung have been exalted as the bible of ideological indoctrination. Chinese Communist publications abound in reports of miraculous results from the study of Mao's words. Young people who complain about their routine jobs are reported to have gained new inspiration and enthusiasm for their work after study. Graduates of schools and colleges who see little relation between their education and the jobs assigned to them after graduation are said to have changed their viewpoint and become happy with their work. People who feel frustrated because they do not attain the distinction and success they have longed for have been so inspired by the reading and rereading of Mao's short treatises that, according to the Communist publications, they feel ashamed of their "individualism" and selfish personal ambition and find meaning and satisfaction in carrying on their work as "nameless heroes."

(5) *Labor and production.* The socialist man loves labor. The Communists exalt labor both for its ideological value and for its contribution to production. The Communists call themselves the vanguard of the working class, and labor is the trademark of the working class. The proletarian society expects all people to engage in labor; there is to be no distinction between manual and mental labor and no place for "white collar" persons who disdain to soil their hands in labor. The Common Program of 1949 provides that reactionary people "shall be compelled to reform themselves through labor so as to become new men." Labor is thus believed to have therapeutic value in ideological remolding.

Labor and production are inseparable. In 1958, the Communist party issued a directive on education which laid down the basic policy that education must be combined with productive labor. The work-study plan is today extensively adopted in schools and colleges. All students are required to engage regularly in productive labor as an integral part of school work. Work and study are combined in different ways. Sometimes, school time is equally divided between work and study so that the school can accommodate two groups of students at the same time, one group attending classes in the morning and working in the afternoon and another group studying in the afternoon and working in the morning. In some rural schools, students work on the farms during the busy farming season and attend schools in the off season.

A radical approach to the integration of study with work is the establishment of factories and farms by schools and the establishment of schools by factories, agricultural cooperatives, and communes. The students work as regular employees of the productive enterprises with full responsibility for their jobs. The variety of enterprises is wide: steel furnaces, iron smelting, tool and machine manufacturing, railway and small airplane construction and design, metallurgical workshops, and so forth. The originators emphasize that these are not merely instructional laboratories where students gain some practical experience; they are regular productive enterprises that take orders and turn out products on a business basis. Schools and universities, it is said, have become centers of production as well as centers of learning.

(6) *Versatility.* The ideal socialist man is a person able to serve in varied capacities. He can be shifted from one productive activity to another in response to the changing needs of the party-state. When the communes got under way in 1958, Communist writers viewed them as a big step in the direction of producing the new socialist man. They said that every commune member should be five-in-one—peasant, worker, trader, student, and soldier at the same time. This idea of the versatile man was emphasized in an editorial of the *Peking People's Daily* on August 1, 1966, summarizing Mao Tse-tung's educational ideas:

> While the main activity of the workers is in industry, they should at the same time also study military affairs, politics, and culture . . . Where conditions permit, they should also engage in agricultural production and side occupations . . .

> While the main activity of the peasants in the communes is in agriculture . . . they, too, should at the same time study military affairs, politics, and culture. . . . They should also collectively run some small factories . . .

> While the main task of students is to study, they should . . . learn other things, that is, industrial work, farming, and military affairs . . .

> Where conditions permit, those working in commerce, in the service trades, and in party and government organizations should also do the same.[2]

(7) *Red expert.* Much of what has been said about the new man can be summarized by the pithy term "Red expert." The socialist man, it is emphasized, must be both Red and expert. Expertness refers to the specific knowledge and skills that enable a person to make positive contributions to production and "socialist construction." It means technical or occupational competence. Redness means the full acceptance of the Communist ideology and the commanding role of politics in all realms of life.

It is the task of all education and training to produce Red experts. Education must combine political training with technical or occupational training, for no man may remain aloof from politics. The engineer as well as the philosopher, the bricklayer as well as the bookkeeper must engage in ideological study to make himself thoroughly "Red."

---

[2] English translation in *Peking Review,* August 5, 1966.

[Since 1949] there have been occasionally short periods of somewhat relaxed political control when professional people and scholars took the opportunity to voice their concern that academic learning and occupational competence were overshadowed by political considerations and that the country was turning out a generation of ill-trained personnel whose political qualifications, however good and "Red," could not compensate for their deficiency in technical knowledge and ability. These were times when some of the practical administrators openly acknowledged that until a new generation of Red experts became available it might be temporarily necessary to make use of "white experts." Such periods of realism, unfortunately, have been brief and soon terminated by a renewed demand for more pronounced political emphasis. Regardless of the occasional shifts in relative emphasis, the Red expert has remained the Communist ideal of the new socialist man.

Difficulties Encountered

What success have the Communists had in molding and remolding the new man? To the outside observer the Red Guards who vow unswerving loyalty to Mao and respond enthusiastically to the call for revolutionary dedication seem to attest to a good deal of success in Communist remolding, at least among the young people. Mao Tse-tung and his followers, however, have reason to be less sanguine. They know that the Red Guards represent only a small fraction of the population. Moreover, the emotions of youth are apt to rise and fall rather quickly, and there is little assurance that their exuberance will last and continue as an effective driving force.

Among other sections of the population old attitudes and habits persist. There are indications that while patriotism and national pride in the achievements of the regime in its first decade have produced a high degree of public enthusiasm and popular support for the government, Communist ideology itself has made little impact in the country. Socialism has not gained popular acceptance, and the all-important concept of the class struggle has not won many ardent converts. The new man envisioned by the Communist has been slow in appearing. While the people work hard, they still expect rewards in the form of material benefits and improved personal welfare. They have resisted collectivization.

Among the efforts to remake man is a campaign to popularize a new concept of "happiness." Communist publications abound in articles dealing with the topic "What is Happiness?" The purpose of the campaign is to attack the old concept of happiness, which considers personal welfare, comfortable living, and private family life to be essential. A Marxist writer has been severely condemned for having written that peaceful living, good food, adequate clothing, and harmonious family relations are important for happiness.[3] Such ideas, the Communist ideologues say, only serve to perpetuate the old man. Nevertheless, after [more than two decades] of Communist indoctrination and remolding, the old Chinese man is still very much alive.

Even young people brought up under the new regime have been found to entertain too many selfish ideas. Many of them want to marry and settle down despite official warning against relaxation of revolutionary effort. Students desire to continue their studies on higher levels instead of obeying the call to serve in industry or farm or other fields of revolutionary work. Those who accept the jobs assigned to them often complain

---

[3]Philosopher Fen Ting wrote the *Communist Philosophy of Life* and other books which were censured during the Cultural Revolution.

about their work conditions. The new spirit of selfless dedication evidently has not taken hold.

The intellectuals continue to be the regime's big headache. They have been subjected to tortuous thought reform and pressured to sign confessions of guilt, but in their hearts and minds many have preserved their independence and intransigence. It is only necessary to mention in passing that the early phase of the Cultural Revolution consisted of attacks on intellectuals accused of revisionist ideas. After many years of remolding, intellectuals who appeared to have fallen in line were actually expressing contrary ideas through satirical and allegorical writings. Some of them used historical figures as objects of criticism and ridicule, but their description of history sounded very much like comments on current conditions.

Resistance to remolding has probably prompted the Communists to step up their demand for the abolition of the old and establishment of the new. But changing man has proved to be far more difficult than changing political institutions or economic systems. The Communists have a long way to go before they can achieve their goal of new men with new minds and new hearts to suit their blueprint of socialist society.

21

Socialization for Self-Management in Yugoslav Schools

Susan Lampland Woodward

In his Third Thesis on Feuerbach, Karl Marx offers an intriguing challenge to students of political socialization in socialist societies:

> The materialist doctrine that men are products of circumstances and changed upbringing, forgets that it is men who change circumstances and that it is essential to educate the educator himself. Hence, this doctrine necessarily arrives at dividing society into two parts, one of which is superior to society.[1]

Despite this admonition, contemporary Marxist societies have not abandoned schools as agents of social transformation. At the same time, it is typical for scholars to reinforce this tendency by treating political socialization in Marxist societies as a form of intended indoctrination: a schoolteacher becomes the indoctrinator in the service of the state and its ideology, and the students become pliable materials to be imprinted with a doctrine which will make them obedient citizens. Any evidence of failure, or even of less than perfect end-products, leads scholars to suggest the interference of other agents—family, peergroup, human nature—with the learning process.

There are at least two difficulties with this approach, both of which are easily evident if one examines the curriculum in Yugoslav secondary schools: First, successful political socialization depends less on indoctrination itself, than on learning the kind of social relations implied by a doctrine. Indeed, learning the values of a doctrine without the behavior which follows from those values may be detrimental to the polity; or, at any rate, "indoctrination" implies an overly restrictive notion of obedience when one confronts societies intent on change. Second, Marx was correct in maintaining that "upbringing" divides society into two parts, one of which is superior. It follows, therefore, that any failure of schools to teach the habits necessary to socialist democracy, at least as it is defined in Yugoslavia, should not be attributed to the intereference of other

---

The research on which this article is based was made possible by a fellowship from Princeton University and its Center for International Studies and with the guidance of Harry Eckstein. Undertaken during 1970 and 1971 in fourteen secondary schools within the Socialist Republic of Croatia, Yugoslavia, the study reports results from interviews with approximately forty teachers and directors, from the responses to questionnaires by 1,488 students between the ages of 14 and 23, and from eighteen months' observation in those schools.

[1]Karl Marx, "Theses on Feuerbach," in Robert C. Tucker, ed., *The Marx-Engels Reader* (New York: Norton, 1972), p. 108.

agents of socialization but rather to the nature of the learning situation in schools itself. Schools are constructed on a relation of authority and, in a society whose doctrine denies positions of superiority to anyone, students learn early to obey their "superiors."

In this essay we shall discuss Yugoslav schools, and what the students are learning that will enable them to become active (or at least not disaffected) members of the Yugoslav polity. Since the Yugoslav polity includes a vision of some ideal towards which its citizens are striving, it is also important to ask in what way students are learning to foster the culture projected for the future in which they will be expected to live. The "upbringing" of youth, then, includes socialization not only to current practices, but also to a not yet fully developed future society—the associationist socialism of Yugoslav self-management. We shall examine political instruction in Yugoslavia from the perspective of her new system of self-management: what do youth need to know to make self-management work and to adapt themselves to this truly radical attempt to restructure society?

Self-management is, at this stage in its development, a *structure* of social relations, which Yugoslav legislators have imposed on every organization in the socialized sphere of their society with the goal of achieving socialist democracy by eliminating hierarchy and thus domination. Its rationale can be easily understood by reference to national liberation movements and the earliest arguments for national self-determination. Just as it is impossible for a country or a people to be free until it is independent—both politically and economically—from colonial status or imperial exploitation, so individuals cannot be truly free until they are no longer dependent on others, either because an inequitable system of property ownership prevails or because some have political domination over others. Individuals live in societies, however, and must in some ways depend on others for their subsistence. To maintain individual freedom, therefore, what collective organization is necessary must be structured so that dependence is reciprocal, and the possibilities of subordination and superordination are eliminated. In other words, to attain a classless, nonconflictive, nonantagonistic society, Yugoslavs argue, one must not only eliminate the private ownership of property, and so the basis of the division of society into opposing classes, but also abolish the division in every workplace between management and workers, between dominant and subservient. As Yugoslav economist Branko Horvat writes, "If the fundamental principle of bureaucratic organizations—the principle of hierarchy—is left to operate, in the course of time two social classes with conflicting interests will again emerge."[2]

The Yugoslav system of self-management views the workplace as the center of an individual's world, alters its nature from a place of employment to a locus of community, transfers effective control of the work organization to those who work in it, and thus attempts to make democratic (equal) participation in decision making a fact of everyday life for every individual rather than an activity assigned to the few elected representatives of the people or the few who control the essential resources of the economy. If no one person or group of persons has more power or influence over the direction of a workplace than any other, the need for a state, as the final fortress of domination, will also vanish, since its sole purpose is to enforce the obedience of subordinates to directives from superiors. ·

Ideally, when this transformation was complete, all collective action in Yugoslav society would consist of freely made, mutually agreed upon arrangements among

---

[2]Branko Horvat, *An Essay on Yugoslav Society* (White Plains, New York: International Arts and Sciences Press, Inc., 1969), p. 20.

workers in an organization and between autonomous, self-governing associations of workers. No more coordination would be required than would naturally result from a willingness to participate equally in the common interest by all those concerned. In sum, a structural rearrangement of decision making in all organizations in society and a concomitant willingness by each member of society to take equal responsibility for the management of his workplace would provide the foundation for socialist democracy, with which the achievement of all other social goals would follow.

The elimination of all forms of antagonistic conflict in society would lead naturally to political equality: with no superiors, people would cease to desire superiority, that is, to have power over others or to acquire excessive possessions. In addition, the consensual, collective structure of self-management would itself provide the obvious arena for, and thus encourage, equal participation in decision making. Simply by using the structure, it is postulated, self-managers would recognize that to work for the collective good was rational and that to be self-interested was irrational.

However, others maintain that this structure is not self-perpetuating, and that youth must therefore be prepared for this new system, and socialized for self-management. Teachers stress their role of upbringing, and educational legislation assigns an important role to schools in the process of socialization. Although a "curriculum for self-management" has not been devised, the following passages from the 1970 federal resolution on education state the task of schools clearly:

> The self-managed, socialist society demands a fully developed personality, educated and capable to perform its functions in the complex conditions of life and work.[3]

The major task of education, then, is to see that young people

> become familiar with the essence of socio-economic relations, political structure, rights and duties of citizens in the self-managed socialist society, and that they become fit for direct decision-making on the conditions and results of their own work, for progressive change of social relations; that they master democratic methods in the realization of personal rights and freedoms and develop a sense of solidarity in work and in communal life.[4]

The theory, then, is that the more educated one is, the more one is capable of self-management. By implication, the more years of formal schooling one acquires, the less he is inclined to accept the word of another in deciding matters; the more he is able to understand the arguments necessary even for technical decisions, let alone the issues in policy decisions, which are to be made by all workers, the less he is willing to defer to authority. Thus, the better educated the general public, the higher the level of education throughout society, and the more widespread the attitudes in favor of continual education throughout one's adult life, the more capable of freedom the population is. Second, it is assumed that the more familiar a person is with the structure, rights, and duties of self-management, and the more he participates in it, then the more he will continue to participate democratically and with an experienced eye to the common good. Through specific learning in schools, youth will come to accept this system as natural, or at least as customary.

---

[3]*Resolution on the Development of Education on Self-Management Basis* (Beograd: Savremena Administracija, 1971), p. 9.
[4]Ibid.

In this evaluation of the effectiveness of political socialization[5] in Yugoslavia, we are going to analyze the actual experience students receive in cultivating the three qualities that have been identified by the law on education as essential to self-management: these are the desire and ability to participate directly in decision-making, a knowledge of democratic methods and how to use them, and a sense of solidarity with one's fellows in work and communal life. In other words we shall examine what students today are learning to *do* rather than to *believe*, when they act politically.

The first important area of self-management is decision-making. By the time a student enters secondary school—and between 80 and 98 percent of the current generation attend secondary schools—he is guaranteed some rights to participate in school management and to join his peers in managing their own affairs as students. The central vehicle of this early experience with self-management, at least formally, is the class association. Recalling that the "self" in self-management properly refers not to individuals but to individuals associated equally in a work unit, it is clear that students would have rights to management as members of a group. The class, or the students' work unit, consists of 30 to 40 students who share a classroom, a homeroom teacher, a set of 13- or 14-year-long courses, and four years (usually) of education together. This class also forms a class association, which elects officers, meets to discuss issues of mutual interest or concern, and is held collectively responsible for the performance—both learning and behavior—of each student within it. Although the parallel is rarely drawn, students are like workers in a factory, in that they are responsible for work performance as a unit, they receive instructions, rules, and specific tasks from forums representing the whole organization (the Teachers' Council instead of the Workers' Council), and they even send representatives to authoritative decision-making bodies of the school, such as the School Council and the Student Association. Unlike workers, however, students are not yet employed and are only preparing for the adult world of work; they are not yet defined as "workers" and so are not granted the full rights to self-management that they will gain with employment. Unlike teachers and other school staff, their "self" is not the school but their class.

The formal introduction of the class association and of some student representation on teachers' councils and school decision-making bodies is itself a crucial step in socialization for self-management. At this stage the organization charts presented in the textbooks become meaningful, and students become familiar with the structure of self-management. Since self-management has been introduced by the League of Communists' platform and implemented through federal legislation, identical management structures and basic rules of working relations have been imposed on all self-managing organizations, regardless of the nature of their specific activities. Therefore, by knowing the structure of one organization, an individual should be able to reorient with ease to any other organization within the socialist (self-managing) sphere. Thus, once a Yugoslav has been to secondary school, even if he is only vaguely conscious of the rules that prescribe management in his school and the ways in which decisions are made, he has, at the very least, begun to learn where to begin to participate in the management of his place of employment. Manipulation of this structure outside the school and discovery of its actual, rather than its formal, operation will then depend to a certain extent on

---

[5]The term "political socialization" means here the learning to play a full role in the Yugoslav system of self-management by participating in the management of one's workplace. The conception follows the Yugoslav notion of the polity, which is wider than the Western notion of politics.

what else he has learned in school about the way to participate and the efficacy of doing so.

If a secondary-school student wishes to participate through established channels in the decision making of his school, either to gain experience in self-management, or to influence the government of his school, he has three possibilities. The first, the activities of his class association, is the only one accessible to the majority of students. Here a student first experiences elections and, more importantly, becomes acquainted with the national concept of good citizenship: that is, only those students who have done well in their studies and have demonstrated good behavior qualify as candidates to represent the whole; a citizen is eligible for leadership only if he first fulfills the obligations of community life. To teach this principle, teachers may interfere with student elections, either by refusing to seat at meetings a student representative whom they consider undesirable or by insisting on a new vote. As one teacher comments,

> It is wrong to give them complete self-management. Students choose representatives who are likeable rather than hard workers; this is a mistake; when the worst students are elected, the homeroom teacher then calls them to task and they take the necessary steps. If a bad student is elected, and acts negatively on the class, then usually they have another election. Usually the students intervene, but sometimes the homeroom teacher does also.

Once a class has elected officers, it is ready for action: it is equipped to discuss mutual problems and resolve them, to form a unit for participation in work projects in the school or the community, or to pressure its teachers to change a student's grade, remove an unpopular teacher, or alter the examination procedure. Although its potential for effective action is great, in practice the class association is most often an instrument of discipline in the hands of teachers. Students soon learn that they must be responsible for the discipline of their group. For example, if a student misbehaves, he is admonished, but the teachers feel obliged to inform the class association; furthermore, they consult the class for assistance in preventing any further lack of discipline. If a student is absent from class, his fellow students are responsible for learning why, reporting the reason to the teacher, and then finding a way to insure his quick return. If a student becomes a serious disciplinary problem or remains a truant, the teachers convene the associated students to learn what the students know about the problem, to determine whether they have been negligent in some way, and then to request their assistance or to admonish them for lack of responsibility. Thus if a student has difficulty with a subject and so receives a poor grade, it is a poor reflection on his fellows who, it is assumed, have not given him extra attention. Grades are recorded both individually and collectively for each class, and are considered the responsibility of the class as a whole. At each grading period the classes obtaining the lowest grade averages in school become the subject of discussion, and the concern for remedy may lead to the convocation of the class association, a change of homeroom teacher, or a collective punishment. As an example of collective punishment, a senior class in one Croatian school was not allowed to accompany the other three senior classes on an excursion to the Soviet Union: it had been obliged to forgo the trip because its grades in mathematics had been considered unusually poor. Despite the apparent severity of this penalty, the students seemed to accept it as justified. The teachers maintain that making grades public, as the law now requires, improves study and behavior significantly. Students respond to the pressure of their peers, either out of embarrassment or because they know it reflects poorly on the group: their peers will learn who is depressing the class average.

Although most attempts to teach students the system of discipline by the group rather than discipline by someone in authority are initiated by teachers, occasionally students will themselves request a change of regime. For instance, if a few students continually disrupt class time or if a teacher is so lenient that some students feel their peers are escaping with preferential treatment, the class association will send a delegation to the appropriate teacher or even to the school director. In addition, an increasing number of schools have begun to assign to the class association the duty of determining the quarterly grade for deportment. Without the aid of the homeroom teacher, the students discuss and assign individual behavior grades to each member of their class and recommend these to the teachers assembled in the class council. Few schools as yet permit students the final word, however.

Although students limited to their class association's activities probably gain more of a sense of community than of participation, there is a small minority in every school who have the opportunity to be more influential. These delegates become representatives of their class association, and as delegates to the various decision-making bodies in the school, they are spokesmen for their peers, and channels of communication between teachers and students. Perhaps the most important decision-making body is the class council: at its meetings all those teachers who instruct a particular class gather quarterly to determine student grades and discuss individual difficulties. Each class council receives one or two student representatives who may influence the teachers by protesting an individual grade or providing information which teachers may lack about a student. In addition, if the agenda includes matters of concern to them, these student delegates will be invited to meetings of the Teachers' Council, which comprises all the teachers in the school and meets monthly.

In actuality, however, most students appear to view their representation as a ritual and only rarely of any real influence. They speak only when addressed—for example, when asked to answer specific inquiries from a teacher or the director—and otherwise remain silent. The teachers, in turn, treat these representatives more as agents, reminding them of failed duties, advising improvements in class behavior, or requesting reports on student opinion and difficulties.

Of the 600 to 1000 students in an average secondary school, only six or seven students have a guaranteed voice in school management. These are the student representatives on the School Council, the most authoritative decision-making organ for a school, and the forum of community control over schools. This organ of social management, rather than self-management, consists of representatives from the three legally defined "interested parties" of education—the community, the teachers and school staff, and the students. Thus, students are given one-third voting membership in an organ of approximately twenty people assigned the responsibility of selecting the school director, approving the school budget and yearly schedule, and hearing and passing on all matters of organizational importance to the community, such as finances and curriculum.

Alongside this small group of students, another type of student participation in school offers genuinely useful experience in self-management and political life: that is, participation in the two school-wide organizations, the Student Association and the League of Youth Committee. The small group of truly active students in a school belong to these organizations, though they are only remotely associated with the organ of student self-management, the class association. In most schools, the Student Association Committee, the pinnacle of student self-management, is not as influential as the purely "political" organization, the League of Youth Committee, which is responsible for engaging students in issues and actions of social and political interest. If these junior politicians are active, they can be very effective indeed. For example, the school director relies on them to organize students for work projects and community actions, he meets with them regularly to sound out student opinion as well as to enlist their aid in various problems, and he usually depends on them to familiarize students with those "rights to self-management" which are not taught in class. Although teachers in some schools remark that the activity of these student organizations is in fact barely noticeable, a more common problem is that these students—often politically ambitious and skillful—can become elites who are considered spokesmen for student opinion and complaints but who have not bothered to canvass their peers first. As one student wrote, "often youth leaders act in the name of students without their knowledge."

The low proportion of active students is indicated in the answers students themselves give about themselves. Most, although agreeing to the importance of self-management and participation in decision-making, state that they themselves do not practice it; they claim they want to participate but admit they rely on the proxy participation of four or five student leaders. For instance, when students were asked whether they were interested enough in how their school was managed to converse with their school-mates about it, 44 percent of the 1488 students questioned replied that they did so often or very often, whereas 20 percent replied that they rarely or never held such conversations. When students were asked if they and their classmates expressed their opinion to teachers or the school administration, however, only 3 percent said that almost all the students did so, and 67 percent reported that this minimal attempt at influence was made by only some or a few of their peers. Teachers concurred with this general evaluation. Also, when students were asked if they attempted to influence their teachers or a school director, a similar pattern of responses emerged, suggesting that the majority rarely, if ever, made such an effort.

Nonetheless, students do not approve of such passivity, and appear to have learned the values of participation and self-management. A strong majority (92 percent) thought students should be more active in expressing their opinions about how the school is run—and more than half thought students should be *much more* active. Many of these students, furthermore, were not satisfied with the opportunities in school for doing so, and suggested that hesitancy, disinterest, or fear of retaliation among students contributed to their apathy. In defense of their nonaggressive behavior, many students argue that they are often consulted and their wishes *are* at least taken into account. Agreeing with many of their teachers, who believe that a student's primary respon-sibility is to study, they say they are satisfied with promises of self-management in the future and with the present degree of participation they have as students. However, when students were asked whether they should decide for themselves on school matters, such as how they perform their own tasks and behave while in school, only 13 percent responded that the present situation was satisfactory; 87 percent of the students wanted to decide such matters themselves.

The difference in students' responses between what they say they would like to do (which they defend with reference to the principles of self-management) and what they actually do and can do in schools, reflects an incongruity between the values to which they have been so well socialized and the opportunities that actually exist for practicing those values. My evidence indicates rather that students are aware of this contradiction from an early age. For example, one student wrote, "In these schools, the future leadership cadres are being created and therefore they should be offered oppor-tunity already, now, to show what they know." Another commented, "Since a majority of the factories are in the hands of the workers, since there is self-management in them, I think that the principle of self-management about which so much is being said lately, ought to be carried out in the schools." Finally, a third stated, "Two years already the students have been told about self-management, but nothing has come of it. The student who has become accustomed to being subordinated in school without thought will never become a useful and progressive member of our community."

In addition to the discrepancy between participatory values and practice, students appear to be concerned about their meager influence over issues which matter to them. Manifesting a pattern that studies of Yugoslav industrial organization have shown to exist among workers, students show little interest in school policy and finances, which touch them only indirectly and about which they are little informed, even though they have representation on the body which decides such matters. But they are intensely interested in such matters as grading criteria and examining methods, the selection of teachers, what extracurricular activities they may join, and what rules regulate their dress and behavior in school, that is, not policy issues but issues that directly affect their lives as students. Nonetheless, teachers classify these issues as "professional" ones to be decided in meetings that students may only observe if indeed they are permitted to attend at all. Most teachers are convinced that students are neither mature enough nor otherwise qualified to participate in decisions on such matters as curriculum or grading.

The second quality that is identified by the law of education as essential for self-management is an understanding of democratic methods and the ability to make use of them to influence decisions. In this area, too, many Yugoslav students are deficient, and exhibit a reluctance to avail themselves of such channels in the schools. Rather, as many as 90 percent elect instead to go individually or in informal groups to a specific teacher for help with a problem. This tendency resembles the behavior pattern of workers, whose attempts to influence a decision in industry have been described as informal appeals to superiors, foremen, and Workers' Council representatives, rather than organized efforts, appeals to the Director, or written communications and petitions.

The predominance of informal, personal means of influence is not only specifically encouraged by teachers, who prefer to leave problems to the resolution of the homeroom teacher, but also Yugoslavia's open, socially egalitarian society as a whole. Such procedures do not provide experience in self-managing relations, however. That such experience is needed is illustrated by a report of a visit that President Tito made in 1970 to a Zagreb factory, where he was besieged by factory workers who complained of many problems, most of them seemingly minor, and requested his help in solving them. His reaction was one of anger that they had not learned to work out their own solutions or to appeal to their representatives in the workers' council or socialist alliance. Similarly, if students rely on individual appeals to persons of authority—such as a homeroom teacher—rather than learning to solve problems by engaging the prolonged participation of everyone effected, or rather than learning to recognize those matters that in fact concern them the most, then socialization to self-management is not being accomplished effectively in Yugoslav schools.

Since Yugoslav secondary students report that they value participation, why is it that they do not in fact participate in school decision making? One of the most common excuses is ignorance of their actual rights for self-management. Students are carefully instructed in rules of study and good behavior—courtesy, dress, attendance, work habits—but the teachers leave instruction in self-managing rules and opportunities to student leaders, the few who already have influence in the school. One reason that some teachers do not inform students of these rights is surely their own concern about losing authority in the classroom, and also many themselves lack information about the rules since the laws regulating self-management change so often. Another excuse for low student participation is unresponsive teachers. If their suggestions are ignored or teachers become angry and threaten harsher grades, students then have little choice but to concentrate on their studies, since the good student attains such rewards as the grades that lead to a good job and salary, and even access to his teachers as a student leader or a trustworthy representative.

Perhaps most damaging to the prospect for increased student participation in self-management is the lack of political efficacy sensed by students. Teachers maintain that students are easily discouraged; and the students themselves are of the opinion that attempts to influence teachers—for example, to initiate a new practice or to change a rule considered unjust or harmful—are futile. Since, at this stage of socialization of the individual, a trust in the rules which are made to bind the association is crucial to the success of self-management, such evidence is not encouraging.

The third quality deemed essential for effective self-management is the "sense of solidarity in work and in communal life." Indeed, it is considered fundamental to the development of the other two qualities—the abilities to participate in decision making and to make effective use of democratic methods to influence policy formulation. Consequently, student acquisition of this third quality is a matter of genuine concern to secondary-school teachers, many of whom maintain that students must learn to manage themselves before they can be considered mature enough to manage others, or an entire institution, such as a school. In other words, teachers believe that students earn the right to participate only by paying the dues of obedience and responsibility first. Although this quality is less easily measured than the previous two, one does observe a strong sense of striving for mutual welfare among students and a spirit of camaraderie. In spite of the doubt expressed by teachers that they do not stress collective spirit enough, their use of the class association, and their frequent reference to the need for collective responsibility appears to have its effect. However, this process of socializing solidarity appears to have unexpected negative consequences such as the following three.

The first negative consequence is that many students acquire a tendency to evaluate themselves and their fellows too harshly. The primary means that teachers have at their disposal for instilling collective responsibility appears to be the system of group discipline—that of expecting students to be responsible not only for their own behavior, but for the collective behavior and scholastic performance of their classmates, and often for actual deliberation on the grade for deportment each will receive.[6] Nonetheless, teachers continue to hold themselves ultimately responsible for decisions on discipline and grading, and also remain concerned about the effect on individual personalities, as indeed their profession demands. Where students have been given full responsibility for the grade on deportment and for evaluating all excuses for absence

---

[6]If one follows Adizes this is consequential. He argues on the basis of his study of two industrial organizations in Serbia that the act of disciplining must be done by the group if the participative system of self-management is to work. He writes, "If executives had power to punish and reward, the hierarchical system would prevail regardless of the philosophy behind the organizational structure. Since this power was withheld from the executives, they actually had to seek support from the workers and rely on them for the adequate management of the company." Ichak Adizes, *Industrial Democracy: Yugoslav Style; the Effect of Decentralization on Organizational Behavior* (New York: The Free Press, 1971), pp. 192–3.

(the second task being perhaps the more important since a student can be expelled for 30 to 35 hours of unexcused absence), teachers complain that students are too strict with themselves, that they tend to value "principle more than personality." And if a homeroom teacher decides his students are grading too severely, he withdraws their "right" to grade for several months until he is able to demonstrate by example the necessity for leniency and for sympathy in individual cases.

Another attitude, which schoolteachers share with Yugoslav adults in general, also interferes with socialization to collective responsibility, a quality that Yugoslav writers at present consider the major weakness in the self-managing system. This concerns the deeply ingrained cultural attitude that, "everyone should be permitted his youth." Youth, it iş believed, should be protected as long as possible from the burdens of adulthood, one being the responsibility for one's actions, and be allowed the frivolity that is a part of the youthful spirit. Perhaps as a consequence of this attitude, teachers appear to spend little time teaching the responsibilities of freedom, except by an occasional post hoc prohibition, and ethical issues are rarely stressed except when an admonishment is being given. Little provision is made for discussion of any kind in the classroom and the weekly Homeroom Teacher's Hour, once designed for wider discussions on the problems of youth, is being eliminated in an increasing number of schools as curricula become more extensive.

Furthermore, although teachers may be correct in assuming that with maturity will come a sense of responsibility, they do little to foster the development of that responsibility. For instance, although Yugoslav children are preparing to be self-managers, they do not visit Workers' Council meetings or parliamentary sessions on their many excursions. One director of a technical school reported that his students had been taken to a workers' council meeting during the early 1960s, but that he did not know why they had stopped the practice. He added, however, that industry would not permit students to visit if any vehement disputes were expected, because it was believed that they should not witness such conflict, but rather only those meetings to be conducted in a respectful, orderly way. The prevailing view, then, appears to be that students, if they are to observe the working of self-management at all, can be exposed only to the procedural administration of responsibility but not the upheaval that takes place when genuinely vital issues are resolved.

Finally, although this socialized solidarity of the collective may de-emphasize individual competition in Yugoslavia and foster a sense of mutual cooperation and support, it also seems to promote group aggression toward other groups or toward an institution. In particular, an active class association can become a weapon of protest and rebellion. Resembling work stoppages in Yugoslav industry, student disobedience is often collective. Deliberate, often spontaneous, and short-lived, it takes the form of such actions as leaving en masse before the hour begins. Although organized attempts to influence policy are desired, these minor and potentially destructive protests are considered detrimental to self-management because they divide people into factions, into "us" and "them." Students rebel against teachers, workers rebel against directors, even though in theory there is not supposed to be a superordinate, or even a difference in group interests, which might lead to antagonistic, that is, political, conflict in society.

Secondary-school students in Yugoslavia are on the whole intensely proud of their country, optimistic about the future of self-management, and supportive of the values of participation and democracy. However, the evidence presented in this article suggests that they are not being socialized to participate directly in the decision making of their workplace, in democratic methods of participation, or even to develop a sense of solidarity with those beyond their immediate group. Rather they are learning to support an oligarchical, personalistic pattern of participation, to leave political action to their representatives. They are taught by experience in school that discipline should be lenient, that they will not be expected to be too responsible until they are employed, and that rights do not always impose correlative duties. Since we also find that students' passivity and their reported lack of opportunities to participate are more often than not encouraged by their teachers, who maintain that students are not sufficiently mature or knowledgeable to take part in self-management, let us examine the teacher-student relationship itself.

Although equality among citizens is essential to self-management, the relationship between student and teacher is by nature one of inequality, arising out of a discrepancy in knowledge, and usually in age.

In Yugoslav schools the social treatment that teachers and students accord one another is remarkably egalitarian, both in practice and in what both value. There is much joking, warmth, directness, and even friendship between secondary school students and their teachers. Judgments of social distance by both students and teachers are almost completely egalitarian.[7] In order to encourage warm relations and to break down the artificial barriers that exist in school, homeroom teachers even take their classes on excursions, such as a picnic or swimming in the country. But those barriers do exist, and teachers often vacillate in their efforts to achieve a balance between social equality and the authority they consider necessary for teaching. One director illustrated the delicacy of this search for balance by saying; "Treat everyone equally, but don't allow a situation students could take advantage of. Friends, yes, but never intimacy; don't confide with students, but maintain confidence between teachers and students."

Inherent in immaturity, and in "upbringing," is the feeling of inferiority, or of being subjected to some form of domination. This distinction is further reinforced because teachers are members of a profession with standards of their own by which they carry on and evaluate their work; like professionals in other fields, they value and demand autonomy as well as their own professional discretion. Unlike other self-managing organizations, such as a factory, in which professional staff serves as advisor to the general working body, the teachers constitute between 75 and 90 percent of the workers in a school, and students are not classified as workers.[8]

In one survey students indicated reasonable satisfaction with their teachers' treatment of them and with the cordial relations existing between teachers and students, but expressed strong dissatisfaction with the degree of participation and influence they had.

---

[7]Students were asked to rank themselves as a group and then their teachers on a scale of ten, the ten symbolizing the best person one had ever known in school, and the zero the worst. Teachers were asked the same. The difference in mutual evaluation between the two groups was less than one numerical point on the scale.

[8]Students are acutely aware of this difference between other self-managing organizations and their own. In Zagreb, the city-wide student organization, Sabor Učenika, waged a major campaign during the discussion of the new Law on Directed (Secondary) Education for Croatia (1970–71) to try to persuade teachers and legislators that the articles regulating students' status should define them as workers, not as objects or subjects of the teaching process. This deceptively simple change would gain them constitutionally guaranteed equal standing with teachers, particularly with reference to school decision making. That this radical attack on the authority of teachers did not succeed portrays the limits of self-management in schools.

They said they wanted fewer rules concerning their personal affairs but *more* rules to regulate their relations with teachers, so that more equality and less arbitrary treatment would ensue. They also expressed the wish to be consulted more, and to have greater say over matters which concern them. Above all, they talked about grading.

This concern should not be surprising, since the system of grading is an overt symbol of the inequality between teachers and students but also one of the areas teachers insist most on maintaining control over, as essential to their task. Furthermore, the system of grading in Yugoslav schools is based mostly on oral examinations, making the teacher an enormously powerful figure, despite the self-managing denial of individual, personal power. If one adds to this the importance of good grades for obtaining advancement, a good job, good salary, and so forth, then it is no wonder that the students' greatest complaints concern arbitrary grading. Although students would like to help determine the grade themselves, or abolish the grading system altogether, they were found to be even more critical of teachers who were capricious in their grading. Furthermore, as a result of the low budgets allotted to schools and the lack of concern with teaching methods, secondary-school teachers have maintained traditional, autocratic teaching methods in the classroom, techniques that are poorly suited to the precepts of self-management, and that also reinforce the inequality because students cannot influence the way in which a teacher exercises the ultimate power of determining the distribution of rewards and punishments.

In conclusion, to the Yugoslav student, socialization means not only learning supportive attitudes but also developing the capacity to be self-managers. Although secondary students have learned to value self-management this does not appear to lead them to participate more. In other countries, similar indications of apathy have even been referred to as a sign of "alienation" among youth. Yet if the Yugoslav society expects schools to prepare youth to be skilled workers (and self-managers) who can aid the economic development of their country, or expects teachers to teach skills at the same time they socialize for equality, or expects students, as the law insists, to study conscientiously and fulfill the obligations of students at the time that they contribute to the development of self-managing social relations in the schools, are these expectations likely to be fulfilled if the students are alienated from that society? Furthermore, should teachers encourage full equality and self-managing attitudes if these privileges are at the expense of values on which an industrializing economy is founded—namely, the acceptance of "rational authority" and selection according to levels of competence and skill?

Students enter a working world, which like the schools, inflicts conflicting demands on them also. They are expected to join an enterprise in which each worker is considered equally capable of making policy decisions, and then they are supposed to resist any inclination to defer to authority. Yet it is also assumed by the society that the center of one's satisfaction and community is the workplace, within which jobs, salaries, chances for promotion, managerial positions, and perhaps even chances for self-fulfillment, are allocated on the basis of formal schooling and grades. This stratification according to education reinforces a teacher's authority and his potential influence on the future lives of his students, and it extends the inequality of competence to the workplace, despite the ideals of self-management.

Contrary to the expectation that education will foster self-managing relations of equality, we find that the more educated one is, the more he is in favor of change in the direction of inequality.[9] We also find that skilled workers dominate in Workers' Council deliberations, not because they are considered better than semiskilled workers, but because it is assumed that they know more and deserve greater say. The workers who support such a system have learned to do so in the schools, where students are taught to be task-oriented, to value rationality and expertise, to view rules as means of self-protection, and to reward merit. Furthermore, it seems likely that this fundamental contradiction between the egalitarian, revolutionary ideals of self-management—embracing a nonhierarchical social structure—and the atmosphere in which students are expected to learn these qualities—the subordinate, efficiency-oriented, and meritocratic conditions suited to economic development—will continue for some time to plague the process of socialization in Yugoslav schools.

---

[9]In a study of India, Poland, the United States, and Yugoslavia, the International Project on Values and the Active Community found, for instance, that "Surprisingly, the *less* educated [a] leader is the *more* concerned [he is] to reduce economic disparities. The educated leader, while espousing change, is committed to *in*equality and differential rewards as an incentive for developmental change. This finding stands out because there are so few other characteristics, personal or environmental, which consistently identify the kind of change to which leaders are disposed, and whether they are change-oriented at all. Most of the demographic and status factors familiarly cited as correlates of progressive or conservative social action have not proved significant in all four countries; few apply in any of the countries." Philip E. Jacob, et al., *Values and the Active Community* (New York: The Free Press, 1970), pp. 316-7.

Selected Bibliography

Soviet Union

Bereday, George Z. F., and Pennar, Jan. *The Politics of Soviet Education.* New York: Praeger, 1960.

Bronfenbrenner, Urie. *Two Worlds of Childhood, U.S. and U.S.S.R.* New York: Russell Sage Foundation and Basic Books, 1970.

Grant, N. *Soviet Education.* London: Penguin, 1964.

Hayward, M., and Fletcher, W. C., eds. *Religion and the Soviet State: A Dilemma of Power.* New York: Praeger, 1969.

Kassof, Allen. *The Soviet Youth Program.* Cambridge, Massachusetts: Harvard University Press, 1965.

Mickiewicz, Ellen Propper. *Soviet Political Schools: The Communist Party Adult Instruction Program.* New Haven: Yale University Press, 1967.

China

Chen, Theodore Hsi-en. *The Maoist Educational Revolution.* New York: Praeger, 1974.

Croizier, Ralph, ed. *China's Cultural Legacy and Communism.* New York: Praeger, 1970.

Goldman, Merle. *Literary Dissent in Communist China.* Cambridge, Massachusetts: Harvard University Press, 1967.

Hu Chang-tu. *Chinese Education under Communism.* New York: Teachers College Press, Columbia University, 1962.

Lifton, Robert J. *Thought Reform and the Psychology of Totalism: A Study of "Brainwashing" in China.* New York: W. W. Norton, 1961.

MacFarquhar, Roderick, ed. *The Hundred Flowers Campaign and the Chinese Intellectuals.* New York: Praeger, 1960.

Mackerras, Colin, and Hunter, Neale. *China Observed.* New York: Praeger, 1968.

Price, R. F. *Education in Communist China.* New York: Praeger, 1970.

Yu, Frederick T. C. *Mass Persuasion in Communist China.* New York: Praeger, 1964.

SECTION EIGHT

STRATEGIES OF ECONOMIC DEVELOPMENT

Communism is more than a temporary and fragmentary reform within an existing culture; rather, it should be considered a *weltanschauung,* or world view of life. Like Christianity or capitalism, then, it is a way of life founded on a particular outlook or interpretation of one's total existence. It should permeate the individual's action, thought, writing, speech and everything that he does in life. But if one is to implement Communist theory effectively in his thoughts and actions, it is essential that he be grounded in Marxian economics, the core and impetus of communism.[1]

It is important to recognize that Marxists, when referring to economics do not mean simply monetary affairs. Friedrich Engels aptly stated the place of economics in Karl Marx's thought in a eulogy spoken at his mentor's graveside in 1883:

> On the 14th of March, at a quarter to three in the afternoon, the greatest living thinker ceased to think. . . . Just as Darwin discovered the law of development of organic nature, so Marx discovered the law of development of human history: the simple fact, hitherto concealed by an overgrowth of ideology, that mankind must first of all eat, drink, have shelter and clothing, before it can pursue politics, science, art, religion, etc.; that therefore the production of the immediate material means of subsistence and consequently the degree of economic development attained by a given people or during a given epoch form the foundation upon which the state institutions, the legal conceptions, art, and even the ideas on religion, of the people concerned have been evolved, and in the light of which they must, therefore be explained, instead of *vice versa,* as had hitherto been the case.[2]

---

[1]See Section One for a more detailed elaboration of Communist philosophy.

[2]Friedrich Engels, "Speech at the Graveside of Karl Marx." In Robert C. Tucker, ed., *The Marx-Engels Reader* (New York: Norton, 1972), p. 603.

To the Marxist, the real world is not ordered by God, a universal Mind or Spirit, or other mystical phenomena; instead, the dominant influences on human events are material forces, which engender man's thoughts and ideas. The Communists believe that no person—whether he is a factory worker, farmer, scholar, painter, physicist, politician, or other—lives independently of the need to make a living and that essential fact determines the life style of all human beings. According to the Communist view, it is not simply that one does everything for money, though money is recognized as a powerful force, especially in the capitalist system. But if the society in which one lives stresses competition, emphasizes individual initiative and enterprise, and accepts private profit and property as an indispensable part of life, the culture of that society, the social relationships of its people, and their economic condition will be determined by that particular mode of economic development. The Communists maintain, then, that all of man's activities are determined by the economic system to which he belongs. Marx himself succinctly expresses this conviction in a letter to a Russian friend, the Russian critic and writer P. V. Annenkov:

> What is society, whatever its form may be? The product of men's reciprocal action. Are men free to choose this or that form of society for themselves? By no means. Assume a particular state of development in the productive forces of man and you will get a particular form of commerce and consumption. Assume particular stages of development in production, commerce and consumption and you will have a corresponding social structure, a corresponding organization of the family, or orders or of classes, in a word, a corresponding civil society. Presuppose a particular civil society and you will get particular political conditions which are only the official expression of civil society.[3]

In building their own economic system during the postrevolutionary period, each Communist government has been largely concerned with efforts first to achieve basic economic survival and, then, to attain economic superiority over the non-Communist powers. Both of these efforts have a long and interesting history.

By tracing the economic histories of the Soviet Union, China, and Yugoslavia, we can discern in each a pattern consisting of two initial stages: one of consolidation and reconstruction; the second, of centralized planning, during which a sequence of intensive and tightly organized Five-Year Plans were instituted in order to attain industrial and technological superiority within a minimal period of time. The first stage, then, the consolidation and reconstruction effort, was carried out by the Communists during the initial years after their assumption of power. Though the internal conditions of each of the three nations were similar—massive destruction as a result of war, extensive poverty and malnutrition, general disorder in industry and

---

[3]Leo Strauss and Joseph Cropsey, eds., *History of Political Philosophy* (Chicago: Rand McNally, 1966), p. 699. See also Isaiah Berlin, *Karl Marx His Life and Environment* (New York: Oxford University Press, 1963), pp. 106–107.

agriculture, and considerable governmental paralysis—the process that each adopted for solving the problems varied.

In Russia in 1917, the task of governing was hardly an enviable one, particularly since an experimental political system was being introduced. Millions of men and land had been destroyed by World War I, and the economic forecast looked grim indeed. Lenin ascertained that the immediate goal of the inchoate Communist regime was the consolidation of its power, and this would be most quickly and effectively accomplished by terminating an unpopular war and placating the masses with food and land. As a result of Lenin's prompting, the Second Congress of Soviets issued the Decree of Peace and the Decree of Land; the one proposed a negotiated cessation to the fighting and the second abolished private ownership of land without compensating the owners, and proclaimed all land the common property of the people. Lenin's immediate goal to end Russia's participation in the War was achieved by the signing of the Treaty of Brest-Litovsk with Germany on March 3, 1918. Though the conditions of the Treaty were harsh, the Soviet government was then able to tackle Russia's serious internal problems.

Though Lenin and the Bolsheviks had won a significant victory in the old capital of Petrograd (the capital was soon moved to Moscow), their authority to enforce their new decrees and laws would be severely tested in the outlying cities and provinces. Almost immediately after the October Revolution, civil war swept through Russia. After more than three years of fighting—and despite stiff anti-Bolshevik opposition and intervention by American, British, French, and other foreign nations—the Communists attained victory and were able to turn their attention to the pressing economic problems.

Caught by surprise by the speed with which the tsarist government and its immediate successor, the Provisional Government, collapsed, the Communists had few centralized and coordinated economic policies for the nation. Consequently, a series of unplanned sometimes irrational, and often unenforceable economic decrees were issued in a confusing array. The disastrous policy of printing money to keep up with inflation only exacerbated the problem. Money became all but useless, farm and factory products neither could be easily purchased nor expediently transported, and internal chaos intensified as Lenin desperately tried to establish communism with non-Marxian alacrity. The Eighth Party Congress of the Russian Communist Party in March 1919, was optimistic that the overthrow of the old regime had laid the foundation for the "dictatorship of the proletariat" at home and proletariat revolutions abroad.

In agriculture, too, the policies seemed to spring from urgency rather than from deliberation. An effort was launched to eliminate the wasteful—and often rebellious—small farmer as well as the richer—and often rebellious—peasants (kulaks). The objective was the transformation of Russian agriculture into a centralized and rigidly controlled system of large co-

operative farms. With one hand the new government seemed to be benefiting the poorer peasant by awarding him land, better equipment, and the
means to distribute his produce more widely, while with the other hand the
government bureaucracy interfered in even the most remote agricultural
areas. The Soviet Central Executive Committee had issued on May 9, 1918 a
strict order by which the storing of surplus grain was forbidden, the prices
on food were rigidly fixed, and the masses were urged to initiate a merciless
fight to exterminate the *kulaks*. Committees of the Village Poor and Food
Requisition Detachments roamed the countryside, ferreting out "criminals"
and any suspicious persons, and assisted in the requisition and distribution
of food. Coercion and violence were the methods of enforcement employed by many; and fear and distrust were too often the by-products.
To evade the confiscatory policies, the peasants, in turn, utilized various
methods, including armed opposition, reduction of the sown area, and
destruction of the harvested grain.

Chagrined but determined, Lenin decided to take "one step backward
to take two steps forward" and introduced a New Economic Policy (NEP)
for the Soviet Union in 1921. Essentially NEP was intended to rescue the
nation from its economic doldrums by appeasing the defiant peasants with
revised policies on grain surplus and state control of all food production.
The peasant was now allowed to keep some food surplus for himself,
though he was required to pay a tax, and he could dispose of the surplus as
he wished. Upon the promulgation of the New Economic Policy, the
Russian economy began to revive.

Throughout the first decade after the Bolshevik coup, Soviet economic
policies were largely trial and error, retrenchment and advancement, and
little better than the final efforts of the tsarist regime. But during this period,
the power of the government had become increasingly centralized under
Lenin, a tendency that would intensify under Stalin, Lenin's successor.
Stalin would dramatically redirect the Soviet economy as well as its political structure.

In China, the Communists came into power under the same kinds of
adverse conditions that had prevailed in Russia before the Revolution.
Their initial years of consolidation and reconstruction were devoted to
eliminating the last opposition of the Nationalist government, expelling
"unfriendly" foreigners, such as Americans, establishing firm cordial relations with the Soviet Union, and placating various economic circles within
the country until the national economy could recover from the destruction
wrought by World War II. Whereas the Chinese Communists had the advantage of being able to use the example of the Soviet Union as a guideline, they had the drawbacks of an enormous population and a less
developed economy.[4]

---

[4]The Chinese economy, by the time the Communists assumed power, had suffered a
reversal. Some economic progress had been accomplished under the Nationalist government during the 1930s and 40s, but the War with Japan and the subsequent Civil War had
destroyed most of the benefits achieved.

Among the first tasks that Mao Tse-tung and the Chinese Communists undertook as the new rulers of China were centralization of political and economic control, establishment of a stable currency, repair of the heavily damaged transportation system so that commodities could move again, and the construction of socialism along the Marxist-Leninist lines. In agriculture, the initial activity was concentrated in the three following efforts: (1) destruction of the traditional landholding patterns, and the landlord-tenent relationship; (2) confiscation of land, animals, farm implements, and other property of the landlord class; (3) encouragement and assistance to the peasants in a variety of ways. In industry, some enterprises of the Nationalist government were simply confiscated; some of those owned by foreign operations were either confiscated or bought for a nominal price; still other capitalists who could not be classified as either reactionaries or counterrevolutionaries were allowed to remain in business so that the entire economy would not be disrupted.

With the odds heavily against him, Mao Tse-tung used stringent but efficient measures, mixed with coercion and ruthlessness, to lead China out of the morass of the 1940s and into an era of accomplishment and hope. By 1952 the Communist government had balanced the budget, reopened extensive miles of roads and railroads, controlled waste, corruption, and much dishonesty by means of the "three-anti" and "five-anti" movements,[5] established much needed popular support in the rural areas, and revitalized industry enough that it once again attained its prewar level of development. These goals were achieved despite considerable external opposition from foreign powers, internal hostility to foreign people and influences, and severe pressures caused by the Korean War. But, as in the Soviet Union, the economic policies of the totalitarian regime were subject to abrupt fluctuation.

In Yugoslavia, when Tito came into power at the close of World War Two, he too inherited a devastated nation. To some degree his problems were even more severe than that of the Soviet Union, because the economic destruction in his country was more extensive and the less developed prewar economy made it more difficult to proceed toward economic recovery. However, Tito's good personal relations with the leaders of the major allied powers brought him and his followers considerable aid during the war. The first efforts at economic recovery were sponsored by the United Nations Relief and Reconstruction Agency (UNRRA). Subsequently the distribution of relief aid, valuable food supplies, seed, animal stock, farm tools, clothing, and medical assistance from the Western nations helped Yugoslavia survive the immediate postwar crisis.

---

[5]These movements constituted organized attacks on traditional officialdom, bureaucracy, and other bourgeois elements in the Chinese society. The "three-anti" campaign in 1951 was launched against corruption, waste, and bureaucratism. The "five-anti" campaign in 1952 was directed against bribery, tax evasion, theft of state property, cheating in labor or materials, and stealing of state economic secrets.

Along with these relief measures, the Tito government itself devised its own policies to stimulate economic recovery. Among the measures promulgated during the consolidation and reconstruction period were the repair and restoration of the railroads, and the "Agrarian Reform and Colonization" law, passed in August 1945, which provided for the confiscation of land belonging to collaborators against the government and other enemies. In addition thousands of acres of arable land were distributed among the peasants and their debts were cancelled. Finally, efforts were made to boost the industrial output and to nationalize all transportation, banking, and wholesale facilities.

By 1947 the combination of these efforts had resulted in partial recovery in several economic areas, although growing tension and dissension between Tito and Stalin diverted some of Yugoslavia's efforts from economic problems to political and military matters.[6] The early years of socialist development were difficult for the Yugoslavs, but in the 1950s official statistics began to indicate impressive gains. For example, in 1938 the real national income per capita averaged $115, but by 1965 it had grown to $480. The overall economy has been expanding at an average rate of 7 percent per annum, and between 1957 and 1960, the growth rate was 13 percent per annum, one of the highest in the world.

It was this inital period—the consolidation and reconstruction stage—in the histories of the three Communist governments of the Soviet Union, China, and Yugoslavia, that was particularly vital for immediate survival. The various emergency measures employed by each to provide the means for minimum economic recovery were successful, but once the crisis was past, the long-term survival of each Communist system was still in question. The real test came during the next principal period in the development of each, the stage of "centralized planning," during which a series of so-called Five-Year Plans were implemented in each regime, the first having been initiated by Stalin in 1928. In the Soviet Union and China in particular, the Five-Year Plans called for strict centralized organization in all phases of the economy, not only in order to achieve rapid economic growth but also to surpass that of their capitalist rivals. In Yugoslavia, too, centralization was an important feature of her economy in the early years, though her leaders began in the early 1950s to move progressively away from the centralized economic system to a more decentralized, self-managed system.

In all three countries, the foremost economic goal of centralized planning, and the Five-Year Plans was to accelerate the nation's technological

---

[6]Relations between the Soviet Union and Yugoslavia were considered cemented when the two nations signed the Treaty of Friendship and Alliance in April 1945. But growing differences between Stalin and Tito over economic aid, Soviet military "protection" in Yugoslavia, and the Soviet Union's role as a model for Yugoslavia caused the rupture of the alliance in 1948 when Stalin had Yugoslavia expelled from the Communist Information Bureau (Cominform).

development as much as possible, and establish it among the world's industrial powers. In each system, therefore, the first of the Five-Year Plans was centered on industrial growth: the major portion of available capital was to be utilized for building industries, constructing factories, training factory workers and plant managers, expanding the needed transportation system, and exploiting the necessary natural resources to achieve rapid industrial growth. The results of the Five-Year Plans in the industrial sector were too often uneven and unclear, however. For example, officially released economic data noting record increases of pig iron, cement, and other such commodities, would not be substantiated with evidence of correlated progress in other areas. At times, Western economic experts would have to adjust such data to allow for inflated statistics (submitted at times by lesser political functionaries who had to meet required quotas), or to compensate for incomplete statistics or information rendered inaccurate by error or a different method of computation. Nevertheless, most economic observers agree that gains in the industrial arena have been most impressive in each of the three Communist systems we are studying.

Agricultural goals were also incorporated in Five-Year Plans, but the picture is not nearly as bright, and at times, quite gloomy during the centralized planning stage. Of course, the agricultural problems faced by the Communists were immense, there being too many people trying to farm, without the proper tools, machinery, fertilizer, and training, on land that had been too long overworked. But these drawbacks aside, the Communist leadership must also share some of the blame for agriculture's generally unimpressive showing: unpredictable and intemperate economic decisions, combined with benign neglect, have contributed to the woes of the farmer. Stalin and Mao, in particular, upset agricultural production and caused peasant recalcitrance on several different occasions by collectivizing too quickly and too extensively, by depriving the farmer of his traditional desire for an individual plot of land (however small), or by promoting personal, military or political campaigns that interfered with farm work.

The results of the Five-Year Plans favored industry more than agriculture, for factories and machines require less human input, and they are more easily directed by economic blueprints than are plants, animals, and soil, which are highly dependent upon the close attention of the farmer and the vagaries of nature.

The reading selections in this section pose, for one's consideration, a number of ideas on the present and future economic status of these three countries, including the following. (1) There is, especially in the Soviet Union and Yugoslavia, an increasing interest in consumer demands and needs: is this concern a drift to individualism and away from the concept of communism? (2) The prices of consumer goods remain quite high, and the quality is generally low, but it is important to recognize that other economic priorities—which can change rather quickly—strongly influence the amount of time and effort put on consumer goods. Consequently, in assessing the consumer's situation in any given system, one must try to determine what priorities currently prevail in that system at that time. (3) A desire for more and diversified foreign trade appears to be growing (more in the Soviet Union and Yugoslavia than in China), leading one to wonder whether closer economic ties between Communist and non-Communist nations will lessen ideological differences. (4) In spite of the technological growth in the three nations, progress in agricultural production, and improvements in wages and other benefits for the individual, continued to lag behind the marked increase in industrial production. Especially in China and the Soviet Union, where the populations are so large, the sporadic declines in agricultural production have been acute. (5) Although agriculture still remains their most difficult problem to solve, in recent years all three Communist systems have increased food production faster than population growth.

As in other areas of socialist activity, the readings on economics clearly indicate that there are "many roads" to socialism. Rather than concentrate on illusive statistics of the Communist countries, the three articles that follow explain briefly what have been their past economic policies, what have been their successes and problems, and what future projections can be made.

Abram Bergson, for example, is concerned with the more general but vital statistic, the gross national product (GNP) of the Soviet Union and the factors that might affect its future growth. He also surveys the past successes of the Soviet economy and explores reasons for recent declines and difficulties. Among the reasons he gives for the deceleration in the Soviet economy are the reduction in working hours, the vicissitudes in agriculture, and the difficulties in the central planning system. The readers will especially want to note Bergson's analysis of how the investment rate and the capital-stock growth will affect the Soviet economy in the future.

Dwight H. Perkins' article on China explains why statistics, especially for that country, are so difficult to work with. First of all, there have been years for which few or no reliable economic statistics were available; furthermore, even when statistics have been available, economists have disagreed about their accuracy and meaning. Perkins does look at the important growth rate statistics in industry and agriculture. While noting the ups and downs of this important economic indicator, he concludes that "China has managed an overall rate of economic growth that has kept well ahead of the increase in population."

Finally, Deborah D. Milenkovitch introduces the reader to the subject of Yugoslavia's economy. She examines the "radical changes" that have taken place in the Communist economic system of Yugoslavia. Of particular interest is her treatment of such aspects as the encouragement of the expansion of private enterprise, the sanctioning of various forms of nonlabor income, and the decentralized, market-type economic system that has evolved.

22

Soviet Economic Perspectives: Toward a New Growth Model

Abram Bergson

An attempt to peer into the long-term future of the Soviet economy is always timely, but it is especially so after the launching of a new Five-Year Plan proclaiming rather novel priorities.[1] Such an attempt should properly rest on substantial statistical projections of a kind that still remain to be made for the USSR. Even on the basis of limited inquiry, however, it is clear that the Soviet economy has for some time been in a high degree of flux. The resulting change in structure may be more profound and enduring that many commentators on the new plan have supposed. Indeed, the famous Soviet model of economic growth that Stalin initiated with the Five-Year Plans appears at long last to be passing from the Soviet scene.

Like any relatively modern economy, that of the USSR consists of a myriad of activities, but the results of all these are summarized in the country's real national income. Hence, the trends that are relevant to the present inquiry may be explored by focusing on movement in that cardinal indicator and particularly its best known variant, the gross national product (GNP).

Inquiry into the future must begin with an analysis of the past. Therefore, let us at the outset look at trends in Soviet national income since the completion of the initial postwar Five-Year Plan in the year 1950.

From Abram Bergson, "Soviet Economic Perspectives: Toward a New Growth Model," *Problems of Communism* (Vol. XXII, No. 2, March-April 1973). [Reprinted with permission from the publisher.]

[1]This article is a revised version of a concluding discussion presented at a symposium on Soviet economic prospects held in Brussels on April 14-16, 1971, and published in Y. Laulan, Ed., *Prospects for Soviet Economic Growth in the 1970's*, Brussels, NATO, 1971. The revision has provided an opportunity, among other things, to correct a transcription error affecting the estimated magnitude of Soviet capital stock in 1970 and to take account of a revision in Stanley H. Cohn's calculations of the Soviet gross national product. These modifications are reflected in Tables 1 and 2 in the ensuing discussion.

Past Trends

After 1950, as is well known, the national income at first increased rapidly, though probably not quite as rapidly as is often supposed. During 1950-58, according to Stanley H. Cohn's well-known calculations, it grew at an average rate of 6.4 percent a year (see Table 1.)* That is somewhat lower than the rates indicated by other Western data, but it must still be much nearer the mark than the official Soviet claim of 10.9 percent. (This figure relates only to "material output," and such Soviet data must for familiar reasons be treated very skeptically.[2])

Even according to Western calculations, the tempo of Soviet growth much exceeded that of the U.S. (2.9 percent). But it is worth noting that the Soviet growth rate was nearly equaled or surpassed by the growth rates of Italy (5.6 percent) and Western Germany (7.6 percent). Moreover, it fell well shy of that for Japan. In these early years, Japan had not quite achieved the economic miracle that is now a hallmark there, but its rate of growth was already an impressive 8.0-9.0 percent.

Since 1958, as is well known too, Soviet growth has slowed. As Table 1 shows, the retardation is manifest in both Cohn's and the official Soviet data (curiously enough, it is more marked in the official figures than in Cohn's). Why the slowdown? The question has often been discussed, but there may still not be general understanding that no corresponding retardation occurred in the growth of inputs of the two principal productive factors generating output—capital and labor. According to both official Soviet and Western data, the available stock of capital increased during 1958-67 at about the same rate as during 1950-58 (Table 1), and the tempo was extraordinarily rapid (a matter to which we shall return later). Similarly, Murray Feshbach's calculations with regard to employment (Table 1) show that it also rose at much the same rate during 1958-67 as during 1950-58.

The slowdown in output growth, then, was due essentially to a decline in the rate of productivity increase. While that is already evident from the trends in output and factor inputs, it becomes even more obvious if we average the rates of growth of capital and labor in a way that has lately become a standard practice in economics. Using this method, we can calculate the rate of growth of output per composite unit of labor and capital together, or "factor productivity" as it has come to be called. During 1958-67, that rate was significantly below the corresponding one for 1950-58 (Table 1). A computation of factor productivity for a non-market economy such as that of the USSR, it is true, is almost inevitably rather arbitrary, but the results obtained are still illuminating.[3]

Why the decline in the growth of factor productivity? There are, perhaps, too many reasons. For one, in 1956 Nikita Khrushchev initiated a reduction in working hours

---

*Readers should be alerted to a very specific usage in the author's presentation of growth statistics. He always includes the base year as well as the years for which performance is being examined: e.g., growth "during 1950-58" signifies output increases in the years 1951-58 from levels achieved in 1950.—Eds.

[2]For a recent appraisal of the official data, including the nature of the Soviet concept of national income, see Abraham S. Becker, "National Income Accounting in the USSR"; Stanley H. Cohn, "National Income Growth Statistics"; and Abram Bergson, "Soviet National Income Statistics: Summary and Assessment," in V. G. Treml and John P. Hardt, Eds., *Soviet Economic Statistics*, Durham, N.C. Duke University Press, 1972.

[3]The arbitrariness derives in part from the difficulty of obtaining for the USSR meaningful factor income shares, such as are generated in a market economy, to use as weights in averaging the rates of growth of labor and capital. This paper employs weights of 0.6 and 0.4, respectively, for the two factors—weights suggested by relevant Western experience. . . .

TABLE 1
Selected Economic Indicators for the USSR, 1950-75 (average annual rates of growth, in percent)

	1950-58	1958-67	1967-70	1970-75 (Planned)
National income, Soviet official data[a]	10.9	7.2	7.3	6.7[b]
GNP, Cohn calculations	6.4	5.3	3.4[c]	n.a.[d]
Capital investment, Soviet official data[e]	12.9	7.6	7.5	6.7
Gross investment, fixed capital, Moorsteen-Powell calculations	11.4	6.9[f]	n.a.	n.a.
Gross investment, Moorsteen-Powell calculations	12.2	6.1[f]	n.a.	n.a.
Fixed capital stock including livestock, Soviet official data	8.3[g]	8.3[g]	7.5	n.a.
Net fixed capital stock, Moorsteen-Powell calculations	10.0	9.4	n.a.	n.a.
Net capital stock, Moorsteen-Powell calculations	9.0	9.0	n.a.	n.a.
Employment, Feshbach calculations	1.8	1.7	1.7	n.a.
Total input of capital and labor	4.6	4.6	n.a.	n.a.
Factor productivity (GNP per unit of labor and capital)	1.7	0.7	n.a.	n.a.

[a] National income "produced" unless otherwise indicated.

[b] National income "utilized for consumption and accumulation." For 1965-70, such income grew at an average annual rate of 7.1 percent. The corresponding figure for national income "produced" was 7.7 per cent.

[c] This figure is for 1967-69.

[d] "n.a." means "not applicable" or "not available."

[e] Investment in fixed capital only; during 1950-58 exclusive of investment in private housing as well.

[f] These figures cover 1958-66.

[g] These figures are for 1950-59 and 1959-67.

SOURCES: Tsentralnoe statisticheskoe upravlenie, *Narodnoe khoziaistvo SSSR v 1960 g.* (The National Economy of the USSR in 1960), Moscow, 1961, p. 85, and subsequent volumes in the same series for 1962, p. 535; for 1967, p. 613; for 1968, p. 49; and for 1970, pp. 60, 478, 533; Tsentralnoe statisticheskoe upravlenie, *Kapitalnoe stroitelstvo v SSSR* (Capital Construction in the USSR), Moscow, 1961, p. 40; *Gosudarstvennyi piatiletnil plan razvitiia narodnovo khoziaistvo SSSR na 1971-1975 gody* (The State Five-Year Plan of Development of the National Economy of the USSR for 1971-75), Moscow, 1972, pp. 62-75, 345, 352.

Stanley H. Cohn, "General Growth Performance in the Soviet Economy," in Joint Economic Committee, U.S. Congress, *Economic Performance and the Military Burden in the Soviet Union*, Washington, DC, U.S. Government Printing Office, 1970, p. 17; Richard Moorsteen and Raymond P. Powell, *The Soviet Capital Stock 1928-1962*, Homewood, Ill., 1966, pp. 323, 341, 360; *Two Supplements to Richard Moorsteen and Raymond P. Powell, The Soviet Capital Stock, 1928-1962*, New Haven, Conn., Economic Growth Center, Yale University, 1968, pp. 11, 18, 24; Murray Feshbach, "Estimates and Projections of the Labor Force and Civilian Employment in the USSR: 1950-1980," Bureau of the Census, U.S. Department of Commerce, February 1970, processed.

which ultimately led to the establishment of an approximately 40-hour week in industry in place of the 48-hour week that had prevailed in the early 1950s. That reform had already had some impact before 1958, but its principal effect came in subsequent years. Thus, it would have tended to reduce productivity growth in the post-1958 period compared with the pre-1958 one.

Another cause lay in the proverbial vicissitudes in agriculture—most importantly, Khrushchev's heroic interventions, notably the great New Lands Program. This innovation had a favorable outcome at first, but progress became relatively slow and uncertain after the great crop of 1958.[4]

Still another element in the slowdown has been the well-known deficiencies of the Soviet system of central planning: the failure of enterprise managers to behave as desired because of ineffective incentives and the often fallible direction and coordination of superior agencies. These difficulties are by no means new. On the contrary, they date from virtually the earliest days of Soviet planning. But, as has often been argued, they may have become increasingly costly as Soviet central planning had to cope with the ever-growing complexities associated with continuing industrialization: the increasing number of plants that have to be coordinated, the increasing number and variety of products whose output has to be determined, etc.

Last but not least, there was the varying impact in the USSR of so-called "catch-up" phenomena in the wake of World War II. As is widely recognized, countries ravaged by the war for a time experienced a speedup of economic growth because of such factors as the restoration of partially destroyed productive capacity at relatively limited investment cost, the acceleration of technological progress through application of innovations made in other countries less affected by the war, and so on. By the same token, the progressive exhaustion of such advantages necessarily proved a source of retardation in later years. By 1950, the USSR had already surpassed its prewar level of national income, but recovery from war damage remained to be completed in some areas. Thus, "catch-up" phenomena still exerted an appreciable influence on growth. By the 1960s, however, such factors no longer were as potent as they had been previously.

Some Alternative Projections

So much for past trends. What of the future? One possible answer may be found in the new Five-Year Plan itself: during 1970–75 national income is to grow at nearly the same rate as it did in the 1960s (Table 1).[5] Interesting as a Gosplan projection is, however, we must seek somehow to arrive at an independent evaluation.

To that end, we ought to begin, I think, with Feshbach's forecast that employment will grow in the 1970s at a rate of 1.2 percent a year, or somewhat less rapidly than during the 1950's and 1960's. What of the other principal input, capital? Can Soviet capital stock still be expected to grow at such notably high rates as prevailed during the 1950s and 1960s?

---

[4]Note, however, that chiefly as a consequence of the New Lands Program the cultivated land area increased sharply during the years 1950–58. If our calculation of productivity were extended to include agricultural land as an input (as might be proper), productivity growth during 1950–58 would be somewhat reduced as compared with 1958–67.

[5]As noted in the table, official rates cited for past periods relate to national income "produced," but that planned for 1970–75 relates to national income "utilized for consumption and accumulation." The growth rate for the latter is only 0.4 percentage point below the actual growth rate of national income "utilized for consumption and accumulation" during 1965–70. Therefore, the projected retardation of growth is even less than a comparison with the rates of growth for national income "produced" in past years might suggest.

A clue is already provided by available data on the rates of growth achieved in the volume of capital investment in those years. According to both official Soviet and Western data, the rate of growth of investment, while fully comparable to the rate of growth of capital stock during 1950–58, fell well below the tempo of the latter in later years (Table 1). During any year, investment represents new additions to total capital stock; thus, the rate of growth of investment is not at all the same thing as the rate of growth of the capital stock itself. Indeed, the two might temporarily tend to diverge widely. But in the course of time they must nevertheless tend to converge. Hence, if investment continues to increase at a reduced rate like that of the 1960s, the rate of growth of total capital stock will inevitably tend to drop also. In fact, if the official data are indicative (Table 1), the latter had already commenced to decline in the late 1960s. Moreover, the new plan apparently projects a tempo of investment growth actually somewhat below that of the 1960s.

Because the question at issue here is central, however, we must again strive to arrive at our own assessment. To do so, let us look at several alternative projections that I have made for the general Soviet economy (see Table 2). While these projections are quite hypothetical and might properly be viewed as exercises, they may help to clarify the implications, and thus facilitate appraisal, of alternative hypotheses regarding the future growth of the Soviet stock of capital. In this way, they may also serve to structure speculation about the future increase of national income.

The projections begin with estimates—sometimes rather crude—of the GNP and its disposition in terms of major uses in 1970, and of the capital stock in that same year,[6] and they assume that employment will grow subsequently at a rate already mentioned of 1.2 percent a year. As for the capital stock, two hypotheses are explored. The first postulates that it will continue to grow at a rate of 9.0 percent a year in the 1970s; the second, that the rate of growth will be only 6.0 percent. In effect, the former assumes that the decline in the rate of growth of investment in the 1960s will prove only transient, while the latter assumes that the decline will persist and indeed become more pronounced.

Under each hypothesis, three possible alternative rates of increase in factor productivity are explored. Specifically, it is assumed that factor productivity will increase at alternative rates of 3.0, 2.0, and 1.0 percent a year (these rates compare with actual growth rates in factor productivity of 1.7 percent in 1950–58 and 0.7 percent in 1958–67). In conjunction with the average rate of growth of inputs of labor and capital combined (a figure calculated in the same manner as previously described), each of these hypothetical rates of factor productivity growth results in a particular rate of increase in GNP (Table 2).

---

[6]The absolute figures underlying the percentages in Table 2 are in 1964 adjusted rubles and are taken or estimated from data in a variety of Western sources, including principally the works of Cohn and of Moorsteen and Powell, cited in Table 1: Abram Bergson, "The Comparative National Income of the USSR and the United States," in Conference on Research in Income and Wealth, National Bureau of Economic Research, *International Comparisons of Prices and Output*, New York, Columbia University Press, 1972; and various RAND studies of Soviet national income. They also draw upon Stanley H. Cohn, "The Economic Burden of Soviet Defense Outlays," in the Joint Economic Committee, U.S. Congress, *Economic Performance and the Military Burden in the Soviet Union*, Washington, D.C., U.S. Government Printing Office, 1970; but it should be noted that the correspondence between the tabulations of GNP by use in 1970 for this paper and those for 1967 in Cohn's essay is to some extent misleading. Cohn's data are in current adjusted rubles, while those for this article, as indicated, are in 1964 adjusted rubles.

TABLE 2
The Soviet Economy in 1970 and Alternative Projections for 1975 and 1980 (in percent)[a]

A. With the Capital Stock Growing at 9.0 Percent a Year

	1970	$\lambda = 3.0$ percent[b]		$\lambda = 2.0$ percent		$\lambda = 1.0$ percent	
		1975	1980	1975	1980	1975	1980
Consumption	56.5	71.1	96.5	65.8	80.0	60.2	65.2
Government and defense	13.3	19.0	27.1	18.1	24.6	17.2	22.3
Gross investment	30.2	52.1	80.2	52.1	80.2	52.1	80.2
Net investment	20.2	36.9	56.8	36.9	56.8	36.9	56.8
Depreciation	10.0	15.2	23.4	15.2	23.4	15.2	23.4
GNP	100.0	142.8	203.8	136.0	184.8	129.5	167.7
GNP, average yearly increase in percent from previous date		7.4	7.4	6.3	6.3	5.3	5.3
Net stock of capital, Dec. 31	290.4	446.9	687.7	446.9	687.7	446.9	687.7

B. With the Capital Stock Growing at 6.0 Percent a Year

	1970	$\lambda = 3.0$ percent[b]		$\lambda = 2.0$ percent		$\lambda = 1.0$ percent	
		1975	1980	1975	1980	1975	1980
Consumption	56.5	81.8	111.0	76.3	96.2	70.8	82.8
Government and defense	13.3	18.0	24.2	17.1	22.0	16.3	19.9
Gross investment	30.2	35.2	47.1	35.2	47.1	35.2	47.1
Net investment	20.2	22.2	29.4	22.0	29.4	22.0	29.4
Depreciation	10.0	13.2	17.7	13.2	17.7	13.2	17.7
GNP	100.0	135.0	182.3	128.6	165.3	122.3	149.8
GNP, average yearly increase in percent from previous date		6.2	6.2	5.2	5.2	4.1	4.1
Net stock of capital, Dec. 31	290.4	388.6	520.1	388.6	520.1	388.6	520.1

[a]All figures except those for average yearly increase in GNP from the previous date are in percent of total GNP of 1970—i.e., total 1970 GNP = 100.0 percent.
[b]λ is the projected rate of increase in factor productivity.

It is also illuminating to carry the projections somewhat further. From the indicated rates of growth of GNP, we can calculate hypothetical levels of output for 1975 and 1980. The stock of capital in these years can also be determined once the rate of increase from that of 1970 is specified; so, too, can the annual net investment in 1975 and 1980 if the capital stock is to rise by the required amount each year.[7] Net investment, of course, must be financed, and in real terms such finance must come from the very output that the mounting capital stock makes possible. Hence, the volume of current output that must be allocated to net investment in 1975 and 1980 can be established. With depreciation allowed for at the 1970 average rate, gross investment can likewise be deter-

[7]See Footnote 8.

mined. To complete the tabulation of the GNP by use in 1975 and 1980, it remains merely to allow for dispositions to government administration and defense. It has been provisionally assumed here that these will absorb the same share of output as they did in 1970. The residual thus represents the volume of output available for consumption.

This residual is of particular interest here along with the growth rate of output. (Note that in Table 2 all data on output uses and on the capital stock, including those for 1975 and 1980, are expressed as percentages of total 1970 GNP. This may seem odd, but it facilitates comparisons of interest.) Under each of the two assumed rates of capital stock growth in Table 2, the rate of increase of both GNP and consumption varies depending on the rate of increase in productivity. For any particular rate of productivity increase, however, the rate of growth of output, logically, is always greater with the capital stock rising at 9.0 percent a year than with the capital stock rising at 6.0 percent a year. On the other hand, the increase in consumption when the capital stock grows at 6.0 percent is always greater than it is when the capital stock grows at 9.0 percent. Although, in the latter case, consumption still rises markedly when productivity grows by 3.0 percent, the gains in consumption are quite modest with lesser rates of productivity growth. For instance, with productivity increasing by only 1.0 percent, there is hardly any gain to speak of in per capita terms, for the indicated growth in consumption would barely exceed the rise in population, which is expected to amount to 3.9–6.1 percent over the period 1970–75 and 3.4–6.6 percent over the period 1975–80.

In effect, then, the extra increments of output produced when the capital stock grows at 9.0 rather than 6.0 percent a year are, in every instance, more than totally offset by concomitant increases in requirements—chiefly those for investment to render possible the higher rate of growth of the capital stock in the first place. These additional requirements are always incongruously large, but they become more and more so the slower the rise in productivity and output.

The inordinate demand on output to meet current investment requirements is but a corollary of a cardinal feature of Soviet economic growth which is already evident but merits underlining: the capital stock has risen not only rapidly but distinctly more rapidly than output. This was already true in the 1950s when output increased at a relatively rapid pace, but it was even more the case in the 1960s when the growth of output had slowed. In any economy, such an incongruously rapid growth of the capital stock can be assured only through the allocation of an ever-increasing share of output to current investment. To be sure, this observation is simply an arithmetic truism, but it does help to explain the rising share of output which, as our data clearly imply (Table 1), investment was already absorbing in the 1950s and 1960s.

We must also see in this light the further projected increase in investment—*i.e.*, from 30.2 percent of 1970 GNP to between 39.4 and 47.8 percent of GNP in 1980—that is indicated when we extrapolate to the future on the basis of a 9.0-percent tempo of growth in the capital stock. At that rate, the capital stock rises more rapidly than output even with the most favorable hypothetical rate of productivity increase, and the disparity between the growth of the capital stock and the growth of output only widens if the rise in productivity is viewed less optimistically.

What about the alternative projection which assumes that the capital stock will increase at only 6.0 percent a year? In that case, the tempo of growth of the capital stock is only matched by that for the GNP when the rise in productivity is 3.0 percent; when the rise in productivity is just 2.0 or 1.0 percent, the rate of growth of GNP will be less than that of the capital stock. In neither of the last instances, however, is the difference nearly as marked as when the capital stock rises by 9.0 percent. Thus, though gross investment as a share of GNP may rise, its projected levels for 1980—25.8 to 31.4

percent, depending on the increase in productivity—turn out to be much lower than those required when the capital stock grows by 9.0 percent a year.[8]

Implications

The foregoing exercises are just that, but they still afford insights into why the Soviet government has lately been acquiescing to a retardation of the extraordinarily rapid expansion of the country's capital stock despite the fact that such expansion has been the primary means by which the government has over the years endeavored to achieve a rapid growth of output. More important, the projections suggest that the retardation will probably be allowed to continue.

To expand the capital stock by 9.0 percent a year has always been an onerous undertaking for the USSR, but it would become even more so should the government seek to maintain that tempo in the future. The chief costs, of course, have been and would continue to be borne by Soviet consumers. But while Stalin freely sanctioned such deprivations, soon after his death the Soviet government avowedly committed itself to a different policy, and that policy has now been reaffirmed in the Five-Year Plan just promulgated for 1971–75. According to its own language, the "chief test" of the plan will be whether or not it assures "the rise of the material and cultural level of life of the population."[9]

---

[8]Note that for 1970–75 the differences between the two sets of projections given in Table 2 with respect to the growth rates of investment and, by implication, of consumption might be deemed to be somewhat understated because of the manner in which net investment in 1975 and 1980 has been arrived at. Thus, net investment in each of those years has been taken as simply equal to either 9.0 or 6.0 percent of the capital stock on January 1 of the given year, the particular figure depending on the rate of growth of the capital stock in question. In effect, then, under each hypothesis regarding the growth of the capital stock, net investment increases from 1975 to 1980 at the same tempo as that of the capital stock.

Such a correspondence of the rates of growth of net investment and the capital stock is to be expected over the long run, but inasmuch as we start with 1970—a year when, at the current rate of net investment, the capital stock rose by 7.5 percent—net investment at least for a time must increase at an even higher rate than 9.0 percent if the capital stock is to grow at an average annual rate of 9.0 percent from 1970 to 1975. Similarly, net investment could rise for a time at less than 6 percent and still assure a 6-percent rate of growth of the capital stock from 1970 to 1975.

While there is no logical bar to the achievement of the rates of investment listed in Table 2, it might perhaps be more reasonable to assume that investment will grow at a constant rate during 1970–75—i.e., at a tempo which would produce the hypothesized rate of increase in the capital stock, on the average, over the five-year period. Under such an assumption, investment in 1975 would have to constitute 40.6 percent of GNP, instead of the 36.9 percent shown in Table 2, to guarantee a rise of 9.0 percent a year in the capital stock; but it would need to be only 19.2 percent of GNP, rather than the 22.0 shown in the table, to insure a growth of 6.0 percent a year in the capital stock.

According to the same reasoning, the calculations for 1975–80 contain an element of bias too, though of a contrary nature. Thus, if we alter investment's projected share of total GNP in 1975 as just indicated above and then apply to 1975–80 the same methodology for computing investment as we just did for the 1970–75 period, we come up with the following results: investment in 1980 would need to be only 53.7 percent of the GNP, instead of the 56.8 percent shown in Table 2, to assure an increase of 9.0 percent a year of the capital stock; however, it would have to be 31.9 percent of GNP, rather than the 29.4 percent shown in the table, to guarantee a rise of 6 percent a year in the capital stock.

[9]*Gosudarstvennyi piatiletnil plan razvitiia narodnovo khoziaistvo SSSR na 1971–1975 gody,* Moscow, 1972, p. 73.

The Soviet people, to be sure, have come to understand that improvements in consumption standards do not inexorably follow government commitments to provide them. Nevertheless, these standards have by all accounts tended to rise since Stalin, and sometimes markedly. It would be surprising if the government in the years ahead decided, except under great duress, to suspend such rewards for any length of time for a population which is now relatively educated as well as conscious of Western living standards, and which has elite groups who themselves have become increasingly materialistic. Such a governmental decision would be especially surprising in circumstances where a full reversion to the techniques of rule of the days of the "cult of personality" no longer appears to be a feasible alternative.

The implementation of the government's commitments to consumers obviously will not be made easier by the 1972 crop failures, still much in the news as these lines are written, but the government's reaction to these failures also underlines that at least a partial shift in priorities has occurred. Reportedly, nearly $2.0 billion of scarce foreign exchange has been allocated for the importation of some 28 million tons of grain. Under Stalin, needless to say, concern for alleviating the impact of harvest losses was hardly so intense.[10]

If the tempo of capital-stock growth is permitted to decrease, of course, the growth rate of output will likely do the same. Our projections only underline the evident at this point. But the government has already acquiesced in a retardation of output growth. Given its heightened concern for consumers, it may well find it expedient to continue to do so in the future.

But what about productivity? Do not our projections show that if productivity grows rapidly enough—say by 3.0 percent—the capital stock, and with it output, could continue to grow at high rates even while the needed improvement in consumption standards is realized? Theoretically, that is a possibility, and the Soviet government, always concerned about raising productivity, has understandably become even more so as the investment costs of sustaining the further growth of the capital stock have become ever greater. As the just concluded U.S.-USSR economic accord underlines, the USSR, once so uneasy about economic relations with the West, is now actively seeking to promote them. It hopes that productivity growth will be helped by the increased exchanges, and especially by the more accelerated importation into the USSR of advanced Western technology that the agreement makes possible. The Soviet government has been trying to speed up productivity growth in other ways as well. Of late, it has placed increasing stress on domestic technological innovation, and at the same time it has sought, through the much discussed planning reforms launched in the fall of 1965, to remedy the perennial deficiencies in economic administration, such as those to which we have already referred, and thereby to increase the efficiency of the system.

---

[10]This, it will be recalled, is not the first occasion since Stalin's death that the government has imported grain on a large scale to offset harvest losses. However, the current imports much exceed even the purchases made in response to the exceedingly bad harvest of 1963 (16.8 million tons during 1963–65), and they apparently will suffice to make good all the 1972 losses.

In the aftermath of the recent harvest failures, the government is also reportedly revising its investment program in order to assure more funds for agriculture. This initiative should be taken into account when we come later to a consideration of the prospects for productivity growth in the economy generally, though its implications in that regard are perhaps not so evident as is sometimes assumed. Thus, while some analysts have argued that any substantial revision of investment allocations under the current Five-Year Plan might in itself tend to impair efficiency, it is also possible that additional allocations to agriculture might be relatively productive in view of the chronic shortage of capital there.

Thus far, however, the planning reforms do not appear to have been highly effective.[11] Moreover, the acceleration of technological progress in any wholesale way in a complex, modern economy such as that of the USSR is not an easy task. While productivity may increase more rapidly in the future than it has recently, that is not saying a great deal. Certainly, the government would have difficulty achieving a tempo of productivity improvement much higher than the more buoyant rates of the 1950s. Should the government seek to sustain a superhigh rate of capital-stock growth at the expense of consumption, big gains in productivity would be all the harder to attain, inasmuch as frustration of consumer aspirations for rising standards of living could not help but affect labor incentives adversely.

Though the changes introduced in the wake of the planning reforms announced in the fall of 1965 were hardly revolutionary, the reforms themselves did represent something of a break with the past. Hence, we should not be too surprised if, in search of additional sources of productivity gains, the government should initiate still further reforms in planning. Perhaps it will at long last even make the kind of wholesale shift to "market socialism" that many thought was being initiated in 1965. But only time will tell just what further changes, if any, might be introduced, and how productivity might be affected thereby.

Our projections have assumed throughout that the Soviet government will devote to public administration and defense a constant share of output corresponding to that of 1970. Defense is by far the more important claimant here, and the USSR could obviously find additional resources for both investment and consumption, should it be prepared to limit allocations to that competing use. While the Soviet government has always seemed reluctant to restrict defense expenditures on purely economic grounds, it might in the future—political circumstances permitting—find such grounds more impelling than it has found them in the past. Indeed, we may wonder whether it has not already found them so in view of the apparently increased flexibility that it has manifested lately in, for example, arms-control negotiations.

To conclude, then, I have referred often to the extraordinarily high tempo of capital-stock growth that has prevailed hitherto in the USSR—a tempo which has surpassed that of output growth even when output was increasing relatively rapidly. I have also discussed a corollary of that incongruity: the rising share of output absorbed by the investments required to sustain such rapid growth of the capital stock. While the pattern of economic growth that emerged in the USSR under Stalin's Five-Year Plans—and has come to be called the Soviet model—has many facets, a central characteristic has been the imbalance manifested in such disproportionately rapid growth of capital stock in combination with a rising share of output going into investment. (The latter phenomenon is perhaps even more familiar in the alternative guise of an inordinately high tempo of growth in "heavy" as compared with "light" industries.) As so characterized, however, the Soviet model has clearly been undergoing a process of erosion lately. Notably, unbalanced growth has apparently been giving way to relatively balanced growth in the very sphere—capital formation—where the imbalance had previously been most striking. The prospect is that this erosion will continue. In the USSR at least, the Soviet model may not survive its dictatorial originator much longer.

---

[11]See Abram Bergson, "The Current Soviet Planning Reforms," in Alexander Balinky et al., Planning and the Market in the USSR: the Sixties, New Brunswick, N.J., Rutgers University Press, 1967; Gertrude E. Schroeder, "Organization and Management as Factors in Soviet Economic Growth in the 1970's," Laulan, Prospects for Soviet Economic Growth.

23

China:
An Economic
Reappraisal

Dwight H. Perkins

Ever since the blackout on statistical data from the People's Republic of China began in the early 1960s following the disruption of the nation's data-reporting services, outside appraisal of China's economic performance has had the character of an occult art. Controversies have raged through the relevant literature over whose estimates most accurately portrayed the state of the economy, and both the estimated figures and their interpretation have differed considerably. One group of analysts, for example, argued that China's total farm output in the mid-1960s was no higher than in 1957—a claim which, if true, would have meant that per capita farm production had fallen considerably, given the intervening growth in population. Another group, however, countered with evidence that agricultural output not only had kept pace with population increases but perhaps had even kept a bit ahead of the number of mouths to be fed.

[At present] the end of controversy about China's economy is not yet in sight—and perhaps never will be. But the raw material that will make it possible to narrow the range of disagreement between contending analysts is once again beginning to trickle out of China, as the PRC government has at last resumed publishing statistical indicators of national economic performance. To be sure, the statistical blackout of the 1960s was never total, and the volume of data now being released is still small, leaving great gaps in coverage. Nevertheless, the contrast between [today] and, say, 1969 in this area is very striking—as indeed it is in many other areas as well.

What is it that the new information tells us, and does it jibe with what we thought was happening in the Chinese economy in the middle and late 1960s? First let us see what fresh light this information sheds on the rates of growth achieved [since the 1950s]. Then let us attempt an analysis of the policies and organizational changes that lay behind this performance.

Growth Rates in Industry

For many years there has been little doubt that Chinese industry, particularly the producer-goods sector, was growing faster than agriculture and production for con-

From Dwight H. Perkins, "An Economic Reappraisal," *Problems of Communism* (Vol. XXII, No. 3, May–June 1973), pp. 1–13. [Reprinted with permission from the publisher.]

sumption in general. Data released during the past two years, however, have made it clear that the differential has been even larger than we had previously thought. It is not that farm output grew more slowly than previous estimates had indicated, but rather that industrial output grew more rapidly. To mention only one key indicator, total steel output in 1970 was 18 million tons and rose to 23 million tons in 1972 (see Table 1), whereas earlier estimates for the middle and late 1960s had generally placed annual steel production at 10 to 12 million tons.[1]

There are still not enough data to come up with a precise estimate of industrial growth, in terms of value added, between 1957 (the last year of plentiful and accurate statistics) and 1972, but a plausible and reasonably narrow range of estimates can be reached. Two kinds of relevant data are now available for the [early 1970s]. On the one hand, there are output figures for several important commodities (a number of these are presented in Table 1). On the other hand, there is an officially-released estimate of the gross value of industrial output in 1970, which can be compared—not without some difficulty—to the official figures for the 1950s.

On the basis of the figures given in Table 1, China's crude steel output grew at an average annual rate of 10.2 percent between 1957 and 1972. It does not necessarily follow, of course, that the close correlation that existed in the 1950s between steel production and the total output of producer goods continued into the 1960s. In the 1950s, steel itself and machinery (a big steel user) accounted for a high proportion of the total industrial development program, whereas in the 1960s chemicals, petroleum, nuclear weapons, missiles, and conventional weapons became the leading sectors. Even so, steel and machinery continued to account for a substantial portion of the growth in producer-goods industry, and in addition there were apparently a number of slow-growing sectors (e.g., coal) which tended to offset the impact of chemicals and the like on the growth rate. Hence, even for the 1960s, it is plausible to assume that total producer-goods output increased at a rate similar to, if not identical with, that of steel—say, 9 to 11 percent per year.

Somewhat similar reasoning can be applied to the industrial consumer-goods sector. Again on the basis of the data in Table 1, cotton textile output between 1957 and 1970 grew at an average rate of 4.1 percent a year, although the failure to report any figures for 1971 and 1972 may indicate that output in those years was below or only slightly above 1970. Since most manufactured consumer goods in China are, like textiles, still heavily dependent on agricultural raw materials, and since, moreover, the overall agricultural growth rate was certainly less than 4 percent a year (see Table 1), it is reasonable to assume that the growth rate for industrial consumer goods as a whole closely approximated the relatively low rate for cotton textiles. On the other hand, output of some consumer items not dependent on agriculture, such as bicycles and cloth made of synthetic fibers, is known to have grown at a much higher rate than the average.

A short article such as this is clearly not the place to attempt to present all the arguments and evidence behind a particular set of estimates. The above figures are presented simply to give some idea of what is involved and what the remaining gaps in our knowledge are. Nevertheless, we can use these figures as a starting point toward arriving at an estimate of overall Chinese industrial growth. Thus, if we apply average growth rates

---

[1]Steel output, according to Chou En-lai, probably did fall to 10 million tons in at least one year during the main phase of the Cultural Revolution (1967–69), but it is likely to have been well above that figure in 1965 and 1966. See Edgar Snow's report of his talks with the Chinese Premier in *The New Republic* (Washington, DC), March 27, 1971, p. 20.

TABLE 1
Selected Output Data for the People's Republic of China, 1957–1972

[Product]	1957	1970	1971	1972
Crude steel (million tons)	5.35	18	21	23
Chemical fertilizer (million tons)	.63	14	17	20
Petroleum (million tons)	.46	20	25	29
Cotton cloth (billion meters)	5.05	8.5	n.a.*	n.a.
Grain (million tons)	185	240	250	240

*"n.a." indicates figures are not available.
SOURCES: The 1957 figures were published by the State Statistical Bureau in various periodicals. The 1970, 1971, and 1972 data are either from Edgar Snow's interview with Chou En-lai (*The New Republic* (March 27, 1971) or from various 1971 and 1972 yearend press releases issued by the New China News Agency.

of, say, 10 percent for producer goods and 4 percent for consumer goods to 1957 value-added figures for these sectors (in 1952 prices), the result is an annual growth rate for industry as a whole (including mining, handicrafts, and utilities) of about 8 percent for the period between 1957 and 1972.

A careful study by Thomas Rawski, using more data (including provincial data) and a slightly different methodology, comes up with a rate of growth for all industry of 9.4 to 10.4 percent per year between 1957 and 1971.[2] The addition of 1972 would lower the rate somewhat, but not significantly. Rawski's figures are for the gross value of industrial output, not for value added, and use of the latter would probably, although not necessarily, lower the indicated growth rate further. The only recent official figure thus far given out by the Chinese for total gross value of industrial output, namely the figure for 1970 ($90 billion) given by Chinese Premier Chou En-lai to American newsman Edgar Snow,[3] also suggests a growth rate of 9 percent per year for the 1957–70 period, although it is unclear whether the figure was calculated in prices comparable to those of the 1950s.

An average annual rate of growth of 8–9 percent in industrial value added between 1957 and 1972 does not, of course, imply that there was steady growth throughout the period at that rate—far from it. Accelerated development in 1958–59 was followed by a sharp decline in 1960, then by recovery and renewed growth in the early and mid-1960s. Subsequently, when the Cultural Revolution was at its height in 1967–69, it certainly disrupted industry and transport for a time. However, it has now become clearer than ever that these disruptions did not have a long-lived impact. All indications

---

[2]Thomas G. Rawski, "Chinese Industrial Production, 1952–1971," forthcoming in *Review of Economics and Statistics* (Cambridge, Mass.).

[3]See Snow's report of his interview with Chou, p. 21. The $90 billion figure was converted into US dollars at the official exchange rate, but Chou did not specify whether it was based on current or constant prices and, if the latter, for which year. Prices, particularly of industrial products, have been quite stable in China since the early 1950s; however, there have been some variations.

are that China's industrial output in 1970 was above that of 1966, perhaps by a significant margin.

In 1971, the gross value of industrial output was officially stated to have increased by 10 percent over the preceding year,[4] and other published data are consistent with that claim. No figure for 1972 has yet been published, however, and all indications are that the rate of output growth fell sharply. The decline stemmed only partly from difficulties in agriculture, as the rates of growth for steel and petroleum—neither of which is dependent on farm-based raw materials—likewise dropped, although still remaining relatively high.

In sum, the recent statistical information from China seems to confirm that the average annual rate of industrial growth from 1957 through 1972 was approximately 8 to 9 percent. It should be added that this rate, though quite respectable, was well below the rates of the First Five-Year Plan period (1953–57), when the officially estimated rate of growth was 19 percent a year. But a decline from that rate was almost inevitable. The abnormally high growth rate of the 1950s resulted from the existence of much unused capacity at the beginning (1952) and an excessive diversion of investment resources away from other sectors toward industry—a diversion that was bound to have a dramatic impact on output performance in what was then still quite a small sector of the economy.

Growth Rates in Agriculture

Our knowledge of the rate of growth is more solidly based for the agricultural sector than for industry. For one thing, we have a nearly complete series for grain output in the 1960s and early 1970s, and grain accounts for over half the output growth in terms of value added for the entire sector. In addition, we also know something about a number of other key crops. For example, since raw cotton output is closely correlated with the production of cotton textiles (with a one-year time lag), and since we now know—as pointed out earlier—that cotton textile output grew at an average rate of 4 percent a year from 1957 to 1970, it follows that the growth rate for raw cotton from 1957 through 1969 must have been approximately the same. By the same reasoning, the apparent decline in cotton textile output growth in 1971 (inferred from Peking's failure to report the production figures for those years) suggests that the same was true of raw cotton output after 1969. As for such other major agricultural crops as soy beans, peanuts, and other oil-bearing seeds, the fact that exports of these items have yet to recover to the levels of the 1950s[5] suggests that their rate of output growth has been slow, perhaps below the rate of population increase.

Finally, we have an official Chinese estimate of the gross value of agricultural output in 1970 ($30 billion), although it is uncertain (as in . . . industry) whether the prices used in arriving at this figure are close enough to the prices of the 1950s to make comparison meaningful. If prices in 1970 and 1957 were the same, then the agricultural growth rate averaged 2.3 percent per year. If prices rose (and it is highly unlikely that they fell), the growth rate would be slightly lower. Either way, the rate of increase in the value of farm output as a whole appears, not surprisingly, to be highly correlated

---

[4]New China News Agency (henceforth cited as NCNA), Dec. 31, 1971.

[5]Chinese trade figures are based on reports of China's trading partners and appear in various places, including A. H. Usack and R. E. Batsavage, "The International Trade of the People's Republic of China," in *People's Republic of China: An Economic Assessment,* A Compendium of Papers Submitted to the Joint Economic Committee, US Congress (Washington, DC, US Government Printing Office, 1972).

with the growth rate of grain output, which averaged 2.0 percent annually between 1957 and 1970, or 1.7 percent if the calculation is carried through 1972 (based on the output figures in Table 1).

Of course, as in the case of industry, production in agriculture did not rise along a steady path. After a bumper harvest in 1958, grain output fell sharply in 1959, 1960, and 1961, and it had only just recovered to the 1957 level by 1963. Between 1963 and 1971, as a result of a major shift of investment resources to agriculture, growth averaged nearly 4 percent, although a decline of 4 percent in 1972 brought the average for the period 1963–1972 down to 3.1 percent.[6]

The improvement in the rate of agricultural growth, though it may seem small, is highly significant. Available evidence suggests that China's population, as in the 1950s, continues to increase at a rate of about 2 percent a year.[7] Thus, the growth achieved in agriculture since 1963 has been enough to enable China not merely to keep pace with the food needs of the people, but also to recover the ground lost as a result of the stagnation in agriculture between 1957 and 1963.

Growth in GNP

Estimating the rate of growth of China's Gross National Product (GNP) is more problematical than estimating the growth rates for industry and agriculture alone. In 1957 these two sectors accounted for roughly 77 percent of China's total GNP; hence, to arrive at a growth rate for GNP over the 1957–1972 period, one must have a figure for the remaining 23 percent, i.e., the services sector. Unfortunately, there are almost no solid data on which to base an estimate of growth in services. About the best one can do is to assume that certain services (finance and trade) grew at the same rate as industry plus agriculture, and that others (residential rents, personal services, and government administration) kept pace with population. On this basis, the annual growth rate for the service sector as a whole between 1957 and 1972 can be estimated at about 4 percent.

Combining this figure with the indicated growth rates for industry (8 percent) and agriculture (3 percent), we arrive at an average annual rate of GNP growth between 1957 and 1972 of between 5 and 5.5 percent. If, however, we calculate on the basis of 1933 prices instead of those of 1952 (because the former give weights to industry and agriculture that are closer to those of other less developed nations), the indicated rate of GNP growth falls slightly, to between 4.5 and 5 percent.[8] In 1971 the rate appears to have risen to between 7 and 8 percent, but in 1972 it fell back to between 3 and 4 percent, mainly because of the poor grain and cotton harvests and the secondary effects of those poor harvests.

In any event, it appears from the foregoing discussion that, in spite of the economic setbacks of 1960–61 caused by the Great Leap Forward and the Soviet withdrawal of technicians, and in spite of the disruptions resulting from the Cultural Revolution [of] 1967 through 1969, China has managed an overall rate of economic growth that

---

[6]The figures for 1971 and 1972 were released by NCNA, Dec. 28, 1972 (see Foreign Broadcast Information Service *Daily Report,* Dec. 29, 1972, pp. 3–4)

[7]No official figures on the growth of China's population have been published since the 1950s, but Chou En-lai has . . . told at least one visitor that the rate is still about 2 percent per annum (see *The New York Times,* Jan. 28, 1973).

[8]These calculations are based, in part, on data for the year 1957, in 1952 and 1933 prices, from T. C. Liu and K. C. Yeh, *The Economy of the Chinese Mainland, National Income and Economic Development, 1933–1957,* Princeton, N.J., Princeton University Press, 1965, p. 66.

has kept well ahead of the increase in population. Most of the rise in per capita product has resulted from growth in the producer-goods sector, but if 1963 is used as a base year rather than 1957, there has also been some increase in the per capita availability of consumer goods.

Investment and Planning in Industry

Let us turn our attention now to the factors responsible for this quite respectable economic performance. One factor of major importance has apparently been the maintenance of a high rate of investment. While there are no official figures on the investment rate, it is possible to arrive at some general conclusions on the basis of what we know about the producer-goods sector. Thus, it is clear from the reasoning in the preceding sections that the share of producer goods in China's GNP has doubled between 1957 and 1972, and we know that these goods are generally used for one of three purposes—i.e., for investment, as inputs into other producer and consumer goods, and for the production of military equipment.[9] Given the much higher rate of growth in the output of producer goods as compared to that of consumer goods, the proportion of total producer-goods output used as inputs into the production of consumer items has undoubtedly declined. As for the military share of producer goods output, even though China's expenditures on military equipment and installations have risen sharply, particularly since 1960 when Soviet military supplies were cut off, it is unlikely that they could have absorbed all of the very marked increase indicated above in the overall share of producer goods in GNP. Hence, the most plausible conclusion is that there was a rise in the proportion of such goods allocated to investment.[10]

A second major factor in China's economic performance over the past decade has been the regime's arrival in the early 1960s—after years of experimentation and changing policies—at settled ways of organizing the economy that have evidently proven effective. Because the organization of the industrial sector is quite different in form, if not in spirit, from that of agriculture, the two will be dealt with separately. Let us look at the industrial sector first.

In the early 1950s, China introduced the highly centralized Soviet system of planning and control, complete with a powerful planning commission in Peking which, in principle, was expected to exercise direct control over all industrial firms above the handicraft level. However, because China had tens of thousands of industrial firms with widely different technologies and, in many cases, with primitive accounting procedures, it was found to be totally impossible for the central authorities to keep track of performance at the plant level in each of these enterprises. To remedy this situation, it was decided in late 1957 and early 1958 to decentralize authority over production and even over investment choices, but this decision was carried out in such a way during 1958 and 1959 that there was in fact no authority responsible for coordinating inputs and outputs. The result was chaos, with firms churning out items that were often of low quality and of little use to anyone.

Beginning in the early 1960s, order was restored—not by recentralizing economic authority in Peking, but by placing it in the hands of provincial and county . . . plan-

---

[9]Producer goods can also be exported, but Chinese exports of such goods have been quite small.

[10]It is also possible, of course, that the share of machinery and equipment in investment rose in the 1960s, but the rise would have to have been very large if the rate of investment remained the same as in the 1950s or fell.

ning and control organs. Individual firms still had to meet essentially physical output targets and stay below targeted levels of input use, but principal responsibility for drawing up these targets was in the provincial and county seats, not in Peking. Only a few enterprises were controlled at the national level, and the number of firms in this category appears to have declined throughout the 1960s. As long as most of a firm's inputs were purchased within a given region and its output sold within that same region, there was no need for coordination on a national scale.

With regard to the impact of the Cultural Revolution on the economic structure, the available evidence suggests that it was largely limited to the manner in which the planning and control apparatus conducted itself, and that it entailed few major changes in the *formal* planning system. How the Revolution affected the behavior of the economic apparatus can be inferred from criticisms that began to appear in the Chinese press in the early 1970s with respect to the conduct of cadres during the 1967–69 period. The criticisms implied that many cadres had failed to distinguish "rational rules and regulations from revisionist practices of controlling, restricting and repressing the working masses" and had taken the mistaken position that "all rules and regulations which obstruct anarchism are no good."[11] Such complaints strongly suggest that the Cultural Revolution witnessed a recurrence of at least some of the excesses that had marked the 1958–59 Great Leap Forward. As indicated earlier, however, the excesses of the Cultural Revolution period slowed growth only temporarily, mainly because they were not allowed to get out of hand as in 1958–59. Thus, the early 1970s were dominated by calls in the press to end anarchy, to strengthen management and accounting, to make more careful inventories of warehouses, to pay more attention to veteran workers, and to emphasize product quality. At the same time, a number of individuals who had been severely criticized during the Cultural Revolution as architects of the economic policies of the early 1960s, most notably Ch'en Yun, were rehabilitated—another possible sign of a return to the main lines of pre-Cultural Revolution policy for the economy.

Other key features of the industrial policies of the 1960s that have continued unchanged into the early 1970s include special emphasis on the development of military equipment industries, on rapid expansion of agricultural support industries (most notably the chemical fertilizer industry), and on a major increase in the number of rural-based small-scale firms of many types.

The effort to expand small-scale rural industry merits closer attention. Rural China has always had small-scale handicraft industries for the processing of food and similar activities, but what is different today is that the concept has been extended to a number of industries that hitherto were not typically either small in scale or rural-based. This effort, too, began during the Great Leap Forward, when there was a drive to develop small enterprises such as the much publicized "backyard" iron and steel furnaces. As in the case of so many other activities connected with the Leap, implementation of the program, though energetic, was poorly thought out and resulted in waste of raw materials and poor quality of output. Most of the backyard furnaces were closed down in the early 1960s, as were many other small plants, but in others an attempt was made to rationalize production procedures rather than to close the plants down altogether. Apparently the effort was deemed successful, for the number of small plants was once again on the rise by the mid-1960s. By 1970, thousands of such enterprises dotted the countryside, and hundreds—perhaps even thousands—more were built in 1971 and 1972.

---

[11]Numerous Chinese radio broadcasts in 1971 and 1972 criticized cadres for behaving in this manner during the late 1960s.

Although there are many kinds of small-scale firms, they are centered mainly in five industries: iron and steel, cement, chemical fertilizer, energy (coal and electricity), and machinery (chiefly farm-machinery repair shops, but also production of simple tools). The development of rural-based cement and chemical fertilizer plants is, perhaps, the most unusual aspect of the program in comparison to what is found in other less developed countries today.[12] In 1971, some 60 percent, or 10 million gross tons, of China's total chemical fertilizer output was produced in such small rural plants, while 40 percent of China's cement output was produced by 1800 small enterprises (the addition of 600 more small cement plants during 1972 brought the percentage of total cement production up to 48).

Unfortunately, we do not yet have enough information to judge whether the development of these small-scale rural plants makes possible more efficient use of China's endowment of productive resources, characterized by surplus labor and short capital. What we do know is that such enterprises have helped to familiarize millions of Chinese farmers with modern industrial technology. This effort seems bound to produce both economic and social benefits, the latter by breaking down the sharp distinction that exists in so many less developed societies between the sophisticated, modernized cities and a primitive countryside.

Agricultural Organization and Policy

It is agriculture, however, that lies at the heart of China's economic problems, for the agricultural sector must not only provide the ever increasing amounts of food required by the country's mounting population but also generate surpluses needed to help finance the development of industry. As pointed out earlier, while the rate of growth in industry has far exceeded that of agriculture, the latter has shown marked improvement since the early 1960s, so that output is now expanding at a pace more than adequate to take care of population growth. Let us now look at the changes in agricultural organization and policies that have brought about this significant improvement.

During the period extending from the start of agricultural collectivization in China in the winter of 1955–56 up to 1962, the Chinese Communist regime experimented with a wide variety of organizational forms. In 1958 and 1959, under the banner of the Great Leap Forward, virtually all remaining noncollectivized farming activities (the peasants' private plots and the small free markets) were abolished, and the farmers were organized into communes of 4000–5000 families each, with control over their activities centralized in the hands of the commune leadership. These innovations, however, contributed to a sharp recession in agriculture which forced a reversal of policy. In the depths of the rural depression in 1961, many areas experimented with something called the "agricultural responsibility system," which was tantamount to a virtual abandonment of collectivized agriculture.

This period of instability in agricultural policy ended in 1962, when China finally settled on a basic organizational structure for agriculture which has not undergone any major changes since. The larger existing communes were split up into several smaller ones, and at the same time authority over the planning and management of labor and crops was decentralized to a considerable degree from the commune to a small subunit

---

[12]A useful first-hand description of a number of small-scale Chinese rural industrial plants can be found in Jon Sigurdson, "Rural Industry—A Traveller's View," *The China Quarterly* (London), April-June 1972, pp. 315–32.

of the commune, the production team. The production team was also made the accounting unit, a change which meant in effect that whatever profits (or losses) the individual team made (after taxes) were no longer pooled and shared with the entire commune but accrued to the team itself. Whereas several thousand families had shared the fruits of their collective labor in the initial communes, now only several dozen families did so. Even before this, moreover, small private plots and rural free markets had been reinstituted in order to revive declining food production, and these institutions were continued after 1962.

There have, of course, been minor adjustments in this basic organizational pattern since 1962. Over the next few years, for example, the amount of land in private plots (which were supposed to be kept to about 5 percent of total cultivated acreage) appears to have increased slightly.[13] During the Cultural Revolution, there was some talk of restricting or abolishing private plots, as well as of recentralizing more authority in the hands of the production brigade (a unit above the team but below the commune), but little if anything was actually done along these lines. The rural areas were generally kept out of the mainstream of the Cultural Revolution, and they appear to have suffered little disruption of any kind in that period—certainly not enough to affect crop output.

As of 1971 and 1972, there continued to be little indication of any major change in rural organization or general agricultural policy. If anything, it is possible that the independence of the individual production teams may have increased, inasmuch as "self-reliance" has been the leitmotif of the "Learn from Tachai" Campaign, which has played such a big role in the Chinese countryside in recent years.[14] The basic idea of "self-reliance" is that all units should try to produce as much of their own needs as possible and thus minimize their dependence on others; however, this sort of self-sufficiency necessarily implies a reduction in the influence of outsiders on decision making at the production-team level. The higher authorities must instead resort to more indirect methods of exercising control.

An interesting example of the use of such indirect methods was the government's decision in 1971 to raise the purchase prices of bast fibers, oil seeds, and sugar. In 1972, in spite of a generally poor harvest, the output of these items increased 20 percent in the case of sugar and rapeseed (a major oil seed) and 40 percent in the case of bast fiber. It is possible that unusually good weather in the relevant regions or, perhaps, even direct orders from the central authorities to emphasize these items were more responsible for the increases in output than the higher prices offered, but the most plausible explanation is that the farm production teams responded with alacrity to the incentive of better prices. In contrast to this experience, major increases in the purchase prices of certain lagging cash crops in 1956 and 1957 had failed to stimulate higher outputs of these items (in 1957, in fact, all declined); however, the farm cadres at that time had been operating under clear directives to emphasize grain output and consequently had not been at liberty to raise the gross income of their units by concentrating on crops yielding higher monetary returns.[15] Now the production teams seem to have enough autonomy to be more flexible in their production decisions.

---

[13]. . . See Shahid J. Burki, *A Study of the Chinese Communes, 1965* (Cambridge: Harvard University Press, 1969), p. 35.

[14]Tachai is the name of a production brigade belonging to a commune in Shansi Province. The brigade was singled out as a model for all of China.

[15]For further discussion of these developments, see D. H. Perkins, *Market Control and Planning in Communist China* (Cambridge, Mass.: Harvard University Press, 1966), pp. 70–71.

TABLE 2
Foreign Trade of the People's Republic of China (in millions of U.S. dollars)

[Products]	1959	1962	1966	1970	1971
Total imports	2,060	1,150	2,035	2,183	2,247
Machinery and Equipment	1,058	52	490	395	495
Metals	248	62	280	560	605
Wheat	0	200+	330	275	204
Chemical Fertilizer	44	27	150	190	180
Total Exports	2,205	1,525	2,170	2,063	2,364
Textiles and Clothing	651	523	470	490	550
Foodstuffs	412	156	595	655	800
Total Trade	4,265	2,675	4,205	4,246	4,611

SOURCES: Most of the data for 1959 and 1962 are from Alexander Eckstein, *Communist China's Economic Growth and Foreign Trade* (New York: McGraw-Hill, 1966). Data for other years were compiled by the U.S. Consulate-General, Hong Kong, and published in various issues of the periodical *Current Scene.*

Autarky in Trade

It is readily apparent from the preceding survey of China's economic performance [since the late 1950s] that the government's overall policy of economic development has been characterized by a strong element of autarky, or an emphasis on achieving "self-reliance" or self-sufficiency both within the economy and on a national and international scale. It may therefore be relevant to see how this tendency has manifested itself in the PRC's foreign trade over approximately the same time span.

Some pertinent trade data for various years between 1959 and 1971 are presented in Table 2. Several conclusions are immediately apparent from the figures. First, China's total trade in 1971 was only $346 million, or 8.6 percent, above the previous peak level of 1959. Since world prices in the meantime had risen by more than the indicated percentage increase, China's trade in real terms was still below the 1959 level. Further, between 1959 and 1972, China's economy had grown considerably, as indicated earlier, so that trade as a percentage share of GNP (X + M/GNP) fell from between 7 and 11 percent in the 1950s to under 5 percent in the early 1970s.[16]

China's declining dependence on foreign trade emerges more clearly in relation to specific items. In the 1950s, for example, the PRC had to import virtually its entire supply of petroleum, i.e., about 3 million tons a year, whereas China produced 29 million tons domestically in 1972 (see Table 1) and may soon become an oil exporter. Again, as seen in Table 2, over half of China's total imports in 1959 consisted of machinery and equipment and included a large number of complete plants, reflecting the fact that the domestic industrial development program was heavily dependent throughout the 1950s on complete plant imports from the Soviet Union and Eastern Europe. In contrast, throughout the 1960s and early 1970s there have been few Chinese purchases of complete plants, and machinery and equipment imports by 1971 were less than half of the 1959 level, with most Chinese investment in new plants and equipment being supplied from domestic sources.

---

[16]It is not possible to calculate the share of trade in GNP with precision because we do not have a single figure for GNP in, say, 1970: equally important, statistics of China's trade are calculated in prices different from those used in estimating GNP.

China also is no longer dependent financially on the outside world. Foreign aid from the Soviet Union in the form of long-term credits ended in the mid-1950s, and all such credits had been repaid with interest by 1965. Since then, although the PRC, like all countries, has resorted to short-term credits to facilitate trade, it has neither sought nor received long-term credits. Instead, in fact, China has become one of the world's major aid-givers, her commitments in 1970 and 1971 averaging about . . . $600 million a year, exclusive of aid to North Vietnam.

The PRC's policy of economic self-reliance, or lack of dependence on foreign trade and aid, does not imply, however, that Chinese trade with the outside world is going to wither away. China's trade in 1971 was slightly above 1970, at least in money terms, and the increase in 1972 was even larger. Nevertheless, there are no signs of a reversal of the basic disposition toward autarky.

Incomes Policy and Growth

One further matter that merits attention here is the rather unusual fact that China has endeavored to couple its pursuit of rapid economic growth with a policy of eliminating inequalities in income distribution. This sets the PRC clearly apart from the rest of the less developed countries of the world. Although a good many of the latter have espoused some form of "socialism" during the past few decades, it has in most instances been socialism for the rich, and particularly for the bureaucracy. Great effort has been made in these countries to find jobs in state enterprises and government offices for the newly emerging elite, but relatively little has been done to keep the incomes of this elite from rising too far above those prevailing among the great majority of the people.

The PRC has deliberately followed a different path. One of the central purposes of the Cultural Revolution, for example, was to prevent or reverse the rise of a new elite class based on the party-government bureaucracy. As a result of this effort, all but a handful of cadres in the various government and party offices are now required to go to the countryside and work at unskilled jobs for considerable periods, and youth, instead of moving steadily up the educational ladder, are expected to spend several years at manual labor before they can even be considered for admission to a university. Numerous other measures have been adopted with a similar purpose.

Apart from such measures to prevent the reemergence of elitist attitudes, the Communist regime set out from the beginning to reduce the range of income differentiation between different types of labor as well as between different levels of skill and responsibility. While substantial disparities in income still remain, these disparities have certainly been sharply reduced in comparison to those that existed in China before 1949 or presently exist in other less developed nations. However, most of the steps in this direction were taken in the 1950s, and there has since been a slackening of efforts to push ahead with income equalization as this policy has come into conflict with the requirements of growth and the policy of self-reliance.

The nature of the problem can be seen most clearly in agriculture. In the 1950s, the newly established PRC government effected a major redistribution of rural incomes by first confiscating the land of landlords and redistributing it to the poor peasants and then incorporating the peasants' holdings into cooperatives in which earnings were based solely on labor and not on the amount of land brought into the cooperative. Welfare funds were set up within the cooperatives; grain was distributed at least in part on the basis of need rather than individual production; and education and health services were provided gratis or at nominal cost to members of the cooperatives. But several sources of inequality remained. Families with more and better workers, for example, received more income per capita than families made up of the old and weak. The continued existence of private plots also gave an advantage to those with relevant farming skills, particularly if their village was near an urban center where produce from the private plots could be marketed. By far the most important continuing source of inequality, however, was the diverse amounts and quality of land in farming units.

Because of these differences, farm incomes varied considerably. A 1965 study of 13 communes, for example, showed that the ratio of income per worker between the richest and the poorest commune sampled was 3.4 to 1.[17] Moreover, this differential obscures the fact that in the poorest communes the income of some production teams was below the average for the whole commune, while some teams in the richest commune earned incomes higher than the commune's average. In effect, the smaller the basic producing and accounting unit, the greater the inequalities of income in the countryside. For the past decade, the basic unit has been the production team consisting of only a few dozen families, and it has been kept small because the initial experience of the communes proved that large units were less efficient.

Measures that could offset the continuing differentials in farmers' incomes have, in general, not been extensively resorted to. No major effort has been made, for example, to move people around so that all units would have lands of equivalent productivity to farm; nor has the agricultural tax been either very large or very progressive (there is a slight progression). Furthermore, investment in agriculture has most often been channeled into the naturally better-endowed areas where it would have the biggest impact on productivity, rather than into the poorer areas where it would help bring about a more equalized distribution of income. For example, in the drainage area of the Yellow River, a generally poor and dry region, grain output rose by only 7 percent between 1957 and 1970, whereas in the rich and wet middle and lower Yangtze Valley, by contrast, grain output in 1971 was 69 percent above the 1957 level; and much the same picture emerges in the case of cotton. The obvious explanation is that it has been the areas that can best use chemical fertilizers—generally the area with plentiful supplies of water—that have received the lion's share of the fertilizer supply.

The policy of self-reliance also is often in direct conflict with a policy designed to redistribute income more equally. If communes and production teams are expected to rely on their own resources, those that save and invest more and that work harder and more effectively will naturally get ahead of the others, and those that are better endowed to start with will often have an advantage over all the rest. It is an obvious point, but one that is frequently overlooked.

Our knowledge of income distribution in China's urban areas in the early 1970s is less solidly based than our knowledge of the corresponding situation in the countryside. In the 1950s, of course, city dwellers as well as inhabitants of the rural areas experienced a major redistribution of incomes. The incomes of the wealthy who remained were sharply reduced, while those of the poorest groups were raised and the basic needs of the latter were guaranteed through the rationing of key commodities. Wage differentials between skilled and unskilled worker and between managers and workers were based on a scale similar to that of the Soviet Union.

---

[17]Burki, *The Chinese Communes,* p. 29. The poorest commune in this sample, it should be noted, was considered a success story by local authorities.

Visitors to China in 1972 . . . reported that the eight-grade wage scale, with the top-grade wage three-plus times the bottom, [continued] to be the basis of wage determination in the larger enterprises just as in the 1950s. Professional and managerial staff [were] generally paid wages equivalent to or a bit higher than those of the most skilled workers. It [appeared], however, that the average wages paid to professionals [had] declined somewhat . . . as younger engineers and technicians [had] replaced those trained before 1949. If this trend is verified by more systematic studies and continues, it would indicate a significant narrowing of income differentials in urban areas.

In sum, China still seems to remain committed to the principle of equalizing incomes, though the pace of such efforts has naturally slowed down by comparison with the rapid and drastic changes of the 1950s. The fact is that the PRC is still a relatively poor country and cannot afford to push the redistribution of income too vigorously at the price of markedly slowing down the rate of economic growth. During the Cultural Revolution the pursuit of social goals closely related to issues of income distribution did slow down or stop growth for a time, and it consequently was an effort that could not be sustained indefinitely. China has not abandoned these social goals in the early 1970s, but it does appear to have given them a lower priority in a generally successful effort to accelerate growth.

What the ordering of China's priorities will be in the future is probably not known even to the current leadership of the People's Republic of China. We do however, know something about the range of likely alternatives.

If the policies in effect today are continued, there is reason to believe that China's rate of economic growth will rise above the levels of the 1957–70 period. A high and rising level of investment should itself be enough to ensure that result. But there is a cloud on the horizon, and it looms in the vital agricultural sector. Expansion of farm output may prove to be more difficult in the late 1970s than it was in the late 1960s when large crop increases were achieved mainly through greater use of chemical fertilizer. China appears to be reaching the limits of what can be accomplished by this means alone, and the next steps are likely to prove either expensive (e.g., harnessing the rivers of the north for irrigation purposes) or uncertain (e.g., the development of new, improved seeds).

There is, of course, always the possibility that a renewed drive toward income equalization and related social goals, particularly if carried out in an atmosphere like that of the Cultural Revolution, or a situation of political instability created, say, by a succession crisis, might cause a departure from the present policies and slow down or halt the pace of growth temporarily. [In] the longer run, however, the only question is whether China's national product will grow more or less rapidly. The elements of continuity in Chinese economic policies since the early 1960s suggest that no set of leaders is likely to stray very far from what has proven to be a successful formula for sustained development.

24

Which Direction for Yugoslavia's Economy?

Deborah D. Milenkovitch

[In the early 1950s] Yugoslavia, in a heretical move, abandoned Soviet-type planning. The central planning apparatus was dismantled, enterprises became autonomous and profit was reestablished as the motive force. In the [last half of the 1960s], Yugoslavia . . . made even more radical changes. In its second major economic reform, Yugoslavia—

—abandoned central planning of investment.
—eliminated taxes on enterprise profits.
—gave enterprises complete control over the use of profits.
—permitted enterprises to lend money at interest.
—created profit-making banks paying dividends to shareholders.
—enabled firms to sell bonds to the public.
—encouraged the expansion of private enterprise.
—sanctioned various forms of nonlabor income.
—invited foreign capital to share Yugoslav profits.
—tolerated an unemployment rate as high as 20 percent.

Whether Yugoslavia has deviated from socialism and whether it is heading toward capitalism depends, of course, on one's definition of socialism and capitalism. Whatever definition is accepted, it is clear that the Yugoslavs are moving in a direction not traditionally associated with socialism and are adopting some mechanisms which have been traditionally associated with capitalism. Specifically, the central features of the traditional socialist economic system—central planning of production; central planning of investment; socialist ownership of the means of production; and distribution of income according to labor supplied—have been abandoned in Yugoslavia. Some of these characteristics are also being modified in some other countries of Eastern Europe.

Exploring why these particular changes have been made in Yugoslavia and what remains of socialism as a result may give some insight as to whether similar economic forces will compel the same developments elsewhere in East Europe. Current economic

From Deborah D. Milenkovitch, "Which Direction for Yugoslavia's Economy?" *East Europe* (Vol. 18, No. 7, July 1969), pp. 13-19. [Reprinted with permission from the publisher.]

reforms in East Europe involve a decentralization of decision making, an increase in the use of market signals and, in some instances, the development of Workers' Councils. These follow the pattern of the Yugoslav reforms of 1950-1954.

Central Planning of Production

We may start with a brief review of the demise of the doctrines of production planning and of the central administration of the economy. Marx had little to say about the economics of socialism. Consequently, Marxists have lacked a socialist blueprint of economic organization. Until recently, most Marxists believed that socialism implied a planned economy in which there would be a rational allocation of national resources. The market was associated with capitalism, the profit motive, irrationality and anarchy. Not until Stalin's death was the role of the market in socialism seriously reconsidered in the Soviet Union.

Despite their ideological training in strict and slavish adherence to Stalin's interpretation of Marxism, the Yugoslavs resolved the doctrinal conflict between socialism and the market almost ten years before the Russians. The 1950-54 Yugoslav reform dismantled the centralized system of administrative planning, eliminated price controls, and made costs more rational by introducing interest payments and repayable investment loans. Within the limits of existing plant and equipment, enterprises could determine what to produce, how to produce it, and at what price to sell it. Having paid the appropriate (and heavy) taxes, the enterprise could distribute the remaining profit as bonuses or could reinvest it in the firm. While it is true that Yugoslav enterprises were not as free as private companies, there was substantial freedom as to day-to-day production details, which were no longer centrally planned.

Why did these changes in the economic mechanism occur? The Soviet type of planning and incentive systems, which relied on exhortation, threat, bonus and promotion to attain physical output targets, may have been effective in raising output, but once bottlenecks were broken, the emphasis on quantity ceased to be rational. Inflexible planning and quantitative indicators caused aberrations—the systematic understatement of capacities and overstatement of input needs; insufficient incentive to provide variety to meet customers' specifications or to innovate; and little pressure to minimize costs—which were detrimental to development. The economic reforms in East Europe and the Soviet Union were designed to improve performance in these areas.

Central Planning of Investment

Just as tautly planned production may be effective in the beginning but later lead to the wrong assortment of goods being produced at high cost, planned investment may initially have great advantages but later may produce an inappropriate structure—an economy operating at excessive costs—and must similarly be abandoned. The Czechoslovaks were especially vocal about the defects of the classic Soviet type of investment planning.

The first Yugoslav economic reform discarded central planning of production. Notwithstanding a strong residual sentiment in favor of centrally planned investment, the second major reform (1961-1965) appears to have marked a drastic reduction of investment planning in Yugoslavia. Starting in 1961, taxes on enterprise income were cut to leave more funds for reinvestment and personal incomes. In 1963, government investment funds were transferred to the banking system. The 1965 economic reform again reduced enterprise taxes, increasing the funds available to enterprises by as much as 40 percent. By 1966 the annual plan ceased to exist. What remains are medium-term indicative plans of four to seven years; their method of construction and operational significance still remain somewhat unclear, however.

With only indicative planning, the initiative for investment originates in the enterprise. The incentive of enterprises to invest efficiently derives from the self-interest of the individual worker-consumer. Taxes which reduced enterprise incentive were eliminated; the many subsidies and privileges which made enterprise profit only distantly related to enterprise efficiency were dropped; the share of consumption goods provided independently of earned income (free or subsidized goods or transfer payments) was cut back. As a result, consumption by the worker is based more closely on earned income, which is now more dependent on his own performance and on the success of his enterprise. Finally, the success of the enterprise depends on its profitability based on current operations and successful investment decisions.

Investments are financed from enterprise profits. The enterprises which have accumulated profits are not necessarily those in which additional investments are essential. For an efficient use of these funds, there must be capital mobility in some kind of socialist capital market. The reform provided for such mobility. Enterprises can reinvest in their own firm, they can lend funds directly to other enterprises or they can become shareholders of banks. Banks, previously administrative agencies for government investment funds, became autonomous profit-sharing enterprises with capital subscribed to by shareholders (enterprises and government bodies) who manage the bank.

Behind the Decentralization Decision

What economic forces, if any, influenced the decision to reduce central control of investment? The market mechanism can work reasonably in a developed economy with many producers and consumers, but in a typical underdeveloped country it tends to produce inferior results. On the one hand, there may be monopolies; on the other, with few buyers and sellers, the consequences of enterprise decisions are less predictable. Under such circumstances, coordination of decisions can be an improvement. According to this reasoning, the misallocations resulting from the use of the market may become less significant relative to the total volume of investment at higher levels of development. At the same time, the planning system itself may become dysfunctional. As technology becomes more complex and as the supply bottlenecks are eliminated, the choices open to the planners multiply. It becomes far more difficult to evaluate alternatives. In addition, the planning bureaucracy may have developed its own information and decision-making biases.

These remarks about the usefulness of investment planning at different levels of development are relevant for all socialist countries. Additional factors seem to have influenced the Yugoslav decision to abandon investment planning. Centrally planned investment may have become impossible in Yugoslavia because of the absence of political agreement about such planning. It appears that the interests of the six republics differed so sharply that no consensus about the objectives of planning or development strategy was possible. What appear to be irreconcilable differences arose from differing levels of development. The developed regions saw investment planning as a burden which transferred resources from their areas, cut seriously into economic incentives and created errors of allocation. At the same time, the less developed regions were convinced that without investment planning they were doomed to remain underdeveloped.

Given the decision to decentralize investment, two possibilities for financing investment may be considered, one based loosely on past Yugoslav experience and the other on projections based on reforms scheduled to take place after 1970. In the former, the chief source of new investment funds is the tax on socially owned capital, which may be regarded as the interest paid to society for use of its capital. The proceeds of this tax are allocated, through the banking system, to the enterprises seeking investment loans. The latter possibility involves no capital tax, and the principal source of investment funds is enterprise profits. The profit-making enterprise invests either in its own firm or makes capital available to other firms through a capital market.

To Tax or Not to Tax

There is no significant difference between the "tax" and the "no tax" versions in allocating investment. There is, however, a major difference between the two versions in the sources of personal income and in the rate of savings. In the "tax" version, the tax rates (given the volume of enterprise capital) determine the volume of saving and investment. In the "no tax" version, savings decisions are voluntary. This change has two effects, each significant for the socialist economy. First, the rates of saving and investment depend on the decisions of many individuals and may be expected to be lower than was previously the case. Second, there will be a significant volume of interest income. Interest income may appear either as explicit interest payments for owned assets or as higher personal incomes for workers in plants where investments have been made. The choice of the "no tax" option sanctions interest income. There seems to be no compelling economic reason to select the no-tax, interest-paying version. This choice also has a number of other implications for personal incomes and the concept of social property.

Socialist economies have gradually been abandoning central planning of production and of investment and have accepted the advantages the market mechanism offers. Concurrently, or perhaps as a consequence, there have been changes in resource ownership and income distribution. Serious questions have been raised in Yugoslavia about whether social ownership of the means of production is necessary and about what social ownership means.

The resistance to private property runs deep in socialist doctrine. Private property has been identified with capitalism and is regarded with distrust because capitalism is exploitative (or because it represents a basis for possible counterrevolution). It has been identified with simple commodity production, a technologically backward remnant of the past which can be tolerated but certainly not encouraged since it is considered outmoded and inefficient. Private property has been held incompatible with socialism because by definition society owns the means of production. Finally, private property cannot be sanctioned because it contradicts the socialist principle of payment for labor alone. Private ownership also means payments for rent, interest and profit. (In practice, of course, private activity has been tolerated, if not sanctioned. An intriguing aspect of the current economic ferment in East Europe is that the socialist tolerance for private activity is increasing.)

The private sector in Yugoslavia encompasses the vast majority of agricultural producers and an important segment of the urban labor force in the service sector. However, the private sector was limited by laws governing the number of employees who could be hired, the size of plots, and other restrictions. The quality of service and quantity of goods remained low.

The balance-of-payments crisis of the early 1960s was apparently instrumental in bringing about policy changes. To reduce imports of foodstuffs, agricultural prices were raised and restrictions eased somewhat, making modern agriculture more accessible than before. Since socialist hotels and restaurants could not satisfy the demand of foreigners for tourist services, individuals were encouraged to augment the supply. There was also a new attitude toward foreign capital. Although Yugoslav enterprises had been operating under foreign licenses for some years and had received loans from foreign firms to make Yugoslav goods more competitive on world markets, foreign capital was invited to invest in Yugoslavia and to share the profits.[1] Domestic consumers also benefited from the new attitude toward private enterprise in the wake of the economic reform. In 1967, retail trade was opened to individuals on a very limited basis. Private persons could obtain licenses to run small shops in certain areas where there were no socialist enterprises already in operation.

Since private activity was no longer ruled out a priori, the Yugoslavs had to determine the limits on private activity. At this point there seem to be no firm policy guidelines covering the private sector. There has been intense discussion about the nature of social property, but the role of the private sector continues to be a sensitive subject. (It should be noted that the changing attitude toward private activity is not peculiar to Yugoslavia. Similar trends are visible in Poland, East Germany, Hungary and Czechoslovakia, some of which have gone beyond Yugoslavia in freeing private enterprise.)

The doctrinal dressing for change has been forthcoming, however. It has been argued that a private sector is necessary even under socialism. The technology of production is such that the social sector cannot provide all services adequately and therefore some spheres of activity should remain open for individual activity. Another approach to the question of private property suggested that the essence of socialism does not lie in legal forms of property relations but in the absence of exploitation. Thus, private ownership need not imply exploitation and exploitation can exist even under the legal forms of social ownership.

Distribution of Income

The changing role of private enterprise is one prong of the assault on social ownership of the means of production. The other is a reinterpretation of socialist principles of income distribution and the tendency to "privatize" the income streams emanating from social property.

The distributional principle of communism is supposedly "from each according to his ability, to each according to his needs." Marx recognized this as a goal, not a prescription for immediate implementation. According to Marx, until full communism is attained, goods and services must be distributed in proportion to the labor supplied. The socialist principle is "to each according to his work."

On the one hand, this means that labor is the only legitimate source of income, since in Marxian economic analysis only labor is productive. All nonlabor sources of income, therefore, represent income appropriated from the workers. Although sometimes tolerated, rent, interest and profit incomes are not recognized as socialist. On the other hand, the socialist principle limits the income differences between individuals. Marx did

---

[1]Although the legal form is a joint venture rather than direct equity investment, the contracts provide for sharing the profits of the Yugoslav enterprises.

not maintain that his principle was egalitarian. He recognized that "one man is superior to another physically or mentally" and would therefore receive a greater share of the goods.[2] He emphasized that the only equality was the right of individuals to receive income in proportion to their labor. Given the knotty problem of measuring the quantity of labor, Marxists have debated such factors as labor time, labor intensity and quantity of output. Regardless of the measure used, if earnings are proportional to the labor supplied, the differences in earnings between individuals will probably be smaller than those that would arise if earnings were proportional to the total amount of privately owned factors of production under private ownership. And, of course, under socialism some consumer goods would be provided free, so that inequality in consumption would be less than inequality in earnings.

The Yugoslavs have departed from the traditional interpretations of socialist income distribution in two ways. First, income differentials have increased significantly (the quantity of free or subsidized goods has been cut as well). The economic reform, as intended, strengthened personal monetary incentives and increased inequality. Second, Yugoslav practice has effectively "privatized" the nonlabor factors of production. The incomes generated by socially owned means of production accrue to individuals. This in turn also affects the distribution of income.

There are several sources of disparity in individual incomes, differences which have increased as a result of the economic reform:

Occupational differentials. The spread in pay for various types of labor grew after the reform, and persons with technical skills improved their positions markedly. Earnings differentials are often closely related to training and represent in part a return on the capital invested in humans by the socialist state. So the returns to social capital accrue to individuals.

Personal interest income. Although citizens have long received interest on their savings accounts, personal interest income became more important after the reform. The reform increased individuals' monetary income, and part of that income was used to purchase bonds or was put into interest-bearing savings accounts or other assets. If those with high incomes save more than those with low incomes and if they purchase interest-bearing assets, the differences between rich and poor are maintained or increased.

Private sector. The new, liberal attitude toward the private sector initially seemed to increase the number of persons earning exorbitant incomes and seemed to sanction various quasi-legal activities often associated with the private sector.

Variations in pay for the same job. Differences in pay arise for several reasons. There are vast differences in income levels between northwest and southern Yugoslavia. Per capita incomes are three to four times higher in the richest republic than in the poorest. Very often those in the south receive lower pay for performing the same work that yields a higher income in the north. If the factors of production are mobile, these differences will eventually diminish. The abundant labor of the south will seek higher wages in the north and the capital of the north will try to utilize cheap southern labor. Labor mobility, in fact, seems closely related to such economic factors as job availability and

---

[2]Karl Marx, *Critique of the Gotha Program* (New York: International Publishers, 1963), p. 11.

rates of pay. Still, language barriers and nationality differences limit inter-regional labor mobility in Yugoslavia. In addition, the higher levels of unemployment since the reform (domestic unemployment averages 10 percent and is over 20 percent if the several hundred thousand Yugoslavs working abroad are included in the ranks of the unemployed) further limit mobility because it is difficult to find jobs. The economic reforms of 1961–1965 attempted to stimulate capital movement by providing for inter-enterprise flows of funds and by revoking previous restrictions on such flows. But capital is not as mobile as had been hoped because of economic, nationalist or political reasons. Despite cheap labor, investment in the south may be less profitable because of the low level of skills and limited supplies of transport, power and other forms of social overhead capital.

Variations in pay for the same job can also occur within the same region. The Yugoslav system of economic organization does not appear to provide an equilibrating mechanism. In a competitive private-enterprise economy, pay differentials for similar work would tend to be eliminated (within a given geographic region) as employers hire at the lowest possible wage and workers try to obtain the highest possible wage. The Yugoslav enterprise functions differently. It is a producers' cooperative in which workers share total enterprise profit. Since some enterprises show greater profit than others (for a number of reasons to be explored below), profit per worker differs among enterprises. Such differences are not eliminated with time. Workers in prosperous firms continue to receive higher personal incomes for the same work than those in less successful enterprises. Although low-income workers in unprofitable enterprises may be willing to move to the high-profit enterprises, the highly paid workers would obviously object, since it would mean sharing profits among a larger number of workers. In the long run, although some additional labor will be employed in the high-profit firm as it expands, the introduction of machines which use relatively little labor will tend to perpetuate the income gap.

The Variations in Profit

Inequalities in personal income arise from differences in enterprise profits. Differences in profits, in turn, can be attributed to monopoly position or privilege, interest income, rental income or the quality of entrepreneurship.

Since the market for some goods is not expansive enough to support many suppliers, a number of producers have become monopolists and profit accordingly. In other cases, subsidies and other privileges have been granted. These factors create substantial differences in enterprise profits. Searching for equity and efficiency, the economic reform of 1965 sought to eliminate privileged positions protected by subsidies and by high tariffs.

In addition to the highly visible interest income from lending operations, there is an important implicit income source. Although the means of production are supposed to belong to society, society makes no charge for their use. The interest rate on social capital (the capital tax), always far below the equilibrium price, is scheduled to be abolished in 1970. If there is no charge to the enterprise for the use of social capital, then the enterprise itself receives the return, that is, part of the enterprise profit is really an implicit interest payment on the social capital society has placed at the firm's disposal.

The difficulty is that socially owned means of production are not distributed equally among enterprises, given their different capital endowments. If firms paid a market-clearing price for the use of social capital, this would present no problem. Capital would be just another factor in production, in this case purchased from society. This is true whether one thinks of financial capital for which the firm pays an interest charge or of capital equipment for which the firm pays a rental fee. The enterprise would receive as profits only what was left after paying for the capital. Such profits could be attributed to the entrepreneurial skill with which the firm put the capital to use. This is not the case, however. No fee is charged. Since enterprise profits include implicit interest income on social capital, and since firms differ in the amounts of capital at their disposal, profit varies from firm to firm.

In a similar manner, some portion of enterprise profits arises from unpaid rental charges for the use of scarce resources. Society fails to collect an appropriate rental fee from the firms using social property. Socialist rents are low on urban land sites and have been nonexistent in mining since 1964. The absence of rent leads to the inefficient use of such properties. It also means that enterprise profits contain implicit rental incomes. Thus, rental incomes arising from exclusive access to scarce resources are distributed unequally among firms.

The concept of profit as used by economists is crucial to the understanding of entrepreneurial income. Economists understand profit as being exclusive of the implicit return on factors of production (exclusive, that is, of interest or rent). Apart from a monopoly advantage, profits so defined can arise for several reasons. The innovative acts of entrepreneurs continually create temporary profits until the adoption of these innovations on a wide scale eliminates the initial advantage and the profits. Yet by its very nature, innovation involves risk. If managers prefer to avoid risky situations, then a price must be paid to induce risk-bearing. This will also appear as part of profit.

The Yugoslav collective is an entrepreneur. It innovates and it incurs risk. Profits are the return for its managerial activities, innovations and risk-bearing. This has long been recognized in Yugoslavia and references to socialist payments for entrepreneurship appeared as early as 1953. Aleksandar Bajt, among others, argued that, just as more productive labor receives higher wages, superior collectives should be given higher entrepreneurial incomes.[3] According to this line of reasoning, differences in entrepreneurship are yet another source of differences in profits among firms.

The traditional socialist principle of distribution—"to each according to his work"— has been revised by the Yugoslavs, becoming "to each according to the factors of production supplied by the human agent or to which the human agent has access, as valued on the (imperfect) market." This principle is scarcely distinguishable from that of private enterprise.

Privatization of Social Property

What has happened in Yugoslavia is that the social ownership of productive factors has been eroded and private ownership has been established. The concept of social ownership of productive factors, always vague, in fact proved vacuous. Gradually, certain members of society acquired effective property rights which prevailed over social property.

The erosion of social property started with the first economic reform of 1950–1954. That reform decentralized the management of existing facilities and gave each enterprise exclusive access to the social property at its disposal. In a reaction against central

[3]Bajt, *Gledista* (IX, No. 4).

administrative planning, no government organ could remove social property from the enterprise. Access to state property initially meant the right to work it; how it was to be used was to be decided by the workers in a given enterprise.

Under a socialist system, all citizens should theoretically have equal access to social property. The meaning of equal access was never made clear, and it was used variously to mean identical productivity of labor, equal personal income, equal capital-labor ratios or equal opportunity to bid for social capital under identical conditions. In fact, of course, social property is distributed unequally among the population because identical capital-labor ratios are neither necessary nor desirable. The unequal distribution of social property per employed person had no major significance for income distribution before the second reform for two reasons. Earnings generated by socially owned factors were taxed away and did not accrue to individuals; and in any event they were a minor source of influence on enterprise profits compared with subsidies, price controls, and other forms of discriminatory treatment.

The Newest Reforms

The economic reform of 1961–1965 brought a number of changes. First, subsidies and other discriminatory devices were reduced. Second, charges for social resources were virtually abolished so that the enterprise acquired exclusive right not only of access to social property but also to the income streams generated by the social property at its disposal. Finally, enterprise members gained the exclusive right to make decisions about the firm's activities and the use of profits.

As a result of these changes, members of the enterprise have acquired an exclusive right to use social property, to receive the income emanating therefrom and to distribute that income as salaries or to reinvest it. The income from social property accrues only to members of the enterprise, who have no obligation toward low-paid or unemployed workers outside the enterprise who have no access to such property. Although title to the asset remains in the name of society, the exclusive rights granted enterprise members amount to private property rights, albeit in group rather than individual form.

The mere establishment of independent enterprises subject to market forces does not necessarily transform social property into group property and impede the harmonious development of the national economy through planning. It is the decentralization of investment decisions, coupled with the reduction of taxes, particularly the elimination of charges for social resources, that make these dire predictions come true. These reforms evolved in Yugoslavia because of general dissatisfaction with the investment planners and the consequent need to provide adequate incentive for enterprise investment decisions. Whether these factors will provoke similar pressures elsewhere in East Europe remains to be seen.

Selected Bibliography

Soviet Union

Bergson, Abram. *The Economics of Soviet Planning*. New Haven: Yale University Press, 1964.

Berliner, Joseph. *Factory and Manager in the USSR*. Cambridge, Massachusetts: Harvard University Press, 1957.

Campbell, Robert W. *Soviet Economic Power: Its Organization, Growth, and Challenge*. Boston: Houghton-Mifflin, 1966.

Nove, Alec. *The Soviet Economy: An Introduction*. Rev. ed. New York: Praeger, 1965.

Schwartz, Harry. *An Introduction to the Soviet Economy*. Columbus: Charles E. Merrill, 1968.

China

Chao, Kang. *Agricultural Production in Communist China*. Madison, Wisconsin: University of Wisconsin Press, 1970.

Chen Nai-Ruenn and Galenson, Walter. *The Chinese Economy under Communism*. Chicago: Aldine, 1969.

Eckstein, Alexander, Galenson, Walter, and Liu Ta-chung, eds. *Economic Trends in Communist China*. Chicago: Aldine, 1968.

King, Frank H. H. *A Concise Economic History of Modern China (1840–1961)*. New York: Praeger, 1968.

Perkins, Dwight H. *Agricultural Development in China: 1368–1968*. Chicago: Aldine, 1968.

Prybyla, Jan S. *The Political Economy of Communist China*. Scranton, Pennsylvania: International Textbook Company, 1970.

Richman, Barry M. *Industrial Society in Communist China*. New York: Random House, 1969.

United States Congress Joint Economic Committee. *People's Republic of China: An Economic Assessment*. Washington, D.C.: U.S. Government Printing Office, 1972.

Wu Yuan-li, ed. *China: A Handbook*. New York: Praeger, 1973.

Yugoslavia

Bicanic, Rudolf. *Economic Policy in Socialist Yugoslavia.* New York: Cambridge University Press, 1973.

Dirlam, Joel B., and Plummer, James L. *An Introduction to the Yugoslav Economy.* Columbus: Charles E. Merrill, 1973.

Hamilton, F. E. Ian. *Yugoslavia: Patterns of Economic Activity.* London: G. Bell and Sons, Ltd., 1968.

Milenkovitch, Deborah. *Planning and Market in Yugoslav Economic Thought.* New Haven: Yale University Press, 1971.

Vanek, Jaroslav. *The Participatory Economy.* Ithaca, New York: Cornell University Press, 1971.

Wachtel, Howard M. *Workers' Management and Workers' Wages in Yugoslavia.* Ithaca, New York: Cornell University Press, 1973.

FOREIGN POLICY AND INTERNATIONAL AFFAIRS

At a time when trade, communication, and even travel between the United States and the Communist countries seem to be expanding, Americans (and indeed citizens of all Western nations) are more interested than ever in the apparent intentions of the Communist states—not only toward the non-Communist bloc, but toward one another. In short, what can we expect of the Communists? As we examine the foreign policies of the various Communist states, and contemplate our expectations of each, a number of questions necessarily come to mind. Are Communist states— say, the Soviet Union, China, and Yugoslavia—dedicated to the idea of world revolution, or have they adopted a policy of peaceful coexistence? If they are pursuing a policy of revolution, is it a strategy inspired and guided by Marxist principles, or is it one determined by the national goals of several self-interested, secular nation-states? If they embrace coexistence, is this shift a consequence of various manipulations of the Marxist faith, or of the protective instincts of an increasingly conservative coterie of leaders whose primary concern is preservation of the status quo? And, whatever the policy, do the Communist nations present a united front, or is there serious dissension among some of them: for example, is the so-called Sino-Soviet dispute really a dispute or merely a ploy to deceive the Western powers into relaxing their defenses?

These and other questions on Communist behavior are of vital importance today. At a time when governments of both Communist and non-Communist blocs are capable of destroying the world, it is essential that we understand the issues surrounding such questions, as well as the facts and forces behind Communist behavior and our responses to them. To do so, we must consider the three systems separately as we ask ourselves if, how, and to what degree the behavior of each is influenced by the two most often cited foreign policy determinants—namely, the Marxist guide to action and the national self-interests of the state.

It may be instructive at this point to review the past foreign policies of Communist states. Let us begin with the Russian revolution in 1917, a time when Soviet leaders and supporters expected the capitalist states of the Western world to fall to the "inevitable proletarian revolutions," and therefore, follow the Bolshevik lead. Thus, from 1917 until the autumn of 1924, the prevailing international policy of the Bolsheviks was based on Trotsky's theory of "permanent revolution" (formulated in 1905) and the subsequent pronouncements made at the Third International Party Congress, held in March 1919. At this Congress, Lenin told the delegates, "It is inconceivable that the Soviet Republic should continue to exist for a long period side by side with imperialist states. Ultimately one or the other must conquer." According to the Leninist and Trotskyite theories, it was impossible for Russia to establish a stable socialist state in an otherwise imperialist world. The Communists expected that the class struggle would express itself elsewhere in the form of other national struggles between the capitalist and socialist camps. They believed that their own camp would win, and all that remained was a small amount of patience and faith in the Marxist dialectic.

However, when the proletarian revolutions and Communist victories failed to materialize (the attempted uprisings in Berlin, Munich, and Budapest proved to be abortive), the Soviets began to turn their attention from international to domestic concerns, as evidenced by Stalin's eventual pronouncement of the doctrine of "socialism in one country." With this policy, Stalin undertook the task of replacing the international and revolutionary approach of Trotsky with a new doctrine that emphasized a domestic goal—namely, the building of socialism in the USSR. After this dramatic break from the more revolutionary international strategy of the past, a conservative force emerged and became increasingly apparent in the foreign policy of the Communist party states.

However, since Communist sympathizers and supporters throughout the world continued to look to the Soviets for international leadership and inspiration, most Communist revolutionaries in other countries gained directives and at least token support from Soviet leaders throughout the 1930s and 40s. The Comintern, designed to provide some unifying organization of the Communist movement, was Soviet controlled and directed. Then, upon the end of World War II, communism became successfully established in other countries—first Eastern Europe, then Asia. Although the Soviet Union continued to adhere to an essentially conservative foreign policy, the international aspect of the Communist movement appeared healthy and growing stronger.

The facade of a strong and united Communist front was short lived, however, and was soon replaced by evident disunity among the Communist states that still exist today. The causes of the disunity were varied and complex, but three events seem to be of central importance. The first was Tito's successful challenge of Stalin and the Soviets in 1947. For the first time, a dedicated Communist leader from a small and less-developed European country successfully challenged and finally disobeyed the Soviets. And what was most damaging to Soviet leadership and Communist unity was that Tito survived and has prospered in spite of his independence from the Soviet bloc. The second event contributing to disunity in the Communist world was Khrushchev's Secret Speech to the 20th Party Congress of the CPSU in February 1956, in which he denounced Stalin and implicitly admitted to the fallibility of the Soviet road to Communism. The third cause was the rise of Communist China and the conflict of interests that developed between the Chinese and the Soviet leaders. The combined effect of these three factors crushed the goal of Communist unity, and ultimately, led to the dissolution of the ideal of a united front. Taking its place was a divided and polycentric Communist world, consisting of many "centers" of Communist power, each with its own patterns of international behavior.[1]

Although we will not attempt to discuss in detail the determinants theoretically affecting Communist behavior, it does seem reasonable to suggest that a good part of Communist behavior results from a combination of the two influences mentioned at the beginning of this introduction—Marxist principles and national self-interest. Thus, if we look at the historical evolution of Communist foreign policy, there is no denying that past and contemporary Communist leaders have traditionally been guided by certain ideological principles when weighing various strategies and policies in the international sphere. However, since their policies in response to similar events can be highly dissimilar, it would appear that national interests can significantly affect and sometimes transcend the "universally accepted" and more ideological motivated prescriptions of Marxism.

If we examine the first influence—the prescriptions of official Marxist-Leninist doctrine—more closely, we note certain common elements to which all Communist states subscribe. At the core of the doctrine is the tenet that the world is divided into two opposing camps, the capitalist

---

[1]There is, of course, one major and important exception to the idea of polycentrism: Eastern Europe. Thus, when referring to Eastern Europe, we can accurately speak of the Soviet "bloc" with the power center being Moscow. At the same time, we should not overemphasize Soviet influence in Eastern Europe, and should draw attention to the various challenges emanating from each of the East European states upon Soviet influence.

and the socialist. It is further asserted that the internal contradictions in the capitalist system are such that these inferior states are destined to a future of inevitable decline. In contrast, the socialist systems can be expected to increase in numbers and strength, owing to the superiority in their social and economic systems. Finally, Marxist doctrine asserts that conflicts between these two camps are inevitable because the capitalist forces are unwilling to acquiesce to the inevitable rise of the socialists. However, these elementary points of agreement notwithstanding, the doctrine neglects to specify details, and a variety of interpretations are possible. For example, the form or nature of the conflicts to occur between the two opposing camps is not indicated: is it to be a peaceful and primarily economic rivalry? or an ideologically based propaganda war (such as the Cold War that began in the late 1940s and endured into the 1960s)? or one erupting into violent confrontations (such as those in Korea and Vietnam) and perhaps ultimately into nuclear conflagration?

There is, then, no one Communist policy. In the history of the Soviet Union alone, policies have varied from the extremely revolutionary approach espoused by Trotsky to the more conservative line advocated by Stalin and followed, at least implicitly, by subsequent Soviet leaders. But as Soviet action turned inward, the Maoist variant developing in China resembled more and more the Trotskyite prescription. While Khrushchev spoke of "peaceful coexistence" during the 1950s and 60s, Mao was espousing the radical slogan "Make Revolution."[2] At the same time, Tito and the Yugoslavs were adhering to a "diplomacy of balance," emphasizing peace and security in an attempt to protect their highly valued national sovereignty. This meant maintaining a delicate balance between the Communist and non-Communist world, while simultaneously attempting to generate a "nonaligned movement" among the countries of the Third World. Without going into further detail on the various approaches by the different leaders today, we can easily recognize that the Marxist guide to action is not of ultimate explanatory value in explaining why certain Communist states behave as they do. If it were, we would observe more uniformity of strategies and policies and certainly less bickering (both within and among the individual Communist states) about their goals. What is it then that accounts for the great variability in foreign policy among the Marxist states?

The second influence on Communist foreign policy—and one that often transcends the first, the ideology—is a particular regime's view of the world from the perspective of its own national self-interest. This world view seems in turn to be influenced by a variety of other factors, such as the historical conditions defining the regime's advent to power, the contempo-

---

[2] In point of fact there was very little Chinese involvement in "making revolution" over this span of years. Nowhere were the Chinese important participants in attempts to overthrow capitalist governments. Recently, the Chinese have softened their rhetoric bringing it more in line with their less revolutionary behavior.

rary environmental realities characterizing the state's existence, and the particular personality types making up the state's leadership organization. These factors combined can be a rather strong predictor of the state's policy in the international arena. For example, it has been proposed that Chinese foreign policy is defined largely by her bitter grievances of the past and the unique Maoist revolutionary experience. That is, such historical humiliations as the Opium Wars, the unequal treaties, and encroachment upon Chinese territory by foreign imperialists, as well as the Chinese revolutionary struggle, guerrilla warfare against the imperialists, political victory through military preparedness—all have affected current Chinese thinking and behavior in international events in the contemporary world. In the Soviet and Yugoslav histories, other factors—for example, the Soviet experiences during the two World Wars, and Yugoslavia's expulsion from the Cominform—have been of vital importance in defining the world view of each, and in rendering that view distinct from the others.

In conclusion, the foreign policies of Communist party states should not and cannot be viewed as a monolithic, united front. One must study them separately, keeping in mind that a variety of factors ultimately affect the final shaping of foreign policy behavior. Finally, although all Communist policy might be viewed as having some basis in Marxist doctrine, all are shaped also by a variety of influences indigenous or unique to a particular national setting.

The readings by Vernon V. Aspaturian, A. Doak Barnett, and Robin Alison Remington contain some salient points that are useful in explaining the present policies of these states toward the rest of the world, and toward one another.

First, there has been an increasing willingness of the three Communist countries to extend the offer of peaceful coexistence to non-Communist nations, including the United States. This is explained by the growing self-confidence of the Communist governments in their own success, their desire to exert their influence among the nonaligned nations (especially by bestowing economic and military aid), and the slow disintegration of the so-called Communist bloc.

Second, their openness toward the United States, on the part of the Soviet Union and China in particular, is directly related to the degree of tension and antagonism they display toward each other. Peaceful coexistence with the United States, then, is a useful approach for China, according to Barnett, as long as she believes Soviet Communism to be a departure from Marxism, and she views a million or so Soviet troops poised along their long, common boundary. Aspaturian sees little change in Soviet foreign policy as long as Moscow believes that "only China . . . poses a direct threat to the Soviet territory and at the same time is in a position to threaten the Soviet Union with means other than nuclear weapons."

Third, all three readings tie the continuation of such policies of peaceful coexistence to the successful operation of domestic affairs in the Communist countries. For example, the direction and degree of involvement in world affairs for the Soviet Union and Yugoslavia may depend upon how successfully they continue to manage the varied and many national minorities in their countries. Another example might be the way all three governments confront any problem of succession to head of state.

Finally, all the authors agree that there is greater suspicion and fear within the Communist countries of aggression by another Communist state than of aggression by a non-Communist nation. This fact may have as much influence on their international policies as any other single factor.

25

Moscow's Options
in a Changing World

Vernon V. Aspaturian

[Since the late 1960s] there has been a dramatic transformation in the fortunes of Soviet foreign policy and a remarkable revitalization of Soviet decisiveness and self-assurance in foreign affairs. The Soviet leadership appears to have overcome much of its previous feelings of inferiority and inadequacy in facing up to the manifold issues that confronted it both as a global power and as the leader of an ecumenical revolutionary movement. Only in dealing with the Chinese do the Soviet leaders fail to exude the self-confidence they have acquired . . . and instead continue to betray signs of irresolution, uncertainty of purpose, and indecisiveness. There are good explanations for these distinctive Soviet postures in dealing with the West and with China, just as there was considerable warrant for the irresolution and demoralization that characterized the Soviet leadership in foreign affairs between 1961 and 1968.

The Period of Defeatism, 1961–1968

Before 1968, the Soviet leadership was divided, hesitant, and confused about its direction in foreign policy. On the global level, its ambitions were blocked by the United States; within its own Communist world, it was challenged by the Chinese, and its East European empire appeared to be in the throes of dissolution as individual countries responded favorably to the seductive siren calls of the Johnson administration's "bridge-building" policy and the Erhard-Kiesinger brand of Western German *Ost-politik*. The Soviet leadership, sitting in Moscow, seemed gripped by paralysis as Czecho-slovakia under Dubcek appeared to be slipping out of the Communist community. But the Czechoslovak Spring was only the latest in a succession of minor and major disasters in Soviet foreign policy since the Berlin crisis of 1961 and the Cuban missile crisis of October 1962. Although the Partial Nuclear Test-Ban Treaty of July 1963 had stabilized Soviet-American relations, the embryonic condominium that it established worked clearly to the advantage of the United States, the most powerful of the dyarchs. The Soviet position in world affairs, instead of being enhanced by the Khrushchev

From Vernon V. Aspaturian, "Moscow's Options in a Changing World," *Problems of Communism* (Vol. XXI, No. 4, July–August 1972), pp. 1-20. [Reprinted with permission from the publisher.]

detente, was diminished to that of a tired, worn-out revolutionary power content with permanent status as "Number 2," while the United States was left free to flex its diplomatic and military muscles all over the world and to undermine the Soviet position in Eastern Europe with subtle policies of "bridge-building" and "peaceful engagement." Although the Johnson administration faithfully refrained from aggressive and overtly hostile moves against the Soviet position in Eastern Europe, its selective enticement of individual Communist states proved to be a device against which the unimaginative Soviet leaders had no defense except military intervention to arrest the growing forces of autonomy. Furthermore, China had been progressively transformed from an alienated ally into a hostile and threatening neighbor, the world Communist movement was fractured and demoralized, and the national liberation movement was deprived of its protective umbrella.

Confident of its superior power and relying on a prudent Soviet Union to refrain from any action that might endanger Soviet-American collaboration, the United States in 1965 massively escalated the war in Vietnam against Moscow's North Vietnamese ally and landed Marines in the Dominican Republic to prevent the establishment of a revolutionary-minded regime. Furthermore, not only in Moscow but also in Belgrade, Cairo, and elsewhere, particularly after the Arab-Israeli war of 1967, the impression that the Johnson administration had been using the detente not to preserve international stability but to mount a cleverly conceived political offensive against Soviet and radical nationalist positions all over the world achieved widespread acceptance. The Dominican affair, the ousters of President Sukarno in Indonesia and of João Goulart in Brazil, the fall of Kwame Nkrumah in Ghana, the overthrow of Mohammed Ben Bella in Algeria, the Greek military takeover, and finally the Israeli attack upon Egypt appeared to many in Moscow as part of an overall United States design. . . .

Only in the Middle East, where Khrushchev's successors embarked upon a bold effort to develop a Soviet sphere of interest in the Eastern Mediterranean through the transformation of Egypt into a client-state, did it appear that the new leaders were making headway. But this effort also culminated in a debacle of substantial magnitude as the tremendous Soviet investment in Egypt was incinerated by Israel in the lightning six-day war of June 1967. The defeat of Moscow's Arab client-states was a humiliating and sobering experience, and it perhaps convinced the Soviet leaders that unless they altered their behavior, they might sink in the morass of defeatism.

The generally defeatist, hesitant, and vacillating mood of the Soviet leadership continued to manifest itself for over a year as Moscow helplessly watched developments in Czechoslovakia (and to a lesser extent in Romania) approach a climax that could prove catastrophic for the Soviet Union. The Soviet leaders opted at this stage to adapt and adjust to the developing situation in Czechoslovakia, not only out of a sense of responsibility and prudence but also out of fear of the consequences of forcible Soviet intervention, particularly if it were to fail.

Revival of Self-Confidence

But in the meantime there had been several developments that impelled the Soviet leaders to risk a reversal of their previous pattern of behavior and to act more militantly. First of all, the gap in strategic capabilities between the Soviet Union and the United States had narrowed considerably, thus diminishing the risk of American counteraction. Secondly, the United States itself was gripped by domestic turmoil that caused President Johnson not to seek a second term, which meant that the United States would be temporarily governed by a lame-duck President less likely to act vigorously in countering Moscow. Third, the U.S. President was psychologically vulnerable because he was anxious to cap his political career by making a state visit to Moscow and was therefore predisposed not to react in a way that might result in the cancellation of his prospective trip. And fourth, the Chinese leadership was involved in a debilitating internal power struggle that deprived it, too, of the capacity to react effectively.

Whereas the Israeli defeat of Egypt in 1967 had had a traumatic impact in Moscow, the successful outcome of the decision to intervene in Czechoslovakia seems to have had an electrifying effect upon the Soviet leaders. Since that time, they have appeared more decisive, self-assured, and confident in the correctness of their judgments. The regime has been considerably strengthened, and although Brezhnev still has his critics and detractors, his position in the leadership has been conspicuously enhanced. The most immediate manifestation of this new self-confidence was the enunciation of the Brezhnev Doctrine wherein Moscow announced in advance that the Soviet Union would no longer tolerate any internal or external challenge to its authority and hegemony in Eastern Europe.[1]

The reassertion of Soviet self-confidence has produced dramatic results in the form of a string of successes in foreign policy since the Czechoslovak occupation, and this has continued to reinforce Soviet self-assurance. The most important practical results have been the reversal by the Brandt government of the Erhard-Kiesinger *Ostpolitik* and the halting of the Western policy of "bridge-building" to Eastern Europe with the formal acceptance by the Western powers of the post-World War II East European status quo.[2] Juridically this has been expressed in the two treaties concluded by West Germany with Poland and the Soviet Union, the Quadripartite Agreement on Berlin signed on September 3, 1971, Bonn's instrument of adherence to the Treaty on the Non-Proliferation of Nuclear Weapons, and other related documents.

Although the original reach of the Brezhnev Doctrine has been contracted somewhat to exclude Yugoslavia, the Soviet sphere in Eastern Europe has been largely stabilized, with the defiance of Romania considerably muted. The reassertion of Soviet confidence may also have been instrumental in impelling the Soviet Union to confront the Chinese militarily on the Ussuri in early 1969—a confrontation which seemingly achieved its immediate aim of frightening the Chinese, but was also instrumental in persuading the Chinese to mend their fences with the United States. Just as the China problem has been an important stimulus to the USSR to reach agreements in the West, the Soviet problem has impelled China to move toward the West as well, given favorable circumstances. To this degree, the Soviet reassertion of confidence may have set in motion patterns of realignment that will have long-range implications.

The revival of Soviet self-confidence has left its imprint not only in Central and Eastern Europe but also in other parts of the world where the Soviet Union has undertaken the commitments of a global power. The decisive nature of Soviet action in Czechoslovakia and its salutary impact (from the Soviet point of view) on West Germany, the United States and NATO, and others, aroused expectations—on the part of Moscow's non-Communist client-states—of more credible Soviet commitments, and these expectations were reciprocated by Soviet willingness to give these commitments

---

[1]For a discussion of the broad implications of the Brezhnev Doctrine, see the author's *Process and Power in Soviet Foreign Policy* (Boston: Little, Brown, 1971).

[2]For further elaboration see the author's "Soviet Aims in East Europe," *Current History* (October 1970).

formal juridical expression. Thus, during [the period 1971–72], the Soviet Union . . . signed no less than three "Treaties of Peace, Friendship and Mutual Assistance" with non-Communist states: Egypt, India and Iraq, in that order. While these treaties are not formal treaties of alliance, they can only be defined as proto-military alliances, since a common feature is that their provisions are so devised that the stronger party can, if it wishes, come to the assistance of the weaker in accordance with the articles dealing with "mutual consultations" and "appropriate effective measures" in the event of attack or threat of attack. Furthermore, each of these . . . Soviet treaty partners is the beneficiary of increased Soviet military and economic assistance. In short, the treaties convert all three countries into *de jure* client-states and *de facto* protectorates of the Soviet Union.[3]

The treaty with India, moreover, effectively eviscerates the legal remains of the Sino-Soviet military alliance in the event of a Sino-Indian war. Indeed, during the Indo-Pakistan war of late 1971 it was revealed that the Soviet Union engaged in "appropriate effective measures" to deter the Chinese from supplying material assistance to Pakistan, including the discrete movement of Soviet troops along the Chinese border. Conversely, the treaty formally involves India in the Soviet encirclement and containment of China, a matter which will be discussed later in another connection.

The Shifting Strategic Balance

What accounts for this resurgence of self-confidence in the Soviet leadership, and how will it affect future Soviet behavior in world affairs? The first question is easier to answer than the second, because the new horizons created for Soviet foreign policy by the factors which have brought about the recrudescence of Soviet self-assurance are many, and the Soviet leaders themselves remain sharply divided as to whether they should use the occasion to exercise self-restraint and magnanimously agree to choices that would reduce international tensions or to opt for policies designed to exploit to the maximum whatever momentary advantage exists.

In any event, the Soviet leaders appear to have become persuaded, soon after their remarkably smooth operation in Czechoslovakia, that the conditions and circumstances that enabled them to act decisively and successfully in that instance were not momentarily fortuitous but represented a condition of flux in the military, political, and psychological balance of power that would continue for some time. The Soviet reappraisal of power trends since 1968 seems to stress three major elements. First of all, it takes cognizance of the extraordinary growth of Soviet strategic and conventional military capabilities, which has brought the armed strength of the USSR up to rough parity with [4] Second, it sees a corresponding decline of the relative strategic power of the United States resulting in part from the costs of the Vietnam war and

---

[3]Full texts of the treaties with Egypt and India can be found, respectively, in *Pravda,* May 28, 1971 and *Izvestia,* Aug. 10, 1971. The chief distinction between the two treaties is that the Egyptian treaty contains provisions relating to "cooperation in the military field." Article 8 reads: "Such cooperation will provide, in particular, for assistance in the training of UAR military personnel and in mastering the armaments and equipment delivered to the United Arab Republic for the purpose of increasing its capability for eliminating the consequences of aggression, as well as for increasing its ability to withstand aggression in general." There is no counterpart to this article in the treaty with India. . . .

[4]See, for the most recent data, *The Military Balance, 1971–1972,* London, Institute for Strategic Studies, 1971; and for a trenchant analysis, Walter D. Jacobs, "Soviet Strategic Effectiveness," *Journal of International Affairs* (Vol. 26, No. 1, 1972).

in part from U.S. volitional restraints on further quantitative armaments expansion. Third, it posits an increasing American infirmity of purpose and weakening of will and commitment brought about by domestic turbulence, by racial and generational conflict, and by the social ideological, and political polarization that has resulted. What in 1968 appeared to Moscow to be perhaps just a momentary upsurge of public demoralization and disillusionment with the Johnson administration over Vietnam now seems to the Kremlin to have the character of a continuing and more enduring condition.

Among other causes of the revival of Soviet self-confidence, one might mention the resurgence of anti-American revolutionary movements, forces and regimes of various hues in the Third World and elsewhere. Although the Soviet reception of such revolutionary movements is mixed because they often represent kaleidoscopic melanges of sectarian and Peking-inspired groupings that at best may be of marginal value to Soviet policy and sometimes may even be counterproductive, the proliferation of these groups is usually accepted by Soviet strategists as further evidence of the disintegration and dissolution of the fabric of bourgeois and feudal societies.

As a consequence of all these factors, there has been a remarkable revitalization of Soviet will and a dramatic expansion of Soviet capabilities. Before World War II, the Soviet leaders possessed the will and were gripped by a fanatic focalized purpose, but they were bereft of capabilities; after the war they possessed both, but unfortunately for Moscow, the United States possessed even more of both essential ingredients, with the result that for more than two decades the Soviet Union was compelled to play second fiddle to the United States on the world stage. Today, there is little doubt that the Soviet Union, if it cannot boast a clear or even meaningful superiority, is at least no longer second to the United States in strategic weapons capability.[5]

If the old bipolar international system were still functioning, with just two players opposing each other in a dangerous sort of zero-sum game, this development would be cause for grave alarm in an immediate operational sense. But the international system is no longer bipolarized, and power is no longer—if it ever was in its entirety—distributed and redistributed within the context of a zero-sum game. Other powers, particularly China, have assumed a greater importance, and although they are not sufficiently powerful to challenge the two global powers, they are sufficiently influential, individually in some cases and collectively in any event, to seriously alter the balance between the two global giants and thus to function as objective and prescriptive balancing actors.

For this reason, while most members of the world community—with only the clear exception of China—are fundamentally interested in a meaningful rapprochement or détente between the United States and the Soviet Union, they share with the Chinese an opposition to any arrangement that would be tantamount to a condominium or dyarchy, with or without a division of the globe into spheres of influence. Today, at least three secondary power centers (Japan, China, Western Europe) and possibly India are too powerful to be subordinated or assimilated into a sphere of influence of the global powers. The United States and the Soviet Union individually still remain in a distinct class by themselves in terms of power magnitude—possessing together perhaps 90 percent of effective operational strategic power in the international community—and could conceivably impose solutions upon the rest of the world if they were able to act in concert and with a unified will. Such a true dyarchy, however, no longer seems possible,

---

[5]While the Soviet leadership shows an awareness of this new state of affairs, Soviet military writers continue to stress the expansion of U.S. strategic capabilities. For example, see Col. V. Kharich, "The Strategic Arms Race in the USA: Reliance of Nuclear Might," *Krasnaia zvezda,* July 16, 1971.

and any attempt by the two global powers to impose solutions on the secondary power centers, increasingly sensitive and alert to any such tendency, could be expected to meet with more intensive and extensive defiance and incur higher costs than previously.

Internal Debate on Global Strategy

These fortuitous changes in the strategic balance create both opportunities and risks for the Soviet leaders. They provide Moscow with a wider range of options, including some that would stabilize the existing situation and reduce international tensions as well as others that would expand Soviet power and influence at the risk of generating greater tensions and dangers. As in the past, these choices can be expected to divide the Soviet leadership, but whereas before 1968 the divisions reflected a condition of relative Soviet strategic inferiority, since 1968 they have revolved around options created by the growth of Soviet power and the contraction of American global commitments. The Kremlin's choices, however, are complicated by the fact that Chinese power has also grown qualitatively during this period. The Soviet Union, unlike the United States, now finds itself vulnerable to nuclear devastation from two directions, and some Soviet leaders tend to see the problem as one of how to take advantage of the new strategic balance while China is still relatively weak. For the Chinese, on the other hand, the question is how to postpone a showdown with the USSR while they are still weak. The immediate resolutions of these interlocking sets of problems have apparently been separate decisions by Moscow and Peking to reduce tensions with the United States. These decisions suggest that both Communist powers no longer see the United States as posing an immediate threat to themselves—or rather that each of them views the other as a greater threat to its own interests than the United States.

The evidence is strong that elements in both the Chinese and Soviet leaderships perceive the lessening threat from the United States as reflecting American decline, although some Soviet commentators warn that the U.S. retreat from globalism, rather than reflecting a crippling of objective potential, is volitional and represents merely a temporary phase of debilitation of will stemming from disappointment and disillusionment over the costs, both domestic and foreign, of trying to police the world. Given the immense industrial and technological capacity of the United States, according to this view, the situation could once again change very quickly if the American public should become sufficiently aroused to resume the arms race. Hence, there have been powerful voices in and around the Soviet leadership arguing that the time is ripe for a stabilization of the arms race at current levels, since it would provide Moscow with ample "sufficiency" to pursue its aims without provoking fears in America that might refuel demands for an escalation in U.S. capabilities. These voices still recall with concern the consequences of Khrushchev's irresponsible bluffing in the late 1950s which gave rise to the "missile gap" myth in the United States and the consequent spurt in American strategic capabilities.[6]

---

[6]For example, in what might be considered a cautionary warning that a policy based on achieving Soviet superiority might simply refuel the arms race and backfire, Georgi Arbatov, director of the Soviet Academy of Sciences' Institute of the USA, points out that during "the very alarming experience of the previous decade, the 1960s . . . the USA's strategic arsenal increased by 10 to 12 times. An aggressive war against the Vietnamese people was started. Israel launched aggression against the Arab states. . . . And in 1962, as a result of the Carribbean crisis, the USA and the USSR found themselves rather close to the brink of war. . . . If the 1970s are merely a repetition of the 1960s . . . peace may be seriously jeopardized." "A Step in the Interests of Peace," SShA—Ekonomika, Politika, Ideologiia (November 1971), p. 56.

Furthermore, a detente with the United States, and with NATO generally, would defuse international tensions, stabilize the status quo in Germany to Soviet advantage, reconfirm Western recognition of Eastern Europe as a Soviet sphere of interest, and open up vast opportunities for expanding trade and commercial relations with the industrial capitalist states. The Soviet leadership is particularly eager to import advanced technology from the United States, especially in the computer realm, and is interested in importing consumer goods which its own economy is unable to deliver in sufficient quantities, as well as entire factory installations. Finally, détente with the United States and the West, in addition to protecting Russia's western flank in the event of a conflict with China, would create the conditions for a shift in economic priorities away from heavy industry and defense to consumer goods, light industry, agriculture, and public services.

The controversy over options in Soviet foreign policy thus merges with the debate over economic priorities. For decades now, the continuing postponement of priorities for the consumer sector has been officially justified in terms of Soviet foreign policy obligations and security considerations. Soviet Premier Kosygin's revelation at the 24th Party Congress that the Soviet military establishment had been absorbing about 25 percent of all funds available for economic development over the preceding five years was tantamount to an accusation that development of the consumer sector of the economy was being frustrated by the terrible appetites of the military, whose chief spokesman at the Congress, Defense Minister Marshal A. A. Grechko, demanded an even larger share of the nation's resources as he continued to emphasize that the United States and NATO were plotting aggressive actions and spending huge sums on armaments in order to dictate to the Soviet Union from "a position of strength."[7]

As Soviet policy has tended to become increasingly oriented toward internal constituencies, various groups, institutions, and personalities have become polarized into two competing constellations: a security-productionist-ideological grouping and a consumptionist-agricultural-public services grouping, which take opposite stands with reference to the distribution of investments, resources, and expenditures on the basis of their conflicting assumptions and/or expectations concerning the likelihood of heightened international tensions or of a relaxation *cum* détente.[8] This issue has agitated the Soviet leadership since Stalin's death, the basic arguments remaining relatively intact as leading political personalities changed sides and exchanged arguments in accordance with their political and factional interests at any given time. Thus, Khrushchev, when he was challenging Malenkov before 1955, emerged as a leader of the security-productionist-ideological forces against Malenkov, but once he became firmly

---

[7]*Pravda*, April 7, 1971.

[8]The conflicting views of these opposed interest groupings have found frequent expression in Soviet writings. For example, an exponent of the consumptionist viewpoint, commending Soviet efforts to lower international tensions and check the arms race, wrote in 1969 that "experience has proven that only under conditions of a relaxation of tensions is it possible to concentrate a maximum of resources for accomplishing plans for the building of communism" (K. P. Ivanov, *Leninskie osnovy vneshnei politiki SSSR* [Leninist Fundamentals of the Foreign Policy of the USSR], Moscow, 1969, p. 50). On the other hand, a military spokesman, writing in the offical organ of the Soviet Defense Ministry, paraphrased Lenin in an effort to imply that no ceiling should be placed on military spending. "Everyone will agree," he wrote, "that an army that does not train itself to master all arms, all means and methods of warfare that the enemy possesses, *or may possess,* is behaving in an unwise or even criminal manner." (A. Lagovsky, "The State's Economy and Its Military Might," *Krasnaia zvezda*, Sept. 25, 1969).

installed in power after July 1957, he switched over to the consumptionist-agricultural-public services constellation.[9]

By and large, Brezhnev and Kosygin have attempted to steer a middle course between the two principal demand-sector coalitions. Although on balance the military and heavy industry groups appear to have increased their influence in shaping Soviet priorities and their preferences continue to be favored over those of the consumptionists, the regime has compromised the issue by simultaneously supporting both détente abroad and a high level of defense expenditures and priority for heavy industry at home in an endeavor to demonstrate that détente policies need not lead to an immediate re-orientation of budgetary priorities detrimental to the interests of the military and heavy industry. However, stepped-up Soviet military commitments to Egypt, stronger political commitments to India, the growing Chinese nuclear capability, the deteriorating situation in Czechoslovakia before August 1968, and the ambivalent character of the defense debate in the United States have all had a part in reinforcing the skepticism of the military and their allies as to the desirability of détente-oriented policies. Furthermore, it is possible that the military's opposition to détente policies is also motivated by expectations of new opportunities for the expansion of Soviet influence as the strategic power balance vis-à-vis the United States becomes more favorable. At the same time, Soviet military leaders apparently perceive that the exploitation of these opportunities will involve risks, and this in turn leads them to keep on pressing for higher margins of safety and hence greater defense expenditures.

The Kremlin's Options

The revival of Soviet self-confidence, the changes in the strategic balance, America's redefinition of its global role, and China's efforts to force her way into the global club have combined to present Moscow with a variety of discrete options in the choice of grand strategy. Some of these, if elected, could plunge the world into a new era of violence, uncertainty, turbulence, and confrontation; others might provide the foundations for mutually agreed-upon adjustments and arrangements of outstanding questions, thus ushering in a long era of negotiation and reduced tensions. Whatever choices are made by the Kremlin, they will inevitably be affected by domestic Soviet interests as well as by the external environment, and all the available options involve both dangers and opportunities for the Soviet leaders. What these options are with primary reference to dealing with the United States on the global strategic level may be briefly summarized as follows:

(1) *Strategic superiority.* This would require the retention of current economic priorities and continuous maximization of Soviet power in order to achieve a permanent, clear-cut superiority over both the United States and China, individually and jointly. Such a policy would be based upon the assumption that the Soviet Union will be more able than was the United States to convert military muscle into diplomatic and foreign policy gains because Soviet power will be consonant with the rhythm of historical processes whereas U.S. power attempted to arrest and reverse the wheels of history and consequently was crippled by the weight of its own internal contradictions. This policy would, in effect, result in the unilateral assertion by Moscow of a role as "world gendarme" with all that that would imply: threats, intervention, imposition of solutions upon local conflicts, and continuous global surveillance.

---

[9]See H. S. Dinerstein, *War and the Soviet Union* (New York: Praeger, 1959).

(2) *Condominium/détente based upon Soviet strategic superiority.* This policy would be similar to the first, except that it would not require the same magnitude of superiority because it would involve a limited détente relationship with the United States. As Moscow would not challenge the security or vital interests of the United States directly, the policy would be less likely to arouse the kind of fears and anxieties that might provoke the American public to support another round in the arms race. In addition, it would envisage expanded commercial contacts with the West, enabling the Soviet Union to exploit the tremendous industrial and technological resources of the capitalist world and thus to lessen the pressures for an immediate shift in internal economic and budgetary priorities; but cultural contacts would remain minimal, and there would probably be a tightening of ideological controls. Finally, this option, which presupposes further and perhaps escalating conflict with China, would permit Moscow to concentrate on the Chinese danger without at the same time forfeiting the right to make gains at the expense of its capitalist American partner at the global level—a right which would be impaired if Moscow were to accept a limited sphere of interest temporarily off limits to Soviet intrusion.

(3) *Condominium/détente based upon strategic parity.* This option would more accurately resemble a condominium or dyarchy based upon an authentic détente relationship. Such a policy would involve formal agreements establishing both *quantitative* ceilings and limitations on *qualitative* development and deployment of weapons; furthermore, it would require agreement on joint measures to keep other powers in check by enforcing the nuclear non-proliferation agreements and obtaining ceilings on the development of capabilities by other nuclear powers (France, Britain and China). Beyond this, there would be a clear though tacit and indirect demarcation of U.S. and Soviet spheres of influence; joint action would be taken to resolve selected local conflicts; agreements would be devised to allow continuing rivalry in marginal and peripheral areas of the world involving minimal risks of direct confrontation and nuclear war. Most importantly, this option—in calling for a wider orbit of cooperation and a more restricted arena of rivalry than does the preceding option—would create the conditions for a drastic shift in Soviet domestic economic and budgetary priorities and a restructuring of the distribution of social and political power in Soviet society; hence, it is vigorously opposed by the Soviet military-industrial complex embracing the military professionals, the defense industries, heavy industry, and key personalities in the party apparatus. Advocates of this policy, on the other hand, wish not only to solve internal economic problems but also to diminish the disproportionate influence of the Soviet military-industrial complex and enhance that of other social and functional institutions and groups in Soviet society. The policy would perhaps allow a wider degree of cultural, educational, and scientific exchanges, but even under this option Moscow would not formally relinquish its broad ideological goals or accept "ideological coexistence" as the basis for agreement.

(4) *Entente with the United States.* An entente would involve radical changes in Soviet attitudes tantamount to agreement on first principles with the United States. It is doubtful that any serious sentiment exists within the inner circles of Soviet power for this option, although some progressive and democratic intellectual groups centering upon individuals like the dissident nuclear physicist Andrei Sakharov advocate what amounts to an entente relationship.[10] Thus, the "democratic movement" in Russia

---

[10]See Andrei Sakharov, *Progress, Coexistence and Intellectual Freedom* (New York: W. W. Norton and Co., 1968).

calls not only for administrative reforms designed to enhance efficiency, but also for drastic political and social reforms that would indeed result in the possibility of agreement on first principles with the United States.

(5) *Triarchy with the United States and China.* This also is not a likely possibility as it would involve agreement with China, which poses insuperable problems for the Soviet Union. It would entail satisfying not only Chinese national demands against the USSR (on territorial boundaries, for example) but also Peking's demand for parity in the world Communist movement. If agreement could be reached with the Chinese on these two vital issues, Moscow would presumably have little use for a condominium or triarchy of any kind with the United States as Soviet policy could then be founded on Sino-Soviet reconciliation, which would in effect present Moscow with a whole new set of possible options. (As indicated earlier, Soviet options relating primarily to relations with China will be discussed later.)

The Case for Détente-*cum*-Parity

These, then, are the broad options that have confronted the Soviet leadership in deciding the USSR's global strategy. The author has discussed at considerable length elsewhere the views and attitudes of different Soviet groups with respect to some of these options.[11] Suffice it to note here that controversy within the leadership has probably centered on the first three options, and . . . the debate has apparently tended more and more to narrow down to the second and third—that is, to condominium/détente based on Soviet strategic superiority versus condominium/détente based on strategic parity. The terms of the Strategic Arms Limitation Agreement signed in Moscow during President Nixon's recent visit suggest that those in the Soviet leadership who advocate détente based on parity have won out in the internal debate—at least for the time being. It may therefore be useful to take a detailed look at the perceptions that appear to underlie this decision.

Although certain members of the top Soviet leadership—notably, Premier Kosygin, President Podgorny, D. S. Poliansky, and G. I. Voronov—can be identified as advocates of the détente-*cum*-parity position, its most articulate public proponents appear to be the Americanologists in the Soviet Academy of Sciences, the most conspicuous of whom are the two doyens of Soviet Americanology, Georgi Arbatov, Director of the Academy's Institute of the USA, and N. Inozemtsov, Director of the Academy's Institute of World Economy and International Affairs. The former is also a member of the Central Auditing Commission, and the latter is a candidate member of the Party Central Committee. Thus, both are members of the outermost rings of the inner circles of Soviet power and have access to the top decision makers.

In a succession of remarkable and audacious expositions of this position over the past several years, Arbatov bases his arguments on a subtle and relatively sophisticated analysis of U.S. domestic and foreign policy. His analysis is extraordinarily nonpolemical in tone and marked by pragmatic realism; yet it is framed within orthodox doc-

---

[11]"The Soviet Military-Industrial Complex—Does It Exist?," *Journal of International Affairs* (No. 1, 1972). See also the author's "Foreign Policy Perspectives in the Sixties," in A. Dallin and T. Larson, Eds., *Soviet Politics Since Khrushchev,* Englewood Cliffs, N.J., Prentice-Hall, 1968; "Soviet Foreign Policy at the Crossroads," *International Organization* (No. 3, 1969); and "Internal Politics and Foreign Policy in the Soviet System," in R. Barry Farrell, Ed. *Approaches to Comparative and International Politics* (Evanston, Illinois: Northwestern University Press, 1966).

trinal parameters, positing the steady growth of Soviet power on the one hand and the bankruptcy of U.S. globalism and continued U.S. domestic turmoil on the other.

Writing in 1970, Arbatov asserted that U.S. globalism based on the concept of "world gendarme" had failed, but at the same time, he gave no comfort to the advocates of Soviet superiority when he emphasized that "no single country can govern worldwide processes."[12] In another roundabout hint that strategic superiority fueled the arms race and created temptations to engage in actions that undermined the possibility of détente and coexistence, he recited his version of how President Johnson—at a time when the United States enjoyed strategic superiority—had converted the policy of "bridge-building" into a ploy to undermine Soviet authority in the USSR's own sphere:

> At the time it [i.e., the policy of bridge-building] was announced, it could still be regarded by many as a kind of response to the challenge of peaceful coexistence hurled by the socialist states. It was no accident that, at the outset, it was subjected to a fire of criticism by the extreme Right in the USA. . . . However, the "bridge-building" policy soon presented itself . . . as a platform for extended subversive activity aimed at dissolving the socialist commonwealth and undermining [its] . . . social system.[13]

In the same article, Arbatov argued that while U.S. global strategy was crumbling and the role of "world policeman" had already been renounced by President Nixon prior to his election to the White House,[14] the collapse of U.S. "globalism" as distinct from its role as a global power not only could create problems for U.S. foreign policy but would confront the Soviet Union and other countries with new, hard choices. The United States, he cautioned, would remain a powerful and formidable power for many years, although its opportunities would progressively diminish. Under these circumstances, Arbatov saw the appropriate Soviet response to be one of continuing to blunt American foreign policy and to deter Washington from residual acts of foreign intervention as the United States retrenched, but at the same time acting to prevent acute local conflicts from escalating or spreading. "The matter at issue," he wrote, "is essentially that of further limiting the freedom of action of imperialism—above all, U.S. imperialism."[15]

More than a year later, in May 1971, Arbatov emphasized the increasing impact of domestic conflict and disturbances as a factor restraining U.S. foreign policy and suggested that a new strategic balance was taking shape as a result of this in combination with the growth of Soviet power:

> The past five-year period confronted imperialism, including American imperialism, with new realities—above all a further change in the alignment of forces between the two world social and economic systems in favor of socialism. Throughout the past few years, this process has grown in two ways, so to speak. It has proceeded both through the further strengthening of the positions of the Soviet Union, the other socialist countries and the international workers' and liberation movements, and through the serious exacerbation of the internal contradictions in the imperialist camp itself.[16]

---

[12]G. A. Arbatov, "American Foreign Policy on the Threshold of the 1970's," in *SShA—Ekonomika, Politika, Ideologiia,* January 1970, as translated in *Soviet Law and Government* (White Plains, New York: Summer 1970).

[13]Ibid, p. 10.

[14]See Richard M. Nixon, "Asia After Viet Nam," *Foreign Affairs* (October 1967), pp. 111–25.

[15]Arbatov, "American Foreign Policy on the Threshold," p. 17.

[16]"American Imperialism and New World Realities," *Pravda,* May 4, 1971.

The United States was thus being forced to adjust to the new strategic equation, and Arbatov went on to pose the logical question: "How should the attempts of the imperialist bourgeoisie to adapt to the new world situation be treated?"

Arbatov's counsel was both measured and prudent. He gingerly warned against resorts to threats and force to take advantage of the situation and explicitly advocated that the Soviet Union should respond positively to any realistic adjustments the United States sought to make in order to ameliorate its difficulties, even though such a course might be attacked by unnamed quarters as "reformist" or "revisionist":

> . . . it does not at all follow from this [new strategic balance] that elements of realism in the domestic and foreign policies of the capitalist powers have no importance and should be rejected on the ground that such attempts express an endeavor to preserve imperialism, to prevent new shocks and political failures for imperialism. Needless to say, any concessions by imperialism, any steps in the direction of adapting to the existing situation, objectively express this kind of class interest of the bourgeoisie. But such steps signify forced concessions under the pressure of the forces of peace and progress and objectively can have consequences that correspond to the people's interests. . . . The peoples of socialist states are by no means indifferent to the direction in which international relations develop—in the direction of preparations for thermonuclear war or in the direction of the peaceful coexistence of states and a political détente which, of course, does not abolish the struggle between the two systems itself but moves it into channels in which this struggle does not lead to military conflict. The significance of these distinctions was emphasized by V. I. Lenin, who pointed out that one should take different attitudes toward those representatives of the bourgeois camp who "gravitate toward the military resolution of questions" and toward those who "gravitate toward pacifism, even if they are of the very worst sort and, from the standpoint of communism, cannot withstand even the slightest criticism."[17]

But perhaps the most ambitious and elaborate examination of the preconditions for, and general configuration of, a détente based on strategic parity was provided by Arbatov in November 1971. Hailing the projected visit of President Nixon to Moscow as a "positive act," he noted:

> The possibility of the normalization of Soviet-American relations, just as the sphere of such normalization, is determined by the interests of the two states. If spheres of common interests exist, normalization is possible. If there are no such spheres, it will be impossible to achieve normalization. How do things stand in this case? Are there problems whose solution would be in the interests of the Soviet Union and the USA and at the same time would not be contrary to the legitimate interests of other countries? There certainly are.[18]

As the "most important" of these problems, Arbatov listed "the prevention of nuclear war," stating that everybody, including "most representatives of the ruling circles" in America, considers thermonuclear war "a 'useless' instrument of policy." This common foundation of concern, he argued, establishes the basis not only for a "normalization" of relations but for détente as well. Alluding to previously signed U.S.–Soviet agreements designed to reduce the possibility of accidental or unauthorized employment of nuclear weapons, including the "hot line" agreement and its various refinements, Arbatov advocated further measures that would involve closer Soviet-American collaboration in order to reduce the possibility of inadvertent confrontation as a result of incremental escalation:

---

[17]Ibid.

[18]"A Step in the Interests of Peace," SShA—Ekonomika, Politika, Ideologiia (November 1971), p. 55.

There is another danger that is less noticeable and therefore perhaps more serious: Even if they do not deliberately want a world thermonuclear war, states may be drawn into serious conflicts whose escalation at some point may get out of control and make war unavoidable. This danger can be prevented only if there is a radical improvement in the international situation.[19]

That the Soviet leaders already accept the wisdom of this view was demonstrated by their refusal to be dragged into a confrontation with the United States over the mining of the Haiphong harbor on the eve of President Nixon's visit to the Soviet Union. When asked at a Moscow lecture on the President's visit why the Soviet navy did not sweep the mines, V. S. Glagolev, a Soviet specialist on arms control, replied that "the sweeping of mines takes a great deal of time, and furthermore *such action on our part would greatly aggravate the situation.*"[20]

In his November 1971 article, Arbatov went on to cite the recent Soviet and Polish treaties with Bonn as examples of settlements which defused crisis situations and relaxed tensions. His general implication was that particular situations, such as that in the Middle East for example, could be defused without the necessity of a substantive or definitive settlement:

Not to stop with what has been achieved, not to rest content with an unstable equilibrium between peace and war, but to seek a more stable foundation for strengthening peace and international security—this is an important common interest of the Soviet and American peoples, as well as of all the other peoples in the world. If this interest finds proper reflection in U.S. policy, the sphere of possible cooperation in international affairs will be expanded considerably. Within the framework of the overall normalization of the international situation, we must extinguish the hotbeds of international crises in the Near East and Southeast Asia, take new steps to improve the situation and set up a reliable security system in Europe, and create conditions precluding the possible outbreak of new crisis situations. Only in this way can really durable guarantees of peace be created.[21]

Arbatov further cited the termination or limitation of the arms race as lying within the sphere of common U.S.-Soviet interest. Emphasizing the onerous drain on economic and financial resources for both countries, he asserted that these political goals are becoming ever more attainable in our era. Then, shifting from "normalization" to more positive measures of "détente," Arbatov stressed that "expansion of commercial, economic, scientific, and technical cooperation can be an important sphere of common interest for the USSR and the USA" and offered these vistas of potential cooperative endeavor:

In conditions of détente, broad possibilities would open up for cooperation in such spheres as the development of science, the utilization of natural resources of the oceans, the struggle against pollution of the natural environment, etc.[22]

It should be noted, however, that in all of his analyses Arbatov stresses the difficult task of reaching agreement on specific points and issues and warns that "it would be unrealistic to close one's eyes to the very serious obstacles blocking improvement of Soviet-American relations." Understandably enough, he points in particular to "influential forces in the USA that oppose such an adjustment and are trying to drag the

---

[19]Ibid., p. 56.
[20]The *New York Times*, May 23, 1972. (Emphasis added.)
[21]"A Step in the Interests of Peace," p. 56.
[22]Ibid., p. 57.

country back to the time of the 'cold war'," but needless to say, he could also have mentioned the "influential circles" in the Soviet Union, including the Soviet military-industrial complex, that would like to resume the "cold war" under conditions of Soviet strategic superiority.

It should further be noted that Arbatov is careful to base his prescriptions on the line laid down by Brezhnev at the 24th Party Congress, thus indirectly invoking the authority of the party General Secretary:

> As for the Soviet Union's position, our line was clearly set forth by L. I. Brezhnev, General Secretary of the CPSU Central Committee, at the 24th CPSU Congress: "We proceeded from the premise that the improvement of relations between the USSR and the USA is possible. Our principled line with respect to the capitalist countries, including the USA, is consistently and fully to implement in practice the principles of peaceful coexistence, to develop mutually advantageous ties and—with those states that are ready to do so—to cooperate in the field of strengthening peace, making mutual relations with these states as stable as possible."[23]

The Brezhnev statement quoted by Arbatov ended with a cautionary declaration that the Soviet Union, while seeking détente with the United States, would still have "to consider whether we are dealing with a real desire to settle questions at the negotiating table or with an attempt to pursue a 'positions of strength' policy." Similarly, although the results of President Nixon's visit to Moscow would appear to confirm that a majority of the Soviet leadership has accepted détente based on strategic parity rather than on Soviet superiority, it must be remembered that there are powerful elements in the Soviet hierarchy that are undoubtedly still wedded to the goal of superiority as expressed in the following statement by a Soviet military writer in 1969:

> . . . Vladimir Ilyich taught that one must pay the closest attention to the enemy's possibilities, study his strong and weak points, and carefully weigh the balance of forces. "Everyone will agree," V. I. Lenin wrote, "that the army that does not train itself to master all types of weapons, all means and methods of struggle that the enemy has or may have is behaving unwisely or even criminally" (Vol. XLI, p. 81) . . . . Here special attention should be given to the words "may have." This means that it is necessary to evaluate the military, economic and scientific potential of a possible enemy on the basis of a careful study both of the existing situation and of realistic prospects. *Only with such a sober and scientific approach can one outline the correct path to the achievement of superiority over the enemy in the balance of forces.*[24]

Moscow's Two Worlds

So far we have focused our attention on Soviet–U.S. interaction and Moscow's strategic policy options primarily in relation to the United States. But Soviet interaction with the United States takes place in only one of the two international environments in

---

[23]Ibid.

[24]A Lagovsky, "The State's Economy and Its Military Might," *Krasnaia zvezda,* May 25, 1969 (emphasis added). See also Thomas W. Wolfe, *Soviet Interests in SALT; Political, Economic, Bureaucratic and Strategic Contributions and Impediments to Arms Control,* RAND Paper P-4702 (Santa Monica, California: RAND, 1971); and Uri Ra'anan, "The Changing American-Soviet Strategic Balance: Some Political Implications," Memorandum prepared for the U.S. Senate Committee on Government Operations, 92nd Congress, 2nd Session (Washington, D.C.: U.S. Government Printing Office, 1972).

which the Soviet Union operates, i.e., the general interstate system and the parallel world system of Communist states and parties. The network of 14 Communist states constitutes a subsystem within each of the two international environments, and thus cuts across the two. Indeed, from the Soviet point of view, the present group of Communist states represents the vanguard of a universal system of such states which will eventually displace the existing international order made up of Communist and non-Communist states poised in varying degrees of protracted coexistence.

While this is the theory, that theory has in recent years foundered on the shoals of both logic and national interests. The world Communist movement has become transformed from an instrument of Soviet foreign policy, first, into an arena of conflict, controversy, and debate among Communist states and parties, and second, into a distinctive international environment in which the Soviet Union and other Communist states must act and react. Instead of assuming the contours of a placid and harmonious community in accordance with the idyllic visions of "socialist internationalism," this distinctive Communist environment now functions increasingly like a microcosmic international countersystem akin to the general interstate system it has penetrated and seeks to displace. Organized into nation-states or national Communist parties that are proto- or potential Communist states, the Communist world, in faithful reproduction of the general international order, is divided along developmental, racial, and geographical lines, structured vertically rather than horizontally, and organized hierarchically rather than laterally, with the Soviet Union at the apex. Furthermore, it is polarized by great-power rivalries, spheres of influence, and constellations of client-states and parties, and it is regulated by an internal balance-of-power mechanism. Its principal mark of distinction from the existing order it seeks to replace is the ideological and sociopolitical content of its constituent states.

Curiously enough, the Soviet Union increasingly occupies essentially identical positions in both international environments, and its behavior in one environment inevitably creates perturbations and reverberations in the other, as imperatives and responsibilities generated in each tend to come into collision, forcing the Soviet leaders to establish priorities not only within environments but between them as well. The contradictory imperatives stem from the fact that in the Communist environment the challenging power is China, whereas in the general interstate system Moscow's principal rival is the United States.

Recently, the situation in both environments has become even more seriously complicated for the Soviet leaders because China has now burst out of the confines of the Communist environment and is demanding recognition and a role as a third global power in the general international system. This means that the Soviet Union is now challenged by two global powers: by the United States in one environment, and by China in two.

In dealing with the Chinese, the Soviet leaders have failed to exude the self-confidence that they have evinced in dealing with the Americans. Indeed, they have periodically given vent to outbursts of irrationality and desperation where China has been concerned. The reasons transcend the mere fact that China shares a 4000-mile-long frontier with the Soviet Union and that her 800 million population presses down like an oppressive incubus upon the Soviet psyche. More important, the Chinese constitute an inside threat to Soviet power and ambition because China is part of the socialist commonwealth and challenges Moscow's legitimacy and power within the world of Communist states and parties as well as in the overall international system. For example, Peking cannot be credibly termed an interloper in the Kremlin's ideological garden, which is roughly congruent with the Soviet Union's regional sphere of influence. Hence, while

Soviet leaders have had a fair amount of success in employing non-Communist states like India as means of countering the Chinese challenge, they have been less successful in achieving this purpose by using the Communist states, which frown on the notion of intra-Communist ideological and military coalitions arrayed against one another. Only Mongolia (which shares a common border with both China and the USSR and fears engulfment by the Chinese) and occupied Czechoslovakia have signed military alliances which could be invoked in the event of a Sino-Soviet war; moreover, all attempts by Moscow to read China out of the world Communist movement or to transform the Warsaw Treaty Organization into a potential anti-Peking alliance have thus far been unsuccessful.[25] Broadly speaking, then, the Chinese challenge within the Communist camp continues to cripple Russia's consolidation of control over Eastern Europe, as well as over nonruling Communist parties elsewhere, and it has been instrumental in facilitating the erosion of the Soviet Union's ideological legitimacy and in forcing her to behave more like an imperial rather than an ecumenical power.

The Dual Threat of China

Thus, of all the states in the international system, only China today poses a direct threat to the Soviet territory and at the same time is in a position to threaten the Soviet Union with means other than nuclear weapons. The American threat to the Soviet Union has always exhibited a synthetic, abstract quality at the olympian level of strategic and global rivalry: U.S. and Soviet troops have never clashed, and neither country has territorial demands against the other. Their rivalry has mainly been one for "world leadership" as champions of contending ideological social systems. And in this contention the Soviet leaders have derived comfort and sustenance from their belief that, no matter how powerful the United States, the civilization and social order that it represents are in the long run historically obsolete, that no matter how protracted and erratic the contest, history and the dialectic will at some point catch up with the United States, and it will inevitably enter into a period of decline and social dissolution.

But the same historical and ideological convictions that sustain the Soviet leaders in their rivalry with the United States have tended to produce irresolution, ambivalence, and cognitive inadequacy in their approach to China, for the ideological prism that they employ to perceive the world provides them with little or no guidance about how to cope with those who use the identical prism but perceive a different rainbow. The Chinese subscribe to the same convictions as the Soviets, yet their prognosis for "Soviet revisionism" is remarkably similar to some of the Soviet predictions of doom for "American imperialism." Moreover, the Soviet leaders view China not as a declining power, but as an ascending one; and their awareness of the tremendous material and human potential of China, combined with their inherent faith in the inevitability of growth and development, can only create in their minds the ineluctability of Chinese paramountcy if they continue to subscribe to their own doctrinal postulates. Thus, their ideological presuppositions lend credence to their visceral fear that Peking's claim to future world hegemony may be stronger and perhaps more warranted by history than their own. Chinese efforts to move the epicenter of the international Communist movement, which the Soviets regard as the historical vehicle for the future transformation of

---

[25]For a detailed discussion of these matters, see the author's "Soviet Aims in East Europe," *Current History* (October 1970).

the world, from Moscow to Peking have further stoked this fear. According to one Soviet commentator,

> The course of the "great leap" pursued the ambitious goal of taking a vanguard position among the socialist countries. This appealed to Maoist hegemonic aspiration. . . . No matter what ultrarevolutionary phraseology was used to cover up this course, its essence remained unchanged . . . to establish hegemony in a world devastated by war. . . .
>
> It [Peking] would like, in implementing its plans, to use the military and economic might of the socialist countries, the strength of the international working class and the possibilities of the national liberation movement, striving to turn these factors into tools of its great power hegemonism. . . . It sees the Soviet Union, the policy of the CPSU . . . as the main obstacle to the implementation of its hegemonic aspirations in the international arena.[26]

Furthermore, as a result of these historical and ideological beliefs, the Soviet leaders have seemed to assume that China's baffling, obstinate, and persistent hostility toward the USSR reflects a Chinese conviction that Soviet power will eventually be destroyed or subjugated to Chinese hegemony on the road to the final Armageddon with imperialism.[27] This assumption, in turn, has caused the Soviet leaders increasingly to regard the military and strategic components of the "balance of forces" between Moscow and Peking as critically important.

Looking at the Soviet position vis-à-vis China from another angle, one can see that Soviet advocates of détente with the United States based on strategic parity have a powerful ideological argument to support that policy, but that the same argument collapses when applied to China. The argument is that strategic parity with the United States is sufficient to achieve Soviet aims and purposes because the natural movement of world social, political, and historical processes is in tune with Soviet goals and because, given a constant military equilibrium, any alterations in the overall "correlation of forces" can only be in a direction detrimental to the U.S. position. It holds further that strategic parity is sufficient to deter any attempts by the United States to intervene in order to arrest or reverse these processes (as was possible under conditions of U.S. superiority), although on the Soviet side it may mean foregoing the option of intervention (i.e., "export of revolution") designed to force or accelerate revolutionary transformations in marginal situations. All these assumptions become implausible, however, in dealing with Peking. Seen from the perspective of the Soviet leaders, China—unlike the United States, which is viewed as a powerful, capitalist industrial nation in a state of decline and on the brink of being consumed by its own developing internal contradictions—is an underdeveloped giant on the rise. Furthermore, and most critical, China's visions and purposes are also in tune with the social and revolutionary processes of history, and while the unfolding of the historical dialectic may be to the detriment of the United States, China will inevitably share some of the benefits. Hence, in its con-

---

[26]I. Aleksandrov, "Slogans and Deeds of the Chinese Leadership," *Pravda*, Sept. 4, 1971.

[27]These Soviet perceptions were undoubtedly reinforced by a Chinese attack on both the Soviet Union and the United States during President Nixon's visit to Moscow, when the central Chinese party organ *Jen-min Jih-pao* (People's Daily) let loose with a blast condemning both powers as the "archcriminals" of the modern world who "are colluding and at the same time contending with each other" for the purpose of dividing the world into spheres of influence. The paper assured its readers that "despite the baring of their fangs and showing of their claws today, the U.S. and Soviet overlords are very weak by nature and nothing but paper tigers," and predicted that both would be swept "into the garbage heap of history." See the *New York Times*, May 22, 1972.

frontation with China, Moscow cannot rely on the assumption that revolutionary forces in the world operate solely to Soviet advantage, for though the "correlation of forces" may enhance the Soviet position vis-à-vis the United States, it may simultaneously weaken Moscow's posture vis-à-vis China.

For the moment, the Soviet leaders can safely accept strategic parity with the United States by freezing weapons at current levels and still enjoy considerable superiority with respect to China. However, some Soviet leaders undoubtedly feel that such a freeze will inevitably create conditions which will allow China to improve its relative military position. This is more crucial for Moscow than for Washington, for while China is in no position to use its developing military capability directly against American targets, it can employ both conventional forces and strategic weapons against the Soviet Union. As a consequence, the Soviet leaders will probably continue to be concerned about erosion of their relative strategic power as long as it remains frozen by agreement with the United States—unless China in the future also enters into arms control agreements placing a ceiling on her military capabilities.

Options Vis-à-vis Peking

What options, then, do the Soviet leaders have in dealing with the Chinese problem? Hypothetically, there are at least three, conceptualized as follows: (1) reconciliation, (2) annihilation, and (3) pragmatic adaptation.

The avowed Soviet preference is *reconciliation*, and there is no doubt that the Soviet Union is willing to make a number of compromises and concessions to achieve it, although so far all these efforts have failed. Apparently, there are factions and influential individuals in and around the Chinese leadership who favor some sort of limited reconciliation with Moscow in preference to rapprochement with the United States, and the Soviet rulers doubtless continue to hope that the death of Mao Tse-tung may bring to the fore new Chinese leaders who would prefer to select the United States rather than the Soviet Union as the "main" or "immediate" enemy. But the Soviet leaders seem to entertain no illusion that any reconciliation would be more than limited and temporary in essence, reflecting the current calculation of some Chinese leaders that China's immediate interest would be better served by colluding with Russia against America rather than the other way around. Still, they would probably accept even a temporary reconciliation as a welcome respite.

On the Chinese side, however, Mao Tse-tung and Chou En-lai are apparently persuaded that under existing conditions, with Soviet power on the upswing and U.S. power on the decline, a Soviet embrace might be more perilous than continued hostility. Furthermore, they recognize that China's leverage with Moscow against the United States is rapidly diminishing, particularly since they believe that the United States is now retrenching and withdrawing from the Asian mainland. Finally, just as the Soviet leaders are determined never again to accept strategic inferiority vis-à-vis the United States, Mao Tse-tung is equally determined that China will never again play second fiddle to Russia in the world Communist movement, and since the Soviet Union is clearly unwilling to accept "parity" with China and China does not possess sufficient capability to assert equality with the Soviet Union in the Communist movement unilaterally, the necessary prerequisite for a reconciliation appears to be absent.

This leads to the second possible option, *annihilation*—i.e., the destruction of China's military capability, especially nuclear and strategic. This option apparently was pressed vigorously by some elements in the Soviet military shortly after the successful invasion of Czechoslovakia and the enunciation of the "Brezhnev Doctrine." Sentiments in favor of administering the Chinese a "bloody nose," as well as the notion of a "surgical strike" to arrest or destroy China's burgeoning nuclear arsenal, became quite current in Soviet circles. But cooler heads prevailed, and Soviet action in the 1969 border conflict on the Ussuri was kept at a level sufficient to provide a warning "lesson" for the Chinese. However, now that China possesses a modest nuclear arsenal and has developed intermediate-range missiles capable of reaching major urban and industrial centers in the USSR, the risks of a Soviet preventive attack have escalated, and annihilation is no longer a viable hypothetical option. The Soviet leaders must thus learn to live with and adjust to the reality of growing Chinese nuclear and missile power and must seek other means to deter the Chinese from attempting to employ that power against the Soviet Union.

This leads to the third option, *pragmatic adaptation,* which of course may cover a wide range of specific policies, depending upon conditions and circumstances. Currently, Soviet strategy toward China appears to involve four separate but interrelated links. The first is a policy of encirclement and containment involving primarily non-Communist powers, the chief of which is India. Moscow would also like to involve Japan in its encirclement strategy now that it can no longer count on the United States as a tacit partner. The second link is an effort to forge an effective, if initially selective, anti-Chinese coalition within the Communist system of states. So far, only Czechoslovakia and Mongolia have been recruited, but the Soviet effort will continue.

The third link is active Soviet reinvolvement in Southeast Asia and stepped-up assistance to North Vietnam. But North Vietnam poses a problem for both Communist giants, who have successively caused concern in Hanoi as each in turn welcomed Nixon to its capital while pledging its own undying support of North Vietnam and charging the other with designs for a "sellout." In both summit episodes, the North Vietnamese have tried to complicate matters by deliberately escalating the war and compelling President Nixon to retaliate, hoping that this would create sufficient embarrassment, first in Peking and later in Moscow, either to cause them to cancel their invitations to the President or to cast a pall over the negotiations. Both Communist giants, however, apparently felt that they had their own fish to fry and gave Mr. Nixon's visits higher priority in their respective calculations than they gave to the feelings of North Vietnam. Since both Moscow and Peking welcomed the U.S. President, neither could gain any advantage over the other in Hanoi on this issue. And since North Vietnam is dependent upon the Soviet Union and China for its military supplies, it is hardly in a position to threaten them, individually or collectively.

Moscow's decision virtually to ignore the mining of Haiphong harbor and other North Vietnamese ports and to extend a warm welcome to President Nixon was a signal to Hanoi that a détente with the United States and the Western powers was of more vital interest to the Soviet leaders than the specific character or degree of Hanoi's victory. As Moscow views the situation, the United States has already conceded virtual defeat in Vietnam and is merely seeking an "honorable" exit, while the North Vietnamese are only delaying the inevitable U.S. withdrawal because of the specific character of the victory they seek. As far as Moscow is concerned, this is a luxury for which Hanoi must be prepared to pay, and the Soviet Union has shown, by receiving President Nixon, that it will not allow Hanoi to complicate its larger design. The initial reassertion of Soviet interest in Vietnam after Khrushchev's ouster was clearly designed to prevent Hanoi from falling completely under Chinese influence, and it is not likely that Moscow anticipates that North Vietnam, once the war is over, will join Moscow's

Chinese encirclement strategy. Instead, Hanoi will probably continue to play its two Communist allies off against one another—and perhaps even engage in its own version of "collusion" with the United States.

The fourth and final link in the Soviet leaders' current China policy is détente with the United States and the West. This détente, which encompasses the new treaties with West Germany, means in effect U.S. and West German acceptance of the East European status quo, and it also creates at the very least a foundation for defusing and managing Soviet-American conflict over the Arab-Israeli question. The détente thus serves to stabilize and secure the Soviet western flank and *ipso facto* strengthens the Soviet Union's strategic position in dealing with a hostile China. Détente with the West is therefore one of the main ingredients—together with the USSR's quasi-military treaty with India, its anti-Chinese alliances with Czechoslovakia and Mongolia, and continued assistance to North Vietnam in order to at least neutralize Hanoi in the Moscow-Peking conflict—in the Soviet leaders' current policy of pragmatic adaptation to China's growing power.

For the long run, Moscow no doubt hopes for an amelioration of the China situation, either through changes in the Peking leadership and the assertion of authority by new generations, or through more "responsible" Chinese behavior as a result of growth and development. But should this not occur, the Soviet leaders envisage that there will be sufficient basis for Moscow to form a common front against China with other major powers in the world, who will presumably become increasingly threatened as China's development extends her strategic reach to all corners of the globe. The Soviet leaders probably anticipate that at some future date China may become the single most powerful state in the world, but surely not sufficiently mighty to overwhelm all the others combined. This also suggests that at some future point the disparate policies which Moscow has been pursuing in the Third World, in Western Europe, with the United States, and elsewhere will be merged and unified. For the time being, the Russians will continue to operate on the dual track of global power and revolutionary power, but at some point these two may be brought into inevitable conflict as Moscow attempts to mobilize both Communist and non-Communist countries against the Chinese threat.

The Impact of De-Bipolarization

In all this, it is apparent that the Soviet leaders have had to revise their strategic thinking drastically as a consequence of the new triangulation of world politics. Originally, they evidently anticipated that a change in the strategic balance between the United States and the USSR would merely alter the power relationship between the two global powers. Thus, it would greatly increase the Soviet Union's freedom of action around the world. But things did not turn out as Moscow expected, for the shift in the strategic balance altered the entire international landscape by encouraging China and the United States to move toward a rapprochement. This rapprochement can be viewed as stemming from the virtually simultaneous realization in Peking and Washington that existing Sino-American animosity strengthened Moscow's hand with both of them, and that, correspondingly, a rapprochement would diminish and even in some respects nullify Soviet gains flowing from the changing balance of power.

From the standpoint of the Soviet leaders, the conversion of the bilateral Soviet-Chinese and Soviet-American relationships, in which the USSR was either clearly the strongest party or on the way to becoming the stronger party, into a triangular relationship has served to reduce the relative leverage of the Soviet Union with respect to both China and the United States, for it has restricted the options and latitude of action that they would have enjoyed in a bipolar or a double-bipolar situation. President Nixon's visit to Peking, in short, has tended to limit whatever gains the Soviet Union made as a result of the change in the strategic balance. In fact, the Soviet leaders were fearful, at least for a time, that Washington and Peking might conspire and collaborate against Moscow, and their fears received wide and repeated articulation in the Soviet press. It should be underscored, however, that the Soviet apprehension was not that a Washington-Peking axis threatened Soviet security or interests directly, but rather that it would ultimately rob Moscow of the possible fruits of strategic parity or superiority.

The impact of the triangulation of global politics is perhaps most readily visible in the Asian context, for it was there that Moscow appears to have entertained the greatest hopes of capitalizing on its new strategic position to expand its influence and to cut China down to size. Let us, therefore, explore the Asian situation briefly.

Before the dramatic escalation in Soviet military capabilities, it seemed clearly in the Soviet interest to keep the United States involved on the Asian mainland for the short term. Indeed, the Kremlin leaders initially sought to use the United States as a tacit part of an encirclement and containment strategy for dealing with China. That strategy relied upon the continuation of China's diplomatic isolation, in which Sino-American animosity played the key role. What enabled Moscow to think in such terms, of course, was the fact that Washington's pursuit of a policy of isolating and containing China placed the Soviet and American positions in tandem—something that the Chinese leaders recognized quite well, as their repeated denunciations of Soviet-American collusion against China demonstrated.

But after the USSR had accomplished its military buildup, Moscow's interests, while not altogether clear, seemed to lie in a quick American departure from Asia. The buildup had already put the USSR in a position to take advantage of a number of situations on the Asian continent to enhance its influence, as the subsequent course of events in South Asia proved. With the United States gone from the region, the Soviet Union would plainly be the most powerful state there, and this circumstance might in itself suffice to persuade Asian states fearful of Chinese hegemonic aspirations to scramble under the protective umbrella of an Asian security system, a scheme which the Soviet leaders have advanced on a number of occasions. The American-sponsored SEATO might thus give way to a Soviet counterpart.

To Moscow, the enunciation in 1969 of the "Nixon Doctrine" and its specific application to Southeast Asia, the policy of "Vietnamization," appeared to be a major step in the desired direction, for the Soviet leaders perceived the action as a signal of U.S. intent to withdraw militarily from the Asian mainland and to allow local conflicts to become indigenized and subject to resolution without benefit of American intervention or involvement. However, the Chinese discerned similar implications, and while one of their more obvious goals has been to expel all external intruders from East Asia and they have consequently welcomed the U.S. policy of indigenization of Asian conflicts, they obviously felt that the premature withdrawal of the United States might simply redound to the advantage of the Soviet Union as long as the latter chose to assert itself as an Asian power. For this reason, they not only have endeavored to reach a measure of understanding with the United States but have shown remarkable patience regarding the American timetable of withdrawal, including the ambiguous matter of the continuing U.S. presence on Taiwan.

The Soviet leaders, then, foresee the possibility that instead of being able to translate their new prowess into political gains in Asia, they will be prevented from doing so by the Sino-American rapprochement. One Soviet commentator has expressed the matter thus:

> Outwardly, the Chinese leadership appears uncompromising in its assertion that the affairs of Asia should be settled by Asians, the affairs of Europe by Europeans, and the affairs of Africa by Africans. It may seem that Peking is really concerned over defending the national interests of the peoples and states of Asia, Europe and Africa against "the 'superpowers' interference." But here, too, this is only camouflage. In proclaiming the slogan, "Give Asians the opportunity to settle their own affairs and eliminate the dominance of the 'superpowers' in Asia," the PRC leadership hopes that China, as the largest power on the continent, will be able to impose its will and solutions on the Asian peoples.
>
> In this respect, the contacts between unofficial American representatives and Chinese leaders in preparing the ground for Nixon's visit to the PRC are indicative. Mao Tse-tung, in an interview with the American journalist E. Snow in December 1970, gave a positive evaluation of the "Vietnamization" policy. According to E. Snow, high-ranking officials in China said that Nixon is "withdrawing from Vietnam and Asia." They saw this as an opportunity to restore the grandeur of the Middle Kingdom and the Asian people's vassal dependence on China.[28]

The Japanese Enigma

The rising power of Japan introduces another complex element into the new triangular configuration of world politics. Japan remains an enigma for the Soviet Union as much as for the Chinese. Both Moscow and Peking respect Japan's mighty industrial and technological base and fear her military potential should the restraining influence of the United States be withdrawn or jettisoned. In immediate terms, both Peking and Moscow recognize that Japan could become the dominant power in East Asia virtually overnight should she choose to transform her tremendous industrial and technological capability into a military one. Each would like to use Japan as a counterpoise against the other, without at the same time exposing itself to manipulation by Tokyo. The Sino-American rapprochement having ruptured a vital link in Moscow's chain of encirclement around China, Japan could become an acceptable surrogate, and in a sense her cooperation would be indispensable to Moscow's design. On the other hand, a Sino-Japanese rapprochement could be disastrous for the USSR in East Asia as such a combine might conceivably force the Soviet Union out of the area, or force it to maintain massive military formations there, draining the Soviet economy and depriving Moscow of the will and energy to pursue global policies elsewhere.

Thus, the diminution of American strategic power, instead of simply creating unambiguous advantages for the Soviet Union, confronts Moscow not only with greater opportunities but greater dangers as well. The most frightening of these dangers might be a Soviet Union faced with a united Europe in the West and a Sino-Japanese coalition in the East, which could effectively and perhaps even permanently seal Soviet power within its present boundaries and create the conditions for its contraction and dissolution in its own developing contradictions. Much of this is sheer fantasy—for the Soviet leaders, no doubt, nightmarish fantasies—but Soviet commentators, particularly

---

[28]G. Kadymov, "Class Betrayal is the Essence of the Maoists' 'Superpower Domination' Thesis," *Krasnaia zvezda,* Dec. 14, 1971.

those who have since 1966 been vocally articulating the fantasy of a Sino-American rapprochement, are now fantasizing along these lines. One recent article put it this way:

> Recently Chou En-lai stated that the Common Market is the "first step on the road to an independent Europe." Peking warmly welcomes Britain's entry into the Common Market. . . . . . This position on the part of the Chinese leaders indicates that they are eager to see a united "Europe for the Europeans" as a counterweight to the Soviet Union and as their possible partner.[29]

China, of course, has comparable fantasies concerning Japan, but fantasies based on concrete historical memories, not simply nightmares. A Soviet-Japanese rapprochement in conjunction with a Soviet-Indian partnership in the South could vitally cripple China's ambition to function on the world stage as a global power. But there are formidable barriers to a Soviet-Japanese rapprochement—some trivial, some symbolic, and others of substantial magnitude.

The first is the territorial issue arising from Japanese demands for the return by the USSR of three small islands off the coast of northern Hokkaido. These islands are of little or no strategic value to the Soviet Union, nor do they contain any important resources. Nevertheless, they have assumed great symbolic and psychological importance for Japan, and the issue continues to agitate Soviet-Japanese relations, having been responsible most recently for Japanese refusal to undertake projects involved in the development of Soviet Eastern Siberia. If the issue did not go beyond Soviet-Japanese relations, there is little doubt that Moscow would willingly relinquish the islands in return for a dramatic improvement in relations. But Tokyo's territorial demands are psychologically connected with other territorial demands against the USSR. In fact, Mao Tse-tung himself, in an interview with a group of Japanese visitors, not only agreed that Japan's claim to the islands was justified, but proceeded to associate Japan's territorial claims with those of Finland, Poland, East Germany, Czechoslovakia, Romania, and China against Russia.[30] Thus, Moscow fears that a territorial settlement involving the return of territories to one country would establish a precedent, arouse expectations, and certainly aggravate many of the muted claims against Soviet territory. More importantly, as the Soviet-Chinese border conflict on the Ussuri over Chenpao/Damansky island demonstrated, the territorial issue is a particularly volatile one in Sino-Soviet relations, and a return of some small islands to Japan might serve to reexcite the appetites of the tigers of Peking.

The dilemma of both Communist countries in their attempt to use Japan against the other is that the chief beneficiary of such a policy might be Japan itself. Unlike the United States, Japan is a regional power, and her interests are more intimately connected with the Asian mainland. A strong United States might be a temporary interloper in Asian affairs, but a powerful Japan would be a permanent fixture, with all that that implies. What the Japanese propose to do with their tremendous capability will in large measure determine the responses of the Soviet Union and the Chinese. The tripolar world is still in embryonic form and could easily be aborted before it achieves definitive or even recognizable configuration, if Japan chooses to play a diplomatic and military role in world affairs commensurate with her potential. Should Japan "go nuclear," for example, and succeed through adroit maneuvering in developing a powerful strategic capability, it would seriously alter the overall balance of power and once again force a realignment among the major powers of the world.

---

[29]Ibid.

[30]*Pravda*, September 2, 1964.

The Outlook for Moscow

Confronted by all the manifold complexities of the drastically altered global distribution and alignment of power, how is the Soviet Union likely to behave? Generally speaking, Moscow will probably prefer to continue along prudent and well-worn paths, attempting to retain the main configurations of the bipolar system and refusing to recognize that a tripolar or multipolar system is already here or on the horizon. Now that the Soviet Union has achieved genuine equality with the United States in the international arena, the Russians are loath to debase their newly-achieved eminence by accepting China as a global power, since this would mean according China a standing of equality not only in the general interstate system but in the world Communist movement as well.[31]

Thus, the Soviet leaders are likely to try to keep membership in the global club restricted to Moscow and Washington. At the same time, however, they have now recognized the existence of a broader nuclear club than they were previously willing to acknowledge. Such recognition was implicit in Moscow's call, issued at the 24th CPSU Congress in April 1971, for the convocation of a conference of the five nuclear powers, including China. Peking, however, has spurned the call and awaits formal recognition as the third global (as opposed to nuclear) power, while simultaneously professing to renounce any such heady ambition.[32]

Meanwhile, Moscow can be expected to keep on refraining from imprudent adventures, but this does not mean that the Soviet leaders do not intend to employ their strategic prowess so as to score diplomatic gains commensurate with the changing strategic balance. Since the United States appears to be ready to make adjustments conforming to the new distribution of power, Moscow will doubtless proceed with the West along the path of limited détente through the negotiation of formal agreements, the postponement of some problems, and limitation of bipower confrontations to certain geographic areas where the vital interests of neither party are likely to become involved. Strategic parity may be sufficient to enable Moscow to make incremental gains in marginal areas of the world, and even marginal gains in more significant regions, particularly in the Middle East at American expense and in South and Southeast Asia at the expense of both the United States and China. Marginal gains may be anticipated in Latin America as well, particularly if more revolutionary regimes of the Allende type come to power constitutionally or extra-constitutionally.

Thus, a prudent Soviet foreign policy is not to be confused with an inert one, but it remains to be seen how successful the Soviet Union will be in converting its new military muscle into diplomatic gains. It should be remembered that the USSR, unlike the United States, is a *revisionist* rather than a *status quo* power, and as long as Soviet revisionist aspirations coincide with the objectives of local revolutionary movements, Moscow may well be able to make more gains with less power than was the United States. For a status quo power simultaneously to deter a powerful revisionist adversary

---

[31]Thus, one Soviet commentator petulantly notes that Chinese rhetoric about the "two superpowers" is merely a smokescreen behind which "the Peking leaders are trying to create an independent ideological and political center (a 'third force') . . . [and] they hope that, relying on this center, they can turn China into a global power and make up for its military and economic potential, which is insufficient for the purpose." Kadymov, "Class Betrayal."

[32]The distinction between "nuclear powers" and "global powers" has been clearly though implicitly drawn in Soviet commentaries. E.g., see the commentary on the Soviet-proposed conference of the five nuclear powers, in *Pravda*, July 30, 1971.

and quash or deter indigenous revolutionary movements around the globe requires clear-cut and overwhelming nuclear superiority, whereas for Moscow to deter intervention designed to quash revolutions requires only parity.

Nevertheless, Soviet adjustment to a de-bipolarized world in which the USSR may be the paramount strategic power will be difficult. The Soviet leaders will be catapulted into a strange world, for they are accustomed in both thought and action to think in terms of bipolarity and zero-sum situations. The world is no longer "we and/or they": a loss in American power is no longer an automatic gain for Moscow. The decline in American power may simply create opportunities for other powers to assert themselves and thus create more rivals and more problems for Moscow to deal with.

26
China and the World
A. Doak Barnett

The interplay of the domestic forces . . . will clearly be the primary determinant of the nature of the Chinese Communist regime and the broad thrust of its policies in the period ahead. But the key question for other nations is how China will interact with the outside world. What will China's priority foreign policy objectives be and how are they likely to be pursued? What impact is China likely to have on the international community, and how should other countries view and respond to Chinese activities on the world stage? If it is assumed that China is now—and will be for some years—in a period of transition, what effect is this likely to have on external relations?

While domestic political developments will have a major impact on Peking's foreign policy, China's relations with the outside world will also be shaped by developments beyond its borders and by the responses of the Peking leadership to these developments. What perceptions have the Chinese had—and are they likely to have in the future—of the international environment and its relationship to China's interests? What specific goals, both long-run and short-run, will shape concrete and specific foreign policy decisions? To what extent will ideological considerations and "revolutionary interests" influence China's foreign policy behavior, or will it largely be shaped by more conventional "national interests"? Are defensive considerations or expansionist aims likely to be more important policy determinants? To what extent is foreign policy likely to reflect Chinese initiatives or to be reactive to forces and developments abroad? Is China, on balance, likely to be inward-looking or outward-looking?

And what can be said about China's probable capabilities—military, political, and economic—to pursue the goals it sets? What Chinese foreign policy strategies and tactics—and style—can be foreseen in the period ahead? Will Peking be inclined to use military force in pursuing its foreign policy aims or will it rely on nonmilitary means? To what extent will foreign policy be constrained by domestic factors? And are differences within the Chinese leadership likely to have a major influence on foreign policy?

China's foreign policies, like its domestic policies, have undergone many changes in direction and emphasis during the past 23 years and therefore cannot be characterized with simple generalizations. At different times since 1949, Peking's leaders have had sharply differing perceptions of the opportunities and the dangers confronting them, have shifted national priorities and goals, and have pursued varying strategies and tactics.[1] Despite all the changes, however, there have been significant continuities,

From A. Doak Barnett, *Uncertain Passage: China's Transition to the Post-Mao Era* (Washington, D.C.: The Brookings Institution, 1974), pp. 245-279. [Reprinted with permission from the publisher.]

[1][For a list of the author's references and suggested supplementary readings on this particular topic see the note at the end of this article.]

and it is important to understand both the elements of change and the elements of continuity.

The Immediate Post-Takeover Period

When the Chinese Communists first established their new regime, their principal goals were to complete their revolution, end all vestiges of Western imperialist and colonialist influence in China, reunify the country, and reestablish centralized control over all areas considered to be Chinese territory. In the flush of victory, both nationalistic sentiment and ideological fervor were at a high pitch, and Peking's leaders were in no mood to be compromising. They proceeded to establish military control over areas such as Hainan and Tibet, and prepared to invade Taiwan. Within China, they applied gradual but effective pressures to eliminate Western personnel and influences.

The image of the international community propagated by the Chinese Communist leadership in 1949—shared at the time with leaders in Moscow and, for that matter, in Washington as well—reflected the cold war views of the time. The world was portrayed in essentially black-and-white, bipolar terms. The crucial fact of international life was believed to be an intense struggle between two blocs or "camps"—a revolutionary "socialist camp" headed by the Soviet Union and a counterrevolutionary "imperialist camp" headed by the United States.[2] The Chinese, like the Russians and Americans, regarded the arena for this struggle as worldwide. Neutrality was said to be impossible. There was no possibility, Mao declared in 1949, of pursuing a "third road";[3] all nations and forces must of necessity be linked to or associated with one side or the other.

Several conclusions followed naturally from this set of premises. The Chinese decided that in such a bipolar world their interests required close alignment with the Soviet Union and the Communist bloc. Ideology was obviously a major factor influencing this conclusion, but Peking's security concerns were also involved. The new Chinese regime considered the United States to be China's prime adversary and the main threat to its interests. Several years earlier, when they were still struggling for power, Chinese Communist leaders had intimated to American officials that they might be prepared to adopt a more flexible posture, less hostile to the United States, and perhaps less clearly aligned with the USSR.[4] Some flexibility may have lasted until 1949,[5] but now, in view of the direct support provided by the United States to the Nationalists during the final

---

[2]The two "camps" idea was elaborated in detail in a long article written by Liu Shao-ch'i in November 1948. See *Internationalism and Nationalism* (Peking: Foreign Languages Press, March 1951), pp. 1–51.

[3]Mao Tse-tung, "On the People's Democratic Dictatorship," *Selected Works of Mao Tse-tung*, Vol. 4 (Peking: Foreign Languages Press, 1961), p. 415. This theme had already been emphasized by Liu in the article cited in footnote 2.

[4]See *Foreign Relations of the United States, Diplomatic Papers, 1944*, Vol. 6: *China* (Washington, 1967), August 23 memorandum on John Stewart Service conversation with Mao Tse-tung, pp. 604 ff., and *Foreign Relations of the United States, Diplomatic Papers, 1945*, Vol. 7: *The Far East, China* (Washington, 1969), March 13 John Stewart Service interview with Mao Tse-tung, pp. 273 ff.

[5]Data recently published in a book by Seymour Topping reveal that U.S. Ambassador John Leighton Stuart was invited to visit Mao Tse-tung in Peking in early 1949. (Ambassador Stuart had been accredited to the Nationalist government but stayed in Nanking at the time of the Communist takeover.) Many students of that period, including myself, have been inclined to believe the Chinese had probably decided as early as 1948 to align closely with Moscow. The new data about the invitation to Stuart raise a question as to whether the Chinese Communists were more open-minded than has generally been assumed and whether they might have been willing to adopt a more flexible and less hostile posture toward the United States if Stuart had made the visit. See Seymour Topping, *Journey Between Two Chinas* (New York: Harper and Row, 1972), pp. 83–90.

years of China's civil war and in the cold war climate of worldwide conflict between the Communist and non-Communist blocs, Peking adopted an overtly antagonistic posture toward the United States.

Despite signs that the United States was gradually disengaging from China during 1948–49, Chinese leaders in early 1950 signed a thirty-year military alliance with the Soviet Union, directed against both the United States and Japan.[6] This was the most important single foreign policy decision made by Peking in the period immediately after 1949, and it established the basic framework for Chinese foreign policy throughout the 1950s. Never before had any Chinese government joined a well defined bloc or signed a close military alliance with a major foreign power. The Communists' decision to do so in 1950 proved to be a mixed blessing. While the alliance reinforced China's defense capabilities, in a period when it was relatively weak and was concerned about a potential U.S. threat, the close alliance with Moscow limited Peking's freedom of action in various ways. Over time, moreover, it proved to be disappointing to the Chinese in other fundamental respects. Before many years had passed, clashes between Moscow and Peking over both ideology and national interests led to open Sino-Soviet competition and conflict, with the result that for all practical purposes the alliance lapsed. In the early 1950s, however, there was no reason for Peking's leaders to anticipate this course of events, and they deliberately chose to make the Sino-Soviet alliance the keystone of China's foreign policy.

At the time of their takeover, the Chinese Communists also made a point of identifying their interests closely with Communist-led insurrectionaries throughout the world, most particularly with those who were mounting efforts in 1948–49 to seize power throughout much of Asia. Peking openly proclaimed its support for these revolutionary struggles abroad, and gave strong moral support to Communist movements in many countries.[7] In short, the revolutionary component in its foreign policy was overt and intense in this period. This was not surprising. As revolutionaries who had just won power in China, Peking's leaders had a self-image that dictated a posture of open support for fellow revolutionaries elsewhere. Self-confidence born of their own success impelled them to hold up their experience as a model for others to emulate.

The revolutionary militancy of the Chinese Communists was largely expressed, however, in rhetoric rather than concrete action. Even though Peking did give support—in the form of matériel and training—to the Communists in neighboring Indochina, and proffered advice to others, it did not back revolutions outside China's borders with its own combat forces. The task of consolidating power at home was Peking's primary concern, and while the Chinese fervently hoped that revolutionaries elsewhere would succeed, they were not inclined or prepared to help them directly with Chinese troops. In sum, Chinese support for revolutions abroad was largely in the form of moral exhortation.

The Korean War: A New Situation

The outbreak of the Korean war and the decisions relating to this war made in both Washington and Peking created a very new situation for China, and for East Asia as a

---

[6]Text in *Sino-Soviet Treaty and Agreements* (Peking: Foreign Languages Press, 1951), pp. 5–8. The text states that each would render military and other assistance to the other if the other were "attacked by Japan or any state allied to it"—a phrase that clearly referred to the United States.

[7]See, for example, Liu Shao-ch'i's November 16, 1949, statement; text, *New China News Agency*, Nov. 23, 1949.

whole.[8] In mid-1950, following the North Korean attack on South Korea, the United States decided to send American troops to support South Korea. At the same time Washington intervened again in the Chinese civil war, sending the U.S. fleet to "neutralize" the Taiwan Strait. Later, ignoring Chinese warnings, the United States ordered its troops to cross the 38th parallel in Korea to pursue the war northward. Peking responded by deciding to intervene in Korea itself, at which point the war became essentially a U.S.-Chinese conflict. From late 1950 until mid-1953, when both sides finally accepted the fact of stalemate and signed a truce, the Korean war was for China—as well as for the United States—a foreign policy concern to which all others were subordinated.

In retrospect it seems clear that both the United States and China made serious miscalculations during the early months of the Korean war, with consequences that were to shape their respective policies for years to come. Both reacted in ways they believed to be defensive against threats they perceived to come from the other side. Washington tended to generalize the very real and immediate threat posed by the North Korean attack in Korea into a challenge posed by the entire Communist bloc to the entire "free world." In the Chinese case, U.S. intervention in Taiwan and Korea revived images of past threats to China's territorial integrity and security posed in earlier years by Japan.

Available evidence suggests that, while Peking from the outset gave moral support to the North Koreans in their attack on the South, it was the Soviet Union rather than China that was initially involved in direct military support of the attack; apparently the Chinese did not envisage or plan for Chinese military intervention.[9] Peking's decision to intervene was probably influenced by several factors. When American troops crossed the 38th parallel, Peking probably concluded that the United States posed a direct threat to China's security, in particular to Manchuria. Chinese leaders may also have believed that, even if no attacks were launched against Chinese territory, defeat of the North Korean regime would eliminate an important buffer area on China's critical northeastern flank and create a security threat for the future. It is probable, also, that the Soviet Union pressed for Chinese intervention to prevent a North Korean defeat, and that Peking concluded that its new alliance with Moscow required China to assist in a struggle that obviously had broad implications for the entire conflict between the Communist and non-Communist worlds. In any case, whatever the specific reasons, Peking decided to send its own troops to Korea in the fall of 1950, even though this involved high military risks. These risks included the possibility of U.S. nuclear attack, although the Chinese doubtless hoped that their alliance with Moscow would help to deter such an attack, as in fact it did.[10]

The Korean war significantly enhanced the prestige of the new Communist regime in China. The recognition that Chinese troops prevented the United States and United Nations forces from defeating North Korea impressed upon the world the fact that China was no longer a helpless giant, but rather a dynamic and highly mobilized nation

---

[8]China's decision to enter the Korean war has been carefully analyzed in an excellent study: Allen S. Whiting, *China Crosses the Yalu* (New York: Macmillan, 1960). For general background on the war, and China's participation in it, see David Rees, *Korea: The Limited War* (New York: St. Martin's Press, 1964, Pelican Books, 1970); see also Dean Acheson, *Present at the Creation* (New York: Norton, 1969), especially Chapters 44, 45, 47–49, 53–55, and 68.

[9]See Whiting, *China Crosses the Yalu*, especially p. 45 and Chapter 4, pp. 47 ff.

[10]See *Current Affairs Handbook,* Nov. 5, 1950, in *Current Background,* No. 32 (Nov. 29, 1950), and the statement made by a leading Chinese general to the Indian Ambassador to Peking, in K. M. Panikkar, *In Two Chinas* (London: Allen and Unwin, 1955), p. 108.

determined to defend its vital interests and assert its place in the world. The war also, however, involved sizable political as well as military costs for Peking. One was a significant delay in China's entry into the international community and the postponement by several years of normal state-to-state relations between China and the majority of the non-Communist nations of the world.

In the period between the establishment of China's new regime and the start of the Korean war, Peking had established diplomatic relations with all of the other Communist nations except Yugoslavia, but it was deliberately cautious and slow about formalizing relations with non-Communist governments. Although fourteen non-Communist nations recognized Peking during 1949–50, the Chinese had established diplomatic relations with only six of them before the start of the Korean war, and with only two more by the end of the war.[11] The Chinese leaders obviously placed a relatively low priority in this period on the importance of state-to-state relations with non-Communist states. In any case, Washington's opposition to recognizing the Communist regime and American pressure on allies to follow the U.S. lead in this policy made it difficult for Peking to expand its relations.

The war created new fears and hostilities in many non-Communist nations that continued long after the war was over, and the image of China as an expansionist aggressive power was a major factor inducing numerous nations to postpone recognition of Peking for many years. Most important, the legacy of mutual hostility between the United States and China left by the war led Washington to use its influence for roughly a decade and a half thereafter to do all it could to try to isolate China and exclude it from the international community, thus creating serious barriers to Peking's subsequent efforts to achieve worldwide recognition and expand its influence by conventional political means.

Post-Korea Trends

Even before the Korean war had ended, Peking was beginning to modify its assessment of the world situation and to adjust its foreign policy strategy and tactics. Whereas from 1949 to 1952 China's foreign policy interests had focused almost exclusively on other Communist nations and parties and closely associated insurrectionary and revolutionary forces, in late 1952, under the slogan of "peaceful coexistence," the cultivation of nonofficial relations with many different kinds of groups abroad was begun. Both Moscow and Peking now recognized the desirability of adopting a more flexible and somewhat less doctrinaire approach to the world—one aimed at creating a broad united front of "people's" forces directed against the "imperialists." It was at this time that Peking initiated an active program of "people's diplomacy."[12]

Soon after the end of the war, it went further and began to show a new interest in expanding state-to-state relations with non-Communist nations, searching for opportunities to broaden China's formal diplomatic ties. Between 1954 and the end of 1958, Peking established relations with thirteen more non-Communist nations, and with

[11] See "Diplomatic Relations of Communist China," *Current Background,* No. 440 (March 12, 1957). This gives information up to March 1, 1957. The later evolution of Peking's diplomatic relations is summarized in Donald W. Klein, "The Management of Foreign Affairs in Communist China," in John M. H. Lindbeck (ed.), *China: Management of a Revolutionary Society* (Seattle: University of Washington Press, 1971), pp. 315–16.

[12] See Barnett, *Communist China and Asia,* pp. 97–98 and 147–71; and Herbert Passin, *China's Cultural Diplomacy* (New York: Praeger, 1962).

Yugoslavia. Three were non-Communist Western European states (including the United Kingdom), but the rest were nations—mostly small—in the developing world.

Chinese policy in the period immediately after the Korean war was still predicated on the assumption that it was essential to maintain extremely close ties with the Soviet Union and other Communist bloc nations, and to coordinate policies among the Communist states in competing against the United States and the "imperialist camp." But by now the Chinese had begun to acquire a somewhat more sophisticated view of the world in general, and gradually recognized that the leaders of most "neutralist" nations could not be viewed simply as "running dogs" of the United States. Accordingly, Peking's leaders decided that to expand Chinese—and Communist bloc—influence and weaken the position of the United States, a major aim of Chinese policy should be to cultivate and woo the neutralist nations, in order to draw them into a broad anti-imperialist, anticolonial united front.[13] This policy soon began to pay limited dividends, despite the fact that adamant U.S. opposition slowed the process of expanding China's international ties. Peking's main diplomatic successes in the middle and late 1950s were in South Asia, the Middle East, and North Africa, areas where in fact China's concrete interests were comparatively limited and its capacity to play a major political and economic role was not great.

Thus, even though China began to shift in the 1952–54 period from a fairly narrow doctrinaire policy based on the concept of a bipolar world toward a more flexible policy aimed at creation of a broader united front to align neutralists with the Communist camp, Peking continued to feel threatened and on the defensive. However, its persistent use of militant rhetoric appeared threatening to many of its neighbors as well as to much of the rest of the world, and suspicion about China's intentions was heightened by Peking's continued use of limited military pressures and probes in pursuit of some of its priority goals in areas immediately adjacent to China.

Two serious international crises involving China occurred in the period immediately after the Korean war. Each intensified fears of Chinese intentions, even though in neither case did Peking intervene militarily to try to achieve its maximum goals. One of these was the Indochina crisis of 1954.[14] Although the Chinese were not the initiators of this crisis, Peking's large-scale material support of the Vietnamese Communists and Western anxiety about the possibility of direct Chinese military intervention led to the Geneva Conference on Indochina in the summer of 1954. At that conference, where for the first time since 1949 Chinese Communist representatives participated actively in a major international meeting, Peking ultimately threw its weight in favor of a compromise settlement which divided Vietnam at the 17th parallel. The Chinese, like the Vietnamese Communists, doubtless asssumed that this agreement would be a prelude to a fairly rapid Communist political takeover in Vietnam; nevertheless the Chinese position at the conference indicated that Peking placed highest priority on the need to forestall the danger of another large-scale conflict involving the major powers and on the desirability of ensuring the survival of a buffer area adjacent to China, rather than on the need to ensure an immediate Communist takeover of all Indochina.

---

[13]The Sino-Indian agreement of April 1954, followed by a joint Sino-Burmese communiqué in June of the same year, highlighted this new approach to the neutralist nations. See *Survey of China Mainland Press*, No. 786 (April 29, 1954), for the text of the Sino-Indian agreement and *Survey of China Mainland Press*, No. 841 (July 3–4, 1954), for data on the Sino-Burmese statements. The "five principles of peaceful coexistence" were articulated on both of these occasions.

[14]See Melvin Gurto, *The First Vietnam Crisis* (New York: Columbia University Press, 1967), and King C. Chen, *Vietnam and China, 1938–1954* (Princeton: Princeton University Press, 1969).

The second crisis in this period, which *was* initiated by Peking, focused on the small Nationalist-controlled offshore islands in the Taiwan area near the China coast.[15] Recovery of control over Taiwan was one of Peking's fundamental national aims, but the presence of the U.S. Seventh Fleet now blocked the possibility of direct attack. Peking undertook to see if Taiwan's U.S. protectors could be dislodged by means short of invasion. Within three months of the signing of the Indochina agreement at Geneva, Peking launched a large-scale bombardment of Quemoy, creating a situation of great tension and raising the specter of possible war. In retrospect it seems clear that Peking was not prepared to launch a full-scale invasion of the islands in the face of strong U.S. as well as Nationalist opposition. Its primary objective was to test whether, by means of limited and controlled military pressures and threats, it could create tensions that might ultimately split the United States from the Nationalists and lead to a withdrawal of the American military presence from the Taiwan area. When Peking concluded that its pressures were not achieving this goal but instead were creating a new danger of major conflict, it backed away from direct confrontation, allowed the crisis to subside, and turned to political tactics to pursue its goals in relation to Taiwan. Peking's military probe in this case did, however, reinforce the image already accepted in many non-Communist nations—and in particular the United States—of China as a militant expansionist power, with effects that were both far-reaching and long-lasting.

The net effect of these developments and of the response of the non-Communist nations to them was to intensify the level of hostility in U.S.-China relations, increase the fear of China among the leaders of many of its immediate neighbors, and stimulate greater efforts by the United States to induce other non-Communist nations to participate in a structure of military bases and alliances on China's periphery designed to "contain" what was perceived to be a dangerous threat of Chinese expansionism. In 1954, the United States not only signed a mutual defense treaty with the Nationalist regime on Taiwan, further strengthening the ties between Washington and Taipei, but also took the lead in creating the Southeast Asia Treaty Organization which, together with U.S. treaties already signed between 1951 and 1953 with Australia, New Zealand, Japan, the Philippines, and South Korea, completed a network of alliances and bases that partially "surrounded" China.[16] Initially the treaties with the Philippines, Australia, and New Zealand were made with Japan in mind, but by the mid-1950s their primary significance was in relation to China.

From Peking's viewpoint, these American initiatives—as well as the cold war rhetoric of Secretary of State John Foster Dulles and other U.S. policy makers in the 1950s—reinforced fears of external pressures, encirclement, and even possible attack by the United States. Peking's security concerns still focused almost exclusively on the United States at this time, and its leaders were acutely aware of China's vulnerability to U.S military action. Even though the Sino-Soviet alliance provided an important counterbalance to the United States and a deterrent against nuclear attack, the Chinese probably felt genuinely threatened—a fact that reinforced their determination to build up their independent military strength.

---

[15]Barnett, *Communist China and Asia*, pp. 102–03.

[16]See Fred Greene, *U.S. Policy and the Security of Asia* (New York: McGraw-Hill, 1968), Part 2, . pp. 71–123.

The Bandung Period

From their position of comparative military weakness and relative political isolation, Peking's leaders increasingly recognized in the 1950s the need to take new political initiatives designed to broaden China's relations with non-Communist as well as Communist nations. Their goal was to break out of isolation and to create a united front that would have substantial Third World support. They also hoped to weaken gradually the international position of the United States, particularly in Asia.

In 1954–55, therefore, Peking adopted a new foreign policy strategy which de-emphasized China's revolutionary objectives and stressed the theme of "peaceful coexistence." Peking now proclaimed its desire to develop normalized state-to-state relations with a wide variety of non-Communist nations, and it adopted many new policies that were notable for their flexibility, relative moderation, and stress on conciliation.

The first important manifestation of this new approach was the signing, in 1954, of a Sino-Indian agreement on Tibet, in which Peking and New Delhi cosponsored the so-called five principles of peaceful coexistence. Then, in April 1955, Premier Chou En-lai attended the Bandung Conference of Asian and African states in Indonesia and attempted to assume the role of peacemaker, conciliator, and spokesman for the Asian-African world.[17] He also proposed negotiations with the United States on "relaxing tension in the Taiwan area" and tried to reassure Asian nations worried about their Chinese minorities that China would not attempt to manipulate the overseas Chinese to subvert the non-Communist governments under which they lived.

During what has come to be known as the "Bandung period," which lasted until 1957–58, Peking worked hard to establish its respectability and responsibility as a major power and to underline its desire for peaceful, friendly relations with non-Communist nations. "Revolution cannot be exported," the Chinese Premier proclaimed.[18] Going beyond mere tolerance for the neutralist nations, Peking in effect became a sponsor of neutralism. In particular, great importance was placed on the need for cooperation between China and India, which under Prime Minister Nehru was perhaps the most influential leader and symbol of the neutralist and anticolonial nations. Peking's efforts after Bandung to expand its state-to-state foreign relations produced gradual and limited, but nevertheless significant, results. Efforts to promote foreign trade were part of the new policy, and China also began in this period its first programs of foreign aid to non-Communist nations, and its program of "people's diplomacy" was greatly expanded.

One can only speculate about how China's international relations might have developed if Peking had pursued its Bandung strategy for an extended period. It seems likely that Peking's policy makers could have made steady progress in obtaining general acceptance of China by the international community and could have increased Chinese influence abroad substantially, primarily by conventional political and economic means. In fact, however, the Bandung period proved to be brief.

---

[17]See George McT. Kahin, *The Asian-African Conference, Bandung, Indonesia* (Ithaca, N.Y.: Cornell University Press, 1956); and A. Doak Barnett, "Chou Enlai at Bandung," *American University Field Staff Reports,* No. ADB-1955-4 (May 4, 1955), pp. 1–15.

[18]*Survey of China Mainland Press,* No. 841 (July 3–4, 1954), p. 2.

Militancy Revived

By late 1957 Peking had abandoned its relatively flexible and moderate posture of 1954–57 and was moving toward a much more militant and revolutionary stance once again. Proclaiming that the "East Wind Prevails over the West Wind," Mao called in November 1957 for greater militancy on the part of the entire Communist world toward the "imperialists" and in particular toward the United States.[19] The causes of this major shift in strategy are still a subject of debate. However, it is clear that several important factors were involved.

In a basic sense, the shift reflected changes in the Chinese domestic political and economic situation. It paralleled the change within China from the relatively pragmatic policies of the first Five-Year Plan to a more revolutionary period of economic and social policy. The Bandung period and China's first Five-Year Plan were mutually reinforcing; both at home and abroad the Chinese leaders gave priority concern to concrete immediate goals and de-emphasized long-range ideological and revolutionary aims. The increased militancy of Chinese foreign policy beginning in late 1957 coincided with Mao's abandonment of the Soviet model for Chinese development and his decision to push new domestic policies that were to be a prelude to the radical Great Leap Forward and Commune Program of 1958. Both Peking's "East Wind" policy abroad and its "Great Leap" policies at home were manifestations of Mao's reassertion of his distinctive revolutionary values and visions.

China's 1957 foreign policy shift also reflected a new assessment by Mao of the overall international situation and the prevailing balance of world forces. Mao put forward his "East Wind" slogan when he was in Moscow to attend a Soviet-convened conference of Communist states and parties, on the occasion of the fortieth anniversary of the Bolshevik Revolution, shortly after the Russians had launched their first satellite and intercontinental ballistic missile. He took the position that these Soviet space and missile accomplishments marked a new "turning point" in the "world situation," and apparently concluded that the world balance had been significantly altered, psychologically if not militarily, in favor of the Communists.[20] Although Moscow did not fully accept this assessment, Mao nevertheless argued that all Communist nations and parties should take advantage of the altered balance to press much harder against the "imperialist camp" to achieve their goals. By this time he had already begun to have doubts about Moscow's leadership of the Communist bloc and world movement, as a result of Khrushchev's destalinization program and the ensuing crises in Eastern Europe in 1956, and he urged the Soviet Union not only to reassert revolutionary discipline and orthodoxy within the Communist bloc but also to adopt a more militant "forward policy" toward the West.

A third and more subtle factor influencing the Chinese decision to adopt a new "hard line" in 1957 may have been simple impatience. Although China's international image had improved, its political influence had expanded, and its acceptance by the world community had increased during the Bandung period, the process was far too slow from Peking's point of view. The United States continued its hardline policy of "isolation and pressure" against China, rejecting in 1955 several conciliatory Chinese

---

[19]For Mao Tse-tung's November 18, 1957, speech in Moscow, see "Mao Tse-tung on Imperialists and Reactionaries," *Current Background*, No. 534 (Nov. 12, 1958).

[20]Donald S. Zagoria, *The Sino-Soviet Conflict, 1956–61* (Princeton: Princeton University Press, 1962), pp. 160–61.

gestures and initiatives, including proposals for trade, exchanges of journalists, and a meeting of foreign ministers. In large part because of American opposition, the majority of non-Communist nations still held back from recognizing the Peking regime, and the Chinese Communists were still excluded from the United Nations and other international bodies. Although the U.S.-Chinese ambassadorial talks started in 1955 still continued, Peking had not made any significant progress in weakening the ties between Washington and the Nationalists. In fact, as Peking saw it, the United States was moving steadily toward a "two Chinas" policy, and the prospect of "liberating" Taiwan appeared to be more distant than ever.

Whatever the explanation for the 1957 shift, it had profound effects. From late 1957 on, Peking demonstrated in one situation after another a renewed commitment to militant revolutionary values. In the spring of 1958, it launched a major propaganda attack on "revisionism" within the Communist world, focusing its criticism on Yugoslavia and pressing the Soviet Union to take a harder line against all "liberalizing" tendencies in Communist nations and parties. In the summer of the same year, when the United States intervened in the Middle East during a crisis involving Lebanon and Iraq, Peking urged Moscow to take strong action, and there was even talk in Peking of sending Chinese "volunteers" to the Middle East; although this gesture had little practical significance, it nevertheless symbolized Peking's new posture. In Vietnam and Laos, in the ensuing period, China gave moral and material support to active insurrection.

In none of these situations, however, did Peking intervene with its own combat forces, and the verbal militancy was not indiscriminate. China continued to woo such countries as Cambodia, for example; and when the situation in Laos reached a critical stage, Peking ultimately threw its weight in favor of the compromise political settlement effected at the Geneva Conference of 1962.[21] Nevertheless, the broad thrust of the new Chinese strategy from late 1957 on made it appear that Peking was again prepared to use threats and pressures to promote its revolutionary goals. Not surprisingly, Peking's new stance tarnished China's Bandung image and intensified fears in many quarters about Chinese intentions.

Although Peking's new hard-line strategy obviously affected China's relationship with smaller powers, the more important result was that the new policies ultimately placed Peking at odds with all four major nations whose interests impinged most directly on China—not only the United States but also Japan, India, and, most serious of all, the Soviet Union. By 1960 China found itself more isolated, in terms of big power relationships, than ever before.

In early 1958, Peking decided to exert direct and intense pressures on the government of Prime Minister Nobusuke Kishi of Japan, to try to influence the outcome of the upcoming Japanese elections and to induce Tokyo to loosen its ties with the United States and adopt a more compliant policy toward China. In perhaps the most blatant attempt that Peking has made to use economic policy as an instrument of political pressure, all trade relations with the Japanese were severed and Peking called for major changes in Japan's leadership and policies. Although the immediate results were clearly counterproductive, Peking kept up the pressure in a continuing effort to stimulate new tensions in American-Japanese relations. It was not until after the U.S.-Japan security

---

[21]See Arthur Lall, *How Communist China Negotiates* (New York: Columbia University Press, 1968), and Kenneth T. Young, *Negotiating with the Chinese Communists: The United States Experience, 1953–67* (New York: McGraw-Hill, 1968), pp. 248–49.

treaty had been renewed in 1960—and after the Sino-Soviet split, which necessitated a basic re-evaluation of China's trade and overall policies, had come into the open— that Peking abandoned its policy of economic and political pressure on Tokyo and began to repair Sino-Japanese relations.

In the fall of 1958, in the midst of the Great Leap Forward, Peking launched its second major military probe against the offshore islands.[22] As in 1954-55, the Chinese Communists apparently did not intend to undertake a major military operation but rather to strain relations between Washington and Taipei and thus weaken U.S. support for the Nationalist regime; but once again the tactic of limited threats and pressures failed to achieve this objective. At the height of this crisis, the danger of war was even greater than four years earlier, and in the end Peking backed down and reverted to negotiations and political tactics. The net effect was to reinforce the American image of a hostile and dangerous China—and to postpone any real possibility of reducing tension in the Taiwan area or improving relations between China and the United States.

The Sino-Indian crisis of 1959 was the next important episode in Chinese foreign policy in this period.[23] Its immediate causes were rooted in the problems Peking was encountering in maintaining political control in Tibet—an area of Chinese colonial rule over which all Chinese leaders, including the Nationalists, have claimed sovereignty, but where the local population has consistently resented and resisted Chinese control. Tibetan disaffection, which had steadily grown for some years, exploded in 1959 in open revolt. When Peking suppressed the uprising with a heavy hand, the Dalai Lama and thousands of other Tibetans fled to India, where the Indian government granted them sanctuary. Bitter mutual recriminations ensued between China and India, with Peking claiming that the Indians had instigated the revolt and New Delhi openly criticizing China's actions and charging publicly that China had for some years been violating the Indian border. Whatever the perceptions and motives underlying Peking's tactics in this crisis, it marked the beginning of the end of Peking's policy of cooperation with India in wooing the Third World, which had been a basic element of Chinese foreign policy since 1954.

Border tensions between China and India steadily grew after the Tibetan revolt, reaching a climax in the short Sino-Indian "border war" of 1962. Blame for this conflict cannot be assigned exclusively to either side. Both countries had an arguable basis for their particular territorial claims, and neither was willing to consider compromises acceptable to the other. Chinese military action, moreover, may have been initiated partially in response to Indian military pressures northward.[24] Nevertheless, Peking's

---

[22]See Tang Tsou, "Mao's Limited War in the Taiwan Strait," *Orbis*, Vol. 3, No. 3 (Fall 1959), pp. 332-50; and Tang Tsou, "The Quemoy Imbroglio: Chiang Kai-shek and the United States," *Western Political Quarterly*, Vol. 12, No. 4 (December 1959), pp. 1075-91.

[23]There had been earlier border incidents, and exchanges of notes over differing maps, but it was only after the 1959 Tibetan revolt and the flight of the Dalai Lama to India that the border disputes became tense and were brought into the open; thereafter, Sino-Indian relations began to undergo fundamental change. See Barnett, *Communist China and Asia*, pp. 313-15.

[24]A thorough study of this is Neville Maxwell, *India's China War* (Pantheon, 1970). Maxwell places a large share of the blame for the conflict on India's "forward policy." See also Kuang-sheng Liao and Allen S. Whiting, "Chinese Press Perceptions of Threat: The U.S. and India, 1962," *China Quarterly*, No. 53 (January–March 1973), pp. 80-97. Not surprisingly, Indian interpretations of the motivations for Peking's policy toward India are substantially different; see, for example, Dutt, *China's Foreign Policy*, pp. 195-271.

attack was a calculated exercise of intense military pressure, which was doubtless designed to, and in fact did, humiliate India and strengthen Peking's political hand. Even though China's forces generally did not penetrate beyond the territories claimed by Peking, the attack highlighted India's weakness and vulnerability.

Between 1959 and 1962, Peking shifted to an overtly hostile political and diplomatic posture toward New Delhi, maintaining pressure on the Indians while cultivating all of India's neighbors. Thereafter, support of Pakistan against India became an increasingly important component of China's foreign policy. Peking not only granted the Pakistanis substantial military and economic aid; in 1965, and again in 1971, China gave strong moral and political support to the Pakistani position in Indian-Pakistani conflicts over Kashmir and Bangladesh. In neither case, however, did China directly intervene, nor was it able in either case to determine the ultimate military outcome.

The Sino-Soviet Dispute

While growing tension in areas to the east and south of China in the late 1950s [was] important to Peking, Chinese leaders increasingly were compelled to turn their attention to the north and west. By far the most important development in China's foreign relations in the late 1950s was the widening rift between Peking and Moscow.[25] Whereas Peking's foreign policy in the 1950s had been premised on the concept of a worldwide struggle between the Soviet-led socialist camp and the American-led imperialist camp and had as its keystone the Sino-Soviet alliance, by 1960 the Communist bloc was deeply divided, and the future of the Peking-Moscow alliance was problematic. This new situation fundamentally changed China's international position and greatly altered the basic framework for Peking's perceptions of the world. Major changes in China's foreign policy strategies and tactics were obviously required.

In tracing the origins of the Sino-Soviet dispute, it can be argued that the causes must be sought in deep-rooted historical, geopolitical, and cultural differences between the two countries and in ideological and policy differences between the Chinese and Soviet Communist parties that long predated any overt signs of conflict in the post-1949 period. There is some validity to this view. The historical record of Sino-Russian relations for centuries has been replete with recurrent conflict, mutual suspicion, and fric-

---

[25]The best single volume on the origins of the Sino-Soviet dispute is Zagoria, *The Sino-Soviet Conflict*. The literature on the dispute and on Chinese-Russian relations is, however, extensive—more extensive, in fact, than on any other facet of China's foreign relations—and only a few of the useful studies will be mentioned here. Zbigniew K. Brzezinski, *The Soviet Bloc—Unity and Conflict* (Cambridge: Harvard University Press, 1960), and Alexander Dallin (ed.), *Diversity in International Communism* (New York: Columbia University Press, 1963), analyze the early periods of the dispute in the broad context of developments affecting all the Communist states and parties. John Gittings, *Survey of the Sino-Soviet Dispute* (New York: Oxford University Press, 1968); two volumes by William E. Griffith, *The Sino-Soviet Rift* (M.I.T. Press, 1964), and *Peking, Moscow, and Beyond* (Georgetown University, Center for Strategic and International Studies, 1973); and Harold C. Hinton, *The Bear at the Gate* (Washington: American Enterprise Institute for Public Policy Research, 1971), focus directly on Sino-Soviet relations and carry the story up to the recent period. Richard Lowenthal, *World Communism: The Disintegration of a Secular Faith* (New York: Oxford University Press, 1964), analyzes broad developments affecting the entire "bloc." Kurt London (ed.), *Unity and Contradictions: Major Aspects of Sino-Soviet Relations* (New York: Praeger, 1962), contains a number of useful chapters on Sino-Soviet relations and competition. A study that is very useful for the historical background to recent developments in relations between the two countries is O. Edmund Clubb, *China and Russia: The "Great Game"* (New York: Columbia University Press, 1971).

tion; and from the 1920s on, there were serious differences on many occasions between Chinese and Soviet Communist party leaders. In the first half of the 1950s, however, the Chinese Communists seemed confident that close cooperation with the Russians was both possible and desirable, and committed themselves to strengthen the alliance in every way possible. During the Stalinist period, and especially during the Korean war, there were some strains in the Sino-Soviet relationship, but Peking subordinated any doubts and dissatisfactions it may have had. In the immediate post-Stalin period, when both Moscow and Peking took steps to cement their relationship, the alliance reached its peak of intimacy.

The Chinese now date the start of their dispute with the Russians to 1956, and from their perspective this dating has considerable logic. Khrushchev's dramatic destalinization moves that year, taken without prior consultation with Peking, raised serious doubts in the Chinese leaders' minds about the Soviet Union's policies and capacity for leadership of the Communist world. During the ensuing crises in Poland and Hungary, these doubts increased, and the Chinese began for the first time to articulate their own independent views about basic issues affecting the Communist bloc and movement as a whole; for the first time, Peking intervened directly in the politics of Eastern Europe. At the Moscow meeting of Communist states and parties in 1957, it became clear that the Chinese and Russians now held divergent views on many broad ideological, political, and strategic issues. Thereafter, differences between Peking and Moscow over such issues developed gradually but steadily until finally in 1960 Peking took the initiative in launching a bitter polemical attack against Soviet "revisionism."[26] Moscow responded not merely with its own propaganda counterattack but by withdrawing all of its technicians and ending all assistance to China.

The arguments in the Sino-Soviet debate as it evolved in this period focused on such broad ideological and strategic issues as the present character of imperialism, the inevitability or noninevitability of war, the nature of "peaceful coexistence," the feasibility and desirability of using violent revolutionary methods, the possibility of disarmament and détente with the West, and many others. On all of these issues, Peking took the more militant revolutionary position and accused Moscow of departing from Marxist-Leninist orthodoxy. The ideological element in the dispute was obviously important and reflected a widening gap between Khrushchev's and Mao's perceptions of the world and their basic policy predispositions both at home and abroad. Underlying the polemical arguments, however, were a growing number of specific policy differences and clashes of national interest that had relatively little to do with ideology. These conflicts of interest, above all, led to the ultimate breakup of the Sino-Soviet alliance.

Overall policy toward the United States and the West was one of the crucial issues on which Soviet and Chinese views steadily diverged. Khrushchev, as leader of a major nuclear power, became increasingly convinced that Soviet policy must be adjusted to the realities of a nuclear world and that he must undertake the quest for some kind of limited détente with the United States to prevent nuclear war. In contrast, Mao, as a dedicated revolutionary and as head of a nonnuclear nation still relatively weak in military terms, refused to acknowledge openly that nuclear weapons had fundamentally changed the world situation, although he was obviously aware of the disaster nuclear war could bring. He feared that any Moscow-Washington détente could only occur at the expense of China's interests. Fearing a weakening of the forces for revolutionary change in the world, he pressed for increased militancy against the West rather than détente.

---

[26]*Long Live Leninism* (Peking: Foreign Languages Press, 1960).

In more specific terms, the Chinese learned, during several crises involving crucial Chinese interests between 1957 and 1959, that Moscow was unwilling to give full support to Peking and in fact was now prepared to oppose certain major Chinese policies. One of these cases was the second offshore islands crisis in 1958.[27] Moscow failed to give the strong, active support the Chinese hoped for, and made it clear that, while it was willing to extend a defensive nuclear umbrella over China to deter a major U.S. attack, it was *not* willing to give positive support to any attempt by Peking to "liberate" Taiwan. Moscow's unwillingness to back Peking in crises involving Chinese territorial claims was also made evident in the Sino-Indian border crises of 1959 and 1962; in the latter case, in fact, Moscow's behavior indicated that it sympathized more with non-Communist India than with Communist China. The Chinese were already disturbed by the substantial aid the Russians had been giving India since the mid-1950s; and now Peking found itself in open competition with Moscow throughout South Asia. By the 1960s, the Russians were giving increasing military as well as political support to the Indians while the Chinese strengthened their backing of the military rulers in Pakistan.

Another extremely important clash of Chinese and Russian interests in this period (although it was not publicized at the time) concerned nuclear weapons. From Peking's perspective, this may well have been the straw that broke the camel's back in Sino-Soviet relations. In late 1957, the Chinese and Russians had signed a secret agreement in which, according to later Chinese claims, Moscow pledged to assist Peking in developing a Chinese nuclear capability.[28] Precisely what differences emerged over the implementation of this agreement in the ensuing year and a half is not known, but Moscow ultimately was unwilling to provide the nuclear assistance Peking desired on terms acceptable to the Chinese. The scanty evidence available suggests that the USSR probably insisted on conditions and controls that Peking believed would compromise China's national integrity. In any case, according to the Chinese, the agreement was "torn up" by the Russians in 1959, and from 1960 on Peking was compelled to pursue a go-it-alone policy in developing an independent nuclear capability.

The limits of Soviet support to China were demonstrated in a variety of other ways in the late 1950s. Although Moscow gave some crucial short-term trading credits to China in 1959, all long-term Soviet economic development loans to Peking were exhausted by 1957, and it became apparent to the Chinese that the Russians were not willing to provide such support for China's second plan. This was particularly galling in view of the increasing amounts of aid Moscow was now undertaking to provide to such non-Communist countries as India. And when Mao abandoned the Soviet model of economic development and launched China on the Great Leap Forward in 1958, Khrushchev's undisguised contempt for the Communes and Mao's other economic and social experiments obviously angered the Chinese.

---

[27]On September 1, 1963, the Chinese asserted that although the Soviet Union had made statements supporting China on September 7 and 19, 1958, during the second offshore island crisis, it only did so "when there was no possibility that a nuclear war would break out and no need for the Soviet Union to support China with its nuclear weapons." See "A Comment on the Soviet Government's Statement, August 21, 1963," in Griffith, *The Sino-Soviet Rift*, p. 382. See also Morton H. Halperin, *China and the Bomb* (New York: Praeger, 1965), pp. 55–62; and the papers by Harold C. Hinton, Malcolm Mackintosh, and George Quester on "Sino-Soviet Relations in a U.S.-China Crisis," in Morton H. Halperin (ed.), *Sino-Soviet Relations and Arms Control*, Vol. 2, *Collected Papers* (Harvard University, East Asian Research Center and Center for International Affairs, 1966).

[28]"Statement by the Spokesman of the Chinese Government—A Comment on the Soviet Government's Statement of August 3," *Peking Review* (Aug. 16, 1963), p. 14.

Eruption of the Sino-Soviet dispute into open ideological debate in 1960 climaxed these developments, marking the end of all pretense of close Sino-Soviet cooperation and the beginning of a period of steadily escalating conflict. Not only did the polemics intensify, but Peking and Moscow began to compete actively for support in other Communist nations and parties, and throughout the Third World as well. The fact that each side regarded the other as ideologically heretical intensified the passions resulting from the schism, but the clash increasingly found expression in differences over national interests and concrete policies. When the Russians decided in 1963 to conclude a limited nuclear test ban with the United States—an agreement Peking viewed as aimed specifically against China—a "point of no return" had been reached in the Sino-Soviet dispute. During 1963 and 1964, the Chinese made a sweeping ideological and political attack on the Soviet leadership, climaxed with a denunciation of "Khrushchev's phoney communism." From Peking's point of view, China and the Soviet Union were now bitter adversaries rather than allies.[29]

The Sino-Soviet conflict basically altered China's perception of and approach to the outside world. Peking now accused the two superpowers of "colluding as well as contending" and of cooperating to establish a superpower duopoly to dominate the international community and ride roughshod over the interests of China and the rest of the world. China now saw itself confronted with threatening adversaries on both its eastern and western flanks. In this new situation, China's priority foreign policy task, in the view of Peking's leaders, was to cope with the threats they believed were posed by both of the superpowers, and to compete against both "social imperialism" (i.e., the Soviet Union) and capitalist "imperialism" on a worldwide basis.

There is ample evidence that during the 1960s China's conflict with the Soviet Union became such an obsession in the minds of many of China's leaders—and particularly in Mao's mind—that the perceived threat posed by Moscow, real or presumed, gradually came to overshadow in Chinese thinking the threat presumed to be posed by the United States.

In the first half of the 1960s, although there were some Sino-Soviet border frictions, as in Sinkiang in 1962, Mao's concern centered primiarily on the subversive influence that he feared the Soviet example could have—in fact, was already having, he felt—in China. This was the period when Mao became convinced that the revolution in China was gradually being eroded and undermined, and when he concluded that an all-out counterattack against "revisionist" thinking was required both at home and abroad.[30]

In the second half of the 1960s, Peking's concern focused increasingly on the danger of a direct Soviet military threat. The intensity of Chinese anti-Soviet rhetoric and hints that the Chinese were reviving claims to large portions of Soviet territory had meanwhile aroused reciprocal fears in the Soviet Union, and Moscow began a large military buildup around China's borders. This buildup reinforced Peking's apprehensions. Then the Russian invasion of Czechoslovakia in 1968 and Moscow's proclamation of the "Brezhnev Doctrine," asserting the Russians' right to intervene to suppress counter-revolutionary trends in other socialist states, heightened Peking's alarm. Shortly thereafter, in 1969, a series of bitter military clashes exploded on the Sino-Soviet border and

---

[29]This joint editorial in *People's Daily* and *Red Flag* was the last of nine "Comments on the Open Letter of the Central Committee of the CPSU," which constituted a sweeping polemical attack on the Khrushchev regime during 1963-64. For text, see *Peking Review* (July 17, 1964), pp. 7-28.

[30]See Barnett, *Uncertain Passage: China's Transition to the Post-Mao Era* (Washington, D.C.: The Brookings Institution, 1974), pp. 6-12.

brought the two countries close to war.[31] By the end of that year, the danger of war had diminished and negotiations on border issues had begun, but the adversary relationship continued, with a high level of fear and suspicion persisting on both sides.

Secondary Effects of the Sino-Soviet Split

The Sino-Soviet split set the basic framework for China's foreign policy in the early 1960s. Peking's opposition to the United States continued, but gradually its principal concern shifted to the Soviet Union. The split reinforced the Chinese tendency, evident from the late 1950s on, to put ever-increasing stress upon the need for complete "independence" and "self-reliance." Since Peking was now at odds with all the major powers whose interests impinged most directly on its own, the policy of self-reliance was, in some respects, a matter of making a virtue of necessity. But there was more to it than that. The policy also reflected a deep conviction on Peking's part, born of disillusionment with its alliance with Moscow, that China must henceforth avoid dependence on any other major power. This did not mean that Peking had lost interest in the outside world. On the contrary, it stepped up its activities in many areas during the first half of the 1960s, competing directly with both the United States and the Soviet Union, and to a lesser extent with India as well, in an energetic attempt to expand China's influence on a global basis.

By 1960, Chinese leaders recognized that if they did not modify the posture of revolutionary militancy that Mao had called for in 1957, they probably could not achieve their aims—particularly without Soviet support. Peking therefore initiated a variety of new policies, which represented a new mix of revolutionary and nationalistic aims and were characterized by considerable flexibility and pragmatism. In part because China was now committed to compete against the Soviet Union on a global basis, and in part because Mao was determined to make Peking rather than Moscow the principal center of inspiration for worldwide revolution,[32] China maintained a fairly high level of revolutionary rhetoric. Peking held itself up as the principal interpreter of orthodox Marxism-Leninism, continued to call for intensified revolutionary struggle and a broad united front directed against Soviet "social imperialism" and U.S. "imperialism," and attempted to mobilize under Chinese leadership all nations or groups dissatisfied with the existing international status quo. In practice, however, Peking now tended to view the enemies of its enemies as potential friends, with relatively little regard for ideology, and to do whatever seemed possible to promote the interests and influence of China as a major power.

Both Peking and Moscow attempted to assert their primacy throughout the Communist bloc and world movement, which, as a result of both the Eastern European crises of 1956 and the Sino-Soviet split, was now characterized by growing polycentrism. Sino-Soviet competition strengthened trends toward more "independent" policies in several Eastern European Communist countries. Broadly speaking, however, the Chinese were handicapped in this competition by the fairly extreme ideological positions Peking put forward. China's closest link with a ruling Communist party in this period

---

[31]Thomas W. Robinson, *The Sino-Soviet Border Dispute: Background, Development, and the March 1969 Clashes,* Report RM-6171-PR (Rand Corp., August 1970).

[32]See Griffith, *The Sino-Soviet Rift,* especially pp. 177–206; Gittings, *Survey of the Sino-Soviet Dispute,* especially pp. 200–11; and Robert A. Scalapino, "Moscow, Peking, and the Communist Parties of Asia," *Foreign Affairs,* Vol. 41, No. 2 (January 1963), pp. 323–43.

was with its tiny Eastern European ally, Albania, which turned to China for support because it too was at odds with Moscow. China's main backing from other Communist parties came from a few small splinter parties that endorsed Mao's distinctive views. Although the Chinese achieved only limited success in increasing their own influence in other Communist states and parties in the 1960s, the Sino-Soviet competition resulted in a temporary weakening of Moscow's control.

Increased Activity in the Third World

Unable to achieve a position of primacy in the Communist world, Peking turned its attention to other areas and stepped up its efforts to expand China's diplomatic ties and influence in the Third World.[33] Some limited successes had been achieved in the Middle East by the late 1950s. In the early 1960s, the Chinese began to focus special attention on Africa,[34] where a large number of new nations had just achieved independence. From 1959 to 1964, Peking established diplomatic relations with nineteen additional countries, fifteen of which were in Africa. It also initiated a number of programs of economic aid to African nations.

The principal Chinese appeal to the underdeveloped world in general, and to the new African states in particular, was the call for a broad anti-imperialist, anticolonial, national liberation movement against the major powers (and in the case of Africa, against the white-ruled nations of southern Africa as well). Peking viewed Africa as a region where, as Chou En-lai indiscreetly put it while touring the continent in 1964, "revolutionary prospects are excellent,"[35] and it threw its support behind a variety of revolutionary movements in the region. Many African leaders, jealous of their newly acquired independence, were inclined to be suspicious of the intentions of Peking as of all major powers, however, and they found such statements alarming. As Peking's activities in the region grew, so too did frictions between China and several governments with which it had only recently established relations; four of these broke diplomatic ties with Peking for various reasons during 1965–66.

The Chinese also began to show increased interest in Latin America in the early 1960s,[36] although there its efforts achieved less success than in Africa. The establishment of formal relations with Cuba in 1960, immediately after Fidel Castro's rise to power, gave Peking its first diplomatic toehold in the region. Before long, however, it

---

[33]Most writing on China and the Third World has been in the form of articles. However, most of the general studies listed in note 1 for this chapter deal with the topic. In addition, there have been several very useful booklength studies dealing with China's relations with particular regions, including Bruce Larkin, *China and Africa, 1949–1970* (Berkeley: University of California Press, 1971); Cecil Johnson, *Communist China and Latin America, 1959–1967* (New York: Columbia University Press, 1970); and Melvin Gurtov, *China and Southeast Asia: The Politics of Survival* (Lexington, Mass.: Heath Lexington Books, 1971).

[34]In addition to the work by Larkin cited in note 33, see Robert A. Scalapino, "Sino-Soviet Competition in Africa," *Foreign Affairs*, Vol. 42, No. 4 (July 1964), pp. 640–54; George T. Yu, "Peking versus Taipei in the World Arena: Chinese Competition in Africa," *Asian Survey*, Vol. 3, No. 9 (September 1963), pp. 439–53; and Zbigniew Brzezinski (ed.), *Africa and the Communist World* (Stanford: Stanford University Press, 1963).

[35]*Peking Review* (Feb. 14, 1964), p. 6.

[36]In addition to the work by Cecil Johnson cited in note 33 for this chapter, see Ernst Halperin, "Peking and the Latin American Communists," *China Quarterly*, No. 29 (January–March 1967), pp. 111–54; and Joseph J. Lee, "Communist China's Latin American Policy," *Asian Survey*, Vol. 4, No. 11 (November 1964), pp. 1123–34.

became clear that Mao's revolutionary line differed significantly from Castro's as well as Moscow's, and in the competition among the three, China made only limited headway. By the mid-1960s, in fact, Sino-Cuban relations were seriously strained. Moscow's ability to outbid Peking in material support was not unimportant in the Cuban situation, but the key factor was doubtless Castro's nationalism, which involved him in some disputes with the Russians as well as the Chinese. Elsewhere in Latin America, Peking's stress on revolution and on the Maoist model inhibited governments in power from recognizing Peking, and except for a few splinter Communist parties, the major revolutionary movements in the region looked elsewhere for their primary inspiration and support. In sum, although the Chinese established new contacts in Latin America and emerged as a definite factor influencing the development of ideological and political forces in the region, its impact was still very limited.

In South Asia,[37] Peking continued the hostile policies it had adopted toward India during 1959-62, but it pursued generally conciliatory policies toward all the other nations in the region. The keystone of China's new South Asia policy was Pakistan, to which Peking gave strong political support and increasing amounts of economic aid. A complex competition for power and influence emerged, with Peking supporting Pakistan against India and Moscow supporting India against Pakistan. Elsewhere in the region Peking attempted to woo all of India's immediate neighbors, and between 1960 and 1963 it concluded important border settlements or friendship agreements not only with Pakistan but also with Afghanistan, Nepal, Burma, and Ceylon. The Chinese hoped this strategy would isolate India diplomatically, weaken its influence, exert pressure on New Delhi to agree to a compromise settlement of the Sino-Indian border dispute, and check the growth of Soviet influence in the region. While Peking did not succeed in the last two of these aims, it did have some success in the first two. It was not until after India had successfully supported the Bangladesh revolt against Pakistan in 1971 that New Delhi emerged, with renewed self-confidence and increased Soviet backing, in a clearly dominant position in South Asia. China's room for maneuver in the region declined thereafter, although Peking has continued to give various kinds of support to the Pakistanis.

In other Asian areas close to China, Peking's policies were extremely varied in the early 1960s. In the states of Indochina, it gave increasingly strong backing to the government of North Vietnam and to the Vietcong in their conflict with South Vietnam as the fighting there intensified, and it continued to support the Pathet Lao as they stepped up their revolutionary activites in Laos. It also continued to endorse several other "revolutionary struggles" throughout the region.

However, the Chinese now found it expedient to adopt a conciliatory stance and to develop cooperative relations with a range of non-Communist nations and groups in Southeast Asia. A major effort was made to promote good relations with neutralist Cambodia and Burma,[38] and Peking's ties with the Sihanouk regime in Cambodia became increasingly close. China's hopes for developing a united front of anti-imperialist forces in the region now centered, however, on Indonesia. Encouraged by the steady growth of the Peking-oriented Communist party of Indonesia, China doubtless hoped

---

[37]For the interaction of China, India, Pakistan, and the Soviet Union, see Bhabani Sen Gupta, *The Fulcrum of Asia: Relations Among China, India, Pakistan, and the U.S.S.R.* (Pegasus, 1970). See also, for background, Wayne Wilcox, *India, Pakistan and the Rise of China* (New York: Walker, 1964).

[38]See Robert A. Holmes, "Chinese Foreign Policy Toward Burma and Cambodia: A Comparative Analysis" (Ph.D. dissertation, Columbia University, 1969).

that Indonesia would soon fall under Communist rule, but Peking's short-run policy concentrated on the goal of forging a close tie with President Sukarno, who for his own reasons was more than willing to collaborate with China. Sukarno adopted a strongly anti-imperialist and pro-Chinese stand, withdrew Indonesia from the United Nations, and exerted strong hostile pressures on Malaysia. He also attempted to take the lead in developing wider cooperation among what he called the "newly emerging forces" in the underdeveloped world. Peking decided that it was in China's interest to support and cooperate with Sukarno in many of these efforts. At one point it hinted at the possibility of trying to mobilize the underdeveloped nations of the world to establish a new international body, competitive with the United Nations. This was obviously a trial balloon, however, and it never really got off the ground.

New Flexibility toward the Developed Nations

The increasing flexibility of China's policies in this period was demonstrated most of all, perhaps, by its efforts to expand trade and political contacts with a number of important capitalist countries, notably Japan, several Western European nations, and the principal grain-producing members of the Commonwealth. Practical economic considerations were obviously a major factor impelling Peking to move in this direction. Following the emergence of the Sino-Soviet dispute, the Chinese decided to shift their foreign trade from the Communist bloc to other areas, in part because the economic crisis after the Great Leap necessitated large-scale imports of food products from abroad. The result was a rapid and fundamental shift in both the direction and composition of China's foreign trade. Whereas in the 1950s more than three-quarters of China's trade had been with the Soviet Union and Eastern Europe and less than one-quarter was with non-Communist nations, this ratio was now reversed. And whereas China's imports previously had consisted largely of industrial equipment and raw materials, now Peking had to use the largest portion of its foreign exchange to purchase grain from abroad. Japan and Western Europe became the main suppliers of the kind of industrial goods China formerly imported from Communist nations, and Canada and Australia were now the main sources of its food imports. Economics took precedence over politics in these important developments and trends. In fact, many of China's largest trading partners now—including Japan, Germany, Canada, and for a time Australia—were nations that did not officially recognize Peking.

Despite the crucial importance of economic factors impelling China to develop more active policies toward the developed nations, political considerations were also involved. Peking's leaders now viewed the world in more pluralistic terms than in the past and decided that there could be political as well as economic advantages for China in expanding ties—and especially trade—with many capitalist nations. The rationale for this new policy was articulated early in 1964 when Peking stated that the "intermediate zone"[39] of the world now included two zones, a first intermediate zone consisting of the underdeveloped nations of Asia, Africa, and Latin America, and a second intermediate zone consisting of the capitalist countries in Western Europe and elsewhere (other than the United States). This was not the first time this intermediate zone concept had been

[39]The first reference to the concept of a second intermediate zone was in an editorial in the *People's Daily*, Jan. 21, 1964. See "All the World's Forces Opposing U.S. Imperialism, Unite!" reprinted in *Peking Review* (Jan. 24, 1964), p. 7.

put forward; however, the new formulation differed from that put forward in the 1950s. Peking now argued that because the interests of the second intermediate zone diverged in many ways from those of the two superpowers, there existed—or should exist—a basis for cooperation between the nations in both zones (with China playing a leading role) in opposing domination by the superpowers. In some respects, this position may well have been a rationalization of China's desire to expand its ties with such nations for economic and other practical reasons; but it also appeared to reflect an increased recognition in Peking that polycentrist trends were altering relationships in the West as well as in the Communist world. In concrete terms, China placed highest priority on the establishment of formal diplomatic relations with France, which under President Charles de Gaulle was clearly working against many U.S. policies, and in 1964 Peking and Paris agreed to exchange ambassadors. This was the first new diplomatic link to be established between China and a Western European nation since 1954.

By late 1964 and early 1965, Peking's more flexible foreign policies appeared to be achieving some successes. The degree of success obviously varied from area to area, but it was apparent that China was expanding its international ties on a broad basis. The 1965 UN General Assembly vote on seating Peking was 47 to 47 with 20 abstentions; Peking was not seated only because the American-sponsored "important question" resolution made it necessary to obtain a two-thirds vote to seat Peking and expel Taiwan.[40] Despite its continued exclusion from the UN, China gradually assumed a more influential global role, and its entry into the "nuclear club" with the explosion of its first nuclear device in late 1964 significantly bolstered its international prestige.

The Retreat to Isolation

Then in 1965 and 1966, Peking experienced a series of major setbacks abroad that undercut important elements in its foreign policy, while at home, during the winter of 1965–66, it entered a period of intense domestic political conflict and turmoil that forced Chinese leaders to turn their attention almost entirely inward. In the fall of 1965 Marshal Lin Piao, in "Long Live the Victory of People's War"—a major exegesis of Maoist thinking on strategy and tactics—made a ringing declaration of Peking's faith in revolutionary struggle, in which he called for the "countryside of the world" (the underdeveloped areas) to unite against the "cities of the world" (the developed nations). This was less an operational blueprint for Chinese policy, however, than an exercise in revolutionary rhetoric.[41] The statement stressed the need for all revolutionaries to be self-reliant and not to expect others to fight their battles for them, and it proved to be a prelude to China's turning inward rather than to a more activist foreign policy.

The foreign policy reverses encountered during 1965–66 were of varied sorts. In Indonesia and Ghana, two countries that Peking had regarded as being of special importance to its strategy in the Third World, military coups brought to power new leaders who were openly hostile to Peking. In Indonesia, the local Communist party attempted to seize power in 1965 and failed. Although the degree of Peking's com-

---

[40]*China, The United Nations and the United States* (United Nations Association of the U.S.A., 1966), p. 21; and Lincoln P. Bloomfield, "China, the U.S. and the U.N.," *International Organization*, Vol. 20, No. 4 (Autumn 1960), p. 673.

[41]See D. P. Mozingo and T. W. Robinson, *Lin Piao on "People's War": China Takes A Second Look At Vietnam*, Memorandum RM-4814-PR (Rand Corp., November 1965).

plicity in the coup is not wholly clear, it chose to back the rebels openly as soon as the revolt was under way.[42] The results—the crushing of the coup, the ouster of Sukarno, and the violent suppression of the Indonesian Communist party—seriously weakened the fundamental basis of Peking's policy toward Indonesia, and in a broader sense toward many other underdeveloped nations.

Another setback with even more far-reaching effects on China's policy toward the Third World was the collapse in 1965 of Peking's efforts to help organize a second Asian-African conference in Algiers.[43] The Chinese attached great importance to this meeting, as a move to broaden and strengthen a Third World united front against the superpowers. But Peking alienated many Asian and African leaders in the preparatory meetings by its rigidity in opposing Soviet participation and insisting on an overt condemnation of U.S. policies, and by attempting to shape the conference to fit its own preconceptions. These tactics helped to torpedo the meeting before it was held.

Perhaps most important of all, the escalation of U.S. intervention in Vietnam in 1965 posed new dangers, from Peking's perspective, in a crucial area on China's immediate borders. This development—apparently unexpected by Chinese leaders—heightened Peking's fear of major war during 1965–66 and precipitated a debate within China over alternative defense strategies including whether Peking's security interests required greater cooperation with Moscow.[44] In the end the Maoist view prevailed, with the result that no steps to improve Sino-Soviet relations were taken.

All of these external developments contributed in some degree to China's dramatic inward turn, but the principal causes of Peking's extreme isolationism during the next two years were domestic rather than foreign. From 1966 through 1968, when the Cultural Revolution was in full swing, China's Foreign Ministry, like the rest of the bureaucratic establishment, was virtually paralyzed, and Chinese leaders were almost totally preoccupied with internal political struggles.[45] For all practical purposes, Peking abandoned normal state-to-state foreign relations for a two-year period. The Chinese continued to give major support to the Communists in Indochina and gave substantial aid to a few non-Communist countries such as Pakistan, Tanzania, and Zambia, but every Chinese ambassador abroad except one (in the United Arab Republic) was called home for political screening and reindoctrination. The Chinese in effect retreated into a shell.

During the Cultural Revolution, China's approach to the outside world was primarily a reflection of ideological and political priorities at home rather than the expression

---

[42]For different interpretations of the coup and China's involvement, see David Mozingo, "China's Policy Toward Indonesia," in Tang Tsou, China in Crisis, Vol. 2, pp. 333–52; Daniel S. Lev, "Indonesia 1965: The Year of the Coup," Asian Survey, Vol. 6, No. 2 (February 1966), pp. 103–10; Arthur J. Dommen, "The Attempted Coup in Indonesia," China Quarterly, No. 25 (January–March 1966), pp. 144–70; and John O. Sutter, "Two Faces of 'Konfrontasi': 'Crush Malaysia' and the 'Gestapu,'" Asian Survey, Vol. 6, No. 10 (October 1966), pp. 523–46.

[43]Charles Neuhauser, Third World Politics (Harvard University, East Asian Research Center, 1968), pp. 49–60.

[44]See Barnett, Uncertain Passage, note 12, Chapter 2.

[45]As Melvin Gurtov makes clear in "The Foreign Ministry and Foreign Affairs during the Cultural Revolution," China Quarterly, No. 40 (October–December 1969), pp. 65–102, the worst period was over by the fall of 1967, and thereafter the Foreign Ministry gradually resumed normal operations; but it was not really until late 1968 or early 1969 that it was operating again with effectiveness comparable to the past and began pursuing an active foreign policy on a state-to-state level.

of any coherent foreign policy strategy. The obsession with ideology and the virtual deification of Mao within China led to a posture of extreme revolutionary militancy toward the outside world. Verbal support was proclaimed for revolutionaries everywhere, but in fact Peking gave them relatively little tangible aid. Local Chinese, inspired by Red Guard fanaticism, instigated political crises in several areas on China's immediate periphery, including Burma, Macao, and Hong Kong, creating serious tension in China's relations with the areas involved. But these outbursts were essentially a spilling over beyond China's borders of the struggles at home, rather than a manifestation of deliberate Chinese foreign policy decisions. Certainly Peking did not attempt to exploit them to the extent that would have been possible.[46] In Peking itself, Red Guard units, incited by radical leftist leaders, ignored the rules of traditional diplomatic practices and attacked several foreign embassies.

The damage the Cultural Revolution inflicted on Peking's international image and on China's relations with many countries in the Communist bloc, the Third World, and the West was substantial. In fact, the image China projected to much of the world during the Cultural Revolution was that of a nation seized by irrational extremism, exhibiting an intense xenophobic isolationism, and almost totally uninterested in normal relations with the outside world.

Post-Cultural Revolution Flexibility and Pragmatism

In retrospect it is clear that, to a surprising degree, the damage to China's interests was limited and temporary. Within three years, China's image had radically changed once again; Peking had adopted a new foreign policy approach, and the world showed a greater willingness than at any point since the Communist takeover to accept China into the international community.

The explanation for this rapid and remarkable turnabout must be sought in the attitudes of other countries as well as in the policies adopted by Peking after the Cultural Revolution. By the start of the 1970s, the international community in general believed that the time had come to try to deal with China by incorporating this vast nation as much as possible into normal patterns of international relations rather than by continuing to exclude it. When Peking began to look outward again, therefore, it found a receptive world. The speed with which the turnabout took place was due in large part to the flexible new policies pursued by Peking. Once again, as in the Bandung period of the mid-1950s, China adopted a relatively pragmatic and moderate approach to the world, concentrating its efforts primarily on the tasks of promoting China's immediate national interests and expanding "normalized" state-to-state relations rather than pursuing long-term revolutionary goals.

China's emergence from isolation began in late 1968 and early 1969, in a gradual and step-by-step fashion. There was no sign that Peking had adopted any new "grand strategy." All the evidence suggested, in fact, that Chinese leaders were for the most part simply responding to the necessities created by the problems confronting China at home and abroad, and cautiously feeling their way. The initial signs that Peking was interested once more in repairing and expanding its normal state-to-state relations with foreign nations were small ones. The Chinese first began to treat resident foreign diplomats in Peking with civility again, and then, one by one, Chinese ambassadorial

---

[46]Anthony R. Dicks, "The Hong Kong Situation I: Impasse" (Institute of Current World Affairs, Newsletter ARD-19, Sept. 5, 1967; processed).

vacancies abroad were filled. The men who were now emerging to take charge of China's foreign relations were professional diplomats, close to Premier Chou En-lai, and not the ideologues who had dominated the scene during the Cultural Revolution. As they began reestablishing relationships in foreign capitals, they acted, for the most part, with professional skill and restraint, muting the revolutionary rhetoric of the previous period.

During 1970 and 1971, China's new foreign policies took clearer shape, and soon Peking was operating more actively and flexibly on the world stage than ever before. A major thrust of the new policies was the expansion of Peking's formal diplomatic ties with non-Communist nations in both the developed and underdeveloped areas of the world. The 1970 agreement with Canada to establish diplomatic relations was both a breakthrough and a watershed. For in agreeing to exchange ambassadors with Canada, the Chinese made a significant compromise; instead of insisting that the Canadians must openly recognize China's claim to Taiwan, a compromise formula was agreed upon in which the Canadians simply "took note" of Peking's claim. This important precedent stimulated many other nations to consider recognition of China on the same terms. After Chile's decision to recognize Peking in late 1970, there was a rapid trend toward normalizing relations with Peking, and by the fall of 1971 China had established formal relations with about sixty nations. By mid-1972 the number exceeded seventy,[47] and by January 1973 it had reached eighty-five. In the new diplomatic drive for recognition, ideological factors played little part; from 1970 on, China showed a willingness to establish formal inter-governmental ties with almost all countries—including monarchies such as Ethiopia and Iran and military dictatorships such as Greece and Turkey—so long as they were prepared to break relations with the Nationalist regime on Taiwan. A climax was reached in Peking's efforts to gain acceptance by the international community when the regime was seated in the United Nations in the fall of 1971 in place of the Nationalists. For the first time in more than two decades, Peking began to play a direct role in the functioning of the world's major international institutions.

What was most striking about Peking's "turning outward" in 1969 was the flexibility and apparent lack of dogmatism that Chou En-lai and Chinese professional diplomats showed. China did not by any means abandon its long-run revolutionary goals, but the immediate foreign policy objective was to expand ties and promote Chinese short-run interests by conventional diplomatic, political, and economic means. Peking continued to hold itself up as a model for revolutionaries elsewhere, to give overt backing to the Communists in the Vietnam war, and to provide moral support and discreet assistance to some other revolutionary movements, but its priority aim now was to develop normalized state-to-state relations with existing governments, whatever their ideological coloring, and to expand Peking's role and influence in the established forums and channels of international political and economic intercourse.

A corollary objective continued to be to work toward a position of leadership among the underdeveloped nations of the Third World, and toward this end Peking took positions on one issue after another in support of those favored by Third World nations and in opposition to the views of the superpowers. Meanwhile, however, it also worked assiduously to improve and broaden China's relations with many industrialized nations

---

[47]*Issues in United States Foreign Policy,* No. 4, "People's Republic of China" (Department of State Publication 8666, October 1972), p. 31, is the source for the mid-1972 figure. The January 1973 figure is based on the author's compilation of data on subsequent developments in China's diplomatic relations.

in the "second intermediate zone," particularly in Europe. While neither of these goals represented any very significant departure from past objectives in conceptual terms, the energy with which Peking pursued them and the degree to which its tactics were now characterized by nonideological pragmatism, or opportunism, was the striking new element. While reminiscent of policy during the Bandung period, China in its foreign policy now showed an even greater willingness than in the mid-1950s to play the conventional roles of a major power and to promote its interests through accepted diplomatic, political, and economic means. Long-term revolutionary goals were clearly subordinate to immediate short-run considerations of national interest.

Détente with the United States and Japan

The most dramatic turnabout in China's approach to the world in recent years was unrelated, however, to its policies toward either the Third World or the "intermediate zone." It was Peking's decision to adopt an entirely new approach toward the United States and Japan. The shift in policy toward the United States, in particular, was an extraordinary development that resulted in a basic change in the pattern of big power relations in Asia and had far-reaching repercussions and implications.

The decision by the Chinese to invite the President of the United States—long regarded as the symbolic leader of the "imperialist camp"—to visit Peking in 1972 demonstrated convincingly that Chinese leaders had decided to give highest priority to the working out of new relationships with the major powers in Asia, for reasons relating above all to national security concerns rather than ideological concepts. While Peking continued to assert that it was opposed to any "balance of power policy" and denied any superpower ambitions, Chinese policy implicitly recognized the emergence of a complicated new four-power relationship in Asia involving China, the Soviet Union, the United States, and Japan, and the need for a high degree of flexibility and maneuverability on China's part in dealing with the new situation.

Many factors doubtless contributed to Peking's decision to adopt a new policy toward the United States. First and foremost, there was the belief that it was now the Soviet Union rather than the United States which posed the greatest immediate threat to China's security. As anxiety about Moscow's intentions grew, Chinese leaders concluded that their interests could best be served by improving relations with both the United States and Japan, even though this would require pushing ideological considerations into the background and adopting a less doctrinaire position on the Taiwan problem and other issues.

In more concrete terms, Peking's new policy toward the United States was undoubtedly a response to several specific developments. During 1968–69, tension caused Sino-Soviet relations to deteriorate to the point that Peking's leaders apparently worried about the possibility of an actual Soviet military attack, perhaps a preemptive strike against major Chinese urban centers or nuclear installations. Chinese leaders probably concluded that improving relations with the United States would be the best way to impose constraints on Moscow and increase Peking's room for political maneuver. Japan was seen to be emerging as an influential new force in Asia, both economically and politically, and Chinese leaders were wary about Japan's future role, particularly after the Nixon-Sato communiqué of late 1969 which hinted that Tokyo might become directly involved in security responsibilities relating to Korea and Taiwan. Peking's warnings at that time about the dangers of Japanese remilitarization probably exaggerated its concern for political effect, but there is little question that it was genuinely anxious about what Japan would do with its growing power. The Chinese may have concluded that if they did not improve relations with Tokyo, Japan might move in directions that would pose new dangers to China. A more conciliatory posture toward Tokyo as well as Washington might help check trends in Japan toward increased militarization, and support pressures for accommodation with China. Moreover, if Sino-Japanese relations could be normalized, this could also improve Peking's ability to deal with Moscow.

A third, and extremely important, influence on Chinese policy was the significant change that U.S. policy in Asia was undergoing. China's sense of immediate threat from the United States apparently reached a peak in 1965–66, when U.S. intervention in Vietnam escalated sharply. Thereafter, its fears declined, in part because Washington took direct steps to reassure Peking that, despite intensified fighting in Vietnam, the United States had no desire or intention to threaten China. Equally or more important, the Chinese perceived that the United States—because of domestic as well as foreign pressures—was moving toward military disengagement from Vietnam, and was now committed to a reduction of the American military presence in Asia. The President's announcement in 1969 of his "Nixon doctrine" promised a gradual but steady pullback of the American military presence throughout the region.

The Chinese apparently recognized that both the U.S. government and American public opinion were moving gradually toward a basic reassessment of China policy. From 1969 on, Washington began to take small but significant steps—beginning with liberalized travel and trade restrictions and removal of American naval patrols from the Taiwan Strait—that were almost certainly seen by Peking for what they were, namely "signals" of increased American flexibility.[48] Peking's leaders now had more reason than at any time in the past for believing that, if China were to adopt a more flexible stance toward the United States, Washington might well be responsive.

Exactly when the Chinese began to reassess their policy toward the United States is not known, but it may have been as early as the fall of 1968. They indicated at that time a willingness to reopen the ruptured U.S.-Chinese ambassadorial talks at Warsaw and proposed discussion with the United States of an "agreement on the Five Principles of Peaceful Coexistence."[49] Little progress was made during the next two years, however. Both Peking and Washington were feeling their way cautiously, and several developments slowed the process. The Warsaw talks were postponed by Peking in early 1969, ostensibly because of the defection to the United States of a Chinese Communist diplomat in the Netherlands. This defection may have been only a pretext, however; the real explanation was probably related to policy disputes within China and Chinese reactions to U.S. policy in Vietnam. In any case, the talks resumed in early 1970. But they were broken off again after U.S. military intervention in Cambodia. Finally, in

[48]For data on recent U.S.-China policy and U.S.-China interaction, see Roderick MacFarquhar and others, *Sino-American Relations, 1949–71* (New York: Praeger, 1972); A. Doak Barnett, *A New U.S. Policy toward China* (Washington, D.C.: Brookings Institution, 1971); and Richard Moorsteen and Morton Abramowitz, *Remaking China Policy: U.S.-China Relations and Governmental Decision Making* (Cambridge: Harvard University Press, 1971). Some of the most useful material relevant to recent U.S. China policy also is in several volumes of congressional hearings, including *United States Relations with the People's Republic of China*, Hearings before the Senate Committee on Foreign Relations, 92 Cong. 1 sess. (1971); *United States-China Relations: A Strategy for the Future*, Hearings before the Subcommittee on Asian and Pacific Affairs of the House Committee on Foreign Affairs, 91 Cong. 2 sess. (1970); and *U.S. Policy with Respect to Mainland China*, Hearings before the Senate Foreign Relations Committee, 89 Cong. 2 sess. (1966).

[49]"Statement by Spokesman of Information Department of Chinese Foreign Ministry," *Peking Review* (Nov. 29, 1968), p. 31.

the spring of 1971, Peking signaled a major change in its policy by inviting an American table tennis team to China—the first such American visit since 1949. A few months later, in July 1971, the President's National Security Adviser, Henry Kissinger, made a dramatic secret visit to Peking, after which the United States and China announced to a startled world that President Nixon would visit Peking.

The Nixon-Chou summit meeting in Peking in February 1972 climaxed this series of events. The resulting "Shanghai communiqué"[50] symbolized, in many respects, the emergence of a new pattern of relations among the major nations of Asia. In specific terms, it called for the development of direct trade and cultural exchanges and improved diplomatic contacts (without, however, opening up formal diplomatic relations). More important even than the specific agreements was the fact that the communiqué demonstrated, in a dramatic fashion, the determination of both Washington and Peking to move toward mutual accommodation. Both sides pledged to work toward eventual "normalization" of relations. Even though long-held positions on many major issues reiterated by both signatories, the results were extremely important, and the communiqué clearly marked the start of a very new kind of Sino-American relationship. On the crucial issue of Taiwan, which for two decades had posed a insuperable barrier to U.S.-China contacts, both sides showed a significant degree of flexibility, without abandoning the essentials of their past positions. In effect, they indicated a willingness to set the Taiwan issue aside for the present. For Peking, this meant reversing a long-held position that no real improvement in U.S.-China relations would be possible until the Taiwan problem was resolved.

The repercussions of the meeting between President Nixon and Premier Chou En-lai were immediate and far-reaching. All nations involved in Asian affairs, large and small, were compelled to reassess their positions and policies, and most of them began modifying their policies in varied ways.

Most important, the groundwork was laid for rapid moves toward normalizing Sino-Japanese relations. Peking began in late 1971, after the initial visit by Kissinger to China and before the Nixon-Chou summit meeting, to play down its propaganda about the dangers of Japanese remilitarization, signaling its eagerness to establish formal relations with whoever might be Premier Eisaku Sato's successor in Japan. In Japan—where the President's trip to China was labeled "the Nixon shock," in part because he had not consulted with Japanese leaders beforehand—pressure mounted in the wake of the Shanghai communiqué for rapid steps to improve relations with China, as well as for efforts to define a more independent Japanese foreign policy. Debate intensified on the appropriate role for Japan in Asia and the world. When elections were finally held in Japan in 1972, and Kakuei Tanaka replaced Sato as Premier, the pace of events in Sino-Japanese relations quickened. In his first major act as Premier, Tanaka made his promised pilgrimage to Peking, and the Chinese and Japanese quickly agreed to establish formal diplomatic relations.[51] Tokyo acceded to Peking's demand that it cut formal relations with the Nationalist regime on Taiwan and proceeded to do so, but Peking indicated that it would not object to the continuation of Japan's economic interests in Taiwan or to the maintenance by the Japanese of an informal mission there.

The Soviet Union responded to these developments by attempting to improve relations with both the United States and Japan. Foreign Minister Andrei Gromyko visited Japan in early 1972; discussions on a Japanese-Soviet peace agreement were reopened;

---

[50]See text in *New York Times,* Feb. 28, 1972.

[51]See Text of "Joint Statement of the Government of the People's Republic of China and the Government of Japan," in *New York Times,* Sept. 30, 1972.

and exploration of the possibilities for Japanese-Soviet economic cooperation in Siberia and the Soviet Far East intensified. In late 1972, the first U.S.-Soviet summit meeting in Moscow was held, resulting in several important agreements on arms control and other matters.

Many smaller nations in Asia also sought to adjust to the new situation in various ways. Several made tentative moves in the direction of accommodation with China. To cite a few examples, Malaysia dispatched a trade mission to Peking, the Thais sent a ping-pong team, and even the Philippines decided to allow increased travel and contacts. Some Southeast Asian nations also began to broaden contacts with the Soviet Union. Most of them already had developed extensive economic relationships with Japan, and in fact were beginning to worry about the dangers of economic dependency on the Japanese. Prime Minister Lee Kuan Yew of Singapore probably set an example likely to be followed in time by others when he adopted a policy of attempting to balance the four major powers' influence against each other. China, on its part, stepped up its efforts to expand its diplomatic and political activities not only in Southeast Asia but globally. With its political position strengthened by its acceptance into the United Nations, as well as by its new relationship with the United States, China rapidly assumed an increasingly prominent and active role in the international community.

References on Chinese Foreign Policy

Several general studies on China's foreign policy and foreign relations since 1949 attempt to analyze the subject in fairly comprehensive terms, and most of them include detail relevant to most of the questions discussed in this chapter. They include Harold C. Hinton, *Communist China in World Politics* (Houghton Mifflin, 1966), and by the same author, *China's Turbulent Quest* (Macmillan, 1970); A. Doak Barnett, *Communist China and Asia: Challenge to American Policy* (Harper, 1960); Vidya Prakash Dutt, *China's Foreign Policy 1958–62* (Bombay: Asia Publishing House, 1964); Peter Van Ness, *Revolution and Chinese Foreign Policy* (University of California Press, 1971); J. D. Simmonds, *China's World: The Foreign Policy of a Developing State* (Columbia University Press, 1970); Ishwer C. Ojha, *Chinese Foreign Policy in an Age of Transition: The Diplomacy of Cultural Despair* (Beacon Press, 1969); Arthur Huck, *The Security of China* (Columbia University Press, 1970); R. G. Boyd, *Communist China's Foreign Policy* (Praeger, 1962); and H. Arthur Steiner, *Communist China in the World Community* (*International Conciliation*, No. 533, May 1961). Among the numerous useful collections of writings on Chinese foreign policy are Tang Tsou (ed.), *China in Crisis* (University of Chicago Press, 1968), Vol. 2, *China's Policies in Asia and America's Alternatives;* King C. Chen (ed.), *The Foreign Policy in China* (East-West Who? Inc. Publishers, 1972); and Jerome Alan Cohen (ed.), *The Dynamics of China's Foreign Relations* (Harvard University Press, East Asian Monographs, 1970). Other major works on China's foreign relations with particular countries and areas, including the Soviet Union, Korea, Southeast Asia, South Asia, Africa, and Latin America, and on specific facets of Chinese foreign policy, will be mentioned in later notes. Among the large number of noteworthy articles on broad Chinese foreign policy, a few deserve special mention. These include Allen S. Whiting, "The Logic of Communist China's Policy: The First Decade," *Yale Review* (Autumn 1960), pp. 1–17; Allen S. Whiting, "The Use of Force in Foreign Policy by the People's Republic of China," *Annals of the American Academy of Political and Social Science,* Vol. 402 (July 1972), pp. 55–66; Allen S. Whiting, "China and East Asian Security," in *Strategy for Peace: Thirteenth Conference Report* (Stanley Foundation, October 1972), pp. 60–66; A. M. Halpern, "Communist China and Peaceful Coexistence," *China Quarterly,* No. 3 (July–September, 1960), pp. 16–31; A. M. Halpern, "The Chinese Communist Line on Neutralism," *China Quarterly,* No. 5 (January–March 1961), pp. 90–115; A. M. Halpern, "The Foreign Policy Uses of the Chinese Revolutionary Model," *China Quarterly,* No. 7 (July–September 1961), pp. 1–16; A. M. Halpern, "China in the Postwar World," *China Quarterly,* No. 21 (January–March 1965), pp. 20–45; Tang Tsou and Morton H. Halperin, "Mao Tse-tung's Revolutionary Strategy and Peking's International Behavior," *American Political Science Review,* Vol. 59, No. 1 (March 1965), pp. 80–99; Michael B. Yahuda, "China's New Era of International Relations," *Political Quarterly,* Vol. 43, No. 3 (July–September 1972), pp. 295–307.

27
Yugoslavia and Foreign Affairs

Robin Alison Remington

Yugoslav opinion on the options open to small states in Europe apparently has not changed since Moshe Pijade's blunt formulation twenty-four years ago: "there is no justification at all for the view that small nations must jump into the mouth of this or that shark."[1] The question of how Yugoslavia will jump, however, is the pivotal unknown for scholars and politicians struggling with future security scenarios for Europe.

In this attempt to sort out the plausible from the possible there is more than a little apprehension. For although Yugoslavia is roughly the size of Wyoming, geography magnifies the strategic importance of the area it covers. Yugoslavia is the heart of the Balkans. It borders on seven states (Albania, Austria, Bulgaria, Greece, Hungary, Italy and Rumania), all of which must calculate their national security in part on speculation concerning post-Tito Yugoslavia. Physically, ideologically, even economically, it has been the dividing line between East and West. Since 1948 both blocs have somewhat grudgingly adjusted to a "nonaligned" Yugoslavia. A Yugoslavia that might be solidly integrated into the other side, so to speak, would be a different matter, keeping in mind the relation of the Adriatic coast to potential escalation in the Mediterranean.

Nor is the concern for Yugoslav stability simply academic futurology. Given the level of ethnic tensions that swept the Croation Communist leadership out of office in December 1971 following the Zagreb student strike (a change of leadership that Tito himself justified as necessary to avoid civil war), and the implications of the reshuffling at the top of the Serbian League of Communists in 1972,[2] the question is no longer primarily "after Tito, what?" but whether, with or without Tito, the League of Communists of Yugoslavia (LCY) can contain nationality conflicts sufficiently to stabilize

From Robin Alison Remington, "Yugoslavia and European Security," *ORBIS* (Vol. XVII, No. 1, Spring 1973), pp. 197–226. [Reprinted with permission from the publisher.]

[1]*Borba*, July 9, 1949.

[2]The chairman of the Serbian Communist Party, Marko Nikezic, and the party Central Committee secretary, Latinka Perovic, resigned on October 21, 1972 under attack from Tito and the party Executive Bureau. The wave of related high-level party and government resignations that followed included foreign minister Mirko Tepavac; the dynamic premier of Slovenia, Stane Kavcic; and even Tito's comrade-in-arms during the partisan struggle, . . . Koca Popovic.

the internal political process. In short, Yugoslavia at this time provides a classic example of the interlocking nature of civil disorder, national stability and international security.

Although research for it focused for the most part on the foreign policy aspects of Yugoslav attitudes toward European security, this article has therefore been written with an awareness that in this maverick socialist state the issues of internal and international security are hopelessly entangled.[3] They cannot be isolated; it is artificial to deal with them separately. This means that despite the risk of confusion at introducing into foreign policy analysis the normal political chaos, which is more a matter of Yugoslav style than a symptom of a chronically ailing political system, to some extent it has been unavoidable.

The Remnants of History

To understand Yugoslav views on security in Europe one must accept the fact that, in the Balkans, yesterday is almost as real as today, sometimes more real than tomorrow. The history of the peoples of Yugoslavia reads like a serialized epic of occupation, repression and wars of liberation. Security has been a scarce commodity in that part of Europe. The first Yugoslav state was born in the ashes of World War I only to be dismembered (parceled out by Hitler to those of its neighbors he wished to woo) at the beginning of World War II. . . .

For the majority of Yugoslavs, irrespective of national (ethnic) identity, political objective number one is the physical security of the Yugoslav state. Considering the methods Moscow used to restore its own version of order within deviant East European socialist states in 1956 and 1968, the Yugoslavs have some reason for doubting that their primary objective can be ensured by the current security system of spheres of influences, represented by military-political blocs balancing one another.[4]

The Nonaligned Alternative

This perception directly ties Yugoslavia's European policy to Tito's broader strategy on the world stage, nonalignment. To many Westerners nonalignment has appeared extraordinarily vague, something of a brand name for Yugoslavia and, like most brand names, more symbolic than substantive. They understand its negative aspect, i.e., that nonalignment meant not choosing sides, refusing to be defined into either of the two camps that dominated Europe during the Cold War of the 1950s. In this sense to be nonaligned was to be nonaligned against. Both East and West viewed it with suspicion.

---

[3]Much of the analysis is based on interviews conducted during two trips to Yugoslavia: first during my eleven months in Serbia as an exchange scholar at the Belgrade Institute of International Politics and Economics, September 1970–August 1971; then again in May–June 1972 when I returned to Yugoslavia to interview in other republics primarily on the implementation of the 1971 constitutional amendments, a project made possible by an American Council of Learned Societies area studies grant. Although I am grateful both to the Belgrade Institute and the ACLS for facilitating my research, neither institution has any responsibility for this analysis, nor to my knowledge would my Yugoslav colleagues necessarily agree with my conclusions. I am also indebted to the research assistance of Rada Vlajinac, whose diligent tracing of documentary sources speeded my work immeasurably.

[4]Although the present system has guaranteed the physical security of the Soviet Union and Western Europe, the East European members of the Warsaw Pact might be tempted to agree silently with the Yugoslav position that their military as well as political security requires reducing bloc divisions.

From both sides of the fence it was seen as a nonpolicy; a slightly immoral nonpolicy, at that.

Conversely, to Yugoslav leaders nonalignment implied buying in, not opting out. One must remember that Tito did not invent nonalignment. He joined an ongoing process in Asia and Africa, whereby newly independent states were attempting to influence international priorities away from the ideological East-West split so that more attention would go to the problems inherent in what in political shorthand has been called a "north-south" division between the "haves" and the "have nots" on a continuum of development-industrialization. To these states nonalignment meant not only refusing to be surrogates in superpower conflicts marginally related to their national interests, but an active policy of commitment to influence events whenever problems of special concern for them were at stake. It was a policy of issue-oriented collaboration, a fact often obscured by the nonaligned countries themselves in the rhetoric surrounding their efforts to find common platforms.

Moreover, Tito did not choose nonalignment. Yugoslavia was quite firmly aligned at the end of World War II. Then, as the Yugoslav-Soviet dispute led to the Yugoslav party's expulsion from the Cominform in 1948, Tito became crushingly isolated in Europe. The ideological self-image of the Yugoslav leadership, and fear of the demoralizing impact on party rank and file, made it unthinkable simply to switch sides. To have done so would have run the risk of precipitating Soviet invasion.

Were the psychological restraints and threat from the East not enough, Tito also may have felt that he had arrived at a jumping-off place with no place to jump. The West's first reaction to the Yugoslav-Soviet break was disbelief. Tito's militant aid to the Greek communists, and his obstinacy on the Trieste issue, had been laid to Moscow's door by some, but even among those who suspected that the Yugoslav leader was more than a Soviet catspaw, he had not made himself popular. The Yugoslav party's attempt to shore up its socialist credentials by intensifying the drive for collectivization dimmed Tito's prospects in the West still more.

In part an outgrowth of Yugoslavia's election to the UN Security Council, where in 1949–1950 she for the first time experienced close, prolonged contact with the new independent nations of Asia and Africa, nonalignment maximized both Tito's influence and his options in an otherwise unpromising political environment. Throughout the early 1950's the need for such an alternative was rooted in European security considerations. With the Korean War, Yugoslav vulnerability increased amid pressures from Moscow and what at that time amounted to Stalin's East European echoes. As the Yugoslav *White Book* shows, nonalignment developed in circumstances where the Yugoslavs felt physically threatened.[5]

Although by 1952 fear of Soviet attack had subsided and Western aid under the Tripartite Agreement of 1951 was repairing some of the damage caused by the Cominform economic blockade, the psychological need remained for ideologically acceptable allies that would not by definition shut the door on future ties with the socialist East. Nonaligned allies had additional advantages. They left Tito free to put forward the alternative of a "Yugoslav" model within the international Communist movement, and they did not seriously threaten to close the other essential door, the door to economic relations with the West. Further, by 1953–1954 Yugoslav security preoccupations

---

[5] *White Book on Aggressive Activities by the Governments of the USSR, Poland, Czechoslovakia, Hungary, Rumania, Bulgaria and Albania towards Yugoslavia* (Belgrade: Ministry of Foreign Affairs, 1951).

had changed direction. The problem was now unfriendly relations with Italy because of Trieste.[6] In the end the issue of Trieste was settled on the West's terms. Its resolution undoubtedly added to any uneasiness Tito may have had about the sensitivity of his Western creditors to Yugoslav interests.[7]

Thus foreign policy and security considerations alike favored nonalignment. Perhaps equally important, such a policy came to meet domestic policy needs as well. [For as Alvin Rubinstein has correctly pointed out,] nonalignment [was a compromise] between those who preferred closer ties with the Soviet bloc and those who favored a more Western orientation. Given the substantially equal position of these forces within the country, nonalignment helped to achieve an uneasy balance. It continues to be the only policy acceptable to all factions of the LCY.[8]

As the postwar bipolar international system evolved into the "limited adversary relationship" of the 1960s—a process complicated by sharp clashes of national interest among the nonaligned states in Asia and Africa—the concept of nonalignment became fuzzier than ever. Nehru and Nasser died. In President Nixon's "era of negotiation," which by spring 1972 seemed to have progressed to a special relationship between Washington and Moscow, at least on the level of crisis management, nonalignment appeared to be a political anachronism. Nonaligned between whom?

Yugoslav spokesmen, too, came to feel that nonalignment might be the wrong word, but they clung to it both for the symbolic-emotional content of past associations and because they firmly believe it continues to be the right policy. In their view, what must be corrected is an image problem in which the negative aspects of nonalignment have obscured its positive content. To them nonalignment has meant and means much more than not participating in military blocs or alliances. At its core is the demand for new rules of the game, i.e., a new international system without spheres of influence, power politics and superpower hegemony.[9] It denies the historic fact that some states are more equal than others and asks for recognition of what could be called the inalienable rights of nation-states no matter how small—rights to independence, sovereignty, territorial integrity and choice of the political-social system most suited to their conditions. It is a policy based on the struggle for independence, the policy of "a state with a strong feeling of insecurity that is not in a position to react forcefully to its larger environment."[10] On this level nonalignment is an exemplar. Few Yugoslavs would defend it as the reality of today or even tomorrow. Rather it is an ideal, they hope, in the process of becoming; an alternative international system being built piecemeal.

---

[6]The fact that Tito went so far as to cancel his visit to Italy in September 1971 after Italian statements to the effect that Rome did not consider the Trieste settlement permanent indicates the continuing importance of this issue in Yugoslav eyes.

[7]Alvin Z. Rubinstein, *Yugoslavia and the Nonaligned World* (Princeton: Princeton University Press, 1970), p. 39. The intensity of feeling about Trieste has been well documented by Tito's official biographer, Vladimir Dedijer, in *Tito* (New York: Simon and Schuster, 1953).

[8]Rubinstein, *Yugoslavia.* With respect to current implications of this split, the divided reactions following Tito's visit to Moscow in June 1972 are instructive. . . .

[9]Interestingly enough, the most explicit statement of this aspect of nonalignment has come not from a Yugoslav but from an Englishman. See John Burton, *International Relations: A General Theory* (Cambridge: Cambridge University Press, 1965), pp. 163–228, and "Nonalignment and Contemporary World Politics," in Ljubivoje Acimovic, editor, *Nonalignment in the World Today,* International Symposium, January 16–18, 1969 (Belgrade: Institute of International Politics and Economics, 1969).

[10]The most exhaustive Yugoslav analysis of nonalignment has recently appeared in English, Leo Mates, *Nonalignment: Theory and Current Policy* (Dobbs Ferry, N.Y.: Oceana Publications, 1972).

Influence Building in Europe

In the arena of practical politics, however, the ideal of nonalignment as a broadly based movement directed toward the democratization of international relations has been less important to Yugoslavia than the diplomatic skills developed in seeking for a common denominator to hold together the wide-flung, sometimes tenuously connected coalition of nonaligned states. The nonaligned conferences (Belgrade 1961, Cairo 1964, Lusaka 1969) and Tito's mini-summits with Nehru and Nasser provided a visible platform for Yugoslav foreign policy and turned Yugoslav policymakers into masters of influence building. These tactics are still another link between that conception and the reality of contemporary European politics. Only today the thrust of Yugoslav nonalignment has changed direction. The target is not the Third World; the target is Europe.

The shift did not begin yesterday. Even in the mid-1960s Yugoslavia was taking initiatives related to European security that were unmistakably directed toward building the same kind of issue-oriented base in Europe that Tito had sought in Asia and Africa. In 1965 nine small states (Austria, Belgium, Bulgaria, Denmark, Hungary, Finland, Rumania, Sweden and Yugoslavia) put forward a resolution in the United Nations General Assembly promoting good neighbor relations among European states with different social and political systems. The resolution failed to pass, yet contacts among the initiating states continued. In the next September representatives of the nine met in Yugoslavia and proposed a conference of all European parliaments to discuss questions of European security. Parliamentarians of the ten (by this time the Netherlands had joined) did in fact meet. Then, as the Soviet naval buildup followed the June 1967 Arab-Israeli war, Yugoslavia became the prime mover in organizing a conference of "progressive parties" on Mediterranean security, held in Rome in April 1968.

This process of applying nonaligned principles to Europe, looking toward the 1970s, meant, as is so often the case in Yugoslav politics, expanding theory to fit the conditions. A search for allies again commenced, a search that took on added urgency with the Soviet invasion of Czechoslovakia in August 1968.

Starting from the assumption that the philosophy concerning the right of small states to sovereignty, independence, territorial integrity and self-determination struck a sensitive chord in many European capitals, Yugoslavs began pushing for a new attitude toward European collaboration. Neutrals were considered natural allies. Indeed, Radovan Vukadinovic has stressed that Yugoslav foreign policy in some cases might be closer to the stance adopted by Austria, Finland and Sweden than to the policy of Third World nonaligned countries.[11] Another level of potential support on specific issues was seen [by Tito] in the "independently minded" small countries within blocs.

In sum, yesterday's Third World nonalignment was to be the model for a European nonalignment in which small and medium states would attain to an unstructured foreign policy coordination, at least with respect to the key question of tomorrow's power configuration on the continent. The idea presents problems for Western analysts used to dealing with a phenomenon that can be defined in either-or terms. Yet, in my view, the Yugoslavs were advocating an issue-oriented coalition (whose membership would presumably shift with the issues) that both was and was not a coalition.

---

[11]Radovan Vukadinovic, "Small States and the Policy of Nonalignment," in August Schou and Arne Olv Brundtland, editors, *Small States in International Relations* (New York: John Wiley and Sons, 1971), pp. 99–114. . . .

The goals of this loose grouping are considerably more concrete than its present or future membership. It was, if not exactly a demand for equal time, to be a reminder that *all* European states wanted a voice in any potential restructuring of the political status quo. High on the list came erosion of the existing blocs, by which Yugoslavs also mean challenging superpower monopoly of European problem-solving. A logical extension of this challenge was a call for small states to engage in collective European security initiatives and to create a "nonaligned" constituency in European public opinion.

Thus at the center of Yugoslavia's European policy is the contention that new names for the old Europe will not do. A system with less ideological jargon in which spheres of influence substitute for camps, client states for satellites, and marginal maneuverability for hierarchical command, does not add up to a Europe in which Yugoslavia would feel secure. For in essence her attempt to transplant her own variety of nonalignment in Europe—even as was Tito's nonaligned strategy of the 1950s—is based on fear.

That fear is neither abstract nor paranoid. It can be understood only in the context of the issue that has dominated Yugoslavia since 1948, when Tito became odd man out in the socialist camp: relations with Moscow.

Trauma of the Prague Spring

Until 1968 there was a growing complacency on the Yugoslav side. Stalin had died. Khrushchev went so far as to recognize national roads to socialism in his attempt to bring Tito back into the fold. True, no one would claim it had been a problem-free process. The polemics see-sawed, sometimes wildly. Still, relaxation in which Moscow seemed to perceive its minimal East European interests in broad outlines lulled Belgrade into a false sense of security. Rumania had achieved an unimagined freedom of maneuver in foreign policy. In late 1967 Brezhnev had refused to intervene in internal Czechoslovak affairs, thereby tacitly sanctioning Novotny's fall; initially Dubcek seemed an acceptable substitute.

Yugoslav enthusiasm soared during the Prague Spring. Despite nervousness at the increasingly hostile response of Moscow and the more orthodox East European regimes (particularly those in East Germany and Poland), the euphoria of the Czechs and Slovaks during those months of liberation existed to some extent among Yugoslavs as well. For Tito, even if less than for Dubcek, win or lose, the stakes were high.

Had the progressives within the Communist party of Czechoslovakia (KSC) succeeded in expanding the notion of what constituted an ideologically acceptable socialist state, the implication for Yugoslavia's future political environment could have been immense. In an Eastern Europe with that degree of flexibility, Yugoslav isolation would have been almost impossible. Rather than being an oddity, the "Yugoslav way" would have been legitimated as one of a variety of roads to socialism, and much more solidly than in any reluctantly signed Soviet-Yugoslav declaration. Tito's opportunities for expanding his influence by "exchanging experience" with his East European neighbors (the in-system euphemism for hawking the Yugoslav model) would have been immeasurably greater.

The aging Yugoslav leader whose craving to play a major role on the international revolutionary stage had not waned under twenty years of limitations stemming from his break with Stalin in 1948, must have felt that once again (as in 1955) history was on the verge of proving him objectively right.[12] It was a heady prospect. Conversely, if the

---

[12]Reportedly Tito had bluntly warned against the consequences of military intervention during his April 28–30 stopover in Moscow on the way back from Tokyo, Ulan Bator and Teheran. *Politika*, August 25, 1968.

Soviets reacted by repeating the Hungarian scenario of 1956, it required little imagination to see the negative consequences for Yugoslav security and policy.

Yugoslavia's involvement in the escalating crisis between Czechoslovakia and the spokesmen for socialist orthodoxy in the USSR and Eastern Europe also had a practical political dimension that fed into Tito's hopes and fears. The Czechoslovak representative to the Budapest Consultative Conference of Communist Parties at the end of February 1968, Vladimir Koucky, may have condemned the Rumanian walkout from that meeting, but in doing so he supported the substance of some of Bucharest's views, reserved the right to return to the matter on "a suitable occasion," and went on to criticize the documents of earlier international Communist meetings as being out of date, especially with respect to Yugoslavia. In this manner Koucky signaled a linkage among Czechoslovakia, Rumania and Yugoslavia on issues of interparty relations among socialist countries which was to become explicit during the hot summer following the Prague Spring.

To use the terminology of the participants, it was surely "no accident" in the eyes of Soviet leaders, obviously divided on whether or not to send in troops to restore their preferred order in Czechoslovakia, that on the heels of the Bratislava meeting at which Dubcek's government ostensibly resolved the "differences" between the KSC and its fraternal allies, Tito (August 9) and then Ceausescu (August 15) went to Prague. The warmth of the welcome for the Yugoslav and Rumanian leaders, in contrast to the cool reception given Walter Ulbricht who was whisked off to Karlovy Vary (August 12), spoke volumes. So did the emphasis placed by both Tito and the new Czechoslovak-Rumanian Treaty of Friendship, Cooperation and Mutual Assistance on the principle of noninterference in internal affairs.

The CPSU had some cause for its conclusion that KSC representatives at Bratislava had agreed on formulations without the slightest intention of reversing the policies in question. Still more important, Moscow—also with some reason—may have had visions of a "Communist Little Entente" directed against Soviet hegemony in Eastern Europe. The Soviets returned to the attack with Ceausescu still in Prague.

Yugoslav trauma at the actual violation of Czechoslovak territorial integrity by allied socialist troops came from the bitterness of shattered expectations intensified by the knowledge that from the Soviet view Tito was both an accomplice before the fact and a willing supporter of Dubcek's deviation from Moscow's version of common socialist principles. The LCY attacked the invasion of Czechoslovakia as a gross violation of socialist norms, offered its support to the KSC and the Czechoslovak people in their struggle for independence, and reminded all parties that in case of need the Yugoslav army was ready to defend Yugoslav borders.[13] Moscow responded by polemicizing against "Yugoslav defenders of nationalism," and more seriously with the theoretical rationalization known to the West as the Brezhnev Doctrine.[14]

---

[13]Resolution adopted by the Central Committee of the League of Communists of Yugoslavia, *Borba*, August 26, 1968; English text in Robin Alison Remington, editor, *Winter in Prague: Documents of Czechoslovak Communism in Crisis* (Cambridge: The M.I.T. Press, 1969), pp. 361–367.

[14]Insisting that the concept of sovereignty among socialist states must not be understood abstractly, the Brezhnev Doctrine holds that among these states international law must be subordinated to class struggle. The Soviet Union reserved the right to intervene militarily or otherwise if developments in any given socialist country threatened either socialism within that country or the basic interests of other socialist countries as defined by Moscow. See S. Kovalev, *Pravda*, September 26, 1968.

Concept of Limited Sovereignty

From the moment of its birth the Brezhnev Doctrine, put forward to justify Soviet troops on Czechoslovak soil, directly threatened Yugoslav national security. Moscow's mini-cold war against Tito was on again. The political climate congealed. Soviet-Yugoslav exchanges sounded remarkably like those of 1948, although in fairness polemics never reached the flood of vindictiveness of the early postwar years.

Any lingering doubts about what the Brezhnev Doctrine meant to Yugoslavia could not have survived Gomulka's detailed restatement at the Fifth Congress of the Polish United Workers Party in November:

> Yugoslavia, while maintaining a policy of so-called nonalignment, can maintain it only in the shadow of the unity of the Warsaw Pact states. If other socialist states followed the steps of Yugoslavia, then, in a situation in which Europe did not have any collective security mechanism, each of these countries would represent an open gate to all kinds of imperialist and reactionary intervention, pressures and chaos. . . .[15]

At a minimum this interpretation returned Yugoslavia to the status of an isolated exception, barred from the mainstream of European socialism. It was a role the Yugo-slavs had learned to handle, if not to like. The maximum interpretation was much more worrisome: contrary to the Belgrade and Moscow Declarations between the governments and parties of Yugoslavia and the USSR in 1955 and 1956, Brezhnev and company were serving notice that when in the Soviet view socialism as defined by Moscow was threatened, Soviet troops might again be used. Today the victim had been Czechoslovakia; yet the KSC had not adopted policies perceptibly more controversial than those daily carried out in Yugoslavia. In analyzing the invasion, if in little else, Belgrade might well be tempted to agree with Peking that what the Soviets appeared to want was not a socialist community but a colonial empire with Russian overlords.

Not surprisingly, therefore, from August 1968 until Brezhnev himself disowned the "Brezhnev Doctrine" as a "Western fabrication" on his visit to Yugoslavia in September 1971,[16] European security in Yugoslav eyes meant primarily Yugoslav national security in the face of an unambiguous threat from the East. The response was an immediate retreat to the tactics of 1948. Tito moved to consolidate his base. Domestically this led to revitalizing the party and reviving the concept of partisan popular resistance.

All People's Deterrence

Known as "General [total] People's Defense," this strategy should be considered an outgrowth rather than a straightforward reincarnation of the theory of "all people's war" which provided conceptual underpinning for the Yugoslav partisans during World War II. It differs in purpose, circumstance and possibilities. The concept of "people's war" as developed by Mao Tse-tung and contributed to by Che Guevara is primarily a recipe for revolution: the struggle against the foreign invader encompasses a struggle to mobilize the people into a militarized mass insurrection designed both to liberate the country and to seize power; simultaneously to destroy the pre-existing system and carry out a social-political revolution.

---

[15]Gomulka, *Trybuna Ludu,* November 12, 1968.

[16]Arrival toast, *Borba,* September 22, 1971. The Soviet leader at no time rejected the principles underlying that doctrine, however. On the contrary, he restated them in his speech at the Zemun factory by saying "the foreign political line of the CPSU is clear and consistent. We firmly protect the interests of socialism against all its enemies." *Peking Review,* September 23, 1971.

In 1968 the Yugoslav revolution, despite heated debates about its content, was a fact. Tito's partisans had taken power a quarter of a century ago. Partly as a result of the integrating myths stemming from the mass nature of the partisan resistance, the Yugoslav Communist party consolidated its position (unlike the other East European parties) with the advantage of both power and authority—i.e., recognition of that power as being based on accepted mutual interests between the party and the people rather than upon the regime's control of superior coercive instruments.[17] The object of "general people's defense" was not to make a revolution but to defend one; not to destroy the existing system but to preserve it.

This difference brought its own duality. On the plus side, the regular armed forces provided a solid core around which irregular guerrilla units could form. The Yugoslav People's Army had an integral place in strategic planning, thereby allowing military planners to think in terms of a "mixed" force combining elements of both traditional and partisan strategies. Second, territorial defense units are more economic than a massive conventional military buildup—a persuasive consideration, given the already extensive demands on Yugoslav resources, the dubious success of the 1965 Economic Reform, and the political undesirability of outside assistance even if it had been available. Third, the extensive decentralization of the mid-1960s added a domestic political limitation in the unwillingness of the republics to see a reconcentration of power in Belgrade.

But apart from the political-economic liabilities of returning to the conventional, large-scale standing army of the 1950s,[18] that kind of buildup offered pathetically little protection against the highly mobile forces that had marched into Czechoslovakia with virtually no warning. Such a threat required an effective mobilization capability with a speed that would leave little time for transmitting centrally made decisions. To the Yugoslavs, recent experience seems to prove that the weakness of modern conventional armies is not in taking territory; the problem is rather in controlling that territory to political advantage. Therefore, the thrust of the deterrence value of total people's defense comes in upping the cost of occupation. In short, unlike the theory of "all people's war," total people's defense was designed primarily to avoid war. The doctrine was based on the belief that if they wish to remain sovereign, small and medium-sized states must be able to defend themselves instead of relying on outside aid. It assumed that with national will and the mechanisms for involving the entire population in resistance, such a state can withstand attack.

There is a minus side to this type of mixed defense, however. For one thing, professional and nonprofessional soldiers do not necessarily "mix" well. Although public material on senior officers' reaction to relinquishing the role of the Yugoslav army as *the* Yugoslav military institution for one in which the territorial units are legally coequal is esoteric enough to permit different interpretations, Dennison Rusinow has made a convincing case that reservations did (and quite likely still do) exist among the traditional military elite. Further, the fact of using regular reserve officers in command posts of the territorial units has ethnic ramifications. Despite efforts to recruit among Slovenes and

---

[17]For analysis of this process, see Chalmers A. Johnson, *Peasant Nationalism and Communist Power* (Stanford: Stanford University Press, 1962), pp. 156–176. The revitalization of belief patterns based on the partisan myth of solidarity is treated by M. George Zaninovich, *The Development of Socialist Yugoslavia* (Baltimore: The John Hopkins Press, 1968), p. 44 ff.

[18]In the early 1950s Yugoslavia had almost half a million men under arms and was spending 22 percent of its national income on defense. . . .

Croats, the Yugoslav army remains 70 to 90 percent Serbian, meaning the Croatian and Slovene units may be unavoidably commanded by Serbs. As nationality tensions rose during 1971–1972, this situation only added to the friction. The upsurge of ethnic hostilities in turn weakened the credibility of "total people's defense," for the success of such a strategy depends on how potential aggressors assess both its workability and the united will of the resistance.

Still, in connection with the strategic posturing going on in the Europe of 1968–1969, the policy had its value. The Soviets may never have intended, in the flush of their "containment" of liberalization in Czechoslovakia, to move against the recalcitrant Rumanians or eliminate the Yugoslav thorn that had punctured more than one of Moscow's East European preferences over the years. Yet neither Bucharest nor Belgrade could have been sure of that.[19] The menacing tone of Soviet polemics was combined with disquieting troop maneuvers along the offenders' borders. Undoubtedly the seriousness with which the Yugoslavs overhauled their military strategy[20] added an edge to Soviet memories of the bitter partisan resistance to German occupation in World War II. The bloodstained history of the Balkans stands witness: pushed to the wall, the South Slavs would fight.

Return to the Conference Route

Be that as it may, "normalization" proceeded with almost dizzying speed despite 600,000 Soviet troops in Czechoslovakia. The violence of polemics subsided. Moscow loudly rejected the implication that its "restoration of order" had in any way changed the balance of power in Europe. Even before Dubcek fell in the wake of his people's enthusiasm at their hockey victory over a Soviet team, the Warsaw Pact had officially resumed its persistent campaign for a European security conference.

Soviet policy appeared to have swung full circle—almost as if in Kafkaesque fashion the embarrassment of occupation and concomitant corruption and decline of the KSC did not exist. Whether Moscow's motives in pressing once again for an all-European conference were to shore up the somewhat tarnished image of peaceful coexistence, distract attention from the aftermath of the Czechoslovak crisis, get U.S. troops out of Europe and disrupt NATO, or were the first step toward its subsequent rapprochement with West Germany, the resumed initiative toward a Conference on Security and Co-operation in Europe (CSCE) dovetailed with quite separate interests of the East European members of the alliance. From the outset the approval of bilateral as well as multilateral consultations in search of European security esoterically legitimized independent contacts with the West. It implied a permissibility of independent foreign policy maneuver to come.

In the Yugoslav view, however, the renewed drive from the East created a number of dilemmas. In principle, Belgrade was already deeply committed to the virtues of such a conference. But the gap between its theoretical support for the project and an active desire to see that conference materialize *now* (late 1969) was as wide as that between Yugoslav and Soviet objectives for the conference itself.

---

[19]At the time, Washington too had some doubts. See President Lyndon Johnson's speech warning that invasion of either of these two small Balkan countries would be viewed with great "seriousness." *New York Times*, August 31, 1968.

[20]The revised National Defense Law of 1969 gave legal existence to the territorial defense units and spelled out the responsibility of every citizen to fight the invader.

Hence, Yugoslavia's formal support for the Warsaw Pact's Budapest appeal to all European states to get moving with respect to the stalled talks on European security showed a tinge of skepticism. The response had the ring of the proverbial saying: "Your actions speak so loud that I can't hear what you say." As one Yugoslav commentator put it:

> The appeal to the European peoples from Budapest, urging the development of peaceful cooperation and the convocation of an all European conference contains ideas and principles, which if mutually adopted, could pave the way for broader initiatives in this respect. In that case, however, the practical conceptions and behavior of the signatory states ought to be brought in harmony with the ideas and principles championed by the latter . . . and thus do away with the objections and mistrust provoked by their recent acts which checked the favorable trend of European policy to a considerable degree.[21]

In July, former Foreign Minister Mirko Tepavac categorically stated that the best way to overcome difficulties to multilateral cooperation in Europe was on the basis of sovereignty, equality, and renunciation of the use of force. He reiterated the Yugoslav position: European security can be based only upon the "irrevocable right" to sovereignty, independence, and free choice of internal development.[22]

Throughout 1969 and 1970 attacks on theories of limited sovereignty and references to the harm done to prospects for European cooperation by the use of force against the Dubcek Government paralleled Yugoslav statements favoring an all-European conference. Not that Belgrade held much brief for Western policy toward the desired goal. Yugoslav criticism of NATO's precondition tying the conference to a Berlin settlement went beyond the tactical need for nonaligned evenhandedness, the critics in this case genuinely believing that such preconditions amounted to sabotaging the project entirely.

Yet Tito's foreign policy has seldom been limited to passive reactions. Granting that 1969–1970, or even 1973, might not be the ideal timing for CSCE with regard to Yugoslav national interests—whenever the conference took place, it would hold dangers as well as prospects—to do nothing meant sure isolation. It was essential to avoid the disadvantage of being the only "nonaligned" country in Europe at a time when mutual and balanced force reduction (MBFR) negotiations seemed more and more likely to be conducted on a bloc to bloc basis. Because CSCE afforded the only table at which they had a chance of a chair, Yugoslav policymakers concentrated on the proposed multilateral preparations and once again set about finding, or when possible creating, a common denominator of interest among small and medium European states in East and West alike.

CSCE, Yugoslav Style

By the spring of 1970 the Yugoslav Foreign Ministry had circulated to other European governments a statement setting forth the Yugoslav view of the problem of European security. It took pains to make the main points publicly until there could be no ambiguity as to Yugoslav preference, and simultaneously proceeded to take them up in a series

---

[21]Ljubomir Radovanovic, "A Few Notes on European Cooperation," *Review of International Affairs* (Belgrade), April 20, 1969, p. 10.

[22]*Politika*, July 29, 1969.

of bilateral discussions, which by November 1971 had involved foreign ministry consultations with virtually all other European countries. Moreover, these views were pushed within party forums as well as on the state level.[23]

In skeleton form, Belgrade's attitude toward European security mirrored the main outlines of overall Yugoslav policy.

(1) European states can be secure only when *all* states refrain from acts of force, threats, and pressure against *all* other states. [A direct slap at the Brezhnev Doctrine.]

(2) The purpose of seeking a new system of security in Europe should not be to perpetuate the present bloc structure but to supersede it with a new (democratized) system of international relations. [The reincarnation of nonalignment.]

(a) Acceptance of the territorial status quo can only be a departure for overcoming the political status quo.

(b) The normative basis for the system in question must involve recognized rules of conduct in European relations—i.e., respect for sovereign equality, independence, territorial integrity, and noninterference in internal affairs.

(c) The material basis must be twofold: free and equal cooperation in all fields and measures of regional disarmament.

(3) On the matter of regional disarmament, Yugoslavs officially favor moving from the simple to the complex, although the concrete measures they have in mind are hardly simple.[24]

(a) Reduction (or freezing) of armaments should

(i) include both nuclear and conventional armaments.

(ii) be "balanced," thereby not endangering the global balance while cutting back the danger of confrontation. [This indicates the reluctance of many Yugoslavs to see American forces leave Europe before a workable collective security system is in existence. Since no one is quite sure what such a system would be, it is fair to say, despite formal support for withdrawal of all troops, that skeptics would feel safer not to have U.S. troops go now.]

(iii) lead to a reduction of pressure on the independence of small countries.

(iv) discontinue or at least limit military maneuvers, where they serve as a pressure technique.

(v) prevent foreign bases from being set up where they are not already established [most likely in response to the undocumented but widely discussed Soviet pressure for a base at Split or Pula].

(vi) effect withdrawal of foreign troops to national borders.

(b) These measures should in turn lead to a nonnuclear zone and zones of limited armaments in Europe.

(4) As for the CSCE itself, it must not be considered either the first or last stage in the search for security.

(a) Even as a step in the right direction, such a conference will be significant only if it is a genuinely democratic gathering in which *all* European states participate as equals. [Aimed at trying to weaken bloc politics, particularly within the Warsaw Pact.]

---

[23]Dimce Belovski's speech to the Moscow meeting of European Communist and Workers' Parties, *Borba,* January 18, 1970. Belovski criticized the fact that bilateral discussions had not preceded the Moscow meeting "at least as far as the LCY was concerned," repeated a demand for noninterference in internal affairs as a prerequisite for security, and stressed the "independent and nonaligned policy of Yugoslavia."

[24]This is a composite summary, but most of the specific points (and some less often referred to suggestions) are included in a provocative two-part article by Major-General Berislav Badurina, "Outline of a Model of European Security," *Review of International Affairs,* December 5 and 20, 1969.

(b) Preparations are as important as [in some cases one had the feeling that this should read "even more important than"] the conference itself.

(i) They can create good political conditions.

(ii) They must not be confined to technical matters.

(iii) All European countries must participate equally at preparation level.

(iv) Bloc to bloc preparations must be avoided, for they tend to consolidate rather than overcome the existing divisions in Europe.

(c) Composition: all European states, "others directly concerned" (i.e., U.S. and Canadian participation), and at least observers from non-European Mediterranean countries.

(d) Agenda:

(i) should not try to accomplish too much, but substantive, if modest, disarmament measures should be initiated. [This is one of the vital Yugoslav differences with both East and West. Belgrade holds that for an all-European conference to be meaningful it must at least have a connection with—by which I think most Yugoslavs would mean some control over—MBFR negotiations.]

(ii) must avoid being a simple ratifying mechanism for decisions already taken by power alignments.

(iii) should be the first in a series of gatherings. [Some politically expedient vagueness is noted here: those Yugoslavs concerned with the issues are well aware that if permanent bodies are set up at the present stage of the game in Europe they will reflect the existing bloc structure rather than weakening it.]

But despite a systematic presentation of these positions, apparently including discussions of the topic at the highest level, there was an offhand, distracted air to much of Yugoslav European policy in 1971, for the delicate balance of domestic-foreign imperatives had suddenly tipped. Three short years after the invasion of Czechoslovakia, it was evident to any political observer living in Belgrade that the security question preoccupying most Yugoslavs was the internal security of the Yugoslav state.

The National Question and National Stability

To many Yugoslavs, the 1971 Belgrade joke, "Yugoslavia is a state with six republics, five nations, four languages,[25] three religions, two alphabets, and one Yugoslav—Tito," appeared fact. This is not the place to debate the merits or dangers inherent in the upsurge of Croatian nationalism that convulsed Yugoslav political life,[26] or to decide whether the leaders of the Croat Communist party were fostering an alternative political organization in the guise of the Croatian cultural organization *Matica Hrvatska*. Despite tacit acceptance of the Karadjordjevo interpretation of "counterrevolutionary activity," that remains an open question even in Yugoslavia. Suffice it to say that during 1971 historic antagonisms among the eight-million-plus Serbs and four-million-plus Croats, the country's two largest ethnic groups, surfaced in such a way that official and ordinary Yugoslavs alike were worried.

---

[25]Until the constitutional amendments of 1971 passed, the official languages were Serbo-Croatian, Macedonian and Slovene. Now Albanian and Hungarian have been added.

[26]For a detailed treatment of these events, see F. Stephen Larrabee, "Yugoslavia at the Crossroads," Orbis, Summer 1972; Alvin Z. Rubinstein, "The Yugoslav Succession Crisis in Perspective," *World Affairs*, Fall 1972; and Dennison Rusinow's four-part analysis, "Crisis in Croatia," *American University Field Staff Reports*, June-September 1972.

Security is as much a state of mind as an actual condition. Political decisions may or may not be based on fact, but they are always based on a political elite's perception of the facts. Seen in this light, the poll showing that 54 percent of high-ranking Yugoslav army officers interviewed thought the main threat to the country came from "nationalism and chauvinism" rather than external aggression had more than marginal significance.[27]

Tito showed himself ambivalent on the question of the main danger; enough so to confuse the republican leaderships involved and leave subsequent political analysts divided as to what he thought or intended.[28] The Croat party was indisputably factionalized. Who supported whom and to what extent is clouded in contradictory statements and ex post facto political expediency. This air of Byzantine intrigue notwithstanding, from the perspective of actual security considerations certain events stand out.

First, tension ran particularly high among Serbs living in Croatia (about 15 percent of the republic's population), where any overt expression of Croat nationalism raked over still painful memories of Serbs massacred during Ante Pavelic's Ustashe government, which Hitler installed to run the short-lived independent Kingdom of Croatia during World War II. Second, the assassination of the Yugoslav ambassador to Sweden, Vladimir Rolovic, in early April brought emotions to a boiling point. Third, claims by Croat émigré extremists in West Germany that the Soviets supported their demands for an independent Croatia added ominous undertones to the already inflammable incident.

The Croatian Central Committee countered with accusations that there was a conspiracy to discredit it by spreading rumors that the LCC itself maintained contacts with separatists abroad.[29] Although there appeared to be an agreement, at least at the top of the party, to contain national differences, after the unpublished, reputedly heated discussion at the special session of the April LCY Presidium, nervousness about Soviet intentions persisted. Whether or not Moscow was aiding Croatian and Macedonian terrorist groups, many informed Yugoslavs believed it likely at the time. Reports of Warsaw Pact maneuvers scheduled for the Bulgarian-Yugoslav border in the summer did nothing to dispel such beliefs.[30]

In June, Yugoslav Foreign Minister Tepavac took a symbolic trip to China. His visit was more for the purpose of political shadowboxing than seeking a credible ally, for Belgrade had little in common with Peking and could expect little aid from that side

---

[27]*NIN*, June 20, 1971. It should be kept in mind, however, that according to conservative estimates 70 percent of Yugoslav army officers are Serbs.

[28]By the spring of 1972, notes of Tito's "unpublished speech" attacking nationalist excesses in Croatia during his July 1971 Zagreb visit had been published. (*Politika*, May 9, 1972.) Whether or not the current version is a rewriting of history, it contradicts his flat statement two months later, at the end of a speaking tour in Croatia, that the stories about Croatian nationalism blooming were "completely absurd." *Borba*, September 16, 1971.

[29]On April 7, 1971, the Croatian CC submitted a report of a plot allegedly organized by centralist forces in Belgrade, particularly those connected with the secret police (UDBA), against the Croat leaders. The report was approved by the Executive Committee of the LCC and apparently discussed at the Seventeenth Session of the LCY Presidium. With the expulsion of the four key Croat leaders, Tripalo, Dabcevic-Kucar, Pero Pirker, and Marko Koprtla, in May 1972, all references to these charges disappeared from the LCC's rewritten history of the events leading to the Zagreb student strike. See Slobodan Stankovic, "Former Top Croatian Leaders Expelled from Party: Tito Attacks Both Croatian and Serbian Nationalism," CAA Research Report 1409, *Radio Free Europe Research*, May 10, 1972.

[30]See *Vjesnik* editorial, August 10, 1971. The maneuvers were canceled, perhaps as a prelude to (or condition of) the Brezhnev visit to Yugoslavia in September.

when the chips were down. As Chou En-lai later warned his Balkan friends, "distant waters cannot quench fire."[31]

Brezhnev's visit to Belgrade in September brought Soviet-Yugoslav relations back to their usual agreement to disagree. Still, the results of these fraternal discussions created not a little apprehension among Yugoslav observers. Some worried that the final document of the unofficial visit read too much like documents of "former times,"[32] others that the Soviet leader's subsequent visits to Sofia and Budapest (reportedly the Yugoslav government was both surprised and annoyed not to have been informed of its visitor's travel itinerary) made the occasion look much like a tour of "the bloc," i.e., a deliberate flouting of Yugoslav nonalignment. Moreover, Brezhnev's disquieting reference to "common principles" of socialism indicated that differences had been papered-over rather than solved.

Although, in general, public criticism of Moscow declined as a sign of good faith on the Yugoslav side, there was open annoyance at the coverage of the talks in Soviet news media. Tensions continued with the Bulgarians on the Macedonian question—a sure sign that Brezhnev had not seriously pushed reconciliation while in Sofia—and the massive Freedom 1971 military maneuvers testing out the territorial defense units signaled that Yugoslav policymakers considered political agreements no substitute for self-defense.

Yet in a sense the situation had been "normalized." After supervising the maneuvers, Tito departed for visits to Washington, Ottawa and London. While he was thus reaffirming his country's nonaligned stance, factionalism in the Croatian party came to a head. As Dr. Vladimir Bakaric, so-called grandfather of Croatian communism, later acknowledged, when Tito came back the Bakaric faction went to him personally for support against the "nationalists" in the LCC leadership. Tito promised that he would "take care of things."[33]

In the words of Czech philosopher Karel Kosik: "Politics is a game for and with power and is always a struggle in which one side tries to force the other side to accept its view of reality and its interpretation of events.[34] How Tito took care of things is now a matter of contemporary history. Through his intervention, the LCC faction opposing the idea that a Communist party had any business allying itself to a "mass movement" won, at least temporarily. Nationalist and reform-minded Croat party leaders Miko Tripalo and Dr. Savka Dabcevic-Kucar became guilty of tolerating a class enemy, of fostering counterrevolution. Striking students in Zagreb became counterrevolutionaries or at best counterrevolutionary dupes; *Matica Hrvatska,* a conspiratorial opposition party. Tito himself talked of the danger of civil war and seriously referred to the threat of foreign intervention. In and outside the country, political commentators concluded that Yugoslavia was weathering the "worst political crisis since 1948."

For the time being crisis was a Yugoslav, and most acutely a Croatian, political reality. Croatian Communists at all levels were swept up in a process that affected their careers, even though the new president of the Croat party, Milka Planinc, admitted, "The resignations are not all for the same reasons, nor are all equally responsible."[35]

---

[31]Interview with a correspondent of *Vjesnik,* August 28, 1971.

[32]The concern was particularly directed toward the reference to "socialist internationalism." Text in *Borba,* September 26, 1971.

[33]See Bakaric interview in *Frankfurter Rundschau,* December 17, 1971.

[34]*Listy* (Prague), November 7, 1968.

[35]*Borba,* January 24, 1972.

For many individual Croats the experience was a return to the fear they had thought a part of their past.

In light of subsequent events, it is safe to say that the reshuffle within the Croatian party leadership was Tito's first major move to cut the Reupblican party leaderships down to size and to purge and reorganize the entire LCY until it became again a revolutionary party capable of protecting his image of Yugoslavia when he is gone. Like the constitutional amendments of 1971, this party reform represents his determination to stage-manage his own succession.[36] He remains a driving, remarkable man—a Croatian locksmith who emerged as the giant of Yugoslav communism and has ranked among the most significant European statesmen for two decades, all the while maximizing his influence in the international Communist movement. In his view a reformed, strengthened and *united* Communist party is Yugoslavia's best insurance policy; the LCY must have the power to "interfere" when necessary, and republican parties must be strictly accountable to the center.[37]

These views explain his current references to dissatisfaction with the historic party congress which in November 1952 had spoken of the party's *educational* rather than *commanding* role. His emphasis that Croatia was only one of the offenders and the seemingly senseless expansion of the purge to other republics pointed to the fact that Croatia was being used as an example. Through it he would force a reform of the increasingly factionalized LCY, streamlining it until the party as an organization could succeed him.

Reducing the LCY Executive Bureau by half at the Second Party Conference in January 1972 can be seen as step two, for it was in a tactical alliance with the new Executive Bureau that Tito forced the resignation of Serbian Communist Party Chairman Marko Nikezic. Serbian Communist resignations of note occurred among high-level Macedonians and Bosnians as well. These events are far too recent and complicated, however, for us to sort out all their implications here. For our purposes who next, what now, is less important than to make a general assessment of the relationship of the domestic upheavals to Yugoslav and European security.

Security Implications for Tomorrow

First, Yugoslavia's military reorganization of 1968–1969 is an ongoing fact, although less emphasis is placed on total people's defense in view of the declining sense of threat from the East and the increasing willingness of all concerned to forget about Czechoslovakia. Territorial defense units exist and are expected to function if needed. But the rise of ethnic tensions that culminated in the Zagreb student strike and the after-effects of the solution (which, one may argue, was more divisive than the students' action), evoke the simple question: Who would be fighting for what?

That such a question seems obvious weakens the value of the overall strategy, for as with all forms of deterrence, its credibility depends on the potential aggressors' assessment of the united will of the defenders. The concept of total people's defense evolved in 1968–1969's optimism about the unity of the Yugoslav state. It was a reflex against a deeply perceived external threat at a time when national (ethnic) differences seemed to have been contained, and the party itself gave every sign of being united. Whether or not such a strategy [will be] sufficiently credible . . .—affected as it is by escalated

---

[36]He had been talking about the need for such reform since May 1971. See Robin Remington, "Yugoslavia—Strains of Cohesion," *Survival*, May–June 1972.

[37]Tito's concluding speech to the Second Party Conference of the LCY, *Borba*, January 27, 1972.

tension, the fall of the Croat party leadership,[38] Tito's statements about the use of the army internally if necessary, and subsequent upheavals within the LCY—remains to be seen.

Second, in Zagreb in 1971, 30,000 students struck peacefully for a foreign currency reform that Tito himself, during his September tour of Croatia, had assured them was a Croatian right; they had been promised that the issue would be settled. This was not a sign of threatening disorder. In a world grown used to more violent student protest, it would not have caused a ripple if the purge of the Croat party leadership had not followed. Moreover, at the end of December 1971 the question provisionally was settled much along the lines the Croats had demanded. The reforms allow enterprises to keep up to 20 percent of their foreign currency earnings, as opposed to the previous 7 to 10 percent. If that issue could be decided so soon after the strike, it could have been settled before (as Tito has often said of factory work stoppages). That it was not, and the means taken to restore order, have left a residue of bitterness which can only worsen national conflicts in the future.

There [was] meanwhile . . . an increase of terrorist activity [in 1972]: one airplane bombed, 28 dead; a train bombing with six injuries; a bomb in a *Borba* plant that killed a father of five. In midsummer 1972 allegedly Ustashe terrorists infiltrated into Bosnia and fought it out with the local militia for several weeks;[39] in October, Croat émigrés hijacked a Swedish airplane. All of this raises the ugly possibility that Tito's handling of what he subsequently ridiculed as a noncrisis in Croatia broadened the Ustashe recruitment base. Seen in the context of Yugoslav history, such low-level violence is far from harmless. Terrorist acts can harden emotions into the kind of hatred that makes political compromise impossible and gives vengeance priority over self-interests.

Third, a fundamental problem would remain even if Tito succeeds in creating, or recreating, the Yugoslav Communist party he has in mind. The yearning to believe there is one answer, a panacea that can end deeply-rooted national tensions, social inequalities and economic difficulties at one blow, is a generic weakness of the Yugoslav revolution. Hopes were initially pinned on the catharsis of the revolution itself; then on self-managing socialism, the Economic Reform of 1965, and constitutional amendments that amounted, in principle, to a withering away of the federation, if not the state.

These amendments were the culmination of twenty years of self-management interacting, since the mid-1960s, with expanding economic and political decentralization. Cumbersome as they were, they represented recognition of the unpalatable truth that Yugoslavia could survive as a democratic socialist state after Tito's death only if it were a genuine multinational federation. As a leading Yugoslav theoretician has pointed out, counterrevolutionary forces are "those that undermine the equality of the nationalities of Yugoslavia, inspiring ethnic hatred and a political behavior that in practice encourages disintegration of the social community."[40] What is needed is a mechanism, not an answer.

---

[38]Ironically, the initial proposal for peacetime, large-scale, territorial defense units had come from Croatia even before the invasion of Czechoslovakia. . . .

[39]For Western accounts of this bizarre incident, see *Le Monde,* July 4, 1972, and *The Economist,* August 5, 1972; for commentary, *Borba,* July 15, 1972. In general the Yugoslav press played it down, although plainly such threats to internal stability contributed to the atmosphere of tension and added plausibility to Tito's demands for a general overhaul of the party.

[40]Dusan Bilandzic, quoted by Dennison Rusinow, "Crisis in Croatia: Part I, Post-Mortems after Karadjordjevo," *American University Field Staff Reports,* June 1972, p. 11.

That Tito became impatient with this process, and remains convinced that he knows best how to protect the future, is understandable. The hero of a personality cult is all too often its victim. Yet the idea that the answer is to turn the LCY into a disciplined Leninist party and return to democratic centralism has its own dangers. Such a party must be headed by someone, and if Yugoslavs can agree on anything at this point it is that there is no one, except Tito, who would be acceptable as spokesman for the genuine interests of the five nations and multiple nationalities making up Yugoslavia.

An unrepresentative leadership divorcing the party from its popular base can only intensify national antagonisms. Worse still, such an "answer" runs the risk of undermining the legitimacy of the LCY itself, thereby increasing the likelihood that repression would substitute for resolution of differences in order to achieve implementation of party decisions. That route was tried in interwar Yugoslavia with disastrous results.

It is not that Tito wants to turn back the clock to the Stalinist Yugoslavia of the early postwar years. He, the new leadership in Croatia, and numerous other official spokesmen have stressed that the reforming of the party does not mean a return to orthodox—for which one can read Stalinist—communism. They have strongly warned conservative, bureaucratic and dogmatic forces not to take advantage of the struggle against nationalism in order to gain power.

A dysfunctional means used for the best purpose, however, is often handicapped by its own inertia. Yugoslav communists may find association with the rhetoric of "counterrevolution" used for suppressing Dubcek's "socialism with a human face" in Czechoslovakia to be just as dangerous as Miko Tripalo's alleged alliance with a "mass movement." The signs are seen in the trials stemming from charges filed in the aftermath of the Croatian crisis, Tito's expression of personal dissatisfaction at the lightness of the sentences, and references to the need to change the code of criminal law so that "enemies" of the revolution can be suitably punished.[41] Intellectuals who disagree are increasingly harassed as "anarcho-liberals"; economic doubters are attacked as "technocrats." If the process goes too far there is the dismal prospect that the Yugoslav road to socialism will become less and less of a genuine alternative.

The real danger to Yugoslav security is not that the ongoing turmoil runs an immediate risk of civil war or foreign intervention but that attempting to solve the national question by purging one side ("Croatian chauvinists") and then the other ("Serb hegemonists")[42] can erode the unique content of Yugoslav socialism until there is

---

[41]Tito referred to the need to strengthen the criminal code shortly after the "events in Croatia." (*Borba*, December 23, 1971.). The point was brought up again by Dolanc, speaking in Split (*ibid.*, September 20, 1972), and [subsequently took] the form of a proposal to the Federal Assembly to reinstate wider police powers. *Politika*, November 27, 1972.

[42]Considerable confusion with respect to the charges against Nikezic led much of the Western press to assume that the leader of the Serbian party was forced out because he was a "Serbian nationalist." Nothing could be further from the truth. Although he was accused of being soft on nationalism, the crux of the power struggle leading to his resignation concerned questions of party discipline and the attempt to establish priorities between shifting values of inner-party democracy and democratic centralism. The Serbian leader was a victim of Tito's determination to re-establish a center than can effectively control its republican party periphery. Since Nikezic was among the Serbian communists most trusted in the more developed republics, the impact of his ouster on the "national question" could easily boomerang. It is unclear whether his and Latinka Perovic's successors—Dr. Tihomir Vlaskalic, an unknown economics professor, and Nikola Petronic, a thirty-six-year-old metal worker—can cooperate with their Croat and Slovene counterparts with anything like equal credibility. Among the best analyses of the situation is that of Viktor Meier in *Tages-Anzeiger,* October 30, 1972. For a somewhat more hopeful conclusion, see Bernard Margueritte, *Le Monde* (weekly edition), December 27, 1972.

nothing left to defend except the power of a token collective leadership. This weakening of the country's internal fiber, combined with pressures generated by increased economic dependence on Moscow, could quietly slide Yugoslavia into the Soviet bloc. The fact that its policy toward European security and its stance during the multilateral preparations for a CSCE are designed to change the nature of that bloc so that members have greater freedom of maneuver would be small consolation to many ordinary Yugoslavs for whom self-managing socialism, with all its flaws, has opened the door to participation in the political process.

Danger number two is tied to the growing impression that an independent Yugoslav foreign policy cannot last without Tito. To whatever extent Yugoslavia's future depends on a general belief that the country can stabilize its internal tensions after his passing, the Yugoslav leader has weakened its chances by contributing simultaneously to the belief that his interventions "save" Yugoslavia and that he is the indispensable kingpin holding the country together. Despite his protests and attacks on the foreign press for misinterpreting his actions, it is Tito himself who has taken a giant step toward convincing the world that Yugoslavia is standing on glass legs.

There [was] no credence, however, for the flurry of Western speculation at the end of 1972 and beginning of 1973 along lines that "the most extensive Soviet-Yugoslav rapprochement since 1948" should be seen as evidence that Belgrade is about to join the Warsaw Pact.

True, Moscow is intent both on winning points with Tito personally and strengthening its position within Yugoslavia after he goes. Take, for example, the red-carpet treatment received by the Yugoslav leader during his June 1972 visit to the USSR.[43] It is equally clear that Tito's campaign to recentralize the Yugoslav party escalated at the very time Belgrade was engaged in credit negotiations with Moscow.[44] One could conclude that instead of financing separatists outside Yugoslavia, the Soviets are now using economic pressure to encourage internal changes that would not only tie Yugoslavia more closely to the East economically but set the Yugoslav party on the road of socialist acceptability from the Soviet view. The extent of Soviet influence on what will be an important part of the country's industrial infrastructure, notably in Bosnia and other less developed regions, is disquieting. Still, Soviet aid is coming piecemeal, and, given the past record, there is no guarantee that it will not be cut off should the political situation swing out of phase with Kremlin expectations.

Yugoslavs are not unsophisticated about such matters nor do they lack experience in balancing between Moscow and other options. Kavcic may have been attacked for leaning westward too heavily. However, no sooner had the economic agreement with the Soviets been signed than Yugoslav economic contacts began to move farther East. On November 16 a Chinese economic delegation headed by the PRC minister for foreign trade arrived in Belgrade for a seven-day visit, a sign that assistance from anti-Soviet sources is still welcome. Further, if pressure on the Slovenes to diversify that

---

[43]Since Tito was awarded the Order of Lenin and presented with a marshal's saber by the Soviet Central Committee, the Brezhnev leadership appeared to have decided on a strategy of minimizing differences—which nonetheless were still being referred to in the Soviet press. *Izvestia*, June 3, 1972.

[44]The final credit agreement, amounting to $540 million worth of industrial equipment to be delivered between 1973 and 1976, with a second installment of $450 million due after 1976, was signed on November 2, 1972. This was shortly after the fall of the reformist Serbian party leadership (October 21) and the resignation of Slovene Premier Stane Kavcic (October 30), who had been attacked for tying Slovenia too closely to the West economically.

republic's economic base was an effort to speed Soviet signing, it also reflected a republican power struggle between Kavcic and Stane Dolanc. As such, it does not signify that Yugoslavia would be unreceptive to balancing Soviet credits with Western assistance should that assistance turn out to be available. Neither does it imply that Yugoslavia would hold back from agreements on European economic cooperation coming out of the CSCE.

The "second honeymoon" in Soviet-Yugoslav relations, in my opinion, is based on a temporary coincidence in Soviet preferences and Tito's deepening obsession with regaining control over the republican party organizations. For once, Tito's objective agreed with the thinking of Brezhnev and his Kremlin associates on socialist problem-solving. Moscow must have been delighted to hear of his attacks on the LCY Sixth Party Congress, and Soviet leaders would find no fault with "strengthening the leading role of the party" as a solution. After all, there are advantages to the Soviet Union if the Yugoslav alternative demonstrates its unworkability to its East European neighbors without any visible sabotage from Moscow. Whether Yugoslavia can pull itself together to stave off interference when the Soviets tire of their waiting game is the question.

After his 1972 attack on the Serbian leadership, Tito shifted the struggle between "national" party leaderships back to the ongoing conflict between reform-oriented forces favoring more inner-party democracy (often rather confusingly called liberals) and conservative hard-liners formerly identified with Alexandar Rankovic, whose forced resignation in 1966 signaled a victory for reform. In this process Moscow will inevitably favor like-minded conservatives. Yet that preference does not mean that the Soviets would find it advantageous to have Yugoslavia join the Warsaw Pact, to say nothing of being forced to "defend socialism" in case of a civil war. At this stage, a Yugoslav civil war would be a nightmare for Moscow and Washington alike.

Given the current climate of détente and Soviet hopes for political gains via CSCE and MBFR, it is far from certain that Soviet policymakers would want to pull Yugoslavia back into the bloc at the risk of jeopardizing the special relationship they have been carefully cultivating with President Nixon. For the time being, a weakened, tokenly nonaligned Yugoslavia, sensitive to Soviet foreign policy imperatives and unable to make problems for the Kremlin in Eastern Europe, would be quite enough.

Should Brezhnev's long-range objectives be more ambitious, it is useful to remember that the wheel of history in Eastern Europe has not always rolled along the path of Moscow's expectations or preferences. Soviet success depends to a large extent on whether the Yugoslavs are given other economic and political alternatives.

Selected Bibliography

Soviet Union

Aspaturian, Vernon V. *Power and Process in Soviet Foreign Policy*. Boston: Little, Brown, 1971.

Bromke, Adam, and Rakowska-Harmstone, Teresa, eds. *The Communist States in Disarray, 1965–1971*. Minneapolis: University of Minnesota Press, 1972.

Brzezinski, Zbigniew K. *The Soviet Bloc: Unity and Conflict*. Cambridge, Massachusetts: Harvard University Press, 1967.

Hoffman, Erik P., and Fleron, Frederic J., Jr., eds. *The Conduct of Soviet Foreign Policy*. New York: Aldine, 1971.

Jacobson, C. G. *Soviet Strategy-Soviet Foreign Policy: Military Considerations Affecting Soviet Policy-Making*. Glasgow, Scotland: The University Press, 1972.

Kanet, Roger E., ed. *The Soviet Union and the Developing Nations*. Baltimore: The Johns Hopkins Press, 1974.

Rubinstein, Alvin Z. *The Foreign Policy of the Soviet Union*. 3d ed. New York: Random House, 1972.

Ulam, Adam. *Expansion and Coexistence: Soviet Foreign Policy, 1917–1973*. 2d ed. New York: Praeger, 1973.

Wesson, Robert G. *The Russian Dilemma: A Political and Geopolitical View*. New Brunswick, New Jersey: Rutgers University Press, 1974.

China

An Tai-sung. *The Sino-Soviet Territorial Dispute*. Philadelphia: The Westminister Press, 1973.

Clubb, O. Edmund. *China and Russia, The "Great Game"*. New York: Columbia University Press, 1971.

Cohen, Jerome Alan, Friedman, Edward, et al., eds. *Taiwan and American Policy, The Dilemma in U.S.-China Relations*. New York: Praeger, 1971.

Fairbank, John K., ed. *The Chinese World Order*. Cambridge, Massachusetts: Harvard University Press, 1968.

Griffith, William E. *The Sino-Soviet Rift*. Cambridge, Massachusetts: M.I.T. Press, 1964.

Hinton, Harold C. *China's Turbulent Quest*. New York: Macmillan, 1970.

Hsiao, Gene T., ed. *Sino-American Détente and Its Policy Implications*. New York: Praeger, 1974.

Huck, Arthur. *The Security of China: Chinese Approaches to Problems of War and Strategy*. New York: Columbia University Press, 1970.

Larkin, Bruce D. *China and Africa, 1949–1970*. Berkeley: University of California Press, 1971.

MacFarquhar, Roderick, ed. *Sino-American Relations, 1949–1971*. New York: Praeger, 1972.

North, Robert C. *The Foreign Relations of China*. 2d ed. Encino, California: Dickenson, 1974.

Van Ness, Peter. *Revolution and Chinese Foreign Policy*. Berkeley: University of California Press, 1970.

Zagoria, Donald. *The Sino-Soviet Conflict, 1956–1961*. New York: Atheneum, 1964.

Yugoslavia

Campbell, John C. *Tito's Separate Road*. New York: Harper, 1967.

Hammond, Thomas Taylor. *Yugoslavia: Between East and West*. New York: Foreign Policy Association, 1954.

Mates, Leo. *Nonalignment Theory and Current Policy*. Belgrade: Institute of International Politics and Economics, 1972; and Dobbs Ferry, New York: Oceana Publications, 1972.

Rubinstein, Alvin. *Yugoslavia and the Nonaligned World*. Princeton, New Jersey: Princeton University Press, 1968.

Ulam, Adam B. *Titoism and the Cominform*. Cambridge, Massachusetts: Harvard University Press, 1952.

SOME CONCLUDING THOUGHTS

The Comparative Approach

The subject of comparative communism is extensive as well as complex. The introductions and articles in this book do not make up a thorough study, but they provide representative statements and points of view on various aspects of communism in the Soviet Union, China, and Yugoslavia. On the basis of these readings, let us now reconsider the meaning and utility of the comparative approach and suggest some conclusions and implications for the rise, development, and future of communism in the three systems. First, why do we compare the Soviet, Chinese, and Yugoslav models of communism? We compare societies and political systems for the same reason we compare foods, wines or other items that we want to know more about. In short, we make comparisons to identify uniformities and differences and to explain them.

If we are to compare political systems, then, we must look into their pasts, study their aging, analyze their contemporary characteristics, and generally contrast them one with another. By engaging in this sort of comparative analysis, we stand a better chance of understanding the intricacies and complexities of modern social, political, and economic life. In our comparative analysis of the Soviet, Chinese, and Yugoslav systems, we began with their founding ideology, Marxism, then studied their pasts, and finally, analyzed the present. Let us now review some of the highlights of this enterprise and raise a few additional topics for further research and study.

Comparative Overview

Section One began with a consideration of Marxism. Most observers contend that though the practice of Marxism has varied from country to country, the theory has continued to be the basis for unity. As a result, a more extensive overview of Marxian ideology and its history is in order here. The readings in this section noted that modern communism is founded more on the ideas of its progenitor, Karl Marx, than on subsequent ideas that inevitably evolved. Even Marx's critics express respect for the force of his ideas and influence. One critic, for example, has noted the following: "[Marx] was, for all his failures, a very great thinker. . . . Like Darwin and Freud he changed the minds of men, even of men who hate him, and like Darwin and Freud he must therefore be treated with respect and keen attention. Even if his system were not the secular creed of one-third of the world, it would be a living force of huge proportions in the shaping of all minds."[1] It is also true, however, that Marxism was the product, not only of the fertile mind of its originator, but also of the historical milieu in which he (and Engels) lived. The influences of the time were substantial and varied. For example, from classical tradition, Marx derived his belief in Promethean man who made, suffered in, and, eventually, would conquer history; from the German philosophical tradition of Kant and Hegel, Marx obtained his belief in the power of reason as a tool to combat traditional ideas and institutions; to Hegel he was particularly indebted for the dialectic method and the concept of alienated man;[2] then the Young Hegelians, in their critical analysis of religion and their proclaimed adherence to materialism, gave Marx still more material to digest and modify; ironically, the failures of the French and subsequent revolutions elsewhere in Europe provided Marx with important case studies for his future-conceived Proletarian Revolution; to a host of socialists and utopians, "scientific" socialism was also indebted; finally, there was his collaborator, Friedrich Engels, who in a number of important ways augmented and modified Marxism after the master's death.[3] Thus, although recognizing the uniqueness of Marx's contribution to human history, a contribution that transcended his time, we must understand that he was also a product of that history and limited by it.

---

[1]Clinton Rossiter, *Marxism: The View from America* (New York: Harcourt, 1960), p. 22.

[2]In the Afterward to the Second German Edition of his most extensive work, *Capital*, Karl Marx acknowledged his debt to Hegel: "I therefore openly avowed myself the pupil of that mighty thinker [Hegel]. . . . The mystification which dialectic suffers in Hegel's hands, by no means prevents him from being the first to present its general form of working in a comprehensive and conscious manner. With him it is standing on its head. It must be turned right side up again if you would discover the kernel within the mystical shell." Karl Marx, *Capital: A Critique of Political Economy*, Vol. I. Translated by Samuel Moore and Edward Aveling (New York: International Publishers, 1967), pp. 19–20.

[3]For elaboration on these themes, see Sidney Hook, *From Hegel to Marx* (Ann Arbor, Michigan: The University of Michigan Press, 1962), George Lichtheim, *Marxism: An Historical and Critical Study* (2nd rev. ed.; New York: Praeger, 2nd ed., 1965); and Edmund Wilson, *To the Finland Station* (Garden City, N.Y.: Doubleday, 1940).

Rooted in a conviction that all past and present economic systems contained the seeds of their own destruction and must inevitably give way to a future scientific socialism, Marxism became a cause and refuge for a motley group of revolutionaries, reformists, nationalists, militarists, visionaries, and cynics, as well as masses of exploited workers and peasants. With such an array of supporters, it is hardly surprising that Marxism has undergone a diversity of proclamations about its meaning, method, and goal. Nonetheless, certain tenets of Marxism are still embraced by the various Communist parties, even if not always regarded as pertinent.

(1) Marxists insist that reality is not the abstract realm of ideas, metaphysics, and other intangible concepts; rather, reality is the productive man, his work, and the forces of production that create the world in which he lives.[4] As history unfolds, a succession of definite and predictable economic stages evolve—primitive, slave, feudal, capitalist, and socialist (Asiatic being a special category)—and it is the particular economic state that largely determines the life-style and culture of mankind at the time. The key to understanding each previous stage is the recognition of who has owned the forces of production, and consequently who has exploited whom.

(2) The dynamic force that creates history is the collision between the exploited and exploiters, the struggle between the owners of the means of production and the workers who do the producing. Even if Marx himself did not employ the term dialectical materialism, which describes the struggle of man in history, there is no denying that all Marxists, whatever their differences, "share the common faith in 'dialectical materialism' as a universal 'science' of the 'laws' of *nature* and history, as supposedly adumbrated in a confused fashion by Hegel and finally given adequate expression by Engels."[5] Since the Marxists believe that man is both creator and object of historical events, the dialectical concept is essential as an explanation of change and movement. Ultimately, however, dialectical materialism is the very foundation of the faith that cements the bond among Marxists. It explains, if simplistically, the phenomena of life and assures the faithful that, after long years of enduring hardships, and after certain conditions within the society are achieved, communism will be their reward.

(3) At each economic stage, two distinct classes—the exploiters and the exploited—can be identified: master and slave, feudal lord and serf, bourgeoisie (capitalist) and proletariat (wage earner or laborer). This distinction is the result of the conflict between the groups performing the two different functions in the production process, that is, the conflict between those who control and enjoy the fruits of production and those who have no control over the forces of production and who do not benefit from their

---

[4]Gustav A. Wetter, *Dialectical Materialism,* Trans. from the German by Peter Heath (New York: Praeger, 1958), pp. 31–32.
[5]George Lichtheim, *Marxism* (New York: Praeger, 1965), p. 246.

own work. This idea too is clearly expressed in the *Manifesto of the Communist Party:*

> The history of all hitherto existing society is the history of class struggles.
> Freeman and slave, patrician and plebian, lord and serf, guildmaster and journeyman, in a word, oppressor and oppressed, stood in constant opposition to one another, carried on an uninterrupted, now hidden, now open fight, a fight that each time ended, either in a revolutionary re-constitution of society at large, or in the common ruin of the contending classes.[6]

(4) The struggle that Marx so vividly described reaches its zenith in the economic stage of capitalism, a stage that societies must pass through to attain communism. It is in the capitalist stage of history that exploitation and class conflict become most acute, eventually causing a dramatic social upheaval. Marxists are particularly denunciatory of the incentive for private profit, so fundamental to capitalism. They insist that it prompts the employer to exploit the worker in order to gain more profit, and the worker, in turn, becomes more oppressed.

(5) Another salient drawback of capitalism, according to the Marxist view, is the alienation of the worker from the system in which he works. Marx believed that, if man is to be fully human, he must come to recognize the value of his labor and production. It is necessary, then, that each human being be able to control and judge the product of his own labor. Not only is this individual control of one's own labor impossible in capitalism, but the system itself frustrates and destroys the individual who would try to attain it. This particular estrangement of man from himself and his labor is summarized by Marx in these words:

> Now, therefore, we have to grasp the essential connection between private property, avarice, and the separation of labour, capital and landed property, between exchange and competition, value and the devaluation of men, monopoly and competition, etc.; the connection between the whole estrangement and the *money*-system.
> We proceed from an *actual* economic fact.
> The worker becomes all the poorer the more wealth he produces, the more his production increases in power and range. The worker becomes an ever cheaper commodity the more commodities he creates. With the *increasing value* of the world of things proceeds in direct proportion the *devaluation* of the world of men.[7]

It is important for the reader to understand that Marx's concept of alienation, even a century after these words were written, continues to vitalize communism and to motivate its followers to revolution.

(6) Marxists believe that, when the dialectical tension between the bourgeoisie and the proletariat has reached the breaking point, revolution

---

[6]Karl Marx and Frederick Engels, *Manifesto of the Communist Party.* Published in *Selected Works.* Vol. I (New York: International Publishers, 1968), pp. 35–36.

[7]Karl Marx, *Economic and Philosophic Manuscripts of 1844.* In Robert C. Tucker, *The Marx-Engels Reader* (New York: W. W. Norton, 1972), pp. 57–58.

will be inevitable. Not only will the Proletarian Revolution free the worker from oppression, but also it will halt the very movement of class history itself.

(7) The primary Marxist goal is to assist the worker in his revolutionary struggle, and the Communist party was organized for this purpose. Although the party may have saved Marxism from passing into oblivion (as did other nineteenth-century reform movements), it is doubtful that Marx ever envisioned the party structure and function found in contemporary Communist states. His original concept of the Communist party was that it was to be directed by the workers that constituted its membership. But under Lenin and Stalin it became a tightly knit elitist organization: organizational unity and operational efficiency were gained at the expense of free participation by the proletariat.

(8) The Marxists conclude that, though it will be a hard-fought battle (since the capitalist exploiters will not give up easily), the worker will triumph with the realization of the classless and free Communist society.

These points, then, constitute the theoretical bases of Marxism, though Marxists might insist that they are objective facts and not just theoretical speculations. Marxists believe they have found a weakness in the capitalist promise that the free-enterprise system, governed by the laws of the market, will insure for all people of a nation a share of its wealth. Marx and Engels argued that overproduction, rising unemployment (as increasing numbers of laborers were displaced by machines), and resultant declining profits followed by increased exploitation of the worker would produce intolerable conditions and the inexorable collapse of capitalism. In its place would arise communism, and the dawn of a new era in the history of man. The accuracy of Marx's predictions will continue to be controversial, but there is no doubt that he motivated the capitalist societies to modify their economic and social systems in order that his prediction of the ultimate death of capitalism would not become a reality.

Section Two raised the issues of the cultural and historical settings that preceded communism. Was there something about the past that could be linked to the advent of Soviet, Chinese, and Yugoslav communism? An examination of the past of each of the three societies revealed very interesting and—at least on the surface—very different backgrounds indeed. We discovered differences in culture, religion, language, and politics. Not only were there differences between the three major societies, but there were profound and complex contrasts within. But were there commonalities in these varied settings that led to the collapse of the preexisting state system? And were there any common factors that led to the success of Communism?

Although Marx can be credited with tracing the relationship of societal change and the economic structure of societies, he had difficulty in accurately predicting the advent of communism in industrialized capitalist states. In the three states studied in this book—and incidentally in all states that have adopted communism with the partial exceptions of the German Democratic Republic and Czechoslovakia[8]—the economic and social structure was in a much less developed stage. The traditional peasant-oriented society of Confucianist China, the underdeveloped condition of Orthodox Russia, and the backward, peasant-based setting of multinational Yugoslavia—all were at least decades away from being industrialized capitalist states ready for a proletarian revolution. But although the economic requisites may have been lacking, certain features were present that appear in retrospect to have been related to both the collapse of the old imperial state systems and the rise of communism.

First, the old state systems were elitist in nature, and the political, economic, and social power was concentrated in the hands of a few. Second, as these elitist systems suffered the shocks of twentieth-century development—the Russo-Japanese War and World War I in Russia; civil wars and World War II in both China and Yugoslavia—they found it impossible to maintain the support and continue to govern these fragile, complex, and slowly disintegrating societies. Finally, these and related events resulted in a loss of political leadership. Given the backward, non-participant nature of the societies which had developed under the elitist systems, there was little chance of a democratic movement filling the ensuing political vacuum. Parochial, traditional, agrarian-oriented societies do not produce mass democratic movements to replace the toppling dictators—and they did not in Russia, China, or Yugoslavia. What did happen during these periods of great instability and war, was the advancement of a new political force. Centralized, militant, and prepared to fight against great odds, the Communists fought, struggled, and assumed power in the hopes of changing the past.

Section Three was concerned with the Communist advent to power within the three systems, and with the concept of revolution. There is no doubt that Marxist theory becomes altered in practice, the type and degree of alteration varying with the situation. For example, consider the Marxist concept of *revolution*. Revolution, as enunciated by Marx and generally accepted by the Communist leaders of the Soviet Union, China, and Yugoslavia, was the principal means by which alienated mankind would release itself from the bonds of capitalism and eventually find total freedom in communism. Logically, the focal point of revolution would be the industrial states of Europe and America. Lenin as Marx's successor, elaborated on the revolutionary strategy to encompass the "weakest links" in capitalism's economic chain, the colonial and less developed countries

---

[8]Czechoslovakia was a rather highly developed state with an established democratic tradition when it turned to Communist rule in 1948. We should also note that certain West European states that are now tending toward communism, for example, Italy and Portugal, fit more closely with the Marxist prediction and therefore diverge from the general pattern being discussed above. When the communists took power after World War II in East Germany, it too had an established industrial base.

of the world. But less than a decade after the Russian Revolution of 1917, Communist intellectuals were heatedly arguing about Lenin's interpretation of revolution and the way in which it might be reconciled with basic Marxism. Joining in the argument with his concept of "permanent revolution" was the fiery Leon Trotsky (1879–1940).

In a sense the idea of permanent revolution had always been an integral part of Marxism, for the dialectic of history, the class struggle, and the efforts of the oppressed to achieve communism were unending. Marx himself had mentioned the idea when he wrote about the Revolutions of 1818; "This socialism [Blanqui] is the *declaration of the permanence of the revolution,* the *class dictatorship* of the proletariat as the necessary transit point to the abolition of class distinctions generally. . . ."[9] While continuing to emphasize revolution in the industrial countries, Trotsky presented his expanded view of "permanent revolution," which in turn supported Lenin's thesis on the validity of upheaval in the colonial areas. He contended that, in the less developed countries, the economic stages, such as feudalism, capitalism, and socialism, could be shortened so that communism would be attained more quickly. Consequently, revolutions, the phenomena by which transition from one stage to another was effected, would overlap, so that a continuing or permanent revolution would be in process. But Trotsky's concept of permanent revolution had yet another interesting facet to it: that the social and economic revolutions of one society were linked to the struggles of the proletariat of other societies, despite differences in economic development or their separation in time and space. The significance of permanent revolution for the world at large is perhaps best explained in Trotsky's own words.

> The international character of the socialist revolution, which constitutes the third aspect of the theory of the permanent revolution, flows from the present state of the economy and the social structure of humanity. Internationalism is no abstract principle but a theoretical and political reflection of the character of world economy, of the world development of productive forces, and of the world scale of the class struggle. The socialist revolution begins on national foundations—but cannot be completed on these foundations alone.[10]

For example, Trotsky maintained that the struggle of the Chinese Communists in the 1920s against the Kuomintang deserved the full support of Soviet Russia. He thus opposed Stalin's cautious "socialism in one country" policy, whereby only after the primary objective of building a strong socialist state at home had been realized would the Soviet Union make a major effort to help the proletariat of other countries in their struggles against the bourgeoisie. In the power struggle that ensued between Stalin

---

[9]Karl Marx, *The Class Struggles in France, 1848–1850.* In Saul K. Padover, ed., *Karl Marx on Revolution.* The Karl Marx Library, V. I. (New York: McGraw-Hill, 1971), p. 226.

[10]Leon Trotsky, *The Permanent Revolution.* In Isaac Deutscher, ed., *The Age of Permanent Revolution: A Trotsky Anthology* (New York: Dell, 1964), pp. 64–65.

and Trotsky, Stalin was victorious, and Trotsky was expelled from the Communist party and the Soviet Union, his very name becoming anathema to the so-called orthodox Communist leaders.

Although the leaders of the Soviet Union, China, and Yugoslavia have certainly not abandoned revolution as a means of destroying capitalism and establishing communism in the world, they have, for various reasons, come to support other tactics for achieving the same end. Among the reasons for their shift of attitude are the following: satisfaction with their growing internal prosperity has dissuaded both the leaders and the people from active involvement in external revolutions; concern for national security and, in particular, fear of an atomic or hydrogen holocaust, have encouraged all nations to be more cautious in their expressions of hostility; finally attempts to win friends and followers among the leaders of the "third world" nations, and to achieve détente with certain powerful non-Communist nations have also caused all three Communist countries to strive for peaceful coexistence.

It is interesting to note, however, that Mao Tse-tung may have added another dimension to the Marxian concept of revolution by maintaining that, among the socialist nations themselves and even within a single socialist society, the Communist revolution remains unfinished. For example, in a speech made before high party dignitaries in 1957, Mao made the following statement.

> Led by the working class and the Communist Party, our . . . people, united as one, are engaged in the great task of building socialism. . . . However, this does not mean that contradictions no longer exist in our society. To imagine that none exist is a naive idea which is at variance with objective reality. We are confronted by two types of social contradictions—those between ourselves and the enemy and those among the people themselves.[11]

Mao maintains, then, that China must always be on the alert and must be ready to engage in struggle to eliminate all serious contradictions, especially the antagonistic class struggles. The Chinese leadership may continue to seek improved relations with her former principal enemy, the United States, but she will also continue to criticize the Soviet Union for adopting what she considers to be the revisionist approach. In her domestic policies, the Chinese leadership has periodically promoted rectification campaigns, such as the Great Proletarian Cultural Revolution, to eradicate thinking that is incompatible with government goals, and to eliminate the class differences that persist.

In the years ahead, therefore, it should be interesting to observe the ways in which the different Marxian societies confront the revolutionary con-

---

[11]Mao Tse-tung, "On the Correct Handling of Contradictions Among the People," speech made at the Eleventh Session (Enlarged) of the Supreme State Conference, February 27, 1957. In Foreign Languages Press, trans. *Selected Reading From the Works of Mao Tse-tung,* V. I. (Peking: Foreign Languages Press, 1967), pp. 350-351.

cept. It would seem highly possible that, unless the people of a country are afflicted by economic or political chaos, during which any change might be welcomed, the Communist leaders will continue to profess belief in the inevitability of the Proletarian Revolution while cautiously avoiding its active instigation in other countries.

In Section Four, the readings describe not only various concepts of Marxism that are shared by the Soviet Union, China, and Yugoslavia, but also the diversification that has occurred as a consequence of Marxist principles being implemented at different times within different countries. Let us look at some of the more important implications of this diversity.

If, Karl Marx—from his writing table in England—was the one to formulate the revolutionary ideology of Communism, such disciples as Lenin and Stalin in the Soviet Union, Mao Tse-tung and Chou En-lai in China, Tito and Edward Kardelj in Yugoslavia, and a host of Marxists in other countries have had the task of integrating theory with practice in actual circumstances. Lenin, in particular, had insisted that, although the writings of Marx and Engels were to be the font of wisdom for party members, the "current moment," "the concrete situation" was to be the guide to their action.[12] Whether because of peculiar economic conditions in a country (e.g., underdeveloped capitalist economy, paucity of proletariat), the strength of traditional cultural forces (e.g., religion, the family system), ethnic and cultural divisions within a country, or a combination of these and other factors, the Communist leaders in the Soviet Union, China, and Yugoslavia (as well as other systems) have repeatedly reinterpreted and revised Marxist ideology. When the question has been one of the attainment and the retainment of power, they have not relied upon predetermined timetables or mechanistic formulas to decide policy. Instead they have determined for themselves which measures would be orthodox and which would be revisionist, given the particular country, time, and set of circumstances. Yet each of the three governments has emphatically claimed to be more orthodox in its implementation of communism than the others. The disputes about these claims, combined with conflicting national and international interests, disrupted Soviet-Yugoslav cooperation in 1948 and provoked a series of mutual hostilities between the Soviet Union and China that has endured since 1960.

Section Five centered on the topic of political leadership in Communist party states. Although some Marxist ideologues may have held utopian visions about the desirability of proletarian rule before attaining power in the Soviet Union, China, and Yugoslavia, it was soon apparent that worker participation would have to wait. In the early years following the Communist victories, political power was concentrated within a party with very few workers, and in the hands of those professionals at the very highest levels. In the immediate post-revolutionary eras, such centralization was

---

[12]Alfred G. Meyer, *Leninism* (New York: Praeger, 1962), pp. 78–80.

probably necessary to put the country back on its feet, to get the economy moving, and to bring stability to private and public life.

But as the three states evolve into more modern, developed societies, the feasibility and future of centralized rule becomes more problematical. In the Soviet Union and Yugoslavia, for example, we see the growth of an increasingly educated, sophisticated population that already has challenged, and will continue to challenge, the advisability of centralized party control. Although there have been definite trends toward the decentralization of power, particularly under the Yugoslav system of "self-managing socialism," the party elite are still unwilling to relinquish ultimate political control. While there may be certain benefits to this policy, such as improved coordination and planning, or centralized political control, certain dilemmas are also suggested.

For example, is it possible to continue to overlook or ignore the diverse interests that exist in pluralistic societies such as the Soviet, Chinese, and Yugoslav? If the leaders of these states are able to eradicate competing interests within their respective societies, then this problem may be resolved. However, evidence suggests that the Communist parties are having increasing difficulties in their attempt to maintain unity and centralization in their leadership activities. The Yugoslav example is perhaps most indicative of what may happen once the party's central role is questioned. As is well known, in the 1960s Yugoslav groups and interests rushed to participate in the opening political process as the League of Communists began to remove itself from power. This development ushered in a new phase of competitive, contentious politics that ultimately threatened the unity of multi-national Yugoslavia. This threat signaled the return of the League of Communists to its more orthodox leadership function. How to resolve competing interests within the framework of a one-party state poses a dilemma for which there is no ready answer.

In Section Six it was observed that the monolithic model of a single totalitarian dictator decreeing all policies for Communist countries is no longer valid today, if it ever was. The power of the head-of-state or the Communist party, of course, is not denied, but numerous interest groups, ranging from the military to the consumer, are contributing their input to decision making. Of particular interest to the reader should be the position and power of the proletariat, in whose hands the success or failure of Marxism may lie. Marx and Engels maintained that it was the proletariat that would finally confront the bourgeoisie and topple them from power, because the laboring people were the only genuine revolutionary class. Although incalculable numbers of laborers, throughout the centuries, have been oppressed by the upper classes, communism would enable them to attain total freedom in the future. One might, in fact, contend that Marxism is the first economic and political philosophy of any consequence in history to promote the power and welfare of the masses. But, again, one must ask to what degree the ideological concern for the laboring people has been applied to the actual policies of government leaders in the Communist countries.

Communist ideology has emphasized the close relationship that must exist between the party and the proletarian:

> In what relation do the Communists stand to the proletarians as a whole?
> The Communists do not form a separate party opposed to other working-class parties.
> They have no interests separate and apart from those of the proletariat as a whole.
> They do not set up any sectarian principles of their own, by which to shape and mould the proletarian movement.[13]

However, what seems to have happened—as admitted even by critics within the Communist nations—is that the party has at times ceased to represent the factory workers, farmers, and other laboring people, and has tended to form a new class of bureaucrats and functionaries. Party membership and loyalty have at times been the sole factors to determine who will obtain government jobs, which children will receive the opportunities for advanced education, and who will receive other benefits to be distributed. Although Yugoslavia and China seem to be making some effort to correct abuses and to engage the participation of more working people in factory councils, revolutionary committees, and other policy-making groups, one wonders whether worker influence is really meaningful as long as the party maintains ultimate control. For example, Milovan Djilas, the noted Yugoslav Marxist, has expressed his concern about the relationship between the Communist party and the proletarian:

> . . . it is as if Communism jinxed itself; at the very moment . . . when the Communists come to power, the working class and communism mutually move apart and become estranged.
>
> Spellbound by ideology and by power, Communists have never anywhere fully understood the working class. It is, by its nature and role, a creative, non-exclusive class. Marx could conceive a world without the bourgeoisie, and we can even imagine one without the ideological party bureaucracy. But no past or present world is conceivable without the working class.[14]

Djilas, of course, is speaking as a theoretician and a rather rapturous one at that. The available evidence suggests, however, that a discrepancy persists between the theoretical worth and position of the proletariat (as expressed by Marxian doctrine) and the value actually attributed to this class within the contemporary societies of the Soviet Union, China, and Yugoslavia. As the authors of the readings in this section point out, pressure and interest groups are at work in all three countries to assure a better

---

[13]Marx and Engels, *Manifesto of the Communist Party. Selected Works*, p. 46.

[14]Milovan Djilas, "A Faceless Mass Called Workers" the second of three articles entitled "Communism: 125 Years Later", *New York Times*, August 1972, p. 33M. The articles were sent from Belgrade, Yugoslavia.

deal for the consumers, the laborers, and the nonparty masses. How much these various measures will become institutionalized so that they cannot be easily ignored is difficult to predict, but there is no doubt that the proletarians are being heard and that they are presently effecting the policy-making process.

In Section Seven we compared the efforts within the Soviet Union, China and Yugoslavia to mold a new socialist man. This new socialist citizen, unlike the selfish, individualistic oriented man of the bourgeois state, is to be guided by the collectivist ethic of comradeship. Perhaps somewhat surprisingly, we found that many of the policies of political socialization and education in these three Communist states seem to be quite similar to those we know in non-Communist countries. Schools, youth organizations, and media are all used to encourage attributes deemed to be desirable and to be in the interests of the optimal development of society. The similarities among different states, both Communist and non-Communist, are not surprising, however, since every political system must strive to develop citizen attitudes and behavior conducive to the maintenance and preservation of the system.

But even though general similarities can be discerned, interesting and important differences can be identified when one looks more closely at the political socialization strategies and policies in the three socialist states. Whereas the leaders of all these states share the same ends, as well as somewhat similar means to achieve the ends, they seem to diverge in a number of important respects. Interestingly, many of these divergencies can be traced to factors explored in other sections of the book. For example, as a result of the cultural and historical conditions prevailing in each state (discussed in Section Two) different traits developed in each population in the course of the centuries. The Confucianist, peasant-oriented nature of Chinese society acquired needs and values different from those found in the Western societies inhabiting the Soviet Union and Yugoslavia. Therefore, the more radical socialization policies of Communist China—highly politicized education, communal life, and ideological study—have been practiced and have proven quite successful, at least to some extent in China, whereas the more Western societies of the Soviet Union and Yugoslavia would be inclined to react quite negatively to such policies. This is not to say that political socialization is not at work in these two socialist states; indeed it is. Rather, somewhat more subtle techniques and practices are utilized to achieve the desired end of a patriotic, unified, socialist citizenry.

Other factors covered in the book, such as contemporary ideology, political leadership, and level of economic development, also have an influence on the nature and success of the process of political socialization characterizing the three states. What is important to recognize, then, is that different factors interact in a way recommending different policies. In all states, the search continues for the most effective means to develop a population that supports and contributes to the state, a means that does not weaken or destroy the vitality so necessary for social and economic development.

In Section Eight we studied the search for economic progress in the three socialist states. Given their position and fate in world history, none of these states enjoyed economic prosperity at the time of the Communists' victory. On the contrary, all were suffering from underdeveloped economies which were far behind the more advanced economies of Western Europe. This dismal state of economic affairs was further exacerbated by the devastation resulting from civil and international wars. Consequently, the task of economic development was perhaps the foremost facing the socialist leaders.

Although adhering to rather similar building strategies during the early reconstruction years, China and Yugoslavia were soon to depart from the Soviet command-type of economic system. Again, there were a variety of determinants that influenced the search for new economic methods and practices. The differing levels of economic development, the structure of the society, the personal inclinations of the leaders—all of these encouraged the Chinese and Yugoslavs to go their separate ways. So while the Soviets have clung rather guardedly to their own approach, the Chinese have experimented with a variety of approaches—ranging from the radical Great Leap Forward of the late 1950s to the more moderate, developmentally oriented practices of the early 1970s. The Yugoslavs have experimented the most, and perhaps gone the farthest away from the conventional Soviet practice. Called by some observers the Yugoslav system of "laissez-faire socialism," this system shows a variety of market and competition mechanisms designed to improve efficiency, production, and overall economic growth. While all pursuing the same goal of economic development, then, each system has taken a somewhat different approach to socialist economics.

Although it is difficult to compare the results of the three economic systems here, attention should be called to their qualified success. Although the consumer has definitely been deprived in all states, at least when compared with Western, non-Communist states, other areas of economic growth are quite impressive. The development of heavy industry, the obliteration of poverty and starvation, and the advancement of medical and health care—all are great accomplishments that should be acknowledged. Even the consumer has some reason for hope and optimism. Recent developments in all three states indicate greater investment and growth in the consumer sector. If the socialist systems can in fact improve this area of economic performance, their record will be quite impressive indeed. In fact, in view of the possibility for success in this area, and the general disorder in Western, non-Communist economic systems, socialist states may pose increasingly tough economic competition for Western nations.

Another topic of competition and change was discussed in Section Nine—that of international relations and foreign policy. In this section, the influence of both historical and contemporary factors were particularly important, and can be clearly identified when viewing the changing foreign policies of the three states. Whereas the central goal of all states has been to maximize their position and influence in both the socialist and international arenas, their policies have not always been predictable. The weighing of ideological, domestic, and international factors and motives by Communist leaders has at times resulted in policy surprises. The 1970s thaw in Chinese relations toward the United States, her greatest "enemy" during the ideological fervor of the 1960s, for example, ensued when certain domestic and international considerations transcended stricter ideological motivations. As in all political systems, the leaders are forced to weigh and balance the importance of a variety of considerations. These can include ideology, as well as political, environmental, and international concerns. Ultimately, however, the leaders have to assess, adopt, and pursue that policy deemed most suitable to their national interests. Such major policy developments as Stalin's "socialism in one country," Brezhnev and Mao's policies of détente, and Tito's policy of nonalignment are consequences of the interacting influence of such factors.

One trend that does seem clear as we approach the 1980s is the evolution of a less hostile, more conservative foreign policy among all major socialist states. Their policy seems to reflect economic motivations, founded on the view that cooperation with non-Communist states may be beneficial, at least in the short run. The general socialist perspective in the present appears to place less emphasis on confrontation with Western states, perhaps with the underlying hope and assumption that the West will collapse irrespective of conflict with the socialist East. Communist leaders seem to embrace the hope that, if they allow Western internal forces to take their course, their own societies may be gaining technology from the West while simultaneously watching over the decline of capitalism and the growth and strengthening of socialism.

Further Considerations

The purpose of this book has not been to contrast Marxism with capitalism, but rather to provide a descriptive comparison of three major countries that profess allegiance to the Marxian way of life. However, in the foregoing discussions of various topical areas, the strengths and the weaknesses of Marxist ideology have also been revealed. What are some of the challenges and opportunities that communism presents to the rest of the world? Is it a viable alternative to other existing economic and political systems?

One need not be a professional philosopher to recognize some important problems inherent in the conceptual content of Marxism. One of the most readily evident limitations of Marxist philosophy is the almost exclusive concern with the materialistic influences on the ideas, ideologies, institutions, and way of life within a given system. Although history demonstrates the significance of the economic structure to the formation of a civilization, it shows that various psychological, spiritual, philosophical, and other physical and metaphysical forces are also important causes of historical events and developments—causes that are largely disregarded in Marxist theory.

The dialectical explanation of development—which asserts that progress occurs in the course of a succession of predetermined antagonisms—may be an even more serious drawback in Marxist theory, because it seems questionable at best that a specific scientific conception of history can be valid and acceptable for any culture at any period. Can it be said that the behavior of complex human beings, within pluralistic societies of vastly different geographic environments, is inevitably and irrevocably subject to rigid patterns of conflict, immutable laws of change, and a predestined goal of attainment?

Other problems are of a more substantial nature. In the Marxist analysis of capitalism there are important problems that should be considered. For example, does Marx explain the history and development of capitalism any more accurately than any other individual with limited historical resources and a deterministic view of history? Is Marxism more useful than the many other contemporary schools of economics in explaining the present and future trends of capitalism? Even more specifically, is Marxist economic theory able to clarify the complex relationship between the labor theory of value, prices, and profits, and the subsequent necessary adjustments contemporary capitalism would have to make with respect to this triad? In other words to paraphrase Professor Paul Samuelson's witty remark about Marx and economics: When we deal with Marx's analysis of economic history and especially capitalism are we to be inspired by his Promethean wisdom or discouraged by his Merlinian chicanery?[15] It has frequently been noted that, though Marx was successful in predicting the movement from small, competitive factories to large, monopolistic industries, he failed to anticipate the mixed economic system that dominates twentieth-century societies. In fact, an examination of the economic structures of contemporary Communist states suggests that the less a country's leadership has insisted that the population follow orthodox Communist economic methods, and the more it has adopted the mixed-economy approach—such as economic incentives for workers, private plots of land for farmers, credit buying in international trade, some decentralized industrial planning and operation of factories—the healthier the economy seems to be. This is not to suggest that certain Marxist countries are simply blending capitalism and socialism; on the contrary, their basic

---

[15]Paul A. Samuelson, "Rejoinder: Merlin Unclothed, A Final Word." A reply to Michio Morishima and William J. Baumol in a "Colloquium: On Marx, the Transformation Problem," *Journal of Economic Literature,* XII, (March, 1974), p. 76.

distrust of capitalism is real. However, it would appear that one should critically question the validity of Marxian economic theory and its results in practice, while at the same time recognizing the legitimate challenges it presents to other economic systems.

In conclusion, let us examine the potential challenges and problems the various Communist systems may pose for the United States in the decades ahead. One obvious challenge concerns an evaluation of our own system, and its values and way of life. For the United States, the years since the early 1960s have been especially traumatic. The disillusionment and bitterness that emerged from the Vietnam war, the deep-seated racial and ethnic hatreds that surfaced in both North and South, the political scandals of the early 1970s, and other serious events have been subjecting this nation to the most rigorous test of its history. It will not be enough to demand greater allegiance to the flag, a return to the "spirit of 76", or better courses on the values of capitalism in our schools, if they are no more than perfunctory actions unaccompanied by analysis of the ills of the nation and by reflections on methods for restoration. Thus the following questions about the American system need to be advanced, whether a Marxist challenge exists or not, but the presence of such a challenge intensifies their urgency: (1) What is our understanding of theoretical capitalism, and how should it be actualized? What are the values and limits of the so-called mixed economic system? (2) What is our conception of such traditionally important values as private property, profit, and personal income? What privileges and obligations does property ownership entail, and what are the duties of the individual to the community at large? (3) Should a job be guaranteed to anyone wishing to work? What spiritual and material returns does an employee have a right to expect from a job? (4) How much should the employees share in the profit, the planning, and the operation of a factory or other enterprise? (5) Should an employer's provision of such benefits as free medical care, retirement income, vacation pay, and so forth be optional or obligatory? (6) Should the nation's wealth be more equitably distributed among the people? How about on an international scale? To what degree should the wealthy nations, such as the United States, share their wealth with less developed countries? What obligations do the richer and more developed nations have to the poorer and less developed ones? (7) In what manner and to what degree are we competing with the Socialist and Communist nations?

Probably all of these questions have been discussed to a limited extent in this country, and most have provoked active response of some kind. But the fact remains that they have yet to be seriously analyzed in the majority of our schools, churches, and legislative chambers. Yet they must be heard by the American people as a whole, if we are to continue to believe that our system can be humane, just, and viable.

But if the beliefs and goals of the United States are to be submitted to stiff trials in the years ahead, so are those of the Soviet Union, China, and

Yugoslavia. Indeed, the period since 1960 has been equally difficult for those countries. The arguments between Moscow and Peking have become increasingly rancorous, and the disputable areas more extensive; Yugoslavia continues to have problems of unifying her half-dozen strong-willed nationalities and must look over her shoulder at her giant neighbor, the USSR; Communist and non-Communist nations alike were shocked by the ruthless use of Soviet military force in Czechoslovakia in August 1968; numerous intellectuals, particularly in the Soviet Union, pleaded their causes before the people of the world, protesting Communist governments' inhumane treatment of their own citizens; and economic woes—particularly poor farm yields—plagued the two most populous Communist countries.

Among the many challenges that all three Communist nations must confront, and that have special interest to the people of the United States, are these. It has yet to be demonstrated that a Marxist system can tolerate a free press, critical intellectuals, religious advocates, and other elements that contribute to a truly democratic state. Yugoslavia seems to have coped more ably with the challenge of freedom, but some would argue that this liberation has impaired the workings of that particular Communist system. Nevertheless, even in Yugoslavia the strong hand of Tito or of the League of Communists remains ready at any time to restrict anyone who seems antagonistic to current party policy. As the educated population increases in all three countries, as the governments in each develop more of an international perspective, and as general prosperity spreads, the Communist leaders may be confronted by yet more demands from their people for more openness and more protection of personal rights.

It may be essential to the world's survival that both the Soviet Union and the People's Republic of China, along with the other military powers, agree to negotiate their differences in order to maintain peace. The Soviet Union and the United States are already engaged in this process and it is entirely possible that when China's leaders believe that their military strength is equivalent to that of the other world powers they too will participate in test-ban negotiations and other measures for restricting the use and accumulation of nuclear armaments. Unfortunately, the possibility also remains that relations of the Soviet Union and China, with each other and with the smaller Communist nations, will be strained and, at times, explosive. Various nationalistic causes (e.g., protection of their borderlands), as well as resistance to revisionism within other Communist nations, may constitute justification for both the Soviet Union and China to continue using military coercion. That Yugoslavia and Mongolia may in fact be subjected to increased pressures, both economic and military, from their stronger neighbors might concern all of us in the future.

It is somewhat ironical, then, that although an increased number of non-Communist nations have come to recognize the diversity in modern Marxism, the Marxist nations themselves, especially the Soviet Union and China,

INDEX